D1430314

World Revolution and Family Patterns

✠✠✠✠✠✠✠✠✠✠✠✠

DISCARDED BY

MACPHÁIDÍN LIBRARY

HQ
728
G59
c.2

World
Revolution
and Family
Patterns

❊❊❊❊❊❊❊❊❊❊❊

William J. Goode

89140

THE FREE PRESS, NEW YORK

COLLIER-MACMILLAN LIMITED, LONDON

Copyright © 1970, 1963 by The Free Press

A DIVISION OF THE MACMILLAN COMPANY

Printed in the United States of America

All rights reserved. No part of this book may be reproduced or transmitted in any form or by any means, electronic or mechanical, including photocopying, recording, or by any information storage and retrieval system, without permission in writing from the Publisher.

The Free Press
A Division of The Macmillan Company
866 Third Avenue, New York, New York 10022

Collier-Macmillan Canada Ltd., Toronto, Ontario

First Free Press Paperback Edition 1970

Library of Congress Catalog Card Number: 63-1538

printing number
1 2 3 4 5 6 7 8 9 10

Preface

✿✿✿✿✿✿✿✿✿✿✿✿

WHETHER or not this book meets contemporary standards of excellence, it must be adjudged presumptuous. For it seeks to describe and interpret the main changes in family patterns that have occurred over the past half-century in Japan, China, India, the West, Sub-Saharan Africa, and the Arab countries, and to relate them to various alterations in other institutional areas. In our era of specialization, no one can claim to be expert in all these cultures; few can even master the relevant languages.

Moreover, in the course of writing this book, I have been guilty of yet another presumption. In a group of related papers and in one book I have called for a new attack on the problems of family sociology. This work must therefore be judged partly by the standards I have myself outlined.

Along with other critics of sociology, I have insisted that our generalizations apply to both primitive and "civilized" societies, to non-Western nations as well as to the urban United States; and in addition, these generalizations must be confronted where possible with historical data. Testing sociological insights by historical inquiry, or "introducing the historical dimension," cannot be achieved merely by a few casual or literary references or events.

I have especially urged that family sociology be given the same rigorous intellectual and theoretical attention received by other such areas of sociological inquiry as stratification, polity, or personality and culture. It is simply irrelevant whether family variables have somewhat less impact than, say, economic or stratification variables; surely what we seek are determinate relations among any important variables, wherever they may be located in the institutional structure.

Since family variables are both important and independent, we may profitably begin with them, knowing that as we probe more deeply into their interconnections, we must wrestle with all the significant problems of social systems. To the extent that any particular society is a network, a web, a system, we are quickly led to the core elements and processes of the larger society, no matter where our investigation begins.

Moreover (as I argue in this work), differences in family patterns probably contributed at certain junctures to the development of capitalism in the West, and almost certainly to its development in Japan.

This book is one of several lines of inquiry that I have pursued over the past five years. In my more purely theoretical works—*Struktur Der Familie*, "A Theory of Role Strain," "Role, Status, and Normative Conformity," or "Horizons in Family Theory,"[1]—I have tried to clarify certain conceptual problems and lay foundations for a better understanding of a range of familial relations.

Now and again—as in "The Theoretical Importance of Love," "Illegitimacy in the Caribbean Social Structure," "Illegitimacy, Anomie, and Cultural Penetration," and "Marital Satisfaction and Instability: A Cross-Cultural Analysis of Divorce Rates"[2]—I have attacked specific factual problems, but within a framework of related propositions that had theoretical implications beyond the data themselves.

Both these lines of inquiry are independent of the present study of family change, but both have of course contributed to it; my attempts to solve the problems of the former have guided my search for the dynamics of the latter.

Similarly, this book draws from, but also contributes to, the Propositional Inventory in the Family that my coworkers and I have been preparing for some years. The Inventory is an organization of most of the propositions that have been enunciated in the field of family research. All propositions have been recorded that have a family variable as one term, whether or not the other is a family or a nonfamily variable.

At the present time, I am beginning an inquiry into the relations of family to stratification and mobility systems, a set of problems that branches immediately into the most difficult obscurities of larger social processes.

I must confess that though the implicitly lofty aspirations exhibited in these lines of inquiry have embarrassed me at times, the research itself has been fun. I have enjoyed writing this volume, the last of many drafts that transformed a lecture into a book.

Along with other sociologists who were at one time students at the University of Texas—my classmate C. Wright Mills, Kingsley Davis, Marion J. Levy, and Logan Wilson—I was invited in 1958 to lecture in a series honoring Warner E. Gettys, who was then retiring as chairman of the Sociology Department. That lecture bore the same title as the present work, and contained many of its major themes. Necessarily, it was laconic. To buttress its assertions, I was propelled on a rather lengthy voyage of learning and, I hope, of some discovery. Many of my colleagues and friends helped me, with scepticism, theoretical suggestions, and a command of data with which I was less familiar than they.

Among them is Walter E. Firey, who wondered whether I could prove my assertions about world changes, and Jacques Barzun, who, in his book *The Social Researcher*, had earlier asked, with reference to my *After Divorce*, whether such sociological descriptions could be applied to other times and places. G. William Skinner, whose intimate knowledge of Chinese social relations was invaluable to me, pointed out more than once that what I supposed was a general social pattern was in fact a regional one and very limited. Ezra Vogel often served as a guide in the complexities of the Japanese family. My friends Irene B. Taeuber and G. Watson Barclay answered many questions for me about the demography of Japan and Taiwan.

Among my colleagues in other countries, I wish to thank Takijo Kamiko of Japan, M. S. Gore (technically, one of my doctoral students, but in his own right one of India's mature sociologists), Pravin M. Visaria of Bombay, Jan Lutynski of Poland, Eric Allardt of Finland, Andrée Michel of France, Gerrit Kooiy of Holland, Leila Shukry and Hannah Rizk of Egypt, Johan Galtung of Norway, and Rene König and Gerhardt Baumert of Germany.

Needless to say the succeeding analyses rest to a considerable degree on the published work of statistical bureaus of many countries, but I wish to note also that many have been generous in answering my individual queries. As a part of this inquiry, I circulated a questionnaire in English and Arabic to the statistical offices of Arabic-speaking countries. The bureaus of England and Wales, Holland, Germany, and Austria were especially helpful in answering questions.

As in my other inquiries into the family, I have repeatedly found help in the writings of Kingsley Davis. Other colleagues have clarified my thinking from time to time: Morris Zelditch, Conrad M. Arensberg, Terence K. Hopkins, Immanuel Wallerstein, Sloan Wayland, and Imogen Seger. Naturally, over the past five years I have engaged in correspondence or conferences with many of my fellow sociologists elsewhere in the United States: Wilbert E. Moore, Arnold S. Feldman, Meyer F. Nimkoff, Robert F. Winch, Marion J. Levy, Alex Inkeles, George C. Homans, Reuben Hill, Frank Notestein, and my close friend Melvin M. Tumin.

I am especially grateful to a handful of devoted graduate assistants who have contributed in many ways to the compilation and analysis of the data presented here: Herbert Bynder, John Western, Nicholas Tavuchis, and Cynthia Epstein. The last two have shouldered the greater part of this burden, and Cynthia Epstein contributed further by her severe editorial pencil.

Finally, it must be remembered that even "library research" is expensive. I could not have carried out this investigation without the generous support of the National Institute of Mental Health. Its flexible policy first permitted me some time to work on purely theoretical problems concerning the family; but later it supported a small part-time staff engaged in gathering data for a series of inquiries not directly related to this book. In addition to directly supporting this book, the Institute also granted funds for the Propositional Inventory. I am also indebted to the Russell Sage Foundation, which twice stepped in to offer strong support when our staff had no money. Both times I enjoyed the rare opportunity of returning these grants when alternative funds became available; nevertheless, their expression of confidence strengthened my belief in the value of this work. As in past research, I am grateful to the Bureau of Applied Social Research, and especially to Clara Shapiro, for help in administering whatever finances I was able to obtain. Lastly, I want to express my gratefulness to my wife Ruth, who was so patient throughout the many revisions of this book.

WILLIAM J. GOODE

New York City
April 1963

The author acknowledges with thanks permission to reprint selections from the sources listed below:

The Athlone Press, Raymond Firth (ed.), *Two Studies of Kinship in London*, 1956.

Crown Publishers, Inc., The French Institute of Public Opinion, Lowell Bair (tr.), *Patterns of Sex and Love: A Study of the French Woman and Her Morals*, 1961.

Institut National D'Études Démographiques, Jean Dirac, "Quelques vues sur le travail feminin non agricole en divers pays," *Population*, 13, 1961; Alain Girard, "Une enquête en France sur le choix du conjoint," International Population Union Conference Paper, 16, 1961.

Milbank Memorial Fund and the author, M. A. El-Badry, "Some Aspects of Fertility in Egypt," *Quarterly*, January, 1956.

Princeton University Press, Irene B. Taeuber, *The Population of Japan*, 1958.

The University of Chicago Press, Wendell Bell and Marion D. Boat, "Urban Neighborhoods and Informal Social Relations," *American Journal of Sociology*, January, 1957.

Preface to the
Paperback Edition

ONCE ANY WORK is completed, it begins an independent existence. Its author becomes irrelevant. It is rare that he wishes to warn possible readers from his book. If he cherishes it instead, colleagues will consider him *gauche* to tell others how excellent it is. He cannot run after it in order to plea with its readers to interpret it this way not that, to overlook this blemish and instead admire especially that little insight. He cannot even alter it fundamentally, though in successive editions (in scientific work, even more than in literature, these are unusual: as Shaw remarked, first editions are rare, tenth editions rarer still) he may enlarge or correct it, but its basic pattern of thought is likely to be unchanged.

Since scientific work requires that the writer tell how he reached his conclusions, in order that others can more easily test them, he may in later commentaries describe further his technical procedures. However, in most inquiries into family patterns (as in this one), such a commentary would be largely superfluous since most procedures used are straightforward and self-evident and the data sources obvious if sometimes shaky.

On the other hand, at least part of the intellectual scaffolding—the intellectual or theoretical orientation that guided the investigation—may not be obvious. In the field of the family, reports typically "stick to the facts," and avoid much explicit or even self-conscious theorizing. Doubtless, this style has had an unfortunate effect, since explicitness in theory will usually demand improvements over time. Thus, it may be useful to comment on at least the general theoretical orientation of this monograph. That is, how and why were these ideas and hypotheses generated, this particular book written, of the many possible monographs that might have been devoted to the broad topic of the changes in family and social structure over the past fifty to one hundred years?

The charge is frequently made that sociology contains no theory, and thus a commentary on the theory in this work might seem to appear pointless. In a narrow sense, the charge is true. In sociology there is no core of explicit assumptions and definitions, postulates and operative rules, together with some fundamental descriptions, from which a network of hypotheses can be deduced, in order to test them. However, the notion that "scientific theory" has such a structure is erroneous, though many scientists (including some sociologists) cherish that ideal. Only physics and a few scattered sub-fields in the physical sciences have achieved such a pattern. Chemical theory is less mathematico-deductive than structural. It would be difficult to claim that there is any general biological theory.

If, on the other hand, theory is a structure of linked empirical propositions that express correlations (often in causal language), then there are at least bits and pieces of theory in sociology. In addition, any investigator is guided in his search for relevant facts by some kind of theoretical stance or orientation, even when he may not be able to articulate it clearly. He is also likely to be alerted to new findings by theory fragments from other sub-fields, which he applies to the phenomena he is studying—for example, he may wonder about the likelihood that a high percentage of multi-gene-rational households could ever have existed in a given society, in view of the organizational requirements of such units.

If no rigorous, general theory is asserted here, then of course it cannot be claimed that a theory of social or family change underlies this research. The former must precede the latter. It does contain many empirical regu-larities about change, and thus may be useful to a theorist who does seek general hypotheses of social change, i.e., statements about *determinate se-quences*. However, with reference to this goal we can learn from our col-leagues in other more advanced fields, where such problems play a minor role indeed. Celestial mechanics reached a high development three centuries ago, but theories about the successive physical states of the universe re-mained until recently the realm of the imaginative amateur or as the hobby of a few physical scientists. Chemistry can hardly be said to have such a theory at all. Biology has at most (in ecology, paleobotany, paleozoology, or general evolution) been able to describe some sequences, without being able to demonstrate their determinateness, the causal laws that created them. Only recently has economics, the most sophisticated of the social sciences, begun to tackle this problem, usually defined as the phenomenon of eco-nomic development. We are hardly likely to outpace these forerunners, by simply calling for a theory of social change.

We can, however, look for correlations among variables that might be observable (or might instead fail to appear) over longer periods of time, and such findings should be useful in the building of such a theory. For example, on the basis of sociological theory (backed, happily, by good common sense) we expect to find that the possession of resources generates authority for some members of a kinship unit. Consequently, we also expect that over even great time spans the upper-class family elders will enjoy more authority than will the family elders in the lower social strata. However, we can also become alert to these additional time-linked possibilities:

Even at a distance, elders may retain much authority, if over time they can keep control over new colonial job opportunities;

A colonial conquest will undermine the authority of the family elders who are ruled, but again not if the colonial rulers administer through the existing chiefly system;

Industrialization undermines the family authority of especially lower-class elders or peasant elders, since lower-class or peasant youth can obtain jobs independently of their parents;

But if (as in Japan) the father continues in fact to control access to such jobs, that authority will not diminish much;

And where (as in a primogeniture system) the younger sons cannot obtain much of the family patrimony (and thus fathers cannot threaten to withhold it), they are less likely to follow in the traditional family patterns.

Such correlations, whether altering much or little over time, must be utilized in the construction of a theory of social change, but this monograph has had no such grandiose aspiration.

Since this norm of science is enjoined upon all students, at least as an ideal, it may mean no more than a demand for good evidence. However, a fruitful scepticism is also based on relevant bits of theory, i.e., specifically a set of guesses as to what kinds of family systems of the past are theoretically possible. For example, when a Frenchman at a cocktail party assures us that all French husbands have mistresses, and their wives are not jealous, we have good theoretical reasons for doubt. For theoretical reasons, I do not believe there was ever a time in the history of Rome when fathers punished their sons with death for disobedience; I suspect the Yugoslav *zadruga* was always rare, and that parents in Western countries did not ever typically decide which son would marry which daughter without consultation with them; and I am inclined to believe that descriptions of Heian court family life, as deduced from *The Tale of Genji*, do not make sense. In these statements, I am not peeking at the cards since I do not know what the facts are. For each of them, however, a sociologist could construct a set of fairly defensible propositions about social behavior that would cast doubt on such traditionally accepted views of those family patterns. For others that I have commented on earlier, such as the belief that at some time in the history of the West people typically lived in extended family households, later findings tend to bolster my scepticism.[1] Reasoning from even good theory may lead us astray, but if we look for the relevant facts we can test both our reasoning and our guesses about the facts.

Theorizing about family changes over time is easier, of course, if we enjoy a firm body of data about the past, and in particular if we know how the family pattern operated at some specific point in time: drawing a curve between only two points is dangerous, but not so unwise as drawing a curve from the present to an unknown and possibly legendary family system of the past. The reasons for the gap are both conceptual and historiographic.[2]

Perhaps the most central conceptual problem is the difficulty of obtaining data that permit us to distinguish among real behavior, real ideals, and *ideal* ideals. The difficulty may be expressed as a sceptical stance: If we discover, say, a contemporary description of Chinese family life under the Sung emperors, or a set of rules as to how family members should behave, we should guess that it really applies to upper-class people first of all, and that it is probably made up of ideal ideals, rather than real ideals, and almost certainly is not a description of real behavior. The distinction is important, because value and normative commitment data are fundamental in understanding family patterns. Values do not, of course, determine real behavior fully, but neither can one infer values from behavior alone. How people genuinely feel about such norms is of more importance than what they state publicly as values—consider for example, contemporary sermons, editorials, parental exhortations to children, etc.—but they are not merely epiphenomenal. The fact that people do support ideal ideals—i.e., what people state others should believe—does tell us something about where people in authority will put pressures for conformity.

Thus all of these are of significance, but historiographically we are most likely to be able to obtain ideal ideals, e.g., public exhortations to virtue; less likely to locate factual descriptions of real behavior; and least likely to find out what people really believed. It is indeed only for the past generation, when systematic interviewing has been widely used in research, that we begin to obtain this last type of datum.[3]

The general historiographic problem in measuring family change, especially over several centuries, is that certain types of information are *typically* missing, which may explain why historians have neglected this institution so much. Specifically, or more positively, only a limited set of voices speak to us from the past: the literate, and the upper class. Missing is the testimony of the young, the illiterate, the women, and the lower social strata.

It is not alone that such people might give us dissident *opinions*, informing us (for example) that a young Chinese bride was not only unhappy under the heel of her mother-in-law, but that she thought it morally wrong to be there. We have only recently begun to obtain such documents from children, women, and the lower strata generally. More important, however, would be the simple factual descriptions, as seen from *their* perspectives. A wife and mother in the Puritan household certainly saw different behavior than did her husband. We can garner comments about the lower classes from the writings of upper-class people, but we do not know how the lower social strata (including, especially, servants) saw their own family life—or viewed the family life of their betters!

Missing also is a major *developmental* phase: We often have information about a society of the past when its kinship system was loosening, when its norms were weakening, when extended kin loyalties were being undermined; but the historical page is nearly blank for the period when great kin or family patterns were growing and building up. Periods of decadence, of high literacy, when a society is flourishing economically and politically, generate many records, and we can at least intuitively grasp how such societies might weaken the traditional family patterns; but what factors created those traditions to begin with? The data will, I think, be missing permanently, but without them our theories about social change will be shaky. Clearly, however, without such sources, it is difficult to reconstruct the family patterns of any given time in the past, and thus to sketch how they have changed during the intervening period. Up to this point, among the most hopeful developments is the work of "village reconstitution," begun by the research team associated with Louis Henry and widened further by Peter Laslett and his Cambridge group.[4] Thereby, at least some of the basic demographic and kinship behavior of an entire village can be traced over several generations or even centuries.

However, if we do not assume we already know what the past was, but attempt patiently to accumulate and collate what data the demographers, anthropologists, historians, district commissioners, journal and letter writers, foreign travelers, and early sociologists have recorded for us, we can begin to approximate an analysis of both specific family patterns of given periods and time phases over generations. Such approximations, in turn, will generate further corrections and thus more accurate analyses. Thereby we gain additional knowledge of theoretical importance. For example, we begin to understand social strains better, as we obtain more precise contrasts between ideals and real behavior—e.g., the Chinese divorce in the face of strong disapproval, or the remarriage of non-Brahmin widows in spite of its prohibition.

We also understand better the theoretical importance of values or norms as bases for predicting family change when facilitating conditions arise. Thus, we predict a decreased illegitimacy rate in both the Caribbean and Latin America with increasing prosperity and social integration. If an Indian caste rose in rank over several generations, we would expect that its family behavior would move toward closer conformity with upper-caste ideas. Because the joint family household was the Hindu ideal over several centuries, but only few families could attain it, we would predict that over any given time period of the past there would be a correlation between economic well being and conformity with this aspiration.

A historical perspective has long been lauded, if not utilized, in sociology for somewhat the same reasons that a cross-cultural perspective has been praised. First, it enlarges the range of variation with which our theories must come to terms. A set of hypotheses that can satisfactorily explain contemporary Western, industrial, middle-class urban family life may well seem skimpy when applied to sixteenth century, agricultural, peasant, Japanese family patterns. Moreover, such a wide range of variation stimulates the analyst to more creative intuitions if not grand theories. We learn that some startling family behaviors *have* been possible, since they did exist: the peculiar marriages of the Nayar of the Malabar coast, whose customs are useful to anyone who wishes to cite an exception to almost any theory about the family; the English upper-middle class and upper-class system of sending their young children to "serve" in other families; the immolation of the Hindu widow on the funeral pyre of her husband; the engagement and/or marriage of noble children; the celibacy of warriors among the Zulu; and so on.

A historical perspective of course emphasizes change, lability, or the disharmonies and strains in any system, but it also highlights a goodly number of relationships which are observable over time and in many cultures. For example, although the specific cultural patterns of classes vary among both nations and historical epochs, a goodly number of class differentials are found rather widely. For most epochs and cultures, the upper classes have a lower divorce rate. If there is disapproval of remarriage for widows or divorcees, remarriage is less common than among lower social strata. The age at marriage among nobles is likely to be lower than the average among other strata. The upper-class household is larger. Males are likely to have more authority than males in other strata.

Similarly, although the cultural content of city and countryside varies greatly among nations and epochs, the differences are usually substantial. This theoretical point is important because sociologists often use these differences to locate and emphasize social or family *change*: e.g., if the divorce rate is higher in the city, we can predict that this expresses the changes going on. If the illegitimacy rate is higher in the city (it may well *not* be), or the father's authority is less, we suppose that the differences show the direction of change, i.e., from the "traditional rural" way to the "modern urban" pattern.

However, such assumptions may well be incorrect. The *same* rural-urban differences may indeed have continued for hundreds of years, independently of other long-term changes going on in these cultural traits. There may be no *trend* at all in the changes, but the rural-urban differences continue; or they may trend together, the differences remaining. In the U.S., we suppose that "urban" means modern, a movement away from the traditional, and so it was in our cities. However, many cities of the Eastern countries, though often in the vanguard of change because the royal courts were there, contained traditions of their own, equally old. Modern cities contain the new industrializing forces, but these were often lacking in ancient cities. A comparison of rural-urban differences at one point in time will not, then, necessarily yield the direction of social change, but almost all historical studies will yield some such differences in family patterns.

A historical perspective may uncover these and other "timeless" relationships, but may also disclose what look like "reversions" to older family patterns. That is, family changes do not move only in a simple, direct line from traditional to "modern." Instead, older patterns may drop out or become less important, but later become more widespread. A small example is the modern upper-middle class pattern of supporting children for a few years after marriage. This is not an ideal, and it is not typical, but it is frequent. It is also, as a moment's thought will remind us, a nearly typical *upper*-class pattern, and may even have been fairly common among wealthy English merchant families of the fifteenth and sixteenth centuries. However, for some generations now the middle classes have taken it for granted that young men did not marry until they were able to support their own families.

Perhaps it is only an historical accident, but the trend in Japan is toward some traits of a much older peasant family pattern. During the past century since the Meiji Restoration, Japanese rulers aimed consciously at inculcating an essentially *samurai* family ideal, and succeeded to a remarkable extent. However, the older peasant system permitted a much freer courtship (reminiscent of the eighteenth century Swedish farmer pattern), much sexual freedom before marriage and a high divorce rate.

We cannot know at present whether it is a *reversion*, or a quasi constant, but the Western conjugal family recognizes a wide network of relatives, and certainly did in the past. Was there a period, during the rapid expansion of cities in Western countries, and even more in the United States, when such networks lapsed? Fifty years ago, social analysts did write of the decline of the family, the rootlessness of family life, the decay of family ties in the city—but by now we are suspicious of such rhetoric as being almost a historical constant! It now seems likely that we shall never know what the facts were during this modern period of history. In any event, these networks are apparently to be found in all the industrialized nations, as of course they are in other nations as well, whether they are to be viewed as reversions to older patterns, or merely continuations of an older system.

This monograph has supported a widespread hypothesis that industrialization does undermine large kin systems, and moves family systems generally toward some version of the conjugal system found in Western countries. However, it has also emphasized in depth both the theoretical gaps in that simplistic proposition, "industrialization is the cause of the modern conjugal family system," and its factual discrepancies. The theoretical arguments in favor of some such hypothesis were presented early in this monograph. It is evident, on the other hand, that much of its truth value arises from including almost everything modern in this deceptive variable, industrialization: the development of science, achievement values, hiring and promotion on the basis of merit alone, individualism, urbanization, etc. Since industrialization includes practically everything, it would almost have to be the cause of everything, including the modern conjugal system. Such a truism is hardly fruitful.

Keeping in mind such theoretical weaknesses leads us to uncover interesting empirical paradoxes. For example, if industrialization is so much in harmony with the simple conjugal family, then we would expect the classes most in harmony with industrialization, i.e., those most successful in it, to create such a family pattern. In fact, however, the upper social strata have larger households and larger kin networks; the male heads enjoy more authority, and parents have more control over their children; and so on. Indeed, the benefits the industrial system has yielded to them generate the influence and authority which they can use to maintain an active extended kin network. We are led, then, to see that with substantial resources, a set of relatives can and do help one another, and thus exploit the industrial opportunities very well indeed. Thus, the restricted conjugal system may not be so fully in "harmony" with industrialization as textbook theory would phrase it—except in the same sense the worker without resources is in harmony with the capitalist system.

We are also led to consider the theoretical possibility that the emergence of the new family system—possibly in the fifteenth or sixteenth century, in England—with a greater emphasis on the husband-wife-children unit was itself a facilitating factor for industrialization, rather than the other way around.[5] Whether indeed it appears that early may be questioned, but it is clear that even the Western family systems of seven to nine hundred years ago are very different from those of Eastern countries. It may well be that neolocality (the couple establish an independent household unit upon marriage) is widespread that early, that couples do not depend on their relatives, the male head does not owe allegiance to an elder male, there is individual not family responsibility for crimes, the fertility rate is low, etc. In any event, much of the change toward a family system supposedly harmonious with industrialization may have taken place before the latter appeared.

Moreover, as is noted early in the monograph, it is very likely that *ideas* about industrialization enter a country first and prepare people for changes both familial and economic. After all, except for England (and with some doubt there) most modern countries industrialized late in the nineteenth century, but family changes had taken place in most of them before that time. Family changes are evident in sub-Saharan as well as Arab countries where only the most modest steps toward industrialization have occurred, and the direction is the same one we *would* predict *under the impact of industrialization!*

Aside from these empirical and theoretical paradoxes in that simplistic hypothesis, we should also keep in mind that family systems were changing long before any thought of industrialization, and that the cliché, "Industrialization causes…""—since it *is* partly true—may lead us away from a wide range of variables that would yield a more precise statement of which influences do alter family systems, not only in the contemporary epoch but in others as well.

This study has used and tested theory, but has not been presented as a "contribution to theory"—and in general I believe this is appropriate within any field. I believe that the guidance from a self-conscious theoretical stance was a prime factor in the kindly recognition given to it by my colleagues in this and other countries.[6] In each of the countries dealt with in the monograph, there are scholars who know that family system better than I, but many have expressed surprise that I could have utilized this or that interpretation which was contrary to traditional analyses but (it is to be hoped) nevertheless correct.

Any theoretical stance is crude, and therefore can lead astray unless constantly guided by whatever approximations to hard facts we can locate. To avoid that danger, several great culture areas were omitted, and at least two major theoretical problems. Although I have been keenly interested in Latin America since my undergraduate days (very likely since junior high school), and indeed expended a substantial amount of energy on the collection of Latin American family data, I believe that as yet they are nearly useless for historical, sociological analysis. The records are historically shallow. Social analysts have written books by the hundreds about the Latin American family, but until recently they were not based on field work, interviews, or historical archives. I am sure that the *trends* outlined here for the Western countries also apply to Latin America, but these are recent. Moreover, we have few adequate historical data on a key family phenomenon, the consensual union.[7] On the other hand, social research is progressing rapidly there, and before long it may be possible to achieve such a sociological and historical analysis of family and society in Latin America.

The Slavic gap is equally striking. I omitted that part of the West with still greater reluctance, though with no belief in my general competence in the area. Here again my efforts to penetrate the murk of even fifty years ago were unavailing, in the specific sense that I could not obtain reliable descriptions, adequate census data, believable demographic materials, and so on. Here I gave up the task somewhat guiltily, since I continued to suspect that my simple incompetence prevented me (or my assistants) from finding the relevant data. Since that time, I have been somewhat confirmed in my decision by conversations with Jugoslav and Russian social scientists. Much more telling, however, is the excellent summary article by Cuisenier and Raguin, who remark that I "curiously" omitted Soviet Russia from this monograph.[8] However, again the time depth is lacking, and they are even forced to use a classic work on kinship terminology as a substitute for real observations of past family behavior. *Opinions* about the past are always available, but since we cannot trust them in our own country we could hardly trust them in another.

Missing also is a time analysis of the relationship between family and social mobility. Two millennia ago, Plato had seen that the family is the key stone of the stratification system, and that in order to ensure equal opportunity for all, it was necessary to abolish the family. For him, the difference in quality among men was too obvious to consider abolishing the class system. Since parents of lower quality might produce a potential "gold" child, and golden parents an untalented child, parents could not be allowed to rear their own children and thus frustrate the natural fall or rise of ability. Women should be trained as well as men. Following Plato, many creators of utopias have seen this connection, and dealt with it in various ways.

In real life, neither family nor the stratification is abolished, but both are sets of theoretical *variables*. Although I now believe that even societies with reportedly rigid social barriers, such as Tokugawa, Japan, did exhibit considerable mobility, societies do vary in the amount of both upward and downward movement. And presumably some types of family systems facilitate or retard this movement. Patterns of socialization very likely affect who goes up or down; class differences in socialization may affect what percentage of that class will strive upward or not. Class differential fertility and survival rates are family variables that affect social mobility rates. It would therefore be worthwhile to analyze this nexus over *time*, i.e., the relations among social structures, social mobility, and family systems. However, here again my theoretical interests were frustrated. As soon as we move from the last two decades of research on mobility, in Western nations primarily, into the past, we are once more without any reliable data.[9] Consequently, this theoretically important time link of family variables with the stratification system must remain unanalyzed for yet a while.

Although this study has dealt here and there with changes in socialization and the relations between parents and children, an adequate time analysis seems as yet impossible even for Western countries. Of course, fine-grained family interaction of any kind, e.g., husband-wife relations, is difficult to recapture over any considerable time span. These are the most ephemeral of data, for. such interactions leave few records. One could, however, claim that husband-wife relations are of less importance for society than socialization practices, since the latter may determine the personality dynamics, achievement motivation, and normative commitment of the next generation.

Unfortunately, it is especially in this area that parents' reports about their own actions are to be given at best a modest credence. For reasons that are clear to both sociologists and psychologists, parents typically do not remember as well as children do how frequently parents use physical punishment or loving as socializing techniques. Complaints and exhortations from parents to children sound remarkably similar from one century to the next. There *are* great changes in advice about childrearing. But only the bold would venture to guess what relationship, if any, such statements—made by Jesus, Locke, Rousseau, St. Augustine, Mill, for example—bear to the reality of parent-child interaction at that time. The imaginative effort by Philippe Aries *(Centuries of Childhood)* is an interesting literary exercise, but can hardly be taken seriously as a history of socializing patterns. I am doubtful that we shall be able in the future to establish the relations between social structures and this area of family life over time, but its theoretical importance cannot be doubted.

This is not the place to summarize the work that has been published since this monograph appeared, but it is appropriate to note that the mass of family research now available in many countries make it increasingly possible both to correct this study in details and to extend its compass, both descriptively and theoretically. With reference to the latter, the field of the family has suffered because its intellectual significance seemed minor compared with that, say, of politics or class, and the ablest of the young scholars entering the field have not been attracted to it. Durkheim, it is true, continued to feel that his work on the family would be a crown to his career, but he never completed the manuscript.[10]

Although I have happily studied three great institutions, work, family, and religion, I have always believed that whether the variables we *start* with are prepotent and causal, or instead dependent and caused by others, cannot be of theoretical significance. We begin to make real progress when we locate *any* nontrivial correlations that are firm and, hopefully, timeless. In the physical sciences, in general, it is irrelevant whether a variable should be labeled causal or dependent. Thus, we might fruitfully begin with family variables, as long as we do not remain there, but follow them *wherever they lead*. Obviously, they lead to and through all the major societal forces. Family processes are one set of phenomena where social forces impinge; and they are in turn generative of some impact on the larger society. Our problem is to locate and demonstrate *any* connections among such social forces, whether they arise from family patterns or military force. Although at the present time I am spending much of my time in the analysis of force, money, prestige, and friendship, not only is the family one of the arenas where such processes can be observed, but it is a locus from which such processes move outward into the larger social structure. Consequently, although my future writings will focus (for a few years at least) much more on those processes, I do not falter in my belief in the theoretical significance of the family.

New York City, 1970   WILLIAM J. GOODE

---

[1]For example, Peter Laslett has recently shown that the size and structure of the household in England varied little over the three centuries, from roughly the middle of the sixteenth to that of the nineteenth century: "Size and Structure of the Household in England over Three Centuries," *Population Studies,* 23 (July, 1969), pp. 199-223.

[2]For a more extended analysis of problems in measuring family changes, see my discussion, "The Theory and Measurement of Family Change," in Eleanor B. Sheldon and Wilbert E. Moore (eds.), *Indicators of Social Change,* Russell Sage Foundation, N.Y.: 1968, pp. 295-348.

[3]For example, Southern whites have always believed that Negroes were excessively sexual and had no norm against childbirth out of wedlock, but as far as I know, there were no field interviews on this point until the last decade, in the North or the South. Judith Blake was one of the first to ask such questions in the Caribbean, and most Caribbeanists, who typically *inferred* there was no norm of legitimacy, from the high rates of illegitimacy (i.e., behavior), have not yet accepted the accuracy of her data. See Blake, *Family Structure in Jamaica*, Free Press, N.Y.: 1961, as well as my "Illegitimacy in the Caribbean Social Structure," *American Sociological Review* 25 (Feb., 1960), pp. 21-30. Edith Clarke also took seriously the Jamaican's *own* normative statements and asserts the normative underpinnings of legal marriage: *My Mother Who Fathered Me*, Allen and Unwin, London: 1957. Obviously, without that datum, analysis of *change* is difficult.

[4]For a description of the technique, see M. Fleury and L. Henry, *Des Registres Paroissiaux* a *L'Histoire de la Population: Manuel de Depouillement* et *D'Exploitation de L'Etat Civil Ancien*, Presses Universitaires de France, Paris: 1956; and Laslett in E. A. Wrigley, *An Introduction to English Historical Demography*, Cambridge University Press, Cambridge: 1966, ch. 5.

[5]For a brilliant analysis of new family patterns among the English nobility, see Lawrence Stone, The Crisis of the Aristocracy, 1560-1660, London, Oxford University Press: 1965.

[6]The book was awarded the MacIver Prize by the American Sociological Association in 1965 and was singled out for special mention in the presentation of the Burgess Award to me in 1969.

[7]On this point, see my generally heretical view in "Illegitimacy, Anomie, and Cultural Penetration," *M. Soc. Rev.*, 26 (Dec., 1961), pp. 910-925.

[8]Jean Cuisenier and Catherine Raguin, *Rev. Franc. de Sociol.*, 8 (Oct.-Dec., 1967), pp. 521-557, "De quelques transformations dans le systeme familial russe." Their bibliography is indispensable.

[9]I did, however, make a preliminary analysis of such recent relationships in "Family and Mobility," reprinted now in Reinhard Bendix and Seymour M. Lipset, *Class, Status, and Power*, 2nd ed., The Free Press, New York: 1966, pp. 582-601.

[10]An Analysis of Durkheim's work in this area is being completed by Eugene Weiner.

Contents

❊❊❊❊❊❊❊❊❊❊❊❊❊❊❊❊

III   Changing Family Patterns in Arabic Islam   87

IV   Sub-Saharan Africa   164

V   Changing Family Patterns in India   203

VI   China   270

World Revolution and Family Patterns

✠✠✠✠✠✠✠✠✠✠

chapter

I

World Changes in Family Patterns

❋❋

FOR THE first time in world history a common set of influences—the social forces of industrialization and urbanization—is affecting every known society. Even traditional family systems in such widely separate and diverse societies as Papua, Manus, China, and Yugoslavia are reported to be changing as a result of these forces, although at different rates of speed. The alteration seems to be in the direction of some type of *conjugal* family pattern—that is, toward fewer kinship ties with distant relatives and a greater emphasis on the "nuclear" family unit of couple and children. In the Western Culture Complex—the New World, Australia, New Zealand, and Europe west of the Urals—where a conjugal family system has already been in operation to some extent, the direction of change seems to be toward its wider spread.

If it is true that the rough outlines of a conjugal system are beginning to emerge in such disparate cultures as China and the Arab world, we are witnessing a remarkable phenomenon: The development of similar family behavior and values among much of the world's population. This inquiry will try to ascertain whether, and why, this process is indeed occurring.

Such an investigation raises a host of complex theoretical problems. But important theoretical problems direct any fruitful study of the facts, just as facts in turn serve to sharpen theory. Therefore, an outline of the broad, relevant, theoretical issues should preface our analysis of family changes in six major world cultures.

1. Even if the family systems in diverse areas of the world are moving *toward* similar patterns, they *begin* from very different points, so that the

trend in one family trait may differ from one society to another—for example, the divorce or illegitimacy rate might be dropping in one society but rising in another.

2. The elements within a family system may each be altering at different rates of speed. While some were greatly strained under the traditional system, others were buttressed by many institutional supports; new influences, therefore, encounter more resistance at some points in the family system than at others.

3. Just *how* industrialization or urbanization affects the family system, or how the family system facilitates or hinders these processes, is not clear.

4. It is doubtful that the amount of change in family patterns is a simple function of industrialization; more likely, ideological and value changes, partially independent of industrialization, also have some effect on family action.

5. Some beliefs about how the traditional family system worked may be wrong. Even to measure change over the past half-century requires a knowledge of where these family systems started *from*. We may learn, for example, that although some family patterns are thought to be new, they have in fact always been part of the traditional system—for example, the reported breakup of the Indian joint family. Reports that the joint family system is breaking up have been prevalent for sixty years. It now seems likely that although most Indian families are "joint" at some phase in their life cycle, they also go through a stage of breaking up when the married sons move away to found their own households. Thus, the "breakup" is really one stage in the process of formation and growth of individual families, and has characterized the Indian family system for decades.

6. Correlatively, it is important to distinguish *ideal* family patterns from *real* family behavior and values, and it is especially necessary to differentiate the social habits of upper-class families from those of the majority of the society.

7. Finally, since the aim of research is precision and understanding, it is necessary to examine carefully whatever numbers and counts can be obtained in order to be sure that they are in fact descriptions of reality and not accidents of poor recording procedures. Especially when inquiring into the past, we must question the validity of the data.

Those involved in the process of social change often exaggerate its radical character. If public opinion polls had been taken in every important historical period, they would probably have revealed that the participants thought *all* the old traditions were dissolving, although from our perspective the alterations of each period seem minor. Western people, for example, tend to believe that morals have deteriorated greatly over the past hundred years. However, the illegitimacy rate has actually dropped slightly; and some evidence suggests that the percentage of women who are pregnant when they marry is about the same as it was in the past—although perhaps not so high as it was two centuries ago.

Unfortunately, the data are not yet available for most of the problems with which we are concerned here—a fact to be noted when considering the opinions of social analysts, who tend to assume that changes in economic or industrial systems are the primary cause of alterations in family systems. This relationship has been taken for granted, but has never been scientifically demonstrated.

Social science developed only one comprehensive theory of family change, one based on nineteenth-century evolutionary ideas. (The science has since evolved beyond that theory without developing a substitute.) Intended to explain both the observable differences among the world's family patterns and their history, the theory asserted that in the course of man's development the family had "progressed" from the primitive sexual promiscuity of a semi-animal horde, through group marriage, matriarchy, and patriarchy in some polygynous form, to culminate in the highest spiritual expression of the family, Victorian monogamy.[1] But growing philosophic doubts that the nineteenth-century family and religious systems were indeed the highest levels reached by man began to bring into question the validity of this sweeping theory. In addition, as knowledge about human societies over the world accumulated, the core of the evolutionary theory— that each advance in technology was accompanied by an advance in family patterns and religion—dissolved. No such correlation actually emerged.

E. B. Tylor, who was otherwise so shrewd in his understanding of human societies, formulated the main technique being used in the nineteenth century, the interpretation of certain social patterns, such as "marriage by capture" or the custom of doffing the hat as a greeting, as "social survivals" or *social fossils*.[2] He claimed that just as we can ascertain what *Eohippus* was like from his fossil remains, so can we learn what Stone Age man was like from the survival of some of his social patterns—for example, the relic of marriage by capture appears in some primitive societies in the form of a mock fight between the kin of bride and groom before the bride is carried away. Thus, by looking at Australian aborigines or Polynesians, we can learn about Stone Age man; and the Hawaiian marriage patterns "proved" for a while the former existence of group marriage.

Curiously, the determined anti-evolutionists never attacked this great reconstruction systematically. But the growing use of social research techniques at the end of the nineteenth century added to suspicions about the validity of such reconstructions of man's past. About the turn of the century the evolutionist approach was being labeled irrelevant, foolish, and amateur, and it became itself a "survival" in the writings of *dilettanti* and Communist apologists through the succeeding half-century. It was seen that "primitive" societies like those of the Australian aborigines might have very complex religious and kinship systems, and that modern stone-using societies do not all have the same social systems. Moreover, since all men presumably come from the same evolutionary line and are equally distant historically from Cro-Magnon men, all societies are *equally* old.

Social scientists came to see, then, that contemporary primitive societies were not necessarily "primeval," nor necessarily closer to the social behavior of Neolithic man than to civilized societies. The family patterns of both Neolithic and Paleolithic man are forever lost to us. We cannot reconstruct them either from the behavior of the gorilla or chimpanzee (about which almost no valid information was available, in any event, at the turn of the century), or from the technologically least advanced societies still in existence.

Technological systems may be ranked as more or less advanced, and, with somewhat greater theoretical difficulty, so may economic systems; but no specific family forms seem to be correlated with the specific "stages" of the economic and technological evolution. For example, the Eskimo types of kinship and that of the United States are very similar.[3] Both religious and family systems seem to vary independently of economic and technological systems.[4] This statement does not imply that family systems have not gone through any evolutionary sequence—that is, some determinate series of changes—or even that there is no set of determinate relations among family and economic or technological variables. At the present time, however, no such set of determinate sequences or relations has been *demonstrated* —although they are often assumed to be well known.

Marx did not aim at a comprehensive theory of family social change; but in explaining the origins of industrial England at mid-nineteenth century he took the trouble to analyze the effects of the machine upon the working class family in a society that accepted rational calculation as the basis for economic decisions.

As Marx pointed out, the essence of the machine is not that it is driven by nonhuman power, but that it can perform the work of the human hand, and can thus be multiplied or speeded up. Consequently, women, children, or unskilled men could be used in the labor force, causing the wages of skilled men to drop to the level of those paid to women or children. Furthermore, since *all* could now work, the wage level could be reduced to the point where a composite family income was needed to produce the wages formerly earned by one male household head. Consequently, either everyone worked or all starved. A manufacturer could pay higher wages only at the risk of being driven out of business by his less scrupulous, but more rational, competitors.

Women were forced into factories and thus separated from their children and households. The results were inevitable: infant and child mortality rates rose, the working day lengthened, children were kept out of school, young girls did not learn the necessary domestic arts, and fathers sold their children's labor on harsh terms.[5] Thus, a century ago, did Marx document industrialization's destructive effect on the lower-class family, using the numerous research reports of his time. In fact, however, the processes were much more complex, as Smelser has indicated. In the earlier phases of the factory system, men were able to supervise their own children and thus maintain their authority as household heads.[6]

But though Marx was able to show a few effects of the factory system on the family, his analysis was limited by his political commitment. One could not have predicted from Marxian theory all the changes in the family that have occurred since his time in both industrial and nonindustrial cultures. Certainly, he failed to prove that particular forms of the family emerge when certain economic or technological stages are reached in the history of a given society.

William F. Ogburn also gave major attention to the process of social change, emphasizing technology's impact on the family. Although he is prominently identified with one version of Marxian theory—that the prime mover is technology ("material culture") and that after a period of time ("culture lag") the nonmaterial elements of culture adjust to it—his analyses are actually eclectic, recognizing a wide range of innovations as sources of family change: ideologies, birth control, urbanism, steam engines, airplanes, etc.[7] Ogburn not only pointed out the probable effects of a given invention or social innovation on the family but also traced specific family changes— the increasing divorce rate, for example—to its various probable causes. According to his analysis, with economic production as well as education, religious training, and protection being taken away from the home, the family in the United States was "losing its functions." This opinion has been widely accepted by family analysts, although its precise meaning is unclear and, for the most part, simply incorrect. Ogburn's contribution was not theoretical, and in any event, our aim here is not to criticize large-scale theories of family change, which could only be premature. Ogburn was particularly effective in aggregating masses of empirical data, or in using his mastery of research techniques to test easy assumptions about some detail of behavior. For example, he shows that although the average United States household dropped from about 5.5 persons in 1850 to 3.5 in 1950, the large household made up of many persons was not typical even a century ago.[8]

Similarly, he was able to ferret out data to show that the "labor-saving devices" in the United States home seem to have saved no labor at all, since housewives who owned them continued to work as many hours per week as those who did not.[9] In his mature work, he no longer held that the machine was a primary factor in altering society, but rather that society was made up of intricately interwoven elements so that almost any part could be linked causally with any other.

Such technically careful summations of fact, however, constitute neither a theory of family change nor even a charting of the effects of industrialization on the family. Ogburn's later expositions are guided not so much by a theory as by a general orientation—that to understand family change it was most fruitful to examine the nexus between a specific technological innovation and its several possible effects on family relations (as evaluated by commonsense expectations). This examination proceeded under the assumption that the acceptance of an innovation was to be taken for granted on grounds of rationality. That the responses of different cultures to such innovations would vary did not constitute an inquiry of research for Ogburn. He saw the upward march of technology as both inevitable and theoretically unproblematic.

This has been a brief summary assault upon the attempts to show a simple correlation between economic or technological development and particular stages or forms of family systems. As against this necessary skepticism, one crude observation derived from modern events seems accurate enough: Wherever the economic system expands through industrialization, family patterns change. Extended kinship ties weaken, lineage patterns dissolve, and a trend toward some form of the conjugal system generally begins to appear—that is, the nuclear family becomes a more independent kinship unit. Modern commentators have reported this process from many parts of the world, some interpreting it as one aspect of the "Americanization" of Europe, or even of the world.

1. Idealization of the Recent Past: The United States

In order to weigh the extent and type of changes now taking place in family systems in various parts of the world, it is necessary to examine the recent past; otherwise no trends can be seen. We then usually discover only idealized or stereotyped descriptions of family systems of a generation ago. We must correct such stereotypes in order to measure present-day trends.

In another context, I labeled this stereotype of the United States family of the past, when *praised*, "the classical family of Western nostalgia."[10] It is a pretty picture of life down on grandma's farm. There are lots of happy children, and many kinfolk live together in a large rambling house. Everyone works hard. Most of the food to be eaten during the winter is grown, preserved, and stored on the farm. The family members repair their own equipment, and in general the household is economically self-sufficient. The family has many functions; it is the source of economic stability and religious, educational, and vocational training. Father is stern and reserved, and has the final decision in all important matters. Life is difficult, but harmonious because everyone knows his task and carries it out. All boys and girls marry, and marry young. Young people, especially the girls, are likely to be virginal at marriage and faithful afterward. Though the parents do not arrange their children's marriages, the elders do have the right to reject a suitor and have a strong hand in the final decision. After marriage, the couple lives harmoniously, either near the boy's parents or with them, for the couple is slated to inherit the farm. No one divorces.

Those who believe we are seeing progress rather than retrogression often accept the same stereotype but describe the past in words of different emotional effect. We have progressed, they say, from the arbitrary power of elders toward personal freedom for the young, from cold marriages based on economic arrangements to unions based on the youngsters' right of choice, from rigidly maintained class barriers between children to an open class system, from the subjugation of the wife to equalitarianism and companionship in marriage, and from the repression of children's emotions to permissiveness.

Like most stereotypes, that of the classical family of Western nostalgia leads us astray. When we penetrate the confusing mists of recent history we find few examples of this "classical" family. Grandma's farm was not economically self-sufficient. Few families stayed together as large aggregations of kinfolk. Most houses were small, not large. We now *see* more large old houses than small ones; they survived longer because they were likely to have been better constructed. The one-room cabins rotted away. True enough, divorce was rare, but we have no evidence that families were generally happy. Indeed, we find, as in so many other pictures of the glowing past, that in each past generation people write of a period *still* more remote, *their* grandparents' generation, when things really were much better.

If, then, the stereotype of the United States and Western family is partially incorrect, we may suppose stereotypes of other past family systems to be similarly in error. We shall, therefore, describe current changes in family patterns while ascertaining, where possible, what the patterns of the recent past were.

2. The Conjugal Family as an Ideal Type

As now used by family analysts, the term "conjugal family" is technically an *ideal type;* it also represents an ideal.[11] The concept was not developed from a summary or from the empirical study of actual United States urban family behavior; it is a *theoretical* construction, derived from intuition and observation, in which several crucial variables have been combined to form a hypothetical structural harmony. Such a conceptual structure may be used as a measure and model in examining real time trends or contemporary patterns. In the ensuing discussion, we shall try to separate the fundamental from the more derivative variables in this construction.

As a concept, the conjugal family is also an *ideal* in that when analysts refer to its spread they mean that an increasing number of people view some of its characteristics as *proper* and legitimate, no matter how reality may run counter to the ideal. Thus, although parents in the United States agree that they *should* not play an important role in their children's choice of spouse, they actually do. Relatives *should* not interfere in each other's family affairs, but in a large (if unknown) percentage of cases they do. Since, however, this ideal aspect of the conjugal family is also part of the total reality, significant for changes in family patterns, we shall comment on it later as an ideology.

The most important characteristic of the ideal typical construction of the conjugal family is the relative exclusion of a wide range of affinal and blood relatives from its everyday affairs: There is no great extension of the kin network.[12] Many other traits may be derived theoretically from this one variable. Thus, the couple cannot count on a large number of kinfolk for help, just as these kin cannot call upon the couple for services. Neither couple nor kinfolk have many *rights* with respect to the other, and so the reciprocal *obligations* are few. In turn, by an obvious sociological principle, the couple has few moral controls over their extended kin, and these have few controls over the couple.

The locality of the couple's household will no longer be greatly determined by their kin since kinship ties are weak. The couple will have a "neolocal" residence, i.e., they will establish a new household when they marry. This is turn reinforces their relative independence, because it lowers the frequency of social interaction with their kin.

The choice of mate is freer than in other systems, because the bases upon which marriage is built are different: The kin have no strong rights or financial interest in the matter. Adjustment is primarily between husband and wife, not between the incoming spouse and his or her in-law group. The courtship system is therefore ideally based, and, at the final decision stage, empirically as well, on the mutual attraction between the two youngsters.

All courtship systems are market or exchange systems. They differ from one another with respect to *who* does the buying and selling, which characteristics are more or less valuable in that market, and how open or explicit the bargaining is. In a conjugal family system mutual attraction in both courtship and marriage acquires a higher value. Nevertheless, the elders do not entirely lose control. Youngsters are likely to marry only those with whom they fall in love, and they fall in love only with the people they meet. Thus, the focus of parental controls is on who is allowed to meet whom at parties, in the school and neighborhood, and so on.[13]

When such a system begins to emerge in a society, the age at marriage is likely to change because the goals of marriage change, but whether it will rise or fall cannot be predicted from the characteristics mentioned so far. In a conjugal system, the youngsters must now be old enough to take care of themselves; i.e., they must be as old as the economic system forces them to be in order to be independent at marriage. (Alternative solutions also arise: Some middle-class youngsters may marry upon the promise of support from their parents, while they complete their education.)[14] Thus, if the economic system changes its base, e.g., from agriculture to industry, the age at marriage may change. The couple decides the number of children they will have on the basis of their own needs, not those of a large kin group, and contraception, abortion, or infanticide may be used to control this number. Whether fertility will be high or low cannot, however, be deduced from these conjugal traits. Under some economic systems—for example, frontier agriculture—the couple may actually need a large number of children.

This system is bilineal or, to use Max Gluckman's term, multilineal: The two kin lines are of nearly equal importance, because neither has great weight. Neolocality and the relative freedom from control by an extended kin network prevent the maintenance or formation of a powerful lineage system, which is necessary if one line is to be dominant over the other.[15]

Since the larger kin group can no longer be counted on for emotional sustenance, and since the marriage is based on mutual attraction, the small marital unit is the main place where the emotional input-output balance of the individual husband and wife is maintained, where their psychic wounds can be salved or healed. At least there is no other place where they can go. Thus, the emotions within this unit are likely to be intense, and the relationship between husband and wife may well be intrinsically unstable, depending as it does on affection. Consequently, the divorce rate is likely to be high. Remarriage is likely because there is no larger kin unit to absorb the children and no unit to prevent the spouses from re-entering the free marriage market.

Finally, the couple and children do recognize some extended kin, but the husband recognizes a somewhat different set of kindred than does his wife, since they began in different families. And the children view as important a somewhat different set of kindred than do their parents: the parents look back a generation greater in depth than do the children, and perhaps a greater distance outward because they have had an adult lifetime in which to come to know more kin. That is, each individual takes into account a somewhat different set of kindred, though most of them are the same for all within the same nuclear unit.

The foregoing sketch is an ideal typical construction and thus must be compared with the reality of both behavior *and* ideal in those societies which are thought to have conjugal family patterns. To my knowledge, no such test has been made. Very likely, the *ideals* of a large proportion of United States families fit this construction very well. Some parts of the construction also fit the *behavior* of a considerable, but unknown, fraction of United States families—e.g., the emphasis on emotionality within the family, the free choice of spouse, and neolocality, bilineality, and instability of the individual family. On the other hand, data from both England and the United States indicate that even in lower-class urban families, where the extension of kin ties might be thought to be shorter (following the ideal type), many kin ties are active. We shall examine this in later chapters. No one has measured the intensity and extensiveness of kin ties in a range of societies in order to ascertain how Western family patterns compare in these respects. It is quite possible that those countries thought to be closest to the conjugal pattern do in fact have a less extended kin network.

Nevertheless, the ideal type conflicts sharply with reality *and* theory in one important respect. Theoretical considerations suggest that, without the application of political pressure, the family *cannot* be as limited in its kin network as the ideal typical construction suggests. Both common observation and theory coincide to suggest that: (1) grandparent-grandchild ties are still relatively intense and (2) emotional ties among siblings are also strong. Consequently (3), parents-in-law interact relatively frequently with their children-in-law,[16] and (4) married people have frequent contacts with their brothers- or sisters-in-law. It follows, then, that (5) children maintain contacts, at least during their earlier years, with their uncles and aunts, as well as with their first cousins. Without question, of all types of "visiting" and "social occasions," the most common, even in the urban United States, is "visiting with relatives."

If no active ties are maintained with the categories of kin mentioned above, the family feels that some explanation is called for, and pleads some excuse ("They live too far away," or "We've never got along well").

In addition, perhaps most families have *some* tie with one or more relatives still further away in the kin network. Those noted above seem to be linked to the nuclear family in an inescapable way; it is difficult to ignore or reject any of them without simultaneously rejecting a fellow member of *one's own* nuclear family. The child can not ignore his uncle without hurting one of his own parents, and reciprocally. A girl may not neglect her sister-in-law without impairing her relationship with her brother. Of course, brother and sister may combine against their own spouses, and social interaction may continue even under an impaired relationship. Cousins are dragged along by their parents, who are siblings and siblings-in-law to one another. The extension of the family network to this point, then, seems determined by the emotional ties within the nuclear family unit itself. To reduce the unit to the nuclear family would require coercive restriction of these ties between siblings or between parents, as the Chinese commune has attempted to do.

3. The "Fit" Between the Conjugal Family and the Modern Industrial System

The argument as to whether political and economic variables, or the reverse, generally determine family patterns seems theoretically empty. Rather, we must establish any determinate relations (whichever direction the causal effect) among any particular family variables and the variables of other institutional orders—not a simple task. Even the relation between the conjugal family and industrialization is not yet entirely clear. The common hypothesis—that the conjugal form of the family emerges when a culture is invaded by industrialization and urbanization—is an undeveloped observation which neglects three issues: (1) the theoretical harmony or "fit" between this ideal typical form of the family and industrialization; (2) the empirical harmony or fit between industrialization and any actual system; and (3) the effects upon the family of the modern (or recently past) organizational and industrial system, i.e., how the factors in the system influence the family.

At present, only the first of these can be treated adequately. The second has been dealt with primarily by researchers who have analyzed a peasant or primitive culture with reference to the problem of labor supply, and who suggest that family systems *other* than the conjugal one do not adequately answer the demands of an expanding industrial system. Malinowski asserted, for example, that although young Trobriander men could earn more by working on plantations than by growing yams, they preferred to grow yams because this activity was defined as required for their family roles. Similarly, a head tax was necessary to force young men to leave their families to work in the South African mines.[17] Men's objections to women leaving the home for outside jobs have limited the labor supply in various parts of the world, especially in Islamic areas. On the other hand, within conjugal or quasi conjugal systems such as those in the West, the strains between family patterns and industrial requirements have only rarely been charted empirically.[18]

This last task would require far more ingenious research designs than have been so far utilized. It requires that the exact points of impact between family and industrial organization be located and the degree of impact measured. Succeeding chapters will devote some attention to this problem. Specific decisions or choices need to be analyzed, in which both family and industrial variables are involved.

Nevertheless, if we are to achieve a better understanding of world changes in family systems, it may help if we can correct the theoretical analyses of the first problem, the fit between the ideal typical form of the conjugal family and industrialization. It seems possible to do this through some reference to common observations about both United States and European family patterns.

Let us consider first the demands of industrialization, which is the crucial element in the complex types of change now occurring in even remote parts of the world. Although bureaucratization may occur without industrialization (witness China), and so may urbanization (for example, Dahomey, Tokugawa Japan), neither occurs without some rise in a society's technological level, and certainly the modern system of industry never occurs without *both* urbanization and bureaucratization.

The prime social characteristic of modern industrial enterprise is that the individual is ideally given a job on the basis of his ability to fulfill its demands, and that this achievement is evaluated universalistically; the same standards apply *to all who hold the same job*. His link with the job is functionally specific; in other words, the enterprise cannot require behavior of him which is not relevant to getting the job done.

Being achievement-based, an industrial society is necessarily open-class, requiring both geographical and social mobility. Men must be permitted to rise or fall depending on their performance. Moreover, in the industrial system, jobs based on ownership and exploitation of land (and thus on inheritance) become numerically less significant, again permitting considerable geographical mobility so that individuals are free to move about in the labor market. The neolocality of the conjugal system correspondingly frees the individual from ties to the specific geographical location where his parental family lives.

The conjugal family's relationship to class mobility is rather complex. Current formulations, based on ancient wisdom, assert that by limiting the extensiveness of the kin network, the individual is less hampered by his family in rising upward in the job structure. Presumably, this means that he owes less to his kin and so can allocate his resources of money and time solely to further his career; perhaps he may also more freely change his style of life, his mode of dress and speech, in order to adjust to a new class position without criticism from his kin. On the other hand, an industrial system pays less attention to what the individual does off the job, so that family and job are structurally somewhat more separated than in other systems. Consequently, one might reason that differential social or occupational mobility (as among siblings or cousins) would not affect kin ties. Yet the emotional ties within the conjugal system are intense, compared to other systems, so that even though there are fewer relatives, the weight of kin relationships to be carried upward by the mobile individual might be equivalent to that in a system with more, but less intense, ties.[19]

An alternative view must also be considered. Under some circumstances the kin network actually contributes greatly to the individual's mobility, and "social capillarity" as a process (that is, that individual rises highest who is burdened with least kin) moves fewer people upward than does a well-integrated kin network.[20] A brief theoretical sketch of this alternative view also throws light on the supposed "adjustment" between the needs of the small conjugal family and those of a modern industrial system.

First, in the modern industrial system, the middle and upper strata are by definition more "successful" in the obvious sense that they own it, dominate it, occupy its highest positions, and direct its future. One must concede that they are "well adjusted" to the modern industrial society. Paradoxically, their kin pattern is in fact *less* close to the ideal typical form of the conjugal family than is the family behavior of the lower strata. The upper strata recognize the widest extension of kin, maintain most control over the courtship and marriage choices of their young, and are most likely to give and receive help from one another.

Consequently, the lower strata's freedom from kin is like their "freedom" to sell their labor in an open market. They are less encumbered by the weight of kin when they are able to move upward, but they also get less help from their kin. Like English peasants, who from the sixteenth to eighteenth centuries were gradually "freed" from the land by the enclosure movement, or nineteenth-century workers, who were "freed" from their tools by the development of machinery, the lower strata have fewer family ties, less family stability, and enjoy less family-based economic and material security. The lower-class family pattern is indeed most "integrated" with the industrial system but mainly in the sense that the individual is forced to enter its labor market with far less family support—his family *does not prevent industry from using him for its own goals*. He may move where the system needs him, hopefully where his best opportunity lies, but he *must* also fit the demands of the system, since no extended kin network will interest itself greatly in his fate. The job demands of the industrial system move the individual about, making it difficult for him to keep his kin ties active; and because his kin are also in the lower strata he has little to lose by relinquishing those ties. In short, lower-strata families are most likely to be "conjugal" and to serve the needs of the industrial system; this system may not, however, serve the needs of that family pattern. This means that when industrialization begins, it is the lower-class family that loses least by participating in it and that lower-class family patterns are the first to change in the society.

We might speculatively infer further that *now*, a century after the first great impact of industrialization on the lower-class family in the Western urban world, family patterns of Western middle and upper classes may be changing more rapidly than those of the lower. (Whether rural changes may not be occurring equally rapidly cannot be deduced from these inferences.) However, although this inference may be empirically correct, the available data demand a more cautious inference: Whether or not the middle and upper strata *are* now changing more rapidly in the Western world, they *do* have more resources with which to resist certain of the industrial system's undermining pressures (e.g., capital with which to support their youngsters through a long professional training) and a considerable interest in resisting them because their existing kin network is more active and useful. We would suppose, then, that in an industrializing process both the peasants and primitives are forced to adjust their family patterns to the demands of industrial enterprise more swiftly, and see less to lose in the adjustment. By contrast, the middle and upper strata are better able to utilize the new opportunities of industrialization by relinquishing their kin ties more slowly, so that these changes will occur only in a later phase of industrialization, such as the United States is now undergoing.

Continuing now with our analysis of the "fit" of the conjugal family to industrial needs; the more limited conjugal kin network opens mobility channels somewhat by limiting the "closure" of class strata. In general, rigid class boundaries can be maintained partly by the integration of kin bonds against the "outsider" through family controls. When the network of each family is smaller, the families of an upper stratum are less integrated, the web of kin less tightly woven, and entrance into the stratum easier. Since the industrial system requires relatively free mobility, this characteristic of the conjugal pattern fits the needs of that system. This general principle also holds for classical China, where an empirically different system prevailed. A successful family would normally expand over generations, but thereby have insufficient resources to maintain so many at a high social rank. That is, the reciprocal exchanges necessary for tightness and closure of the kin system could be kept up only by a few individual families in the total network. If all the families in the network shared alike as kinsmen (which did not happen), the entire network would lose social rank. If the few well-to-do families helped their kin only minimally, and maintained ties with other upper stratum families, the integration of the stratum was kept intact and the stratification system was not threatened.

The modern technological system is psychologically burdensome on the individual because it demands an unremitting discipline. To the extent that evaluation is based on achievement and universalism, the individual gets little emotional security from his work. Some individuals, of course, obtain considerable pleasure from it, and every study of job satisfaction shows that in positions offering higher prestige and salaries a higher proportion of people are satisfied with their work and would choose that job if they had to do it again. Lower level jobs give little pleasure to most people. However, in higher level professional, managerial, and creative positions the standards of performance are not only high but are often without clearly stated limits. The individual is under considerable pressure to perform better than he is able.

The conjugal family again integrates with such a system by its emphasis on emotionality, especially in the relationship of husband and wife. It has the task of restoring the input-output emotional balance of individualism in such a job structure. This is so even for lower strata jobs where the demands for performance are kept within limits by an understood quota but where, by contrast with upper strata jobs, there is less intrinsic job satisfaction. Of course, the family cannot fully succeed in this task, but at least the technological system has no moral responsibility for it and can generally ignore the problem in its work demands.

Bilateral in pattern, this family system does not maintain a lineage. It does not concentrate family land or wealth in the hands of one son through whom the property would descend, or even in the hands of one sex. Dispersal of inheritance keeps the class system fluid. Daughters as well as sons will share as heirs, and a common legal change in the West is toward equal inheritance by all children (as is already the situation generally in the United States). Relatively equal advantages are given to all the sons, and although even United States families do not invest so heavily in daughters as in sons (more boys than girls complete college), the differences in training the two sexes are much less than in other family systems. Consequently, a greater proportion of all children are given the opportunity to develop their talents to fit the manifold opportunities of a complex technological and bureaucratic structure.

The conjugal system also specifies the status obligations of each member in much less *detail* than does an extended family system, in which entrepreneurial, leadership, or production tasks are assigned by family position. Consequently, wider individual variations in family role performance are permitted, to enable members to fit the range of possible demands by the industrial system as well as by other members of the family.

Since the young adult is ideally expected to make his own choice of spouse and the young couple is expected to be economically independent, the conjugal system by extending the adolescent phase of development, permits a long period of tutelage. For example, it is expected that the individual should be grown up before marrying. Note, however, that it is not the family itself that gives this extended tutelage, but public, impersonal agencies, such as schools, military units, and corporations, which ideally ignore family origin and measure the individual by his achievement and talent. This pattern permits the individual to obtain a longer period of training, to make a freer choice of his career, and to avoid the economic encumbrance of marriage until he has fitted himself into the industrial system. Thus, the needs of the industrial system are once more served by the conjugal family pattern.

The *different* adjustment of families in *different* classes to the industrial system emphasizes the *independence* of the two sets of variables, the familial and the industrial, as well as the presence of some "disharmonies" between the two. Further points where the two do not adjust fully may be noted here. The modern woman is given little relief from child care, which is typically handed over to one person, the wife, rather than to several women, some of them elders, who are part of the family unit in more extended systems. Adjustments in modes of child care, which seem to accompany industrialization, are in part a result of the decline of a family tradition handed down from older women to the younger. With the weakening of ties with the older generation younger women depend increasingly on the published opinions of experts as a guide for child-rearing practices.

Even the substantial development of labor-saving devices and technology has not lightened labor in the modern United States home, contrary to both advertising in women's magazines and the stereotyped notions of Europeans. Most of these devices merely raise the standards for cleanliness and repairs, and allow the housewife to turn out more "domestic production" each day. Every study of the time allocation of mothers shows that housewives work extremely long hours.[21] For those who have assumed otherwise, let me remind them that the washing machine brings back into the home a job that an earlier generation delegated to lower-class labor or the laundry; that the vacuum cleaner merely raises standards without substantially speeding up work; that the electric sewing machine is exactly analogous to the washing machine. On the other hand, the organized activities of children have become so complex, and the number of objects in the house so numerous, that even the middle-class housewife must spend much of her time in essentially administrative activities when she is not laboring with her hands. Marx, commenting on John Stuart Mill's doubt that mechanical inventions had lightened man's toil, asserted that lightened toil was not the *aim* of the capitalist use (for the modern scene, read "industrial use") of machinery.[22] While one might quarrel with Marx's concept of *deliberate* aim, it remains true that it is difficult to release even well-trained women from their household tasks, and especially from their emotional tasks; there is no one to substitute for that labor, unless new agencies such as communal nurseries are created. In addition, since the amount of work is great and there is presumptive equality of husband and wife, the husband generally has to step in to help after work, which in turn diverts some of his energy from his occupation.

Ignoring the question of feasibility of additional time, it also remains true that for women, the roles of wife and mother are their central obligations. For this reason, and because there is no one else who can be given the care of house and children, over the past half-century in the United States, women have not become much more "careerminded" than they were, and polling evidence suggests that a similar conclusion may be applied to Europe.[23] Even though an increasing percentage of women in the United States are in the labor force, as in some countries of Europe, there has been over the past few decades (in the United States) only a very slight increase in the proportion of mothers of small children who are in the labor force, and these are predominantly in the lower income groups, where the economic pressure to work is great. Much of the recent great increase in female participation in the United States labor force has been concentrated in the older age groups. Toward the higher economic strata generally, a lower proportion of women work.

Unlike men, women do not as yet think of job-holding as a *career*, as a necessary and intrinsic part of their destiny. From 1910 to 1950 in the United States, while the conjugal family was spreading beyond the city, the proportion of women in the established professions did not change greatly. The number of women physicians increased from 6 per cent to 6.1 per cent. In dentistry, the proportion decreased slightly. In law, engineering, architecture, and the ministry, the increase was substantial, but in none did the proportion rise above 4.1 per cent. In college teaching there was a slight increase, so that women constituted 23.2 per cent of the total in 1958, as compared with 19.8 per cent in 1899–1900.[24] The proportion of college-educated women who have gone into the established professions has dropped during the past half-century, although of course the percentage of women has increased substantially within a range of technical or semi-professional jobs in the natural sciences. Clearly, the "needs" of industrialization are not in easy adjustment with the role obligations of women.

Although the preceding and following sections do show that in spite of some disharmonies the conjugal family fits the needs of industrialization and urbanization relatively well, we cannot thereby assume that we have located precisely the factors in industrialization or urbanization that "cause" the conjugal family to arise (if, indeed, they are its origin). Of central importance to this hypothesis is the need for placing individuals in their jobs on the basis of individual merit rather than family position, so that the family gives way before industrializing forces. However, we should not accept *this* relationship as proved, and perhaps it would be useful at this point to present material which cannot yet be fitted into any simple relationship of adjustment.

Doubtless the past thousand years have seen several periods of relatively high class mobility in the Western world, but certainly one of the more striking occurred in Europe during the twelfth and thirteenth centuries. This was an era of marked economic expansion, much building construction, and the founding of hundreds of convents, churches, and monasteries. The proper basis for job placement was merit in administration, organization, and learning, and many men of modest social position rose high. Then, as in perhaps all epochs, a large proportion of the upper clerical jobs doubtless went to members of the privileged classes, but the great expansion of economic opportunities inevitably allowed considerable class mobility. We have no evidence, however, that there were any remarkable changes in the family system during this period and unquestionably there was no substantial move toward a conjugal family system.

At this point I risk offering an important hypothesis which will guide later analyses, although admittedly the hypothesis lacks adequate proof. The lower strata in *most* societies live in small households; one should not, then, expect family systems closer to the conjugal type to change much in a period of economic expansion. However, most crucial to the question of the impact of merit systems or economic expansion on the family is: *Who controls the new jobs?* If, as usually happens, it is the upper-strata elders who create conditions, institutions, as well as the new opportunities (colonial administration, war, nunneries, monasteries), then they can continue to control their young, and the latter will find it to their interest to conform to old family tradition and obligations. This was so for the European expansion of the twelfth and thirteenth centuries.

Whether the percentage of the population that *can* move into new jobs is equally important, we are not certain. It seems likely that if the European expansion created only few jobs in total, so that only few people could ever obtain jobs on their own merit and independently of their families, then its impact on the family system would have been little.

The same hypothesis can probably be applied to Chinese class mobility, on which data are much more reliable than for the high Middle Ages of

Europe. Each past Chinese dynasty has written the biographies of the men in the preceding dynasty, and though these biographies are formalized, they do contain sufficient information to permit at least rough guesses about the amount of mobility in various dynasties from the T'ang on. Each of these studies has shown that a large proportion (from one third to three quarters) of the men of considerable position in any one generation were "new men"; that is, they did not come from an upper-class background. Using biographies from local districts, Hsu found that only about one fifth of the men had three generations of higher-class positions behind them.[25] Mobility in the Ch'ing Dynasty, however, may not have been as great as that of the twentieth century in the United States, because the relatively high rate of turnover may have existed only in the top stratum. We lack information on the society's *general* mobility, *outside* these highest levels of mandarin life.

In any event, there was much mobility in and out of that stratum, and it was based on military or literary achievement. At the same time, positions were thought to be properly given only to people with whom one was linked by kinship ties. A man could not rise easily without taking many of his kin upward with him, and he could not obtain the necessary education to move upward without their help. Thus, although "new men" obtained opportunities and got jobs on merit, at many points in the intertwining of economic structure and family the family elders directly or indirectly *controlled* the new opportunity. Consequently there is no evidence, during this long period when high occupational position was somewhat, if not mainly, based on merit, that any movement toward a conjugal family system appeared.

Nevertheless, a fuller examination of these and other examples of high mobility based on merit may help us understand better which factors in industrialization help create a conjugal family system.

INDUSTRY, IDEOLOGY, AND FAMILY

The seeming "fit" between certain industrial demands and the structure of roles in the conjugal family in the West should not be permitted to obscure either the importance of ideological factors or the independent influence of the family on the industrializing process.

No adequately precise theory has yet shown *which* influences and processes the industrializing elements in modern societies (perhaps transmuted into political and economic factors) *now* influence family structures. Nor do we know yet through which processes the apparent fit took place in the *past*. Neither contemporary nor historical processes have been sufficiently identified, and they may be very different. Even the common assertion that many countries are now becoming "Westernized" may obscure our view of these processes by leading us to believe the countries are changing only under the impact of Western influence, whereas often the most important pressure is nationalist and indigenous.

One important source of change is the *ideology* of "economic progress" and technological development, as well as the ideology of the conjugal family, and spokesmen for both appear in non-Western countries before any great changes are observable either in industrial or family areas of life.

Elders may deplore both ideologies, but both appeal to the intellectuals, often trained in Western schools, and to the young, to women, and generally, to the disadvantaged. The ideology of the conjugal family is a radical one, destructive of the older traditions in almost every society. It grows from a set of more general radical principles which also arouse these groups *politically* in perhaps every underdeveloped country. Its appeal is almost as universal as that of "redistribution of the land." It asserts the equality of individuals, as against class, caste, or sex barriers.

The ideology of the conjugal family proclaims the right of the individual to choose his or her own spouse, place to live, and even which kin obligations to accept, as against the acceptance of others' decisions. It asserts the worth of the *individual* as against the inherited elements of wealth or ethnic group. The *individual* is to be evaluated, not his lineage. A strong theme of "democracy" runs through this ideology. It encourages love, which in every major civilization has been given a prominent place in fantasy, poetry, art, and legend as a wonderful, perhaps even exalted, experience, even when its reality was guarded against.[26] Finally, it asserts that if one's family life is unpleasant, one has the right to change it.

Obviously, no actual conjugal family system genuinely lives up to these principles, but they express family values which, at some levels of consciousness and in many strata, arouse people the world over, just as in their political form they exhibit great power to move men and women. This is not to say that the majority accepts the ideology in either its political or familial form, but rather that people everywhere have *some* resentments against and objections to their family or social system, for which this ideology presents a beguiling alternative. The philosophy of the conjugal family enters each society as a set of general value assertions rather than as a specifically "Western" ideology, and though Christian missionaries have also preached most of these notions, the effect of the ideology is independent of its ultimate origins. Its principles are sometimes attacked *because* of these origins, but their acceptance stems rather from the opportunities they offer to men and women who feel their family ties bind them harshly.

The ideology of the conjugal family is likely to enter the society through some spokesmen *before* the material conditions for its existence are present, but the ideology does prepare individuals for adjustment to the demands of the new society. Debates about the new philosophy of the family weaken the self-evident rightness of the older system. And although its first spokesmen may be the elite, debates soon take place at *all* levels of the society. The ideology of the conjugal family is one expression of a political ideology, while changes in court decisions and laws implement both of these new sets of principles. Such legal actions in turn shape both custom and the *terms* of the ideological debate.

Nowadays, in the more revolutionary countries, new legal codes become a major lever for initiating change. We must not forget, however, that similar pressures in the same direction existed in the past epoch of colonial rule. Granted, European governments did try, almost without exception, to execute policy and to adjudicate through natives, at least at the lower levels of decision and especially in the area of family law (except where Christians were concerned). But at higher levels the administrators and judges were often European, and increasingly the natives who replaced them were Western-trained. Revisions of codes were typically shaped by European practice and theory (e.g., the Swiss Code was especially important in China). Sometimes native social patterns, such as widow inheritance, were weighed by the standard of "civilized custom,"[27] And proposals for new legislation, arising out of such custom, then intensified the ideological debate about family patterns. It seems likely that legislation and court decisions over the past generation in independent, but formerly colonial, countries have generally pressed toward some conjugal form of the family and have been in advance of actual family behavior.

EGALITARIANISM

One principle in this family ideology is egalitarianism, and the spread of the conjugal family is accompanied by a trend toward "equalitarianism" between the sexes. The main causes of this trend are probably outside the family system. Many factors are relevant, and it seems impossible to disentangle cause from effect.

The reality of the trend in the Western world, however, is certain. Women may hold almost any kind of job, including administrative positions in which they supervise men. They may make contracts, buy and sell on their own account, and own property. They may vote and serve on juries. Such economic and legal rights parallel other social liberties that women have acquired, such as the right to take part in important decisions within the family. Granted, Western jokes about this trend exaggerate it, just as Western commentators, observing the apparently obsequious wife elsewhere (especially in Asia), have generally failed to understand that she might have great influence within the home. Nevertheless, the Western trend over time seems clear, as does the Western family's difference from most other family systems. This change toward egalitarianism has been especially dramatic in the Western Communist countries.

The most fundamental set of causal factors derives from the needs of an industrializing system—specifically, the demand for skill wherever it may be found. Racial, ethnic, and sex barriers weaken before this requirement, which gains added force from a long ideological debate about equal rights and opportunities. Perhaps the first full-scale exposition of this philosophy is found in Plato's *Republic,* where a plea is made for the full development of everyone's potential, of whatever class or sex. The modern debate is not based on Plato, of course, but on John Locke, whose psychological ideas and economic philosophy so profoundly influenced both the French and American revolutions. Thus, one major theme in Western ethics and philosophy asserts that all men have a right to an equal opportunity to develop themselves, that talent may be found in any segment of society, and that when education transforms talent into skill this should be put to use. Consequently, both industrial needs and ethical assertions press toward equalitarianism.

A result of these forces is that there is now a smaller discrepancy between the education of men and women than in the nineteenth century, and this change is taking place rapidly in Asian countries as well. An expanded economy offers new jobs, and women are better trained for them than they were. As a consequence, an increasing proportion of women can live independently from their own earnings. In middle- and upper-class families, the discrepancy between a husband's earnings and the potential income of his wife remains great, which probably accounts for the resistance (noted earlier) in these strata to industrializing forces as expressed in the lower rate of participation of these women in the occupational sphere. Similarly, the men seem to have a stronger voice in important decisions within the family than in the lower strata. (Of course, women *work* in all societies; but until recently they did not earn money independently of their men.)[28]

At the same time, certain factors *within* the conjugal family also press toward a greater degree of equalitarianism. The first is the woman's right to choose her own husband. A second related factor is the "love pattern," under which, at least in the earlier stages of the marriage, the woman has some influence over her husband simply because he is in love with her.

Perhaps more important, however, is the emphasis within the family on the uniqueness of each individual, so that sex status and seniority are less relevant than the "human" qualities of warmth, emotionality, character, and so on, which are not based on age or sex. These emphases reduce the sex- and age-based inequalities among children as well as adults, and also undermine to some extent the traditional subordination of the young to the old.

Since at present this philosophy is most strongly held among the better educated segments of the population, and among women more than among men, two interesting tensions may be seen: Lower-class men concede fewer rights *ideologically* than their women in fact *obtain,* and the more educated men are likely to concede *more* rights ideologically than they in fact grant. One partial resolution of the latter tension is to be found in the frequent assertion from families of professional men that they should not make demands which would interfere with his *work*: He takes precedence as *professional, not* as family head or as male; nevertheless, the precedence is his. By contrast, lower-class men demand deference as *men*, as heads of families.

In succeeding chapters, we shall examine this trend and ideology in several great cultures of the world.

FAMILY AS AN INDEPENDENT FACTOR IN INDUSTRIALIZATION

But just as the ideological factors must be considered independently of the technological demands, so must the family itself be judged to have an independent effect on industrialization. Earlier, this independence was asserted in a negative way by noting that no one has yet succeeded in stating the determinate relations between family systems and economic or technological systems. We can go further, however, and assert that Western family systems have had an effect on industrialization. To make an extreme comparison, Western industrialization would have developed more slowly if those family systems had perhaps been patriarchal and polygynous, with a full development of arranged child marriages and a harem system.

For the past thousand years, the Western family systems have been very different from those in China, India, Japan, and the Arab countries. There has been no clan system or lineage pattern. There has been no ancestor worship, and individuals rather than families have been held responsible for crimes. Arranged marriages have been common, but youngsters have had a greater voice in the final choice, in part because (except for the upper strata in Latin countries at various times) young women have not been segregated from young men even when they were chaperoned. Although child marriages did occur, they were never the ideal or the statistically usual. Doubtless there was an ideal, if a weak one, that a large kin group should live together under one roof, but the more dominant pattern, which actually caused a fairly *late* average age at marriage among farmers, was that the young couple should have land enough to support themselves independently. There was no polygyny or regularized concubinage. The eldest male was not even ideally the leader of the family, though he was of course paid deference.

We cannot, then, view non-Western family systems as basically similar to the Western system at some undefined earlier historical phase just before industrialization. In fact, their differences extend for centuries back into time.

Moreover, the differences seem to have become increasingly sharp *after the Protestant Reformation*. It is not mere chance that the crystallizing incident in Henry VIII's break with Rome had to do with his right to make an *individual* choice about his *marital future*, or that a century later it was a Puritan, Milton, who, in "The Doctrine and Discipline of Divorce" in 1643, made the first serious modern plea for the right of divorce.

The part which ascetic Protestantism played in the development of science, industry, and capitalism has been amply documented.[29] Its impact on a developing philosophy of antitraditionalism, freedom of speech, equalitarianism, political liberty, and individualism was less direct but perhaps no less weighty. Its contribution to the gradual transformation of that philosophy into an ideology of the conjugal family seems equally important, but historical inquiry has not yet turned its attention to those connections. It is at least suggestive that serious debates about *laissez-faire* economics, political liberty, industrialization, and the new family system all had their roots in that same *individualistic* philosophy, rooted ultimately in Protestantism, and that these debates began to take place toward the end of the eighteenth century. Economic individualism found its prophet and analyst in Adam Smith. Although no analyst of Smith's stature appeared to discuss the family, there were enough prophets to expound a new philosophy of individualism: Mary Wollstonecraft, Rousseau, Godwin, Goethe in his Romantic phase, and, of course, their successors, the Romantics.[30]

The impact of ascetic Protestantism could be seen in the family life of the Puritans in the United States.[31] The Puritans defined husband and wife as loving companions rather than as links in a family network, and even in the early period of colonial settlement in the United States their children began to insist on choosing spouses independently of parental arrangements. However important or unimportant ascetic Protestantism may turn out to have been for the development of the conjugal family ideology, some changes in the family had taken place between the sixteenth and eighteenth centuries. When English factories were begun in the eighteenth century, peasants felt free to work in them; where they resisted the influence or the demands of the factory, it was *not* because they ranked the values, role relationships, and enterprises of an "extended family" higher than wage earning in an impersonal, individualistic job system, but because of wages, unemployment, or working conditions; factory owners were thus generally able to obtain enough disciplined workers. It must be conceded that in modern work enterprises in underdeveloped countries there is also no general shortage of labor *if* wages and working conditions are adequate, but instances abound of workers returning to their villages and families when they were needed at the factory, or earning enough for a family obligation and then quitting, or exhibiting a low commitment to the factory job because their primary commitment lay with their extended kin and its obligations.

Not only did the English peasants adjust quickly to the factory, but the thesis has also been presented that much of the opposition to the factory (in this instance, textile manufacture) came only after considerable mechanization had taken place, and was due to the impact of industrialization on the *internal* structure of the individual family unit.[32] It seems possible, then, that by the early period in the industrializing Western world some changes in family patterns had already occurred which, to some extent, prepared lower strata workers for industrialization.

A final index of the independent influence of family form on industrialization may be found in the efforts of Communist China to destroy the old "feudalistic" family system and to go *beyond* the conjugal family, so that a greater technological effectiveness may be achieved.* In analyzing the fit of the conjugal family system with the demands of an urban, bureaucratic technology, we left open the question as to whether an *alternative* family system might meet those demands still better. If that earlier theoretical analysis was correct, then there *is* an alternative, some variant of a communal "family" pattern. Plato's variant was of course even more radical than the present-day ideal Chinese version, but in both, as in the more extreme forms of the kibbutz, the aim is to reduce the claims of kin on one another, and especially to weaken the emotional ties of parents with children; in short to reduce the family to, at most, a weak tie between parents and children. Then, each individual may be used as best fits the needs of industrialization, not those of his family (or his own).

Western criticism of China, like the earlier attacks on similar actions in Russia, has largely ignored the basic technological function of a communal family system. True, as the criticism alleges, the State in such a system may more easily indoctrinate the young with its totalitarian philosophy. Indubitably, however, totalitarianism is viewed in China, as in Russia, as a means to the end of rapid industrialization and economic progress. Not only was the older Chinese family, with its approval of nepotism, its clan system, and its cult of ancestors, a definite hindrance to such a development, but even the Western conjugal family is not the most useful family form. What is needed, as was pointed out in our earlier theoretical comments, is that the choice of industrial personnel be made purely on the basis of achievement. But this type of choice runs against deep family values: It is ultimately *individual* in character, for talents and skills are individual, not family, traits. By contrast, members of the conjugal family are obligated to help one another because they are *kin* and love one another. A system which sets the goal of a most rapid industrialization, or of a most efficient utilization of its members, would therefore strive to reduce the scope of family ties as much as possible.

We are not here arguing the *value* of such a goal or denying the perhaps high psychological costs of such a system. If Plato had succeeded in establishing his Republic, the competitive atmosphere would undoubtedly have been at least as psychologically destructive as that of New York City. Though we shall not concern ourselves with such psychological dimensions, perhaps new social arrangements in the commune might be created to substitute for the solace of family supports. However, no communal family pattern in the modern world has ever evolved naturally, without political force and revolutionary fervor, and both Russia and Israel have already

* This will be treated in greater detail in Chapter VI.

retreated toward the conjugal family after considerable communal experience. It seems likely, then, that complete domination of a society by industrial and technological criteria is impossible and that China too has eventually had to compromise somewhat on this matter. As we shall show later, it has not even succeeded as yet in wiping out the traditional Chinese family.

Nevertheless, both the contemporary innovations in China and the retreat from this pattern in Israel and Russia emphasize the *independent* influence, whether negative or positive, of family form on industrialization.

The foregoing analysis emphasizes the independent effect of family variables. This means that they, too, have their effect; that family patterns cannot be predicted from a knowledge of economic or technological facts only; and that even when family variables are overwhelmed by other sets of forces, they do resist and thus prove that they must be taken into account in any adequate analysis of society. Yet we do expect to find order in these social forces.

Even though the larger trend toward some type of conjugal family system is under way, family systems differ among themselves. Thus, they will exhibit very different trends with respect to such matters as age at marriage, proportion ever married, illegitimacy rates, or the ratio of divorce to marriage. Their systems *began* from very different points; even if they *converge* toward the conjugal family, their various characteristics might move in very different directions within different systems. Some family systems may change easily; others may resist strenuously. Certain traits persist while others weaken swiftly. The elements which change first in one family system may hold firm in another. Moreover, when we look beneath the surface, we may find that, although old forms are breaking down, new ones are emerging which might in some cases be as stable as the old once were.

In very specific terms, we cannot expect to find a simple transformation of all family patterns from a "primitive" system—i.e., high birth rate and a high rate of growth, a low divorce rate, a low age at marriage, a high proportion of people ultimately marrying, great control by the elders over the sex lives and romances of the young (with a resulting low illegitimacy rate), family harmony and unity, and extended kin living under one roof—to a new "modern" family system, *opposite* in all ways.

In analyzing changes successively in the West, the Arab world, Sub-Saharan Africa, India, China, and Japan, we shall try, where possible, to utilize survey, census, and registration data. Of course, mass statistics are rare for Africa, China, and Arab countries, but they can be supplemented at times by more restricted community surveys. In the West, time trends may be obtained only for the few countries, such as Sweden, England, and France, in which adequate census and registration systems have been in existence for generations. For others, such as Italy, Latin America, and the

United States, important gaps face us. It is not possible to compare the same characteristics in each world area. The data vary in validity.

Nevertheless, the attempt can be made in a tentative way by accepting the data's limitations and formulating the apparent changes clearly enough to permit later correction.

Throughout, our focus is on the *institutional structure,* the sociological forces that create any given statistical measure or trend.

chapter

II

Family Changes in the West

✠✠✠✠✠✠✠✠✠✠✠

A WIDE RANGE of changes are now apparently taking place in the family systems of the Western Culture Complex.* In certain important respects, the New World south of the Rio Grande is a special case. The changes that seem to be taking place there parallel those of Europe, but the particular situation from which they began would require lengthy exposition. At any rate, we must keep in mind two related, but different, results of our comparisons: (1) The direction or trend in a given pattern may run in contrary directions, as between two countries or cultural patterns, but nevertheless (since they begin from a different point) be moving toward a similar future. (2) Family patterns in different societies may also exhibit similar *directions of change*, but remain very different from one another. For example, in both Europe and Africa, love relations are of increasing importance, but in African societies the proportion of marriages based on love is doubtless still relatively small, while in European courtship and marriage love has played a large role for several generations, and the pattern now is simply being extended and consolidated in strata or regions where it was once somewhat less common. Thus, we cannot expect to find spectacular changes in Western family patterns; indeed, it is very likely that journalistic treatments of these changes have exaggerated the degree of alteration. Unfortunately, relatively few studies have seriously attempted to measure the degree of change in central family characteristics, even over the past half-century.

* Includes the New World, Australia, New Zealand, and Europe west of the Urals.

1. Entering Marriage

The process of entering marriage begins in the Western family system, as in all family systems, from the moment of the first socialization experiences. These impress on the child his duties as well as rewards in assuming his status as male or female. The experiences prepare the child, by anticipatory socialization, for the adult roles of date or fiancé, husband and wife, kinsman, and so on. The youngster comes to take for granted that marriage is the eventually proper state for all adults, and gradually (or by sharply defined rites of passage) the young person is moved into the marriage market.

The marriage markets of different societies vary somewhat in the characteristics which are highly valued (beauty, intelligence, family honor, wealth, charm, courage), in who has control over striking the bargains, and in the rules by which agreements are made.

In all large civilizations, there are several relatively closed marriage markets, separated from one another by geographical distance, by race or ethnic group, by religion, and by class. In the United States, Negroes and Whites do not "buy and sell" in the same marriage market, nor do United States citizens of Greek and Japanese backgrounds; and Catholic-Jewish marriages are uncommon. Naturally none of these markets is completely closed. Some Whites marry Negroes, perhaps a third of Catholic marriages are to non-Catholics, and at least a third of the people marry outside their class *origin*. And an individual may participate in more than one such market. Of course, most people are not conscious that they are engaging in market operations. The girl in Marseilles does not *refuse* to marry a boy because he lives in Calais. She simply has a low chance of ever meeting him in a dating situation.

Nevertheless, the *norms* of most classes and social groups relative to the eligibility of partners create the limits of the various markets. Thus, a Negro girl is ineligible in almost all White marriage markets. These norms, and the market of "eligibles" that they create, are the foundations of the "rule of homogamy" or the rule of "assortative mating," nearly universal in its application, according to which "like marry like." Simply put, the norms of evaluation or eligibility determine who shall associate on intimate terms and who are likely to be acceptable as marriage partners.

The result of these definitions of acceptability can be seen in the many studies of marriage choice showing that there is some rough correlation between husbands and wives with respect to an extremely wide range of both important and trivial characteristics.[1]

More than likely, *within* the group of eligibles the psychological factor of "need complementarity" determines to a considerable extent who will fall in love with whom. The theory of complementary needs states that each individual seeks the person who offers the greatest promise of providing maximum need gratification, so that, in general, one person's need must harmonize with the other person's wish or need to grant or to give that kind of satisfaction. Thus, a maternal woman is likely to be attracted to a young man who wishes to be mothered.[2]

The system of implicit bargaining contains a further kind of "likeness" or "equality." Even two individuals in the same market may differ substantially in characteristics that are valued by their social group or family. Thus, a girl may be relatively poor, but beautiful. The boy may not be so well-to-do as the girl, but he may have excellent prospects for the future. There is thus some rough equality in the exchange: A girl of great charm and beauty may be able to move entirely outside the marriage market in which she was born, exchanging her qualities for money or prestige. We therefore cannot think of "homogamy" as simply implying that the bride and groom have exactly the same rating on every characteristic. Indeed, it seems likely that there will be many differences between them, and in effect these valued characteristics are being traded for one another.

In the West, this part of the process has changed greatly over the past century. Several marriage markets are not so closed now as they were, but the modern analyst is likely to exaggerate the closure of rigidity of class lines in the past. Every historical study of class systems shows a considerable amount of mobility from one generation to the next, and this is reflected in the system of marriage choice.[3]

To the extent that parents no longer arrange their children's marriages, the final decision in these bargains has been transferred from the older to younger generation. However, by emphasizing the apparent "irrationality" of love we should not suppose that young people do not typically weigh all these relatively rational factors. Parents, peer groups, and many years of prior socialization mean that young people of roughly the same backgrounds are likely to meet one another to associate on intimate terms, and to choose one another as marriage partners.[4]

Geographic mobility in the modern world has enlarged the area from which eligible partners might come. This process of geographic enlargement began in England in the late sixteenth century, when "a nation-wide marriage market centered on London" developed. "For the peerage the marriage-market had become nation-wide before the middle of the seventeenth century and even took Ireland into its scope."[5] But the widening of the geographical range does not necessarily mean a breakdown of class lines. In England, for example, it merely meant that nobles from the north began to marry nobles from the south. It is unlikely that there is a Western country in which this process has not taken place.

Nevertheless, every detailed study shows that most partners live rather close to one another. For example, several studies in the United States have shown that about half the urban couples studied lived no more than a mile from one another before they married.

The results of a recent study on choice of spouse in France show that even when place of birth is used (instead of location immediately prior to marriage, which would show even less dispersion), 52 per cent of the spouses came from at least the same *arrondissement*.[6]

The percentages are presented below:

	Place of Birth of Two Spouses	Residences of the Two Spouses at the Time of Marriage
Same commune	22	57
Same canton	32	12
Same arrondissement	52	12
Same departement	63	7
Same region	72	3
Other	100	9
N = 1646		

The study also reports, however, that the areas from which spouses now come are geographically more widely dispersed than formerly: 81 per cent of the previous generation came from the same region, as against 72 per cent of this generation. In another study the percentages of marriages involving a person from a village outside the *departement* rose from 10.7 per cent to 25.2 per cent, from 1870 to 1954.[7]

The geographical "mixing" that has taken place in all Western countries extends, in effect, the range of eligibles—that is, to those who have similar social characteristics but live in different areas. However, at least in the United States, and probably in every other Western country, there has also been an increase in the number of marriages between groups who formerly considered each other ineligible. At least some Englishwomen marry Negroes and Indians, and some Frenchwomen marry Algerian men. In the United States, Jews, Catholics, and Protestants marry one another to a much greater degree than they did two generations ago. An intensifying egalitarianism doubtless plays a role in this apparent breakdown of the barriers between marriage markets.

But some part of the apparent breakdown is not real, for those who cross the more rigid lines of religion, caste, or class are also much more likely to be similar in their own tastes, styles of life, education and attitudes, even though their families of origin may have been very different. In the United States, for example, Catholics who marry Protestants are likely to be less devout than those who marry within the Church, and Protestants who marry Catholics are probably not as devoted to their religious doctrine. If an Englishwoman marries a Jamaican Negro at all, her husband is almost certain to be a well-educated Jamaican Negro whose tastes and attitudes are very much like hers. Even without adequate data to guide us in understanding this change, it seems likely that the social characteristics of the families of origin now play a lesser role in mate choice and the characteristics of the marrying *individuals* a greater role.

2. Dating

The mobility of individuals over great geographical distances is paralleled by the freedom of young persons to leave the house alone to go to dances or places of recreation. This change seems certain enough, even without quantitative data. In Spain and Italy, a respectable girl no longer requires a chaperone when she goes out. The behavior of late adolescence is probably more "advanced" than the adults who respond to public opinion polls would prefer. In most Western countries, there is considerable conflict between parents and young daughters as to how early girls may go out alone with boys.

Parents generally lose the battle, however, and in part because they themselves have conflicting attitudes. For example, the Darmstadt study[8] reported that 52 per cent of the urban population (54 per cent of the rural) thought that 18 years of age was the proper time for girls to be permitted to go to dances; 61 per cent (65 per cent in rural regions) gave 18 years as the appropriate age for boys. Only 11 per cent of the urban and 20 per cent of the rural sample (very likely the rural sample reflects the assumption that the community as a whole will attend the dance) thought that 16 was a proper age for girls to go to dances.

A study asked French women a slightly different question: "At what age should a girl begin going out alone with boys?" The answer—generally conservative—is presented in Table II-1.

On the other hand, in answer to the question whether parents with a daughter aged 17 or 18 should encourage her to go out, or at least not in-

Table II-1
Question: In Your Opinion, At What Age Should a Girl Begin Going Out Alone With Boys?*

Age	14–15	16–18	19–20	21 or Over	With Fiance Only	No Answer
All Women Interviewed	5%	39%	35%	7%	10%	4%
According to Age						
21–24	9	50	29	3	5	4
25–29	8	43	31	5	9	4
30–34	5	39	35	7	11	3
35–39	5	41	39	5	6	4
40–44	2	26	42	11	15	4
45–49	2	29	33	11	20	5
According to Population of Place of Residence						
Under 2,000	7	33	35	8	14	3
2,000–5,000	3	35	34	11	14	3
6,000–20,000	5	43	37	4	8	3
21,000–100,000	3	41	37	4	8	7
Over 100,000	7	46	32	6	4	5

* Patterns of Sex and Love: A Study of the French Woman and Her Morals (New York: Crown Publishers, 1961), p. 59.

terfere, 70 per cent answered either "don't interfere" or "encourage" (28 per cent). Only 24 per cent said that the girl should be forbidden to go out at that age. Some evidence of change may be found in this distribution of answers by age: 29 per cent of the interviewed women aged 45 to 49 said that the girl should not be interfered with, as against 54 per cent of women in the 21 to 24 age range.[9]

Of course the greater independence of the young has been reported for all Western countries.[10] One consequence of this greater freedom is that the young people who marry are more likely than before to have met outside the circle of the family. Even when they meet at a dance, the circumstances are different from what they used to be. Two generations ago the young couple might well have met at a dance, but their parents had *brought* them there and their parents *remained* to take them home afterwards. In Girard's study of choice of spouses in France, 11 per cent stated that they had known each other as neighbors, through family connections, or from infancy. An additional 6 per cent had met each other through a family get-together. A further 11 per cent had met through a formal introduction. Almost *all* of the remainder had met under more informal circumstances, although in most cases, before actually speaking, the young person knew something about the other individual—through club meetings, work, or school. Some 17 per cent met at a dance and 10 per cent met at a "place of recreation."[11] Girard comments on the dance as meeting place by noting that it has been discussed in other French studies.[12] He notes that the authors of *Nouville* claim that the dance was not to be properly identified with a "love market." Rather, young people who had already met elsewhere came to know one another better at the dance. In Girard's sample, however, 40 per cent of the younger respondents say they met at a dance or at a place of recreation, whereas only 20 per cent of the older had done so. By predictable contrast, 29 per cent of the older respondents say they met through family relations and formal presentation, but only 16 per cent of the youngest.

A Warsaw public opinion poll, taken in the late 1950s among a sample of young people, reported that only 7 per cent of the respondents met through their own family or family friends, while 22 per cent met through their own friends and acquaintances. Public recreation and dancing accounted for another 18 per cent, and work and school contacts included 32 per cent.[13]

The freedom to date and to form one's own friendships necessarily means that a higher proportion of marriages are based on love and are independently made—within the sociological limitations already noted. However, we do not know how far these patterns are different from those of half a century ago. I suspect that the urban proletariat has had this freedom for centuries in the West, but in Europe this freedom probably was not obtained by the upper middle class or aristocratic strata until World

War I. On the other hand, it is very likely that this freedom was obtained in the United States at least by the middle of the nineteenth century in most classes, and shortly afterward in the upper strata. Nevertheless, just as modern parents do play some role in their children's decisions to marry, so did they influence these decisions fifty years ago. Freedom, after all, never means absolute freedom.

Finally, many regional differences in the freedom of youngsters have doubtless existed for generations. One study of a small village in Andalusia, conservative by most contemporary European standards, reported that parents have little influence over the children's choice of spouses. Courtship is prolonged and the young man spends a great deal of time with the girl over many months. As the author comments, "One might well *marry* to please the parents, but one could hardly pursue a *courtship* such as I have described in order to please them."[14]

Wylie similarly states, in his study of a small French village, that "all the people of Peyrane whom I questioned on this point agreed that the most important condition for marriage is love."[15] By contrast, the arranged marriage seems to have been common in rural Serbia (Yugoslavia) before World War I, "and all negotiations were carried on between the heads of the two *zadrugas* concerned."[16] Furthermore, some marriages are still arranged by the parents of the couples.

A survey in Belgium among a relatively educated young group asked "Are arranged marriages frequent?" The answers to the question were as follows:

There are no arranged marriages any more	51%
Arranged marriages are very rare, they are no more than 1%	16%
1 to 3% of marriages are arranged	28%
5 to 10% of marriages are arranged	5%[17]

These Belgians' answers to the question, "Do young people take account of the material difficulties that they will encounter after marriage?" proved to be interesting in view of the limits once placed on the freedom of young people because it was thought they could not decide such matters rationally.

Thirty-nine per cent admitted that young people do not pay attention to material considerations, but all the rest (61 per cent) agreed that young people do take them into account before they marry.[18] On the other hand, 61 per cent stated that parents do not intervene in the choices made by their children, while 39 per cent said that young people are guided either by the attitudes they have acquired from their parents or by the direct intervention of the parents.[19] In the earlier stages of a courtship, parents sometimes do not intervene simply because they do not know what is going on; 27 per cent of these Belgian respondents stated that parents did not know about the engagement intentions of their children.[20]

3. Economic Controls Over Marriage Choice—Dowries and Inheritance

Until industrialization, parents in the West could control their children's choice of spouse largely through control over inheritance, for land was almost the only potential source of income. The farm youth could not marry without his father's permission, because by his own effort he could not gain enough money with which to buy land. Throughout most of the West a dowry system was followed, so that the girl's chances of marrying were negligible unless her family was willing to present her with a sufficient marriage gift. Where land was cheap, as on the United States frontier, or where the standards for subsistence were low, as in Ireland during the period when the Irish potato was being introduced, the dowry could be small, and some farmers could marry without a dowry if they were able to obtain land independently.[21]

In 1952, 65 per cent of a sample of married German women said they brought a dowry to their marriage.[22]

The dowry apparently continues to be important in the underdeveloped areas of southern Italy. In such circumstances, of course, the parents can maintain great control over who marries whom. Banfield comments, "Without a dowry, a Montenegro girl cannot make a satisfactory marriage."[23] On the other hand, the idea of a dowry is a recent development in rural Serbia. The traditional *zadruga* attitude was that the girl's family should be compensated for the loss of a working member.[24] Of course this "new" development will disappear relatively quickly.

Several elements can be seen in interaction in this change. Since land is not now the primary source of wealth, and the occupational position is not in the hands of elders anyway, they have far less ability to withdraw important support if their wishes are not consulted. Furthermore, the growing power of decision in the hands of young people and the relative instability of marriage mean that the elder generation is unwilling to make a substantial investment in the marriage. Precisely the same elements seem to be in operation here as in Africa. Baumert, reporting on the German upper-strata marriage, claims the girl's parents are much less able and willing to give her a sizeable dowry, but she has a much better chance of being independent through her own occupational activity.[25] Schelsky has commented, "Formerly one could not marry except on condition that he had already a good situation (an essential factor of security) while now one marries in order to construct an existence together, to create a certain security."[26]

In the same colloquium Boudet asserts that prior to World War I, among the French bourgeoisie, the revenue from the family wealth might well be two to four times as much as that from the occupation.

The dowry is now almost unheard of in the United States and has disappeared from most of Europe except among the upper social strata. Some guess as to its current prevalence may be obtained from data on the percentage of marriages in which a marriage contract is made. Of the 67 thousand marriages in 1952 in Belgium, 30 per cent had a marriage contract,[27] a high proportion of which, however, were among farmers who insisted upon a clear legal understanding about the status of the land. The trend in France has been downward for nearly a hundred years. Between 1856 and 1880, 38 to 41 per cent of marriages were accompanied by contracts; over the years, however, the percentage dropped, and by 1931 only 17 per cent of marriages were accompanied by contracts. (The economic crisis of that time may have affected the proportion somewhat, since it rose to 20 per cent by 1945).[28]

4. Sexual Patterns Before Marriage: Opinions and Behavior

A common journalistic assumption about the decline in the functions of the family in the West is that part of the cause lies in the increased sexual freedom of the past thirty years. This assumption raises a number of questions, implicit or explicit. First, has this increase actually occurred? Are there differences in premarital sexual patterns among different class levels, and can these differences be related to changing economic patterns? Does growing opportunity for economic self-sufficiency tend to encourage greater premarital sexual freedom among women?

If we assume, as the data indicate, that expressed attitudes are at considerable variance with actual behavior, we can turn to illegitimacy data as more accurate indicators of premarital sexual behavior. In examining these data, however, we must correlate illegitimacy rates with a number of other factors in Western cultures that affect attitudes toward illegitimacy—some of these factors being economic or sociocultural. In any case, the primary question remains: Has there indeed been a great change in sexual attitudes and behavior in the direction of greater premarital freedom, and is there any evidence to suggest that this greater freedom, if it does exist, is affecting family patterns?

True, in no part of the "civilized" world have so many pleas for sexual freedom been openly expressed as in the West, and young persons have not been given so much freedom elsewhere. The modern generation is much more liberal in its *definitions* of appropriate sexual behavior than its grandfather's generation. How great the changes have been we shall never know. Changes in public behavior of the upper classes are striking, but the private behavior of other classes escapes our knowledge. The area of sexual freedom is one in which private attitudes may contrast with public attitudes, just as behavior in public and private may contrast.

For example, in a 1939 survey in the United States, 80 per cent of a national sample of men stated that it was either "unfortunate" or "wicked" when "young girls have sexual relations before marriage." Eighty-three per cent of the women gave the same answer with respect to young men having sexual relations before marriage. In 1937, 56 per cent of a national sample asserted that it was not right for either party to a marriage to have had previous experience.[29] In 1943, a survey of women in the United States aged 20 to 35 reported that 59 per cent of them believed that most men require virginity in the girl they intend to marry.[30] Furthermore, a French survey shows similar results: 60 per cent of a recent sample of French women said they disapproved of girls who "give themselves to their fiancés before marriage."[31] Sixty-nine per cent of Girard's more recent and technically more rigorously drawn sample stated that it is either "no less important (36 per cent) or very important that young girls guard themselves before marriage."[32] On this point, as on other major issues, the same percentage of men as of women took this position. The women *believed* that men very much prefer the woman they marry to be a virgin (64 per cent *vs.* 21 per cent); and 60 per cent expressed disapproval of premarital intercourse with the fiancé.

By contrast, however, the DIVO Institute found that only 22 per cent of a German national sample asserted that virginity was either necessary, or that they themselves would marry only a virgin. Twenty-five per cent of the men said that virginity was a definite disadvantage, while 53 per cent were undecided. Here again, the answers were similarly distributed among the women in this sample of the 1950s; 27 per cent gave the first two answers and 48 per cent gave the last answer. On the other hand, 37 per cent thought that virginity might be a definite disadvantage. However, a fairly clear increase in the proportion disapproving this view can be seen with increasing *age,* indicating that older attitudes were less liberal.

It is tempting to suppose that such data reflect the values of the respondents, and to deduce that in the United States and France, the basic attitudes regarding sex have not changed, whereas in Germany they have changed substantially. The few data on *behavior* would suggest otherwise, however. In Girard's sample, 30 per cent of the married women said that they *had* in fact had sexual intercourse with their fiancés prior to marriage. In addition, Kinsey has reported that the greatest changes in the patterns of sexual behavior between older and younger generations of American females were in the areas of premarital petting and premarital intercourse, with the percentage of those reporting premarital sexual experience of some kind increasing with the generations born after 1900.[33]

In the DIVO Institute's German survey, 70 per cent of the women and 89 per cent of the men said that they had had intimate relations with a person of the opposite sex before marriage. A sample of Norwegian students was asked about the "degree of intimacy considered proper for different relations, ranging from first date to engagement," and 81 per cent of the males (39 per cent of the females) asserted that full sexual relations were proper. This may be contrasted with the percentages for an American sample on the same question: 33 per cent for the men and 14 per cent for women. Observers seem to agree that in the Scandinavian countries, sexual relations are accepted as a matter of course between engaged couples, whatever their answers on public opinion polls.[34]

We cannot assume, however, that these data prove any great change from the past. Cautiously stated, it seems likely that a considerable increase has occurred in the toleration of certain kinds of sexual or premarital behavior, such as petting or even sexual intercourse, before and after marriage with someone other than the marital partner. With respect to sexual relations with the future spouse alone, it is not at all clear that *any change has occurred.*

ILLEGITIMACY

Without more rigorous surveys we cannot be certain of the actual sexual behavior even of the present generation, but one reasonably definite datum can give us some insight: illegitimacy. Available studies indicate that recent illegitimacy rates in some Western countries range as high as 18.5 per cent (*excluding* the New World countries where the percentages range from 5 per cent to 70 per cent). The percentage of first-born children conceived outside marriage has ranged as high as 58 per cent in European countries.[35]

Nevertheless, disapproval of illegitimacy seems still to be very strong in England, France, Holland, Belgium and the United States; in the German and Scandinavian countries attitudes are more tolerant. The DIVO Institute found that 33 per cent of the sample cited earlier would not disapprove of an unmarried woman who had a child, and that an additional 39 per cent thought that approval or disapproval would "depend upon circumstances."[36]

Although illegitimacy and premarital conception do not give us an index of general sexual behavior or values, an illegitimate birth is clear evidence that premarital sexual relations have taken place at least once. The available data, however, show relatively little change over time.

Table II-2 presents official illegitimacy rates in selected countries since 1890. In countries, areas, or regions in which data collection has been poor in the past, a slight rise in a rate may only be an indication of better reporting of illegitimate births; it may not signify that a real increase is taking place. For example, it is almost certain that most Negro births in the South were "illegitimate" in the latter part of the nineteenth century and perhaps for the first two or three decades of this century. Since they are now being reported fully for the first time, some *increase* in the *official* rate is apparent. We have no way of ascertaining what the true rate was, but it was certainly higher in the *past* than at present.

Table II-2
Illegitimacy Per Hundred Births in Selected Western Countries, 1890–1956*

Country	1890	1900	1910	YEAR 1920	1930	1940	1950	1956
United States				2.3	3.3	4.0	3.7 (1949)	4.5 (1955 est.)
Germany	9.1	8.7	9.1	11.4	12.0	9.8 (1931–1935)	9.7	
England and Wales	4.4 (1890–1892)	4.2	4.1	4.7	4.6 (1929)	4.3	5.1	4.7
Sweden	10.2 (1881–1890)	11.8 (1901)	14.3	15.7	16.3	11.8	9.8	9.9 (1955)
Australia		6.0 (1901)	5.8 (1906–1910)	4.8 (1921)	4.6 (1929)	3.8	3.9	4.1 (1955)
France	8.5	8.8	8.7 (1912)	10.0 •	8.4	7.3 (1936)	7.0	6.6 (1955)
Italy	7.3	5.9	4.9	4.7	4.9	4.1	3.4	3.1

* All data taken from official sources.

Moreover, if there is any general trend, it is toward a lowering of illegitimacy rates. Relevant to these rates is the practice of premarital intercourse in a small circle of eligibles, with marriage following conception. This is an old European pattern. Delays in marriage sometimes cause an illegitimate birth, although there is little social stigma attached to it. Thus in areas like Sweden, the official illegitimacy rate can be very high while the *social* illegitimacy rate is very low, since almost all girls who get pregnant eventually marry (although they might have the child before the marriage takes place).

There may therefore be a relative tolerance of premarital sexual intercourse but a low tolerance of public illegitimacy.[37]

Three great time processes interact to produce the varying rates of illegitimacy and premarital conception, and to some degree their pressures are in different directions. One is the relatively widespread European "farmer pattern," which more or less permitted intimacy between eligible young people who nevertheless remained under the control of parents and peers. As this rural pattern declines in the West, the rate of official illegitimacy from that source tends to drop. Second, among the urban proletariat and the New World populations of Negroes and Mestizos, who have been to some degree barred from the advantages of full cultural assimilation, there is a much lower commitment to the absolute value of being married. Consequently, their rates of illegitimacy and of extramarital or premarital coitus, as well as *consensual unions* (living together without legally marrying), *are* high, but they have been high for generations. Where there is rapid urbanization, and large populations are thrust into a culturally new situation where they are not committed to the dominant values, these rates may rise for a while. I have applied such an analysis to the New World population, including United States Negroes. The ambivalence toward different sets of values is common. P. Chombart de Lauwe has reported that lower white-collar French workers are attached to the notion of civil marriage, but that workers consider it rather a formality without great importance. He relates this difference to the fact that workers are less likely to believe that upward socioeconomic mobility is possible.[38]

As the excluded populations of the Americas are given the advantages of full society membership, they will come to accept the dominant values more fully, and illegitimacy rates will drop.

The third great process is the interaction between the higher toleration of sexual activities outside (or prior to) marriage, the even greater increase in toleration for a woman who deliberately has a child outside marriage, and the spreading use of contraceptives. A Gallup Poll in Norway in 1946 found that 70 per cent of the sample believed that it is all right for an unmarried woman in public office to keep her position if she bears a child.[39] In the DIVO German sample, 53 per cent said it was all right for an unmarried woman to become a mother deliberately, and 12 per cent said it "depended upon circumstances." The first two factors lead to an increased risk of illegitimacy, and the third to a decrease in illegitimacy. The apparent increase in freedom of sexual relations does not seem to be accompanied by any philosophical conviction that the basic structure of marriage should be changed. Rather, it seems to express the conviction that having sexual intercourse or some sexual intimacy short of intercourse *does not irrevocably commit oneself to an enduring relationship.*

5. Marriages With Kin

Western norms of eligibility and preference have never stated that an individual *should* marry a specific relative (such as a mother's brother's daughter), but they have *permitted* marriages between certain relatives. Moreover, because the marriage market was limited *geographically*, and because relatives often are at the same class level and of similar backgrounds, a sizeable *minority* of marriages used to occur between relatives, usually between first or second cousins. However, fewer young people meet each other at family gatherings now, due to a wider geographical dispersion of friendship and social relations; and there are fewer advantages in marrying within a kindred since there is now less desire to keep property within it. Consequently we would expect a drop in the percentage of marriages with consanguineal or affinal relatives. The amount of decline varies from region to region within each country, but where data are available the decrease seems certain over the past fifty years.[40]

6. Age Differences

The greater freedom of choice of spouse and the lessened importance of *having already* accumulated substantial property before marriage have led to a drop in age *differences* between husband and wife and to an increase in the proportion of marriages between young people of the same age. In Baumert's Darmstadt sample of 1950, 47 per cent of the men under 30 years of age had married women of the same age, as contrasted with only 10 per cent of the men aged 40–49 years. Seventy-four per cent of these older men had married younger women, but only 40 per cent of the men 29 years or younger had done so. With reference to this point, Baumert comments: "Before the first World War it was widely believed that the man should be 5 to 10 years older than the woman; especially in the middle classes other behavior was viewed as a deviation."[41]

Since the 1876–1880 period the age difference between the husband and wife has also dropped in France.[42]

AGE AT MARRIAGE

Ideally, the analysis of trends in age at marriage should be based on average age at *first* marriage, or perhaps the proportion of all first marriages which are entered into by men or women in some specified younger age bracket, such as 15–19 or 20–24 years. This can be done only when marriage registration procedures are excellent. Secondly, the proportion *ever married* in some specified young age bracket should be compared over successive *censuses*, separately for each sex. In many countries, only the second comparison is reliable. In countries in which marriages at younger ages are rare, a comparison of both age groups mentioned may be wise, since the average age may drop over several decades, without any great increase in the proportion marrying in age brackets defined in those countries as extremely young.

Until recently, it was the belief in most Western countries (and certainly in the United States), that at some indefinite period in the past, marriages had occurred very early, but that age at marriage had increased as industrialization occurred and more people began to stay in school until a later age. The belief in another form has been that in rural areas people married at a very early age, but that in urban areas marriages took place somewhat later. In other words, urbanization brought with it a rise in the age at marriage. In the United States this belief may have arisen from frontier experiences, for reasons that will be noted later.

In truth, in the United States, there has been a long trend toward "earlier" marriages, so that the average age for first marriages now is about 22.3 years for men and 20.2 years for women. The change has been most striking during the last two decades, although Monahan also has shown that the data from which the long-term trend has been ascertained contained many errors.[43] Furthermore, this decrease in age at marriage apparently has occurred generally in Western countries.

It seems likely that toward the end of the nineteenth century Western attitudes did alter toward a belief that very young girls should not marry. Prior to the twentieth century, marriages of girls aged 15–17 were not disapproved of providing that the man was sufficiently well-to-do. In the absence of sufficient data my hypothesis is that chronological maturity as a prerequisite for marriage was not an important focus of social attention in the West until about the turn of the century.

Let us consider this point. Prior to the French Revolution, the legal minimum age for marriage in France was 14 years for boys and 12 years for girls.[44] These were also the legal minimum marriage ages accepted under both the older English law and Roman law. In most cases these minimum ages—the assumed ages of puberty for each sex—probably permitted parents to arrange the marriages of their children whenever it seemed suitable. Children of so young an age could not marry independently, and marriage in many Western nations without the consent of parents is even now forbidden to young people under 21 years of age. In the West, there has generally been a substantial difference between the legal minimum age for marriage and the minimum age at which young people might marry *without* parental consent. Since one youngster may be forbidden to marry because of parental refusal, and another of the same age may marry *with* parental consent, it is clear that Western laws concerning minimum ages at marriage were aimed at maintaining the power of the parent, *not* at enforcing a "right" age at marriage. Over the past generation, a typical legal change has been to narrow the gap between the two age minimums by raising the age at marriage *with* parental consent, or establishing a lower age at marriage without consent.

Since marriage was not thought in the West to be properly based on free courtship until late in the nineteenth century, "maturity" as measured by years was given no great weight. If a good match could be made for a girl of 15 or 16 years, her age was no barrier, and there were indeed many youthful marriages. Within noble or well-to-do rural families, a young couple could be married precisely because they did *not* have to support themselves or assume the responsibility of a profession.[45]

In contrast to upper-class families, farming families in regions without free land did not ordinarily permit their children to marry until much later, when the parents were ready to relinquish control of the property, or had accumulated sufficient money to afford the marriage. Without land, marriage was not possible. And, of course, servants and apprentices might not marry at all, since their status was viewed as a semi-familial one, and they had no right to introduce a spouse into the family circle.[46] However, a "proper" age was not the question. Instead, it was whether there was adequate land or income available. Until the end of the nineteenth century the couple had either to wait for land or, if the productive unit was large enough, to become part of a larger kin group, taking part in its economic activities and sharing from the common store. Thus, age in itself was of little importance.

We must therefore conclude that in most parts of the West, until some time in the nineteenth century, marriage came relatively late for the bulk of the population, and the myth that marriages occurred extremely early as we go back in time comes from the fact that the many marriages at very young ages occurred among the most conspicuous classes. The delay in marriage, and even the nonmarriage of farmers in France before the Revolution, has been well analyzed by Duplessis-LeGuelinel. Additional data for the medieval period have been assembled in part by Krause, and of course the excellent study by Homans describes this pattern very well. Indeed, the pattern of the thirteenth-century English villager is strikingly similar to that of the Irish countryman in the 1930s as described by Arensberg.[47]

Similarly, where land or job can be obtained easily, or independently of the parents, as on the North American frontier, youthful marriages may become relatively common. The point to remember, then, is that precocious marriages of the epoch prior to the nineteenth century *do not* show that young people were independent of their parents (indeed, the opposite is true); whereas in the modern period, marriages at early ages do represent an independent decision. To that extent (although the proportions involved may be small) the two changes have moved in opposing directions. The lessened control of upper-class parents has prevented them from arranging the marriages of their children, which may have worked toward later marriages, but the increasing economic independence in other classes has permitted younger marriages.

The same set of forces can be seen at work in eighteenth-century Ireland. Apparently, premarital chastity was the norm in Ireland in the eighteenth century and perhaps in the seventeenth century as well.[48] Contraceptives were not used, and illegitimacy was rare. Marriage occurred relatively early, and though accurate population data are not available for the period when the new crop, the Irish potato, was introduced in the eighteenth century, it is clear that at that time age at marriage was early compared to other countries. (The new potato produced far more per acre than any previous Irish crop.) Marriages occurred at a still earlier age during the period when the crop was becoming widely accepted, but nuptial age again began to increase in the late 1830s when the first great potato famines began (i.e., when the possibility that a young couple could establish themselves independently was once more reduced). As a consequence, in 1839, after some years during which it had become increasingly difficult for a couple to find sufficient capital to enter marriage, 70 per cent of the brides in first marriages in rural districts were under 26. Nine years before, the percentage of brides under 26 years of age had been 76.5, indicating that marriages during that period were occurring earlier.[49]

In other words, a young man and woman, finding it easy to make a crop from potatoes, and finding new lands available higher on the mountains or in the bogs, could set up a household without waiting for the approval (and financial help) of their parents. That period in Ireland, then, was equivalent on a small scale to the situation on the United States frontier in the late nineteenth century.

In the contemporary West, however, a "proper" age (varying from country to country and from class to class—higher in the upper strata[50]) has now come to be accepted, since, under the conjugal family system, a couple must be self-sufficient. The young couple cannot be extremely young, since they have to take care of themselves; on the other hand, they do not have to be very old, because they can be independent.

Here, we encounter an empirical puzzle. It seems likely that in the early period of England's industrialization, the age of marriage would not have changed greatly because, although they did work in the factories, for the most part children were given their jobs through relatives and often were supervised by their own male parents. They were not independent workers, and the traditions of the times dictated that they should give their pay to their parents. It was only when they obtained jobs on their own, without the intervention of parents or relatives, that they could make their own decision about choice of spouse or age at which to marry. However, the age at marriage did not change substantially until still later, i.e., in this century, and now seems to be tied at least in part to the independent participation of *females* in the labor force. The job becomes the young girl's "dowry" in the unskilled and semiskilled white- and blue-collar strata, where, in fact, the highest proportion of women are to be found in the labor force.

The interpretation of labor force data is an extremely complex matter. Even if it is true that a crucial variable in the drop in age of marriage in Western family systems has been the participation of women in the *industrial* (as opposed to agricultural) labor force, it seems equally clear that this factor has an effect only under specific circumstances and perhaps under the potentiating impulse of other value or philosophical elements. In the United States, women certainly participated to a great degree in the labor force during World War I, but it was not until their participation during World War II that any change in age at marriage became substantial. Evidently, both an ideological factor and the sheer material factor must work simultaneously. Moreover, it is not merely that the female *works*, but that she works outside of agriculture and in a social context that defines her work and income as independently her own.

The basic empirical data seem to be clear—that in the West the age at marriage has been dropping for men and, to a lesser extent, for women. This can be seen in Table II-3. The age of men at marriage is affected more than women's by exterior factors operating on a wide scale, since they have the primary economic responsibility for the family and when to marry is

Table II-3
Percentage Ever Married—Males 20–24 Years, Females 15–19 Years— in Selected Western Countries, 1890–1956*

Country	Sex	1890	1900	1910	1920	1930	1940	1950	1956
United States	M	19.4	22.4	25.1	29.3	29.2	27.8	40.9	
	F	9.7	11.3	12.1	13.0	13.2	11.9	17.1	
Germany	M	8.6	9.1	8.3	11.1	9.5	13.7	16.6	
					(1925)	(1933)	(1946)		
	F	1.5	1.6	1.4	0.6	1.0	1.9	2.8	
England and		19.5	17.4	14.3	17.7	13.9	17.4	23.8	27.8
Wales	M	(1891)	(1901)	(1911)	(1921)	(1931)	(1939)	(1951)	
	F	1.9	1.5	1.2	1.7	1.8	2.9	4.4	5.5
Sweden	M			6.8	6.5	7.1	7.0	15.5	
	F			1.1	1.1	1.4	1.9	3.7	
Australia	M		11.7	12.1	15.0	13.5		22.8	25.4
			(1901)	(1911)	(1921)	(1933)			(1954)
	F		3.1	3.9	4.0	4.2		5.7	6.9
France	M	23.9	10.3	33.4	39.6	45.8	44.8	43.1	45.0
		(1896)	(1901)	(1911)	(1921)	(1931)		(1952)	(1954)
	F	4.6	6.5	6.4	5.7	7.1	6.2	5.8	5.4
							(1936)		
Italy	M	10.7	15.8	13.4	14.2	11.6	9.0	9.3	
		(1882)	(1901)	(1911)	(1921)	(1931)	(1936)	(1951)	
	F	4.8	2.6†	4.5	4.0	4.1	3.8	3.8	
Denmark	M					11.0	15.0		
	F					(1935)	(1945)		
	(20–24)					32.0	41.0		
Czechoslovakia	M					12.0		15.0	
								(1947)	
	F					38.0		46.0	
	(20–24)								
Holland	M	45.3	47.0	48.9	50.5	50.1	50.3		
	(25–29)	(1889)	(1899)	(1909)			(1947)		
	F	21.4	22.5	22.5	25.2	24.6	28.5		
	(20–24)								
	F	55.9	57.6	57.6	60.0	62.0	66.3		
	(25–29)								
Hungary	M				24.6	18.8	72.3	24.1	
					(1921)	(1931)	(1941)	(1949)	
	F				10.2	9.0	9.6	11.4	
	(20–24)								

* From official Census of relevant countries. Data not available for all years.
† Age cohort for males is 21–25 years and for females 15–18 years.

their choice. Which *age* of females they choose might depend far more on ideological factors.

If female participation in the labor force is crucial for the lowering of age in marriage, then more refined calculations are required. Intuitively, I would guess that in those countries in which the male has extremely strong social control over the female the least change has occurred, or there has been even a slight *increase* in age. In these countries, however, the female labor force participation has probably dropped, especially in the *industrial* sectors. Even in France, the nonagricultural sectors still include substantial amounts of home industry where the young girl is under the control of her family or father. In 1901, 32 per cent of Italian females were in the active labor force and in 1951 only 25 per cent of the females were working.[51] Later, we shall take up separately the problem of working women.

Clearly, the relevant factor is not merely the percentage of women in the labor force, but the percentage who are active in secondary or tertiary occupations and have some *independence* in the allocation of their income, so that their salary can furnish the equivalent of a dowry when they get married. Nevertheless, this factor does not seem sufficient to explain variations from country to country.

Let us now consider a further variation in the age of marriage. We noted earlier that laymen commonly believe that industrialization and urbanization led to later marriage. Data for the past half-century do not show this except for a few countries. On the other hand, a few data covering a *longer* time period suggest that there may indeed have been a slight rise with industrialization and urbanization in the West in the nineteenth century. The data for England and Wales show that the age of marriage rose during that period even though it has now dropped again. (See Table II-4.)

Table II-4
Mean Marriage Age for Spinsters and Bachelors and Number of Minors Married per Thousand Marriages in England and Wales, 1876–1956*

Year	MEAN MARRIAGE AGE M	F	NUMBER OF MINORS (UNDER 21 YEARS OF AGE) PER THOUSAND MARRIAGES M	F
1881–1885	25.9	24.4	73.0	215.0
1891–1895	26.6	25.0	56.2	182.6
1901–1905	26.9	25.4	48.3	153.1
1911–1915	27.5	25.8	39.2	136.6
1921–1925	27.5	25.6	48.2	149.2
1931–1935	27.4	25.5		
1941–1945	26.8	24.6	33.8	163.8
1951–1955	26.6	24.2	65.0	271.1
1956	26.2	23.7		

* Data available in the Registrar-General's Office, from Table B in its 58th and 59th Reports, 1876–1884 and 1885–1895. For the years 1896–1920, Registrar-General's Statistical Review of England and Wales, N.S., 1930, Text, pp. 112–3 (H.M.S.O., 1932); for 1921–1956, ibid., 1956, Part II, Civil, p. 76 (H.M.S.O., 1958); see also Census of England and Wales, 1911, vol. VII, Ages and Condition as to Marriage (London: H.M.S.O., 1913), Table 24, p. 428.

In the United States, a parallel pattern seems to emerge, although reliable data do not reach back as far as in England and Wales. Registration data, even at the turn of the century, are worthless for our nation as a whole. Recent computations suggest, however, that in the United States there was a change in the marriage pattern about the turn of the century. At that time, the marriage rate began to *rise* once more; it had decreased from about mid-century until immediately after the Civil War.[52] These data do suggest that the lay notion may have been correct as to at least a *slight* rise in age at marriage when the West entered the modern period—though it does not seem to correlate well with the *phase* of industrialization in the various countries.

The data for France, for example show that in the 1911–1913 period, the average age of males at first marriage was 28.0, with the figure dropping irregularly to about 26 years by the mid-1950s.

However, French figures available for a still *earlier period*, 1853–1881, suggest that the apparent trend may be no more than a normal fluctuation, and that, from 1853 until the World War I years, there was an insignificant drop in the age at first marriage for both males and females.[53] To complicate matters further, much of France was economically depressed during the 1850–1900 period. Finally, to cause additional difficulty, the female percentage of the labor force decreased by about 9 per cent from 1911 to 1954:[54]

On the other hand, the data for Sweden, paralleling those of England and Wales, indicate a slight rise for the latter half of the nineteenth century (see Table II-5).

Table II-5
Sweden: Percentage Married, Males 20–24 Years of Age and Females 15–19 Years of Age, 1751–1910*

Year	Males	Females
1751–1775	13.6	4.1
1776–1800	12.0	3.7
1801–1825	11.6	2.7
1826–1850	9.9	1.4
1851–1875	7.3	1.0
1876–1900	7.8	1.1
1910–	6.8	1.1

* E. G. Sundbärg, "Demography," in *Sweden*, 2d ed. (Stockholm: J. Guinhard, 1914), p. 130.

It may be supposed that industrialization and urbanization did not cause a great change in Norwegian life until very recently. But whatever the general impact on social life, the age at first marriage has not changed substantially since the 1886–1890 period. At that time, the average age of males in first marriages was 28.3, and for females 26.4 years. The changes were extremely minor over the succeeding decade, and by 1955, the average age was 28.2 for males and 25.2 for females. For both males and females there is a drop in average age after the 1936–1940 period, but this may be merely a fluctuation.[55]

Table II-6 shows the ages at marriage in selected Western countries, drawn from marriage registration figures. It seems likely that the age at marriage among the urban working classes has changed only little over the past half-century.

Table II-6
Average Age at First Marriage in Selected Countries*

YEAR

Country	Sex	Before 1900	1900	1910	1920	1925	1930	1935	1940	1945	1950	1955	1958	1959
Norway	M	28.2 (1891–1895)	27.8 (1896–1900)	27.9 (1906–1910)	27.6 (1916–1920)	28.1 (1921–1925)	28.7 (1926–1930)	29.1 (1931–1935)	29.3 (1936–1940)	29.2 (1941–1945)	29.3 (1946–1950)	28.2		
United States	F	26.4	25.9	25.7	25.4		25.9	26.3	26.4		26.4 (1947)	25.2		20.2
	M	26.0	25.0	25.0	24.0		24.0		24.0		23.7 (1947)	23.2		22.3
Sweden	F	22.0	21.0	21.0	21.0		21.0		21.0		20.5	20.4		20.2
	M		28.0	28.0	29.0		29.0		29.0			28.2		
	F		26.0	26.0	26.0		26.0		26.0			25.1		
Finland	M	27.3 (1881–1890)	27.1 (1891–1900)	26.0 (1901–1910)	26.6 (1911–1920)		26.6 (1921–1930)		27.2 (1931–1940)	27.4 (1941–1945)	26.0 (1945–1950)	24.9 (1953)		
	F	25.2	24.8	23.6	23.8		23.8		23.4	24.3	23.6	23.2		
England and Wales	M	25.8 (1876–1880)	26.6 (1896–1900)	27.2 (1906–1910)	27.9 (1916–1920)	27.5 (1921–1925)	27.4 (1926–1930)		27.5 (1936–1940)	26.8 (1941–1945)	27.2 (1946–1950)	26.6 (1951–1955)		
	F	24.4		25.6	25.8	25.6	25.5			24.6	24.5	24.2		
Poland	M				25.8	26.3 (1927–1929)	25.5		25.4	28.0 (1946–1948)		25.5 (1956)		
	F					23.1 (1927–1929)								
Belgium	M				21.8	25.4 (1927–1929)		26.0 (1936)		25.5		22.7 (1956)		
Hungary	M							29.5 (1938)				29.3	29.0	
	F							24.9				25.3	24.8	

* From official sources.

One interesting change—the increasing number of student marriages —indicates the strength of family ties in the middle-class conjugal family. A generation ago students did not often marry, and in Germany a common aphorism was *Ein Student verlobt sich nicht* ("A student does not become engaged"). In the United States, one index of this change is the inclusion of "married students' housing" in plans for college construction. In France, a recent comment notes that the proportion of married male students had increased from 9 to 12 per cent between 1946–1951.[56] Such a pattern can occur only to the extent that the conjugal family continues to accept responsibility for its grown children while they prepare for a profession. Indeed, it might be suggested that the middle and upper strata have begun to follow a pattern that was characteristic of the highest social strata in former generations: It was not expected that the younger generation be independent when they married, or be able to discharge adequately their social responsibilities. They were to be protected by the family, even after marriage, until they could assume their adult positions in society.

7. Proportion Eventually Marrying

The changes in the proportions eventually marrying in selected Western countries are presented in Table II-7.

In general, the data show a slight rise over the sixty-year period, but the changes are *very small*. In considering these small changes, it should be remembered that even in the earlier period something like nine out of ten men and women were married by age 45–59 years. That the proportion moves upward slightly may show that "free" courtship is effective in getting people married; nevertheless, a *large* change upward is not possible. A change from, say 90 to 98 per cent would require an important alteration in the system of mate choice in the West (diametrically opposite to that which has in fact been taking place) in which mate choice would be decided upon by elders with a strong interest in founding marriages and a weak interest in the personal preferences of the youngsters marrying.

The amount of variation between one census year and another is small enough to be due, in some cases, to the changing possibilities of marriage under different age-sex distributions of the population, and to differences in the quality of census enumerations. For example, at the time of the first Australian Census in 1901, there was a shortage of women—a common phenomenon under frontier conditions. Almost all of them could marry, but not all the men could marry. As the sex ratio approached equality, however, men came to have as good an opportunity to marry as women. Thus the increase of the ever-married is greater for the men over the half-century. The change is not due, then, to a change in social customs. The data also show how *little* one Western country varies from another in the proportion

Table II-7

Percentage of Age Group 45–49 Ever Married in Selected Western Countries, 1890–1956*

Country	Sex	1890	1900	1910	1920	1930	1940	1950	1956
United States (45–54 years)	M	90.9	89.7	88.9	88.8	88.6	88.9 (1941)	91.5	
	F	82.1	92.2 (1901)	91.5	90.4 (1921)	90.9	91.3	92.2	
Germany	M	91.3	90.4	91.5		93.8	93.6	93.2	
	F	89.5	88.3	89.0		87.8 (1936)	86.8 (1946)	88.5	
England and Wales	M	89.6	88.6 (1901)	87.3	87.6	89.2		90.2 (1951)	91.1
	F	87.1 (1891)	85.8	83.5 (1911)	83.2 (1921)	83.2 (1937)		84.8	86.9
Sweden	M			84.7	82.4	82.5	83.4 (1945)	85.9	
	F			78.5	70.0	79.5	79.1	81.5	
Australia	M		76.4 (1901)	77.9	80.5	84.9 (1936)		85.7 (1947)	88.2 (1954)
	F		90.2	86.3 (1911)	83.4 (1921)	85.4		87.0	89.5
France	M	86.3 (1881)	89.1 (1901)	87.4 (1911)		91.1 (1931)	89.9 (1936)	88.3 (1949)	88.7 (1954)
	F	86.1	88.3	86.8		88.2	86.7	89.5	90.2
Italy	M	86.3	87.3 (1901)	88.6	88.9 (1921)	89.3 (1931)	89.6 (1936)	90.6 (1951)	
	F	87.2 (1882)	88.0	88.7 (1911)	87.8	86.2	85.0	85.0	
Ireland	M						65.9 (1941)	67.0 (1946)	
	F						74.0	74.0	
Hungary	M							.97 (1949)	
	F							.96	

* Data from official sources.

eventually marrying.[57] The Western countries differ much less when the proportions ever married by some *mature* age are compared than when the 15–49 age groups are compared. The latter group proportion is a conglomerate and shows mainly *when* people marry rather than *whether* they every marry. On the other hand, countries having lower average ages at marriage will ordinarily show a higher proportion eventually marrying (compare the United States and Ireland).

In general, a slightly higher percentage of men than women marry in the West. As the sex ratio of Western countries decreases, a slightly lower proportion of women and a slightly higher proportion of men will eventually marry. On the other hand, in a system of free marital choice, an irreducible minimum of men will not want to marry, so that the proportion of men ultimately married will increase only slightly.[58]

FERTILITY

Since the conjugal family produces for its own needs, and the West has had a declining proportion of its population in agriculture, where children might be useful, there has been a continual decline in the birth rate in most countries since the decade from 1870 to 1880 at the latest. The general decline is well known so that no more is necessary here than an illustrative table of changes in the birth rate of several European countries.

Table II-8
Crude Birth Rates Per Thousand Population in Selected Western Countries (1866–1961)*

Country	Year	Birth Rate Per 1000 Population
Norway	1898–1902	29.8
	1960	17.4
Germany	1890	35.7
	1960	17.7
France	1881–1885	24.7
	1959	18.4
Belgium	1898–1902	28.8
	1960	16.9
England and Wales	1881–1885	33.5
	1959	16.5
Yugoslavia	1898–1902	38.5
	1960	23
Italy	1881–1885	38.0
	1960	18.4
Czechoslovakia	1920–1924	26.7
	1959	16.0
Bulgaria	1920–1924	39.6
	1959	17.6
Hungary	1881–1885	44.6
	1960	14.6
Sweden	1891–1895	27.5
	1960	13.6
Finland	1866–1870	31.8
	1960	18.5
Denmark	1866–1870	30.7
	1960	16.7
United States	1880†	39.8
	1961	23.5

* Data from official sources.
† The above figure is based on census data. The first figure that could be taken from vital statistics data was 25.0, in 1915.

The decline began at different periods in different countries since the larger processes of social and economic change moved at different rates. In the early period of English industrialization, for example, when "domestic industry" existed and the entire family might work at home at weaving or spinning (or even in the beginning of the nineteenth century, when women often brought their young children into the factory), a large family could be economically profitable—or at least, by a summation of all their wages, they could survive.[59] As noted previously, the introduction of the highly productive Irish potato in the late eighteenth century and the reclamation of less-desired lands in Ireland made it possible to support a large family on a small plot, so that the birth rate continued to be high well into the 1840s.[60]

However, it must be admitted that sociology has not as yet determined the major factors in the long-term changes in Western birth rates. Certain connections with economic variables are clear:

1. In general, the upper strata have had lower birth rates than the lower strata.[61]
2. Within any given class stratum, the upper income segments within it have more children than the lower income segments.
3. With industrialization, the birth rate drops.
4. The birth rate increases during prosperity and immediately after a war.
5. The birth rate decreases during depressions.
6. The fertility in rural areas is higher than in urban areas (even in Ireland), where it can be supposed that additional children can be supported because of their contribution to farm production.

But though economic variables of this kind may correlate reasonably well with the differences in birth rates, we cannot suppose that they are the prime *moving* variables, and it is fairly certain that parents do not have children for *economic motives*. A more general statement seems relevant at this point, although it does not solve the problem. Kingsley Davis[62] has pointed out that in all human societies a high evaluation is placed upon fertility, *and* that human beings are socialized from early childhood to marry and beget children. In contrast to the socialization experience emphasizing fertility, there is a lack of emphasis on mortality: a society expends little effort in persuading individuals to save themselves from death. Since people want to stay alive anyway, it is quite easy to get them to change patterns leading to high mortality. But to persuade them to change their fertility patterns is more difficult because these patterns are deeply rooted in a lifetime of socialization experiences that evaluate fertility highly.

In general, then, people are socialized to *want* children as a value in itself, and when they are economically capable of supporting children, they will have them. Economic deprivation may, under certain conditions, have a distinctly adverse effect on the birth rate. In Western Communist nations, where women feel a need to supplement their husbands' income, where they are officially encouraged to work, and where the birth control and abortion policy is lenient, there is a distinct drop in the birth rate.

Correspondingly, no simple "economic" interpretation seems applicable: at the most cautious, viewing most periods of Western history over the past two hundred years, it seems unlikely that one could prove that many parents actually made a profit from their children. If, in fact they did not, then the prime moving variable cannot be economic; the economic merely becomes a facilitating, retarding, or intervening variable. Certainly one could not prove that lower-class parents have more children because they find them more profitable than do middle-class parents. Economically, children must be generally classified as a *loss*. Within a given social circle, social and cultural definitions specify how many children are desirable, and economic factors may facilitate more or less the achievement of this goal.

Our failure to understand this process adequately led to striking errors in predicting Western birth rates after World War II. In conformity with predictions, birth rates went up immediately after the war, but then—unlike any previous experience—the birth rates in many countries *remained* high—for example in the United Kingdom, Austria, the United States, and France. The sociologist cannot be content with any simple economic explanation when he sees that the highly industrialized and urbanized United States has a higher birth rate than the relatively more rural, less industrialized, and Catholic Spain (about 23.6 as against 21.9 births per 1,000 population in 1960).

The changes in the postwar period do, for the most part, fit the patterns we have described up to this point in our analysis of world changes. We may summarize these changes by saying that the groups and strata which formerly had very *different* birth rates have gradually been approximating one another. That is, rural rates have dropped so that the difference between rural and urban birth rates is far less in the more advanced countries than before. The better educated and more prosperous strata, in which birth rates were relatively low prior to World War II, have increased their birth rates somewhat, while the less advantaged strata have decreased theirs. The proportion of families having a large number of children (five or more) has declined, and at the same time the proportion of families with only one or two children has also decreased. In the United States, there has been an increase in the fertility of young women, but a decline in the fertility of older women. That is to say, young wives have their children somewhat earlier, and *complete* their childbearing at an earlier age.[63]

BIRTH CONTROL AND ABORTION: LIMITS ON FERTILITY

Newer contraceptive techniques have of course been the *means* through which these differences between strata, social circles, or regions have been reduced. Here again, however, we must not confuse an intervening variable with a causal variable. It is now well understood that the West has for centuries controlled its reproduction somewhat by various forms of contraception, abortion, and infanticide.[64] Until very recently, the most widely used technique in most European countries was undoubtedly *coitus interruptus*. In Slater and Woodside's admittedly nonrandom British sample, 50 per cent of the respondents reported using this method; even in the report of the Royal Commission on Population the "nonappliance methods" were said to have been more commonly used than any other in marriages contracted before 1935.[65]

Of course, modern contraceptive devices permit a more complete control over conception, but even less effective techniques would have kept birth rates at a low level had they been used consistently by all the Western peoples in a determined effort to keep births at a minimum. Had any such attempt been made, the population of Europe would not have risen so substantially during the eighteenth and nineteenth centuries, since mortality was high during much of this period. We must instead say that the modern *demand* for better control has led to the *development* of more adequate techniques, i.e., has created a large market for the new, improved devices. The wish to control conception has become strong enough to keep the birth rate relatively low in all Western countries, even where modern contraceptive devices are not widely used. The great change, then, is in the value system which has made the new devices more acceptable.

The important change is *not*, therefore, that the birth rate has dropped in the last generation. Its decline had begun in France by the last quarter of the eighteenth century, in the United States by the early nineteenth century, and before 1875 in England and possibly Sweden and Belgium.[66] Rather, the change is in the general acceptance of the opinion that husband and wife may *control* the number of their children if they wish to do so; as a consequence, *both* decline and rise may occur more quickly than in the past as rapid adjustments to alterations in the life situation, such as prosperity or war, or the particular experience of special segments of the population. Within a country or a social group, the *average* level of fertility about which such a movement fluctuates will vary according to the respective social definition of the proper number of children to have.

Certainly, however, if the curve of birth rates towards the latter part of the 1950s is a hint of the future, the average will be relatively low in all Western countries.

It is not clear how much change has occurred in Western attitudes toward abortion. A United States conference on abortion concluded that "a plausible estimate of the frequency of induced abortion in the United States could be as low as 200,000 and as high as 1,200,000, depending upon the assumptions made . . ."[67]

More than 100,000 applications for legal abortion were approved in Czechoslovakia in 1960.[68] In Hungary the number of legal abortions exceeded the number of live births for each of three years from 1958–1960. Certainly a large factor in the extremely low birth rate of the Communist countries in the 1950s was the control over birth by abortion.

It may be impossible to demonstrate that any change in behavior has taken place in the past half-century in the West, and the only good indicator of social change in *values* regarding abortion may be found in the fact that the subject can be openly debated in most European countries, while in Communist countries after World War II, the laws regarding abortion were liberalized. This liberalization occurred in Russia after World War I, but was followed by a tightening of these regulations. However, ideological considerations alone do not account for the low birth rate and high abortion rate in the Communist nations. The severe housing shortages have made large families not only impractical but almost impossible. Married people often cannot live together,[69] the imbalance between wages and prices puts pressure on wives to supplement the family income by working. Thus women often resort to abortion to end pregnancies which might interfere with their occupational demands.[70]

A close analysis of Western rural cultural patterns in a given region usually discloses that there is knowledge about abortion and some resort to it—how much numerically, it is impossible to estimate. In one study of a rural Serbian village, this comment is made:

The most widespread type of birth control, however, is abortion. It is not at all uncommon for a healthy woman to have three or four abortions. Most of them are achieved with the assistance of a midwife, by means of both internal and external manual treatment, or by self-imposed paddling with a plank . . . In a survey of 20 women taken before the war in a village near Belgrade, it was found that the total number of abortions were only a little less than the total number of living children of the same women.[71]

In the national German sample taken by the DIVO Institute, 55 per cent of the respondents were in favor of doing away with the German law punishing abortion severely, or for liberalizing it. Only 36 per cent were in favor of keeping the law, and 8 per cent were in favor of making it still more severe. In the United States, public attitudes seem to support officials who are vigilant in prosecuting physicians who help women to abort, but there remains a large demand for those services by parents and pregnant women who face the problem of an unwanted child.

8. "Equalitarianism" in Society and Family: Values and Behavior

To discuss "equalitarianism" is to discuss a popular topic, "the status of woman." It is, however, almost impossible to analyze fully the position of the female within the entire social structure. Any status must be defined by its relations of obligations and rights with respect to other positions in the society. Hence, when the status of the female changes, so does that of the male; if the woman gains greater rights of choice and decision in many areas, the male must necessarily lose some of his former power in those same areas. Whether we analyze contraceptives and fertility, or the remarriage of older people, we cannot avoid analyzing to some degree the more general question of equalitarianism and the rights and obligations between statuses.

We shall, however, try to restrict our attention to a smaller number of areas that seem crucial, and which have only been touched on up to this point. Specifically, we shall focus on an area that is important to the larger society—work—and an area that is central to the woman's position within the family—the authority of her husband. These areas, interwoven with other areas of interaction, pose difficulties for exposition and analysis. We begin, therefore, with some general comments on equalitarianism in behavior and attitudes within the larger society. This priority appears to be a *causal* priority, since we believe that it is the changing position of women with respect to men in the larger society that has changed woman's position within the family.

CIVIL AND SOCIAL RIGHTS OF WOMEN

Perhaps the most striking change in the movement towards equal rights may be found in a legal datum: in 1900, two generations ago, women were permitted to vote only in New Zealand, and in four states of the United States. By 1954, they had obtained the right to vote in sixty countries (including non-Western nations), and only seventeen independent countries denied them the vote. Women have been permitted to occupy high supervisory positions, and seats in national legislatures. They hold posts in the national cabinets of many countries; they may become ambassadors. Although perhaps the Communist countries are in many respects ahead of the non-Communist ones, most Western countries have permitted women a wide range of freedoms once denied to them: entrance into universities, the ownership of property, making independent contracts under certain conditions, equal inheritance with brothers, and many others. It is no accident, of course, that many of women's rights are to be found in the area of economic freedom, but these in turn are determined by changing attitudes and values.

The West is the first major civilization to give such equality to its women. Even the period of great license of imperial Rome during its decline did not give women a similar position. In Rome, women had great freedom with respect to sexual behavior and divorce, but no range of important tasks was defined as open to them. Indeed, we may perhaps speculate that had Rome put its women to work, the society might not have fallen. Yet neither Rome nor any other society prior to our epoch has ever attempted this solution of its social and economic problems. Why is the West different?

"Machine technology" has been offered as a simple explanation to the question of why women were permitted to earn a living outside the home. Under the processes developed by Western technology, tasks are broken down into small parts with machines carrying out segments of the work. Thus, women and children, or unskilled men, may supervise machines although they lack the strength or skill to carry out alone the task performed by the machines they attend.

But such an explanation is unsophisticated. Few tasks, even in ancient

Rome, required great strength, and women can learn—and in our society have learned—any skill whatsoever, from writing novels of the first rank to performing surgery, from driving an automobile to operating a giant computer. (Millions of brain-hours devoted to the task of isolating and demonstrating *specifically* male skills and talents, motivated in part by a male desire to prove his own innate superiority, have established no conclusions of this kind.) Differences there are, and we owe much of both our sorrow and joy to them, but they apparently do not lie in the realm of those innate abilities which can be trained into skills. With a different set of cultural values and social structure, many of Rome's factories could have been run by women, and its immense bureaucracy of colonial administrators could also have utilized women. Apparently the Romans, the forebears of our Western civilization, saw eye to eye with their descendants in the Western Middle Ages on this point: women were not to be permitted to do important tasks outside the home.

One cannot, then, make a defensible case for the thesis that it is modern technology, with its division of labor, that creates the statistically unusual status of women. Nor can we find any better proof for the notion that it was the desire for economic profit that made woman useful to the West and thus gave her a new position. In all great civilizations, women could have discharged most jobs adequately, had they been trained for them, and all civilizations would have been wealthier had they done so. However, those tasks were culturally defined as impossible for women. I believe that the crucial crystallizing variable—i.e., the necessary but not sufficient cause of the betterment of the Western woman's position—was *ideological:* the gradual, logical, philosophical extension to women of originally Protestant notions about the rights and responsibilities of the *individual* undermined the traditional idea of "woman's proper place."

I do not see at present how such a thesis can be demonstrated, though it would be easy to make a *plausible* case for the idea. Unquestionably, in the Communist nations of Europe, the immediate impulse has been ideological.

It appears more certain, however, that the social *implementation* of this change in values—and all great changes in values must be supported (when they are not caused) by changes in the social structure—was the development of a free labor market, in which the individual was hired for his own skill, with little or decreasing regard for his family position. Using Parsonian terminology, this is a change from ascription to achievement, from quality to performance; or, in Sir Henry Maine's terminology, a change from status to contract. The woman, like the child, no longer needed to depend on her family elders or males when she wanted to work. Consequently, she achieved an independent basis for her own existence, so that she could, in the larger society as well as within the family, drive a better "role bargain." That is, she could achieve a better set of rights and obligations with respect to other statuses.[72]

Men have not, however, yielded their ancient prerogatives willingly. After all, no ruling status group readily relinquishes its powers. We have only to view the battle of colonial peoples for independence over the past few generations, or the attempt by ethnic groups within European countries to gain equal rights, to understand how strong are the resistances to equalitarianism. Journalistic accounts of the position of women in Western nations typically exaggerate their equality, but precisely because this is new and thus worthy of notice. We should, therefore, take a serious look at the extent to which this movement has not yet been full accomplished in *any* Western nation, Communist or non-Communist.

Perhaps a useful point of departure would be an analysis of the implicit values, even of "family experts" in the West. Let us focus on France, since this country seems to fall between the ideologically rather conservative Latin countries (Italy, Brazil, etc.) and the more liberal Communist countries.

The best summary of this position can be found in Andrée Michel's qualitative content analysis of much of the current family literature.[73] She points out that their implicit *value* judgments, often *expressed* as empirical judgments, contain three important themes: (1) the notion of the emancipation of both women and children is seen to be identical with the idea of a "destructive evolution" or "disintegration" of the family; (2) the concept of "the strength" or "solidarity" of the family is viewed as identical with the authority of the father; (3) the "unity" of the family is identified with the prerogatives of the husband and father.[74] Let us consider each of these briefly.

The "menace" of disintegration, destruction, and individualism seems to be equivalent, in the minds of many French writers, to the loss of masculine privileges. Such a menace seems to be found wherever liberal legislation is proposed to grant woman her own voice in such matters as maternity and the choice or exercise of a profession. Secondly, whenever the authority of the male seems to diminish, many of these experts seem to suppose that thereby the family itself has been weakened. Indeed, Rouast seems to be pleased that the French laws of 1938 and 1942, which emancipated the French woman somewhat further, were in fact no more than verbal formalisms which left intact the prerogatives of the husband within the household.[75]

Third, the notion of a family hierarchy in which the male is the final authority is viewed as necessary for the unity of the family; the husband should have the right to decide the place of residence, to give his name to the woman, and to decide on the education of the children. That is, the law is viewed as correct in giving the power of decision to the man with respect to all the affairs of the common conjugal life.

As Michel properly notes, such opinions rest upon myths, and frequently upon debatable or erroneous facts and logic. Here, however, we are not concerned with the *correctness* of these ideas. After all, they are value judgments, and cannot be proved or disproved empirically. For our purposes, they are data. They are especially interesting because they demonstrate that even among an intellectually emancipated group, whose field of interest is the analysis of the modern family, much of the movement to give equality to the woman is interpreted as disorganizing.

We have not located a comparable analysis for other Western countries, but we believe that such an analysis in the United States would locate a substantial number of family experts who would similarly identify women's rights with "the modern disintegration of the family." American experts would less frequently express their own philosophy about the family, and a smaller percentage would accept the French value position just noted.

In a recent study of relatively well-educated Belgian (French-speaking) adult men, excluding the clergy, it was found that their answers conformed to the values expressed by the experts already noted. For example: 32 per cent thought it perfectly all right for a woman with a school-aged child to work away from home, and 42 per cent said it was good that women were allowed to follow all the university courses of instruction, including those of lawyer, surgeon, and engineer. But 26 per cent thought that men should never be under women's supervision as, for example, in an office. Only 25 per cent thought that women would be as capable as men in occupying all higher management posts in industry, finance, and the state, and only 12 per cent said that a husband should not have more authority over his wife than she over him. Ten per cent thought a woman should be less educated and cultivated than her husband, and 10 per cent said that a woman could never become a great scientific genius like Pasteur or Einstein, and 29 per cent thought it contrary to nature for a young woman to take the initiative in openly declaring her love to a young man.[76]

In the actual study, women form about half the sample. Here, I include only the opinions of men, which are more strongly antifeminist than those of the women. The answers are scaled items. I have reported only those percentages agreeing to the most extreme antifeminist responses.

In general, the answers of women are more strongly in favor of giving greater respect or equality to women than are those of the men. The answers given by respondents having a university education are also more strongly favorable. The young are more favorable than the old, but here the study, without being able to make exactly the same comparison, at least suggests the general conclusion of Kirkpatrick a generation ago: that though the young are more favorable toward the woman's position than the old, when *education* is held constant the difference is *not* significant.[77] That is, the differences among the age groups are not great in this Belgian sample. Nevertheless, what concerns us primarily is the simple fact that in spite of the general belief that women have indeed achieved equality, it is clear that even among those who supposedly form the vanguard of opinion, this equality has not been conceded.

Since the attitudes are even less favorable to the equality of women in less educated strata one might interpret all such values as remnants of an outmoded philosophical position, which will eventually disappear along with racist and other similar attitudes. After all, a man may be unwilling to concede equality to a woman, but if she is the manager of his office, he must obey her instructions just the same. Or a university professor might well prefer that his wife stay at home, but she may nevertheless hold a job. Consequently, it might be held that the more important datum would be the extent to which women have come to occupy *important* positions in the occupational sphere, *independently* of men, so that eventually their greater scope of freedom will be conceded in value patterns as it is in behavior.

At first glance, indeed, such a view seems tenable. Certainly women now hold many more high posts in government and industry than they did sixty years ago. And, within the highly industrialized nations, women form a large part of the labor force.

However, the change seems to be more qualitative than quantitative, and perhaps in this fact is to be seen the portent of the future. Women have always worked, in the field and in the home. Even in the cities, only a tiny minority of women were allowed to avoid work. In Western countries that were extremely poor, such as Italy, a high proportion of lower-class women also engaged in *paid* employment, and thus by technical definition were part of "labor force," i.e., formed part of the economically active population. On the other hand, most of these women were engaged in domestic employment or in agricultural work, and in both types of work they were under the supervision of men. Even more important, their jobs were obtained through male kinsmen. If we consider only the 1910–1950 period, most Western countries did experience an increase in the percentage of all females engaged in such "economically active" work.[78]

Few countries, however, show much of an increase. Most increases are less than 4 per cent. Indeed, one must conclude that the work participation rate tended to rise in countries where it had been low, and to fall or remain stable where initially it had been high. If we look only at the nonagricultural work force, the picture is complex. Table II-9 shows that for the 1900–1950 period in some Western countries, although female participation did increase, at most it increased very little; and in Switzerland, the Netherlands, Portugal, Norway, France, and Italy there was a decrease. Of course, the exact percentages are influenced by various technicalities of labor force definitions. In sheer quantitative terms, the changes have not been spectacular.

For example, in Italy at the turn of the century, there were many women engaged in paid employment in agriculture, and the majority of workers employed by the textile industry probably were female. However, there has always been a labor glut in Italy with accompanying unemployment. The small expansion of Italian industry has not kept pace with the decline of female employment in agriculture or in domestic industries of a relatively unskilled type. The resistance of Italian males to their women

Table II-9
Per Cent of Women in the Total Nonagricultural Labor Force
1900–1950*

	About 1900		About 1930		About 1950	
Germany†	(1907)	27	(1933)	30	(1950)	33
Belgium	(1900)	32	(1930)	27	(1947)	25
Denmark	(1906)	36	(1930)	35	(1950)	37
Finland	(1900)	27	(1930)	38	(1950)	41
France	(1906)	37	(1931)	34	(1954)	35
Great Britain	(1901)	32	(1931)	31	(1951)	32
Italy	(1901)	32	(1931)	30	(1951)	28
Holland	(1899)	27	(1930)	26	(1947)	25
Sweden	(1900)	28	(1930)	35	(1950)	31
Switzerland	(1905)	36	(1930)	37	(1950)	34
United States	(1900)	23	(1930)	26	(1950)	30

* Jean Dirac, "Quelques vues sur le travail feminin non agricole en divers pays," *Population*, 13 (January–March, 1958), 72.
† East and West combined.

working away from home has been strong and until recently there was official Catholic Church opposition to female labor outside the home.[79] Even the numerous laws to "protect" women have worked against their employment: since male labor was so cheap, and laws designed to improve women's working conditions increased the cost of hiring them, it has not been generally cheaper to hire women. Consequently, the female participation in Italy's labor force has dropped slightly since the turn of the century.[80]

A study of German working mothers indicated that a large majority worked merely because of financial pressures and that 90 per cent of the female laborers and 80 per cent of the salaried employees would drop out of the labor force immediately if they were no longer under financial stress. However, few women professionals in the same sample said they would leave their work.[81]

In Holland factors at work limiting the participation of women in the work force include the Catholic Church's official prohibitions of employment of married women; these lasted until 1958 in government employment and still remain in force in provincial and municipal regions. In the southern regions where Roman Catholics predominate, many employers agreed directly either with the clergy or with the Catholic trade unions not to employ married women except for minor, menial, or part-time jobs.[82]

Most feminine employment in Norway has been in farming, handicrafts, and industry, and the percentage of women in paid employment has decreased from 35.2 per cent in 1910 to 26.0 per cent in 1950.[83] In the United States, the apparent increase has been very great since the turn of the century, but partly because few women were then engaged in paid agricultural employment, although of course they were engaged in agriculture as members of a family group.

The changes that have occurred in the United States may be noted briefly:

1. In 1890 women in paid employment accounted for about one sixth of the working population; in 1961 they comprised over one third of the labor force.
2. At the end of the nineteenth century, about half of the adult women never entered paid employment; now at least nine out of ten women work outside the home at some time in the course of their lives.
3. Women who reached adulthood about the turn of the century participated in paid employment on the average for 11 years during their lives; today's school girls are likely to spend 25 years or more at a job outside the home, over their lifetime.
4. About two out of every five mothers whose children are of school age are now in the labor force. Over eight out of ten employed women not working on farms in 1890 were in domestic or personal service, teaching, or in the clothing and textile industry; now less than one out of ten employed women are in domestic service, 29 per cent are in clerical work, 17 per cent are semi-skilled operators, 11 per cent are professional and semi-professional workers, and 8 per cent are in sales occupations.
5. The most striking increase in employment has been among married and older women; today the peak participation in paid employment occurs at ages 18–19 years and the proportion working then declines until after age 30, when the percentage of women in the labor force rises for each successive age group. Now, the chances of a woman of 60 working are as high as one of 40.[84]

These changes are not, however, to be found in all other countries, though perhaps they can be found in most countries in which there has been a decline in domestic service, in home and handicraft industries, and in agriculture. We would suppose, even without being able to obtain adequate data at this time, that these changes would be parallel in the European Communist countries. On the other hand, the employment of married women has actually declined in Norway, and in the 1950s it was only 3.5 to 5.6 per cent for the age groups under 60.[85]

Sociologically, it would be much more interesting to compare the percentage of *higher*-level jobs occupied by women over the past half-century. We have not found such a comparison, and believe that existing data would permit only spotty comparisons, since most earlier employment data give employment by type of industry but not by *level* of job. Even in Italy and Spain such a comparison probably would show a marked increase in the percentage of women who hold higher-level positions in most types of occupations. Such a comparison can be made, for example, among French teachers, where the number of women per hundred men in the higher levels has increased markedly since 1900. At that time there were twenty-one women out of one hundred men teaching in secondary schools; in superior schools the ratio was ten women for every hundred men. In 1930, secondary school teachers were 44 per cent women; in technical and superior schools the percentage of female teachers was 25 and 28 respectively. And finally, in 1954–1955, the percentages of women teaching in secondary, technical, and superior schools had risen to 95, 56, and 56 respectively.[86]

In the Soviet Union the reported proportion of women professionals to all professionals was 53 per cent in 1959 as compared with 23 per cent in 1928.[87] One might question the reliability of the data here since even 23 per cent is a surprisingly high figure for as early as 1928, before far-reaching changes had been effected in revolutionary Russia's social system. It is also true that this figure is largely made up of people listed as physicians, and women constitute 75.5 per cent of the medical profession. However, even though women appear to dominate medicine it might be assumed that this number includes medical practitioners at lower levels of competence than we in the United States normally consider qualified as physicians. That is, the figure may include such lower-ranking occupations as medical technicians.

Women in the Soviet Union also seem to comprise a greater proportion of the traditionally male professions than in other Western countries (although, again, caution must be exercised in appraising the percentages). Available figures show that in 1959, 29.6 per cent of engineers, and 32.1 per cent of jurists were women.[88] Even allowing for imprecision in the categories and the possibility of exaggeration in the percentages, there is no doubt that in the Soviet Union and other Communist nations, there are increasing percentages of women in the prestige occupations.

About one in four graduate students at Polish universities is a woman[89] and, according to the 1959 Soviet Census, out of 3,778,000 people who completed higher or university educations, 49 per cent were women.[90]

State encouragement and support of higher education for women, the availability of child-care centers and institutions, and the still unrecovered loss of manpower suffered as a result of World War II,[91] all contribute to the situation of women in the Communist world as a special case within the West.

One might hypothesize that where women have been in a socially and economically underprivileged position, and where men are unable to provide for them at a level viewed as adequate, they are willing, like the young men with few opportunities in tribal life, to seize new career opportunities. Women in Communist China, for example, have had less to lose and relatively more to gain from work than Western middle-class women who expect to be provided for. Western women receive support and encouragement for *not* assuming a career and have a substantial investment in the *status quo;* the women in Communist nations receive propagandistic encouragement at the least, and often material benefits in addition.

Without doubt, the direction of change toward women assuming a place in the professions can be paralleled in every Western country. We must not, however, exaggerate the differences. The percentage of women professionals in the United States has increased substantially over the past eighty years, but the percentage of women in the professions of highest prestige, such as medicine and law, has increased hardly at all. In fact, the percentage of female college graduates who go into the professions is probably lower now than half a century ago, since at that time almost *all* women who went through college went into serious work. In every occupation, even that of social work (which is predominantly female), the percentage of women decreases as one moves up in the administrative hierarchy.

Such an observation can be made throughout the Western world. Although, as has been noted, a majority of Soviet physicians are female, as one moves up through the levels of training and prestige of university and hospital staff appointments, the percentage of women declines. It is likely that this broad pattern—i.e., the higher the level of the post, the higher the percentage of posts in the hands of men—will not change in the coming generations. What has changed, and what will continue to change, is the *proportion* of women in such higher level positions.

It cannot be supposed that all the resistance to these changes comes from the "prejudices of men." Most studies of employment show that women are somewhat less committed to their jobs, are absent more often than men, and, of course, are generally less well trained.

The resistance to equalitarianism may be seen especially in the social assumption that whatever job the woman takes, she should nevertheless continue her responsibility for homemaking tasks. Her husband may help somewhat, but the prime obligation is hers. No one assumes that by taking a job a man is "neglecting" his homemaking tasks. No alternative arrangements or services are available, except to the very rich. Consequently, the burden a working wife assumes is great, and her motivation to continue working is reduced. Possibly, if alternative services were available, more women would express a desire to work, and would feel free to develop career-oriented attitudes.

With reference to women's lack of commitment, even in the United States the young man is much more likely to receive a university education than is the young woman. Of course, the American woman's chances have increased over the past generation, by contrast with Great Britain where the percentage of women among full-time university students has not changed since 1921–1922.[92] More important, a substantial proportion of both women and men prefer that the woman stay at home and not follow an occupation. Norway may be viewed as one of the more equalitarian nations, but three quarters of Norwegian housewives in one sample preferred to stay home rather than work at a paid job.[93]

Chombart de Lauwe has brought together data from studies in several countries on this point and comments, with respect to France, that half of the women in a working-class neighborhood wanted to stay home while 40 per cent preferred to work outside the home. In another and larger sample, 56 per cent of men and women preferred the woman to stay at home.[94] In a public opinion poll, 69 per cent of men and 67 per cent of women said that it was best for a woman to devote herself to her home.[95]

In a sample of working wives in Germany, the women were asked whether they would give up their job if they could; 63 per cent said that they would.[96]

A Belgian public opinion survey done in 1950 reported 71 per cent of the respondents as saying that women should stay home even if there were no children.

Ishwaran reports that girls in Holland are generally disinclined to work outside the home and very few envisage a career aside from that of housewife. They seemed to reflect the attitudes of their mothers (of a sample of 415 mothers, nine worked part-time and only six worked full-time outside the home) and did not seem to think it proper to work unless absolutely economically necessary.[97] Even university girls seemed unsure of their career goals, although boys in the same situation seemed relatively free of tension in the matter of choosing a career.[98]

A more restricted Detroit sample of women *already* in the labor force was asked whether they would work if they did not have to, and 34 per cent said that they would not. Although 66 per cent said that they would work even if they did not have to, more than half gave "noncareer" reasons for working, such as escape from the household or obtaining luxuries. This last group did not work because of any strong career orientation.

Many variables enter into these opinions. Since women are expected to continue to discharge their domestic duties even when they work—and this is true in Russia as well[99]—a woman who works takes on a great burden. As the studies of time budgets have shown, the working woman has to work more hours per week than one who stays home. For example, in a careful study of time budgets of French wives, it was found that the married woman with a job had to work from six to well over twenty hours per week longer than the married woman without a job.[100]

It should be kept in mind that in some countries a pattern began to be accepted, as much as a generation ago, that wives should work a few years in order to get established, or that young girls should get some training in case their marriages did not work out satisfactorily. Baumert claims that even in the higher social levels girls must now earn their own dowry.[101] A survey carried out among an extremely conservative group—French-Canadian Catholics—reported that half of 45 thousand such couples believed that brides should continue working after their marriages.[102] Forty-two per cent of the future husbands and 37 per cent of the future wives said that the bride should work "more than one year."

This change in the definition of appropriate wifely behavior, and its emphasis upon establishing the home through the additional earnings of the wife, means that the wives of lower-class husbands are much more likely to be in the labor force than wives of husbands in higher social strata. On the other hand, it seems likely that the middle- or upper-class wives more frequently *prefer* to work than do lower-class wives,[103] which would tend to support my earlier speculation about the influence of economic factors on women's attitudes toward work.

A recent study of German working mothers indicated that a large majority worked merely because of financial pressures and that of this group, 90 per cent of the laborers and 80 per cent of the salaried employees would drop out of the labor force immediately if they were no longer under financial stress. However, few women professionals in the same sample said they would leave their work.[104]

A few comments on these points will attempt to sharpen some of the issues involved in this area of change. First, it seems possible that there is some relationship between the drop in age at marriage in many Western countries, and the extent to which young or older women have entered the nonagricultural labor force. Secondly, unquestionably a higher proportion of the upper-level jobs in most occupational sectors of Western countries can be attained by women, as compared with fifty years ago. This change is most striking in the Communist and Anglo-Saxon countries, although it is apparent in all. Of course, such changes are to be found in the *intermediate* levels of competence and supervision as well. Thirdly, women have not, on the other hand, moved very rapidly into the upper levels of jobs over the past generations, certainly far less quickly than should have been supposed from their movement into universities, the opening of curricula and training opportunities, and the seemingly strong feminist movement of a half-century ago. For example, though it is true that some women have become physicians in the United States, over the past half-century women have not *increased* their share of this highly prestigious profession. They have, of course, come to occupy many quasi-professional jobs such as laboratory technicians. Even when they have become medical specialists, their specialties have primarily been the "female" specialties, those associated with traditional womanly activities like psychiatry, pediatrics, and gynecology.

Fourth, in most Western countries, women can now obtain training, and can, under some handicaps, enter almost any occupation, including those traditionally open only to men. But, fifth, their *motivation* to do so is undermined initially by a socialization that still emphasizes that certain jobs are *male* tasks, and that a woman should not take a career seriously. In addition, their motivation is continually undermined by the acceptance in all Western countries of the idea that a woman must choose between two exclusive alternatives—work *or* home—an idea demonstrated best by the fact that the married working woman is still expected to carry on all her domestic duties, regardless of job demands. By contrast, a man's motivation to work is never undermined by such a choice: he *has* no choice. Even in Communist countries, it must be remembered, women can stay at home and much propaganda is devoted to persuading women to take outside jobs.

Finally, in spite of the great percentage of women working in the United States and in some other Western countries, it can be supposed that only a small fraction of adult women have a serious career orientation. This lack of career mindedness is not necessarily sex specific, however.

Many men, as well, have only a modest interest in their jobs: in a Detroit area survey,[105] although 83 per cent of the men and 66 per cent of the women said that they would work even if they did not have to do so, three fourths of those men gave "negative reasons" for working, and in addition, 17 per cent of the entire male sample said that they would not work if they did not have to do so.[106] Every study of men's satisfaction with their work shows that the percentage who like their work increases with the level of challenge, prestige, and income, and we can suppose the same pattern applies to women. Thus, the lower-class woman is much more likely to have to work, but is much more willing to stay home if the man's income rises sufficiently to permit her to give up her job.

WOMEN'S POSITION WITHIN THE FAMILY

If the Western trends towards equalitarianism in work and the larger society cannot easily be shown to have the same pattern in all countries, the position of the woman *within* the family is still more difficult to assess, because even fewer quantitative data are available. Perhaps both the paradoxes and aspirations inherent in this question were captured by the statement of a Yugoslav analyst about the modern family in his country: ". . . the creation of the socialist family type [is] founded on *individual* and *reciprocal sexual love* and on the *true equality of the spouses*. It is necessary to confess, however, that in Yugoslavia this type of family is found rather rarely at the present time, especially with respect to the latter characteristic."[107] The paradoxes may also be seen in the problem created by West Germany's new constitution, which asserted that there was to be full equality of the sexes in all fields without any qualification, and that legislation had to be made to conform with this new provision before March 31, 1953. However, when the legislators went to work, they could not reconcile this legal mandate with the attitudes, values, and practices of the German family. Indeed, they did not succeed in rewriting the legislation, and eventually had to leave specific decisions to German judges in particular cases.[108]

The central problem is an empirical one: What *was* the past? What is the present? There is general agreement that the woman has obtained considerably greater freedom than she possessed a half-century ago, and that the old "patriarchal family" is uncommon in Western countries; but in many specific areas of conduct, the husband is dominant in every family system of the West. Moreover, and more important for an analysis of time trends, we can ascertain, at least intuitionally, from a reading of books of advice, philosophical discussions, speeches, and diaries from the past that the *ideal* of the dominant male used to be much stronger than at present, but anyone who has had personal experience with a wide range of older families knows very well that women often had great power, and that even when she deferred to the man publicly, she often managed to have her way just the same.

In spite of the apparently equalitarian answer given by the British sample as to who manages most of the money, Michael Young's study, as well as other observations, suggests that in the lower strata of the English family, the husband manages to retain many privileges denied to others. Even when the French woman draws up a marriage contract which permits her full freedom and control over her money, she is likely to leave it in the hands of her husband.

The findings get paradoxical, and this may well result from the *intellectual* equalitarian bias which is not necessarily expressed in practice. For example, in a national German sample, 79 per cent of the men and 87 per cent of the women responded favorably to the statement, "Men and women have the same rights and the same duties." In response to two epigrammatic phrasings, one of which emphasized the dominance of the man and the other the dominance of women, a majority were positive to *both*.[109]

	Per Cent Men	Per Cent Women
Dienen lerne beizeiten das Weib.		
("A woman should learn to serve.")	59	53
Der Mann denkt, die Frau lenkt.		
("Man proposes; woman disposes.")	64	73

A Berlin sample was asked in 1946 whether, within a family, a girl should have the same rights as a boy, and over 90 per cent said "yes."[110]

On the other hand, when a Dutch sample of families was asked about decision making at home, it was found that although most couples said that the mother and father made decisions together, the father actually participated in a greater number of decisions than any other person in the household. In money matters, particularly the acquisition of "costly objects," 75 per cent stated that the mother and father decided together and 6.5 per cent stated that the father decided alone. It was felt, however, that the males actually did exercise the greater influence among the percentage answering both. Where it was answered that mothers made the decisions (5.5 per cent) these decisions were mainly in such household matters as food buying.[111]

We do not believe that at the present time a precise judgment can be made as to how far the Western countries have moved in their *values* concerning the place of the woman within the home, and perhaps it is not possible to weigh adequately how much her behavior has changed over the past half-century. As noted previously, it seems likely that in general, male attitudes are somewhat more conservative than female attitudes, and that the upper-stratum male maintains more authority than the lower-stratum male.

Without comparable data from fifty years ago, it is impossible to prove how much change has occurred. It does seem likely, however, that where traditionalist opinions are reported approving the man's right to decide these matters no great changes have occurred.

The claim has been made that the German worker gives his salary to his wife and that the same pattern is to be found in France. The East German migrant miners who work in the Ruhr do not follow this pattern. Some research has been devoted in England to the problem of the maldistribution of income within the family caused by the husband's refusal to give more than a fixed sum of money to his wife, thus reserving the disposal of all the rest to his own decision. On the other hand, the pattern of giving all the money to the wife seems to be found in the north of England.[112]

The following disagreements according to sex and country are interesting. Although the data refer to a period that is now half a generation past, at the same time they apply mainly to countries which are reputed to give rather great freedom to the woman in handling family matters, especially the use of money. Thus: 69 per cent of the Australian women but only 51 per cent of the men (1943) thought that the woman should own whatever housekeeping money remained unspent. Twenty-five per cent of the Australians polled thought that both sexes should have equal say, while 5 per cent thought the decision should be the husband's. Of the remainder, 7 per cent thought the leftover money should be spent on the home, and 3 per cent were undecided.

In the United States (1946), 27 per cent of the men, but only 11 per cent of the women, thought that husbands should have the most to say in deciding how family money is to be spent; and 16 per cent of the men and 23 per cent of the women thought the decision should be left to the woman. About half (men—46 per cent, women—55 per cent) said both should decide.

On the other hand, 32 per cent of a United States sample, but 54 per cent of a British sample, reported that the wife managed most of the money in the household. In general, however, in these and in other such questions, there seems to be a strong "egalitarian bias." That is, where respondents are permitted an answer which seems to be "decide together," they are likely to choose that answer, perhaps even more frequently than the truth would determine. For instance, 24 per cent of the British sample and 39 per cent of that of the United States chose this answer.

It is interesting to note that in Great Britain (1943) 75 per cent of those polled thought that wives should be allowed to keep savings out of housekeeping money and that 72 per cent of the men told their wives how much they earned a week. In general, the majority of both men (48 per cent) and women (43 per cent) around the world seem to think the husband should decide where the family is going to live. Thirty-five per cent of the men and 11 per cent of the women thought the choice should be up to the wife.[113]

Baumert reports that the dominance of the male was greater in the independent professions and generally in the higher levels of each class stratum than in the lower[114] Some of the data for both Darmstadt and Paris are presented in Table II-10.

Both Baumert and Fougeyrollas generally find that the woman's position is stronger when she has a job. Similar conclusions may be drawn from American data, based on experimental situations in which the husband and wife are faced with a decision problem.[115]

Although much popular sociology has been devoted to the supposed relationship between German authoritarianism and the German patriarchal family, analysis not only shows that the patriarchal family in Germany has been weakening for a half-century or more but suggests that other family systems in Western nations have in fact been fully as patriarchal as the German.[116]

Far more data on authoritarianism or patriarchalism in the German family exist than data for other western family systems, but the differences among European nations do not seem to be profound on this point. Without comparative data, however, no conclusion can be reached. (For example, a 1946 German survey found that 73 per cent of an American Zone sample stated that "the father should be unquestioned law in the family,"[117] but we do not know how many Swiss, Spanish, or Danish fathers would give a similar answer).[118] For example, 52 per cent of a Danish sample in 1944 said that husbands do not even "occasionally help the wife with domestic work other than washing pots."[119]

Baumert reported that in 32 per cent of the German households in his sample, husbands did help their wives in domestic duties. Eighteen per cent of the wives stated that their husbands helped, but had reservations in doing so. On the other hand, 27 per cent said that he should help and 21 per cent said that he should help under certain conditions. However, 41 per cent of the men and 68 per cent of the women said that he should *not* help in such duties.[120] A more recent study gives a still more patriarchal picture of

Table II-10
Who Determines Family Expenditures*

Darmstadt	INCOME			
	Under 200 DM	200–400	400 and Over	No Answer
Husband decides	19%	14%	32%	31%
Wife decides	35%	33%	24%	10%
Both	46%	53%	44%	59%
Number answering	103	180	75	29

Paris	TYPE OF OCCUPATION					
	Ouvriers	Employees	Fonctionnaires	Prof. liber	Commerce Artisans	Milieux d'affaires
Husband decides	8%	11%	14%	21%	36%	95%
Wife decides	77%	61%	59%	58%	28%	0%
Both	15%	28%	27%	21%	36%	5%
Number answering	98	57	38	24	65	18

* Gerhardt Baumert, *Deutsche Familien Nach Dem Kriege* (Darmstadt: Roether, 1952) p. 148; and P. Fougeyrollas, "Predominance du Mari ou de la Femme dans le Mènage," *Population*, 6 (January–March, 1951), 91.

household duties, but it contains a liberal sprinkling of equalitarian attitudes as well.[121]

The rapid acceleration in the proportion of working women has brought ambivalent attitudes about family role patterns in Poland as well. The press has reported that young husbands of working wives who leave the house-cleaning and even cooking to them grumble that " 'progress' may have come too fast."[122]

After evaluating the conflicting comments and data published by Shaffner, Rodnick, Schelsky and Wurzbacher, Baumert comes to the conclusion, which seems eminently reasonable, that claims of fundamental equalitarianism in the German family (or in any other European family) are not correct and that an unequivocally equalitarian family is rarely to be found. In the final analysis, only few family relations are not determined by the male. It is not possible at present to state just how well such a statement could be applied to other countries. In reality, in all countries there are many women who manage to dominate the men, but it seems likely that in most countries, when the husband tries to dominate he can still do so. Even when the husband performs household chores, his participation means that he gains power—the household becoming a further domain for the exercise of prerogatives in making decisions.

Perhaps the crucial qualitative difference is to be found in the extent to which, in one country or another, the male can still dominate *without* a definite effort to do so. It may be this which distinguishes the present period from fifty years ago, and on this point we do not believe that data are available.

9. The Disintegration of the Extended Kin Network

A major thesis of this volume is that most family systems of the world are moving toward a conjugal system, but that because their traits are very different, each may exhibit different trends in a number of areas. For example, the divorce rate may rise in some systems, but drop in others. However, an equally central thesis is that *no* family system as a whole may be called "nuclear," if by that it is meant that the family system is reduced to the unit of parent and children. At a *minimum*, the members of each unit are tied to other units through a common member of a given nuclear family. For example, the brother has continued social relations with his sister, and thereby with his brother-in-law and nephews; the father continues to have social contacts with his daughter and thereby with his daughter's family, his son-in-law and grandchildren. Thus, even in theoretical terms, a "nuclear" family system seems impossible without a great expenditure of ideological fervor and social energy and we may more properly refer to the *conjugal* family. Consequently, the widely held thesis that in the most highly industrialized nations, a genuinely nuclear system has come into existence, or is emerging, seems doubtful at best. If it *is* appearing, and if the extended kin network is disappearing, then a fundamental change in family patterns is taking place in the West. Can this change be demonstrated?

Since we have not found adequate comparative data on this point, we shall confine ourselves mainly to England and the United States. These countries presumably have moved furthest toward the conjugal system and are the most industrialized of all countries. The state has intervened relatively little, either to "rebuild" an old family system or to establish a new one. Of course, no comparable data exist for half a century ago. On the other hand, if in these countries the extended network is still functioning, and if it includes a wide range of kin, then we can at least conclude that *not* much change has taken place—and in an analysis of social change, this is an important conclusion. We shall consider this problem with respect to the following four main areas:

1. The size of the kinship network according to various criteria.
2. The frequency of interaction with extended kin.
3. The kinds of activities engaged in with the relatives.
4. The areas where relatives attempt to exert control.

Although the size of the kinship network reported varies from study to study, the number of intimate, "familiar," relatives recognized by the respondents casts much doubt on the supposed isolation of the conjugal family. In a still unpublished sample of 182 "nuclear" Jewish families in the New York City area, a tabulation was made of the "familiar" kin and the effective kin (those with whom Ego maintained *some* kind of contact, such as those seen at large family gatherings or even more frequently). Table II-11 shows the blood kin (affinal kin excluded) for these two categories.

In an intensive study of a small number of families in London, the Firth group tabulated *recognized kin* (recognized by informant as related to him by consanguinity or affinity, whether or not known by name) and *nominated kin* (whose names are specifically known), as presented in Table II-12.

In a similar presentation for a set of London families with Italian background, the number of recognized kin ranged from 123 to 386, and the number of nominated kin from 107 to 260.[123]

In a sample of 728 Detroit families asked about their frequency of contact with relatives, it was found that 67 per cent saw their relatives once a week, 20 per cent once to a few times a week, and 13 per cent a few times a year or less. No person interviewed said that he *never* saw his relatives.[124]

A sample of San Francisco families was categorized as having either high or low family status (social rank), and high or low economic status. Their frequency of participation with relatives is reported in Table II-13.

As can be seen, these data suggest a somewhat high frequency of participation with relatives and also indicate the extent to which social rank by prestige or economics is correlated with frequency of interaction. An-

Table II-11
Number of Familiar and Effective Cognatic Kin*
(in per cent)

Number of Familiar Kin	FAMILIAR COGNATIC KIN—CLIENTS[a]					
	Nuclear Family		Wives		Husbands	
0	—	(0)	7	(13)	7	(12)
1–15	34	(62)	75	(136)	80	(145)
16–30	49	(90)	16	(29)	12	(21)
31–45	13	(23)	2	(4)	2	(4)
46–60	2	(4)	—		—	
61–75	2	(3)	—		—	
	EFFECTIVE COGNATIC KIN[b]					
0	—		1	(2)	—	
1–15	11	(20)	46	(83)	34	(61)
16–30	27	(50)	41	(74)	49	(90)
31–45	32	(59)	11	(20)	15	(27)
46–60	20	(37)	2	(3)	1	(2)
61–75	7	(1)	—		1	(2)
76–90	1	(2)	—		—	
91–105	1	(2)	—		—	

* Hope Jansen Leichter and Candace Rogers, unpub. ms., 1961. Leichter also uses the term "cognatic kin," in a way that cuts across all kin categories included in her study, and refers to the fact that no affines are included; i.e., they are all blood kin.
  [a] Kin with whom Ego maintains some form of contact. Includes kin seen at "Big Family Gatherings" or more frequently. This arbitrary criterion was frequently given in interviews as an operationally defined boundary for minimal interaction. Figures extracted from *ibid.*, Table 11. Filial kin—children, grandchildren, and great grandchildren—are excluded.
  [b] Kin with whom Ego maintains *frequent* contact. As defined, it is an "interaction" criterion, although it would probably overlap with a "sentiment" criterion. These are kin that Ego sees more frequently than familiar kin—at weddings, funerals, Bar Mitzvahs, etc. *Ibid.*, p. 2.

other Detroit sample also reports frequency of association with relatives, and the results are as follows: 49 per cent saw their relatives at least once a week, 13 per cent a few times a month, 12 per cent about once a month, 22 per cent less often, and 4 per cent not ascertained. Seven hundred forty-nine people were interviewed.[125]

Table II-12
Range of Kin for Twelve Households, London*

Households	Recognized Kin	Nominated Kin
A	246	176
B	231	140
C	223	53
D	209	162
E	167	137
F	160	122
G	157	144
H	126	96
I	113	99
J	52	43
K	45	34
L	37	14

* Raymond Firth (ed.), *Two Studies of Kinship in London*, London School of Economics, Monographs on Social Anthropology, No. 15 (London: The Athlone Press, 1956), p. 42.

Table II-13
Frequency of Social Participation with Relatives† By Family and Economic Status, San Francisco*
(in per cent)

Frequence of Participation By Group	Low Family, Low Economic Status	Low Family, High Economic Status	High Family Low Economic Status	High Family High Economic Status
About once a week or more	33	30	45	42
A few times a month	10	15	13	13
About once a month	13	13	14	11
A few times a year	10	16	14	19
About once a year	8	12	4	6
Never	26	15	10	8
Total per cent answering	100	100	100	99
Number answering	172	191	170	168

* Wendell Bell and Marion D. Boat, "Urban Neighborhoods and Informal Social Relations," *American Journal of Sociology*, 62 (January, 1957), 294.
† Relatives other than those living with the respondent.

Equally high percentages may be found in a report on 312 Los Angeles families.[126] In the San Francisco sample, respondents were asked on whom they could call to take care of them if they were ill for as long as a month. Table II-14 shows that relatives and friends are the most frequently named groups, and that relatives are far more important.

Table II-14
Reliance on Individuals for Help in Illness, by Status,† San Francisco*

Whom Could You Call on for Help If You Were Ill for Even as Much as a Month	PER CENT NAMING AT LEAST ONE MEMBER OF THAT GROUP			
	Low Family Low Economic	Low Family High Economic	High Family Low Economic	High Family High Economic
Relatives	71 (172)	84 (191)	81 (170)	85 (168)
Friends	60 (172)	65 (191)	53 (170)	73 (168)
Neighbors	34 (172)	29 (191)	45 (170)	40 (168)
Co-workers†	40 (145)	46 (166)	24 (149)	44 (156)

* Bell and Boat, op. cit., p. 396.
† Unemployed persons are excluded. Parenthetical numbers are those upon which percentages are based.

The Detroit Area Study also asked about the type of help received or given by wives. It listed the major types of help, and out of 723 wives interviewed, the results were as follows: 46 per cent said they had received help with baby sitting, and 47 per cent said they had given such help; for help during illness, 54 per cent gave and 50 per cent received; 34 per cent had received financial aid and 30 per cent gave it; for help with housework, 26 per cent received and 27 per cent gave; 12 per cent received business advice and 10 per cent gave it; 12 per cent helped in finding a job and 8 per cent got such help; and 11 per cent received valuable gifts and 8 per cent gave them.[127]

Although parents and siblings are the most frequently named relatives, other relatives also help. Whether they have a high or a low income, they give and receive about as frequently. In answer to the question: "Considering friends as compared to relatives who don't live here, which would you say are most important to you?" Seventy-nine per cent of the wives answering the question said that relatives were most important, and only 17 per cent named their friends.[128]

The close links between children and parents are related to the maintenance of a kin group outside the nuclear family. American attitudes concerning parent-child ties were tested by questions in a National Opinion Research Center survey that dealt with the duties of adult sons and daughters toward aged parents. Answers showed that a majority of older persons and a majority of the American public believe that responsibility toward one's parents takes precedence over other responsibilities. Fifty-one per cent of older people and 50 per cent of other persons expressed the opinion that when faced with a choice between visiting his parents on Easter and entertaining his wife's relatives who had just come to town, a man should visit his parents. Questioned concerning other similar dilemmas, most respondents indicated that they felt strongly about adult sons and daughters making every effort to accommodate to the demands of aged parents.[129] Sons, daughters, and other relatives of older persons—the ones who would actually have to assume responsibility toward them—were less certain that "parents come first."

The frequency of parent-child contacts was probed in a comparison of London and San Francisco samples taken among daughters, in which it was ascertained that 42 per cent of the San Francisco sample (Menlo Park), 41 per cent of the Woodford (London) sample, and 45 per cent of the Bethnal Green (London) sample saw their parents once a day. The percentages of sons seeing their parents once a day in the same samples were 22 per cent, 19 per cent, and 26 per cent respectively.[130]

Actual reliance on kin to care for children was indicated by four-fifths of a sample of recently married German working women.[131] In Poland, in spite of the availability of state-run nursery schools, Lutynski found that only 11 per cent of the mothers in his sample took advantage of them while 30 per cent preferred to let grandmothers care for children. (He noted that white-collar people particularly disliked using the state child-care agencies.)[132]

Litwak attempted to determine whether social and geographical mobility are correlated with a low intensity of family ties. Although his data do not show to what extent ties with families or origin are *maintained*, he was able to show that a high percentage of those who are socially or geographically mobile do have extended kin ties.[133]

Finally, Sussman made a study of an urban, middle-class, white Protestant, economically prosperous, and well-educated sample of ninety-seven families in the New Haven (Connecticut) area, who had 195 married children living away from home.[134] Ninety-two of the ninety-seven parents said they did not expect financial support from their children, but 154 of the 195 children had established a pattern by which they received help and services from their parents, including gifts of furniture and household equipment, financial assistance, services in gardening or house construction, or care of grandchildren at various times. The parents did not, however, give regular monthly contributions except during emergencies.[135]

Parents seem to give moderately and in special situations in order not to conflict with the authority of the new head of the family, but at the same time they try to obtain a strong tie with their children and grandchildren.

The pattern of kin assistance and involvement existing in England and the United States also seems evident in Poland with reference to help and contact between parents and children. Parents maintained ties with the newly-married pair through mutual help. Some economic support was given by the wife's parents in 58 per cent of the cases and by the husband's parents in 35 per cent of the cases.[136] Couples helped parents with no apparent distinction between the wife's and husband's parents; 20 per cent helped the former and 20 per cent aided the latter.[137]

Returning to the subject of mate selection, we can speculate that parental desire and pressure to have children marry into their own class is aimed at protecting conjugal ties. Parents of young people studied by Lutynski generally favored their children's marriages to white-collar mates, although this was especially true of white-collar parents.[138] Social origin of prospective mates was important to blue-collar parents who thought in terms of their own future relations with the future in-laws of their children.

Sussman's study found that, among his ninety-seven families, 166 of 195 married children had been expected to make class-endogamous marriages, and 145 of these 166 children did so. The parents tried to control the setting of their children's dating and courtship by residence in class-typed neighborhoods, stressing family and clique expectations, and arranging recreation and social activities for their children. Eighty-one per cent of these parents admitted that they had used economic threats toward their children at some time to influence their behavior. In thirty-six cases, they were able to discourage unfavored marriages.[139]

Thus, the few available studies seem to show that no matter what index is used, the family in the most industrialized nations has not taken on the supposed characteristics of the nuclear family system. The extended kin network continues to function and to include a wide range of kin who share with one another, see one another frequently, and know each other. Moreover, if we consider the difficulties of transportation and communication of a hundred years ago, and the numbers of relatives in interaction compared with their frequency of interaction *now*, common sense suggests that the frequency of social participation between the average modern nuclear family and its relatives may not have been reduced at all.

The data also suggest that the higher social strata maintain a more vigorous kin network than do the lower strata. Naturally, the contacts of upper-strata families with their kin form a smaller proportion of their total social interactions, since the higher strata belong to more voluntary organizations, clubs, and formal groups than the lower strata. On the other hand, they have more resources with which to maintain their ties with kin, and because of these means, mutual exchanges are also more frequent than in the lower strata.

In addition, though the ideal of independence for the young couple seems to be overwhelmingly accepted in those countries, parent-child ties in fact remain very strong, supported by visits and exchanges that may be only a little less frequent, if there has been a change at all, than those of fifty or one hundred years ago.

Large family gatherings, however, seem to be less frequent now. Instead, individuals, or their nuclear families, usually visit a related nuclear family. Cumming and Schneider suggests that the predominant "style" of interaction among kin emphasizes the sentiments of kinship—i.e., ritual activities, friendliness, and sociability—but lays less stress on mutual aid or instrumental activities.[140] Indeed, kin are likely to be embarrassed at asking for help unless they have previously been in close personal association with one another.[141] It is likely that the recognition of reliance among kin for services was more frank a hundred years ago.

Several studies also suggest the importance of women in maintaining these kinship relations since families in both Great Britain and the United States seem to emphasize the woman's more than the man's side of the family. Intuitionally, it seems likely that a hundred years ago the contacts would have been maintained far more by the men than by the women, since the ties would most frequently arise from work obligations, the ownership of land, and plans for settlement and transportation.[142]

Finally, we suppose that a qualitative change, impossible to measure, has taken place—that, to a considerable extent, relatives are now assimilated to the status of "ascriptive friends." That is, one has an obligation to be friendly to them, but they, in turn, have an obligation to reciprocate, and they may not intrude merely because they are relatives. Perhaps another way of phrasing this is to say that in spite of the perhaps lessened intensity of extended kinship ties, the ascriptive character of kinship greatly increases the chances of relatively frequent contact and thus the chances of reciprocal services and sentiments.

RELATIONS WITHIN THE NUCLEAR FAMILY

Beyond the area of role relations of husbands, wives, and parents, still fewer conclusions can be demonstrated. The relations of brother-brother, sister-sister, mother-daughter, mother-son, father-son, and father-daughter were not described with much exactitude fifty or one hundred years ago in the

West. We have no precise analysis of either the real or ideal behavior of the period, since the moralistic books and articles of that time do not tell us what people actually believed was proper behavior. After all, in our generation as well, we can see the discrepancy between sermons or the platitudes of advisors to the young, or etiquette books, and the values and attitudes to which young and old people are really committed. Perhaps the discrepancy was greater then, but we cannot even be sure of that.

We do not believe that any scientific purpose would be served by a speculative assessment of the changes in these relationships. Hundreds of essays have been written to describe these alterations, and we suppose that they do not err greatly; rather, we simply do not know how to test them.

Most of the specific comments may be subsumed under the large categories already treated: the lessened authority of parents over children and the liberalization of standards of sex behavior.

It might be useful, nevertheless, to list briefly many of the changes that are thought to have taken place in Western families. Doubtless, some countries have changed less than others, and for that reason I shall focus primarily on changes which are thought to have taken place in the United States. A cursory reading of European literature suggests that all of these changes are thought to have occurred to a greater or lesser extent in all Western countries. Although I do not doubt that these changes have actually taken place, the data necessary for proving that they have do not seem to have been collected and analyzed by the social historian. It still may be useful to note them here, with the thought that they may become the object of serious investigation.

Just as husbands can no longer command unquestioned obedience from their wives, so parents seem to have lost part of their authority over their children during the past half-century. As in any role relationship, the change occurs on both sides: children are less willing to comply with parental orders, but parents themselves have also lost the secure faith that their orders should be obeyed. Parents do not even support one another in the effort to control the young as rigorously as they did in the past. Modern children are described as "spoiled," but after all, parents spoiled them. Grandparents sometimes bemoan the breakdown of family standards, but no observer can fail to see that grandparents contribute their share to the change when they are caring for their own grandchildren.

The modern doctrine that members of the nuclear family should love one another, and that permissive love is "psychologically healthful" for the child,[143] has given ideological support to the normal pressures of children toward greater choice in all matters, and to the greater opportunity to be free economically at an early age. This change may be seen in the reportedly greater amount of affection between parents and children, and the less formal behavior expected between them. Terms of respect and social distance are less commonly used by youngsters, and elders are likely to become a "pal" or "partner" to their children and may be on friendly, equalitarian terms with them. The lessened formality may express greater intensity of emotionality between parents and children, but this is not at all certain. Even in the Puritan family of the seventeenth and eighteenth centuries in the United States there was considerable emphasis on love between parents and children.

Parents are also thought to allow their children to be exposed to a wider variety of experiences, though older children are permitted a wider experience than are younger children. In addition, younger children are allowed freer expression of their own views about most subjects than in the past, at least ideally. For example, 61 per cent of a sample of German adults gave positive responses to the statement, "Children have their own views, correct for their own world, which should be respected and not corrected by the person who rears them."[144] When asked about decision making, only 17 per cent of the German youths said that their fathers did the deciding, while 29 per cent of the older generation said that their fathers did so. Correspondingly, it is no longer considered necessary for children to be called upon as frequently as in the past for minor services or errands, although in all Western countries young people are supposed to be responsible for various household chores. On the other hand, in all countries for which data are available, most children report that they receive corporal punishment (even when the parents deny that they administer it).

This set of reported changes links very closely with the supposed alterations in the relationships between parents and their *adult* children. A recent study of relations between parents and married children reveals a number of ideals which would presumably have been different two generations ago.[145]

Ninety per cent of the parents and their adult children questioned said that after marriage a person's main loyalty was to his own family, and only secondarily to his parents. Although about half the parents had lived with their adult children at some time or another (often the children had lived with them at the beginning of the marriage), 94 per cent of the small sample of parents said that this was not a good idea.[146]

Although an overwhelming majority of both parents and adult children rejected the notion that parents *should* live with children, only 7 per cent of the children said that they *would* not permit it at all, and an additional 8 per cent gave no answer. All the rest agreed that under some circumstances, they would accept their parents into their homes.[147]

The attitudes of adult unmarried children conform to those of their parents. They wish to live separately even before they are married. This comment has also been made for the Netherlands.[148] Older parents do not want to participate in the household of their married children, and the children prefer to live away from the older people.

In industrializing areas generally, the trend is toward neolocality.

However, under certain conditions, such as during the postwar housing shortages, married children are often forced to live with parents. Japan, Czechoslovakia, and Poland are examples. In the Polish cases, 33 per cent of a sample of young people lived with parents.[149] Of these, 21 per cent lived with the wife's parents and 11.7 per cent lived with the husband's family. In general, blue-collar families more often lived with their parents than did white-collar families (45 per cent *vs.* 35 per cent), and then most often when the parents belonged to the same socio-occupational category.[150]

With the smaller family of our time, and the longer lives of the population, there are *fewer* adult children to take care of *more* older parents. Consequently, the burden of old age has increased somewhat. Nevertheless, the movement toward independence seems to arise from *both* parents and children. In the United States, the older generation seems increasingly to seek *their* independence from the young. One aspect of this is the smaller emphasis given to the idea of "building up an inheritance." The older generation comes to believe that they have the right to spend their own money on their own pleasures. They may choose activities, recreations, and even clothing to suit their own tastes rather than conform to the behavior considered appropriate by their adult children. In recreation especially, they feel free to take part in any active sport, if they desire to do so. They may therefore refuse, more than in former times, to "act their age."

On the other hand, as noted earlier, adults give a considerable amount of support to their children, and in turn children are expected to help the old folks whenever it is necessary. The willingness to live without any aid from one's adult children is partly dependent on the *need* for help. In a French sample, 50 per cent of the adults still in the labor force, but only 40 per cent of those retired or about to retire, intended to live away from their children.[151]

Of those who expected to live with their children, 23 per cent were still in the labor force as compared with 39 per cent of those in the category of retired or about to retire.

The pattern of independence may be seen in one further facet, perhaps of no great intrinsic importance: The young boy or girl who earns money outside the home is now much less likely to contribute much of that money to the family income. For instance, Baumert observes that lower-class German youngsters do not give their earnings to their parents as frequently as they once did.[152] In some families, the money may be taken from the young person and placed in a separate account or, as in the United States, "saved for your college education." It is not expected, however, that the young person will make a continued contribution to the household income, and with each succeeding year of adolescence the expectation grows smaller. A somewhat similar pattern is exhibited by young Spanish bachelors working in France, who send all their earnings to their mothers to be saved for their eventual marriage—as they would do if they lived near home.[153]

In the United States the pattern reverts when the person is adult, and very frequently a contribution to the older household is expected if the younger adult still lives in the parental home. This applies, however, to adult children only. For example, although a majority of upper middle-class adolescents in the United States work for outside income, this only means that they have much larger incomes to spend, since earnings are often supplemented by an allowance from the parents.

The apparent changes in the relations among brothers and sisters parallel the patterns just noted. Independence is expected. Love is also expected, and so is support when it is needed. Age grading has little significance. The older brother may no longer command obedience from the younger brother. Girls may engage in activities which were once thought proper only for boys, such as sports or dating without a chaperone at an early age. In the contemporary United States it would be thought a ridiculous posture for a brother to "protect his sister's honor" by demanding that her date "explain his intentions." Equality of inheritance is expected, a change which has become typical in Western Europe. Even in the Netherlands, a relatively conservative country, boys and girls inherit equally, and there is no primogeniture.[154]

Much has been written about the growing "parent-youth" conflict of our times. Newspapers and magazines are replete with articles about "Teddy boys" in England, the "Chuvaki" in Russia, and similar groups in the United States, Poland, France, and other countries. The feeling is widespread that adolescents are in considerable revolt. That there is much parent-youth conflict seems to be certain. We should, however, view it in a broader perspective. In any era of social change, parent-youth conflict will be intense, since the values and attitudes of the adult were acquired in a situation which the younger generation no longer experiences. The more rapid the change, the greater the discrepancy between the values and attitudes of the two generations: It is perhaps at a maximum between an immigrant generation and their assimilated children.[155]

Even at a minimum, some conflict between the generations necessarily appears because the older generation must combine affection with authority and must teach both ideals and reality. Conflicting authorities try to guide the young, and there are always psychosocial and physiological differences between the generations.

The question is, how much *above* the minimum is the level of the present conflict between generations? And, perhaps more important, where is the conflict greatest? For example, in the contemporary United States, there is undoubtedly greater conflict within *rural* families than urban families, for the rate of social change is unquestionably greater in rural areas. On the other hand, at the turn of the century, much more parent-youth conflict was found in cities, especially among immigrant groups.

Finally, much of the "rebellion" is a myth. The adolescents of our time have taken on the external semblance of rebellion—the "D.A." haircut, motorcycle jacket, and bluejeans in the United States; the Edwardian costume in London; and so on. However, studies of attitudes among such groups and their parents do not show great differences of values between the generations. Yesterday's rebels usually succumb to their parent's socialization, and the revolt of adolescence is discarded when they become married adults. Although at any *given* time, there usually is such a population of adolescent rebels, this group is replaced by *new* adolescent rebels; they themselves become ordinary married couples.

10. Divorce

Even marriage analysts are likely to consider divorce a misfortune or tragedy, and high divorce rates evidence that the Western family system is becoming disorganized. Actually, divorce must be viewed as an important element in Western family systems, an escape valve for the tension which inevitably arises from the fact that two people must live together. A majority of the world's societies have evolved this solution, which is used under varying circumstances and with varying consequences.[156] Divorce differs from other solutions for tension, such as annulment or polygyny, in that the women are free to find another husband.

The most striking change in this area of family relations is, of course, the lessened social stigma attached to divorce. It is safe to say, even without quantitative data, that at the turn of the century almost everyone who divorced was viewed as having lost respectability to some extent, and from many circles the divorcee was excluded. The change may be seen through another index, which is very likely paralleled in Western countries other than the United States: Alterations in laws during the past half-century in the United States have made divorce only slightly easier; it is rather the *attitude* and definitions of both judges and the society which have allowed easier divorce by interpretation of old provisions in a new way. For example, "cruelty" as grounds for divorce formerly was narrowly defined as harsh behavior—physical cruelty—but now is interpreted as almost any behavior that either spouse does not wish to tolerate.

One may say, with reference to the rise in the divorce rate (in all countries that permit divorce), that it is based upon (1) changes in the *value* system, (2) lessened emphasis by the *circles* of friends and kin on the necessity for marital stability, and (3) new *alternatives* to the existing marriage. For instance, the wife can now support herself, even if poorly, by her own effort. In addition, since there are many other divorcees, both husband and wife can almost certainly remarry. In most adult age groups in the United States, the chances of eventual marriage are higher for divorcees than for single people of the same age.

It is unfortunate that for most countries, we must be content with the ratio between marriages and divorces in any given year; those divorces, of course, do not all come from the marriages contracted in that year. Such a comparison creates spurious relationships in more refined tabulations. For example, such a ratio among older persons who are receiving pensions or who are retired will show an extremely high ratio of divorces to marriages simply because, while there are very few marriages, there are *some* divorces (though few). A better comparison, of course, is to compute the number of divorces per thousand *existing* married couples. However, for most countries, this datum is not available.

Table II-15
Divorce Rate Per Thousand Marriages in Selected Western Countries, 1900–1960*

Country	1900	1910	1920	1930	1940	1946	1950	1956	1960
United States	75.3	87.4	133.3	173.9	165.3	274.4	231.7	246.2	259.0 (1959)
Germany	17.6	30.2	40.8	71.4	125.7	125.5	145.8	89.2	88.7
Switzerland		55.8	64.1	84.7	95.2	110.9	114.3	106.0	111.9
England and Wales		2.2 (1911)	8.0	11.1	16.5	77.3	86.1	74.4	69.5
New Zealand	14.5	18.6	47.1	55.9	60.7	103.9	98.9	82.6	87.2
Australia	13.5	12.9	22.6	41.7	41.9	91.0	98.2	90.4	88.9
Belgium	11.9	18.5	20.6	34.8	50.5	62.2	70.8	62.8	70.4
Norway	12.6 (1901– 1905)	22.6 (1906– 1910)	33.0 (1916– 1920)	46.4 (1926– 1930)	43.3 (1936– 1940)	69.5	85.4	82.3	88.5 (1958)
Denmark		30.0 (1901– 1910)	44.0 (1911– 1920)	79.4	98.5	186.3	176.8	193.0 (1955)	186.1
Yugoslavia			42.8 (1921)	42.1	57.4	101.6 (1947)	96.1	123.6	131.4
Sweden	12.9	18.4	30.5	50.6	65.1	116.0	147.7	175.4	174.6 (1959)
France	26.1	46.3	49.4	68.6	80.3	207.2	106.2	100.5	82.4 (1959)
Netherlands		21.5	41.8	48.2	46.3	147.5	77.7	60.1	57.7 (1958)

* Data from official sources.

Because divorce has aroused such moralistic fervor, few objective studies of its place in Western family systems have been made. Many pretended "analyses" begin with the well-known rise in the divorce rates, and then use selected anecdotes to describe the unfortunate consequences of divorce. Almost no studies exist that have attempted to chart the real consequences of divorce in the lives of those affected.

There is some hope that from the demographic data and a few survey materials collected over the past half-century some patterns of changes in divorce behavior can be abstracted. At the present time, I am engaged in collecting necessary data for whatever cross-national divorce patterns may be evident. Unfortunately, many of these are in fugitive publications or government publications, which are difficult to locate even in major libraries. Such items as average length of marriage or age at marriage can be obtained but, beyond such small matters, I cannot at the present time predict what will emerge, or even whether the findings will be sufficiently interesting sociologically to be reported.

On the other hand, I am willing to state some hypotheses about the changes in divorce patterns that have been occurring in the West over the past half-century. It must be emphasized that most are based on theoretical deductions for family sociology, although all can be supported somewhat by specific data. I shall touch them briefly with no more than a passing comment. The future will disclose to what extent any of these are correct.

The first item is the change in attitude towards divorce, which can be documented only by content analysis. However, it seems useful to present here some data on divorce attitudes in various countries of this generation. The permissiveness of present attitudes is apparent, and can be supposed to represent a real change from attitudes at the turn of the century. Permissiveness, of course, is only one factor in the rise in the divorce ratios themselves.

In Italy during the late 1940s and early 1950s the majority of people were still against divorce. According to a national sample in 1947, 68 per cent were "probably in favor" or "certainly in favor" *against* a law instituting divorce. By 1949 this figure had been reduced to 61 per cent. Males were more in favor of divorce than females; 40 per cent were probably or certainly in favor as against 28 per cent of the women.[157]

There is some suggestion of change in the rise of the percentage favoring divorce among younger ages. Another index of change is the higher percentage in favor among urban segments. In 1949, 34 per cent of the national sample was certainly or probably in favor of a law instituting divorce, but 38 per cent in cities over 100 thousand in population and 63 per cent in Milan. Even in Rome 39 per cent were in favor.[158]

Another survey taken in May, 1955, shows that 40 per cent were generally favorable by that time and about 60 per cent in favor for certain extreme situations (such as attempted homicide of spouse, abandonment of family for fifteen years, etc.).[159]

In general, when *cross*-tabulations of these results are presented, they show what the sociologist would expect them to show: A greater acceptance of divorce by urban than by rural people, by men than by women, by those with more rather than less education, and by the doctrinally less strict in religion as contrasted with Catholics or Calvinists. Without great error, one may suppose as a secondary aspect of this change that over time, the *differences* in degree of acceptance have become narrower and will shrink even further in the future. That is, the segments already accepting divorce will not change their views towards still greater liberalization, but those which now are strongly against divorce will come to accept it more.

In countries (e.g., Italy) having no legal divorce (that is, permitting remarriage by both parties) marital disharmony is not missing. Perhaps one index of shift in *behavior*, where no change of importance has occurred in

89140

Table II-16
Attitudes Toward Divorce, Various Western Countries
(in per cent)

Should divorce hearings be speedier, or should it take more time for a case to be heard in court? (Great Britain, 1946)	Speed up	49
	Take time	36
	Don't know	15
Should divorce be made easier or more difficult? (Australia, 1945)	Easier	27
	More difficult	53
	No change	19
Should divorce be easier to obtain in your state (United States, 1936)	Yes	23
	No	77
Do you think the divorce laws in this state are now too strict or not strict enough? (United States, 1945)	Too strict	9
	Not strict enough	35
	About right	31
	Undecided	17
In your opinion is it too easy to get a divorce in this country or not easy enough? (Canada, 1943)	Too easy	27
	Too hard	24
	About right	32
	Undecided	17
Do you believe it's all right that people can get divorced? (Germany, 1949)	Unconditionally yes	79
	Conditionally yes	7
	No	9
	Undecided	5
Are you in favor of making divorce easier, harder, or are divorce laws all right now? (Germany, 1949)	Easier	29
	Harder	13
	As now	43
	Don't know	15
Should divorce be made difficult or easy? (Germany, 1954)	Difficult	66
	Easy	26
	Indifferent	6
	Don't know	15
Should divorce be permitted in this country? (Brazil, 1946)	Men:	
	Yes	70
	No	22
	No opinion	15
	Women:	
	Yes	48
	No	37
	No opinion	15
Should divorce be permitted in this country? (Italy, 1949)	Yes	36

the divorce laws, is the great rise in the number of Italian *separations*, from 4,523 in 1933 to 10,912 in 1947 (the peak of the divorce rise in most Western countries), and then a drop to 8,152 in 1952. Indeed, Deputy Sansone, in a 1955 speech, proposed five grounds for divorce and commented: "One can assert, then, without any error, that a considerable number of couples, perhaps no less than 40,000 each year, break the matrimonial bond."[160]

The most important consequence of the change in absolute number of divorces and in the lessened stigma attached to divorce is that the re-marriage of divorcees has become the rule rather than the exception. In *After Divorce* I asserted that an increase in the divorce rate is correlated with an increase in the rate of remarriage. This conclusion seems to be roughly correct. Of course, the second (or later) marriage is accompanied by less fanfare, and the divorcee cannot command quite so high a price on the marriage market as can the single person. An exact test of this trend is not easy because of the procedures for recording marriages in various countries, but in the countries where the datum is available the proportion of divorces among those marrying seems to rise. In Australia, for example, the percentage of male divorcees among those marrying increased from 2.0 per cent in 1931–1935 to 6.6 per cent in 1951–1955.[161]

Another consequence is that divorces now occur *earlier* in the marriage, in part because alternatives to the existing marriage may be found, and the stigma is not so great. Those who find a marriage difficult to bear will now try to get out at an earlier stage than before. Thus, we would expect the *average length* of marriages in Western countries ending in divorce to have become shorter.[162]

Next, divorces are more common among childless couples, although American analysts have generally agreed that this association occurs be-cause couples who are likely to divorce are also likely not to have children, rather than because children "prevent" divorce. However, when calcula-tions of the trend over the past half-century are made, they will probably show that the difference in divorce rate between the childless and couples with children is *not* so great as it once was.[163] (In 1900–1904 50 per cent of divorced Dutch couples were without minor children; the percentage had dropped to 40 in the 1925–1929 and 1951–1955 period.)

These data constitute merely one aspect of a more fundamental change in divorce patterns to be expected in Western family systems over the past half-century, and in the future as well: Divorce occurs not only among *deviant* families or couples who are nonconformists but also among the normal population.

Moreover, partially as a result of the former changes, we would suppose that the consequences of divorce have become less harsh for the children as well as for the husband and wife. In the United States at least, it seems clear that children of couples who did *not* divorce, but who remained to-gether in disharmony, are more likely to have subsequent histories of personal difficulties than children of divorced parents (although, of course, these latter will experience more difficulty than children of happily married families).

Finally, over a longer period of time, a change in the *class* distribution of divorce can be expected. Since family law has been typically made by governmental authorities to solve the problems of the middle and upper strata in most Western countries, the divorce rate *was* higher in the upper strata when permitted at all. That is to say, it was impossible for any but the well-to-do or the powerful to obtain a divorce, and even difficult for them. This was not necessarily true in societies in which divorce procedures were *not* specified by governmental authorities (for example, in the Arab countries). In the West, as divorce procedures were liberalized and made economically available to all, the normal difficulties of lower-class family life were permitted an expression in divorce.

At the present time, the divorce rate in countries with liberal divorce provisions is higher in the lower social strata, and lower among the upper strata, whether the index of rank is education, occupation, or income.[164] For all Western countries, then, a gradual shift in the *class distribution* of divorce should occur, from a positive correlation between class position and divorce rate, to a negative one.

One final change, less certain than the previous ones noted, is the shift in the sex distribution of plaintiffs in divorce suits. We suppose, without having adequate data, that there has been, or will be, a change from a majority of suits being filed by men to a majority being filed by women, simply because this solution to marital difficulties was once primarily in the hands of men and it has come to be expected that women take the initiative.

chapter

III

Changing Family Patterns in Arabic Islam

░░░░░░░░░░░░░░░░░░░░░░░░░░░░░░░░░░░░░

ANTHROPOLOGISTS and sociologists have given little attention to the Arab family over the past half-century. There has been far more *systematic* field research among the Bantoid peoples of Africa. In the absence of detailed field observation of the family (which Arab male jealousy might have greatly impeded) scholars have had to rely too much on essentially literary and legal sources, although the statements of ideal domestic behavior gleaned from these sources, and eloquently expressed in the Koran, cannot be ignored in any analysis of the family. Adequate analysis requires, however, that they be compared not only with the actual social behavior but also with the ideals and norms of the less literate—e.g., peasants and desert Bedouins—who may not know or accept all the doctrines of the culture's great philosophical tradition.

It seems likely that a flood of sociological studies in the major Arab countries will appear in the next decade, and lists of recent books suggest that the task is already under way. The rising sense of destiny expressed in the nationalistic fervor which has freed them from foreign domination has also stimulated the beginning of economic planning for the future, with the aim of enjoying the benefits of industrialization. These developments have created a recognition of the need for facts on which to base adequate planning and are already stimulating some surveys and studies; these are attracting the attention of foreign scholars who will carry out additional research. Many of the present gaps in our knowledge of the Arab family will probably be filled within the next decade.

The pride and self-assertion of nationalism have created a minority body of elite public opinion which asserts that progress should proceed without violating the ideals of the Arab cultural heritage. Another group, equally proud of this heritage but more sensitive to the widespread disapproval of Arab family customs among the "advanced" nations, has reinterpreted the Koran to prove that the "true Islam" had been distorted (e.g., with reference to polygyny) and that in fact many improvements in customs would be in conformity with the Koran.[1]

Moreover, some assert with reason that (as in India) the British and French colonial policies, in supporting the *status quo*, had prevented a natural evolution of family patterns from ancient ways under the ostensible policy of not interfering with "native custom."

The official propaganda of Arab nations shows great sensitivity to the opinions of the West, especially to Western disapproval of traditional Arab family customs. In attempting to prove how far the Arab world has progressed, it emphasizes the family legal codes, promulgated over the past fifteen years, giving far greater privileges to women. In speeches, pamphlets, and publicity photographs it suggests that Arab women have now achieved equality in the political and occupational realms. This propaganda exaggerates the amount of change by focusing on a minority of Arab women and thus hindering an accurate evaluation. Nevertheless, the propaganda is itself a social datum, an index of the attitude and aims of the Arab leaders who are guiding the direction of modern change. Consequently it yields a clear picture of the future and is not to be ignored.

To what extent the Arab world may be treated as a cultural unit is open to debate, and indeed Arab leaders fiercely argue about which nations ought to be included. Morocco might be excluded, "because after all they are Berbers." Lebanon is more than half Christian. Even Egypt has been called non-Arab; Desert Bedouins call *themselves* (but no one else) Arabs. Turkey is admittedly non-Arab, as witness the fact that it uses the only authorized translation of the Koran into a foreign tongue; elsewhere in the Moslem world, as far East as Indonesia, its Arabic purity is maintained. Eastward of Iraq the Islamic world stretches, but it is not Arab.

Here we shall try to ignore both the grandiose, all-inclusive dreams of pan-Arab leaders and historical hair-splittings so that we can focus on those nations and groups in which the Arabic heritage has been dominant. These include Morocco, Tunisia, Algeria, Egypt, Syria, Jordan, Lebanon, the Arabian Peninsula, and Iraq. Within each, we shall ignore where possible the Jewish, Christian, or European groups. Comparable data within these limits cannot be obtained for most family patterns. Arabic Islam is one of the important world cultures, and it will be useful to assess the changes now going on so that later research may build on these findings or correct them where necessary.

1. Choice of Mate

Ideally, the Arab groom *could* not choose his own bride, since he never had an opportunity even to see her until the marriage contract had been concluded; he usually waited until the wedding day itself. The accumulation of the bride-price was outside his power since he had no wealth of his own. Both families, but especially the girl's, insisted (in conformity with Koranic prescription) on equality of rank, so that every effort was made to prevent those emotional attachments between a young girl and boy which so often frustrate the wiser decisions of elders.

The elders aimed at maintaining the power of decision in their own hands primarily to achieve two important goals. First, the Arab family was—again, ideally—an extended family system, made up of the married couple, their unmarried sons and daughters, and married sons and their wives and children; in other words, the unmarried females in the direct line, the females who married into the agnatic line, and the males in the direct line. Beyond this, but important in matters of political dispute or power, was the lineage. Beyond that was the subtribe or *ashira*, and still beyond that the "tribe" or *qbila*. These larger kinship structures will be treated later in this chapter.

At no point in this ideal extension of kin was the husband-wife relationship a central focus. The extreme fragility of the marriage bond undermined still further the importance of the conjugal relationship. Economically and socially the man remained secure in his familial network. Women came and went. The network was linked by kinship, not by husband-wife bonds. The choice of mate reaffirmed the significance of the extended family: A marriage brought in a female to produce more family members, to adjust to the larger family, to create wealth for it by her work, but not to found an independent nuclear household with her husband.

Of nearly equal importance, however, was the great emotional attention given to the sexual purity of the female. In a curious sense, her very insignificance in most areas, which prevented her from having much value no matter what she did, increased her weight in this one area in which she could express her will. To prevent any assault on her purity she donned the veil at age 10 or 11 years at the latest, and she remained with females in the harem until she ventured forth to marry. She was not even present at the conclusion of the marriage contract, where her guardian or father represented her. No effort was too great to assure her chastity both before and after marriage. Any social arrangement that permitted choice would also have increased the likelihood of "shame"—shame for her father and brothers more than for her husband. He could repudiate her on the marriage night if she was not a virgin, or later if she showed any tendencies to stray, but the obligation to avenge the shame by killing or otherwise punishing her and her lover was the obligation of father and brothers: She was their *'ird*, their "honor." The focus of the family's attention was on preventing all the actions that might lead to any transgression of chastity, real or symbolic, rather than on preventing choice as such,

The real, rather than ideal, situation was somewhat more complex, since it varied by class and region as well as changed over time. It may be granted that young men cannot choose invisible women, but some women could be seen. Among Syrian Bedouins and peasants, the veil was not used except for the well-to-do. Even in the Arabian peninsula a generation ago, the *burqa* (a mask completely covering the forehead and face, with slits for the eyes) was worn only south of Kuwait, and even then not all the tribes there wore it. Northwards, a transparent black veil was worn. In the general region from Iraq to Palestine in the late 1930s, the veil was not worn in the villages (though it was in the towns).[2] The veil was common in Egypt a century ago, but many lower-class women "even in the metropolis, never conceal their faces."[3] In villages and towns of North Africa, the identity of young girls might be a mystery to a passing English or French traveler, but not to the local marriageable males who had watched them for years. Overtly, they were supposed to look aside when passing young women, and to avoid social interaction with them, but within those limits a young man could indulge in some observation. Males in all cultures learn to make acute judgments about what is underneath, from the cues made by swishing clothing. And Arab women were always noted for their walk. Even in the cities, which contained the extremes of advanced tolerance and of highly guarded surveillance, a young man might glimpse a face through a lattice. And, of course, young women could easily look at men.

A girl was permitted to go unveiled among some men: for example, a man who had suckled at the same breast (a "milk brother") or, in general, with any relative with whom marriage was forbidden.

It would be unwise to understate the restrictions on free social interaction among eligibles. By Western standards, they were severe until very recently. However, fiction and imagination have so seized on the Moslem harem that a more moderate evaluation should be stated here. As is obvious on sober thought, only a tiny minority of Arabs ever lived in the classical harem of Western fantasy. Polygyny was uncommon, the costs of such a cloistered establishment were enormous, and, in fact, most women had to be given at least enough freedom to work at agricultural tasks or urban crafts. The majority of Arabs were, and are, poor, and the male cultural ideal asserted that fighting was for men but work was for women. Such a "male vanity culture" required that women be given modest freedom. Although the Bedouins were fiercely jealous, their women had to work long hours in the encampment, doing everything from preparing food and keeping the tent in order to watering the stock at some distance from the camp. Certainly the male ideal was to immure the women, but few men had the power or the wealth to achieve it.

In addition, though few women felt any strong resentment against the veil itself until recently—indeed, as in India, it can be manipulated with skilful seductiveness—many women did object to the lack of freedom it symbolized and resisted its extreme forms. Women wished, for example, to visit one another, and most were able to do so. Some were persuaded by the arguments of Moslem reformers, beginning with Qasim Amin at the turn of the century,[4] or by the Western example to resist further, and they achieved still more freedom of decision and movement. We shall discuss later some of the events in the history of that emancipation, but at this point it is enough to insist that even in "traditional" Arab life not all young girls and women were guarded by eunuchs behind an iron grillwork. By a generation ago a goodly minority of educated women in major cities were not only obtaining freedom from the veil, already enjoyed by most of their less privileged sisters, but also some freedom in social interaction.

In Syria during the late 1920s, "in the large cities, and especially in the modern quarter, Moslem women who go out unveiled are becoming increasingly numerous."[5] Moreover, the young girl, "especially in rich and cultivated families of the large cities, can take off the veil, not only before the men of her family, but even in the presence of almost all her distant relatives"[6] With reference to being secluded and guarded, "it is not customary today in Syria." Girls go to school after puberty and go out "freely and often, without being watched or accompanied . . . the young Moslem teachers who leave their family and go to the most distant villages and *cazas* to instruct their female coreligionists are no longer rare."[7]

In the 1930s a new custom was beginning in the large cities: some educated young Moslems were insisting on seeing the girl and visiting her to make her acquaintance.[8] Among peasants, in the 1920s and 1930s, the young man himself might express his choice, since he had had some opportunity of seeing the girl; this was also the practice among Bedouins,[9] even though among some of the wealthier ones the use of the veil was beginning to *spread*.[10]

But although a young man might express his choice, neither the girl nor the young man had any *right* of choice. A young man could ask his mother or an adult friend of his father to persuade his father to *permit* him to marry, or to select a particular girl, but he himself could not finance the marriage and thus the decision was not in his hands. As an adult, if he was economically independent, he might make marriage arrangements himself for a second or later wife.[11]

Under some circumstance, he might make arrangements for a first wife. Of course, the woman had almost no right of decision. If she was a widow or divorcée, she had some small chance of freedom in this matter.

In the towns and cities, once the decision was made that the young man should be married, the elder women of the family instituted a search for the girl. In the villages, of course, they would already know all the possible eligibles. Lane's description of the search in Egypt of a century ago is little different from that of Daghestani in the Syria of a generation ago. After obtaining information about houses in which there were girls and eliminating those families who ranked too high or low, the women as a group began their visits. They did not explain the reason for their visit and it was not necessary to know the family visited. In fact, Daghestani claims that sometimes they did not even give their names.[12]

In Lane's account, a female matchmaker was often used, but one important detail may be in error. He claims that the women ask the visited family what property the girl possessed. This is unlikely. Their task (and pleasure) was to evaluate the girl's personal qualities and those of her family. The economic and political arrangements belonged to the males. The girl served them, spoke with them, and was dressed well for them, since her family wished to find a good match for her. Having left one house, the women would go to another until they had examined all the prospectives mates, so as to be able to describe them to the young man.[13] Nothing in the Koran forbids a young man to see the young girl before marriage, but his choice was based on their reports and counsel, and upon the decision made by his father and paternal uncles.

The actual marriage arrangements were made between the males of the two families. If their rank was high, the haggling over bride price or dowry was done by elders or men of position, who accompanied the two fathers. Within the same class level, a girl would command a higher bride price if she was beautiful, if she was talented, if she had a sweet disposition, if she had much property of her own, or if her family was unwilling to give her up. In middle- and upper-class circles, in most Arab regions, one half to two thirds (usually the latter) of the bride price was paid at the time of signing the marriage contract. The remainder had to be paid if a divorce occurred.

Among Bedouins, all the bride price was usually paid when the contract was concluded. Middle- or upper-class families used the bride-price to purchase a trousseau of jewels, furniture, etc., and added to that sum whatever their generosity and local custom required. As will be noted later, this property belonged to the girl and remained hers during and after the marriage. Among the urban and rural poor, as in China and Japan, the girl's father was likely to keep the money and give only a token present to the bride. A father did have that right, but a man of standing risked censure (it was milder in rural areas than in urban) if he was not generous in his gifts to his daughter.[14] This fact is the source of the misunderstanding among some that "each bride has a dowry which the groom must match before the wedding"; that many men remain unmarried because they cannot "match the dowry" of an acceptable bride; or that the boy's father must know how much "dowry" she will bring.[15]

The Hanafite sect of Mohammedanism claimed that the consent of both parties was necessary, but not that of the parents; the Malekites took the position that the man's consent was necessary, but not that of the girl, unless she was no longer a virgin.[16] In practice, however, the consent of both bride and groom was taken for granted. The conclusion of the marriage contract did not require the presence or the response of either, although in fact the groom was sure to be present. The legal code in force in Syria in the early 1930s, like the later codes in other Arab countries, required that the girl's and man's consent be obtained, but also that of the parents. Nevertheless, the underlying social fact was that no marriage would take place without a marriage contract and the payment of a bride price; there was no courtship, and the young man and woman had no basis for implementing an independent decision.

A further structural element in the Arab kinship system was of central importance for freedom of choice: the preference for marrying father's brother's daughter. A man had the *right* to marry her under a wide range of varying circumstances (differences in education and talents, social rank, etc.) which might otherwise make a match between the two people unlikely. This unusual limitation on freedom of choice, patrilateral parallel cousin marriage, has been discussed so frequently in the past that only little comment on it is necessary here.

The pattern was found throughout the Arab world and at all class levels, especially in upper-stratum families. It was reported about 150 years ago and apparently did not change much until a generation ago.[17]

The exact form it took varied from region to region, primarily by whether the *girl* had a reciprocal right, whether the marriage was a *duty* incumbent on the boy, and how far the right could be claimed. For example, in some regions the man could claim the right to be paid if he gave up the girl; here and there, the claimant felt he could kill a man who tried to marry her. It is reported that in most regions the girl's family could not successfully oppose the marriage if the boy's family insisted on it.

Although no adequate cross-cultural explanation has been given as to why this pattern became so firmly entrenched in Arab family life, some of its consequences are clear. Since in such a marriage brother would be giving money to brother, the bride-price was much lower. Since both sides were interested in maintaining the honor of the same lineage, the husband could be sure that her chastity would be guarded adequately after the marriage. Land and any other property would remain in the same agnatic lineage. Children of brothers would have about the same social rank, and the Koran enjoined the marriage of equals.

These statements, it must be kept in mind, are not "reasons for" the creation or the maintenance of a custom. They are consequences or the rationalizations that people might give for the custom. However, the same sought-for consequences can be found in many other cultures in which this mating pattern was not found.

This custom, then, limited the choice of both the younger and the elder generation. In common with other barriers to freedom of choice, this one has weakened and almost disappeared except in the more remote country districts.[18]

How common was it? In an area of high fertility and where sons were highly valued, it could be supposed that almost every girl could be claimed by *some* father's brother's son. On the other hand, the willingness to accept such a claim varied in intensity. Lane noted a century ago that in Cairo the custom was not followed so much as in other parts of Egypt, but that such marriages were less fragile than other types of unions.[19] It is likely that this urban-rural difference was found elsewhere in Arab countries even at that time. In the 1920s in Syria this cousin-right had begun to weaken in the large cities, and it was no longer customary for a rival to pay off the agnatic cousin in order to wed the girl.[20] In the 1930s, it continued to exist among peasants and the Syrian aristocracy (though somewhat modified).[21] Patai himself notes that in the Arab middle class up to 1947 there had been a decline in the strength of the claim,[22] and Daghestani's similar comment from the 1950s was cited earlier.

Reports differ as to the frequency of conformity with the norm, and nearly all of them come from rural or isolated areas. In addition, Daghestani's complaint of a generation ago—that observers do not always specify precisely who is marrying whom—is still accurate, so that an inflated figure may rest on nothing more secure than bad classification. De Montety found that 80 per cent of Bedouins and 70 per cent of urban people in Tunisia married "within their family," but he does not specify the limits of either the population or the kinship relation. He does note that the middle class is now marrying outside the family circle, but that some magazines are denouncing interfamily marriage, from which we may deduce that the custom may still be prevalent.[23]

In the outlying region of Djebel Ansarine in Tunisia, a survey disclosed recently that some change is even under way there. Seven eighths of the older generation had married within the *qbila* (tribe or sib acknowledging the same sheik and claiming the same name), four fifths of the younger generation, and two thirds of the most recent adult generation. "True endogamy," i.e., marrying an agnatic cousin, amounted from 40 to 50 per cent of the cases.[24] It is not clear, however, that the agnatic cousin is *only* father's brother's child, or that the cases noted above are only the most recent generation. He notes (p. 424) the *opposition* to such matches as well.

In presenting her own data on a Lebanese Druze village, Miss Ayoub summarizes the quantitative data from other sources. Hilma Granqvist had found that 13 per cent of 264 marriages in a Palestine village were with father's brother's daughter. Barth had found 13 per cent in a feudally organized village, but 43 per cent in a tribally organized village.[25] Within her own village, Miss Ayoub found that about four fifths married within the same major lineage, but 8 to 11 per cent seemed to have been marriages between father's brother's children. Yet she also states that 63 per cent of the marriages were with women "claimed as kin," that is, with the "daughter of a man one would call FaBro"[26] (father's brother). Here, the looseness of usage and classification suggests that a wide range of cousins of the same generation in the agnatic lineage would be called father's brother's child. A 1944 survey of five Palestinian Arab villages reported that over half the marriages were within the large extended family, the *hamula*, and an additional 18 per cent within the same village.[27] This tells us little about agnatic parallel cousin marriage, but does emphasize the endogamy characteristic of Arab marriage.

The discrepancy between the clear preference for marriage with father's brother's daughter and the actual frequency, and the discrepancy among the various numerical frequencies reported, call for at least one further comment. Fredrik Barth has presented some descriptive data which explain part of the discrepancy.

The preference for this type of marriage has been most intense in the rural and outlying areas of Arab countries, especially among the Bedouins. It is especially among such groups that the political importance of the large kin group extensions, whether called lineages, ramages, or sibs, becomes important. Any adult has greater political power if he can command more men, and one way of obtaining such loyalties is by foregoing the usual bride price (in Barth's area from £ 30 to 100).

The paternal cousin has the right to the girl. If he exercises that right, and obtains the girl (for no more than wedding expenses) he owes support to his uncle (her father) in any factional fight. The uncle, in turn, gains a supporter, on whom he can especially count, since the young man is already part of the agnatic lineage though perhaps not part of the segment which his uncle may begin or continue.

Consonant with this interpretation, Barth found that in a village organized in the traditional tribal way, in which there was a considerable amount of fission or segmentation, 43 per cent of the marriages were between father's brother's daughter and father's brother's son.[28] On the other hand, in a nontribal village, the bride price might be relatively low or almost nonexistent, or marriages might be based upon the exchange of women; and paternal-cousin marriages were only 13 per cent of the total. Barth also points out that though the traditional rationalization of this marriage is that it "keeps the wealth within the family," in fact the daughter rarely inherits anyway. These villages are based upon class and land ownership, as against the tribal villages based on descent. The latter now survive primarily among the nomads in more isolated territories in Iraq. Since most villages do not now fall into this category, the percentage of conformity with the norm of marriage with father's brother's daughter is not likely to be very high.

Even when the educated Arab ridicules this form of "right" as obsolete, he may continue to have a vague preference for marriage within the male line. It is apparent from the few quantitative data that in the recent period the strict rule has not been ordinarily followed even in outlying regions. Since it cannot be supposed that in such groups industrialization has changed the norms, we must conclude that many other factors are likely to make some other kind of marriage possible. Moreover, now that some type of courtship between a young man and woman has become common among the educated groups in the cities, the likelihood of cousin marriage has declined.

The limitation on choice of mate that is inherent in the bride-price system seems not to have been weakened as yet, although attacks are being made on it. In the relatively liberal family code promulgated in Tunisia in 1956, the contract and bride-price system remain the basis of the marriage. It is true that here and there an elopement may occur when a man is poor and can persuade a girl to marry him before civil authorities without such a payment.[29]

The burden of a bride price has, at times, been very heavy. It is not possible to estimate what the real value of such exchanges was in the past, especially since they occurred in an economy partially based on barter, and with money that varied in value from one region to another. De Montety cites bride prices of fr. 600 to 2,000 in about 1940, and claims that in Tunis itself the amount was as high as fr. 10,000 within the bureaucratic strata where a man earned fr. 30,000 a year.[30]

When, in 1960, President Nasser mentioned a village near Alexandria as the "true" Egypt, a reporter visited it and wrote that the bride price was $12 to 50.[31] Since the average income per person *including,* of course, the urban population at that time was $146 a year; such a figure would have been a considerable burden for the village peasant.[32]

We predict that the bride-price pattern will begin to disappear among the educated groups in Arab countries over the next ten years. A hint of the movement under way may be seen in an Egyptian student organization that encourages marriages without dowry or without exchanges of wealth. Moreover, this organization was commended by H. El-Shaffy, Minister of Social Welfare.[33] Western norms disapprove of the bride price, even when it is understood that the bride is not actually "purchased." Many of the younger generation will find it distasteful and undignified, and a barrier to a free expression of their own choice. The change anticipated, however, is not from a *formal* system of bride price and contract to their total *absence.* After all, throughout the Western World, where the marriage contract and dowry have all but disappeared (remaining only in a few peasant families and among the highest social strata), almost all marriages are accompanied by some exchanges of gifts, and custom dictates that both sides of the family shall give as lavishly to the young couple as they can afford. The gifts, as well as the wedding reception itself, are an expression of both the pleasure of the group and the social rank of the two families. There is no chance that this pattern will disappear from either the Western or Arab system.

Several significant elements in the bride-price system among the Arabs should be emphasized here. First, although the wedding was an occasion for great display of wealth, not all the wealth was actually given to the couple or formed part of the bride's trousseau. Apparently in all of the Arab world a century ago, the procession from the bride's house to the groom's house was marked by entertainment, dancing, and music, and even now by somewhat more restrained expressions of merriment. The jewels, costumes, and wealth that were part of this procession, and still are in much of the Arab world, were often borrowed by the bride's or groom's family, to be returned to the owner after the celebration. And in Syria, a generation ago, there was some movement to lower the bride price, with some success. The pattern of evasion at the time was to demand a small bride price, but to stipulate a much larger amount to be paid later; or to announce publicly a larger figure for the bride price than was actually paid.[34] A relatively fixed amount was often agreed upon by custom.[35] Very likely both these patterns were relatively widespread.

Of equal importance, however, is the fact that although the girl did have inheritance rights, she generally gave them up, especially if these were rights to land. Thus, the bride price formed the equivalent of a kind of inheritance. Since the woman had no opportunity to earn money by working, the trousseau which the bride price bought, together with the amount that had to be paid upon a divorce, gave her at least a small amount of economic independence or source of support. It also formed a small barrier to divorce itself since the husband had to consider whether he could indeed afford to pay his wife the one third or one half of the bride price he had not paid at the time of the marriage contract. Finally, although this point is not usually brought out in analyses of the Arab family, in most exchange systems there was a near equivalent of value, either because the girl's family contributed as well, or because (in the lower classes) the money that was received for the girl was then used to obtain a bride for her brother within the same circles. Marriage by sister exchange was relatively common, and permitted two families of young men to marry them off without any great expenditure of money.[36]

As the system moves from a formal bride price system to one of informal exchanges and gifts, the bride price will become less of a barrier to the free choice of a mate. Since World War I, the demand for this freedom has been growing. To the Westerner, the beginnings of this demand a generation ago seemed most modest. In Syria, one of the more advanced countries, the demand simply took the form (among the better educated) of wishing to make each other's acquaintance after the marriage contract had been signed but before the final wedding ceremony.[37] Some men in the more sophisticated circles of Syria would actually pay court to the girl, in Western fashion, after the conclusion of the contract (which was almost irrevocable).[38] As noted before, in villages where veils were not common, the young boy had probably known or even seen the girl before marriage. Furthermore, there was at that time a very small feminist movement, confined primarily to a segment of the disenchanted and those of fairly high social status.[39]

In Tunisia in 1930 there were only a few dozen emancipated females— educated women who had decided to oppose some of the old customs. Some of them were influenced by Tahar El Haddad, who reinterpreted the Koran and argued that the immurement of women was not demanded, but that women would be the better for equality in social treatment as well as in education. However, his opinions were considered a scandal and his theories condemned as heretical.[40]

In attempting to chart the changes in the demand for freedom of choice, it must be emphasized that we are not basically concerned with the legal requirement of free consent. In most Arab states at the present time a marriage is not valid unless both parties have given free and full consent to it. Under the Tunisian Personal Status Law, both parties as free agents must give consent to the contract of marriage if it is to be valid.[41] Under the new Algerian law, the girl must give personal and oral consent to marriage in the presence of two witnesses of full age.[42] In Syria, of course, that consent has been part of the legal code for over a generation.

It is now rare within the urban wealthy or middle classes for a marriage "to be contracted without the two parties concerned having previously become acquainted, at least by sight," and Daghestani suggests that one factor contributing to this practice is the decline in the use of the veil.[43] A similar statement is made for contemporary marriages in Iraq, although it seems to be derived from Daghestani.[44] Perspectives differ, of course. To the Western eye, permitting engaged couples to see one another "at least by sight" before the engagement hardly seems a radical step; but to many Arabs it may seem shocking or shameful.

Although the Lebanese girl seems still to have little voice in the decision, in this relatively advanced Arab country she does have the opportunity, as in the West, of meeting boys while swimming or playing tennis or at the movies; in short, while engaging in the usual activities of middle-class girls in other metropolitan areas of the world. The major decisions remain in the hands of elders, however.[45] After the engagement, which is socially defined as an irrevocable commitment, the couple's behavior may well resemble that of a Western engaged couple in their relative freedom to see one another.

Since the boy always had the right to take more initiative in these matters than did the girl, it is not surprising that middle-class young men, even in Iraq, are tending to seize that initiative now.[46] However, as in Japan, the crucial factor is the lack of any established system by which young men and women can meet one another socially, and on relatively informal terms, without any commitments for the future. In Jordan, for example, there are a few mixed public parties at which young boys and girls can know or date one another, but, except in a small segment of the population, the girl cannot go home alone after dark.[47]

Perhaps the most radical statement of change has been made about Algeria, and it deserves some attention, since without any question the revolutionary fervor in Arab countries over the past fifteen years has been a prime mover in the changing position of the woman and the changing structure of the family. In a nearly pornographic analysis of the French motives in trying to persuade Algerian women to remove the veil, Fanon claims that this previously indifferent element took on a taboo character for the Moslems, hence their resistance to its removal.[48] However, from 1956 on women began to participate substantially in the Algerian revolution. They first took off the veil in order to dress like Europeans, and thus move in the European sector, carrying messages or weapons. They were able to face their brothers or fathers, who were shocked to learn that their female kinsmen had been seen without the veil, because they were engaged in a great enterprise. Later, however, many used the *haik*, the typical body covering, with the veil, in order to keep their hands free and even to carry heavy weapons beneath the garment. This became so frequent that the French began to take veils off the captured women, despite the taboo, in order to ascertain whether they carried arms.[49]

When Algerian women then began to put the veil *back on* as a gesture of the rebellion against the French, it had lost its old meaning of guard and reserve against men and became a political symbol. Moreover, according to Fanon, in the course of this short period young girls were able to develop their personalities and discovered both responsibility and liberty; indeed, they began to identify the liberty of their country with the liberty of women. Revolutionary cells of women began to develop, and women engaged in the revolution would sometimes have to hide out or escape from the French,[50] living apart from their families for a while. When the young girl was risking her life for her country, the typical male worry about her honor began to seem ridiculous. As Fanon comments, "To ask a woman who was daily confronted by death whether she is 'serious' (that is, virginal) becomes grotesque and derisory."[51]

Among the guerillas, girls became acquainted with young men and then made plans to marry. The F.L.N. became, in effect, a substitute guardian for the young woman, and marriages took place in the absences of real guardians or fathers. Formerly, the girl would avoid facing her father for a month or two after her marriage, out of shame for her recent sexual experience. Now, instead of being passive and compliant and denying her part in the marriage process, she actually takes part in the contract, signing it herself, and generally feels much freer in her relations with men in her own family.[52]

Although this description seems somewhat extreme (for example, many women in Algiers wear the veil today), the revolutionaries in Arab countries have typically led the way toward emancipation and freedom, and some elite groups have also begun movements toward equality for women. Even in Jordan, the royal family has led the way toward greater participation by women in the life of the nation. In Tunisia, the veil began to disappear after Bourguiba took power, and women were permitted to vote only if they abandoned it.[53] Tunisia had not advanced far toward emancipation under the French. With the current changes, however, young men increasingly want to establish independent households and choose their own brides.[54]

A questionnaire survey done in Iraq during the 1950s suggests the direction of present-day forces, if not a clear picture of how far they have moved. At that time, the veil was rapidly disappearing from the three major cities of Baghdad, Mosul, and Basra. Some mixing of the two sexes was increasingly taking place in Baghdad where, in addition, coeducation had begun in the higher schools.[55]

Among the married men, 27 per cent claimed they had married on the basis of a love relationship, and 38 per cent claimed to have at least made the acquaintance of the girl before marriage. The remainder married in the traditional pattern, often because of a kinship tie (for example, father's brother's daughter).[56] Among the married women, 37 per cent claimed their marriage had been based on love, and 24 per cent said that it had at least been preceded by acquaintanceship. The remainder had arranged marriages on the basis of a kinship tie without any love relationship or acquaintanceship. Nahas wisely explains the higher percentage of women who claimed they married for love as being simply a difference in the sentimentality of the two sexes. That is, the women, not having had much prior experience with men, accept as love whatever sentiments they feel.[57]

These 300 respondents were well-educated, and thus a minority in Iraq. Among the *un*married, the preference was strong for love as a basis for marriage, which is simply a way of stating a wish to make one's own choice. Seventy per cent of the men and 64 per cent of the women expressed a preference for entering marriage on the basis of love, or love plus some other desirable qualities in their partner. Thirty per cent of the men and 36 per cent of the women still expressed the opinion that the marriage should be based only on the good qualities of their potential mates. This difference between the reality of those who were already married, and the preference of those who had not yet married, is also to be found in Japan. On the other hand, it does give a clear index of the emerging norms among the educated peoples in this relatively undeveloped Arab country.

In another study a small sample of educated Egyptians was asked how they had entered their marriage, or how they would prefer to enter marriage. The sample is too small to be treated as representative even of educated Egyptians, but the direction of preference is clear. Seventy per cent of the married sample claimed that they had made the choice "alone," and another 27 per cent said that they had made the choice but with their parents' counsel. I suggest, however, that even among the first category there was some indication that parents had taken part in that decision. Among the eleven unmarried respondents in the sample, an overwhelming majority (85 per cent) stated that they preferred to make the choice alone.[58]

Such changes among the educated are also reinforced by persistent Arab propaganda in favor of the emancipation of women and their fuller participation in social and occupational realms. The independence created by achievement of their personal rights, and the independence that participation in activities outside the home engenders, will lead increasingly to a strong demand that they also be permitted to choose their own husbands. More important, these new experiences lead to emotional attachments that parents will increasingly find it difficult to oppose. Moves in the direction of freer mate choice will also reduce the importance of the bride-price as a formal part of the marriage contract or engagement, since elders will be less willing to invest money in agreements over which they no longer have control.

It is interesting that one limitation of freedom of choice (though perhaps of little numerical importance now), is still maintained in the new Tunisian Code of Personal Status. The boy and girl who have been suckled by the same mother may still not marry one another. The "foster child" in this connection is treated as a natural child when the foster care has occurred during the first two years of life,[59] so that a marriage between foster brothers and sisters would be "incestuous."

2. Polygyny

Under Koranic doctrine, a man is permitted to have as many as four wives. However, this tantalizing freedom was hedged by an important restriction—that a man treat all of them equally. Recent Moslem reformers, intent both on altering custom and improving the standing of Arabs in the eyes of the West, have argued that this meant, in effect, that polygyny was forbidden. It was argued that before Mohammed there was *no* limit on the number of wives, and that his limitation was a step forward. The new exegesis is resisted in some circles, since the text itself (Sura 4, Verse 3) seems to be clear enough, and presumably the equality of treatment meant merely that the man should see to it that all his wives received equal material benefits. The verse in question says nothing about giving all of them equal emotional attention. It enjoins a kind of impartiality which presumably could be assessed prior to a marriage; otherwise there would be no point in setting that condition at all.[60]

The Egyptian Ministry of Social Affairs, set up in 1939, considered as one of its first projects the restriction of polygyny and some limitation on divorce. Both of these were generally agreed upon by educated opinion, but the religious leaders objected immediately and pointed out that the ministry could use its time better by paying attention to other social evils denounced by the Koran rather than by attacking an institution it approved.[61]

Nevertheless, although polygyny was specifically approved in the Arab social structure—as it was not in Japan, China, or India—as in other polygynous systems, few men ever managed to obtain more than one wife at a time. A hundred years ago, Lane made the shrewd estimate that in his opinion no more than one out of twenty Egyptian men had two wives.[62] His further comments are equally perspicacious, and may be applied to the Arab world since the turn of this century. A man might acquire a second wife because his first wife was barren, but "fickle passion is the most evident and common motive." Even at that time, fathers did not generally consent to their daughters becoming a second wife, and might demand that the first wife be divorced.

Although the law required strict impartiality between wives, compliance with it seemed to be rare. Common opinion was (and remained throughout the twentieth century) that a polygynous household was hard to manage; it was full of quarrels and difficulties.[63] In one particular, Lane's observations seem to contradict those of twentieth-century observers. He asserts that a poor man was more likely to have two wives than a well-to-do one, because the former could have both of them working. They would thus provide nearly all of their own subsistence. However, most twentieth century analysts have claimed that polygyny was confined primarily to two groups; the great Bedouin sheiks, whose wives formed in part the basis of political alliances, and the traditionally-minded well-to-do land owner. In neither case would the women actually be producing their own food or wealth.

Daghestani asserts that one reason for polygyny's decline is the decline in the burden of household work, so that a large number of women is no longer needed to take care of it.[64] In a survey made in the 1950s, it was claimed that polygyny was declining in the Syrian urban middle class but still continued in rural areas, where women were an asset as field workers. However, no numerical data were presented to show to what extent the custom was being maintained.[65] By the mid-1950s, the custom had practically died out in Lebanon.[66]

A generation ago in Syria, the estimate was made that about one out of twenty men was polygynous, and these were found only in certain strata. The well-educated were not likely to be polygynous because they were Western educated and because parents would not ordinarily permit a daughter to be married as a second wife. It was even common to specify in the marriage contract that the marriage could be dissolved if the man did not remain monogamous.[67] On the other hand, small merchants and artisans in the rural area were more likely to take a second wife. This was not common among small farmers, but those in the middle and upper classes might well do so.[68] By the 1940s, Weulersse asserted that among the rural Syrians polygyny could be found only among the great Bedouin chiefs and rural bigwigs, for whom it was still a sign of success.[69]

The *trend* over the past generation or more is clear and can be stated here in quantitative terms. It seems evident, however, that the change has come about, not because of substantial industrialization, but because of a change in publicly supported ideals, largely adopted from the West. In most Arab countries at the present time, some substantial move has been made to abolish or severely limit polygyny, although it cannot be supposed that it is a moral problem for most of the population in any of these countries. It is worth noting that even a generation ago a considerable body of Syrian public opinion was not in favor of polygyny.[70]

Very recent data are not available, since census materials are generally published slowly, but Table III-1 gives the prevalence of polygyny for recent periods.

Table III-1
Polygyny in Arab Countries, Census Data*

Country	Year	Percentage of Polygynists Among Married Men
Algeria	1958	1.9
Egypt	1947	3.6
Tunisia	1946	4.5
Morocco	1952	6.6
Iraq	1947	7.8
Urban Jordan	1952	5.3–6.9
Five Moslem Palestine villages	1944	11.0

* Mahmoud Seklani, "La Fecondité dans les Pays Arabes: Données Numeriques, Attitudes et Comportements," *Population*, 15 (October–December, 1960), p. 846. Data for Iraq from the 1947 Census cited by Fahim I. Qubain, *The Reconstruction of Iraq: 1950–1957* (New York: Praeger, 1958), p. 10. The survey of Jordanian towns and those on the five Arab villages of Palestine are cited in Raphael Patai, *The Kingdom of Jordan* (Princeton: Princeton University Press, 1958), pp. 136, 139.

Another estimate for Jordan suggests that about one out of ten Jordanian men has two wives and a very small minority has three or four.[71] Census data, of course, tell us how many men are living in polygynous households at a given time. The data on marriages in any given year tell us what proportion of marriages are *entered* into by men who are already married. For Egypt, the percentage was 8.4 in 1951.[72]

But though these data tell us roughly the extent of polygyny in recent Arab life, they do not tell us about any changes that might be taking place. A generation ago, Dahgestani asserted that polygyny was disappearing among the rich and was rare among the poor. Folk opinion singled out its central problem: in rural areas, a rich farmer who did not marry more than one wife was viewed as "avaricious and cowardly"—avaricious because he was not willing to pay the large costs of maintaining a second wife, and cowardly because dominating such a household took great courage.[73]

He also noted that the second marriage was likely to be with a poor woman, without much ceremony, and somewhat clandestine. The man tried not to let his first wife know that the marriage was to take place until it had already occurred, and he would sometimes even go through the wedding ceremony in another house. His first wife was likely to respond by going to her parents' home for a while, returning only after her husband pleaded with her and gave her a present.[74] This suggests that whatever the male norms about polygyny may have been, the informal forces against it were strong and its economic advantages minimal. One may then suppose that the propaganda and legal pressures over the past half-century have borne some fruit precisely because the Arab family structure was not really based on polygyny.

In Egypt, the decrease had begun well over a generation ago. By one estimate, though perhaps a dubious one, the number of polygynous husbands dropped from 62 per 1,000 in 1907 to 48 per 1,000 in 1927.[75] The estimate is dubious since Mboria rests his assertion on the number of "surplus" wives in the census—that is, on the number of married women reported in the census as against the number of married men. Even if this datum is not correct, census data from 1927 show a drop: 4.8 per cent of the married males in the 1927 Census were polygynous, but the figure was 3.4 per cent in 1937, and remained around that figure, 3.6 per cent, in 1947. The percentage of polygynous *marriages* formed 11.0 per cent of the total number of marriages that took place in 1937, 9.6 per cent in 1947, and 8.4 per cent in 1951.[76]

A somewhat better measure can be obtained from Algeria, where, in 1903, 4.0 per cent of the men who entered marriages were then already married. By 1955, this figure had dropped to 1.55 per cent.[77] As would be expected from such a change, the polygynous males in the population are older.[78] During the period from 1886 to 1948, the number of polygynous males in Algeria dropped from 89 thousand to 39 thousand, although during that time the total population continued to grow.[79] The proportion of polygynous marriages remained higher in Algeria's southern territories, the more outlying and rural areas where the older traditions have changed less.[80]

When polygyny was outlawed by Tunisia in 1956 (effective January 1, 1957) and a violation was made subject to criminal penalties, there was little outcry against this break with tradition. The Syrian law of 1953 was somewhat less radical than the Tunisian law, since it requires prior judicial approval of polygnous marriage in order to protect the first wife financially. If the *qadi* judges that the man cannot really support two wives equally, he will not be permitted to marry. On the other hand, it is not clear just who is to furnish this proof. For example, if it is the first wife who must bear this burden, then very likely the man's domination will prevent the law from being effective. Nevertheless, the trend is so clear that, whatever the exact procedure followed in the Syrian marriage law, the abolition of polygyny in the near future seems relatively assured. On the other hand, it seems unlikely that there will be any substantial change in the Arabian peninsula, Iraq, or in the more isolated regions of the Arab world for the next few years.

3. Age at Marriage

In traditional India, the young girl was supposed to be married, at the latest, *by* puberty, whereas the Arab tradition dictated that she was to have *attained* puberty. This condition was not measured by years, however, and was defined rather flexibly. As a consequence, Western travelers in Arab countries have reported that many girls were married at 9 or 10 years of age. In fact, there were no judicial procedures to hinder such a union, and, as in China and Japan, foreign observers sometimes confused the betrothal or marriage contract ceremonies with the actual wedding, concluding that marriage occurred somewhat earlier than it in fact did. Referring to the Egypt of a century ago, Lane remarks that "many marry at the age of 12 or 13 years; and some remarkably precocious girls are married at the age of 10. But such occurrences are not common. Few remain unmarried after 16 years of age."[81] Lane, in common with other Western observers of the past century, believed the widespread myth that puberty came earlier to people in Southern climates.

A system that permits marriage just before puberty or in the earlier years of adolescence fits well with a system of high control by elders over mate choice. If the young girl or boy can be kept from members of the opposite sex so that no emotional attachments can be formed, and marriages are arranged early, the bride and groom have neither independent emotional nor independent socioeconomic resources with which to oppose such decisions. Thus it was to the interest of elders who wished to maintain the traditional family system to arrange the marriage at as early an age as possible.

Actually, many factors converged to make the age for marriage, at least among men, not very different from that in Western countries in recent times. Parents of daughters were not under the pressures experienced by Indian parents, who believed it to be a religious duty to marry their daughters before puberty, whereas the father of a *son* had a relatively strong wish to arrange the marriage in order to continue his lineage. The young Arab wished to marry a relatively young girl in order to guarantee her virginity, however, and indeed both sets of elders concurred in wishing to avoid any scandal. On the other hand, the father of a daughter obtained some goods or wealth when she married, whereas the son's father had to accumulate enough wealth for the wedding ceremony and the bride-price. Thus, there was likely to be far more delay in marrying off the boy than in marrying off the girl. Furthermore, there was no feeling that a wide age difference between the two was improper, and indeed there was some feeling that a young girl was a delight; thus a wide range of choice was available to the young man when his father finally decided that the time to marry had arrived.

Moslem laws did not specify any particular age for marriage, and when there was such a specification the ages were likely to be rather low (for example, Ottoman Law specified 12 years for males and 9 years for females). Moreover, since the emphasis was on puberty, there have usually been some regulations that permitted younger ages if the *qadi* would agree that the girl or boy had achieved puberty.

Egypt was perhaps the first Arab nation to require ages within the range of years that might be deemed acceptable by Western nations: 18 years for males and 16 years for females. This law was passed in 1923, before any but the most minimal industrialization had occurred, and largely represented the impact of Western ideas on the Egyptian legal code. It was recognized at the time that the law was widely violated, although it undoubtedly had some effect upon the ages that families *claimed* their daughters had achieved. On the other hand, as with most such regulations, some effect seemed to be visible by the 1930s.[82] As we shall note in a moment, the age at marriage in Egypt has certainly risen over the past generation.

The Syrian family code operative in the 1930s required the young man to have completed his eighteenth year and the young woman her seventeenth, and defined as invalid any marriages between people of a lesser age. Chatila comments that before World War I, city girls married between the ages of 13 and 15, and city men between the ages of 18 and 20. He asserts that in the 1930s in the upper strata of Syrian cities, the ages for marrying had increased to 20 to 25 for girls, and 25 to 35 for young men. Among the educated bourgeoisie, he says, girls were married between 17 and 22 years and boys between 25 and 30 years,[83] whereas among the more traditional urban dwellers (bourgeois merchants and clergy) the age for girls was more likely to be 15 to 17 years, and 20 to 25 years for the young men. In the urban working class, the age of girls was likely to be from 13 to 16 years, and those of men from 17 to 20 years.

Thus, although quantitative data for that period are not available, Chatila's estimates at least suggest that the age at marriage in Syria a generation ago was not so spectacularly low as Western commentators have suggested.

Because present laws at least indicate the *attention* which Arab countries are giving to the problem of youthful marriages, a summary of the legal age stipulations for a valid marriage seems worthwhile. Table III-2 presents these ages, with no illusions that they are accepted as *normative* rules by the Arab populations. Certainly Bedouins would view these ages as far too high. For example, a recent study of sedentary Bedouins reported that in eight out of eleven reported marriages the girl was 15 years old or less. Moreover, when the respondents were asked what the ideal age of marriage was, thirteen out of twenty said 15 years or less.[84] Only nine out of fifteen males had been married at 20 or less, but fifteen out of twenty believed that to be the ideal age.

It should be remembered that in the Western world the ages stipulated by law generally serve the function of preventing extremely young people from marrying *without* parental consent. Often, the legal age *with* parental consent is not much higher than the ages shown in Table III-2, and the average ages at marriage in Western countries are much higher than the legal minimum permitted. Implicit in this Western legal structure is the notion that below a certain age mate choice must be approved by the parent. It is safe to venture, however, that the intention of the laws is to

Table III-2
Minimum Legal Age Required for Marriage, Islamic Countries*

Country or Group	Males	Females
Algeria	18	15 (test of maturity and medical certificate)
Druze-Lebanon	16	15 (with guardian's permission)
Egypt	18	16
Iraq	Guardian must permit a marriage if either is 16–18 years old.	
Jordan	16	16
Lebanon		12–16, depending on religion
Sudanese Moslems	Puberty for both sexes	
Syria	Completed 18 years	Completed 17 years
Tunisia	18	15

* Data assembled from UNESCO: *Observations of Governments on the Draft Convention and Draft Recommendation on the Minimum Age of Marriage, Consent to Marriage, and Registration of Marriages,* January 13, 1961; UNESCO: *Consent to Marriage, Age of Marriage, and Registration of Marriages,* Commission on *Status of Women,* 14th Session, December 21, 1959; Millicent Ayoub, *Endogamous Marriage in a Middle Eastern Village,* Ph.D. diss., Radcliffe College, 1957, p. 95; Kazem Daghestani, "Evolution of the Moslem Family in the Middle Eastern Countries," *UNESCO International Social Science Bulletin,* 5, no. 4 (1953), 686; *News from Tunisia,* Bulletin No. 51, January 15, 1960; (Algeria) *Newsletter on Status of Women,* No. 19, September, 1959; personal letter.

prevent too early marriages, not to give parents control over choice of mate. The purpose of the new age requirements in Arab countries is somewhat different; the aim is to raise the actual age at marriage because of various new beliefs about health, fertility, human dignity, or the changed definition of the meaning of a husband-wife relationship—but they do not as yet aim at giving freedom of choice. The laws do not permit marriage at these ages *without* parental approval of the specific choice of mate. Since parents take an active part in arranging marriages, almost no women, and few men, will be mature in years, unmarried, and independent enough to have no need of parental consent. Thus, the Western category of "marriage without parental consent" is given little attention except for the traditional right to be married at all by a certain age.

Without doubt, the age at marriage is rising in all Arab countries; however, the general suppositions about marriage age for females in the past was probably as erroneous as that concerning the age of males. Western observers have concurred with Arab commentators in asserting that the laws specifying minimum age of marriage have been widely ignored—a correct assertion that suggests an incorrect inference. There have always been *some* very early marriages in Arab countries, but *most* marriages took place at ages which would not have been thought improper in the West during the late nineteenth century, if we consider *averages* rather than a few striking cases.

We can select two items of information to bolster such an interpretation. At the turn of the century in Algeria, there was no serious pressure to report female ages at marriage incorrectly. Since there was no government restriction of any consequence, we can suppose that the ages reported were at least roughly correct. In 1903, there were 856 out of 14,230 marriages in which girls under 15 were married—only 6.6 per cent of the total. At the same time, 13.5 per cent of the males were under 20. In this instance, then, a small minority of girls married at very young ages; indeed, although 46 per cent of the 14,230 girls were 19 years old or less, 86 per cent of these were over 15,[85] hardly a striking deviation even from contemporary United States data (almost two fifths of United States brides in 1959 were 19 years old or less). This is a far cry from the stereotype of the Arab marriage of a half-century ago, according to which all the brides were at best barely adolescent.

Two additional items of information are somewhat closer to the traditional picture, though still perhaps less dramatic. An actual survey carried out among Palestine Bedouins in 1946 found that one half of the women had been married by age 17, and about four fifths by age 19. Considering the data carefully, the author of this survey reports that the true average age at marriage was 17 years.[86] On the other hand, among the Bedouins, who had little contact with urban or industrial forces, the tradition of early marriage was perhaps stronger than in any other Arab subgroup.

The next item is also somewhat closer to the traditional picture of early ages for marriage, although once more it does not conform exactly. A survey carried out in Beirut in 1952–1953 ascertained the ages at marriage of both the present heads of households and their parents. Twenty-nine per cent of the women of the *previous* generation had been married at ages 15 and under, and 44 per cent at ages 16 to 20. That is, some 72 per cent of the previous generation of mothers had been married by age 20, a figure that was approached only by one of the less developed Arab countries, Morocco, in 1952 (61 per cent ever married by age 15 to 19).[87]

On the other hand, a survey carried out in five Arab villages in Palestine during the 1940s found that 12 per cent of the Arab females were married by ages 13 to 17, and 89 per cent by ages 18 to 22. For all Palestine Moslems, data for a generation ago are available: In 1931, the average age at marriage for females was 20.2 years, for males, 25.8 years.[88]

These data would seem to be more reliable than census data gathered by governmental employees, to whom many Arabs might fear to give correct information even if they knew it. They have the merit, moreover, that they do not give exaggerated emphasis to a few striking cases observed, but instead yield some statistical averages and distributions. (We wish to emphasize here that we are aiming at no more than a correct assessment of the *extent* of early marriage in the past or, currently, in more isolated areas.)

As to more recent data, two sources are available. A few countries now publish data on the ages *at* marriage. In addition, census data yield the percentage of people who are in the category of "ever married" (widowed, divorced, or married) at any given age group. These do not yield the same percentages of course, since in any census a person who is now 20 years old and married may actually have married at a somewhat earlier period.

The small educated Iraqi sample noted earlier had an average age at first marriage of 25.1 years for men and 21.8 years for the women.[89]

In 1953, 3.9 per cent of all Egyptian marriages involved males under 20 years old. This may be contrasted with the figure of about 13 per cent for the United States in 1959. In those Egyptian marriages, 47 per cent of the women were under 20 (39 per cent in the United States in 1959).[90] The average age *at* marriage was 19.1 for spinsters and 25.3 for bachelors.

Table III-3 presents census data from several countries to show the percentages *ever* married for both males and females in several age categories. They do not, of course, represent the latest data on average age at marriage since they are for *censuses,* taken over the past fifteen years.

Table III-3
Percentage Ever Married in Young-Age Categories, Selected Arab Countries*

		15–19 Years	20–24 Years	25–34 Years
Algeria (1954)	M	5.8	34.6	77.2
	F	37.9	79.1	93.6
Egypt (1947)	M	12.7	30.8	74.9
	F	40.8	80.1	95.1
Morocco (1952)	M	7.4	40.9	81.0
	F	60.7	91.7	97.4
Tunisia (1946)	M	6.6	27.6	65.2
	F	29.5	72.4	89.9

* Seklani, op. cit. (in Table III-1), p. 843. Taken from recent censuses.

In Jordan in 1960, only 2.2 per cent of the women who entered marriage were under 15 years; 60 per cent of those who married were in the 15 to 19 age group.[91]

The use of census data to measure the degree of change in the Egyptian marriage age is fraught with problems because of the technical deficiencies in the earlier censuses. In Arab countries, people have shown a tendency to round off their ages to the nearest five years, and among illiterates, who have constituted a majority of these populations, age has not had the fixed and definite quality that Westerners ascribe to it. As the Director of the 1907 Census commented, "The data given by age periods must be regarded rather as specimens of the *ideas* prevailing concerning the ages of individuals rather than as a faithful reflection of the actual facts."[92] In addition, there is likely to be some upgrading of female ages if the age requirement for marriage has been violated. Also, the age categories used from one census to the next have changed. Nevertheless, as Table III-4 shows, there is a clear movement toward a somewhat higher age at marriage for the 1907–1947 period. That is, because of the extent to which a *smaller* percentage of the ever-married are to be found in the very *young* years, we must conclude that a rise in age at marriage has taken place.

Vital statistics for Egypt do not extend back so far in time as the

Table III-4
Percentage Ever Married By Given Ages,
Egypt, 1907–1947*

	1907	1917	1927	1937	1947
Male					
10–14	1.0		1.0		—
15–19	8.7		4.1		3.1
0–19	5.6	1.1	0.9		0.65
20–24					69.1
20–29	60.8	43.2	53.1	44.8	45.8
Female					
10–14	5.6		1.6		—
15–19	51.8		37.9		25.96
0–19	9.1	8.2	7.4		5.3
20–24					78.9
20–29	93.7	92.6	92.3	88.4	86.4

* Data calculated from successive Egyptian censuses.

censuses. Cleland used registration data for a limited area, however, and calculated that from 1907 to 1927 the number of "child marriages" (marriages of females under 15) was reduced from 55 to 15 per 1,000 marriages.[93]

It is not possible to ascertain the trend by decades in Moslem Algerian marriages, since for much of the period since the turn of the century the published data have not separated Moslems and non-Moslems. However, as noted previously, of the Moslem marriages in urban areas in 1903, 13.5 per cent involved males under 20 years of age; 46 per cent, however, involved females under 20, and 856 girls were married under 15 years of age. By 1955, the figure for males under 20 had dropped to 4 per cent. That for females had also dropped, but proportionately less so, to 37.5 per cent who were under 20. No marriages recorded in 1955 indicated a bride under 15.[94]

Finally, the 1952–1953 survey carried out in Beirut, Lebanon, also yields generational data and shows a clear trend toward higher ages at marriage.

These generational data show clearly that the age at marriage has been rising in Lebanon. Additional evidence of at least potential change is to be

Table III-5
Per Cent Married at Given Ages in Two Generations,
Beirut, Lebanon, 1952–1953*

Age at Marriage		Former Generation	Present Generation
15 and under	M	8.0	0.3
	F	28.9	18.2
16–20	M	24.0	11.2
	F	44.0	44.8
21–25	M	20.0	27.3
	F	14.0	
26–30	M		28.4

* Charles W. Churchill, *The City of Beirut, Lebanon* (Beirut: Dar El-Kitab, 1954), pp. 32–33.

found here and there in the apparently higher ages of marriage in urban areas than in rural areas—although it must not be forgotten that such an age difference may well have been as traditional in Arab countries as in many others. In addition, the evidence suggests that university people marry at relatively mature ages, and this, too, we would expect to find as the population moves away from traditionally arranged marriages.

We would also expect to find the change noted in other cultural areas —that is, a narrowing of the age difference between husband and wife. This should be especially notable in the Arab world, since the age difference was substantial in the past. It was always considered proper for a mature man to marry a girl in her teens. If this is true, the age difference should be greater in rural areas than in city areas, but we have been able to obtain this datum only for Algeria, where the relationship does seem to hold.

Although the average age of marriage in Arab countries seems to be rising, the percentage *eventually* marrying has probably not changed at all. Under a system of arranged marriages, almost everyone gets married eventually. Comparing this system with the free choice pattern of the West, people in the Arab world still marry at somewhat younger ages than Westerners do. By maturity, only a slightly higher proportion of Arab than European men or women succeeds in getting married.

Breil has made this comparison from the 1948 Census for Moslem and European men and women in the *same* country, Algeria. From age 30 onward, some 22 per cent of Algerian Arabs are unmarried as against 25 per cent of the European men. At 50, the unmarried form 3.6 per cent of the Arabs and 7.4 per cent of the Europeans. Among females, the difference is somewhat greater. Only two per cent of the Arab women in Algeria failed to marry by 45 or older, as against 9.3 per cent of the non-Moslems. The difference by sex and culture seems to result from the two types of marriage processes discussed earlier. Among non-Moslems, some females cannot marry because they cannot compete adequately on a relatively free marriage market, while elders arrange marriages for the Moslem women. Among Moslem males, some men fail to get married simply because neither they nor their elders can accumulate sufficient wealth to permit them to do so.[95]

4. Fertility and Contraception

As in other peasant societies, the Arab culture gives a high evaluation to having children, especially sons. The Biblical injunction, "Be fruitful and multiply," is also Mohammedan. To refuse to have children because of economic considerations was to express a lack of faith in God, who would always provide. Mortality was, and is, high. For example, in the major Egyptian cities during the 1901–1936 period, the death rate ranged between 21.7 per 1,000 population to 39.7 (an influenza year); infant mortality in Cairo and Alexandria in the same period ranged between a high of 376 and a low of 199 per 1,000 infants born, although the trend was generally down-ward during that generation. As a consequence, high fertility was necessary to insure survival of several children.

Sons especially were desired. They were viewed as a source of support, not only in a father's old age, but also in his maturity. A man could super-vise his sons on his plot of land as soon as they could work well. There was no moral injunction for a man to keep working to the last; but there *was* a strong moral injunction for young sons to relieve their father of his bur-den. In addition, the father was normally the major person to decide when the young son would marry and found a family of his own. Consequently, he could keep the young man unmarried until fairly late in life if he wished to do so. Thus, outside the advantaged classes in the Arab world, sons were economically valuable.

Having sons was also politically important in the less settled areas. But even in settled areas a man with many grown sons, or perhaps an extended kin network based upon the son's children, would have support in the potential conflicts that were likely to be decided on a personalistic, informal, or even forceful basis, rather than on formal principles of law with due re-gard for equity. Consequently, having many children was generally viewed as an advantage.

Given such a set of values and beliefs, it is not surprising that the young bride was rewarded if she produced many sons who stayed alive. The mar-riage tie was relatively fragile, but not so for a woman who had produced a living son. It has always been viewed as improper to divorce a woman with living children, unless there was a serious reason for doing so. After all, an additional wife could be added to the menage without discarding the first. Barrenness was, and is, viewed as a shame and a burden, and many women would go to great lengths in the search for medical or magical remedies in order to conceive children.

A further cultural factor also seems to have kept the birth rate high in Arab countries, although its exact effects are difficult to evaluate. In the socialization process, a great effort was expended to keep the female chaste, and much attention was devoted to teaching her to avoid all the various ways in which she could bring shame on her family or husband. This em-phasis is relatively common in a patriarchal culture. The male side is some-what more complex, however, and differs from the cultures we have con-sidered up to this point. The delights of the flesh have been a major theme not only in the folk wisdom of the Arab world but in its literature as well. One of the *hadiths*, the moral lessons derived from Mohammed's comments or actions during his lifetime, states that every time a man engages in sexual intercourse he carries out an act of charity. The man was enjoined to take his pleasure whenever he wished to do so. Far more support to male sexual-ity was given in the formal and explicit Arab culture than in other major cultures. Of course, nearly all cultures emphasize the pleasures of sex at the level of folk wisdom and joking, but none has given it such religious or literary approval.

One would suppose that such an emphasis would lead to a higher frequency of sexual intercourse in marriage, although the evidence for this is not available. Higher frequency of sexual intercourse would undoubtedly raise the birth rate to some extent. Here again, the evidence is not entirely clear, but several studies have reported this to be the result. It is doubtful for example, that because the sperm count is lowered somewhat with high frequencies of sexual intercourse, fertility also is lowered.[96] In a recent study in Lebanon, 18 per cent of a sample of more than 600 women reported that during the first year of marriage the coital frequency per month had been more than thirty. An additional 33 per cent reported twenty-one to thirty times per month, and another 33 per cent reported eleven to twenty times per month.[97] During the first year of marriage, the median frequency of sexual intercourse per month among uneducated village Moslems was 24.5, and 18.2 among Christians in the same category. Among educated urban Moslems the median frequency per month was 21.2 times, and 17.9 among Christians in the same category. The uneducated urban Moslems and Christians differed almost not at all, reporting, respectively, a median frequency of 19.8 and 19.1 times per month.[98] These frequencies are considerably higher than those reported by Kinsey, and suggest that the high evaluation given to male sexuality in the Arab culture may indeed affect frequency and thus possibly the crude birth rate.

The total fertility would also be increased by the generally early marriages among Arabs, and by the fact that almost all females do get married eventually, so that all are exposed to pregnancy. Of course, a girl married at age 11 to 13 years will not bear any more children than one married 14 to 17 years, since there would be a period of adolescent sterility in the earlier years of exposure.[99]

Thus, a wide variety of the Arab world's institutional arrangements and cultural values served to keep the birth rate at a high level, and indeed birth rates among some selected Moslem groups have been among the highest ever reported for any group. As can be seen in Table III-6, the birth rates are at about the level of India's fertility level, somewhat over forty births per thousand population each year. It is generally asserted by responsible demographers, both Arab and Western, that many of these figures are *under*-estimates, since an unknown but substantial percentage of births (on the order of 10 per cent) may be unregistered.

Weulersse estimates that the birth rate among Syrian peasants during the 1940s was between forty-five and fifty per thousand, although exact data are not available.[100] The "official" birth rate for Syria as a whole in 1957 was 24.3, according to the *United Nations Demographic Yearbook*, but this applies to both Moslem and non-Moslem populations and is not generally accepted as correct. As might be expected, the birth rates of the Europeans in these countries is much lower than that of the Moslems. In

Table III-6
Number of Births Per Thousand Population
Selected Arab Countries*

Name of Country	Year	Birth Rate
Algeria	1948	45
	1954	48
Egypt	1954	50
	1947	49
Iraq	1947	49
Jordan	1957	39.7
Lebanon	1957	38
Morocco	1952	45
Moslem Palestine	1939	49
	1946	53.6
Tunisia	1946	39
	1956	42

* Seklani, op. cit. (in Table III-1), p. 841. These figures do not correspond to the crude birth rates presented in the *United Nations Demographic Yearbook*, but are rather recalculations of the birth rate in the light of available census and vital statistic data.

Algeria, for example, during the 1948–1956 period the European birth rate was roughly half the Moslem birth rate (that is, 18 to 22 per thousand).

A special study of fertility in 3 thousand Arab households in Palestine was made in 1946. For the entire sample the estimate was made that the Arab women aged 45–49 years had had an average of 6.7 children. The sedentary Bedouins had had 8.8 children, and the sedentary Moslems (presumably non-Bedouins) had had 7.3 children. However, the investigators suspected that these figures were somewhat inflated by memory errors or perhaps by a wish to exaggerate the number of children born. Of the children ever born, 4.8 were still alive in the households of the sedentary Moslems and 5.6 in those of the sedentary Bedouins at the time of the study. A more intensive inquiry was made of a sample of 525 women, who had come to the clinic to have their children vaccinated. These women had averaged about seven children, but this, too, may not be used as an average for the entire group, since all of them were fertile.[101]

These birth rates are high enough to suggest that little change has occurred in the fertility patterns of Arabs over the past fifty years. Although studies of urban and rural birth rates show that the latter are somewhat higher than the former, the difference is small, has undoubtedly existed for many decades, and cannot as yet be viewed as an indication that the processes of declining fertility have made much headway. In Egypt for example, calculations based on census age distributions, rather than on the somewhat doubtful vital statistics registration, show that in the 1917–1946 period the birth rate did not drop at all. In the 1917–1926 period it was 41.8 and in the succeeding decade rose to 43.6. From 1937 to 1946 it remained equally high at 41.7 and in 1946 was estimated to be 42.7.[102]

Mboria carries his estimate back still further to 1901, and shows that in the 1901–1936 period there was no change at all in the Egyptian crude birth rate.[103] Cleland made a comparison of the birth rates in the Egyptian cities as against those in Egypt as a whole, which was, of course, mostly rural, and showed that from 1908 to 1931 there was not only no trend in the two series, but that there was very little *difference* between rural and urban rates considered year by year. The urban rates are somewhat higher, primarily because of better registration.[104] El-Badry has analyzed fertility carefully in the light of the last Egyptian census, and was able to show that the rural regions do not have a higher fertility than the urban—perhaps at most 0.1 child higher per married woman.[105] As already noted, the officially reported Egyptian birth rate was 39.2 in 1954, and one demographic estimate suggests that from 1955 to 1957 the rate was 45.1.[106]

The birth rate of Palestine Moslems was estimated to be 50 per thousand population from 1921 to 1925 and 47 per thousand in 1938.[107]

Breil has recalculated the crude birth rate of the Algerian Moslem population in the 1921–1950 generation, and has shown that little or no change has appeared (see Table III-7). He has also calculated a corrected birth rate for Algeria's urban area. During the 1950–1953 period, the corrected birth rate ranges between 44 and 46, high enough to suggest no trend at all.[108] Moreover, he finds no real differences in the birth rate among the large cities, the smaller cities, and the rural area, again suggesting that there has been no change at all over the past generation, at least if we consider only Moslems.

Table III-7
Corrected Birth Rate of Algerian Moslems, 1921–1950*

Period	Corrected Birth Rate Per Thousand Population
1921–1925	38
1926–1930	43
1931–1935	44
1936–1940	42
1941–1945	44
1946–1950	42

* Jacques Breil, La Population en Algerie (Paris: Imprimerie Nationale, 1957), p. 110.

If any perceptible changes in the fertility pattern were beginning to take place, presumably they would occur among those who have had Western educations and have occupations based on "Western" education. These are in the vanguard of leadership in the modern Arab world. A test of this possibility can be made from the 1947 Egyptian vital statistics data, which give the *order* of birth of children born to fathers in that year, by occupation. As Table III-8 (drawn from that source) shows, there is very little dispersion among the varied occupational groups. The highest fertility is to be found among the various *religious* occupations, and following close behind are merchants, who of course include the small shop keepers who have always been viewed as being among the more traditional occupations. However, teachers have a fertility almost as high. It is true that the lowest fertility is to be found among the technical occupations, but even so the difference is relatively small, since these fathers have had about 3.5 as against the 3.9 children of agricultural laborers.

Table III-8
Average Number of Children Ever Born Per Thousand Fathers
of 1947 Births, Selected Occupations, Egypt*

Occupational Group	Average Number of Children Born Per Thousand Fathers Who Had a Child Born in 1947
Agricultural laborers	3,899
Nonagricultural laborers	3,879
Merchants	4,105
Religious employees	4,407
Teachers	4,124
Lawyers, prosecutors, judges	3,814
Administrative officers	3,806
Engineers, doctors, technicians	3,455

* M. A. El-Badry, "Some Aspects of Fertility in Egypt," Milbank Memorial Fund Quarterly, 34 (January, 1956), 37.

These data suggest that Ammar's comment, based partly on his 1951 field work in an Egyptian village, would therefore seem to be essentially correct.

There is no policy of any kind for limiting birth, either by spacing it out or by practicing birth control. Birth control in the modern sense is unheard of, and in any case it is considered as a religious sin and deemed an interference with god's creation. A part of the married male ethos is not to regulate his sex desires, but to give them full play whenever the need arises. Continence is not a desirable thing for a married man . . . The writer heard of no woman who has practiced any devices to confer sterility on her.[109]

However, writing in the 1930s on the Egyptian population, Mboria commented (without specifying the technique used) that the well-educated elite of Egypt had begun to limit birth rates somewhat, although this development was barely perceptible at that time.[110] Daghestani, basing his comments on observations in the late 1920s and early 1930s, asserted that although the peasants and those living far from cities had no thought of controlling the number of children they would have, the idea of "limiting the number of children in order to give them more care is spreading more and more among urban parents who belong to the upper or middle class.[111] Nevertheless, the crude birth rates during the 1950s did not show any effects of such a change.

Since this harmony between Arab cultural patterns and family structure has created high birth rates, many Westerners were startled when, in the spring of 1962, President Nasser of Egypt made an "about-face" by repeatedly emphasizing "family planning as a necessary means of averting a possibly disastrous population rise in over-populated Egypt."[112] This emphasis was, however, merely a later stage in a development that had begun in the early 1950s. The National Commission for Population Problems of Egypt was asked in 1953 to outline a population policy which would achieve the greatest amount of prosperity for the greatest number of citizens. One of its measures was the establishment of family planning clinics, of which eight were established in 1955. The Egyptian government's official position was made known in 1954: that, essentially, a reduction in the birth rate was a social necessity if the country was to achieve prosperity.[113] The success of the clinics between November 1955 and March 1956 led to a decision to increase the number of clinics to twelve. By the mid-1950s many Arabs had at least heard of contraceptives, even if they had not used them. Lichtenstadter comments that she frequently heard birth control discussed even by illiterate fellahin.[114]

In 1958 the editor of the influential newspaper *Al Akhbar* appealed for the establishment of birth control in view of the country's economic situation. Various people in favor of birth control "demanded the introduction of sex education in all the Egyptian schools and a widespread campaign throughout the radio, press, cinemas and theatres, in order to combat the widespread belief . . . that every child brought into the world has his living guaranteed to him."[115]

In this decade, a considerable debate has taken place between the defenders of the old and the proponents of the new. To counteract the proponents of the new in *Al Akhbar*, another Egyptian newspaper made an impassioned attack on birth control proposals. In one land-reallocation project, only families with fewer than four children were taken in, but religious leaders have generally been strongly against birth control of any kind.

Of course, Arab folklore knew of contraceptives and abortifacients. In the nineteenth century, contraceptive folklore was reported even from the sacred city of Mecca. There is general agreement that at least one form of contraception is permissible: *coitus interruptus*. More important, a *fetwa*, or religious interpretation, handed down by the Grand Mufti of Egypt, the highest judicial authority under Moslem religious law, has sanctioned the use of contraceptives under a wide variety of circumstances, from ill health to economic difficulty.[116]

Although the Koran does not forbid birth control, whether it permits all forms has been debated among religious leaders; and many of the *ulemas*, or religious leaders, have expressed themselves strongly against even *coitus interruptus*.[117] Perhaps it is fair to say that by now most important religious leaders have taken the position that the use of contraceptives, or some form of birth limitation, is proper.[118]

Thus, even before Nasser's recent announcement, the government had permitted, encouraged, and even paid for some development of birth control policies and the offering of procedures and apparatus through Egyptian family planning clinics. Indeed the success of the diaphragm and jelly method by the mid-1950s had led to the establishment of local firms who manufactured these products.[119]

Although the differential fertility data given earlier were derived from a period that is now fifteen years past, the crude data for these nations as a whole continue to show very high rates. However, it is entirely possible that over the past generation some changes in fertility have occurred, even in the crude rates, but have been concealed by the increased effectiveness of birth registration. Thus, if the birth rate was 43 per thousand population in 1930, and was still at that level in 1955, the real rate may have dropped somewhat, but the recorded rate remains the same because now a higher percentage of infants are registered than a generation ago.[120] Only a study of the fertility in different *segments* of the most advanced Arab countries, Egypt, Lebanon, or Syria, could be expected to show any differences in fertility rates predictive of changes in fertility practices in the near future.

Two recent studies have reported fertility differences showing what the future trend in Arab countries may be. The first was carried out by Rizk in Egypt, with a sample of 8 thousand.[121] The second, cited earlier, was done in Lebanon, and followed Rizk's model.

In his study of 8 thousand Egyptian wives, Rizk ascertained that nearly one fourth in certain urban areas had tried some method to prevent pregnancy, but in rural areas only about one per cent had ever made such an attempt; among these, from about 40 to 50 per cent thought that the number of children a woman bore was a matter of God's will.

Yaukey's Lebanese sample included both rural and urban wives at different levels of education. The findings generally support the pattern that has occurred in the West—first the more educated and urban populations begin to decrease their fertility, followed by the less educated and rural strata.

As in previous data cited, there were no differences between generations in the fertility of the sample of women considered as a whole. Moslems have a higher fertility than Christians, but there was almost no difference in the fertility of urban and rural Moslems.[122] Among *rural* people, as in Rizk's large Egyptian sample, there were no significant differences in fertility by education, occupation, or religion.[123]

Both Yaukey and Rizk found some socioeconomic differences in fertility among the *younger urban* Moslems (total fertility rate of 7.05 children when neither husband nor wife possesses an elementary educational certificate, as against 5.85 when either possesses it).[124]

Among the uneducated rural Moslem wives, only 2 per cent had ever used any method of conception control at all, none of these being standard contraceptive appliances. However, 60 per cent of the urban uneducated Moslems and 83 per cent of the educated had used some type of method, usually a nonappliance method like abstinence, withdrawal, or the rhythm method. Forty-four per cent of the uneducated and 51 per cent of the educated urban Moslem women had at some time used nonappliance methods; 34 per cent of the uneducated and 60 per cent of the educated Moslems had at some time used some kind of appliance (mostly the condom).[125]

A parallel class difference appeared in two Indian cities, Lucknow and Kanpur, in a study of birth control. Fifteen per cent of the Moslems in class one (the highest) and 14 per cent in class two had practiced contraception at some time, but none in the other classes had ever done so.[126] From the viewpoint of cultural comparisons, most interesting is the fact that the favorite methods used were those in which the *male* took direct action. One would suppose, reasoning from data on Puerto Rican family limitation, that the Arab male emphasis upon his own virility and the expression of his status through conception would lead him to avoid such methods. It may be, however, that the difference is to be found in the fact that such methods were not part of the cultural background of these Lebanese Moslems, so that no special attitudes existed with regard to them. In the Western world the condom especially has been rejected by the male as being somehow a barrier to the free expression of male sexuality. Consequently, the method chosen among Moslems was simply the easiest to use. Withdrawal, of course, has been the most common method in the West until perhaps two decades ago.

It is also interesting that although almost none of the uneducated village Moslems had induced an abortion (only 0.2 per cent), 2.5 per cent of the uneducated urban Moslems and 13.7 per cent of the educated urban Moslems had done so. We would suppose that the higher rate among the educated Moslems shows not so much a preference for abortion as such, but rather a serious interest in controlling fertility. Since the methods used were often ineffective, abortion was induced as a solution. Far more educated urban Moslems used abortion than did their Christian counterparts (8.2 per cent), but many of these Christians were Catholics of one sect or another.[127]

This study, then, corroborates most of Rizk's Egyptian findings on a larger sample, and suggests that in this most advanced of Arab countries the transition to fertility control is well under way among at least the most advanced strata, following the experience reported in Western countries. As Yaukey comments, "The least fertile of our Lebanese social background types tended to marry their women latest, were most willing to advise specific (limited) family size, were most likely to have used either induced abortion or conception control, and were mostly likely to have initiated conception control at early parties. The similarity between the modern Western model and the behavior of the least fertile types of Lebanese is strong."[128]

Additional evidence may be found in the two tiny samples alluded to before. In a sample of well-educated Egyptians, 49 per cent of the respondents said that three children or *fewer* was their ideal, although 39 per cent wanted four. Both categories, however, expressed a wish for a smaller number of children than is currently the fact in Egyptian family life.[129] Another Egyptian sample made the distinction between *expected* and *desired* number of children. The small sample of women expected 3.2 children but desired 2.7; the men expected 4.3 and desired 3.5. Even the number expected would create a substantial drop in fertility if it were carried out in practice.[130] We can expect then that in the next decade these efforts at controlling fertility will begin to show results in at least the more advanced Arab countries, and possibly others as well.

5. Illegitimacy

As the Arab world moves away from arranged marriages and high family control, and toward greater freedom of courtship, an increased illegitimacy rate would be expected. At present, no such process is in evidence at all. In no Arab country at the present time does the rate rise above 2 per cent, and in most it is one per cent or less. In the village of Silwa, Ammar heard of no cases of adultery or illegitimacy for the previous thirty years.[131] The Statistical Department at Cairo has given me figures for the years from 1935 to 1957 which show an apparent drop from 3.8 per cent to 1.0 per cent; but so swift a change, especially unaccompanied by other apparent alterations of so large a magnitude, cannot be taken seriously, and probably must be ascribed to the vagaries of Egyptian registration procedures. As might be expected, the rates are somewhat higher in urban areas than in rural. (For example, in Algeria during the 1950s, the Moslem urban rate was 2.2 per cent, but about one per cent elsewhere.) Higher rates are also found along Egypt's coastal regions, whereas in upper Egypt, the rates are lower.[132]

In the Arab world, as in China, some births which the Western world would classify as illegitimate were not treated as such socially, and would not, therefore, have been so registered. A man could recognize as his own a child who was born less than six months after marriage, and under some interpretations a child born as much as four years after the end of cohabitation could be considered legitimate as well. A child born to a man by his concubine or slave was also socially accepted as his own.[133] Indeed, it was difficult for a child of any but an unmarried girl (who of course was closely guarded) to be considered illegitimate. There was much variation among the different Moslem sects as to the definition of the time period (after divorce or widowhood) within which a child could be considered legitimate. According to some, pregnancy could not normally last more than ten to eleven months; "The Malekites permit four and even five years; the Hanafites permit six months for the short term basis, nine months for normal pregnancy, and two years for the longest."[134]

Of course, the Moslem religious leaders had no illusions about the exact duration of a pregnancy, but the aim was to diminish the number of people who were declassed or disinherited, especially in a culture of high marital instability. The status of a concubine's child could not be assured merely by the existence of a concubinal relationship. An inquiry into paternity or maternity was necessary.[135]

In spite of the very great power of the male in this society, a man could not simply repudiate his wife on a charge of adultery and thus evade responsibility for his illegitimate child. The husband had to witness the adultery and have four male witnesses to support his testimony.[136] However, the Koran also contains a procedure of anathema, permitting the husband to repeat the charge on five different occasions. If she responded by five denials, she was not condemned, but he could nevertheless disavow the paternity.

In the contemporary Tunisian family code, for a child to be considered illegitimate, the husband has to disavow the child and the child must have been born one year after the absence or death of the husband, or the date of divorce.[137]

Thus, as in Western legal codes generally, the law is interpreted to minimize the possibility that a child may be classified as illegitimate if his mother has been married. On the other hand, the Arab system gave little protection to the unmarried girl. There could be no inquiry into possible paternity, and the father had no responsibility for a child thus born prior to marriage. Nevertheless, since no young man could approach a young female, and can do so only rarely now, except under the strict supervision of her kinfolk as well as his own, there was, and is, little possibility of a clandestine relationship prior to the marriage.

6. Infanticide

Mohammed's strong condemnation of the custom of burying a newborn daughter, like the recurring Japanese attacks on infanticide, tells us mainly that the practice once existed, but gives us no quantitative data on its prevalence. Informal comments by Middle Eastern observers suggest that there is a widespread belief that Arabs neglect infant girls, and some suspicion remains that the custom of infanticide has not completely died out. As is true of all peasant cultures, such a suspicion dies hard, since in fact some cases may exist here and there and become exaggerated, Unfortunately, as in other societies where males births are welcome, the suspicion cannot be put to a test, since there is a strong tendency to omit the registration of female children. Official figures may simply show an absence of female children.

We believe, however, that a few data can be assembled to show with relative clarity that neither neglect nor infanticide runs to any great proportion, and possibly may not exist at all. It is at least true that many Western observers have by now insisted, in answer to the common charge, that in fact Arabs welcome female children, and the relation between father and daughter is often tender and protective, and that between mother and daughter is likely to remain firm throughout the young woman's lifetime. That is, although male children are more desired than females, the difference is not so great as to permit one to suspect the kind of neglect that would create a higher death rate among females.

Perhaps the most careful attempt to inquire into this question was made by Jacques Breil, who notes that the sex ratio is much higher in the more outlying regions of Algeria, indicating perhaps some neglect of girls. If the infant dies in the first few days, the parents do not feel it is necessary to declare either the birth or death.[138] He also notes from 1939 to 1952 there was a correlation between the sex ratio and the rate of infant mortality. When a higher number of males per hundred females was reported, the infant mortality rate was also higher, suggesting that both the death and the birth of females had not been registered. Even upon closer examination, however, he was unable to do more than show a failure to register; he found no positive indications of infanticide. In 1951 the sex ratio in Egypt was 109 males for 100 females, suggesting an overly high number of males born. However, the number of male deaths in the first year of life is about 13 per cent greater than that of females.[139]

Similarly, in Algeria in 1958 the number of male deaths at ages under a year was about 11 per cent higher than the number of female deaths, again suggesting that there is apparently little neglect of females. A half-century ago, Raymond Pearl carefully analyzed fertility and mortality in Algeria, and in his examination of the mortality curves of males and females in early as well as late years for the 1911–1913 period he shows no important differences; he does not suggest any interpretation of infanticide or neglect.[140]

On the other hand, in Jordan in 1960, the sex ratio was 109, and the number of deaths for females under a year was higher than for males. A higher number of deaths is also recorded for females in the 1–4 age group. Since Jordan has only recently developed an adequate statistical department, it is not clear whether these figures represent any more than the usual problems of registration.[141]

A special survey of several traditional groups was carried out in 1960 in Morocco, one of the less developed Arab countries. It found a gap in the female population aged less than one year, and a large gap aged one year; but by the 2-year age group the sexes are in a predictable balance, and this also applies to the 3–7 age group. This merely suggests that the very young females are not counted, since they show up eventually in subsequent years.[142]

Mboria has also compiled the sex ratios for the 1917–1936 period in Egypt. These ratios are all extremely high—far higher than a normal sex ratio would be in any human population—106–109. But though he does not have the data on deaths in the first year of life, which would be the more relevant figure, he does have the number of female deaths per thousand deaths for the entire female population for these years. In each year, the number of male deaths is higher by 17 to 41 per cent, which leads him to the obvious conclusion that the result arises from the simple failure to declare female deaths.[143]

It seems fair to conclude that whatever may have been true of the past, the available data do not suggest infanticide, nor even any perceptible neglect of females which might cause their mortality to be higher than that of males. All that seems evident is a failure to register female births—an obvious expression of the lesser evaluation of female children in the Arab world.

7. The Extended Family

It has been generally supposed that the extended family is the predominant family system among Arabs. Thus one report states: "A typical household consists of husband and wife, unmarried children, married sons and their wives and children."[144] Similarly, Patai states, "The Syrian family is *extended*, that is (under traditional circumstances which prevail in the majority of cases) the family constituting one household consists of an elderly man, his wife (or wives), his unmarried daughters, his unmarried as well as married sons, and the wives and children of the latter."[145]

This common belief may be accepted (as in other major family system considered in this study) if we view it as a description, not of reality, but only of *ideals*. Certainly the ideal Arab family was a large extended family under one roof. Ideally, there would be no divorce; there might be a second and third wife; and all the wives would have many sons. These sons, in turn, would be married at a relatively early age to fertile women who would produce more sons. The father would continue to supervise the work of the family, or perhaps the care of camels or other stock. The brothers would live in harmony, with some authority given to the eldest son. After the father's death, the eldest brother would continue to handle the family finances, but would deal equitably with all his brothers. If a married sister was divorced or widowed, or had trouble with her in-laws, she might from time to time be found in the household. Ideally, a man became a patriarch in his elder years, full of wisdom and authority; he would be supported by his married sons.

As we have suggested before, however, the facts of fertility, mortality, and finances have prevented all but a few men in most major civilizations from attaining this objective. High fertility societies have also been high mortality societies, so that by the time some children have become of marriageable age, others have died. Again in contrast to the ideal, most families have both sons and daughters, and the daughters leave for other households. Most men do not obtain several wives, and the fertility of wives in polygyny is lower than that in monogamy. In any event, it takes great managerial skills to hold together a large ménage, so that with increasing numbers the likelihood of fission, or conflict causing one or more subunits to break off, becomes more likely. Finally, but perhaps of most importance, in most of the great societies of the world, and of course in Arab countries as well, average wealth and income is small. Plots of land are tiny, and physically maintaining a large household in most Arab families has simply never been possible, in the past or in the present.

On the other hand, it is likely that many Arabs have lived at *some time* in an extended family. Either they did so as adolescents, or as adults who continued to live with their parents for some time after marriage before finally breaking away and establishing a productive unit of their own; or, as married adults, they kept one or more married sons with them for a time, perhaps even until death. That is, the extended family was a stage in the life cycle of the individual and the family unit as well. On the other hand, a survey at any given time of a cross-section of all the families of a given region would probably show that a minority of the families were joint.

Thus, we see two basic patterns. One is the *traditional* and continuing process by which larger family groupings develop and dissolve through sons who live with their parents after marriage for awhile before breaking away. The other is a *secular* trend, accelerated in the last decade, in which a young couple breaks away from an extended family and establishes their own home, but does not then develop another extended family made up of their own married sons and grandchildren. And, in urban areas, it is more common now that a bride and groom have not grown up in an extended family, and do not establish one in their later years.

As long ago as the 1920s, the number of sons in urban Syria continuing to live with their parents after marriage was diminishing. These larger joint families continued, however, among the large merchants and among rural families with a considerable amount of property. (Even in the large cities of Aleppo or Damascus, one could still find large houses in which forty or fifty family members were living together.) It was typical for the young married Bedouin to have a tent of his own (but close to his father's) either immediately upon marriage or very soon afterwards, but this was not a break from the extended family, since the father maintained his power.[146]

Among the Syrian peasants in the late 1930s, the most common form of the family was the "restricted patriarchal family," which simply meant that the father maintained his power until he died,[147] whether or not his children remained in the household.

By the 1950s, Daghestani could write that the "paternal" family was only found in small towns or among conservative circles, and that "the large houses which at the turn of the century sometimes contained thirty or forty family members . . . are divided into separate units for several conjugal families, or rented out as schools, institutes, etc."[148]

If our line of reasoning has been correct, we should expect to find that the average or *typical* family was relatively small in the past as well. A 1937 study of one Egyptian province throws some light on this matter. In 1887, Sharquia had an average family size of 5.5 members. In 1917, about 60 per cent of the families had from one to five members, and 33 per cent from six to ten—far removed from the traditional picture of the patriarchal, extended Arab family. In 1937, at the time of the survey, the average family had 5.04 members. This may represent a slight drop over time, but the data do not lend themselves to so refined a calculation.[149]

In the 1947 Egyptian Census, the average family size was 4.8 members.[150] As noted earlier, in the village of Silwa Bahari, Ammar found an average of four members per household.

In the 1946 study of the Palestine Bedouins, the average number of children still alive among women from 45 to 49 years old was approximately five. This included both males and females, so that about half of this number would be female. The investigators also suspected that some fictitious children were reported. An average of 2.5 living sons, if married and with children, could create a sizeable family unit.[151] However, it was rare for the Bedouin married man to live with his father in the same tent.

Another survey (1950) of several small population groups in Morocco found that the average number per household was 4.0. These households had an average of 1.4 youngsters under 13 years old.[152]

Seklani, in citing several studies of North African *proletarian groups* in Algiers, Meknes, Tunis, Casablanca, and eight mining villages of Morocco (among whom one would expect the extended family to be *least* common), found that the average number of children per household was small. For example, in the Algiers *Bidonville* or slum, the average number of children was 1.9; in the Tunis slum, 2.2.[153] With so few children, it would be difficult to expect the eventual formation of any substantial extended family. Among such proletarian groups the advantage to the son of remaining with his father is minimal; in turn the father typically does not have sufficient land or work to utilize fully the services of his adult sons.

For Algeria as a whole, the average family size was 5.1 members in 1954.[154] A somewhat higher result was obtained in a 1952 census of Jordanian towns: The average size of a family from one town to another ranged from 5.26 to 6.94.[155] A 1953 Lebanese survey (Kasmie Rural Improvement Project), showed the average size of a household to range from 5.5 to 8.3.[156] The five Arab villages in southern Palestine that were studied in 1944 had from 5.2 to 7.4 members per family.

A special survey made in Beirut in 1952 attempted to draw a random sample, but obtained a somewhat disproportionately higher number of upper-strata households. The average number of persons per household was 4.04, and there were 2.77 children per family. This means, of course, that there were families headed by a single adult. For example, 9.2 per cent of the heads of households were women.[157]

Moreover, over 97 per cent of the children residing in the sample households were *not* married. This, of course, is an index of the tendency to set up individual households when marriage takes place. As we noted earlier, parents in modern urban circles are increasingly likely to stipulate in discussions about marriage arrangements that the couple must set up their own household. It is the bride's parents who do this, in order to prevent the kind of disagreement and quarreling which has always been thought typical of the Arab mother-in-law–daughter-in-law relationship.

It might be thought that the "extended patriarchal family" has at least been preserved in the villages. Once more, however, the data are negative. To the data from the Kasmie Rural Improvement Project in Lebanon may be added a survey of villages in the southern Bequa's valley of Lebanon. Here the households average 4.4 persons each, but perhaps more important is the general lack of *differentiation* in the size of household and number of children among different occupational and social strata. As we would expect, the largest average household was among those with the most land (4.93 per household). The smallest size of family was found among the nonagricultural workers—the lowest stratum not linked to the soil.[158]

Similarly, in a Druze Arab village of Lebanon, 106 of the 171 households in the village were composed of husband, wife and unmarried children. Only eighteen families were composed of married sons and their families as well. Twenty-one additional units also contained one or more members of the husband's female kin.[159]

These data do not, however, throw any light on the more significant question as to the continuing relations between a man and his married sons, if they do not live within the same household. Nor do they throw light on the life cycle of the family. We would suppose that in the *past* a majority of the Arab families had at least one period in which there was a minimum of one married son in the household, but on this point we have not found any information at all.

It is also useful to consider the internal stresses and strains within the extended family of the past and present. Nowadays, the opportunities for independent existence are greater, and public opinion is much more favorable. On the other hand, there is no doubt that pressures towards fission always existed.

Among the Bedouins, grown siblings established a separate tent upon marriage; when the father died, the property was simply redistributed among all the sons with a small portion going to the women surviving.[160]

But the Bedouins' situation was different in certain crucial respects from that of Arabs who tilled the land. Since the Bedouin family owned camel and sheep herds rather than land, the division of labor could easily follow a simple division of flocks. The property fell into clear units of stock so that the adult siblings could live relatively independent lives even before the father's death, as indeed they did.

The process of fission in the families of farming Arabs of a Palestine village was studied intensively in the 1950s. Their economic situation at that time was similar to what the life experiences of the majority of Arabs were until fairly recently. They engaged in agricultural labor, working the land with a relatively undeveloped technology that required everyone to participate. There was little specialization of skill, and great energy was needed to obtain sufficient water, to mill the grain, to build, and to obtain sufficient fuel for cooking and eating. The markets were distant and undeveloped. A man's labor had little monetary value, and much exchange was simple barter. Absentee landlords commonly owned most of the land, so that taxes or payments to the landlord took up to 50 per cent of the produce.[161] The father ruled over his sons, and either made all purchases himself or had to approve them.

In this village, the overwhelming majority of families were nuclear or conjugal. Two hundred and five families were conjugal families, seventeen included the adult couple with all their married sons, and an additional twenty-seven included both married and unmarried sons. Twelve additional families were composed of married and unmarried brothers working together.

At the time of the survey, fifty-seven married sons had left thirty-two of these families; and sixty-four sons from forty-nine families had stayed. Moslems were more likely to stay (one half of the Moslem sons left as against two thirds of the Christian sons).[162]

Here again it should be noted that *time-data* are needed to ascertain how many sons leave in what period of time. Although the 1944 survey of social and economic conditions in Arab villages in Palestine reported that in one village one third of the sons left after marriage, the important question is how many left after what period of time. Presumably, one third of the sons left shortly after marriage, but it is likely that a majority might have left eventually.

The dynamics of fission are more interesting than the statistics. As noted earlier in the discussion on choice of mate, the young man is dependent upon his father for both his sustenance and the bride price with which the young man can marry. In Rosenfeld's village, only one villager left his father before marriage. Because the son typically has no independent source of support, he cannot leave while his other brothers are unmarried. He must contribute to accumulating the bride price necessary for their marriages, although one half of the sisters' bride price remained in the father's hands for such purposes. On the other hand, after the father dies, there is no single authority who can maintain this unity. Some half-brothers may avoid the obligation to help their younger half-siblings marry.[163]

Landlessness or poverty may still, however, mitigate equally *against* the large family, as it did in the past. There may simply not be enough land to support all the children, and some brothers may leave to seek work elsewhere on the land or in the cities. In the contemporary period, the son who leaves the village early in order to take a job elsewhere is likely to begin keeping the money for himself. Also, the older sons may sometimes begin to leave because the father has married a second time and has additional children with whom they feel no great emotional tie and for whom they do not care to work.

There are built-in strains in the system, if we consider only the siblings. The sons will have nothing in their father's lifetime and they may feel increasingly that they are contributing far more than their share. After their father dies, they may wish to have their share independently. It is striking that in Rosenfeld's village, fourteen out of seventeen married sons who continued to live with their fathers are *only* sons. They are not then contributing to the support of other siblings. Moreover, no *only* son has left his father.[164] As Rosenfeld comments, "Joint labor is demanded and individual property is the fact."[165]

We should also remember that sometimes the father with grown sons may not yet have left *his own* father, so that he may find it very difficult to arrange the marriages of his own sons. If the father with grown sons dies before his own father dies, *his* sons do not inherit at all. The aspiration of a married man, then, is to have a household of his own with sons of his own whom he can supervise.

But the tradition of brotherhood and of joint family action is strong, and men feel guilt at breaking off from their family; we note a similar phenomenon in India. Consequently, the blame is put on the women, not altogether without justice. After all, the entering women have little interest in maintaining the extended family. The woman's family begins with her husband, and she gives her emotional attention to him and to their children. She is not mistress of her own household as long as her mother-in-law, who retains all authority, is in charge. Added to this conflict is that between sisters-in-law, who, for the same reasons, have little interest in the extended family as such.

Consequently, although some brothers work together after their marriages, and even after the death of their father, all contributions by each conjugal unit are carefully weighed. If a man cannot work, he must hire a worker, and a similar substitution is maintained even for women's work. The siblings here are all equal with respect to *rights* to the produce of the land, although the elder brother will usually be manager. The careful calculation by each adult member in each conjugal unit as to who is contributing or consuming the most often makes relations within the extended family strained. True, it is difficult to split the property (especially since often the land is already made up of tiny strips); but the pressures to do so increase with time and with alternative sources of support that will permit one family or another to obtain additional income outside the land and use the small bit of the estate as an economic base. The stages in the pattern then move away from the collective operation of the family land, toward rational cooperation among the brother's conjugal families, and finally to private ownership.[166]

Thus, the industrializing and urbanizing forces, especially of the period since World War II, intensify the internal strains that were always found in the extended family, and, in addition, offer alternative sources of support for those who finally decide to set up conjugal households of their own. Among the educated urban people, such a household is viewed as a normal aspiration, and the traditional extended family is seen as old-fashioned. The young man who obtains a job on the basis of his education does not want to remain dependent upon his father; his interests and those of his wife run parallel. This does not mean that the relations among such conjugal units are strained when they are independent. The intensity of family ties even among educated Arabs remains strong. On the other hand, the pressure toward independence that is visible in the wish to choose a mate of one's own is also expressed in the desire to have a household of one's own. Consequently, in addition to the forces which always produced a high proportion of conjugal families (even when the *ideal* was the extended family) modern pressures have appeared that move both to establish such conjugal units and to defend them ideologically.

8. Larger Kinship Structures

The ratio between the amount of published sociological material based on actual field work to the amount based on previous publications and literature is higher for Arab countries than for any other great culture area analyzed in this inquiry. This ratio is still higher for the subfield of Arab kinship structure, where even the best of recent scholars feel they must call for authority on such shades of the past as Burckhardt or Doughty; and for lack of adequate anthropological field work they must accept the writings of travelers, political advisers to sheiks of Arabic kingdoms, "Old Arab Hands," and so on. Estimable and useful as these writers are, when describing particular events, they cannot be considered adequate observers of the *larger* family structures, which are not readily seen with the untrained eye. Unraveling these connections and delimiting all the units and loyalties are tedious, rewarding only to those who can experience an aesthetic pleasure from an elegant kinship chart laboriously derived from a mass of native comments, rationalizations, and actions.

If I believe that most kinship analyses of the past are deficient because they only rarely grew from painstaking field work, I fall victim to my own criticism, since I must base this next section on published materials alone. However, my aim is not a full exposition of the technical complexities of the Arab kinship system, but a discussion of only one aspect of family behavior, the extension and linking of kin ties into larger groupings. Second, although I shall avoid a textual criticism of previous authors, I believe that a fair integration of conflicting statements in various sources can be made, laying at least a groundwork for more adequate inquiries in the years to come.[167]

Even though the extended family as a *residence* or household unit been numerically exaggerated by observers of the Arab world, it has been and to some extent still is important as a building block for much larger kin groupings in Arab life. These, like the Chinese clan or the Japanese *dozoku,* are the functional equivalents of governmental and financial agencies which displace them in urban areas. All contemporary observers of Arab life report the gradual disappearance of those groupings, as more Arabs leave nomadic or village life, take new jobs, and acquire an education.

Though this secular process is going on, it must be separated from the urbanizing of particular *individuals* or families that migrate to the city, a process which antedates industrialization proper, and which doubtless has been important in Arab life for centuries.

Larger kin groupings are social structures that evolve to take care of legal and political problems that the extended family cannot handle. The unit made up of the elder couple or siblings, with their married sons and grandchildren, cannot, for example, defend itself adequately against raiders, or adjudicate a quarrel with a comparable unit. It cannot work out and execute a rational or equitable irrigation plan for a large farming area. It is always engaged in some market activities, and these sometimes require cooperation, loans, and protection against injustice beyond the limits of its strength.

Without a centralized state authority, societies have created large kin organizations having some family functions but serving primarily to solve problems beyond the capacity of the single family. In the city, these groupings are still based on family membership, but precisely because their main activities are taken over by the state or by other urban social agencies they weaken and lose their meaning. In the past this has happened again and again in the complex population movements of Arab countries.

Consequently, when an observer of a generation or more ago suggests that the *hamula* or the *khamseh* is "disappearing" he may be reporting a recurring difference between urban and rural, or urban and nomadic, kinship patterns, rather than a recent, long-term trend. If one had visited Baghdad 200 years ago, one might also have reported that the *hamula* is disappearing, or "the tribal organization is no longer important."

It is therefore necessary to distinguish between the kin groupings of urban Arabs, peasants, and Bedouins. It is also important to recognize that linguistic differences abound in Arab countries, so that terms may be used in different regions for the *same* groupings, and that the various higher levels of kinship organization may not be present at all, though the *terms* used for them elsewhere may nevertheless be known. Let us begin with the most complex set of groupings:

"The tribe (*qabilah*) is usually subdivided into two or more sub-tribes (*ashirah*); each sub-tribe, in turn, is commonly divided into two or more sub-divisions (*firqah*). The *firqah* comprises two or more further divisions (*fakhdh*); the *fakhdh* is divided into two or more *hamulah,* and finally the *hamulah* into two or more related extended families."[168] Each tribe usually claims that it is made up of descendants of a single ancestor, whose name they all bear. Sometimes, this ancestor is a fictitious figure.

However, we immediately run into the problem encountered at every step in analyzing these larger kinship structures: "It is doubtful that the ideal six-level tribal structure can be found in any Iraqi tribes today; even the largest and most complex groups probably do not show more than four levels—extended family, lineage (*hamulah*), sub-tribe, and tribe."[169] Moreover, even when a large group is divided into several levels, the levels are not symmetrical. One part of the group may be built on two sublevels and other parts may contain three or four.

These comments also apply to the ideal structure outlined by Patai in his discussion of Syrian tribes.[170] Here again, we are told that "Many tribes do not have this six-story structure." A similar ideal description and caution is to be found in Patai's analysis of Jordanian tribes.[171]

It is notable that no such description is given in the Human Relations Area Files Survey of Egypt,[172] nor is any such description to be found in Lane's account of Egyptian life a century ago, confined as it is to urban and village life. Thus, we see that where tribal life has disappeared, little of the larger kin structures remains.

Perhaps one of the more striking aspects of these traditional larger groupings of kinship is the very small place they occupy in Moslem law. Although the law is concerned in great detail with the family, from the formation of the marriage to its dissolution, as well as the problems of affiliation and succession, for the most part it deals almost entirely with the small family and has not typically recognized the larger kin groupings as being of legal significance. Written law was not characteristic of the tribal society or among sedentary Bedouins, so that where larger kin structures were more common, they did not figure in such legal scholarship as was taught in Koranic schools. Nevertheless, the contrast must be made with both Japanese and Chinese law, which concern themselves with the rights and duties of individuals in their relations with these larger structures.

There is general agreement that the two highest levels are *qbila* (tribe) and *ashira* (subtribe). However, no delineating criteria of these have ever been agreed upon. Daghestani believes that the origin of the term *ashira* is the Arabic term '*ashira* for "ten." That is, it meant all the members of the same group who were relatives within the tenth degree. The *qbila* is headed by an independent sheik, while the sheik who rules the *ashira* presumably owes allegiance to such an independent sheik. However, some *ashayer* claim to be independent, and sometimes a *qbila* has no paramount sheik. In any event, all the members of these divisions claim kinship, even when their origins lie in adoption, simply because they are progressively built up from lower levels of family organization. However distant the relationship between any two members may be, ideally it should be possible to trace out the family links joining them.

In spite of some omissions from one description or another, there is also some agreement at the *lowest* level. First, the general term *bet* is used rather widely. It refers to the household, hearth, or "house," meaning all those persons with the same name—normally the extended family as a resident unit. It includes the parents, the married sons and their children not yet living apart, unmarried sons, and unmarried daughters; essentially all the people for whom the head of the house is responsible. The more technical term is *'ahel*, or *ahl*, its essential characteristic being a family group living together.

When a relatively large family group includes one or more sons who have a family of their own within it, such a subunit may be called a *'yal*. Such a *'yal* would be called an *'ahel* when the son leaves the houshold to live apart with his family. Among the Bedouins, a married son would normally have a separate tent, so the term *'yal* would be uncommon. The son's family, living apart, would simply be called an *'ahel*. Similarly, in some rural regions where the pattern of house construction did not permit several generations to live together, almost any conjugal unit might be referred to as an *'ahel*, and the term becomes in effect synonymous with *'yal* and *bet*.[173]

Weulersse found three levels of groupings among the Syrian peasants in the late 1930s: the conjugal family (parents and children), the patriarchal family (usually made up of conjugal families, headed by the older father who maintained his authority over his married sons), and the *ashira*, or "tribal family," which could extend as far as the tenth degree of kinship.[174]

With reference to the middle levels of groupings that we have been considering, it is not possible to reconstruct a clear-cut set of terms from the existing literature. As Bräunlich has remarked, "Lexicologists have tortured themselves with the fixing of the nuances of meanings of these terms wihout success."[175] Different terms may have the same meaning, but may be used with very different frequency in the same group, or not used at all in one group but used in another.

These middle levels of organization are the source of the greatest disagreement, because Arabs in one area may have only part of the total "ideal" organization, and in any event may call its parts by different names.

The main point of disagreement between Daghestani and other reliable scholars is the exact place of the *hamula*, a term which is nearly universally reported, and is sometimes called a "clan" or lineage." An alternative term for it is *samiyah* or *summiyeh*. Patai places the *hamula* just one step higher in size and inclusiveness than the basic family unit, and asserts that it is "composed of two or more families."[176] Similarly, it is asserted that among the Bedouins of Iraq the *hamula* is next to the extended family in size, and "consists of several related extended families with a common ancestor."[177] In Patai's discussion of social structure in Jordan, he asserts that the *hamula* is next to the smallest subdivision, and "is composed of two or more families."[178]

By contrast, Daghestani's usage is much closer to the usage of those who refer to this family grouping as a clan, kindred, or lineage: He asserts that it "Embraces all the members of a family, men and women who are linked among themselves by a male kinship tie, real or fictive, who all bear the same name and claim to descend from the same ancestor."[179] He does not specify whether this ancestor is real or not. In all of the instances he gives, however, the ancestor was real. Presumably, this would separate the *hamula* in most instances from the *qbila*, or the *ashira*.

The basic disagreement is essentially that Daghestani believes the *hamula* to be a relatively *higher* level of family organization, just under the *ashira*, while the six-level pattern of organization places the *hamula* at the next to *lowest* level of social organization.

We do not believe it is possible to solve these problems definitively on the basis of the existing data. We are willing, however, to express our views. The six-level "system" appears to be a composite or conglomerate of terms and levels used in different regions by very different groups. All the actual charts seem to have four levels or less. On the other hand, if one obtains a term from one region, one may well combine it with a term used in another region, and thus arrive at a more complex set of levels for a *hypothetical* social organization.

Second, where authors suggest the six-level system, the *hamula* is defined in rather minimum terms, not corresponding to its apparent importance in Arab social life. This suggests that some of the terms may have been *interpolated* between top and bottom, as being somewhat higher levels, simply because it was difficult to fit them in—especially so since nowhere can one find adequate descriptions of the criteria or characteristics used by the Arabs themselves to delimit one of these levels from the next. One can obtain concrete instances or terms, but not the *bases* on which the division is made. Consequently, one cannot be sure that a division found in one region means even roughly what it seems to mean in another.

On very general theoretical grounds we are inclined to suspect the six-level system of never having existed at all, because even very large Western formal organizations often do not have six clearly defined levels. This does not mean that six levels are not possible; I am only expressing the bases of my skepticism about their existence.

In Table III-9 I attempt to judge the relationship of these levels of organization in different types of social structures. On only one of these levels do I still feel some doubt, the place of the *fendeh* in the levels of organization.

In general, the peasants living in outlying regions are likely to have a social structure very close to that of the sedentary Bedouins. As would be expected, these various levels begin to disappear as groups are incorporated more and more into the national and urban social patterns in the Arab

Table III-9
Arab Organization
LEVELS OF FAMILY STRUCTURES IN VARIOUS SEGMENTS OF THE SOCIETY

Bedouins	Sedentary Bedouins
Qbila (tribe)	'Ashirah, sometimes called firqa, ferka
Ashirah (subtribe)	'El 'abou, or fakhed, hamula, or samiyeh
Hamula (clan, kindred, lineage)	Small fakhed, or fendeh,
Fendeh	'Ahel, bet
'Ahel, bet (family, house, extended family)	

Peasants in Contact with Cities	City Dwellers
Hamula—term not used	'Eleh, Al, 'a'ila ("House of . . ." descendants
Large hamula called ashira	from same stem agnatically)
Bet, 'yal, 'ahel	Bet, 'yal (conjugal or extended family in same residence)

countries. The nomadic Bedouins become sedentary, and the sedentary Bedouins become village merchants or even farmers. A constant trek to the city is going on in all Arab countries, and although, for a time, the early migrants congregate together within the city and keep alive their feeling of kinship with distant relatives (partly because these are the only city people with whom they can feel any kinship), the effectiveness and utility of these larger organizations decline. Other organizations and agencies substitute for them, although perhaps inevitably yielding less emotional satisfaction in the process.

Our concern is not so much with naming or delineating these structures as with asking what the changes are that have taken place within them over time. Before doing that, however, three further divisions based on kinship must be noted, somewhat different structurally from the foregoing levels.

The first of these is the *khamseh*, designating all people within five degrees of patrilineal relationship. These form the core and perhaps the origin of the *hamula* grouping, and comprise all those who can be counted on when blood vengeance is called for, just as they are the persons against whom blood vengeance is directed when another *khamseh* feels wronged.[180] Since any individual counts from himself five kinship steps beyond, upward or in any other direction, the *khamseh* is different for each person, depending upon his generation or location within the kinship structure. Thus, a man's grandfather's brother's grandson is in the man's *khamseh*, but because this grandson is distant from ego laterally, the grandson has a slightly different *khamseh*, although it still includes ego in turn. Like the "Kindred" in the West it is therefore not a *group* having a membership and boundaries that are the same for all.

The *khamseh* no longer functions within the city, and almost not at all among peasants in contact with the cities. In Arab countries, individual responsibility for crimes is the law, and except among some Bedouin tribes in outlying regions, this is the fact as well.

Another type of division noted by some observers is the *bani'am*, which, strictly speaking, seems not to be an organization of families of a higher order or a *group* or even a political unity. It has no chief. It may include several subtribes or sections of a tribe, and among some groups is defined rather strictly, since these subtribes carry the relationship to the seventh generation of male ascendants. However, it seems to be more properly viewed as a *relationship* of brotherhood requiring certain reciprocal duties. For example, a man must not seize and bind another who is in such a relationship, nor attack him in war by a dawn assault, nor raid his camp after midnight. Between *bani'am* the blood vengeance can be settled by payments.[181]

The extension of this relationship may go very far. For example, the Rwala, one of the largest of the camel Bedouin tribes, belongs to a still larger group of tribes called the *'aneze*, divided into two great branches, North and South. All of these tribes and clans are *beni al'anam* to one another.[182] Outside of tribal areas, however, this relationship has lost its significance.

Patai calls our attention to a third type of division, again *not* a group but a duality among the nomadic tribes. Its meaning remains somewhat obscure. He notes that there is often a "dichotomy into two equivalent moieties (halves), or a bi-partite division."[183]

Since they are not really exogamous, they are not moieties, strictly speaking. Just what consequences division may have is unclear. Granqvist notes a similar division in her Palestine village of Artas in the 1930s, and it is interesting to note that Ammar, without commenting on the point in detail, reports it also for Silwa Bahari anud Silwa Kibli. He notes, for example, that the extended families are grouped into "clans," which seem to be given a term (*kabail*) like that of "tribe." But the nine clans in turn are grouped into two great sections, North and South.[184]

Returning now to the meaning of larger kin structures, the social system of Silwa Bahari may be taken as illustrative of at least the Egyptian peasants. In Silwa Bahari, in conformity with our analysis up to this point, there is "no institutionalized cooperation between the members of an extended family if they are not living in one house."[185] On the other hand, the *large* land-owning families are more likely to have a stronger or more effective economic unity. Unity *is* expected on formal or public occasions, and some social control over members is maintained. The clans no longer have formal heads but there are natural leaders. Each clan has a guest house where disputes are settled, gossip is exchanged, and feast ceremonies are celebrated. Thus, the *hamula* still has some functions in the Egyptian village.

The broader kinship units also continue to have some political functions in the tribe. The eldest son does not inherit the position of sheikh. The incumbent sheikh may attempt to name an elder or a favorite son as his successor, or attempt to give responsibility to his chosen son so that the young man may exhibit his qualities of leadership and thus have a better chance of being selected. However, there is no rule of clear succession, except that the elders must choose the sheikh from a particular family line. Thus, the elder sheikh knows that his successor will come from his family line even if he cannot insure the succession through his own will.

The feeling of kinship and fellowship among peasants or village dwellers who at least know that they are related to certain other people may play a role in the modern political system, where votes are counted by individuals rather than by senior men of a tribe. Ammar analyzes the election pattern in Silwa to show that "kinship relations, and not party politics, decide the issue of the election in this community."[186]

Membership in the *hamula* is also likely to affect which quarter of a village people inhabit,[187] and some villages may still be primarily composed of one *hamula*. In Syria, the quarters of the town are not based on the *hamula*, but rather on religious or ethnic membership.[188]

These larger kinship structures were of great importance in Jordan, Iraq, and Northern Syria because of the prevalence until recently of *musha'a* a type of landholding which was also common in Palestine. In the Arab world, there are four main types of landholding. One of these is owner-ship in fee simple, the ordinary type of ownership found in the Western world, called *mulk*.[189]

A second, and still the most common type of land ownership in the Arab world, is *miri*, which is land owned by the government but rented to tenants for a definite, or sometimes indefinite, period. The "tenant" pays taxes and has the privilege of bequeathing his rights to use the land.

A third type of land holding is *wakf*, which is also tied to the tradi-tional and legal family structure. This was the Moslem solution to the problem for which laws of entail were developed in the Western world. That is, since land was to be divided upon the death of the father and the father sometimes wished to maintain the property intact, the legal solution was to will the land to a pious enterprise, such as the maintenance of a mosque, but specify that the fruits of a land were to go to a man's family until the family itself died out.

The original purpose of the *wakf* was entirely pious, and corresponds to the pattern of willing land and wealth to the Church in medieval Europe. The *wakf* for family purposes followed this legal model, however. The existence of such property created a number of problems in the Arab world, notably the fact that the land was not typically under the control of the family itself, and thus was often mismanaged. In addition, the system tended to freeze the class structure, and a substantial amount of the land in some areas was *wakf* land.

A major change in the Arab world has been the abolition of many *wakf* holdings, or a serious attempt to reduce them as well as to rationalize and control their administration. In Egypt, for example, there is a Ministry of *Wakf*,[190] and its counterpart may be found in other Arab countries.

Musha'a land was collectively owned and was the standard tenure system in the 1940s in Northern Syria. This type of land is also declining in the Arab world, but where it still occurs it is based on *hamula* memberships. Ideally, each man was entitled to one share of the land collectively held. This was not a particular piece of land, but merely a unit of ownership. From time to time, there was a rotation of the actual land held. Of course, the shares could be inherited, and in many areas over time an individual could acquire a substantial part of the *musha'a* land in a given place. In the 1940s in the Northern Plains of Syria, 70 to 80 per cent of the land under this system was owned by absentee landlords. The shares were rotated according to the usual principles, and farmed by people who succeeded previous members of the family on the land, but a large share of the produce was given to the landlord. In one district, 110 out of 114 villages belonged to landlords, and eighty-six of these belonged to only four landlords.[191]

The change that has occurred in this type of holding is due not to changes in family patterns but to the peasants' political and economic demands, and the responses to those demands by the new Arab leaders. In any event, the *consequence* of those changes is that membership in a larger kin grouping is less important than it was in the past for acquiring or maintaining ownership in the areas where *musha'a* land was important. As late as 1933, *musha'a* land was extensive in East Jordan; it has been reduced since then, lapsing along with this type of holding in Palestine and presumably West Jordan.[192]

In view of the complexity of the topic, a final comment regarding the main levels of kinship structures is in order. It is clear that most of the confusion about the higher levels of the traditional or tribal kinship structure and how to distinguish them, derives from two basic processes in Arab life: (1) growth and fission of the family units themselves, and (2) the exigencies or opportunities of political amalgamation. A sheikh who has not been very successful in war, whose tribe was not successful in gaining adequate sustenance or who was thought not to be wise in counsel might lose a part or much of his following, which would then join other subtribes or groupings. Consequently, a tribe might sometimes number only twenty tents, whereas other tribes might have hundreds or even thousands of tents at an especially important gathering. With reference to the growth process, a family or a *hamula* might very well grow to large proportions and begin to break off in smaller units, still tracing their ancestry back to a common ascendant but gradually assuming more and more independence from the others. Thus, a *hamula* might include all the descendants of a common ancestor for as much as seven or eight generations in the past, or it might instead contain no more than two tents.[193]

The next important principle seems to be that kinship and blood relationship are central for the *hamula*, and that the *hamula* is typically thought of as connoting blood relationships. Beyond that point, however, the considerations which arise are primarily political. Indeed, one of the reasons why the *ashira* (or subtribe) and the *hamula* have sometimes been used interchangeably is that they may in many instances refer to the same grouping of people although *viewed in different contexts*. In a *family* context the grouping might be called a *hamula*; in a *political* context, the same grouping may be referred to as an *ashira*. As Bräunlich comments, "The tribe is only a political, not a somatic, unity."[194]

Just as the *hamula* and the *ashira* (or *bedide*) sometimes appear to be indistinguishable from one another, so the *hamula* and the *fendeh* (or *firqa*) also seem to be indistinguishable at times. These higher levels of organization or political systems are often based on artfully constructed genealogies so as to link up all the various *hamula* into a tribe, to utilize the *vocabulary* of a kinship—and thus to elicit a type of loyalty that might otherwise be absent.[195]

The tribal genealogies and higher levels of kin structure then have a primarily political foundation, important for law and order. Among the Bedouins, right and wrong have had only a conditional validity, as between two men, one of whom is outside the tribe. Within the tribe, law and custom are well known and applied, and indeed, observers have always remarked that the Bedouin was extremely sensitive to comment and criticism from his fellow members. Beyond this foundation of law and order, the family foundations were of some importance in arousing the loyalty that was important for raiding and war.[196]

The basic kinship grouping, then, was the individual family in a tent sometimes belonging to a married son still under the authority of his father in a larger tent close by. Beyond that was found a grouping which differed from each individual to another since it was made up of all the relatives from male ancestors counted five steps from ego. This was the core of the kin folk within any *hamula*, which was always larger. Within the *hamula* everyone traced his ancestry to a common ancestor for as much as six to ten generations. When it reached such a size, the unit would probably begin to take on the characteristics of a political confederation and might be called *fendeh, ashira, firqa,* etc.

Beyond this level, however, several additional possibilities emerge, although all of them seem to be of little family importance. They are simply larger and larger confederations of unions of tribes and subtribes. As noted already, they utilized a family *vocabulary* simply because this had an emotional appeal and became a basis, readily understood by everyone, for unity, law and order, sharing, and common defense against the outside enemy. Beyond the level of *hamula*, it is very likely that all such organizations or units had aliens within them—that is, adopted people not related by blood.

In the city, the larger kinship structure disintegrates, as all observers have noted over the past fifteen years, but two great allegiances (besides the immediate family) remain even among the educated. (These have some importance in the West as well.) The three-generation link of grand-parents, married children, and grandchildren continues to be important. Beyond that, there is still a consciousness of belonging to a particular kindred, even when it is no longer organized clearly on a lineage basis, with a definite head or lineage council.

9. Relations Internal to the Family

There are no contemporary studies of the changes in the relations among the various members of the Arab family, except for a few comments here and there on the husband-wife relationship. Obviously, the contemporary educated Arab wife has much more freedom than she used to, as do adolescent children. It is to be hoped that in the near future studies on all these relations will begin to appear. In spite of this paucity of data, a few comments concerning contemporary Arab family relations can be made.

The Arab family was patrilocal; the girl joined her husband at his house. True matrilocal residence was apparently the pattern in Egyptian Silwa Bahari; and in Kuwait during the 1920s, a bride spent her seven-day honeymoon in her mother's house.[197] And Daghestani notes that sometimes a boy might live with the girl's family if she was an only child.[198] The standard pattern, however, was patrilocal residence. Thus, as a rule the wife had to adjust to her husband's peculiarities and to those of his family.

The traditional lore about mother-in-law-daughter-in-law relations in Japan and China are exactly paralleled in the Arab countries and need not be reported here. The mother-son relationship was intensely emotional, and the mother viewed the young bride as an interloper. Moreover, the bride was usually young, so that she could be dominated, and the chances of divorce were high.

However, several elements in the husband-wife relationship among Arabs were different from those in Japan, China, or India. Perhaps most fundamental is the Moslem rule that the woman could have some property entirely her own. Depending on her class position, she would bring more or less dowry or wealth with her in the marriage. These might be jewels or household effects and might even be property or other wealth. Her husband did not acquire the property through marriage. If she sold any of it, the money became hers. She could lend money to her husband. Granted, the husband would usually manage her property, especially since she would not have the right to move about in the financial world. Nevertheless, she did have a certain independence of at least a small sort.

Although it would be unwise to minimize the high control by the Arab husband over his wife, we must continue to note the points at which this control seems to have been at least different from, if not less than, some other patriarchal systems. In addition to the property which she might hold in her own right, the wife typically had insurance in the fact that nowhere in the Arab world did she completely sever her ties with her own family; she never became part of her husband's lineage. This has several structural ramifications. Essentially, it meant that if the wife found life in her new household too difficult, she could always return home. This was not morally scandalous, and she could set conditions for her return to her husband, who would always need her services more than she needed his.[199] Moreover, if we assume that the number of stories Arab men have invented over the centuries to suggest that the women's gesture of defiance was *not* successful indicate a simple psychodynamic process of denial, we would guess that indeed the woman's lot was often bettered in her home situation by virtue of this right.

This possibility was also a feasible one since most marriages took place within the village or tribe, often with father's brother's son, so that the woman did not have to travel far, nor was the road dangerous. This pattern, it must be emphasized, was not merely found in villages, but was common among the Bedouins as well. The possibility of at least a mild rebellion was further intensified by the fact that, although in Moslem law a daughter did inherit one half a brother's share, typically she did not take that share. Thus, she always had a certain vague legal right to sustenance from the family land or property.

It seems clear, on the other hand, that in the Arab countries (as we have noted elsewhere) the upper-stratum woman was likely to be controlled far more, to be kept more rigidly in seclusion, and to have less right to move about than those in the lower strata. Moreover, she would have been more likely to have joined her husband from some distance, so that she could not easily go back to her family.

It is perhaps for these reasons that Winifred Blackman, writing of the fellahin of the 1920s, commented, "Indeed, I am often inclined to think that it is the poor oppressed Egyptian *man* who has a claim to my sympathy and that the overruled, oppressed wife is somewhat of a myth." She describes many concrete instances which show, not that the woman had great power over her husband, but that she did have some basis for counterattack, defense, or resistance.[200]

It is true that the woman could be divorced easily, but the fact of easy divorce also meant a relatively easy remarriage for the woman as well as for the man. Indeed, if the woman returned to her home divorced, her family could obtain another bride price for her, so that her welcome was twice assured.[201]

In addition to these sources of possible support, the existence of a marriage contract system always made it possible for the girl's parents to make some stipulations regarding maintenance, support, type of treatment, the right to divorce if the man married a second time, and so on. As noted earlier, even life in the harem was not equivalent to being in jail. Among the upper strata, women of one harem would visit those of another even a hundred years ago.[202]

In the small cities of Syria during the 1920s, a woman might have to ask for permission before going out, but she could go out of the house on errands and even on visits. On the other hand, even at that time many urban husbands thought it somewhat shameful to go for a walk with their wives, although some would do so in spite of the opinion of others.[203] When Daghestani inquired into the relations of husband and wife in villages close to Damascus a generation ago, he thought he found that their freedom was much greater than that of women peasants who lived at a much greater distance from the cities.[204]

Ideology was sometimes at war with emotion. It demanded domination of the wife, and in rural regions, for example, it was thought *weak* to be tender or sweet to her. But the Arab tradition that sexual relations with the wife were a great pleasure and were to be enjoyed undoubtedly created a considerable amount of emotion in the husband-wife tie and colored to some extent the husband-wife interaction. Granted, the aim was not at all to give pleasure to the wife, but she was nevertheless always viewed as one source of solace. Perhaps it is not at all inappropriate to note that the ritually appropriate remark in initiating sex relations with one's wife was, "I seek refuge in God from the accursed Satan; in the name of God the beneficent, the merciful."

There is general agreement that the work tasks were unequally divided between the sexes. Once the sowing was done, the men left most of the work to the women until harvest. Work, was, and is, looked down upon. Even the fellah, for whom actual fighting in war was unlikely, continued to share the Bedouin attitude that women should do the work; it was enough for men to be brave and valiant.

Almost every observer of Arab life up to World War II gives a similar report: The Arab men took great pleasure in one another's company, engaging in discussions and talk at great length and leaving all but the heaviest work to the women. Wood was rare and had to be gathered or carried great distances. Water was often rare or distant and required constant carrying of water pots. Among Bedouins, the women not only wove the tents but set them up and took them down when making or breaking camp. Although the Artas women in Palestine rejected the following proverb because of its cynicism, saying it was not true of their village, it does express one view of the Arab wife: "By night my wife—by day my she-ass."[205]

On the other hand, Weulersse makes the shrewd observation that in somewhat more *prosperous* areas the inequality between the sexes has diminished somewhat, simply because men have more to do: With each new technique, each new demand of the job, the amount of free time given over to ease diminished.[206]

Perhaps the relationship might be better phrased by saying that, at least in the early years of marriage, the Arab husband was not expected to share much with his wife, and that there was relatively little interaction. The important kin ties in village and tribe were those among men. The young bride was directed by her mother-in-law rather than by her husband and a good bride would see her husband primarily at night. Although Western women are likely to think of marketing as a chore, in the Middle East it did afford (and still does) an occasion for friendly social intercourse and leisurely discussion. As a consequence, much or most of the marketing was done by men, especially among the better classes.[207] In Syria a generation ago, only the proletarian or lowest-class woman went to market; the ordinary poor or middle-class woman did not.[208]

In describing the changes in behavior of nomads who moved from a rather rigidly controlled family life in the oasis to the city, Miner and DeVos note that in the city there are new reasons for women to leave the house. In the oasis, almost every family produces most of its own food, and for the few remaining market purchases there will always be a male relative who can be sent. In Algiers, by contrast, the men have to be away during their definite work hours, and food must be shopped for constantly. Since men *must* grant their women somewhat greater freedom in the matter of marketing and going out, they gain confidence in their women—but as might be supposed, they have not yet adjusted emotionally to the amount of freedom they have to give.[209] Nevertheless, the change in attitude which can be seen in Algiers is probably the usual result of urbanization, rather than merely a modern change. The greater freedom of the urban woman was noted long before any changes due to industrialization or to the entrance of Arab women into new occupations.[210]

The separation of husband and wife was extended to dining as well. Although among the poor the wife would dine with her husband, and the men with the women, this was not generally true for farmers or the ordinary middle class. The educated *urban* men, however, began to dine with their wives a generation ago, and now this is relatively common.

It was formerly taken for granted that if a woman committed adultery, her father or brothers would kill her. They were the guardians of her honor and remained the instrument of social control after she married. A husband could, and sometimes did, kill his wife, especially if he caught her in the act. However, as the power of formal state authorities has grown (and for many decades this has been especially true in the cities), this response is increasingly viewed as outmoded. Doubtless, the male attitude is much more severe than in the West, but we should keep in mind that even in the West (take, as an extreme example, the southern United States) a husband is not likely to be convicted for such a crime or, if convicted, is not likely to receive a severe sentence.

The most extreme description of changes in the husband-wife relationship has been offered by Fanon, who describes the reorientation of husband and wife toward one another under the demands of the Algerian revolution. Even if this is an exaggeration, it at least points to the underlying *processes* which are going on in Arab countries generally. From a more generalized view the cause of change is not so much the Algerian revolution itself as the need to break rules in order to solve new problems: the woman had to become independent in decision, in action, and even in spatial mobility. New choices were offered, and since sometimes the woman was the more fervent and ardent revolutionist, the man was forced to give her additional respect. She was no longer the passive servant, but often the initiator of a new solution. Her relationship to the larger family became less important, but as that tie became less intense, husband and wife might actually come closer to one another emotionally.[211] Women whose husbands were away had to run the household alone and could not be treated as ignorant, since in fact they were taking a responsible part in the new society.

Perhaps one tiny index of a change in this relationship may be found in Article 23 of the new Tunisian Code of Personal Status, according to which the wife is now required to contribute to the support of the family if she has property of her own. In Lebanon and Egypt as of 1958, the absolute separation of the wife's property was still maintained.[212] Another index may be found in the fact that in most Arab countries it has become increasingly difficult for the man unilaterally to decide on a divorce; the woman has a greater voice in the matter, and gradually the grounds for divorce become the same for both.

The relation between Arab mother and son was an extremely intense one. Aside from the expected love of a mother for her son, she had some reason to find in him a major center of her being. By producing a son, the woman helped to build up her husband's house, both symbolically and in fact (since a son became part of her husband's work force). She was unlikely to be divorced if she bore a son, and he represented her primary link with her husband's line. Basing their conclusions in part on Rohrschach materials from Bedouins, Miner and DeVos comment, ". . . the erotic attachment of men to their mothers and sisters is very strong . . . nor are these feelings one-sided."[213] Although a girl baby is likely to continue nursing for as long as one or one and a half years, the boy is nursed until he is two or two and a half, and gets far more tender treatment. Here, as in Japan, one is struck by the reports of rather great permissiveness in child-rearing at the earliest years, when the youngster is (by Western standards) apparently spoiled—but at the same time the child is taught to show great deference to both parents, and especially to the father. The Arab boy was taught not to sit down when his father was standing, and to get up when his father approached. If he had begun smoking, he could not do so in his father's presence (nor, in many regions, in the presence of his elder brother). He could not dispute with his father in an argument.

To some extent this respect pattern extended to the eldest brother, who, in some families, became the manager of the common property. In some Bedouin tribes, the father might attempt to make his eldest son his successor. According to Ammar, brothers were expected to show great solidarity, but to preserve some social distance after the age of 11 or 12.[214]

Actually, the structure of the Arab family would suggest a gradually increasing amount of sibling rivalry between brothers as the years advanced. If, in addition, they had different mothers, some conflict between them was expected, and Arab folk tales emphasize this hostility, just as it emphasized the hostility within the polygynous household generally.

Since the mother was a major source of solace and tenderness for a boy, who increasingly spent most of his time with adult males, so was the relation with the mother's side of the family likely to be a warm one, uncontaminated by severe demands. This side of the Arab family has not been adequately described, although references to it are sufficiently frequent to justify inclusion here. Moreover, this pattern is what one would expect in a strongly patrilineal society.[215]

Among the nomadic Bedouins, who wanted their sons to become strong and warlike, independent behavior in the young male was tolerated, and the relation between father and son was tender.[216] An aphorism among the seminomads of North Palestine ran, "When your son begins to have a beard, treat him like a brother."[217]

It is not possible, with the available data, to chart the changes now going on among the various relationships within the Arab family. They can be predicted, and one might cite contemporary observers who have recorded the changes that the sociologist would view as predictable. These do not constitute studies, however, and such comments are likely to be only interesting, anecdotal impressions. A few are worthy of brief comment.

Some of the changes that are taking place grow from changes in the place of the woman in the larger society to be discussed in the next section. Both the young boy and the young girl are likely to spend much more time in school, where they are less exposed to customary socialization and more exposed to teachings that contradict what their fathers or mothers learned a generation before them. A majority of Arab youngsters will remain illiterate, so that it would be foolish to exaggerate the importance of school education, but formal education becomes increasingly recognized as a way of moving out and up, thus bringing to the attention of the young Arab the possibility that there is a different pattern of life.

Increasingly, the home is neolocal, so that some of the strained relations between mother-in-law and daughter-in-law will become less intense. Among the educated Arabs, the ideology that demands respect for the woman from the husband is more accepted, even when traditions and social pressures have not as yet given a secure institutional basis for this new relationship. The greater respect which the younger brothers were supposed to pay to elders continues to decline, in part because the younger brothers do not depend on the elders for their future, although we would expect that fraternal solidarity will be a characteristic mark of Arab culture for generations to come.[218]

The brother-sister tie will remain strong, although one would expect that the brother will become far less of a refuge in time of trouble than before simply because the changed relationship of husband and wife will make that source of refuge somewhat less necessary. We would predict that the intense tie between mother and son, will not lessen to any perceptible degree. There is no serious ideological attack on this relationship, and, in a highly competitive urban and industrial world, it may remain a solace, just as it was a solace even in Bedouin tribes against the somewhat harsh and implacable demands of the adult males' warlike existence.

We would suppose that the relation between father and son, as well as between father and daughter, may change somewhat to permit the expression of greater tenderness. As the female becomes less a symbol of pure sexuality in the Arab world, and can be treated more and more as a person, the father can begin to feel more comfortable with his married daughter and she with him. On the other hand, the mother was always a center of the daughter's affection, especially since the girl was not in love with her husband nor part of his lineage, and it was partly to be with her mother again that she wished to return often to her father's house after marriage. Under the new, gradually emerging conditions of married life, the young wife will be closer to her husband and have less motivation to flee his house and the conflicts with sisters-in-law or mother-in-law. Thus, the relationship with her mother can become a much more personal one, instead of a partial counterpoise to the difficulties of her new home.

Finally, we would expect one area of discord to increase in the near future, although it may decline eventually: When young Arab men have moved to the city in order to make their own way, they have in the past sent money to their parents and continued to feel somewhat dependent upon them emotionally; in many instances they have even expected to go back to their village or small town. Nevertheless, as Ammar reports, they often resent the excessive demands their families make upon them, and envy those who have always lived in the city and who seem to be somewhat freer of those demands. In the near future, we would expect the differences between village and city to increase rather than decrease, and the greater number of migrants to the city to augment the number of instances of family discord because of differences in mobility and success, together with the typical, gradual refusal of the more successful to share their greater wealth with their less successful kinsmen.[219]

10. The Position of Women in the Larger Society

A nation cannot directly change the social interaction in the family, but it can change important variables that will inevitably lead to internal change. The Arab countries, with few exceptions (Bahrein, Saudi Arabia, Kuwait) seek economic and political aims that are viewed as inconceivable without altering the position of women: Women must become literate, they must contribute economically to the wealth of the country, and their help is needed even in political reconstruction. Thus, to the slow effects of urbanization and a minuscule industrialization are added the intensifying consequences of major propaganda campaigns. These have opened the doors of political and economic opportunity to tens of thousands of women; more subtly, they carry the new and intimate message to both men and women that they must re-evaluate each other, as well as their family values and behavior, courtship patterns, socialization of children, and the authority of ancient family traditions. The new opportunities make it possible for an able Arab woman to find a new realm for using her talents, but in turn the Arab father or husband cannot so easily force her to follow the old patterns; nor can they easily find justifications for such pressures. Not only can she point to other women who are emancipated, but the Arab national leaders have called to Arab women to come forward and take part in building a new epoch.

The pace of these changes has accelerated during the last decade, too recently for research reports to have been made about them, but the new laws both express these changes and serve as an index of the direction of future alterations. Similarly, changes in education tell us what has been going on and what is to come.

As noted before, the Arabs have been sensitive to the Western criticism that they have treated their women like chattels, kept them subjugated, and given them little respect. One Arab answer has been to alter these conditions. Another has been to move forward, but to insist that the charges were exaggerated or untrue. This debate, it should be noted, has been going on for decades.

Some view of the ideological conflict can be obtained by considering briefly the paraphrased argument by one Moslem apologist that Islam had always granted the women great freedom and equality, or at least as much as she deserved.[220] Kotb's thesis, reduced to its simplest terms, runs somewhat as follows: Islam always gave more freedom of property to women; it denied them only the sexual license permitted to them in the West. While the West permits women to work, the circumstances in which they perform their jobs are unsavory—". . . a form of slavery and servitude in an atmosphere of incense and opium."[221] He suggests also that the underlying reason for the apparent generosity of Western men in the matter of permitting women to work is really the unwillingness of the men to take care of their women. Finally, he leans upon differences in biological endowment to explain the Islamic insistence upon the natural right of men to act as overseers of women.

But by claiming that Islam always *was* in favor of equality, the apologist is in effect *conceding* it to the modern woman; by setting equality of skill and responsibility as a reason for *in*equality, the apologist implicitly makes an agreement to grant those rewards when she earns them. Thus, the apologist is often moving in the same direction as the explicit feminist radical, even while looking backward nostalgically.

Some changes should be viewed as progress by any standards of equality, although the Westerner may be shocked that the step was not taken long ago. Perhaps the most striking of these best measures the great distance yet to be traveled: Nasser's decree of April, 1958 that the practice of clitoridectomy was to be punished by fine or imprisonment. This was the culmination of a press campaign of several years. The Cairo government thus attacked a well-rooted custom, especially widespread in Egypt (although no numerical data on the percentage of women who underwent the operation are available). It was common among the lower strata, but also followed among many bourgeoisie families, sometimes even among the relatively emancipated.[222]

The ablation of the clitoris was justified by Islamic tradition, based upon the belief, repeated here and there in many commentaries, that women's sexuality was much greater than that of men.[223] Berque claims that popular belief held that women's sexuality was twenty times greater than men's. By removing the clitoris, it was felt that temptation was being removed from women; and certainly their pleasure was removed, leaving it all to the men. It cannot in any way be treated as the ritual equivalent of circumcision. There was no such religious meaning to the operation, which was usually carried out by mid-wives. Nor was it, of course, anatomically comparable to circumcision. Whether the various schools of Islam made this operation a duty or a permission has been debated, but the debate itself shows that the practice was taken for granted. It expressed the wish of the male to keep women in subjection.[224]

Major changes have also been taking place—for example, women's suffrage. In 1944, the Arab Women's Congress in Cairo demanded the right to vote; by 1956 they had gained that right. Syrian women have had the vote since 1949, and Lebanese women since 1952. In Tunisia, women first voted in the 1957 municipal elections, but the Tunisian Constitution of June 1959 granted them the right to vote and to be elected to national office. In Morocco, women were permitted by law in September 1959 to vote and to be elected to the *Conseils Communaux*. Moslem women in Algeria voted for the first time in the referendum on the proposed new French constitution.[225]

Typically, these laws continue to make distinctions between men and women. In Egypt, voting is compulsory for men but optional for women. In Syria, a woman has to have at least a primary school education to vote, whereas men do not. Nevertheless, the movement has been dramatic, and even in the countries where equality in the right to vote has not been completely achieved, it seems assured in the near future.

This great change can be illustrated in several countries, but the sequence of events in Egypt is perhaps more striking. An Egyptian Feminist Union was founded in 1923, but it had little impact and confined most of its activities to social welfare work. Under the monarchy women had no political rights. The Egyptian revolution took place in 1952, and in that same year the jurists (that is, the interpreters of Moslem law) of the great

University of Al-Azhar issued a *fetwa* which, "In the name of God and Mohamet, formally condemned the granting of political rights to women."[226] In that same year, however, the Official Studies Commission decided to grant the vote to all women who could read and write, and the 1956 constitution not only granted those rights but recognized women's rights to employment. By 1956, several *ulema,* or religious leaders, had conceded that Islam does not forbid political rights to women.

It seems likely that the lesson of Israel has not been lost on the Arab nations that have been in closest interaction with it. In spite of the Arab hatred of Israel as a state, the Israeli success in war and economic production is evident to any thinking Arab. Moreover, it is equally clear that the Israelis have effectively used their women in military as well as productive activities.

If these ideological changes have their source in education, they also contribute to it by strongly urging the creation of new educational facilities and opening them to women. The expansion of these opportunities has been one of the most spectacular changes in the contemporary Arab world. Although it was possible for an Egyptian girl to attend secondary school forty years ago, only forty-three were actually in attendance in the year 1921–1922. By 1953, there were over 19 thousand attending secondary schools. In 1921–1922, 653 girls were taking teacher-training; in 1953, the number had increased to 3,700.[227]

The total enrollment in all schools rose from approximately 25 thousand in 1921–1922 to over half a million in 1953. One small element in this change is a by-product of the change in class structure and economic conditions which has been taking place over the past generation, and has been accentuated in the last decade. There is less certainty that a girl of high social rank will be able to find an adequate husband and lifetime security as a wife, even without education. At least a few people have begun to feel that she ought to have some training, if not to make a contribution to the state then at least as a form of social insurance for herself. The changes may be seen over time in a group of selected countries in Table III-10, which presents only the elementary school enrollment of girls over the past generation.

These data are especially striking by contrast with Daghestani's observations of a generation ago. He noted then that well-to-do urban families sent their male children to school, but sending girls to school was not yet approved. However, at that time the situation had already improved. It was taken for granted that girls might go to schools for a modern education, and some even took advantage of the few facilities available for higher education, against much social opposition.[228]

An equally important change is to be found in the secondary schools, since formerly the number of females enrolled in elementary schools was partly illusory. Although a substantial number of girls enrolled during the first year, half or more dropped out by the second year and within two

Table III-10
Elementary School Enrollment of Girls in Arab Countries, 1937-1960*

Country	1937 Number of Thousands	1937 Per Cent Female	1950 Number of Thousands	1950 Per Cent Female	1960 Number of Thousands	1960 Per Cent Female
Jordan	1	18	16	21	18	43
Syria	82	33	74	28	111	25
Egypt	439	36	472	35	997	38
Morocco					224	28
Tunisia					113	about ¼
					(1961)	

* UNESCO: *Access of Girls to Elementary Education* (January, 1962); E/CN.6/396; *Women of Tunisia*, Secretariat of State for Information and Tourism, Tunisia, April, 1961. Also, Paul Sebag, *La Tunisie* (Paris: Editions Sociales, 1951), pp. 181–182.

or three years the number left was only a tiny fraction of the original number. Now, a substantial proportion remains to enter the secondary schools. Table III-11 shows the percentage of the total enrollment made up by girls in secondary schools.

As can be seen by comparison with Table III-10, the proportion of girls in the total enrollment of secondary schools is about as high as that in the primary schools, suggesting that girls are actually being given the opportunity to take advantage of education in the major Arab states. At

Table III-11
Percentage Female of Total Enrollment in Public Schools,
Arab Nations, 1954*

Country	Secondary Schools
Egypt	38
Iraq	26
Jordan	25
Lebanon	41
Syria	31

* Berger, *op. cit.*, p. 151; Data from: *Compulsory Education in the Arab States* (Paris: UNESCO, 1956), p. 68.

still higher levels, at least some of the Arab states offer educational advantages to girls. In 1958, 12 thousand young Egyptian women (of the 83 thousand total) were in higher education, including teacher training. In Iraq, 1,784 of 8,334 students were young women; and in Lebanon, 849 of 3,999 in 1956.[229] In addition, a newly created university in Tunis enrolled 381 young women, while 238 were enrolled in foreign universities.[230]

A still more dramatic index of change may be found in a three-generational comparison made in Egypt. Five hundred girls in Alexandria's secondary schools were interviewed. Among the *mothers* of these girls, two fifths were illiterate and another two fifths had only completed primary school. In the preceding generations—these girls' *grandmothers*—almost three quarters were illiterate and only one tenth had finished primary school.[231]

This enormous expansion in educational opportunities for women has not taken place at the cost of male education, although the facilities for girls have generally increased faster than those for boys. The task, of course, is enormous. During the 1950s, slightly more than a fourth of the Egyptian population, about 10 per cent of the Moroccan population, and 6 to 7 per cent of the Algerian population were literate. It goes without saying that in all these countries, a higher percentage of men than women were literate.

The following comments on Morocco would apply to several of the Arab nations during this period:

> During the disturbed years of 1953–55, women were thrown on their own re-sources for the first time, as men were fighting. . . . Once peace came, this pattern of participation was carried into matters outside the family domain. Women set up organizations for the spread of literacy and fundamental education. Those who had received some education become monitresses to the first students who enrolled and devoted themselves in their turn to the educative work and to the emancipation of women. . . . It was recognized that the education of women was one of the factors in the country's social evolution.[232]

Together with the campaign for male literacy in 1956, the Princess Lalla Aicha inaugurated a similar campaign for women, in which some 30 thousand girls and women were taught how to read and write. In 1958, some 15 thousand women were reached in a literacy campaign in five regions including Casablanca; and in 1959 another 15 thousand were included, in the northern part of Morocco and the Riff.[233]

Egyptian women have become physicians, journalists, and lawyers. Syrian women are enrolled in the faculties of medicine, law, engineering, the arts, science, and pedagogy.

Although the Arabian peninsula lags behind the rest, the winds of change are to be found even there. In 1962, some 150 thousand pupils were enrolled, and new schools were being built at the rate of a hundred a year. Some education of girls was finally beginning, according to one report, because the educated sons of wealthy men had begun marrying Turkish or Egyptian girls who had been through school. By 1962 there were eight schools for girls in Saudi Arabia.[234]

These facts also suggest a change in the *attitudes* of Arabs toward female education. In one sample of middle-Eastern Arab students in colleges and high schools in the 1950s it was ascertained that 50 per cent of the mothers of these Moslem girls had had no primary education, so that there was a great discrepancy between the generations. Ninety-five per cent of both Christian and the Moslem girls in this sample agreed that girls should be allowed to go through college, a more extreme demand than was even found in the American student sample used for comparison. Almost all were in favor of equal education.[235]

Without any question, the more educated respondents are far more intensely in favor of the emancipation of women than are the less educated, and the urban more than the rural. We must not forget, however, that the cultural base from which these people begin—often the culture in which the college students themselves were reared—accepts far more restrictions on the personal freedom of both young men and women than is the case in the West. A few further data from the study just cited are a useful corrective to any premature judgment, based upon superficial observation of Egyptian or Syrian women who work in laboratories as professionals, that somehow the entire culture has been transformed in a decade.

In this sample of middle-Eastern students in secondary and higher education, 80 per cent of the Moslem girls agreed with their parents that girls should not be permitted to go dancing. Sixty per cent of the Moslem men had the same opinion. Seventy-five per cent of the girls and 70 per cent of the boys agreed with their parents that girls should not be permitted to go to movies alone, since they might be molested there. As against these opinions, conservative by Western standards, only 12 per cent of their parents now insist on girls wearing the veil.

Forty-six per cent of the Moslem men (as against 20 per cent of the United States men) thought that girls should not be allowed a free choice of friends. Sixty-two per cent of the Moslem men thought that girls should not be permitted to go out with mixed groups, and 50 per cent thought they ought not to be permitted paid work. On the other hand, only 20 per cent thought that girls should *not* be permitted to have the kind of job they wanted after graduation. In general, the girls' opinions were about as strongly against such freedoms as those of the boys.

Perhaps as an expression of dissatisfaction with such restrictions, and in spite of this apparent agreement with the conservative male opinion, 53 per cent of the Moslem girls, as against only 28 per cent of the United States girls, sometimes felt that they would be happier if they were boys.[236]

In this connection, a generational change of importance ought to be noted. As we suggested earlier, girls and women generally had *less* freedom under the traditional Arab social structure if their family had a higher class position. By contrast, among the Moslem daughters with some education in *this* generation, the degree of emancipation and freedom *increases* with the higher income and education of their fathers.[237] As Berger remarks, in the former generation the middle class was the core of the emancipation movement, and "thus emancipation and education of women seemed to have spread upward and downward from the middle class."[238]

In Tunisia, too, the middle class had an important role in the emancipation of women, although the revolution itself was perhaps the greater catalyzing force over the last decade. Of the girls in Tunisian colleges in 1956, 90 per cent were veiled, but by 1959 only 5 to 10 per cent were veiled, and female personnel had become common in administration, hospital, and schools.[239]

Women will not be permitted out of the home to take jobs if the men strongly object to it. Arab men have generally objected to women obtaining jobs that paid them money independently, in part because the ancient tradition of Moslem law always gave the women far more control over her own wealth than the Western woman was permitted under traditional law. But in Arab countries, as in all other cultures we have considered, the women with poor families always worked, although they did not ordinarily obtain independence, wealth, or control over money.

If a job is defined as inappropriate for women, or if there is no expansion of economic opportunities, women are not likely to be given a chance either for the inappropriate job or for jobs in general. Although the high *rate* of growth in the modern Arab world means an expansion of new jobs, it does not necessarily mean that a large number of jobs in *absolute* terms becomes open to women. In 1956, only 12 per cent of the gross national product of Egypt came from manufacturing. In the late 1950s, only about 30 thousand workers in Iraq were to be found in modern factories. Only 34 thousand Lebanese were engaged in manufacturing in 1955. Thus, although there has been some change in values and attitudes and some expansion of opportunities, most Moslem women have not as yet begun to take a place in the occupational world.

Recent surveys have thrown some light on the attitudes of Arab women about independent jobs. In one study of middle-Eastern students (both Christian and Moslem) all women in Iraq, Egypt, and Lebanon were in favor of working before marriage, and 97 per cent of the male students had no objection to their doing so. On the other hand, 41 per cent of the young men objected to the girls working *after* marriage, while only 24 per cent of the girls had such objections.[240]

This result shows a pattern that we have noticed in other cultures— the generally great objection of men to their women participating independently in the occupational world at least as a matter of *right*.

Further relevant data on attitudes toward women working come from Morocco, one of the less advanced of the Arab countries. As part of the background for these data, it should be noted that a *fetwa* of the *ulema* of Al-Azhar stated in 1952 that women ought not to take jobs in public life "because of their femininity which makes them likely to quit the path of reason and moderation," but that it was all right for them to work at jobs where "strength of judgment and will are not required"—that is, as teachers, or as physicians or nurses for females.[241]

As has happened in other Arab countries, not only has the number of female students increased, but the curriculum itself has changed from traditional female subjects to modern Western education. In this sample, which is part of a larger middle-Eastern sample, only 23 per cent of the young men and 14 per cent of the women say that women should *not* have the same education. Such opinions are expressed against the background of change in the jobs which women have had in Morocco. There were only 54 Moroccan women teachers in 1947, 819 in 1958, and 2,352 in 1960.

With reference to the *values* in favor of work, 75 per cent of the men and 85 per cent of the women approved of young girls working; 60 per cent of the men as against 75 per cent of women approved of married women with children working. The small differences need not be interpreted as conservatism on the part of women, but may rather be a recognition on their part that they would have to assume double responsibilities (like their sisters in the West).

Even if the girl is not going to work, her value to her fiancé's family rises if she becomes educated. Consequently, the boy's family is now more willing to wait for her to finish her education.[242] In this connection, a Koranic prescription is relevant: A man is required to pay for a woman's expenses and those of the family even if she has money. If he does not pay for these expenses she could demand a divorce. However, this duty ceases if she takes refuge with her parents *or* if she works all day outside of the house. Thus, some readjustment of legal and religious formulations is required.

A class difference is also apparent: although 90 per cent of the educated in the same sample approve of married women without children working, only 33 per cent approve if she has children. That is to say, they have learned from their courses something about the noneconomic problems of child-rearing. Factory women, much more accustomed to allowing their children to run unsupervised, are somewhat more inclined to approve of the woman working if she has children: that is, they believe that a woman would ordinarily *have* to do so.

Nevertheless, the feeling still remains that it is not quite respectable for women to work. Men, for example, are much more likely to approve of their *daughters* entering occupations that are part of the traditional female duties: For example, it is all right for them to be nurses, but not physicians. By contrast, *women* are likely to approve of many occupations (embroideress, secretary) which, in fact, they do not want their own daughters to follow. That is to say, as against the greater respectability of such occupations, they feel that they are greatly restricted.

A prominent worry is that of promiscuity. The traditional attitude among Arabs has been that if a woman is not supervised or watched, and is working independently of the males of her household, she is open to an approach by other men. As a consequence, while half the women believe they could work anywhere with men, only 18 per cent of the men held that belief. Some 71 per cent of the men thought it was all right for men to work with women, but set various kinds of conditions of job or circumstances—for example, the women could be secretaries or nurses, or hold jobs where they would have few contacts with men or where outsiders would not *see* them in contact with men. Thirty-five per cent of the male sample believed that working women "play around with men." Half the women have heard of this belief, but 17 per cent say it themselves. It would be interesting to know just what percentage of American men and women would give the same opinion since, although in the United States there is disapproval of such relations, it is nevertheless widely believed that they *can* and do happen at times.

Consequently, an Arab husband is likely to disapprove of jobs that the Westerner would consider excellent, both because his wife would be under another man's authority and because she might be independent. He would prefer her to have an active social life (with women) and work without remuneration in charitable or philanthropic activities.[243] The Western attitude might well be that the Arab man does not, in fact, have reason to be confident of a woman who, after all, did not marry for love.

Finally, it is interesting that this Moroccan survey elicited few responses that showed any doubt of women's *ability;* rather, the emphasis was upon ethical responsibilities or temptations, the rights and obligations of women, and the great differences in the social definitions of appropriate activities for men and women.[244]

In light of these *socially* restrictive attitudes, the remaining *legal* restrictions on women's occupations and activities must be viewed as relatively unimportant. The governments of Iraq, Jordan, and Lebanon claim that women are recruited to civil service positions on an equal basis with men, although diplomatic and consular posts are not open to Jordanian women.[245] In Tunisia, most jobs follow the principle of equal pay for women, except for a few classifications where no less than 85 per cent of a man's wage is permitted.[246] Syria has ratified the United Nations convention regarding equal remuneration.[247]

In speaking of "emancipation," we are largely talking about opportunities that are gradually being opened to the *educated* Arab woman. Although these changes already have had some impact on the family life of other women, for the most part the rural illiterates have not changed their position much in either the family or the larger society. As one generally optimistic comment notes, most Egyptian women belong to the peasantry, "four million in number, but largely unorganized, uneducated, and neglected."[248] Consequently, even her right to vote is limited, since most peasant women are illiterate and thus ineligible. Women in the middle and working classes have created many organizations to establish greater rights and freedom for women; for the most part, however, the mass of rural and illiterate women have been given few new opportunities. Nevertheless, the great changes of the past decade cannot be reversed, and the immediate future should see changes equally important. The improvement of the position of Arab women in a larger society both grows from and contributes to her position within the family and kinship network itself. The direction of the present movement seems clear enough to both Arab women and men, and their motivation to move steadily toward the goal we have been describing is evident.

11. Divorce, Widowhood, and Remarriage

The Western male searching for the erotic in the exotic customs of the world has for centuries been titillated by three elements in Arab family life: the Arab male's frank delight in women as sexual partners; his right to a harem; and his right to divorce freely. The first attitude was shared by Western man when privately talking among men, but was viewed as improper by theological and moral doctrine and moreover was marred for him because of a childhood rearing that made sex pleasurable but dirty. The second and third elements made into reality the fantasy that the individual male whim might dominate over the religious and legal prohibitions of a repressive Western society.

Without question, free divorce permitted a range of marital partners denied to the Western male, and the wider choice was blessed further by carrying little stigma. Especially for the poor, divorce was the Arab's polygyny, and the right to divorce a woman at will gave the man an excellent bargaining position in conflicts with his wife.

Alas for the fantasies of the Western male, most Arab men could not afford a second wife, either tandem or in series. Moreover, even if he could afford it, he would be as limited in choice as men in other cultures by his economic and social rank, his power, and his personal attributes. Finally, having chosen a substitute for his first wife, the problems of living with a woman might have changed little. The Arab family system is, and was, different in important respects from that of the other cultures we have been examining. But no system has made automatically pleasant the adjustment to the needs and demands of a person of the opposite sex.

The Koranic tradition did not evaluate divorce very highly: "Of all that he has permitted, God detests nothing more than divorce."[249] However, custom and law gave such complete freedom to the husband that he could divorce his wife by simply saying "I divorce thee," three times before two witnesses. The ethical injunctions of the Koranic tradition assumed that a man would not express this formula three times at a single conflict, but might say, "I divorce thee," and then retract that divorcement. That is, it was assumed that only after successive trials would a man finally and irrevocably divorce a woman. Having divorced her irrevocably, the first husband could not change his mind and marry her again until she had married and actually cohabited with another man, who then might divorce her. As might be expected, various subterfuges were developed in all Arab countries to avoid this awkward solution. Sometimes a mock ceremony was carried out, the man chosen as "husband" not really cohabiting with her. Sometimes, to confound the problem still further, a man so selected and paid to do this service, might insist not only on cohabiting with the woman, but even on continuing to live with her. Or, the woman herself might prefer not to go back to her former husband.

If a man divorced his wife finally, he was required to pay her that part of the dowry which had been held back at the time of the marriage (generally one third). She then returned to her father's or brother's house, from which she would be remarried.

After the first or second declaration of divorce, a man could take his wife back without any formalities at all. She was not allowed to marry during a period of three lunar months (that is, menstrual periods), necessary to see whether she might be pregnant, and during this period she stayed in the man's house—or at least ideally so, since she had the right to maintenance during that period. If she was pregnant, she could not marry again after the 'iddh of three months; rather, the period was extended until forty days after her delivery. It will be noted that nothing prevented a man from taking an additional wife during any of this time.

A woman could not divorce a man against his will, although under extremely cruel treatment or neglect she might apply to a *qadi* for an order to her husband to divorce her. If the man was impotent, she might make such an application, such applications, of course, being actually made by her family. In addition, she might for various reasons ask to be divorced, forfeiting the dower that he still owed; but in that case he could not remarry her without her own consent or without a new marriage contract.

Another type of divorce was known, essentially the "bed and board" divorce of the West. If a woman refused to obey the lawful demands of her husband, he could lodge a complaint against her in the *qadi's* court. If she was declared rebellious, then the man did not have to maintain her, nor was he obliged to divorce her finally. Consequently, she could not marry another man and he could insist that she become obedient before taking her back or perhaps before even divorcing her.[250] It was, of course, more likely that under conditions of severe conflict her family would make charges against her husband in order to protect her.

In addition, a woman might goad a man into stating the formulation for a final divorce in order to be free of him.[251]

Because of the peculiarly revocable character of the Arab divorce, and the inevitable folk interpretations of the conditions for irrevocability, a man might promise to divorce under all sorts of circumstances. A Bedouin might say to his guest that he would divorce his wife if the guest did not partake of a feast. This would bind the guest to stay. Or a man might say that if what he was saying was not true, then his wife would be divorced. On the other hand, in instances of "accidental" divorce the woman did have a refuge and often demanded presents and blandishments before returning to her husband's house. Many cases arose in which a man did not mean to divorce but was divorced just the same.[252]

When a divorce took place, the children, of course, belonged to the husband's family, although the man was required to support them in his wife's father's house until the son was 7 and the girl 9, or until puberty —but he was not required to give such custody to his wife for that period.

Nor was he required to give her alimony at any time, aside from the maintenance in his own house during the period of waiting after the divorce.

Under the Arab institutional structure, the wife's family had little reason to pressure her to remain in an unsatisfactory marriage other than the traditional and firm belief that a woman should be subordinate to her husband and to all adult males of her family. The sons she bore did not belong to her family. When she married, she did not take her rights of inheritance with her, but implicitly ceded them to her brothers. If she returned irrevocably, her family could obtain another bride price for her (but, of course, not so large a one as the first). Since it was not scandalous to divorce, the family was not ashamed.

And indeed, looked at from the woman's side, at least a few Arab women thus experienced a rather interesting married life. Dickson gives the example of a handsome, wilful sister of a Bedouin sheik in the 1930s, who married seven times at least, three times to King 'Abdul 'Aziz Al Sa'ud.[253] He goes on to comment that "nearly every woman, by the time she is 30 years old, has had two or three husbands." The freedom of these Arabian Bedouin women was great; the woman could simply go back to her parents and refuse to return at all, so that the man would have to divorce her.

Thus, although the man had the basic legal power in his hands, he had to pay for it, especially since he was required to produce not only the one third of the dower not yet paid, but also the additional bride price for his next wife. On the other hand, he might cleverly manipulate his wife so that she would leave on her own initiative and agree to let him have this part of the dower if he would divorce her. One further factor kept divorce from being entirely a matter of the man's whim, at least among the middle and upper strata. Here, a marriage was viewed more often an alliance between families, and, of course, was sometimes a marriage between two first cousins. Divorce was not socially so acceptable as in the lower strata. Consequently, a divorce, with all its attendant emotional problems, might well estrange the two families. A wise man, then, might think twice before divorcing.

One of the demands of the 1944 Arab Women's Congress in Cairo was for the right of women to divorce and for prohibition of divorce without a court decision.[254] In the 1950s in Egypt, women increasingly came to include the right to divorce in their marriage contract.[255] These two points have indeed been one focus of the changes in marriage laws in Arab countries over the last decade. The requirement that a man must go to court and give his reasons for a divorce became effective in Egypt on October 1, 1960. Furthermore, the reform gave women certain rights to separation, divorce, and alimony when there were specific abuses. And although the limit of four wives was still retained, first wives were given the right to divorce a man who took an additional wife.[256]

Under the new Algerian law, divorce can be decided only by the courts, which also will decide questions of maintenance and the custody of any children from the marriage.[257]

Under the new Tunisian code, the judge may not grant a divorce decree until he has examined the causes of the conflict and failed to bring about a reconciliation. Moreover, the judge can take any measure to persuade the spouses to adjust to one another, and can make decisions about their maintenance and the rearing of the children.[258] This means the judge may decide the wife has the right to alimony, contrary to previous Moslem tradition, and he may grant her custody of children.[259]

As to the actual rate of divorce, there is no question but that it was high by Western standards. Doubtless in many farming villages the divorce rate was relatively low. Jane Fuller asserts that divorce was "uncommon in the village" (Buraij).[260] Hilma Granqvist reported that among 264 marriages in Palestine, only 4 per cent experienced divorces. She does not, however, give any time period within which the 4 per cent occurred.[261] A more recent study of an Arab village in Palestine gives a similar report—only 2.2 per cent.[262] Seven out of thirteen divorces in this village were instigated by the wife or her family. Nevertheless, when regional and class differences are averaged, the number of divorces per hundred marriages was, and remains, relatively high.

In conformity with the line of reasoning followed throughout this study, we would expect the Arab countries to exhibit a *declining* divorce rate as they move toward industrialization. However, the amount of industrialization has been so small as to lead one to expect little impact upon the divorce rate. On the other hand, as we have repeatedly affirmed, the effects of a new ideology of the family may well have some consequences long before any substantial amount of industrialization, so that in some countries we might expect a small decline in the divorce rate. Alternatively, as we have been able to show now and again, the indigenous developments within a country may raise or lower the rate of some family occurrence.

To test any of these we need time data for periods longer than are available for any country but Algeria. The Egyptian divorce ratio may be calculated only from about 1935 onward, but since the time series begins during a depression, when the divorce rate would normally be lower, and ends in prosperity, when it would rise somewhat, it is not possible to obtain a clear picture of any real trend. We shall, however, present the data that we have available.

In the 1931–1934 period, divorce data were collected in Egypt for Alexandria, Cairo, and the major cities. During those four years there were 53.6, 49.8, 46.6, and 47.8 divorces per hundred marriages. A somewhat lower rate in villages was ascribed to under-registration.[263]

At that time, it was claimed, widows and divorcees made up more than half the women who married each year. For Egypt as a whole, the ratio of divorces to marriages was much lower, as may be seen in Table III-12.

Table III-12
Ratio of Divorces Per Hundred Marriages, 1935–1957*

Year	Ratio
1935	26.9
1940	27.2
1945	32.3
1950	31.1
1957	24.8

* Data supplied to me by Statistical Department, Cairo, September, 1960.

If one considers the problem of registration during this period, it is not possible to conclude that any trend has developed as yet. I am willing to predict, however, that the relatively low figure for 1957 as against the figures of the previous decade will be maintained, and that there may be a slight drop in the next few years. Very likely, this figure already represents a decline, because the registration precedures have improved greatly since the 1930s and the actual ratio has not increased.[264]

In contrast to the reports of Granqvist and Rosenfeld, the 1944 survey of five Palestine Arab villages found that 31 per cent of women aged 38 and over had been married twice or more.[265] Table III-13 presents divorce ratios for selected Arab countries.

For Algeria, we can test our expectation that the ratio of divorces to marriage has dropped, although once again the data contain many problems. The marriage figures for 1949 onward simply reflect a regularization of marriages which had not been previously registered officially. Consequently,

Table III-13
Divorce Ratios, Selected Arab Countries*

Country	Number of Divorces Per Thousand Marriages			
Iraq	121	(1950)	97	(1957)
Jordan	169	(1951)	104	(1957)
Lebanon	75	(1944–1945)	53	(1957)
Syria	156	(1944)	80	(1957)

* Calculated from official sources.

the much lower ratio is not part of the trend. On the other hand, these unregistered marriages do inflate the divorce rate in earlier years.

As to whether the incidence of divorce is distributed as we would expect it to be—that is, whether the rate is higher toward the lower strata —we have not yet been able to demonstrate. For Syria, this expectation does not seem to hold, since the liberal professions make up approximately one sixth of the divorces in 1960, but (depending on how the classification was made) the number at that job level cannot possible amount to that large a fraction of the working population.[266]

Similarly, in Jordan in 1960, 65 per cent of the divorced males were

Table III-14
Algeria: Ratio of Divorces to Marriages, Algeria, 1897–1955*
(Moslem population only)

Year	Number of Divorces	Number of Marriages	Per Thousand Marriages
1897	12,267	32,897	370
1900	12,310	34,863	352
1905	14,569	35,877	410
1910	10,288	35,689	288
1920	9,007	22,949	396
1930	6,985	24,281	256
1940	7,675	31,648	292
1948	6,434	35,661	180
1949	7,753	58,161	133
1950	11,223	319,332	35
1951	13,549	161,536	84
1955	13,910	86,095	162

* 1897–1905 figures from *Marriage and Divorce 1867–1906*, U.S. Bureau of the Census, Washington, D.C., 1909, p. 451. Where these figures overlap in time with years for which I was able to obtain official Algerian statistics, they are the same. From 1906 to the present, data are presented in *Annuaire Statistique de L'Algerie*, N.S., vol. 8, Service de Statistique Generale, Alger, 1955, p. 40.

literate as against 77 per cent of the males who married.[267] Whether such a figure is vitiated by the likelihood that literate men are more likely to have their divorces registered is not clear.

As in the West, divorces are most apt to occur during the first few years of marriage, and are likely to occur in marriages without children. In Jordan in 1960, 14 per cent of the marriages ending in divorce had lasted less than a year and 15 per cent had lasted one year. An additional 13 per cent had lasted two years, and 11 per cent had lasted three years. Thus, over 40 per cent of the divorces had occurred during the first two years. Sixty-three per cent of all divorces occurred in marriages with no children at all.[268]

In Syria in the same year, 15 per cent of the divorces involved marriages that had lasted less than a year, and 22 per cent resulted from marriages of one to two years, a total of 37 per cent within the first two years.[269] Sixty-two per cent of the divorces resulted from marriages without children.[270]

Somewhat higher percentages of marriages of short duration seem to be found in Egypt, though perhaps partly because of different registration procedures, since Egypt seems to record revocable divorces (*raga'a*). In 1951, 16 per cent of all divorces came from marriages lasting under six months. An additional 13 per cent occurred to marriages lasting from six months to a year, and 20 per cent to marriages lasting from one to two years. Thus, over 49 per cent of all divorces resulted from marriages lasting less than two years.[271] I have not been able to find an official figure for the percentage of divorces coming from childless marriages, but Wakin asserts that for 1955 eight elevenths of Egyptian divorces were childless.[272] Nearly a generation ago, Mboria had estimated that more than half of the divorces occurred to childless marriages.[273]

In Rosenfeld's Palestine Arab village during the 1950s, there were children in only three out of thirteen divorces.[274]

On the other hand, it must be remembered that many marriages resume even after a divorce, and sometimes with no cognizance of the divorce. Considering only those coming into official notice in Egypt, about one fifth of the divorces occurring in 1951 were *raga'a*; that, is, they were revocable. About three fourths were in the category of *binina sogna:* that is, in order for the couple to resume married life with each other, a new contract had to be made. Of the just over 75 thousand Egyptian couples divorced in 1951, nearly 5 thousand resumed their marriages that year. Of the nearly 75 thousand in 1950, over 4 thousand resumed in 1950 and nearly 3 thousand in 1951. The number resuming marriage with one another after the second year following the divorce dropped substantially. Out of approximately 75 thousand divorces occurring in 1948, about 11 per cent of the couples resumed marriage. (We have not found a comparable figure for the United States. In one sample of divorced mothers, about one tenth *wished* to remarry their former husbands.)[275]

We have not been able to find any data on the trend of remarriage over time, although we do not suppose any substantial change has as yet occurred. For those who divorce relatively early, it seems likely that almost all—perhaps over 95 per cent—eventually remarry. This would be so for the United States as well, where in the 20–40 age group as high a percentage of divorcées as single people will marry. In Egypt in 1951, the average age for divorced women who remarried was 27.8 years, and for divorced men, 33.6 years.[276]

A final point with reference to remarriage ought to be noted here. An ancient Semitic tradition encouraged the levirate. Apparently it has persisted in village life, although we have not found any data to permit us to make a numerical estimate. In Rosenfeld's Palestine Arab village, twenty-four Arab widows with children remarried in the village, eleven of them marrying their husbands' brothers. The remainder remarried outside the village.[277]

Hilma Granqvist describes six such cases in Artas. In her analysis she goes on to note the advantage of such a marriage. The widow can thus keep her children with her instead of going back to her father's household and leaving the children with her husband's family. Her husband's family would not, in any event, take responsibility for protecting an unmarried woman, and they cannot marry her off.[278] The advantage from the side of her husband's family is also clear. If she leaves that household, she may demand some property from it, but her brother-in-law might wish to have that property. Moreover, her husband's family has already invested the bride price in her. The bride price is lower for a widow, and it is even less for a leviratic marriage. By that time, too, there may be close personal relations between her and her husband's brother. Finally, if her brother-in-law marries her, he can use her children's property inherited from her husband until they are married, and also can take advantage of their labor.[279] In Egypt, too, local opinion may approve of the leviratic marriage.[280] Daghestani commented on the levirate in Syria a generation ago, noting that it called for only one half the normal bride price, and it is also reported for the seminomads of North Palestine.[281]

Under Koranic law, a man could not marry two sisters, but under some circumstances he might marry a sister-in-law after the sister's death. On the other hand, since it is likely that the younger sister would have already married and would not be divorced or widowed at the time, this would be a lesser statistical likelihood than the levirate.[282]

12. Final Comment

It is clear that, in the main, Arab family institutions had not changed very much until the decade of the 1950s. In this decade, however, a substantial number of legal and social innovations were inaugurated whose consequences in marital and kinship life will not be fully evident until the succeeding decade, when an increasing number of empirical studies may be expected to report them. The most striking changes have, of course, occurred in the position of women in Arab public life. These were partly a response to Western opinion, but the more fundamental origin is the political revolutions which have taken place throughout much of the Arab world. Arab leaders have generally recognized the importance of women's contribution to the nation, and even their potentially greater contribution to marital life if they are permitted to take part in the occupational sphere and obtain the education to prepare them for it.

It should be noted, furthermore, that these changes have occurred without the impact of a substantial amount of industrialization. That is to say, the changes have occurred first of all as a political and ideological revolution, in anticipation of, or perhaps in preparation for, the changes that are beginning in the economic sphere. Moreover, these changes had been preceded by a generation of work on the part of a minority of Moslem leaders, both men and women, who had strongly urged that the position of women inside the family as well as in public life be improved. It also should be kept in mind that the European administrators who ruled much of the Arab population until fairly recently did not make great efforts towards changing social customs. As in India, they left the administration and the maintenance of these customs in the hands of traditional or conservative Moslem leaders, partly to maintain order and social stability. They did not enter as reformers, nor did they take that role after they had established their administration. There is, as a consequence, some bitterness against the West on the part of Arab leaders who feel that their countries would have moved much faster had they been allowed to be independent. This must remain an unanswered historical question.

Nevertheless, in most major particulars, one can observe only the beginnings of change. We have noted, again and again, that although the leaders of Moslem life, and especially the educated middle class, have a clear vision of the alteration in family life—such as freedom of courtship, the equal and easy interaction of young men and women, equality of education, the opening of opportunities to women in the occupational sphere, the protection of women against the power of the male to divorce at whim, and so on—the opinions and actions of the intellectual and ideological leaders are far ahead of ordinary customs, and the laws are far ahead of public opinion. The majority of Arabs are rural and illiterate. Although they are increasingly drawn into the swirl and ferment of urban and industrial ways, and especially toward the new ideology of the Arab revolutions, they have not yet accepted those attitudes and behavior patterns which are, to some degree, forced upon them by the new circumstances of their lives.

Nevertheless, although the changes over time which we have been able to evaluate have been few (and in many instances the changes have been small), the recent alteration of family life appears to be the beginning of major changes that are already observable even to casual investigators, and will be measured more fully within the next decade.

chapter

IV

Sub-Saharan Africa

BECAUSE of the enormous physical size and cultural diversity of sub-Saharan Africa, its peculiar history, and the rapidity of its social transformation, it is only with great uncertainty that even a sketch of its family patterns can be made. West Africa alone is equal in area to the continental United States. More than eight hundred languages are spoken in Africa, and the exact relation of its various linguistic groups to one another is still under debate.[1]

Little of Africa was explored by Europeans until the beginning of the nineteenth century, but within the next hundred years the final invaders had completed its subjugation. Every political unit south of the Sahara is now, or recently has been, a colony. The continent is once again seeing vast rapid change: Although the last battle in the colonization of the Ashanti by the English occurred in 1901, the territory has already become part of a new autonomous nation, Ghana. Mauritania became a nation in 1960; it was finally pacified as late as 1938. These processes—the movement from tribe to nation, from conquest to independent state—are going on in every part of the sub-Saharan area at different rates of speed, and under varying conditions. As a social scientist recently commented, "Black Africa is undergoing a vast process of acculturation . . . there is no population of *evolués* which may be set against an immobile mass; rather, there is an entire continent undergoing evolution."[2]

1. African Family Patterns

There are wide variations in religions, technologies, and family and political systems among the hundreds of sub-Saharan African tribes. Urban areas have existed for centuries in West Africa, but great new waves of urbanization are now taking place. Consequently, although several summary descriptions of sub-Saharan family systems exist, as well as summaries of changes in these systems,[3] such attempts at summary are open to sharp criticism. Generalizations about these patterns and changes are difficult to make or defend because detailed information is limited.

The main reason for postulating a unity of some kind among the societies of Africa lies in their geographical contiguity and historical relationship over millenia. The great differences between such tribes as the Ashanti and the Watussi, the Dahomey and Pondo, for example, can be bridged only if one assumes that these differences are simply gradations from one tribe to the next. Even leaving aside the arguable idea of unity of race, it may be wondered whether any such unity would be attributed to the African peoples if they lived in scattered areas remote from Africa: if the Pygmies came from an isolated area in Micronesia, and the Masai stemmed from a mountainous region of Afghanistan. We might be able to reconstruct or guess at the "unity" through linguistic data, but perhaps not through a comparison of social structures. Merely because all these societies are bound within the same continent, we cannot suppose that common patterns would be easy to find. A similar conglomerate could be yielded by lumping together all the pre-Columbian New World Societies, or even those in North America.

Every society is, after all, like all others in some respects. No descriptive generalizations that begin, "All family systems in sub-Saharan Africa, unlike other systems elsewhere . . . " can be considered valid. But though the diversity of family systems renders most systems containing the words "all" or "none" unsafe, a few safeguards exist. The problem, particularly with respect to Africa, is primarily an analytic one; we must find ways of singling out those elements in the various African cultures which clearly establish shared patterns. The research done on groups of African societies during the past generation has already established similarities in linguistic characteristics and additional agricultural, technological, and historical links, as well as similarities in family patterns. We can expect, for example, a number of characteristics to be shared by the African societies that form what has been called the "matrilineal belt" across central Africa.

Moreover, work already completed and in process will yield tabulations or distribution of family patterns similar to those developed by Murdock a decade ago.[4] In a few years we can expect to see the publication of such items as which bride-price or groom-service pattern is associated with patrilateral cross-cousin marriage in a matrilineal system; or which family patterns seem to yield first under the impact of industrialization. Even now we can describe a few family patterns that are shared by a wide range of African societies and which, when taken together, distinguish the African region from other great cultural areas, at least in degree.

Before attempting that description, however, a further analytic problem should be mentioned. Without a complete tabulation of family change in *all* African societies for which any data are available, only two modes of presentation can be chosen: (1) One might organize the data by societies or groups of societies, describing in each instance both their social structure and the changes now underway. The kinds of changes may not, however, correspond to the groupings by social structure, and such a classification does not fit the categories which seem most fruitful for analyzing social change outside Africa. (2) The second mode of presentation would be to analyze such areas of social change as divorce, marriage exchange, arranged marriage, and the like, without attempting to classify societies. However, this is reminiscent of a bygone age when the "shotgun" type of synthesis was popular. Theorists stated a speculation or hypothesis—for example, "woman's status is low in a warlike culture"—and then cited examples or illustrations from many societies.

Of course, closely analyzed, the first mode of presentation is open to the same objection, for *within* each category or class of social structure the analyst is forced to cite all the relevant cases, so that the result also appears disorderly.

More fundamentally, however, if the data are properly marshalled, *neither* mode is wrong. If no *contrary* cases are excluded, the conclusions will stand until further data are available. The logical advantages of presentation by topic remain.

The fact that we cite only a few societies for most topics means that in the following analysis of change, (1) we have excluded *no* contrary cases, but (2) we have excluded many *confirming* cases because these added no new or interesting qualifications of the generalization. For example, the pattern of arranged marriages may seem to be weakening in societies for which data are available, although at present no tabulation of this change is available for *all* African societies. Doubtless some family systems have changed little in this respect. Change, being dramatic and obvious, is more likely to be reported than stability, but when "stability" is reported in the literature that contrary fact *is* noted here. For that matter, if, for example, there had been reports of African societies in which the pattern of arranged marriages was *emerging* where *none* formerly existed, such instances would have been presented here. The cases cited, then, are not merely *illustrative,* they are *representative*

Keeping in mind these difficult and subtle problems of method, let us examine at least some of the main African family patterns. One element— the high emotional significance of the son-mother relationship—seems to be salient although the Africanist might deny it as either debatable or applicable to only matrilineal societies. If I may dare to intuit more deeply its peculiar quality, it appears to be different from the domination of the mother by the Japanese son or the emotional enveloping of the son by the Indian mother, and rather contains an element of veneration and a high respect for the mother, even in African patrilineal societies. Certainly related to this feeling on the part of the son is the rather widespread political pattern, in both matrilineal and patrilineal societies, by which the queen consort or Great Queen had considerable power and prestige, even outside the confines of the royal family.

If I may venture a step further in this nearly untestable speculation, the tie is in part an outgrowth of the impact of polygyny on the son-mother tie: the son was emotionally dependent on his own mother whose uniqueness was emphasized by the existence of other mothers and other sons in the same family. Thus, to affirm his own existence the son had to invest the relationship with great meaning. At the same time, however, the mother could not be merely an "expressive" figure,[5] acting mainly as a source of solace, a mediator of conflicts, and an emotional support. Because of the great social distance between father and son she had also to act to some extent as "instrumental" leader, advising, analyzing, teaching techniques, and so on. Most African men did not live polygynously as adults, but a fairly high percentage of children grew up in polygynous households, and (more important) the prestige of polygyny—associated as it was with wealth, with nobles, chieftains, and kings—shaped family assumptions, traditions, and values. Perhaps, if these speculations are correct, Murdock's hypothesis, shared by others, that African societies were once largely matrilineal is relevant.[6]

The importance of the mother may be observed in another pattern to which the Africanist would agree more readily. In no African society so far uncovered does the bride bring a sizeable dowry with her. Almost always the groom pays a bride price, or serves the bride's family for a period of time, although, of course, the bride's family furnishes some gifts in exchange. Moreover, this area of traditional African family law—how much marriage payment should be paid, how much owed if the marriage cattle die, who in the bride's family is to benefit from these cattle, etc. —is highly developed and thousands of disputes in the past have focused on it. Of course, no serious student any longer views these payments merely as a "purchase." The bride's family used the cattle they received to obtain brides for the sons of the family, and as a consequence no profit was possible over the long run. Counter-gifts were also made and in many societies the successive exchanges continued over so long a period that marriage cannot be thought of as occurring at a specific point in time, but as a *process* by which two extended families or lineages were gradually united more closely.

The importance of this element is usually interpreted by still another pattern which, although worldwide, is rarely of the intensity that one encounters in Africa. The marriage payment or groom service points to the great concern with the legal possession of children, often overriding the concern with biological fatherhood and with the woman as a bearer of children. The historical and striking fact that Africa has a low population density, although it is the probable cradle of man and certainly has been inhabited by man or his man-like ancestors for a million years, offers us a puzzle.

But, this fact at least suggests that a high value has been placed on children because there were few of them: fertility was low or mortality high, or both.[7]

Fertility is a highly valued attribute in all peasant societies, and barrenness is a shame in all societies. But societies can evaluate fertility highly without evaluating women highly, and in China, India, Japan, and the Arab countries high value was placed only on the production of *male* children. There is also great concern in these countries over whether the father actually is the genitor of the children: On both points Africa differs.

This focus on the birth and possession of children, on the importance of legitimate descendants, creates, as Mair comments, the most distinctive features of African law.[8] So closely related to this pattern as almost to be a corollary is the rarity of what Radcliffe-Brown calls "informal marriages" like those of the Navajo or Zuñi—that is, when little public attention is paid to any ceremonies, when there are easy shifts of spouses, and when there is little legal attention paid to the exact definition of marital status.[9]

The fact that lineages and clans are widespread does not differentiate Africa, except in degree, from many other culture areas. They are common, however, and thus the choice of spouse, gift exchanges at marriage, and the subsequent attention paid to marital behavior by the clan has a corporate character. The corporate pattern can be specified further: bilateral descent is rare and almost all kinship systems are unilinear, a few combining both matrilineal and patrilineal systems into double descent. As in other parts of the world, polyandry has been rare. Most African men have had only one wife, but polygyny has been more common as an ideal (in 88 per cent of the 154 African societies for which we have data)[10] than in any comparable part of the world.

The modal physical arrangement has been to keep wives and their children separate from one another, not in the same house.

Whenever societies form large concentrations of population, the link of kinship creates wards or neighborhoods in which the primary bond of association is descent.

These major configurations of family behavior set the stage for the social and political ferment that characterizes contemporary sub-Saharan Africa.

2. Factors of Social Change in Africa

It is impossible to sketch the main factors in social change in Africa without once more facing the problem of defining "urbanization and industrialization." But under any reasonable definition of these terms, the case of Africa conforms strongly to a thesis central to this book; that factors other than industrialization and urbanization may change family patterns, and that these other factors, as well as ongoing changes in family patterns, may facilitate both of these two great processes.

The usual definitions of urbanization or industrialization include so many factors that they are illogical candidates as factors of social change. If urbanism as a way of life includes anonymity, impersonality, heterogeneity of social contacts, separation of one set of social relations from another, and a developed technology, then we cannot easily use such a complex as a "cause" of social change in a primitive or peasant society. The whole complex itself *is* social change, and we are reduced to analyzing the impact of this great complex on the *individuals* who come to the city or within its orbit. We cannot, however, use "the city" to explain broad societal processess: to the extent that the city exists already, those processes are already underway.

The same illogicality is to be found in the use of "industrialization" as a "cause." Many of its factors are precisely those called "urbanism." In addition, various other factors are usually added—those found in the factory situation, such as a free labor market, freedom to improve one's occupational position if one can do the job, a breakdown of feudal restrictions, increase of scientific and technological knowledge and attitudes, and so on. Again, to the extent that such a complex has been established, it cannot be used to "explain" large scale societal processes; it *constitutes* those processes.

With reference to the modern world, it does not seem possible or useful to distinguish clearly between the *separate* effects of urbanization and industrialization. It is likely that whatever effects industrialization has within a social structure *include* all those which are traditionally thought of as caused by urbanization, although the converse proposition may not be entirely correct. At least we can assert more cautiously that cities never develop without improvements in technology, but the specific form and type of city life that emerges may vary, depending on the type of new technology that has come to dominate that area.

Any definition of industrialization ought to be applicable cross-culturally. In order to assess the contribution of industrialization to social change, one must place various societies with high or low technologies along some continuum of industrialization. When we attempt to do so, the most conspicuous phenomena of modern technology, such as the Ruhr Valley and other great industrial complexes, give us a scale on which it is difficult to place Africa accurately. For, if such complexes were a prime criterion or measure of industrialization, we would have to say there has been no industrialization in Africa, and we could not speak of *degrees* of industrialization. Earlier, it was suggested that the core element in industrialization is a *social* factor, *the freedom to use one's talents and skills in improving one's job.* Obviously, this notion includes many subvariables. We cannot, however, use the existence of "factories" as a major variable since, when considering African industrialization, one must consider the very different development of plantations and mines, communication and transport networks, and oil drilling. The factor of individual freedom implies that performance, not ethnic traits or class origins, is crucial in deciding who gets rewards and jobs. It implies job mobility; the individual can move from job to job within a given industry, across industries, and even over geographical regions. It implies also, although by a complex social process, that the employer and the employee have rather narrow limits to their mutual responsibilities *off* the job. One owes wages and certain types of protection, and the other owes performance and some dedication to the work, but neither has the right to control the other's life outside those areas. Such a social complex seems to be found in a *high* degree only where the technology itself begins to be based on nontraditional and nonmagical solutions to the problems of production and the conquest of the environment—that is, when solutions are not simply handed down from the elders, but are based simply on rational efficiency. On such a basis, a considerable division of labor and a high level of expertise develops. Finally, in this more complex system the products of the system are sold to strangers in at least an approximation to a free market, instead of being retained simply for the self-maintaining needs of a community.[11]

It is not at all clear how many of these characteristics must be considered in placing a society along the variable of industrialization. What is clear, however, is that in the modern world, as in the recent past, the level of industrialization starts with small beginnings—a cocoa plantation, a railroad complex, a diamond mine—and it is at such small beginnings that we must look for any possible impact.

The *specific* point of impact can, I believe, be located. It is best understood by reference to current role theory, most clearly in the notion of "role strain."[12] In this conception, in any ongoing role relationship between two or more individuals, each person owes obligations to the other, and in turn has both a cognitive and a moral expectation of some counter performances from that person, both punishments and rewards. This relationship is supported by "third parties" who are in the social network of those individuals.

Crucial to this conception is the notion that in *all* role relations, and in the total set of role relations of *all* individuals, there are many role strains —difficulties in meeting the obligations expected by others. Indeed, the entire social structure may be viewed as a set of relationships continuing under considerable tension. Within the limitations set by the third parties and the possible rewards and punishments from each individual, people are attempting to achieve the best possible role bargain in any given situation. Consequently, when the external situation changes—when new opportunities are offered by new individuals, new possibilities of rewards or punishments develop, or escapes are created by the protection offered by other third parties—then many changes in this role bargain appear to be possible.

As one conspicuous example, illustrated throughout much of sub-Saharan Africa: To the extent that the new job opportunities are not under the control of either tribal or family elders, they cannot sanction the younger generation for failure to meet their expectations, as they once could by refusing to give support, rewards, or even concrete assistance (such as helping to obtain cattle for marriage). Consequently, members of the younger generation can make new bargains and need not accept the authority of the older generation. This general conception can be detailed in many areas of social change in contemporary African life. In any event, it is apparent that the complex of industrialization noted above changes basically the kinds of role bargains that *had* existed previously, and has a great impact upon family relations. We shall explore this in more detail later within this chapter.

Before industrialization, great forces began to weaken some African family systems and move them in the same direction as did the pressures of industrial life later. Most of these great earlier forces can be classified under the headings of colonialism and missionary work. Under colonialism, as Wallerstein expresses it,

... someone imposes in a given area a new institution, the colonial administration, governed by outsiders who establish new rules which they enforce with a reasonable degree of success ... all those who act in the colony must take some account of these rules, ... indeed an increasing amount of each individual's action is oriented to this set of rules rather than to any other set, for example, the tribal set, to which he formerly paid full heed. The reason for this shift in orientation is very simple. Colonial administration, as opposed to the mere presence of European traders or missionaries, meant precisely that ultimate power lay with this new government, and that this government tried systematically to inculcate in its subjects a feeling that this new power was legitimate.[13]

The expansion of trade and production in the colony required manpower and the maintenance of civil order and peace over a wide area. By various devices, especially the head tax, young men were either persuaded or forced to leave their villages, and to experience urban and urban-European influences for the first time. Urban centers were created in order to centralize and rationalize trade, communication, transportation, and administration. Within this environment were to be found all the attractions that cities have always offered to people; i.e., according to Wallerstein, "The relative freedom from the pressures of one's neighbors, the opportunities for social advancement, the possibility of participation in a wider range of social activities. And . . . material comforts, a longer and healthier life, contacts with a wider world."[14]

Peace also meant civil order in a wider area than the tribe controlled, so that the rebel or the individual who did not wish to conform to the plans of his elders could move outside their control. It meant, too, that for a large number of African tribes, the young male no longer had the option of becoming a warrior, and was in effect without function. He was thus free to try some of the new jobs available.

In this era, when we see the new African nations attempting to reassert their own identity in history as a reaction to their immediate past subservience to European powers, we should not forget that the earlier conquests and the achievements of colonialists created a desire to emulate European patterns in many ways, especially among the African elite and among the Africans who had direct contact with the European influences. Whether or not all these ways were appropriate to the African culture, the changes nevertheless had an impact on existing African custom.

Of perhaps still greater import for family change was the fundamental alteration in the legal and power structure of African tribes imposed by colonial administration. Although the French and Belgians tried a semblance of direct rule, and the British more often attempted some form of indirect rule, both policies put ultimate power in the hands of the colonial administration, not the tribal chieftain. The latter was subject to removal, and at times *was* removed. Important too was the fact that both his administrative orders and his judicial decisions were subject to review by nontribal standards.

The colonial administration of Africa attempted to avoid substantial changes in customary family law, but over time the decisions of tribal courts began to follow the European pattern, often by processes which would now be very difficult to trace for lack of adequate records. One reservation was widely accepted: that the European administration would not tolerate practices which seemed "repugnant to common decency" or contrary to natural human justice. Such a rule is, of course, difficult to apply. Colonial courts disapproved of but tolerated polygyny, but felt much less tolerant of widow inheritance or even infant betrothal. At an earlier period, many courts even rejected the bride price, since they interpreted it to mean the actual purchase of a wife.

Any rule rejecting repugnant acts, or indeed any new rule imposed from another culture, necessarily creates *logical* problems calling for decisions. These decisions came increasingly to follow the European pattern. For example, since courts generally held that a widow might choose her next spouse freely, then cases arose in which the widow was still a *minor*, and the courts eventually came to define the young widow as an adult.

Similarly, an African man might marry under statutory European law and then might attempt to appeal to customary law to justify his behavior in a family problem. Here, generally, courts have come to hold that he could not make such an appeal. In addition, there are quite *new* situations of which the new courts must take account, whether these are European courts or customary courts under the influence of colonial decisions. For example, a man and his family may create an inheritance by their own efforts in the city. If the man then dies, can his lineage claim their usual rights to that property? Moreover, in new legislation, the territories have come to promulgate new marriage laws on the model of laws in the European countries formerly administering those territories.[15]

At the present time, as Phillips' survey shows, the legal aspects of family behavior in Africa are exceedingly complex, but it is quite clear that though many African customs still have legal standing, where modifications *have* occurred, they have been in the direction of European patterns or of a compromise or rationalization of conflict between the two systems.[16]

In order to permit Africans to attain skills necessary for administration and production, colonial offices organized schools which were supplemented by the efforts of missionaries. Since any education was European, so were the models of family conduct set forth there; still more intensive influences of this kind were experienced by the young men who went on to higher education. A more pervasive influence may have been missionary education, because missionaries paid most attention to the women and young girls. Here too, because of the close association of Christianity with European family customs, missionaries attempted actively to inculcate these customs in their schools. Moreover, they took an active part in pressing colonial administrations to legislate or adjudicate against many African practices such as child betrothal, bride price, polygyny, widow inheritance, and initiation customs with a sexual content aimed at impressing upon the young their duties as husbands and wives.

The period of conquest was short and missionary activities were relatively meager, so that the Christianization of Africa is not at all comparable to that of Iberian America in the sixteenth and seventeenth centuries. Toward the Sahara, and also in East Africa, Islam is making many converts. Nevertheless, the influence of missionaries has been strong even when their failure at conversion has been conspicuous. Both they and their disciples have often been leaders in social change, and even when they have failed to convert, they have often managed to persuade Africans or colonials to accept many of their attitudes and rules in family behavior.

The African religions have also lost much of their force, partially under the political and religious impact of missionary activity. Thus, where those religions once would have supported native custom, they no longer can do so. For example, Christianity reduced the customs of sacrifices and cut down the number of occasions when kin would assemble to re-establish their religious unity and influence over the young. Since usually only a part of any tribe became Christian, religious belief frequently divided kinfolk from one another, again reducing the unity of custom and social sanctions.

These forces began under colonialism, but they still continue under independence because of the establishment of mines, trade centers, factories, and cash crop plantations. These accentuate the pressures toward impersonality, freedom from family influence, the power to make decisions without consulting elders, and the ability to rely upon one's own talents.

The development of urban complexes has continued apace, and housing also affects family customs. The African must take a dwelling where he can get it, and although tribal and family ties create some clusters within cities, these may not be large; consequently, the individual will often not be able to remain in contact with his kin[17] even if he would like to do so. As Balandier has remarked, "The feeling of belonging to an ethnic group is intense enough to create or maintain antagonisms and to hamper the development of groupings that would be able to transcend the pluralism of the city; it is not strong enough to impose any effective organization within this urban society."[18] Neighbors may not even be of the same tribe or kin groups, so they cannot reaffirm their family customs or enforce them on the young.

These broad forces take a somewhat different form from one society to another, and we shall examine some of them as we look at specific family patterns. Viewed as a whole, they have generally moved most African family systems somewhat closer to a conjugal pattern, without changing all family systems equally or even in the same direction. There is no reason to doubt that this movement will continue during the next generation. If anything, it will become intensified, since colonial administrators will no longer find it to their advantage to prevent part of the African population from assimilating values and customs that are effective for industrialization, or from enjoying the rewards of that assimilation.

3. Freedom of Courtship

Although romantic love played a larger part in traditional African family systems than is generally conceded, most communities were successful in preventing it from weakening the power of elders to arrange marriages for the young. A large number of tribes had some form of institutionalized "sweethearting"—the Pondo, Masai, Nuer, Hausa, for example—and in some tribes this phase of life led directly to marriage. On the other hand, the sweetheart relationship often was socially defined as irrelevant to marriage. Thus, among the Kanakuru (Plateau Nigerian Chadic) the girl could not become the wife of the boy with whom she slept on the nights of initiation; and among the Somba (Voltaic-Bargu Cluster) a girl might have a lover, but this did not alter the fact that her marriage had been arranged when she was a child

Child betrothal was found in a substantial number of societies. Among the Tswana (Bechuanaland) the betrothal of mothers' brother's daughters and fathers' sister's sons was especially likely to be arranged when they were young children.[19] Many West African societies arranged infant betrothal for girls, and in the northeastern part of central Africa some tribes practiced prepubertal betrothal. In West Africa, for example, the Kilba, Jirai, and Bura practiced infant betrothal of girls (to older males), and the Kilba also practiced infant betrothal of boys. Betrothal was likely to occur before puberty in the Nuba Hills. A similar pattern was found among the Dogon, among the wealthy Mende, the Akan-speaking people generally, and also among (at least) the Nsaw of Bamenda Province and the Somba.[20]

Although infant betrothal is frowned upon by European authorities, and is declining, the influences on its decline are indirect. Children cannot, after all, oppose such arrangements. When the time comes for marriage, however, young men and women may reject the arrangements or, once married, may leave the partner chosen by the parents. Modern courts, increasingly based upon some version of European legal conceptions, will generally at least support the refusal to enter the marriage. Consequently, since parents cannot guarantee the fulfillment of the contracts they may make with each other, they have less reason to agree to such betrothals of their children.[21]

Whether or not infant betrothal existed, marriages were arranged by elders in practically every African society. This pattern has become a major point of resistance and evasion on the part of young people. Some marriages are still arranged by parents among the Iteso (Uganda, Eastern Province) but nowadays the young man and woman usually arrange their own marriage.[22] Early arranged betrothal is still common in the Edo-speaking villages of Benin but there is a growing tendency to allow both males and females free choice in selecting marriage partners. Among the pastoral Fulbe (Northern Nigeria), however, although the decline of the clan has weakened the power of parents somewhat, the girl must use several extreme methods if she wishes to escape an unpleasant marriage, such as threaten to become a prostitute, marry secretly, or even attempt suicide.[23] Forced marriages are not uncommon among the Banyoro, but increasingly the young men and women have taken matters into their own hands by simply informing their parents after they have chosen, so that proper marriage procedures may be initiated.[24]

In Freetown it is the laboring classes, as opposed to "native people of good standing" who make their own choice.[25] Against the usually greater power of the more respectable classes to control their young is the increasing education of the younger generation in those classes, which makes them less willing to agree to a decision made by the elders. Thus, for example, among the Mende of Sierra Leone, individual wishes of girls who have attended school are increasingly taken into account, while nonliterate women are also beginning to press their preferences.[26] As long ago as the 1930s, the Bemba girls in Broken Hill were strangers to their husbands at the time of betrothal, although they often were persuaded by other young men to break the engagement when they came to marriageable ages. There, the girl's parents still had the right of consent, as they did in southern Nyasaland and among the Fort Jameson Ngoni, but in all three of these central African areas, the young people had a considerable voice in the matter of choice.[27]

In the urban areas of southern Africa the influence of parents has been reduced to very little, and often the couple will establish their union and then inform their parents later.[28] It would be expected that there be considerable freedom in the choice of mates in the urbanized locations of the

Union of South Africa, but data in a recent report on West Africa permit a more interesting interpretation. Although 96 per cent of a literate female sample claimed to have personally chosen their husbands, it is likely that their families had consented to these marriages. Seventy-five per cent of the men's marriages had occurred with their families' consent and partial payment of the bride price, and 22 per cent with their families' consent but without a bride price.[29] What such figures seem to show is that although the younger generation does make its own choices, the ties with the parental generation are close enough to elicit at least some agreement and harmony. Relatives can, after all, still register objection by refusing help at the time of marriage or later.

Almost all observers have asserted that the basic cause of the increased independence, particularly of the young man, lies in his new ability to obtain sufficient wealth by his own efforts to pay the bride price, or to run off with the girl should his economic efforts be insufficient. The pattern whereby young men were economically dependent upon their elders may in fact reverse itself, so that the senior relatives, or the young man's father, may even become dependent upon him.[30]

For example, among the Bantu Kavirondo, the eldest son, who is the father's heir, has lost some of his prestige and power since his younger brothers no longer depend upon him. They can leave to work elsewhere and may eventually establish themselves economically and choose their own mates.[31] This change has been noted so widely, that it is hardly necessary here to note more than a few instances where it occurs. The Keiskammahoek Rural Survey found the bride price still in effect but noted that an unwelcome match is seldom forced on the girl, and the young men now earn wages in town and thus become less dependent on their kinship group.[32] A similar pattern has been noted for the Nyakyusa, the Kpe (British Cameroons),[33] and indeed for almost all areas for which data are available.

Freedom of choice and the independence of the younger generation are changes of such fundamental importance that a full explanation of them would require an extensive analysis of each society. Several of these implications will be dealt with in successive sections of this chapter. For the moment, however, a few items are especially relevant. Perhaps the most fundamental point to be noticed is that the pattern of *lobola* (a form of bride price), continues in spite of considerable urbanization and industrialization. Even in the apparently disorganized urban locations of South Africa, the traditional payment or some approximation to it seems to persist[34] Clément comments that "marriages without payment or with a dowry for the girls are still too rare to encourage speculation on their outcome."[35] It must be kept in mind that bride wealth did not go to the bride, but to her family, so that this sum of money or capital could not be viewed as equivalent to the former Western pattern of "saving up enough to get married on." The bride and groom did not enjoy the fruits of this saving, just as the groom himself did not produce the cattle, stock, or other gifts which were handed over to the bride's parents. What is striking about the continuation of this pattern is that some type of exchange is considered necessary to validate marriage except by the most educated Africans, although alternative modes of contracting marriage, either through church or civil ceremonies, are found in all jurisdictions.

Almost as important as the shift of the economic burden to the groom's shoulders is a change that is taking place in the *meaning* of the bride price. It is unlikely that the economic meaning of these exchanges escaped any Africans who took part in these transactions.[36] After all, the amount involved, at least in patrilineal societies, was substantial. Much discussion of a purely economic character took place to decide on either the accumulation of the necessary wealth, or its redistribution after receipt. Apparently the bride price remains as a form of social validation, as an answer to the problem of finding some type of ceremony possessing cultural importance in industrialized or urbanized areas. On the other hand, precisely because of the decline in importance of kinship ties, the bride price has come to have a more clearly commercial meaning and in many areas has become inflated in price. Africans themselves may now be heard complaining that they are "buying a bride," and girls have come to object that they are being treated like chattels.[37] Reports from many areas suggest that there has been a transformation of the traditional payment into cash. Among the Bwamba (Western Uganda), for example, cash payments have come to substitute increasingly for goats and sheep.[38] In urban Baumanville, *lobola* was passed in 90 per cent of all types of marriages, but a tabulation by period of marriage (before and after 1930) shows that the percentage of marriages involving money payment alone was increasing.[39] The Ashanti Social Survey also tabulated marriage payments by time of marriage (1910–1945), and showed that an increasing percentage of marriages were accompanied by payment in cash.[40] Although many reports state that the amount of bride price has actually increased, it seems unlikely that this is a universal pattern, and in any event it would seem to be temporary at most. To the extent that the sum becomes a cash payment and is no longer distributed within the network of the girl's kin, it may become a token payment, especially in the urbanized areas. Moreover, the educated African increasingly disapproves of the custom, missionary doctrine opposes it, and at least some legislation, by permitting individuals to make their own decisions about marriage, has undermined its influence in the marriage process.[41]

Since now the bride's male kinfolk often do not distribute the bride wealth, permitting their young males to obtain wives with it, the meaning of the system begins to break down still further. In many systems, the initial bride wealth was only one stage in a continuing series of payments and gifts which once formed part of the ongoing relations between the two kin lines. These, too, begin to diminish or disappear.

This change, and the conflicts arising from it, must be seen in its African context. Marriage was not generally an event but a *process,* in which visiting, services, and gifts were exchanged over a period of time, as the marriage relationship was gradually strengthened, and each spouse was more fully accepted by his affinal relatives. The process now is accelerated, so that the husband is likely to make his claims earlier, or to translate the demands made upon him into a form which he can quickly discharge, such as money. Because of bride wealth claims, there has been a marked increase in litigation among the Shilluk of the Upper Nile. Young men now may start the processes of marriage but abscond with their brides after some initial payment of chattel and then refuse to honor any further obligations.[42] Among the Tallensi in West Africa, elopement may be used as a substitute for a formal marriage, but it seems to be less an escape from a forced marriage than a method by which the son-in-law claims his independence from his father-in-law. Among the Somba, a young man may now try to obtain a faithful wife by establishing a relationship with a prenubile girl. In that case, the relationship depends upon the attachment between the young man and the girl rather than upon father's authority; consequently the husband may cease giving any service to his father-in-law as soon as he believes the attachment is secure.[43]

Opinion data from one group of Zulu women show that urban women accept the notion that a man should be free to choose his own wife without his parents' consent: 56 per cent of a stable urban sample gave this opinion, as against 6 per cent of a rural sample.[44]

It is not possible to summarize all the rules of preferential marriage in Africa, but a frequent preference in many tribes is with a cross-cousin—in a patrilineal society, marriage with mothers' brother's daughter for example; and, for secondary wives, marriage with the sister of the first wife. However, with a more open courtship system, in which the parental generation has a lesser voice, the number of potential eligibles for a mate increases greatly, so that the statistical chance of marrying one's cousin is less and the alliance serves no important goal of the kinship unit. The frequency of marriages following the ideal pattern is a result of the degree of control by elders over marriage arrangements; however, if the ideal has been strongly inculcated in the young such a union might still be felt as desirable. This is less likely to occur within the socialization experience when freedom of choice comes to be taken for granted by the young.

One would expect such marriages to be more common among noble families where the advantages of following the older generation's advice are greater. For example, about half the noble marriages among the Tswana in one sample occurred between people connected genealogically, as contrasted with one fifth among commoner marriages.[45] Tswana informants also claim that in former times a boy's parents nearly always tried to find him a wife among the daughters of their own brothers and sisters.[46]

Cross-cousin marriages are now declining elsewhere as well: among the Ashanti,[47] the Cewa of Nyasaland, the Thonga of Southern Mozambique, and in the urban areas of South Africa, where, one report states, "the younger generation opposes preferential marriages vehemently, claiming that such unions are essentially incestuous."[48] Hopen states that among the Fulbe (Northern Nigeria) the breakup of the clans has reduced the frequency of traditional cross-cousin marriage, although it still remains common.[49] All rules of mate choice are both endogamous and exogomous; while requiring marriage to be *within* certain group limits it is required that they cross other group lines. Incest rules force the individual to go *out*side his nuclear family and usually outside a still wider circle of kin, but they assure that the choice will be with*in* the same tribe and social rank. People may not marry within the clan, but it is assumed they will marry within the tribe, and sometimes within a narrow circle of blood and affinal kin as well. Most of these rules, except incest rules, may come to be viewed as restrictions imposed by old-fashioned tribal ways. For instance, Phillips has stated that in East Africa the younger generation is beginning to oppose the strict rules of exogamy.[50] On the other hand, an overwhelming percentage of Doob's sample of Zulu women (96 to 100 per cent stable urban, urban, and rural) were against a woman marrying someone from her own clan.[51]

We do, however, have reports on cross-tribal marriages for all urbanized areas. Many Africans prefer to live near members of their tribe when they move into the city, and there are wards made up predominantly of people from the same tribe. But individuals often cannot find housing where they want it, and there are those who wish to escape the restrictions posed by kin living in close proximity. In any event, the young African increasingly chooses his spouse according to personal preference, sometimes having met her in a church, where tribal membership is less important than religious affiliation. Consequently, more and more young men and women decide to marry even though they are from different tribes. Banton has reported a definite increase in cross-tribal marriages in Freetown, as ascertained from the recorded tribal origins of parents registering the birth of children; and Little has reported the same trend for the Mende within the same country.[52] It is also important to remember that the sex ratio of males to females is extremely high in most African cities and it is not possible for men to find enough wives within their own tribe. In Broken Hill, 30 per cent of marriages were between persons of different tribes. In Langa, a location in Cape Town, 31 per cent of the married couples belonged to different tribes, and in a Johannesburg slum (Rooiyard) the proportion was 51 per cent.[53]

4. Age at Marriage

With respect to changes in age at marriage, the African situation is not clear. Age at marriage is not known accurately for the past, since observers did not keep such records. In addition, some assumptions about the trend do not conform with the few reported statistical data for recent periods. Some African elders, for example, seem to believe that men and women marry later than in their own elder generation. For Africa, this notion may be based on several observations. One is that under urban conditions, a man may now live in concubinage or promiscuity for some years, so that his first *legal* union comes late. Second, some young people now go through several years of formal education, thus actually delaying their marriage. Perhaps more significant is the fact that under the older systems, many men and perhaps most women did marry rather young. However, because the young men who did marry early were likely to be from wealthy or noble families, their marriages were most visible and thus the actual total number of young marriages may be overrated.

It does not seem likely that young men *generally* married early under the older African family systems, although certain systems are exceptions. I am inclined to believe that the age of marriage of most young men was not greatly different from that of the rural United States two generations ago—about 25 years.[54]

By contrast, the age at marriage for young women was undoubtedly low in Africa. In most tribes, the marriage of a girl meant *her* kin group *received* cattle; the marriage of a young man meant that his family *gave* cattle. Moreover, his labor was worth more to his kin group when he remained single.

Reports are contradictory concerning the trend for men. Among the Ngoni, Tongo, and Yakö, indications are that the age may be dropping; among the Kgatla and the Pondo it seems to be increasing.

Table IV-1 presents the reported estimates of ages at marriage for various tribes over the past generation. These tell us little about trends, but give us base points from which to measure trends in the present and future. Contemporary changes in family patterns do tell us, however, the *direction* future trends from these figures should take: (1) To the extent that young girls once were married at very young ages, the average age of females at first marriage will increase. (2) The age of the elite men at marriage has increased, since once it was low and marriage is now likely to be preceded by education. (3) A few women go through years of formal education now, so that their age at marriage will be higher. However, most males did and do marry later than women. (4) To the extent that men do not have to wait for their elders' decision, their age at marriage may drop somewhat in the future. On the other hand, (5) the greatest alteration occurs in the cities, where there are not enough women to go around, and many men live in casual unions as adults, before settling down in a formal marriage (whether tribal or statutory). To this extent, little change in age at marriage may be taking place at present. Finally, I venture to predict that (6) as the sex ratio becomes normal, with more Africans earning an independent living, the age at marriage will eventually begin to drop for males.

Table IV-1
Age at Marriage, Africa, 1930–1953*

AREA OR TRIBE	Males	Females	Publication or Field Work Dates
East Africa			
Kenya: Luhya	late 20s	18–20	1930s
Hehe	16–22, most single men		1933
Kipsigis	20–22	16 (probably a minimum)	1930s
Nyamwezi: Birwana	16–20	14–18	1930
Junam	22–30	16–22	1950s
Nyakyusa	25 18, eldest son 30, younger sons	just after puberty	1930s
South Africa			
Pretoria (urban)	30	23–25	1936
Langa (urban)	59% by 20–30	36% by 15–20	1947
(rural)	74% by 20–30	70% by 15–20	
Pondo		22; formerly 16–18	1936
Kgatla	18% 25 under 54% 26–30 20% 31–35 8% over 35	18% 20 under 64% 21–25 16% 26–30 2% over 30	1930s
Stanleyville (urban)	49% single, 16–25 11% single, 25–35	12% single, 16–25 2% single, 25–35	1952
Baumanville (urban)	3% 15–20 20% 21–25 46% 26–30 24% 31	34% 15–20 49% 21–25 14% 26–30 9% 31	1955
	Later age at marrying for both is a recent phenomenon. Urban males and females marry later than rural.		
Keiskammahoek (rural)	Average age at first marriage: Before 1890: 24.3 1930s: 28.6 1940s: 30.1 Average over period: 27.1	Average age at first marriage: Before 1890: 19.3 1930s: 22.3 1940s: 23.6 Average over period: 22.4	1952
	Average age at second marriage: Before 1890: 19.5 1930s: 30.0 1940s: 32.0 Average over period: 44.1	Average age of bride at men's second marriage: Before 1890: 19.5 1930s: 30.0 1940s: 32.0 Average over period: 28.1	
Central Africa			
Lele	Until recently, 35–40 if bride a widow, otherwise 20–25		1951
Yao	20–30	Most women before 20	1953
Ngoni	18–25 (formerly 26–28)	About 17 on (formerly 20–25)	1951
Plateau Tonga	formerly 25–30, now 22–25	Now 16–18	1953
West Africa			
Ashanti	25–30 (20–25)	15–20 (16–18)	1945–1946
Tallensi	Rarely before 25	16–17	1949
Hausa	About 25	13–14	1950
Gold Coast (urban)	Those marrying under ordinance, over 30	Late teens; early 20s	1950s
Mende	Formerly 30–35, now late 20s		1951

Table IV-1 (Continued)

AREA OR TRIBE West Africa	Males	Females	Publication or Field Work Dates
Ghana (Cape Coast)	90% still single at 20 30% of 21–30 married	58% married before 20 Nine out of ten, 21–30 married	1956
Freetown	Two out of a total of seventy-eight, 16–24		1950s
Creoles	Sample of twenty-six: Five 18–20 Fourteen 23–31 Seven 34 or later	Sample of 55: Forty-nine before 27 Four 28–29 Two after 30	1959
Lagos	40% married in 15–34 age group 90% married in 35–44 age group	80% married in 15–34 age group 90% married in 35–44 age group	1959
Accra	More men marry between 30–40 than between 20–30		1959
Sekondi-Takoradi	Late age of men marry- ing under ordinance: most men, over 30		1959
Nsaw (Bamenda Province)		Betrothed before puberty, married year or two later	1952
Tiv	May have to wait until 40		1939

* Data drawn from the following sources: A. Phillips (ed.), *Survey of African Marriage and Family Life* (New York: Oxford University Press, 1953), pp. 34, 57, 59, 91, 136, 149; V. G. Pons, "The Growth of Stanleyville and the Composition of its African Population," in UNESCO, *Social Implications of Industrialization and Urbanization in Africa South of the Sahara* (Paris: The International African Institute, 1956), p. 264; Wilbur C. Hallenbeck (ed.), *The Baumanville Community: A Study of Family Life of Urban Africans*, mimeo (University of Natal: Institute for Social Research, 1955); Monica Wilson, Selma Kaplan, Theresa Maki, Edith M. Walton, *Keiskammahoek Rural Survey* (Pietermaritzburg: Shuter & Shooter, 1952), pp. 89, 90; Margaret Read, *Children of Their Fathers* (London: Methuen, 1959); Michael Banton, *West African City: A Study of Tribal Life in Freetown* (London: Oxford University Press, 1957), p. 198; Kenneth Little, "Some Patterns of Marriage and Domesticity in West Africa," *The Sociological Review* 7 (July, 1959), 70; Kenneth Little, *The Mende of Sierra Leone: A West African People in Transition* (London: Routledge & Kegan Paul, 1952); and I. Schapera, *Married Life in an African Tribe* (London: Faber & Faber, 1939), p. 71.

5. Fertility

The precise effect of industrialization and urbanization on African fertility is not clear, since it is very difficult to ascertain what the level of fertility was in the past. Although children were desired and contraceptives were not used, a number of common African practices may have kept fertility to a modest figure.[55] If fertility was high, mortality must have been almost as high, since the population density in Africa was low at the time of the European invasions.

It is also fairly certain that polygyny reduces fertility. Dorjahn has compiled data from twenty-three studies, most of which suggest that women in polygynous households have a lesser fertility. He also notes the various factors which might reduce fertility in the African systems.[56] Muhsam also attempted to measure the fertility of polygynous families and found that the ratios of children to married women were about 33 per cent lower for first and second wives of polygynous husbands than for wives of monogamous husbands.[57] Some reasons offered for the low fertility include the widespread pattern of a long period of sexual abstinence after childbirth; low nutritional standards; long visits of wives to their own relatives; and possibly the age differentials between husband and wife.

In addition, the divorce rates in many African societies were extremely high; and in the past, unstable marriages kept fertility lower than it otherwise would have been. In recent times, however, the increase in divorce in some tribes now has had a lowering effect on fertility. The increased amount of nonmarriage or consensual unions will also tend to lower the pregnancy exposure rate of women. Eventually, of course, as some approximation to a Western conjugal family becomes widespread in Africa, one might expect some control of fertility, but whether this will be lower than in the past is impossible to ascertain.[58] For the immediate decades ahead, however, we would expect an *increase* in fertility.

6. Illegitimacy

Illegitimacy was rare in the old African marriage system, and indeed among both matrilineal and patrilineal peoples the revelant arguments and court cases often centered about the question of who had the *right* to a child born under deviant circumstances, rather than who had the responsibility for it. A high value was placed on children, and far more emphasis on the social than on the biological continuity of a lineage; consequently, many children who might be considered illegitimate by Western standards were simply accepted as part of the kin line. Girls married young and almost everyone eventually married. Even when the marriage was not at a young age, the girl was likely to be under considerable supervision until she married. If a premarital pregnancy occurred, the parents could arrange for a girl to be married quickly; where custom demanded it, a young man could be held responsible. However, the declining control on the part of the kin network, and its lesser interest in these matters, means that a young couple is increasingly free to establish a relationship that may well issue an illegitimate child; and there are now fewer social forces to adjust the matter.

In the new circumstances of urban life, or in plantation settlements like the sisal regions of Tanganyika or the sugar areas of Uganda, several factors unite to raise the illegitimacy rate. Foremost among these is the high sex ratio of males to females. In Salisbury there are seven men to every woman, and in Nairobi five men per woman. The ratio is about two to one in the Rhodesian copper belt, in Mombasa, Kampala, and Brazzaville.[59] Such a sex ratio initiates a number of complex processes, although the main direction of change is clear. A preponderance of men certainly raises the evaluation of women. This happened on the United States frontier, and among certain groups of immigrants to the United States (Japanese, Chinese, Filipinos, etc.) in the early part of the twentieth century. Under these conditions any woman who wants to get married can do so. (The suggestion has been made that the liberal legislation of Western states regarding the rights of women in the United States in the latter part of the nineteenth century was due primarily to the high evaluation of women at that time.)

On the other hand, this kind of sex ratio also seems to lead to a widespread practice of prostitution and a breakdown in sexual controls. Precisely because the woman is given a high evaluation, if she transgresses the accepted sexual norms she is not only more likely to be forgiven, but some men will be able to offer her more benefits outside marriage than she might get within it. Moreover, under the economic circumstances which are characteristic of new settlements, the male typically has little stability in his economic position, so that the woman may not achieve security even within marriage. And, from the male's point of view, at least some of the benefits of marriage can be had through a temporary liaison, concubinage, or prostitution. The cost of engaging in promiscuity is not high, for when men obtain wealth, they often can free themselves from entangling social relations by simply paying for damages. For these reasons, a high percentage of men must remain unmarried for a large part of their early adult life, the stability of marital unions is relatively low, and the rate of illegitimacy is high.

It seems safe to say that on the whole there is a substantial increase in the number of unsanctioned unions, including many households set up without marriage ceremonies.[60] In urban Abomey, the number of free unions is on the increase, and some parents try to resist the loosening of traditional customs by sending their children back to their tribal homes.[61]

The failure of family controls over sexual matters is equally evident in the widespread reports of prostitution or semiprostitution in Sierra Leone, Kampala, Potopoto, and elsewhere.[62]

The kinship structure's inability to perform its normal activity is a far more fundamental sociological factor in illegitimacy than the one created by an unbalanced sex ratio. Precisely because many members of the kin network are simply not there, they cannot control the young couple before they get into trouble, or press them into a legitimate status afterwards. The young man does not need to approach the young girl through a set of norms imposed by elders, and the two make an essentially independent "role bargain" with one another. This is dictated primarily by the immediate individual advantages either can dispose of, and is unregulated by the social norms and values usually emphasized by the kin network. The situation in many urban African areas is precisely like that which has been described for Caribbean countries, and for many of the countries in the New World generally. Essentially, the girl must enter a consensual union, and thus risk pregnancy, in order to get a husband.[63]

This is *not* a mere matter of young people having sexual intercourse, since many societies having such a pattern insist that pregnancy must be followed by marriage. A basic origin of high illegitimacy rates lies rather in the failure of the kin to impose the normal social controls on young people and adults. This failure is intensified in many of the African towns because of an interesting difference between men and women in their migration patterns. Fewer women migrate, and the men migrate a greater distance. Consequently, "in most towns, women of the neighboring tribes form a much higher proportion of the total female population than men do of the male."[64] For example, in Kampala, Ghanda women formed 57 per cent of all women, but Ghanda men only 26 per cent of all men, in the suburb of Kisenyi; the local Soga women in Genga constituted 31 per cent of all women, but the Soga men only 18 per cent of all men. Moreover, apparently women are likely to stay longer once they have migrated, and at least one study suggests that a higher proportion of women intended to settle *permanently*.[65] This means that the men are even less under the supervision of their kin than if they had migrated from local areas, and may mean that escape from kin was at least one reason many women migrate.

These potential consequences are much less extreme, however, where the social networks have fairly strong roots in towns, such as in many of the older West African cities. For example, the Luo Welfare Association has as one of its functions the prevention of Luo women "from becoming prostitutes or concubines to men of other tribes."[66] These broad changes, and especially the development of the pattern of consensual unions, require one further comment. From many areas, reports have been published that in certain segments of the population "there is no stigma attached to illegitimacy." Judging from similar reports for many of the New World populations, I am inclined to suppose that this is an inaccurate statement of the situation. Though there are some women who derive more profit from prostitution than they could from marriage, no large segment of the population is likely to *disapprove* of marriage, or evaluate a consensual or concubinate union more highly than a proper marriage. There are many reasons why a couple might enter upon such a union, but in comparable social structures in the New World, close examination of real attitudes shows that most people would prefer to get married, prefer to have their children marry, and eventually do get married if it is at all possible.[67] Thus, one cannot suppose that even in the apparently anomic areas of the large African cities the ideal of marriage has been dropped. An appropriate prediction, then, would be that, although the rate of illegitimacy in the great African cities will probably rise for a while, in the next two decades it will begin to drop substantially.

7. Elders and the Younger Generation

The lessened parental control over choice of mate is only one manifestation of the generally greater freedom of the young. To some observers, the relationship between parents and children appears similar to that reported for United States immigrants and their children over a generation ago. African parents are said to lack control "partly because it is comparatively simple for young people to become economically independent of their parents, partly because, having been brought up in town, they have learned more of European ways than their parents, and therefore feel 'superior'. . . ."[68] Granted, the elders often cannot protest against their children's new ways simply because they are not in the area: In one small Stanleyville sample, although families objected to marriages in *only 19 per cent of the cases,* for some 70 per cent in which no objection occurred, no parents or near relatives were in close contact with either or both of the two parties concerned.[69]

One set of processes by which wage earning and labor migration affect the relation between elders and parents in South Africa has already been described. Complaints were widespread in the Keiskammahoek Survey that children were not so obedient as they once were and that daughters-in-law were not so hard working or obedient as they used to be. The wages now earned by the young were of more monetary value than was the produce of the land and thus the father loses the economic hold over the child and cannot compel him to turn over his wages, or demand support from him in his old age. When the sons wish to establish their own homestead, instead of turning to the older generation for assistance, they can obtain the support of their wives who have some migrant wage earnings before marriage and do not wish to submit to a mother-in-law."[70]

No matter how parental control manifests itself, it must ultimately depend upon close and frequent interaction between the older relatives and the younger generation. Urbanization particularly undermines this control since parents are likely to be separated from the children, and even when they live in the same locality, urban living quarters are usually not large enough to include the older relatives. The father's work may take him away from the home a great part of the time. Mothers also often work. In one urban South African sample, 45 per cent of the women worked away from the home, some all day, and some all week. Children were left with neighbors, or perhaps with an elder child, leaving most children without supervision.[71]

Some of these children may be sent away to relatives or to the native reserve. Many urban African families send their children to relatives in the country for lengthy periods, often until they are adults, for a variety of reasons. Sometimes, as when the husband is from a patrilineal society and the wife from a matrilineal tribe (for example in Ghana), each parent will attempt to send the child back to his or her own people in order to gain full custody of it. At other times, the goal is to instill proper traditional values in the child, or even to avoid the burden of the child. In the Sellgoods' survey, over half of the dependent children of the workers were living in the country. In Orlando township, Johannesburg, a 1949 survey showed that 31 per cent of the dependent children were living away from home.[72]

A similar pattern is reported for Brazzaville where there are insufficient schools, the father or uncle works, and the mother is often looking for additional sources of income. Many of these youngsters simply live on the street, according to Balandier.[73]

In addition, of course, *older* sons and daughters may be working in other towns, and the current African experience seems to be that although it is still considered a duty for such young people to give help to their parents, they often do not in fact do so.[74]

8. Polygyny

Women's increasing freedom of choice and the gradual shift from a subsistence agricultural economy to a market or industrial one has meant a steady decline in polygyny. Philosophical and economic factors against polygyny have been supported by the pressures from both political and religious leaders.

One must bear in mind, however, that although polygyny was an ideal of most African males, it was not their usual destiny. Men of wealth and the nobility could have extensive households, but the average man would have only one wife for most of his life, simply because of the shortage of women. No reliable evidence has ever been presented to show that any human society produces an excess of females at birth. As a consequence, polygyny cannot be the usual experience of adult males unless warfare substantially reduces the number of males available for marriage during each generation, or the society can obtain excess women by force or purchase from other societies (which, in turn, leaves an even greater imbalance in the groups that are conquered or which sell their women). The chances that men will take an additional wife may increase somewhat if females are married very early, and males marry relatively late, as seems to have been the situation in tribal Africa. Such an arrangement can yield about ten extra marital years per female, to be distributed among the males who are able to purchase additional wives. In a recent careful evaluation of some demographic aspects of polygyny, it has been suggested that about one out of three married sub-Saharan African males are (or were) polygynous, and that the mean number of wives per married man was 1.5.[75]

In Africa's urban industrial areas, polygyny has become relatively rare: Statutory marriage generally imposes legal obligation of monogamy, while urban life confers on the women none of the benefits that polygyny has in tribal areas.[76]

In addition to the antagonism of the women, who are growing in individualism because of their increasing capacity as independent wage-earners, local authorities will generally not let houses to polygamists so that, at any rate ostensibly, the latter are not found in urban locations. Christian morality as embodied in Western culture is also making some impression, and above all there is the economic factor: not only is urban marriage expensive in itself, but the high cost of married life in the towns usually precludes the African from supporting more than one wife, even when she is working between periods of childbirth.[77]

But although acquiring additional wives is a burden in an industrial area (in tribal areas each wife could generally support herself), it is safe to say that polygyny as a value, or even as an "attitude," still maintains some strength in African society. Certainly the male has greater freedom to participate in sexual unions outside legal monogamous marriage than before, and to a degree not tolerated in European society. Those who are more likely to believe in monogamy, the better educated and the Christian Africans, are certainly under greater pressure to live monogamously. The less educated are more likely to be polygynous.[78] Little notes Crabtree's finding that over 90 per cent of 113 educated men in Accra had been monogamously married as compared with about 60 per cent of their fathers; but he comments also on Banton's finding (noted above) that few men in Freetown had more than one wife, by reporting that in the up-country town of Bo, he (Little) had found over half of the literate husbands to be polygynously married—many of them, of course, married by native, not statutory, law.[79] And Mair states that the Ashanti Social Survey reported that a comparison by generations showed no substantial change in the number of wives accumulated in marriages begun before 1909, 1910–1929, and 1930–1945.[80]

In a few places polygyny may be on the increase; or at least it has not changed. Hopen has reported that the incidence of polygynous marriage has increased among the Fulbe in recent years.[81] A report on what used to be the Belgian Congo suggests that polygyny is as common today as it was among the older generation—even among those who have been exposed to Christianity. Indeed, it is argued that it is precisely because of the increase in wealth that many men can now afford a second wife.[82] In attempting to interpret the reports from the Congo, Mair expresses his puzzlement, since the arguments as to the causes involved seem somewhat contradictory.[83]

It seems unlikely that in the new nation-states emerging in Africa the generally favorable attitudes of African men toward polygyny will be changed quickly. Even so, it will, without question, eventually almost completely disappear as a pattern of behavior. The new legal codes are gradually moving toward its abolition, women will avoid it where they can, and men will not generally be able to afford it.

9. Size of Extended Household and Kin Network

Housing opportunities in urban areas generally prevent the existence of the large households that were common among many African tribes. Although, as in Western cities, kinfolk do try to live close together, it is not always possible; housing facilities are in such short supply that very large households are difficult to arrange. Every survey made thus far shows a relatively small number of people living in the same household; where comparison can be made, this is a smaller number than in tribal areas. Banton comments that households in Freetown are normally much smaller than those in the Protectorate, adding: "In the urban setting a large household is unnecessary and expensive."[84] In the Sellgoods' Johannesburg survey among 171 workers, 72 per cent had households made up of husband, wife, and children only, with no other relative living with them. In 1936, Hunter found that households in Pondoland averaged four to five adults and four children—in other words, extended kin households were common. In the more recent Keiskammahoek survey, the homestead averaged 5.95 persons. Similarly, the Orlando survey showed a household density of 5.38 people, and another taken in Springs township found an average of 5.02 persons.[85] When the averages are so small, extended kin households cannot be common.

The educated Gã in West Africa were found to have on the average 3.75 children in the household, compared with 6 in the preceding generation, and of the 4,989 households in the Accra survey, 2,846 had five persons or less in them.[86] In the Sekondi-Takoradi survey the household had an average size of 3.5 persons. A similarly small household has been reported for Brazzaville.[87] In these studies there has usually been an association between household income and size of household: the household is larger if the income is greater.

Even though the size of households has undoubtedly decreased (and there is no reason to believe that there will be a return to the large households of traditional Africa), the present distribution of size conceals several interesting processes. The most notable of these is the extent to which the extended kin still figure importantly in the family arrangements of Africans in urban and industrial areas. This phenomenon occurs even though the network cannot function as a *unit* in traditional ways. Its coherence is destroyed because some of the people are missing from the network, being in other towns or perhaps still remaining in the tribal areas. Hopen is correct in his assertion that "It is the mobility of households which is most clearly linked with the reduction in the strength of the ties of kinship and clanship for these bonds cannot survive spatial separation indefinitely.[88]

But although the kin network cannot function in the new environment as it did formerly, individuals who come to the new areas need one another since they may not be able to obtain help from strangers. Furthermore, emotional and economic ties continue to bind them to the tribal areas. Consequently, kin ties remain alive to some extent within the urban environment and the tribal areas. The process by which these ties are maintained can be observed in the Yoruba town (although it must be granted that the disorganization of urban life is much less in Yoruba than in many other areas). Here, the ties continue to exist because the Yoruba kin group still has rights to land for building and farming. If the man breaks the extended kin ties, he loses his rights to land.

The educated Yoruba is not likely to develop alternative social roots in a town distant from his kin group, since he may be transferred from one post to another, and even from town to town, so that he has little chance to develop strong ties in any one place. Consequently, his ideal is to retire to his home town where he can supplement his pension (if he has one) by farming and trading.[89] Moreover, the title of chieftain is still a great honor among the Yoruba; in obtaining it a man must have the support of his kin group.

A similar process may be observed among the Batonga on Lake Nyasa, who mostly work in the Rhodesias and in the Union of South Africa. At any one time, between 60 and 75 per cent of the adult males are working abroad, leaving their families behind. These men object to taking their families with them because they fear the disorganizing impact of industrial areas on family relationships. In addition, both because of the level of wages and the unsteadiness of employment, they do not earn enough to maintain a family adequately. Men continue to send money to their familes in the tribal areas, and to take as much part as they can in political and social events. They generally plan to settle in Tongaland when they are older, or when they become unemployed for a lengthy period. Finally, the Tonga tribal structure is used by the official administration of the area, so that the adult men have a real political interest in keeping their ties intact. Thus, although the men may spend a considerable time abroad, at least some part of their kin network is maintained.[90]

Public opinion also strongly supports the claims of kin upon one another within the urban area. This is true to such an extent that, "Public opinion and sentiment may still support the indigenous law that the claims of kin come before those of wife and children. This is so strong as to make the 'problem of family parasitism' so often mentioned in the African literature (Busia, 1950; Comhaire-Sylvaine, 1949; Hellmann, 1948; Capelle, 1947; R. E. Phillips, 1938). Thus a man's resources are continually drained away from his conjugal family, and distributed to his kin."[91] This expectation is so strong that some individuals can, and do, refuse jobs paying only the standard wage rates, under the expectation of help from kin, thus depressing still further their relatives' level of living.[92]

This "parasitism" should not be viewed as merely a disorganizing factor, however. The dependency may be part of a process by which an individual becomes established. Thus, certain members of the extended family may be sent to the city with the obligation of increasing the family income. During the period of becoming established, the rural people may sell and exchange produce and goods with their urban relatives.[93] Moreover, the established person may receive his relatives from the tribal area, and help them get an education or become established.[94] Nevertheless, in the city these economic and social relationships do not force the individual to submit to all the demands made by his kin, and he may at least begin to *choose* which obligations he will accept and how far he will carry them out. As a consequence, it may be said that the ties are not completely broken. Balandier found that only nine out of one hundred families had made complete breaks of this kind, but that the ties were not maintained in either their intensity or their extensity.

10. Husband-Wife Relations

The eighteenth-century eloquence of Rousseau intensified an old bias of Western social analysts: that in the rural past, spouses lived in a state of harmony which disappeared with urbanization and industrialization. Modern analysts holding to this bias have often been supported by the reports of elder tribal members who bemoan the present and look back to a happier time when men and women were aware of their marital obligations and fulfilled them.

However, the high divorce rates in primitive societies are evidence that marital happiness has *not* been the common lot of the men and women excluded from the debated benefits of civilization, and African data do not contradict this judgment. An increase in the rate of marital dissolution may not mean a much higher frequency of discord between husband and wife; it may only mean that standards of what is a *tolerable* level of conflict, or public attitudes concerning appropriate behavior for a couple in conflict, have changed. Yet it is sociologically likely that when either of these two cultural factors change, the norms of proper marital behavior have also been altered, and the husband and wife are, in fact, less likely to agree on their mutual obligations than in tribal times.

Without adequate measures, a sure judgment cannot be made, but it is reasonable to conclude that the amount of conflict increases if husband and wife no longer agree on what is proper marital behavior. In any event, it is more important to sketch some of the changing relations between husband and wife than to speculate at length about whether married life today is more pleasant than it was a generation ago.

Certain of these changes were described in the preceding section and need not be repeated here; but one primary structural change is implied which is particularly appropriate here: To the extent that husband and wife choose each other, without becoming involved in a full kin network, they are more dependent on one another for emotional satisfaction and their relationship becomes more important to each other. When the size of the great household decreases, as among the Pondo, spouses may be better able to enjoy one another's companionship. Or, as among the Fulbe (Northern Nigeria), there is increased interaction between husband and wife, since homesteads are isolated from one another or form very small clusters and the man cannot always find a male with whom to share leisure time at the camp.[95]

But this is only one aspect of the structural change noted above. Although the spouses may interact more frequently when they are together, a high percentage of adult men in many African societies are away from their families for years at a time, as has been true for decades in South Africa. Between 1930 and 1940, the number of men working away from their homes trebled, and it has been estimated that, at any one time, about 40 per cent of the married men under 44 years of age are away from home. Since in most areas men are more likely than women to migrate to the cities, a varying but large proportion of households in their region of birth must lack a male head of household. This absence affects both relations with wives and family discipline within the home.

Equally important is the fact that, because of the increased safety and ease of travel, the women who stay behind are *not* necessarily controlled by their in-laws or relatives. They themselves object to being without their men. They do not usually obtain sufficient support from husband or relatives and thus must become somewhat more independent. In addition, the widespread African feeling that the woman's reproductive powers should not lie dormant also increases the likelihood of involvements with other men. Thus, as already noted, even when official divorces are rare, women may nevertheless begin to live with men other than their husbands.

Furthermore, women also move to the city, often without their husbands, and are given an opportunity "to re-phrase their position."[96] New opportunities for economic independence are open to them, and they can compare their lot with other women.[97] Banton notes that Freetown women migrate and settle in almost the same numbers as men, and these women are more independent then those who remain in villages.[98] The greater independence of women has been noted among the Buganda (where a woman can leave her husband and travel to another village to make money by growing cotton), as well as among the Iru of Ankole.[99]

Since it is characteristic of any role relationship that individuals in it accept new rights more easily than they concede new privileges, this increasing feminine independence creates some conflict. Balandier asserts: "About 60 per cent of the cases submitted to the tribunal of the Commune Mixte relate to family conflict. The economic conditions, the abnormal sex ratio, the participation of women in activities which create monetary income, a great amount of liberty vis à vis the husband, a greater amount of leisure time, far more interaction and easier interaction with other people explain the freedom which the female has been able to choose within the limited family system."[100]

Just as extended kin cannot control married women so fully as in the past, wives in turn cannot count on support from those kin. This, coupled with the urban African male's inability to assure continuous and adequate support, means that wives must substitute the legal protection of courts and official authorities for traditional tribal ones, voluntary associations for traditional social relations, and economic self-support for the support by kinsmen and husbands.

A primary factor in this relatively complex set of relationships is the widening jurisdiction of official courts over family affairs. This has been so well documented that it needs only brief comment. In most jurisdictions now, women may appear in their own right as parties before European courts or formally constituted African national courts. Both, at various levels, are coming to substitute for the informal advice and counsel of tribal elders. In South Africa among the Kxatla, women can now share in the inheritance of their fathers' possessions, and may even succeed as principal heir if there are no sons.[101] Wives can go to the police if they are treated badly. The most commonly accepted view in British colonial courts has been that a statutory marriage places the husband and wife outside native customary law with reference to property rights, so that women, as well as men, can own land, inherit property, and dispose of it.[102] It is perhaps safe to assert that in most respects the formalization of statutory law in the emerging African countries will override customary tribal law with reference to the rights of women.

The development of voluntary associations, especially among African urban women, has been the object of considerable study. What is relevant here is that these associations substitute to some extent for the help that the woman in the tribal situation ordinarily could obtain from her kinsmen or in-laws. They serve economic as well as social functions. The vitality of such organizations shows the extent to which the woman in urban Africa is ordinarily deprived of sufficient security or help within her own household to handle all her social and economic problems. In a survey of Accra, it was estimated that there were some 26 thousand members in the mutual benefit societies, of whom over 23 thousand were women; and 75 per cent of all females 19 years of age or over were members of some association.[103]

As noted above, women's financial independence can be seen to be the result of new freedoms and opportunities. But there is another side to this phenomenon, which make it less innovating than appears at first glance. In all African tribes women worked; in most agricultural tribes the wife produced most or all of the food necessary for her own family. Women thus underwent a socialization experience that impressed upon them the notion that as adults they would earn their own keep. Thus, the urban situation merely offers nontraditional means for fulfilling a traditional role. And, as noted above, the man is frequently unable to earn enough to support a family in the urban situation. In any event, the peculiarities of both the polygynous heritage and the urban dislocation require her to earn money.

Even though the social trend toward having only one wife is strong and will continue to be so in the future, both men and women have been reared under a system in which polygyny is not only tolerated but approved. Men sometimes will marry a woman under traditional law, and later marry an urban, literate girl under the statutory law without terminating the relationship with the former wife. Often, after having married one woman, a man may court another; under statutory law he cannot officially marry her, but he can set up some sort of household with her. The variations in pattern are many; some women are concubines, others are mistresses, and some are "outside wives." The fact remains that whatever the designation or status of the new woman, the man is contributing to more than one household when he may not be able to support even one adequately. When the legally married wife cannot call upon popular support to force the man to have only one legal household, she must have some outside earnings. For these reasons, it is clear that although the so-called "independence" of the woman is real enough, it is to some degree forced upon her. That is why urban women sometimes complain about their "low status" as against the situation found in tribal areas where females at least had a wide range of support and a clearly defined position.[104] In an urban situation that does not offer increased economic opportunities, woman may even lose somewhat economically.[105]

11. Trend Toward "Patriliny"

If, as numerous reports attest, lineages throughout urban and industrializing Africa are weakening and losing their force, one cannot then say that *patrilineality* is on the increase. Nevertheless, it is clear that among matrilineal societies, the father is increasingly able to assert new rights against the traditional rights of the matrilineage, and that eventually, as in the West, the male line will take precedence. The details of the processes by which this occurs have already been presented here; and, as noted, the general problem of maintaining a matrilineal system have been outlined in detail by Schneider and others.[106] To the extent that a man's property is acquired by his own efforts, and not from his mother's brother, he is less willing to pass it on to his sister's son. The usual father-son sentiments are strong in matrilineal systems, as they are in others, and under modern conditions matrilineal kin lines have less political, social, or economic power to enforce their claims. Although land is still inherited through the mother among the Akan in Ghana, self-acquired property may be bequeathed freely.[107] The trend toward strengthening the father's claims has also been reported for what used to be the Belgian Congo.[108]

Among the Yakö, too, the male side of the family is coming to take precedence. Thus, Forde notes that "There has been a general tendency in recent years for sons to lay successful claim to at least a share of the movable goods left by their father which, by former custom, passed entirely to matrilineal heirs."[109] Forde further comments that "cumulatively in the spheres of economics, politics, and religion the bonds of matrilineal kinship and the role of the matrikin groups are being reduced."[110] The matrilineal principle is being challenged directly and indirectly by the European bias in favor of "patriliny" and also by the processes of Westernization. Patrilineal ties in the correct sense of a strong corporate lineage are weakening, too, but the personal, emotional ties between father and son may be strengthened.

In a parallel fashion, the Ovimbundu father (Angola) is increasingly able to arrange his daughter's marriage, thus displacing the girl's mother's brother, who in the past received the bride price.[111] A similar report comes from the Yombe (Congo).[112]

Mair's summary of this process in Central Africa states that "The trend is everywhere in the direction of a greater recognition of the father's position in these matrilineal societies."[113] In some societies, children stay on with their parents, although they have no claim to land of their father's lineage. In schools, children are often taught that their first duty is to their father. Even native courts will frequently support the father's claims, in part because the personnel of the judiciary have been educated along Western lines.

The process now under way seems to be clear enough, but the *degree* of change should not be exaggerated. In the more urban of the two Ashanti villages which Fortes studied, the husband was increasingly able to assert his claims against those of the wife's relatives. Nevertheless, even in that village, just under half the women between 30 and 40 years of age were still living with their maternal kin.[114] It is possible that from our Western bias the degree of change seems greater in the matrilineage simply because this type of family structure seems so alien. On the other hand, although it is clear that *both* types of lineage are weakening, and that no lineage will replace them, these family systems are definitely moving toward a pattern in which the father's line of descent will be given precedence, just as it is in the West.

12. Divorce

Divorce is a widespread method of dealing with the inevitable, ubiquitous disharmonies of married life. But it is not the only one. Societies also attempt to lower people's *expectations* about marriage, to socialize spouses to "adjust" to its disappointments, or, by laying less stress on the husband-wife relationship and more on relations with the larger kin network, to attempt to reduce the impact of husband-wife conflict. Should the tension rise to a level considered unbearable in the society, divorce may be an acceptable solution. Nevertheless, when the wife or husband fails to meet obligations, families may break up without actually divorcing. Unfortunately, the rates for such breakups can at best be only estimated for any country. We cannot, for example, know the real rate of marital dissolution in Spain, a country where divorce is permitted only to non-Catholics. Similarly, although divorce has been rare among the Nuer and Zulu, many husbands and wives do not continue to live together.

Since we cannot quantitatively measure the extent of marital breakup even for European countries like Spain and Portugal, we should not expect to be able to do so for African societies. At best, we can say that some have "high" divorce rates, and that some have recently *come* to have high divorce rates. This statement requires a prefatory comment on African divorce and family structure.

At present, the most fruitful perspective is to separate the domestic and sexual rights of the husband (uxorial rights) from the rights of the lineage to the offspring (genetricial rights).[115] A fuller analysis would require still further classifications of rights—for example, the right of the clan or lineage to the woman's loyalty. What is crucial in African divorce is that in matrilineal systems the husband obtains certain domestic and sexual services from the wife, but her other loyalties and her offspring always belong to her lineage. If there is a divorce, the lineage will care for her and her children. She is not "absorbed" into her husband's lineage. In such systems, divorce is common, and the amount of bride wealth is small, since it would be unlikely for a custom to develop which made a heavy investment subject to so fragile an arrangement.

By contrast, if the man gains his wife's services, and his lineage gains all her children no matter who may be the biological father, she cannot easily leave the marriage, and official divorce will be less common. The amount of bride price will also be relatively higher. If the wife returns home, her kin must return the bride price, always an awkward and sometimes impossible thing to do, and she returns without children for her lineage.

In a bilateral system, as Mitchell writes,[116] "Kinship alone cannot be the basis of corporate kin groups and therefore the possession of rights over a woman's reproductive powers is not a live issue." Unfortunately, this theory implies that bilateral marriages are of short duration, which does not coincide with the fact that until recently there was a historically stable marriage pattern in the West, with bilateral marriage. On the other hand, bilateral societies are rare in Africa, and for our immediate purposes we need not find an adequate solution.

When life in an urbanizing or industrializing milieu begins to weaken kinship systems, the effects on the stability of marriages under matrilineal and patrilineal kinship systems should differ. Added supports and pressures from clan or lineage members would diminish or disappear, and all the reported disorganizing factors of modern urban locations would begin to increase the official divorce rate, as well as the rate of unofficial breakup. If the procedures for divorce were not easily available, couples would nevertheless cease to live together.

In clan systems where the woman was *not* incorporated into her husband's clan, or the matrilineage had included her and her children as permanent members, the urban weakening of the corporate lineage bonds would remove a factor which once made divorce *easy*.[117] It cannot be said, as Mitchell suggests,[118] that urban life would *lower* divorce rates in matrilineal systems. Overriding disorganizing factors may continue for many years, and will maintain high rates of marital breakup. Perhaps it would be more cautious to predict that in the industrializing areas these rates may be about the same, but that *eventually* when a stabler social structure has been developed in such areas, these rates will be lower than they once were in tribal areas.

It is clear that the marital instability in the areas undergoing industrialization is great, even when many couples do not go through official (tribal or statutory) procedures for divorce. Since divorce *was* rare in many patrilineal systems, a high rate under the new conditions would mean that the rate has *increased*. Since tribal divorce rates in matrilineal systems were usually high, however, we will not be sure whether the rates have *increased* in urban and industrial areas until numerical comparisons are available. In succeeding pages, we shall take note of instances in which observers have commented that although the divorce rate is high, possibly it has not *risen* beyond the former level in the tribal areas like, for example, the Plateau Tonga (Northern Rhodesia).[119]

In Stanleyville districts A and B, well over half of those who had been married had also been divorced.[120] According to one calculation, Hausa women average about three marriages between puberty and menopause.[121] Of course, Hausa are influenced by Islamic customs. Eight out of ten persons over 40 years of age in a Yao village (Nyasaland) were found to have been divorced.[122] The Yao are matrilineal and affected by Islam.

In industrialized Broken Hill, women were usually living with their second or third husbands. Bemba marriage was apparently somewhat unstable during the early years, but divorce became more difficult after children were born because then the Bemba man could look forward to using his rights over his children to gain an independent economic status.[123] In a parallel study on the Copper Belt, Mitchell found that only 38 per cent of bridegrooms and 45 per cent of brides were marrying for the first time.[124]

Among the Bakweri (Kpe) of the Southern Cameroons, who have a double descent system, females can now inherit property and obtain sufficient money by their own efforts to repay the bride price in order to be free.[125] This is a plantation area, having, in effect, a rural pattern of industrialization, with a higher divorce rate as a resultant. Although life in Lagos among the Yoruba seems to be far less disorganized than in the industrializing regions of South Africa, the rate of divorce seems to have risen. One factor seems to be the difficulty of maintaining polygynous households, so that the husband is likely to leave his first wife rather than simply acquire another one.[126] The number of divorce suits has mounted among the Lunda (Northern Rhodesia), representing an increase in an already relatively unstable marriage pattern.[127]

In the Voltaic group of the Mossi the rate of marital dissolution has increased. Here the possibility of migration has affected the stability of marriage. Wife stealing was common before the Europeans came, but freedom of movement permits alternatives that formerly did not exist. Now the Mossi woman may run off with a man who is migrating to a job elsewhere. A substantial percentage of these women have gone to Ghana, and even if they do not find a stable relationship with the man who accompanied them, it is apparently easy to find a Mossi man in Ghana who wants a Mossi wife. These men may establish households with the Ashanti women, but avoid marriage, because of the Ashanti matrilineal descent pattern (the men could then not take their own children back with them).[128] Moreover, these Mossi women have knowledge of their civil rights in the new areas, and will not submit to pressures from their relatives or even from district officers.

On the other hand, although the divorce rate in Ghana and among the Tallensi is high, it was undoubtedly always high. The Ashanti Social Survey found that two thirds of the men under 60 years of age had been divorced, but this seemed to represent no change in this matrilineal group.[129] Similarly, Fortes found no reasonably hale Tallensi man over thirty years of age who had not experienced one or more unsuccessful marriages, but instability was normal among this patrilineal group.[130]

A content analysis of letters to a Ghana newspaper's advice column shows that the young men writing these letters understand fairly clearly the main factors affecting the stability of marriage in the urban area.[131] They note the influence of new patterns of living, under which relationships are threatened or broken as they might not have been under traditional social systems, and they are concerned about facing problems of emotional entanglements and of approaching girls in the more romantic courtship patterns of today. In addition, they note the differential rates of change among young and old. The elders remain attached to old standards, and although the younger people have taken on new outlooks they are not able to ignore their elders' objections or pressures—after all, the young man may still need help from his kin. They are also aware of the cross-tribal attachments in urban areas, together with the geographical mobility that lies at the basis of such attachments. Finally, they are concerned with the acceptance of Western patterns, which often means that greater discrepancies may grow up between husband and wife on the basis of class and educational differences than once were possible.

Changes in law express the changing conditions of the society, and thus at least suggest alterations that have taken place in East African societies which would press toward higher divorce rates. For example, Phillips has pointed out that African courts may now claim authority to hear matrimonial disputes, as against the claims of clan or family elders, and (as

noted earlier) married women may actually appear as independent liti-
gants.[132] In addition, although a wife's adultery was formerly considered
very serious, it was not regarded as grounds for divorce. Now, however,
many such proceedings are heard in African Courts. Customary law seems to
be changing among the Busoga (Uganda) relative to both marriage and land
holding, but considerable divergence and uncertainty are created by the fact
that there are no procedures for obtaining consistency among the various
native courts.[133] Where the local lineage groups of the Busoga have been
weakened or dispersed, divorce rates seem to be higher.[134] Men of Jinja are
freer now to choose their own spouses because they can pay the bride price
themselves, but the woman is also freer to leave her husband, because in
town she is sometimes able to return the marriage payment herself.[135] The
marriage systems of the various tribes in Kampala differ in details, but most
of them seem to have been influenced, like the Ganda, toward a higher
frequency of marital dissolution.[136] Among the Nyakyusa (Lake Nyasa),
the divorce rate seems to have risen.[137] The Teso, too, have experienced
a rise in the frequency of divorce.[138] Divorce has also become of comparatively common occurrence among the Nuer, where once marriage seems
to have been relatively stable; now, there is legal machinery for divorce.[139]

These changes in the trend in divorce should not, however, obscure the
various factors of stability in any society. Thus, for example, in Mombasa,
although temporary liaisons are frequent in urban areas, intertribal marriages are still the exception. Moreover, as against the various undermining
factors in urban life, the tribal associations often help to maintain some continuity. In Kampala the Luo Union has sometimes repatriated women who
attempted to break away from family and tribal controls.[140]

13. Widow Inheritance

In traditional African family systems widow inheritance was a form of
social security for the elder wife. Whether she was inherited by her husband's relatives, or whether the specific custom of the levirate existed, the
woman could at least count on being cared for by some man. Among the
Plateau Tonga it is still considered proper for the deceased man's family to
find a replacement for him.[141]

Moreover, the fertility of African women was always highly valued
and widow remarriage was generally taken for granted. Now, even without
adequate statistical data, it may be supposed that there is some decline in
widow remarriage. Some widows refuse to marry, whereas before they had
no choice. A more important change has been the gradual disappearance
of the *custom* of inheriting the widow. It is increasingly recognized that
such matters as the levirate or indeed any pattern of widow inheritance
should be determined by the free choice of the individuals concerned. Here,
as in other aspects of African family customs, the European "principle of

repugnance" is applied—the custom is evaluated by the European view of human rights.[142] In Uganda, the importance of the social security function of the older custom can be seen in striking contrast with one current change (not of course typical) by which the husband's clan still takes all of his personal possessions, but no longer takes responsibility for the widow.[143] A further remnant of the older tradition may be seen among the Busoga in the Eastern Province of Uganda, where widow inheritance cannot now be forced upon a woman, but if she fails to marry her husband's brother he may claim a refund of the bride wealth originally paid for her.[144]

What is occurring here, as in other areas of African family life, is that women increasingly feel free to make their own choice rather than to follow a customary pattern of marrying designated heirs of the husband. The increasing safety of travel and the possibility of independent income mean that widows can travel farther to be free of local pressures, while the kin group itself may not wish to assume the burden of caring for her. The number of widows in some areas may be relatively large because of the high mortality of African men. In the Keiskammahoek Rural Survey about one fourth of all women over 20 years of age were widows. Although this figure may be inflated somewhat, the authors concluded that most of them were in fact widows but that they had not remarried because thereby they would be separated from their children by the first husband, and would lose any rights they or their children had to the former husband's stock and land.[145]

In spite of these personal difficulties, however, it seems safe to say that the custom of inheriting the widow is declining in all areas that have been affected by urban and industrial pressures, and in which missionary doctrine and governmental rules oppose the custom.[146] Doob's small sample of Zulu women perhaps illustrates the trend: 81 per cent of the rural respondents agreed that a dead husband's brother should marry his brother's wife, but only 22 per cent of the urban and 39 per cent of the "stable urban" sample agreed.[146]

14. Conclusion

A summary of so complex a body of material is not possible, but a final comment is in order. The changes in African family systems are difficult to interpret adequately because comparable data do not exist for most societies, and the sheer diversity and number of tribes offer too many details to permit simple conclusions. On the other hand, the general trend seems unequivocal, since with respect to every major family element the movement is definite, and there are no *reverse* trends.

The *amount* of change is arguable, however. It seems great, in part because the traditional systems are so different from those followed by the Europeanized Africans, and thus the steps being taken are large ones. Perhaps nowhere in the world is the disparity between "rural" (here, *tribal*) and "urban" (Europeanized, Western) people so striking. Since the latter are the rulers and leaders, the direction of change is clear, and the kinds of changes dramatic; but the percentage of Africans following the new ways is doubtless still low. We emphasize the point, since by focusing on change its degree may be exaggerated.

So subtle a judgment is difficult to defend and perhaps impossible to prove, but I believe that much of the African industrialized and urbanized population is living in a state of social disorganization. The meaning of this statement can be specified: (1) Many accept both urban and tribal values, although with little moral commitment to either (e.g., polygyny and monogamy). (2) The society gives insufficient means for achieving certain values (e.g., the assumption of full male honor and position for the ordinary African). (3) The individual or group moves in two or more disparate social systems, having a fully legitimate place in neither (e.g., the tribal members in urban employment).[147] The data on illegitimacy support such a judgment. The opinions and attitudes elicited by Jahoda in Ghana buttress this evaluation, too, since the value or behavioral choices in a large number of questions were contradictory.[148]

Such a judgment does not mean that Westernization is only superficial in Africa, or that educated Africans are simply Westerners. Life in the industrial complex is much more complex than such *salon* evaluations, as this survey will show at many points. Very urbanized families may maintain intense and active kin ties, while even in villages only slightly touched by the new currents there will be nuclear families having only few ties with an extended kin network. Some educated Africans pay a mere lip service to the new family values, whereas others not only assert them but also live by them. Nevertheless, the direction of change is clear.

These points are well illustrated by Jahoda's question as to what the respondent would do if he had just returned from leave and could not obtain permission from his boss (with a threat of dismissal) to attend the funeral of an uncle, who was a chief. First, only 11 per cent of the men with elementary school education accepted the kin obligations as primary and felt that they should go to the funeral. Second, those with more education did not differ in this respect: 12 per cent felt they should go. Third, there was general acceptance of the view that the job demands were paramount, in part because only with a job could a man continue to fulfill his continuing family obligations. On the other hand, there was little *rejection* of these obligations, since various compromise solutions were offered, such as letters of explanation, a generous donation, etc. Finally, the reciprocal acceptance of the situation by the tribal family was assumed.[149] The imperatives of both occupational and familial systems were taken for granted, and various kinds of adjustments to them were seen by different respondents as permissible.

If the new African nations follow the path of many other emerging nations, the next decade will witness an accentuated move away from tribal family patterns, and toward a conjugal system. The resurgence of pride in the indigenous heritage will not buttress traditional family patterns, because the effort to be accepted by older nations as "modern" or "civilized" will create continuing social and legal forces in line with "progressive" family sentiments and behavior. The new legal codes will be ahead of both the contemporary values and the behavior of the average African, but they will become forces in their own right, supporting the emergence of the new family systems. The economic and political plans of African leaders will not aim at strengthening the traditional family ways, partly because their tribal core or foundation would hinder the desired intensification of loyalties to the *nation*, made up of many tribes. The ideologies of economic growth and family "modernism" will continue to shape the next decade of change in sub-Saharan Africa. The removal of European administrators will not remove the effects of ideas and socioeconomic processes, originally European, which are now integrally part of the African world.

chapter

V

Changing Family Patterns in India

INDIAN observers, asserting that their country is changing rapidly, have warned Western analysts that its peculiar cultural heritage may lead to an industrial and family pattern very different from that of the West. Both the assertion and prediction may be wrong, and an inquiry into India's family patterns should be especially fruitful for an understanding of social change there, because such patterns embody or express most of the factors that have impeded its social development.

Although the *direction* of family changes seem clear enough, any measurement of the *amount* of change faces nearly insuperable obstacles. Not only was India divided into hundreds of tribes, societies, and states, with a bewildering multiplicity of languages and literatures, but each city and village was subdivided into caste communities. If only the *major* subcastes are included, the number exceeds 2 thousand, and the subcastes follow different family patterns in different regions. These were not fully described and mapped a half-century ago, nor are they now. Even more important, the historical problems of studying family changes are accentuated in India. The publicly acknowledged values and ideals of the recent past can be gathered from literary, philosophical, and religious sources, but we know neither how fully the "average" Hindu accepted these ideals, nor how well he followed them in practice.

These difficulties are compounded by India's internal divisions, which, in turn, have made difficult any organized attack on India's two great interrelated problems—the need to slow down the steady growth of its population of about 500 million, and to industrialize so that its per capita income may increase. To solve these problems, India has chosen neither the road of dictatorship or authoritarian planning—almost the only means by which industrialization can take place swiftly—nor the road of lassitude and apathy, by which these problems can be ignored.

The Indian aspiration of welding its variegated social systems into an effective whole is conceivable because there is one broad cultural pattern common to almost all of the Indian population, however differently each community may interpret its details. Indeed, because these multifarious communities generally share a similar culture, it is fruitful to attempt this analysis of family change in India as a whole, focusing on the main family patterns, but trying as far as possible to take into account some of their deviations.

India's family patterns have not changed as rapidly as those of Japan or China during the past decade, although they have changed faster than those in the West. However, if industrialization and urbanization were the only important variables in family change, we should not expect rapid alterations in the area of domestic life. Although no procedures exist for quantifying with precision the contributions from industrialization, as against those of new ideological elements, the modest amount of change in Indian family patterns seems far greater than could be imputed to industrialization and urbanization alone. Thus, to the extent that much change has taken place, it seems likely that a good part of it can be ascribed to ideological influences internal to India or coming from the West.

Let us first consider urbanization. India's city dwellers differ considerably from rural people. Cities in India were developed long before any were built in the West, and most are ancient by United States standards. But for much of their history they followed settled social traditions and during most of that time the rural migrant to the city would not have had to change his life style much.[1] Even now, Indian and Western cities are quite different, and many agglomerations of populations numbering more than 5 thousand are not classified as cities even by the Indians.

Aside from the differences between the two patterns of living, however, urbanization has not as yet gone far or fast. According to the 1951 Census definition, 17 per cent of the Indian population was urban, that is, living in places having a population of 5 thousand or more (with some exceptions). This is a modest rise over the 13 per cent in 1941, the 11 per cent in 1931, the 10 per cent in 1901, and the 9 per cent in 1881.[2]

In 1951, 12 per cent of India's population lived in cities of 20 thousand or more, and about 7 per cent in cities of 100 thousand. This figure, however, is lower than that for Asia as a whole (about 34 per cent in each size of city), and indeed lower than that for any other major geographical area except Africa, Central America, and Oceania.[3] Thus, although the urban population of India has indeed been growing faster than the population as a whole, only a small minority of the population lives in cities.

As for industrialization, India began this process in the early nineteenth century; at present its industrial output in *absolute* terms places it among the major nations, but its industrial growth has been slow and its *per capita* output extremely low. In 1951, 11 per cent of the working force was to be found in industry (including mining, construction, gas, water, etc.); and in 1952, about 2.5 million people were working in factories, mainly in the cities.[4] Although India's industrialization began before that of Japan, and continued to be ahead of it until about 1890,[5] in 1958, 50 per cent of its gross domestic product was derived from agriculture, forestry, and fishing—one of the highest percentages of any nation in the world— while only 16 per cent of the product came from manufacturing and construction combined. At about the same period, the net food supply per person was only 1,800 calories per day. If we exclude all "factories" except those with installed power equipment, and having twenty or more employees, the total number of industrial workers in 1957 was only 1,813,000 out of a labor force of 101,000,000. Its production of electrical energy and consumption of energy sources (in terms of coal equivalents) is one of the lowest per capita among the nations of the world.[6] Certainly, India can boast high achievements in science, industry, and intellectual work, but these represent the activities of an extremely small minority of the population.

Since here we are only concerned with pointing out how small a part of the Indian population has entered an industrial environment, only a brief summary of these factors *retarding* industrialization is relevant. They are presented here as Davis has outlined them.[7]

First, the caste system, relying heavily on rigid custom and rejecting qualification by achievement, limited competition and accented a type of specialization that could not be fitted into a production line—for example, the lowest castes were allowed to work at only menial tasks, and they were not even permitted inside higher-caste households. By making cooperation difficult, the caste system hampered the development of large-scale cooperative enterprises which might have united many people, largely strangers, of different skills. The joint family, coupled with the village-based caste system, lowered the geographic mobility necessary for increased competition. It also forced some of its members to support other members, even when the latter had nothing to contribute, thus undermining the younger generation's independence and initiative. The seclusion of women prevented their widespread education and utilization which might have increased industrialization.

As Weber has noted, the Hindu religion, emphasizing the moral virtue of accepting one's place and offering rewards in later incarnations for the individual who adjusted to his position in the present one, effectively lowered aspirations. The proscriptions of religion also made it extremely difficult to use the outcastes, who comprised a large part of the population, in the work force. Among the various Indian social groupings, only the Jains and Parsis had beliefs and a social orientation which might have encouraged industrialization.

Beyond these factors in the family and social organization, India was hampered greatly by its political and economic dependence. The Indian rulers could see no great gains to them from industrialization, and the British were engaged in exploiting India's human and natural resources, while hampering the growth of factory systems. In addition, there was little support, even by the Indian government, either for progressive utilization of capital and labor, or for the wise exploitation of natural resources for long-term national interests. Since labor was always cheap, the individual capitalist found it more profitable to exploit labor than to invest in machines. The same holds true today. Only with considerable guidance could there have been any substantial investment in capital equipment which might have eventually led to a higher per capita income through industrialization.[8] One very important way in which the English hampered industrialization was their refusal to alter India's social organization and family customs. The British colonial administrators were also mostly men who had neither training in business nor sympathy with its development. It must be emphasized, however, that even though British rulers, the various Indian governments, and the people themselves were not strongly motivated to industrialize, it is doubtful that India would have industrialized as fast as it did if the British had not been there.

The fact remains that industrialization has not proceeded far in India; if, then, there are substantial family changes in this country, they can be ascribed only in small part to the effects of an industrialized life.

If we consider the state of literacy, the same conclusion is apparent: if entrance into the industrial world and the changes it creates are dependent upon access to the printed word, then the Indian has had little opportunity to become industrial. In 1891, 6 per cent of the Indian population aged 10 and over was recorded as literate. This figure rose steadily to 9 per cent by 1931. At that time, India was less literate than China, Egypt, or British Malaya. The 1941 Census figures contain only an estimate. By 1951, nearly 17 per cent of the Indian population aged 10 and over was literate. It is interesting that over a comparable period of time almost all the Japanese population had become literate.

The problems in making India literate illustrate the vicious circle in which its population was entangled. The country was desperately poor and thus did not have the surplus product with which to invest in so long-term an investment as a school system. It was precisely because the people were illiterate, however, that industrialization was nearly impossible. Although learning itself was honored (the honor accorded the Brahmins was partly based on their learning, primarily their mastery of the philosophical and religious literature), the masses had no motivation for learning to read and write since the rewards from such learning were negligible, one reason being that jobs were not available for them. Even now, there is a great surplus of college graduates who do not have jobs or who have jobs far below their intellectual training because industrialization has not proceeded far enough to utilize their skills. Moreover, a large part of the population had no *right* to read the Vedic literature, and since they generally had no motivation for learning, the drop-out rate in schools was extremely high. During the 1920s in the Punjab region, one of India's most progressive provinces, half the boys and three fourths of the girls dropped out between the first and second years of primary school.[9] Until recently, this same pattern, in a less exaggerated form, could be reported for every part of India. Since it was not upward mobility but adjustment to the society and to one's place in life that was the major aspiration, education seemed a useless luxury at best. At the present time, 25 per cent of the males and 8 per cent of the females aged 10 and over are literate. The percentage of literate women is rising faster than that of men, but the relation between individual success in life and education is still not so self-evident as to create a massive pressure toward the education that is indispensable for a fully industrialized country.

1. Choice of Mate

The importance of the impact of urbanization, industrialization, and literacy on social relations rests specifically on the possibility they offer to the individual for building an independent base for his own decisions relative to the family. These factors have not as yet been powerful in India. In the generation from 1921 to 1951, the number of agricultural cultivators *without land*, per thousand cultivators *with* land, increased from 291 to 706. That is, by 1951, 40 per cent had no land. These landless people, usually illiterate and untrained, are the first to seek jobs in the cities.[10] Since they are at the bottom of the economic structure in the cities, their chances for employment are poor. Their wages are low because their productivity per capita is low. Thus, they have to lean on the village and their joint family as a form of social insurance. For about half a century up to the mid 1950s the occupational structure of India remained relatively static.[11] An index of this condition may be found in the fact that although India's fertility was lower in the cities than in rural areas, this ratio remained the same over the half-century between 1891 and 1941.[12] Men migrated to the cities without their families, so that by 1951 the sex ratio in cities of 100 thousand or more was 127. This means that men frequently left their families with extended kin while they tried to find a place in the urban economic structure.[13] Because male labor was always cheap, even cheaper than machines, there was little demand for an independent female labor force. Thus, the women failed to develop an individual basis from which to implement their own decisions.

Nevertheless, India exhibits more change in family relations than would be expected if industrialization were the sole moving variable. Even in mate choice, the winds of change may be felt, and there is a movement in the direction of giving greater freedom to the young. This change is especially important because the Hindu arranged marriage was the keystone to all the other family patterns that characterized Indian society for so long. Of the eight traditionally recognized forms of "marriage," only four were approved as being acceptable from a religious point of view, and in none of these did the bride or groom have any real voice in the decision.[14] Marriage was both a religious and a social duty for Hindu men and women. For the Hindu man, it meant an important ritual, necessary to him personally because only his son could carry out the *shradda* ceremony, without which his soul would not complete its transmigration and reincarnation. If a man failed to produce a son, he thereby condemned his own soul to hell.

Women were much less important, and marriage was the only occasion in their lives marked by religious ceremonies. From about the beginning of the Christian era, marriage has been considered woman's obligation,[15] stemming partly from man's need to produce heirs for spiritual salvation, and partly from the belief that it was the only way to protect her from the dangers of her own sexuality.

The maintenance of the caste system, the main outlines of which were more or less settled by about the tenth century A.D., depended completely upon the arranged marriage. Maintenance of caste was too important a matter to be left to the young, who might well fall prey to the temptations of love and thus ignore caste requirements. To prevent any serious opposition, youngsters were married early enough to ensure that they could not acquire any resources with which to oppose adult decisions. The joint family, in turn, offered an organization which could absorb a young couple who could not yet make their own living. As noted earlier, this pattern of marriage has always been common among the nobility, but in India it developed not only among the wealthy, who could afford early marriages and whose unions might mark an alliance between two families, but also among the poor, who had nothing to share but their debts.

Even among the Nayars of Malabar, whose matrilineal customs are often used to prove that some commonly accepted generalizations about the family are not correct, and whose sexual freedom after marriage was notorious, the young girl did not choose her own first mate. The devadasis (temple prostitutes), were also obliged to marry, and marry young, without any voice in the decision. This was so settled, even though it might be decided that they marry a ritual object, like a sword (not a human being).[16]

Freedom of choice presupposes a relatively adult age at marriage and a system of courtship where the individual has time and opportunity to know a variety of potential spouses before making a choice (although choice *is* generally limited to a group of people at about the same class level). Until very recently, however, freedom of choice under India's social conditions would have been meaningless without alterations in many other elements of the marriage system. For one thing, choice was restricted to the individual's subcaste, not merely his great caste or *varna*. Some exceptions were permitted—for example, the *hypergamous* marriage, by which a woman might marry a man from a higher section of her subcaste, but not entirely outside of it. Even in this instance, the man's marriage to such a woman was likely to be polygynous; either his primary marriage was to a woman in his own subsection, or his own prospects were poor: for instance, if he were a younger brother with no claim to his family's properties.[17] Even the Harijan or outcaste marries within his subcaste.[18]

There were also several exogamous restrictions. The individual could not marry within his own *gotra*. This rule was defined very differently from one caste and region to another, and is variously referred to as "sib," "clan," or "lineage." In general, it recognized the existence of a patriline, descended from a distant ancestor and carrying a particular name.[19] This patriline was the widest kin group, and although Brahmins claimed exclusive possession of this tradition, in fact other castes were also divided into *gotram*.[20] The rights and duties of membership were not spelled out in detail, but Kapadia comments that ". . . exogamous restrictions based on *gotra* . . . were tenaciously adhered to down to the 4th decade of the present century."[21] But although *gotra* restrictions continued to be observed, and custom has not yet rejected them, actual marriage practice sometimes violated them, as we shall see later. Moreover, under recent laws they can no longer be enforced.

The Bombay Hindu Marriage Disabilities Act of 1946 removed this restriction in law, stipulating that if the marriage was otherwise valid, membership in the same *gotra* did not render it invalid. The Hindu Marriage Act of 1955 made this ruling on a national basis. Thus, the legal barrier was removed, even though there was little public outcry against the restriction. Indeed, in the area of family customs, it must be kept in mind that the legislators represent an elite attempting to move the nation in certain directions which they hope or believe the populace will eventually approve. All that the legislature can do about many of the old practices is to forbid the punishment of those who violate ancient customs that the vanguard think are outdated. The problem of social change has always been to alter the attitudes which are remnants from the past. As Singer has commented: "We know that Nehru is a 'modernist' who feels the 'burden of history' not merely as an obstacle to progress which must be shaken off. The past is rather a burden because it is for him a living presence compelling his mind and heart which must be reconciled with the demands of reform."[22]

Since the *gotra* rule may, in an extremely orthodox version, take the form that a man may not marry into the *gotra* of any of his four grandparents, it may at times overlap with another exogamous rule: that an individual may not marry another belonging to the same *sapinda*. The *sapinda* is not so much a recognized group with its own social organization as a category of kin who are related within a defined boundary of closeness, roughly analogous to the Chinese "mourning relatives." The ancient rule in the northern zone of India was that marriage was not possible with someone removed by less than seven degrees from the father and five degrees from the mother, and this rule "is quoted by all castes from the highest to the lowest when asked about marriage practices."[23] The more common rule prohibits marriage with relatives who are linked to a common ancestor within five generations on the father's side and three on the mother's. The counting itself is simple. On the father's line one counts the father as one step, and then counts back to the first ancestor who is a common ancestor with the other individual. If the number of generations is as many as six, they may marry. The same counting for the mother's line is followed, except that the counting begins with the mother and continues through her direct male line to the common ancestor, and the number of generations must be four or more.[24]

Although the Hindu Marriage Act of 1955 removed the bar of caste and *gotra* from the requirements for a valid marriage, it stipulated that the parties must not be *sapindas* of one another, "unless the custom or usage governing each other permits of a sacramental marriage between the two."[25] Thus, the rule still holds, although there were important exceptions here and there in Hindu marriage choice, as we shall note later.

Another exogamous rule still in use is that the bride be sought in a village that does not border on the groom's village. However, a further rule rejects a potentially eligible spouse who unfortunately lives in a *gotra* village (a village dominated by a *gotra* within which the individual may not marry). The fact that an astrologer must be consulted to find out whether a given match is propitious merely constitutes an additional restriction.

Although there are many divisive elements in Indian society, perhaps no other single rule has helped more to integrate India than these exogamous family patterns. This may be seen in microcosm from a survey of Rani Khera, a north India village. The 266 married women there came from about 200 different villages, the average distance among them falling between 12 and 24 miles. An additional 220 women who married *outside* this, their native, village went to some 200 villages. Consequently, this village of 150 households is linked with 400 other villages in its general area.[26] Thus, by successive steps, almost every village is ultimately linked, at least indirectly, with every other village.

The fit between these rules and adult control over marriage is clear. The young person could not be relied upon to follow the rules exactly. With limited social experience and no opportunity to travel, he or she could not locate the few eligibles to be found in a population of several thousands distributed among many villages. Even if this were possible, the individual might not respond emotionally to the eligible person or be able to persuade him to agree to a marriage.

The combined weight of the rules made freedom of choice unthinkable as a practical procedure. Only adults could initiate and effectively carry out all the negotiations necessary for a valid marriage satisfactory to both sides. The focus of the small minority of reformers in Indian society, from Raja Ram Mohan Roy to Gandhi, was not on freedom of choice *per se*, but on the objectionable elements in the family system, such as caste restrictions, child marriage, and so on, which made freedom of choice impossible.

Although age at marriage is treated in the succeeding section, its importance for freedom of choice must be noted here. The traditional rule, apparently adhered to with much rigor, was that a father committed a sin by not marrying off his daughter before puberty. Even if he had no wish to lose his daughter at so early an age, the elder women of his household would nag him until the negotiations were under way. The preparations for marriage and the attendant social interaction were occasions for visiting, planning, and excitement, in which the women had a central role. Choice of the girl was of more importance to them than to the men, since she had to be incorporated into their group. Restricted as women were in their range of activities and decisions, marriage was a welcome high point. This key role of elder women as prime movers in getting the marriage process under way may be observed in China, Japan, and the Arab countries as well. Finally, of course, elder women and men in India both shared the basic ideal, that the girl ought to be married early, because any sin she committed due to a late marriage was their responsibility.

Obviously, if preadolescent girls were to be brides, they could not be entrusted with the choice of a husband.

The lack of marital freedom in India is related to the unique qualities of Hindu civilization, in which the refinements of both asceticism and eroticism have been pursued farther than in other great cultures. Western civilization had its ascetic moments but never fully accepted the spiritual renunciation of the world as a major duty of the middle-aged man. In Imperial Rome, the elaboration of brutality was carried to a high pitch, but its eroticism never achieved the flamboyance to be found in the Indian sexual cult of Tantricism and the sculptures at Konarak and Khajuraho.[27] The institution of *purdah* was quickly accepted by the Hindus from the Moslem conquerors (although the custom remained weak in the south) because it well fitted the wish of Indians to protect their women from exposure to men. Throughout the last thousand years of Hindu history, not only was woman viewed a temptation to man, but she was attributed with having great lusts. Thus, for her own protection as well as the protection of others (who might otherwise sin) she had to be married early.

As noted earlier with regard to the West and sub-Saharan Africa, a bride price or dowry system is undermined when freedom of choice is given to the young. Such a system is dependent on the ability of adults to ensure that the marriage they agree on will in fact take place, and that it will be relatively stable. If the elders cannot guarantee to one another the security of their financial investment in the union of the succeeding generation, then they are less able to demand either dowry or bride price and less able to ask their kinsmen to contribute by loan or gift to the union. Young people who want very much to marry one another are not likely to bargain for money.

Since both the bride price and dowries are systems of exchange within a relatively closed circle, and any given family line produces about as many males as females, the money received for spouses of one sex will be roughly equivalent to that for the spouses of the other sex. Over the short run, of course, a family might be impoverished by the need to provide dowries for several daughters, if there were no sons to bring in dowries themselves.

It is not yet clear why the dowry system has been found in some societies, whereas others require a bride price. In Indian society there were three *immediate* structural elements that supported a dowry or groom price system: the pressure to get the bride married by puberty, caste, and hypergamy.

The traditional Hindu philosophical and religious literature contains many exhortations to marry the young girl early under various severe penalties. Unmarried, she goes through no ritual purifications and is no better than a Sudra, a member of the lowest caste. According to one formulation, if she does not marry before puberty the parents and eldest brother go to hell. Although men also were obliged to marry, they could afford to wait. This meant that the institutional structure placed the parents in a poor bargaining position. They had to seek out a groom for their daughter, and because in marrying her he saved them all from sin, they owed him gratitude and deference, a pattern which is still observable today. The parents of the potential groom could thus make heavy demands in the form of a groom price.

Caste and hypergamy operated together to enlarge the number of potential brides for a man of a given subcaste, as well as the number of grooms available to a girl; but if her family wished to marry her to a groom somewhat higher in the caste system, again they were required to produce a dowry or groom price. Thus the parents of young men in any higher section of a given subcaste could obtain a larger dowry from the parents of girls in a lower section. At the apex of this system were the Brahmins, again divided into sections. In addition to the bargaining advantages conferred on the Brahmins by these structural elements, they also controlled the philosophical and religious literature and in many discussions condemned as both crass and sinful the notion of *bride* price (i.e., the *groom* bringing money to the bride's family); that is, they objected to the development of any ideas which might have undermined their own bargaining power.[28] Altekar asserts that "in ordinary families . . . the amount of the dowry was a nominal one" and "it is only during the last 50 or 60 years that the amount of the dowry has begun to assume scandalous proportions."[29] However, he himself notes that Rajput families had come to be successful in demanding large dowries by about the thirteenth or fourteenth century A.D.

In addition, the phenomenon called "kulinism" was widespread in the early part of the nineteenth century, and certainly continued well into the twentieth. The Bengali Kulin Brahmins carried out their priestly ceremonies but did not earn their living from them. If the parents of a Brahmin girl in a lower section (those who earned their living by carrying out religious rituals) wished to marry her into the higher section, the Kulins, they had to pay a substantial groom price. Surveys and comments in the early part of the nineteenth century assert that some Brahmin men married fifteen or twenty wives, and occasionally cases were found of those who married as many as eighty. In these cases the husband did not ordinarily live with all these women, but, instead, visited them at their parents' homes, where he was received at each visit with a gift, expressing the caste deference embodied in the marriage itself.

A succession of legislative acts extending back to 1872 attacked polygynous marriages, while the Hindu Marriage Act of 1955 prohibited second marriages under the penalty of prosecution for bigamy. The particular pattern of kulinism is no longer to be found, but a well-educated groom may command from 5 thousand to 50 thousand rupees as a dowry.[30]

In contrast to this pattern, the Harijans or outcastes, constituting about one fourth to one fifth of the total population, followed a system of bride price. Since there is ordinarily no property or money to be conserved in the family line, the bride price bears little relationship to the value of the bride and is mainly fixed by custom,[31] although among some castes high bride prices are found. The bride price may also be found at times among higher castes, generally when an older man wishes to obtain a young wife.[32] Groom service is also found among the Harijans, this being the equivalent of a bride price.[33] Marriage by exchange may also be found when families are very poor, so as to economize on both the expense of the wedding and on the dowry.

It is to be noted that in the preceding discussions many of the descriptions are couched in the present tense. Except where specifically noted, the evidence suggests that these patterns continue in the present. The question can be raised as to the extent to which sentiment in favor of freedom of choice, the abolition of dowry, and the elimination of the traditional restrictions on whom one may choose are now evident in the Indian population.

Of course, the development of attitudes in harmony with freedom of choice does not mean that young people are now demanding that choice with any great success. The sentiment, as in Japan, may be somewhat ahead of the young person's bargaining power. For example, in urban Bangalore, the young middle-class girl is still chaperoned, and if she goes out alone in the afternoon she must be back by 6 P.M. There are few opportunities for young men and women to meet one another, and no opportunities, aside from a college campus, to talk to each other alone. There may be greater freedom in northern India, and among urbanized Hindus, Christians, and Anglo-

Indians, but these still constitute a minority and even their behavior is restricted.[34] The average Hindu girl simply cannot afford to adopt the modern system of courtship because her reputation would be ruined and thus the very aim she was seeking, freedom of choice in her marriage, would be destroyed.

Nevertheless change *is* evident even in this respect. As a striking contrast to the present-day utilization of women in government and teaching, Gray notes that it was nearly impossible during the 1920s to obtain teachers for village schools because an unmarried woman or widow could not live alone in a village.[35] On the northwestern frontier some unmarried women were teaching, but they were accompanied by elderly chaperones. Some argued that an unmarried woman or widow could live alone if she was well-known, elderly, of approved character, and frequently visited by the organization for which she worked.

In interpreting the data on contemporary values relating to caste, the primary bar to freedom of choice, as well as other data relative to freedom, several points should be kept in mind. First, none of these surveys is based on a genuine national sample, or a technically random one. Moreover, the sampling biases are fairly clear; the samples contain a disproportionate number of Western-educated, middle- or upper-middle-class persons. Outcastes, women, and rural populations are not excluded, but current sampling conditions make it difficult to give them their proper weight in studies of values and attitudes.

In addition, as noted earlier, we have no comparable data for a generation or two generations ago. We are forced to compare contemporary expressions of values, made by people high and low, uneducated and educated, with the *published* philosophical or literary comments of an educated group of previous generations. Thus we are really comparing the "ideal" patterns and attitudes of fifty years ago or more, with the actual ideals and values today. If, for example, a high proportion now say that they are in favor of intercaste marriage, we must conclude that this is a substantial change from fifty years ago, when presumably almost none would have been in favor of such marriages. Nevertheless, this is an assumption based upon reasonable inference, not upon empirical surveys. The uneducated, the outcastes (Harijans), women, and rural people generally did not express their values on such matters a half-century ago. It seems reasonable to suppose that they firmly believed in the adults' complete control over mate choice, in prohibition on intimate intercaste social relations as well as marriage, and in very youthful ages at marriage for the girl. Until adequate data to the contrary are presented, this assumption seems most cautious.

If, as Ghurye claims, caste untouchability almost disappeared in the twenty years between the first and second editions of his analysis of Indian social institutions, we should expect that a large proportion of at least the educated groups in Indian society should have come to accept the propriety of intercaste dining—the intimacy of eating together being a first step toward social acceptance—or intercaste social relations generally.[36] The first legal freedom to marry across caste lines was granted by the Special Marriage Act of 1872, which permitted marriage outside caste if the individual asserted that he had no religion or caste. This act was not amended until 1923, but even with new amendments the parties were required to sever their connections with the joint family (thus losing any coparcenary rights). In the 1930s a few states adopted legislation forbidding reprisals by a caste against someone who married outside, and it was not until the Hindu Marriage Disabilities Removal Act of 1946 and the Hindu Marriages Validity Act of 1949 that the bars of religion, caste, subcaste, and sect were finally removed—at least in law.[37]

In Kapadia's sample of teachers, 68 per cent of the 457 answering the question affirmed that "caste is dying out," but about one third of these qualified their statement greatly so that the actual proportion is only about 48 per cent.[38] Only about 11 per cent can be said to be absolutely in favor of eliminating caste considerations in marriage, while some 42 per cent believe that the rigidities should be relaxed considerably.[39] In a village sample of the 1950s, 42 per cent of the villagers and 81 per cent of the "Mill Elite" (holding higher-level jobs in a factory) said that they would be able to be good friends with a person from a lower caste, but 93 per cent of the villagers and 78 per cent of the Mill Elite said that they could not marry a son or daughter to a member of the lower caste. Moreover, 75 per cent of the villagers, 44 per cent of the Mill Elite, and 58 per cent of the Brahmins said that they still believed that a lower caste person was in such a low position because of the sins he committed in a previous life.[40] In a study of 513 university graduates, Kapadia found that 51 per cent claimed to be willing to marry their children outside their own caste, and Patil found a similar percentage in his study of lower-income groups in Bombay.[41] In Ross' educated sample, three fourths of the men were in favor of intercaste marriages, as were about 43 per cent of the women.[42]

As might be expected, in general the urban groups, the educated, and the young are most in favor of dropping these restrictions.

About the same percentages were obtained by the Indian Institute of Public Opinion, which polled samples in Calcutta, rural and urban West Bengal, and Delhi. The polls were designed to ascertain to what extent the fundamental rights of the Indian constitution in Section 15 are actually accepted by the populace. These stipulate the equality of man without regard to religion and caste. The implication of both Sections 15 and 16 would be that women have the same rights as men. The broad conclusion of that poll, relating to widow remarriage, the equality of the sexes with respect to property rights, caste intermarriage, and caste interdining ". . . is not calculated to produce good cheer. In the first place, the Fundamental Rights of the Constitution remain very much a legal fiction."[43] Delhi, the location of the central government, was revealed as the least "progressive" of these areas, while rural West Bengal was revealed as the most progressive.[44]

With reference to dining with members of another caste, an indispensable condition for freedom of courtship, 56 per cent of the rural West Bengali and 34 per cent of the urban said that they would take food and drink from a lower caste, but only 23 per cent and 18 per cent respectively said that members of their family would do so. The corresponding percentages for Calcutta itself were 66 per cent and 36 per cent.[45] In Delhi, 44 per cent said that they would do so, but only 33 per cent said that members of their family would.[46]

With reference to the more intimate step of approving the marriage of a near relation into a lower caste, 33 per cent of the New Delhi sample, 38 per cent of Calcutta, 30 per cent of the urban West Bengali, and 28 per cent of the rural West Bengali said that they would approve a near relation marrying into a *lower* caste.[47] Of course, the percentages are somewhat higher for dining with or marrying into a higher caste.

These are expressions of opinion by a broad section of the populace. Thirty-five to 45 per cent of Kapadia's sample of teachers approved the idea of marrying their children outside caste.[48] He also shows that there are numerous inconsistencies in these opinions. These are, of course, hypothetical questions, and at best express a set of ideals that has come to be accepted in certain circles as "educated and progressive." In fact, however, almost no intercaste marriages take place even now, and most of the few that do occur take place only across the boundaries of subcastes, and not across those of the four great varnas. Morrison reports from his Badlapur study that the thirty-five endogamous castes did not traditionally intermarry or dine together. Dining together is slowly coming to be accepted, but the rule against intermarriage is "strictly adhered to even today."[49] In a survey of 2 thousand urban Hindu households in Bangalore, only nine were found to contain an intercaste marriage, although an analysis at that time of 400 matrimonial advertisements from four English language Indian newspapers showed that one fourth of the males stated that caste was *not* a barrier.[50] In spite of the geographical dispersion of families from Kumbapettai, no intercaste marriages had taken place by the early 1950s.[51]

Indeed, as in the granting of equality to United States Negroes, the laws are passed long before equality is granted, even in public matters like voting or going to school; and, of course, rough equality of opportunity or acceptance in purely work relations and occupations precedes the acceptance of men in more intimate social relations for their personal achievements. Since the 1950s in India are dotted with incident after incident of the refusal by caste Hindus to grant public rights to other castes, it is not yet to be expected that any substantial number would care to go so far as to marry across the caste line.[52]

A majority of the educated Hindus seem to be in favor of freedom of choice *in general*, although under the current social conditions there is little chance of implementing it. Just under half of the single men in Ross' small sample said that they wanted complete freedom of choice, and about half said that they wanted *some* choice; however, only about one third of the women fell into these two categories.[53] Among Kapadia's teacher sample,

152 out of 407 claimed that they had selected their own spouses, but after analyzing the answers he concludes that "the whole data failed to give any idea about the freedom an individual has in the selection of his marriage partner.[54] In the larger Indian Institute of Public Opinion sample, 29 per cent of the rural West Bengali, and 31 per cent of the urban, said that a man should follow his own inclinations if he wished to marry a young woman of his choice. Thirty-eight per cent of the Calcutta sample agreed, but only 12 per cent of the Delhi sample was willing to concede this freedom.[55] Another survey by the Institute in 1955 asked whether the respondents approved of a son or daughter marrying his or her own choice. Thirty-one per cent did not object to granting this liberty. Only 15 per cent of the poorly-educated approved of granting this much freedom, and a fifth of all female respondents agreed. About half of the younger group wished to allow freedom of mate choice to the individual.[56] Since these questions tap only a very general sentiment in favor of freedom, and do not pose even hypothetical reality conditions, we must suppose that the active sentiment in favor of freedom of choice is still fairly low, and the reality of its expression most minimal. Under the traditional system, the caste *panchayat* or council reviewed most important matters of familial concern including marriage, so that even if a parent was willing to permit his son or daughter some freedom in marriage, the family would be under penalty of severe reprisals if that choice were judged to be wrong by the caste group. The girl, of course, would have no opportunity to make a free choice, and the young man would not have even been able to find someone to carry out the necessary rituals for marriage. Caste councils are losing their power, especially since the national government has become increasingly successful in establishing village councils to handle village affairs, thus bypassing not only the separate *panchayats*, but especially the dominant power of the Brahmins. Of course, the success is not complete, but the movement in the direction of cross-caste councils is notable, and the village councils are gradually establishing their rule throughout India. Although the parents need not fear the caste group so much as formerly, and the young men and women can at least sometimes establish an economic base independently, in fact their social relations are so structured that they have little opportunity to mix in an equalitarian way with a wide range of people of similar tastes and education.

These restrictions have developed, in fact, in answer to the breakdown of caste that is visible to the observer. Within the factory, the machine knows no caste, but social relations may be dominated by it, and company housing may be arranged by caste groupings. Informal organizations spring up within the factory to enable those of the same caste to engage in recreation together. Social and philanthropic organizations of many types make it easy for the individual to find a fairly complete world within his own caste grouping, even though he has moved from his village of origin. Those who vaguely favor intercaste marriage and freedom of intercourse between castes nevertheless seem to be in favor of caste charities and philanthropies, caste associations, caste socials, and even caste magazines—the very social organizations that maintain its closed character.[57] Ghurye, too, speaks of "caste-patriotism," by which the caste develops new methods of controlling their members or asserting their rights in the new world in which some of the old caste controls have weakened.[58]

The relevance of these developments is not so much that caste inter-marriage remains rare, as that the opportunity of coming to know other individuals of similar tastes, talents, and achievements, and to choose one's spouse on that basis, will continue to be hampered in the future. We wish to emphasize, however, that we believe these developments to be essentially *transitory*. We do not believe that the castes will succeed in maintaining their hold over freedom of choice indefinitely. Now, however, little control has been lost by the caste groupings and the elders who are their representatives within the family; the loss of control occurs mainly among the highly educated where the elders concede rights to the young because of their own ideological position.

The dowry system is another restriction on freedom of choice. It was officially abolished in May, 1960 by a bill which actually provides punishment in fines or imprisonment for giving, taking, demanding, or abetting in the giving or taking of a dowry.[59] But it is very unlikely that this bill will be implemented immediately. In November, 1955 the Indian Institute of Public Opinion asked a sample of over 11 hundred respondents whether they approved of the dowry system, and whether they thought it should be abolished. Sixty-five per cent said that they did not approve of the dowry system, and the same proportion said that it should be abolished.[60] As might be expected, *females* show less approval of the dowry system than males (76 per cent do *not* approve of it as against 60 per cent of the males); after all it is the dowry that often becomes a barrier to their marriage.

Interestingly enough, however, the poorly educated are far more strongly opposed to the dowry system. Ninety per cent of those below 35 years old are in favor of its abolition, as against 58 per cent of the well educated above 35. Presumably the educated person is less opposed to the dowry system because its present day pattern of operation confers advantages on the individual: educated males command a higher dowry.

On the question of arranged marriage, a small middle-class sample was interviewed in 1935. Fifty-six per cent of the sample of 345 were in favor; among women, 65 per cent were in favor, although the sample included only sixty-six women. As can be seen in the other survey data which follow, some change in these opinions has taken place since that time.[61]

2. Marriages With Relatives

It can be predicted that any movement toward a conjugal family and freedom of courtship is likely to reduce the percentage of marriages between close relatives. The range of possible eligibles becomes much wider, and freer social intercourse reduces the simple statistical chance that a given individual will fall in love with and marry a close relative. So simple a prediction cannot be easily applied to the Indian case, however. In certain ways, the problem is analogous to that of China. If one were to predict marriage patterns from the traditional and ideal limitations on marriages in *gotra* and *sapinda*, one might suppose that marriages with close relatives simply did not occur. Then it would follow that any movement toward freedom of courtship would *expand* the number of possible spouses among both kin and nonkin. Indeed, Indian legislation has moved in that direction, by removing traditional restrictions.

If, however, as in China the bars against marrying close relatives represent a set of "public values," while a less formal and domestic set of values approves the marrying of certain close relatives, then expansion of the total range of eligibles would *reduce* the actual number of marriages with close kin. The latter seems closer to present-day reality.

Under some extremely orthodox religious formulations, marriage into any of the four *gotram* of the grandparents is forbidden, so that a man could not marry any cross cousin. For example, mother's brother's daughter would belong to his mother's *gotra* (before marriage). If the *sapinda* rule (of five degrees from the father or three degrees from the mother) is followed, the mother's brother's daughter would not be a possible spouse, because she would be separated from a common ancestor by only two degrees (that is, the boy's mother's father and his mother's brother's father are the same man, so that the girl's mother is separated from the common ancestor by only two degrees). Even if the more relaxed limitations that Karvé cites as "the actual rule of marriage" are followed, one may not marry the children of mother's siblings.[62] Then, the daughter of mother's brother or sister is eliminated. The daughter of father's brother and father's sister is, of course, eliminated because they are in the direct patriline.

How closely are these provisions obeyed? Quantitative data are not available, but a selection of qualitative materials suggests that matrilateral cross-cousin marriage has in fact been fairly common and some other forms of cousin marriage are also to be found here and there in India.

No survey of the issue is aimed at in these brief comments, but rather the specification of a problem in social change. In assessing the amount and direction of family change, it is necessary first to ascertain the actual family patterns, and, where possible, the real values of various groups, not merely the values expounded by philosophers of ethics and religion. China and India seem to be alike in that the public tradition appears to have forbidden cross-cousin marriage, while folk custom either tolerated or approved it. Indeed, we suppose that in many peasant societies with geographically immobile populations, some form of cousin marriage is common and given some approval.

Dube found that 18 per cent of 340 Hindu marriages in his village were cross-cousin, and that it was the preferred form of marriage. Nearly half of the Moslem marriages were cousin marriages (both parallel and cross). However, the *gotra* rules, as Dube explains them, did not forbid such marriages.[63]

In analyzing traditional writings, Altekar notes that in the Deccan area, marriage with mother's brother's daughter was "long established . . . though it conflicted with the rule of sapindata."[64] Kapadia cites two eleventh-century commentators: one asserted that southerners married their mother's brother's daughter *or* father's sister's daughter; another stated that a similar pattern (that is, marrying a kinsman three degrees removed) was also found in Saurashtra (that is, in the north).[65]

Kapadia also asserts, again referring to the *past*, that "cross-cousin marriage seems to have prevailed over a large area in Northern India," as well as in the south.[66] He later cites Ghurye as asserting that cross-cousin marriage continued outside of India's "middle region" long after it had ceased to be practiced there, and as asserting that except among the Marathi-speaking peoples, cross-cousin marriage has become relatively rare.[67] In a more recent publication, Ghurye lists six groups among whom "marriage is permitted in the line of one's mother's sister," but says that elsewhere in India such marriages are prohibited.[68] Apparently this custom was also found among the Dravidians (supposedly the original inhabitants of India). As noted earlier, the 1955 Hindu Marriage Act still permits this type of marriage if local custom allows it.

However, Karvé's summary shows clearly that cross-cousin marriage is more widespread than these comments imply. The following list gives only a small sampling of the many regions and groups in which this pattern is still found:[69]

CENTRAL ZONE

Rajputs
Kathiawad and Gujarat among the Kathi
Ahir, Gadahva Charan, and Garasia
Maharashtra, among peoples of the Maratha-Kunbi complex*
Orissa, among some of the agricultural castes

SOUTHERN ZONE

Havig Brahmins of Karnatak
Kallar of Tamilnad
Reddi of Telingana*
Karnatak, most agricultural and lower artisan castes
Gonds
Koyas†

* Note also the variation in the Maratha-Kunbi region, especially with reference to patrilateral cross-cousin marriage.

† Karvé, *op. cit.*, pp. 172, 191–192, 221, 228, 231–232, 247. She notes however that in some instances one subpart of the same caste cannot participate in cross-cousin marriage.

Karvé relates this pattern to hypergamy by noting that if a woman married into a higher-class family, she might hope eventually to bring another girl (e.g., her brother's daughter) as a bride to the heir of the family (who would thus be marrying his mother's brother's daughter). She also notes that cross-cousin marriage as well as uncle-niece marriage "is beginning to be considered as outmoded and a thing to be ashamed of among those groups who have come in contact with the Northern Indians and the English speaking people."[70] We are not competent to explain why this pattern is so widespread in the face of generally accepted public prohibitions, but we do not believe that it is a simple "deviation" from approved practice. We rather suppose that these behavior patterns are supported by local values. Moreover, we believe that some structural elements in India's patrilineal kinship system give it emotional support. First, the marriage of a mother's brother's daughter to a father's sister's son repeats the relationship of deference and respect which is due from the matriline. The woman's parents are expected to be grateful to the man's family for marrying her, and this harmony is created in the next generation if the daughter moves in the same direction. By contrast, if a daughter from the father's line were to be married to the mother's brother's son, the deference would be reversed and disharmony would be created. More important, however, is the ease of social relations between a boy and his mother's brother, as contrasted with the patriarchal respect in his relations with the father's brother or the father's line generally. The permissiveness on both sides makes for a closeness and simplicity of social interaction in which a further union of the two lines may come to seem desirable.[71] It must be emphasized, however, that though such a line of social-psychological reasoning helps to explain why such a union might seem desirable, it does not explain why it would develop as a *preferred* social arrangement—that is, an explicit part of the system.

Without pursuing still other forms of kin marriages in detail, it seems clear that matrilateral cross-cousin marriage is socially accepted in many regions and among many peoples of India, although it is not generally approved in publicly accepted formulations about mate choice. Since these customs were followed in the past, we would suppose that greater freedom of personal choice among young Hindus will gradually tend to reduce not only their number but also local approval of the customs.

3. Polygamy

Both polygyny and polyandry exist in India, but as in the other major civilizations considered in this study both are declining in importance. Polyandry was most common in societies outside the dominant Hindu cultural patterns, such as the Todas, Coorgs, the Central Nayars (not, apparently, the southern and northern Nayars) of the Malabar Coast, the Khasis and Garos of Assam, etc.[72] In Hindu society, polygyny was rare, and in modern times monogamy has been the ideal. Polygyny was perhaps more acceptable in India than in China, where monogamy was the only legal form of marriage but concubinage was institutionalized. Socially, concubinages aroused little or no criticism, and the concubine could even have an approved position in the household. On the other hand, polygyny was not so acceptable a marriage pattern in India as in the Arabic countries.

Several indices suggest that the Hindu cultural ideal of marriage was monogamous. The Vedic gods are monogamous. The rules for the performance of domestic religious rituals do not allow for the possibility of an additional wife. Mutual conjugal fidelity is emphasized in the wedding hymn and in philosophical discussions of marriage. Rationalizations of an additional wife are often based upon the barrenness of the first wife, and the necessity of a son.[73] That the preferred pattern was monogamy was also suggested by the fact that the additional wife or wives were likely to be from a lower caste. That is, there was not a full equality of social position between the second wife and husband, so that his relationship to the two wives was not the same. Perhaps the most extreme polygynous pattern was found in Bengal, where the Kulin Brahmins had many wives, but these were accepted from the Maha-Brahmins, a lower-ranking section of Brahmins.

Traditional discussions of polygyny often refer to the second wife as "superseding" the first wife, rather than simply joining the household. Prabhu, Altekar, and Kapadia cite the conditions permitting a second wife, which are often simply rules for a type of divorce or supersession: the barrenness of the wife, bearing a child to another man, drinking, disease, etc.[74] In such a household, the first wife seems to have had an ambiguous status, rather than (as in most fully polygynous societies) being the "first wife" or the chief female in the household. As in other major civilizations, it was only the rich and powerful men who ever had more than one wife at a time, and it is not clear that all the later women who formed a harem were indeed *wives*. The poor did not have more than one spouse. In modern times, however, the attitudes of Indian leaders, in the vanguard of public opinion, have steadily moved toward Western opposition to polygyny. Consequently those who have practiced it have generally been the less-educated, rural men who had the wealth to afford more than one spouse.

The extent of polygyny cannot be ascertained from census data of the past century. The 1901 Census comments, "The rules which in theory govern polygamy are well known, but in practice, except among wealthy Muhammadans, a second wife is very rarely taken unless the first one is barren or suffers from some incurable disease; even then, in the case of Hindus, a man has frequently to obtain the consent of his caste *panchayat* and occasionally that of his first spouse also."[75]

At that time, there were (taking all religions together) 1,011 wives to 1,000 husbands, but the normal errors of census-taking do not permit a precise inference that these 11 wives were all secondary parts of a polygynous household. A prostitute who had entered into a ritual marriage, or a woman whose husband had cast her out, might nevertheless claim to be married; or a married man might deny that he had a wife.

The 1911 Census Report comments, ". . . Sometimes polygamy is a regular practice, as with the Kunnuvans and Kaikolans of Madras. But most castes object to their members having more than one wife, except for special reasons, such as the failure of the first wife to bear a son, or her affliction with some incurable disease or infirmity. In such cases the consent of the caste *Panchayat* must generally be obtained." Sometimes the second wife is a younger sister of the first and in one caste it was the practice for a man to obtain an additional wife when he succeeded to landed property. And, of course, some polygyny occurred because of the levirate.[76] However, these comments and the data on civil status do not permit any inferences as to the number of polygynous marriages per thousand men.

In his north Indian village, Dube found only seven polygynous Hindu households out of approximately 500,[77] and comments that "childlessness and inability to produce a male child" may lead to a man establishing a polygynous household. In an Agri village (south of Bombay) Kale found only five households out of 564 in which wives shared a common household, and fourteen additional instances in which only the second wife lived with her husband.[78] In this village, one progressive group had attempted to imitate the educated classes and eradicate polygyny some ten years prior to the study, but they were unsuccessful. Many of the cases Kale cites would be counted as "divorces" by a Western observer.

During the nineteenth century, one minor force pressing toward a reduction in polygyny came not from Western influences, but from caste mobility: Castes that attempted to rise would sometimes refuse to continue giving their daughters to a higher subcaste. That is, they would in effect deny that it *was* higher, now that they were laying claim to a better social rank. Such hypergamous unions meant often, though not always, polygynous marriages, since families from an equal caste would not usually wish to give their daughters as second wives. Thus, a source of extra wives was cut off from the formerly "higher" subcaste; and the formerly "lower" group became endogamous.

A succession of laws in India has indicated the growing rejection of polygyny as an accepted marriage arrangement, although the laws began long before any substantial influence from the modern complex of urbanization and industrialization.

Under the special Marriage Act of 1872, it was required that neither party to a marriage have at the time a husband or wife living, and further provided that a polygamous marriage could be dissolved under the Indian Divorce Act of 1869. This legislation had little effect, because the Divorce Act required that the person attempting to avail himself of its provisions be outside any Hindu caste or religion (that is, most commonly, a convert to Christianity). Successive amendments did not improve matters much; under the Amendment of 1923, the individual had to forego his connection with his joint family (and thus with joint family property). Consequently, no remedy was actually available if a party felt injured by a polygamous arrangement.[79]

Madras passed laws to prohibit polygamy among the matrilineal societies (primarily Nayar) in 1932, and among the Nambudiri Brahmins in 1933, although the 1933 Act permitted a man to take a second wife if his wife had become an outcaste, had not borne a child within five years of marriage, or had been inflicted with an incurable disease for more than five years. In the 1940s and early 1950s, several states (Bombay, Madras, Saurashtra, etc.) passed laws prohibiting polygamy. Some castes also forbade polygyny.[80] The 1955 Hindu Marriage Act stipulated that neither party may already have a living spouse when a marriage takes place, and that any marriage which violates this condition is void. Moreover, bigamy is punishable under the Indian Penal Code.

It can be supposed that some polygynous households may be found here and there in rural India, but this kind of marriage arrangement has been on the decline for a long time and is now disappearing entirely.

Public opinion data on this matter were obtained in 1955 from people of Bengal and Delhi. Sixty-seven per cent of the west Bengali and 80 per cent of both the urban west Bengali and the Calcutta respondents stated that they disapproved of polygamous marriages. In Delhi, 73 per cent disapproved. For an overwhelming majority, disapproval was based on grounds of morality.[81]

Polyandry is generally supposed to have been customary among the pre-Dravidian or Dravidian indigenous peoples of the Indian subcontinent, but few full-scale descriptions of them are to be found. For centuries, these systems fascinated British administrators and other foreign visitors, who have bequeathed to us a host of observations, inferences, and suppositions, some of which seem rather unlikely. Any summary of these societies must rely on old travelers' and administrators' reports rather than on studies by professional anthropologists. There are only a few studies of polyandrous systems, focused almost entirely on the system as it once existed or almost entirely on its present state, but these do not attempt to describe how the system has been altered over time. Contemporary Indian sociologists have not tried to measure changing public opinion among polyandrous groups.

In 1901, polyandry was already falling into disrepute among the Nayars.[82] At that time it was still found among the Todas of the Nilgiri Hills described in Rivers' famous report. Since that period there has been a gradual shift to polygyny and monogamy, with some persistence of polyandry.[83]

Polyandry was "still more or less common along the whole of the Himalayan area from Kashmir to the eastern extremity of Asia" in 1901.[84] Even at that time, the suggestion was made in the Census Report that in Sikkim there appeared to be a gradual transition away from fraternal polyandry. Generally, the well-to-do men did not follow the polyandrous system. No data exist as to the actual percentage of polyandrous households in the outlying areas, where most polyandrous systems were found. In the 1911 Census Report, Gait notes that fraternal polyandry was supposed to have been common "a few years ago among the Gujars of the *United Provinces*," but by the time the Report was written it had died out.[85] Gait also includes some notes from the Superintendent of the Punjab, which describes polyandry among the hill people as well as among some lower castes, but which also includes a newspaper report from the Simla Hills showing clearly the cooperation between those natives who wished to persuade polyandrous groups to follow the traditional Hindu laws (against polyandry), and the British commissioners of the time.[86]

According to Kapadia, polyandry has almost died out among the Khasas (in Dehra Dun, United Provinces) except for a few small areas.[87] Probably, a closer examination of several supposedly polyandrous societies will disclose that they were not actually polyandrous, nor that they have changed. The reports of travelers, explorers, administrators, and clergymen often reported as "polyandrous" any system in which there was some tolerance of sexual access to a brother's wife. As we shall see, however, this was a widespread pattern in India.

Even without full reports from all of India's relevant, outlying societies, the gradual disappearance of polyandry seems evident, wherever such a society has gradually been drawn into the mainstream of Hindu social organization. Doubtless this change would occur under industrialization, but in nearly all of these instances, the change began to take place before any considerable amount of industrialization in India as a whole, and usually before any industrialization among the groups in question. On the other hand, both Westerners and Indians who followed traditional laws and rituals found this behavior shocking and, where possible, objected to it by law, criticism, and religious persuasion. At the present time, of course, the 1955 Hindu Marriage Act makes polyandry as well as polygyny illegal, but this merely sets the seal on a process which was well underway before the law was passed.

4. Fertility and Contraception

When the religious dogma of a culture proscribes the existence of sons to guarantee the father's entrance into heaven, a high mortality society* requires that many children be born.

Gandhi asserted, in agreeing to the necessity of birth control in India, that it was superstitious to suppose that the *religious* tradition required large families. But although the religious proscriptions have not required high fertility, many social patterns have created it, and there were no cultural proscriptions to counteract it. Almost everyone in the society married, and married early. The wife obtained a higher position in her husband's family

* In 1900, 232 out of a thousand infants born died within the year.

only after the birth of sons, and couples with many sons were admired. Contraceptives were not used, and abortions were rare. As in all societies, some social and cultural patterns kept fertility below the possible maximum, but on the whole these did not contribute much. According to Hindu philosophy, there were four religiously proscribed stages (*Ashramas*) of life. In the third, the man and wife were supposed to live in a forest close to their home and presumably not engage in sexual relations; in the fourth, the man was to become a wandering beggar. Few, however, followed this ideal, and in any event the couple would have been middle-aged by the time of the third *Ashrama* so they would not be having children anyway. Some men, but almost no women, were permanently dedicated to an ascetic life, but asceticism was probably a small cause for reduced fertility. Both polygyny and polyandry reduced it, but few Indians had these kinds of marriages. Fertility was reduced by the long visits of the wife to her family, but since these often coincided with pregnancy and childbirth, again the effect on fertility must have been negligible. Thus, as in the past, the main thrust of the Hindu social and cultural pattern is in the direction of high fertility.

The situation of the past half-century can be summarized briefly. The "official" birth rate dropped from 1911–1920 to 1941–1950, but when these figures are corrected to agree with census and mortality data, the trend disappears. Table V-1 presents corrected figures.

Table V-1
Corrected Birth Rate, India, 1911–1950*

Decade	Corrected Birth Rate Per Thousand Population
1911–1920	45.5
1921–1930	42.4
1931–1940	45.2
1941–1950	38.3
1950	40.0

* A. Ghosh, "Demographic Trends in India During 1901–1950," *Population Studies*, 10, no. 3 (1956), 217–236; and "The Trend of the Birth Rate in India, 1911–1950," in *idem*, 10, no. 1 (1956), 53–68. Ghosh presents in these articles the procedure of correcting the official birth rates. He asserts that there has been a "consistent deterioration in registration throughout the period." For 1950, see S. Chandrasekhar, *Population and Planned Parenthood in India*, 2d ed. (London: Allen & Unwin, 1961).

Chandrasekhar also presents a recalculation of birth rates from 1901–1910 to 1951–1956. His figures for the earliest decade are somewhat higher than those obtained by Ghosh (in the range of 45 to 48 per thousand), but they are close. For the 1951–1956 period, he gives the figure of 40.7 per thousand, which suggests little or no change from the previous decade, but a very slight drop from prior decades.[88]

On the basis of these data, the major conclusion about fertility patterns is that there has been little or no change. The national government has recently begun to introduce contraceptive techniques, however, in a serious effort to forestall the inevitable catastrophe the continuing population growth must create. Since the Indian leaders took over the government from the British, they have generally come to agree that a net addition of 7 or 8 million in population every year cannot be taken care of by the slow growth of industrialization, and, in order to raise the level of living (whatever the growth of industry), a cut in population expansion is necessary.

Before considering the changes in behavior and values regarding fertility control, let us look more closely at the stability of India's birth-rate differential. The spread of contraceptives in certain segments of the population has followed the pattern familiar in the West: They have come to be used by urban people more than rural people, by middle- and upper-economic strata more than by the lower, by the better-educated more than by the illiterate, and by higher castes more than by lower castes. Correspondingly, the birth rates are higher in exactly the segments of the population where the Western observer would predict them to be. There is no evidence that contraceptives are very widely used among even the more progressive strata, or that use of them has begun to trickle down to the less advantaged. It seems likely that only in the last decade has the movement toward contraception begun to gather speed.

At least some fertility differences were caused by indigenous social forces. As an illustration, Davis shows that fertility lowers with increased size of city, and furthermore demonstrates that the differences cannot be attributed to the lack of women in the cities. Even when only the currently married women are considered, the difference between rural and urban, or between small and very large cities, remains. This does not prove, however, that contraception can be expected to spread to the rural area, since these differences have remained stable over the fifty-year period from 1891–1941.[89] In other words, the differences cannot be attributed to contraceptives.

Davis also attempted to ascertain whether Brahmins and other caste Hindus had a lower fertility than those of lower castes. As expected, the higher castes do have a lower fertility, but the differences among castes are very small when only *married* women of fertile ages are considered. The lesser fertility among these higher castes seems to come from their ability to prevent widow remarriage.[90]

A similar analysis shows that fertility is lower as the percentage of female literacy increases. But here again, the difference seems to be due to the higher proportion of widows among the more literate, indicating that the more literate groups were also more successful in keeping their widows from remarrying. The differences are almost eliminated when the fertility of only the *married* women is considered.[91]

When fertility differentials seem to grow from the social forces indigenous to a traditional civilization, and not from the spread of contraceptive practices, we would expect to find a slightly higher fertility toward the upper-income strata, if only because of better chances of survival among married adults and the greater fecundity among women owing to their being better fed, better protected, and so on. In the Poona Survey of 1951 and the Kolhapur study of 1945, a slight correlation between income and fertility was found. The first analysis of the Kolhapur data suggested that there was no difference, but this conclusion was based on the use of too many income classes. In both studies, when only two large income classes were used, the fertility of the groups with better incomes was slightly higher.[92] This relation merely illustrates a point made earlier in a discussion of the Western pattern—that within a given cultural group with an accepted norm for the proper number of children, those with larger incomes will have a higher fertility. On the other hand, where the norms do not as yet proscribe low fertility, then various cultural and social factors *not* explicitly concerned with fertility may determine the differences in birth rates among various groups.

Indian leaders, aided and encouraged by Western social scientists, have made a serious attempt to lower India's fertility. Since it was generally assumed that the Indian population would find any use of contraceptives or any propaganda in favor of their use distasteful and offensive, a handful of studies have attempted to ascertain the extent to which various segments of the population are willing to learn about contraceptives, and to accept and use them. Different types of birth-control propaganda and contraceptive techniques have been tried in different areas in an effort to ascertain the optimum system. Of course, most of the research work has been carried out not by the Indian government, but by Indian and Western social scientists, supported by both Indian and Western funds.

At this time, when millions of women in the world have already begun to use a contraceptive pill with apparent success, it is tempting to suppose that many physiological and physical problems have been solved, and that it is now only necessary to make the pill available. As Davis so pungently expresses it: "From a purely physical point of view birth control is easier than death control. It involves the management of only one type of germ and only one kind of contagion, as against hundreds of types in health work. It involves only one period of life, as against all periods subject to disease; and only one type of medical specialist, as against dozens in fighting sickness."[93] However, the social and cultural problems in persuading a peasant, largely illiterate population to *use* contraceptives are far greater than that of *developing* an adequate contraceptive. We have only to look at the slow, steady decline in birth rates of France and the United States from the early part of the nineteenth century, to know that even the crudest contraceptive technique will have a profound effect on the general fertility of a nation.

Japan has been able to reduce its birth rate quickly through the use of both abortion and contraceptives, but the idea of birth control had been acceptable to both urban and rural Japanese for hundreds of years. The notion of birth control in India was simply not part of the cultural tradition, although there were no specific rules against it. Most people accepted their children as the will of God.

This is not to say that contraception movements were entirely absent in the Indian context. A few Indian leaders began to press for instruction in birth control even a half-century ago. By the 1930s, centers for the dissemination of birth control information had been set up in several Indian cities.[94]

By 1946 the Health Survey and Development Committee had agreed that contraception was necessary and the first Five Year Plan (1951–1956) envisaged a full program of family planning.[95] The second Five Year Plan aimed at establishing some 300 urban and 2 thousand rural birth control clinics. This goal was not reached, but by 1961 there were over 600 urban and some 1 thousand rural family planning centers.

In 1951, one of the first experiments in family planning was undertaken through the offices of the World Health Organization. This experiment attempted to ascertain whether rural Indian women could learn the rhythm method, since at that time the Ministry of Health was "unwilling to consider any other type of family planning."[96] The experiment was not a success. But this was primarily because of technical difficulties. The method required some observation of the menstrual cycle over several months, but often the women had become pregnant during the observation period.

The many studies of attitudes toward family planning over the past decade do show that there is little serious *moral* objection to the use of contraceptives. The main reason for their restricted use is that most people do not know anything about them, and are not seeking to find out about them.

In a study of Bengali women in the late 1940s, C. Chandra Sekar and Mukta Sen found that some 38 per cent of the upper-class urban Hindu women had tried contraception, whereas 60 per cent said they had no desire to do so. The rural women and the lower-middle-class Moslem women overwhelmingly expressed no desire to use contraceptives.[97] Earlier in the 1940s, Desai had asked a small sample of middle-class Gujarati women in the city of Bombay about their attitudes on birth control. Twenty-one per cent were against it and 38.5 per cent were in favor of it, but an additional 31 per cent were in favor of "self-restraint"—the method that Gandhi approved.[98] In an enquiry into the attitudes of lower-middle-class salaried persons in Bombay during the 1950s, only about 12 per cent under 35 years of age said that contraceptives should not be allowed to married persons even if they desired to use them. Among those 35 years and over, some 31 per cent expressed this opposition. As in many other areas of family customs, the young are somewhat more radical.[99]

The Poona Survey in the early 1950s found "no strong organized and widespread opposition to birth-control on religious, moral, or other grounds."[100] Of 850 urban males, only nine thought contraceptives were immoral and fifty-nine believed it to be against the will of God. Among 855 *non*city males, eight believed them to be immoral and eighty-five to be against the will of God. A study in the cities of Lucknow and Kanpur found that some 40 per cent of high-caste Hindus in the upper income levels had *ever* practiced contraception. However, only one fourth of those in a slightly lower economic stratum had done so, and about 12 per cent of a still lower group, which they call "class III." Almost none of the lower-class Hindus had done so.[101]

A more recent study has attempted to pose an extremely negative question to university students. It asked whether they approved of the statement that it is "unwise and against our religion and culture" to use any means to control birth. Sixty per cent of the men disagreed or strongly disagreed with this statement, and about 70 per cent of the women did so. It must be kept in mind, however, that these are university students in one of the most progressive of the former native states.[102]

Morrison, in a summary of the surveys made up through the mid-1950s, notes that studies in Bombay State, urban Poona, Kolaba district, Nasick district, and Satara North, covering both urban and rural populations, show that from about 20 to 30 per cent of the rural people were favorable to the idea of contraception. In two further studies in Uttar Pradesh and Mysore, about three fifths of the mothers wanted to *know* about contraception, and, in Mysore, about the same fraction of the couples were willing to *use* them; but these percentages are higher than in other studies and the sample is rather indeterminate.[103]

Morrison's own study in a Maharashtrian village focuses on the more important variable, the number of *sons* that a given couple *already* has. The importance of this could be seen from a World Health Organization study in the 1950s in New Delhi, since in an upper-middle-class area (Lodi Colony) eight tenths of the women who were not pregnant but who already had three or more children did *not* desire any additional offspring. The importance of the variable may also be seen in the fact that young couples do not use contraceptives consistently, even when they are generally favorable to their use, because they have not had enough sons. Morrison found that 47 per cent of those with two living *male* children did not want any more children, and that 75 per cent of those with three to seven did not desire any more.[104] The desire to have no more children also increases with age, so that some 95 per cent of those over 35 years of age did not want more children. About two fifths of these wanted to know about an effective contraceptive. Women with more education show more willingness to use contraceptives.[105]

Over 90 per cent of the uneducated males had no interest in learning a method of avoiding another child. In general, the outcastes and the agricultural castes were less willing than other groups (14 per cent and 17 per cent respectively were willing to learn about their use).[106] An ironic sidelight on this matter is that, due to a misreading of the Law of Manu, the village technique for avoiding unwanted children was to practice self-restraint for the first fifteen days of the menstrual cycle. Thus, when they did engage in sexual intercourse, both the women and the men were likely to be most fertile.

In 1958, the Indian Institute of Public Opinion made a survey among 400 residents of Calcutta and 100 residents of villages just outside the city. Unfortunately, this sample was taken primarily among the middle class, so that it exaggerates the degree of acceptance and use of contraception among the general population. Since its findings parallel those of other studies cited here, only a few findings from this study need to be cited: Four fifths of the urban residents said that they knew something about contraception while 44 per cent of the rural residents said that they didn't. An overwhelming majority, over 95 per cent in both areas, said that "a planned family would give relief."[107] Slightly less than a third in both areas knew of the existence of family Planning Centers, and only 12.5 per cent of the urban respondents and 6 per cent of the rural had actually visited such a center. Surprisingly enough, three fourths of the urban women and 59 per cent of those in rural areas claimed that they had talked with their husbands about the number of children they would like to have.

Half the urban women and 11 per cent of the rural women said that they had used some method of family planning at some time. Among the urban residents who had ever used any method at all, about 85 per cent claimed that they still practiced some method, but only one third of these were using a method which could be described as reliable.[108] Apparently rural respondents were not asked about the method employed.

Several conclusions emerge from a consideration of these and other related studies: [109]

1. The more educated and the economically well off groups approve the use of contraceptives, but the majority do not use them as yet. No large segment of the Indian population actually uses contraceptives regularly.

2. Although a majority of those with many sons are in favor of limiting birth *when they are asked,* only a tiny minority from the vast multitude of the lower castes and classes are *actively* in favor of contraception, and almost no one follows any modern contraceptive practice. Most do not even know such techniques exist, and in many cases the necessary materials and appliances are not yet available.

3. The government has been pursuing a vigorous policy of promoting contraceptives, but the thousand rural clinics are distributed among some half a million villages, so that their influence is negligible at present.

4. If Morrison's general position is valid, about half of the women with two living sons are *willing* to use contraceptives. However, a willingness to use them is not the same as *using* them regularly. Moreover, even granting the willingness is equivalent to regular use, this would mean that on the average only half the Indian couples would begin to be *ready* to use contraceptives before they had an average of four living children. This would still mean an extremely high fertility, perhaps about as high as at the present time.

The generally optimistic tone of reports on attitudes toward contraceptives comes primarily from the fact that there seems to be no strong ideological opposition to their use. On the other hand, the amount of apathy is very great, and the planning of births has not yet become a normal part of Indian family life.

The uneducated Hindu, like his counterpart in other countries, sees no *immediate* advantage to limiting births, and indeed he is correct. His standard of living does not go up as soon as he begins to use contraceptives. Indeed, at their present cost, his living standard would immediately drop. He cannot rationally be shown that by limiting births *now* his income will *increase* in the future. The obstacles against the success of these campaigns are many, and there is no reason to expect a quick alteration of the birth rate. Nevertheless, pressures toward the use of contraceptives are increasing. There is a process of education going on owing to the word-of-mouth spread of knowledge about even sporadic efforts to lower the birth rate and to disseminate information about contraceptives. Moreover, the mobility strivings of Indians at all caste and class levels are no less strong than in other countries, and the upper strata's example is not lost on those in the lower strata. We would expect, then, that a corrected birth rate for the present five-year period will show that some drop has occurred since ten years ago, and we predict that there will be a further decrease in the next five years.

5. Age at Marriage

Preadolescent marriage of daughters was the ideal for caste Hindus. Apparently a majority actually succeeded in accomplishing this. From 1860 to 1890, for example, the "proper" age at marriage was 8 for girls and 12 for boys.[110] The mean age at marriage around 1890 was reported to be 12.5 years for girls and 19.6 for boys. Since these figures were calculated from the ages reported to the 1891 census takers, it is safe to assume that the real ages were somewhat lower because the census takers were representatives of the British Government, which was known to disapprove of child marriage.[111]

In a study of 515 teachers, whose families may be expected to have been most affected by the ideology of later marriage, 55 per cent of those married before 1920 had done so *before* age 13.[112] Although there are great variations by caste and region, the Brahmin ideal of early marriage was followed equally closely by the untouchable harijans or outcastes. A generation ago, 42 to 57 per cent of the Bengali untouchable girls aged 7 to 13 were widowed or married; 26 to 46 per cent of those in the United Provinces; 53 to 55 per cent of those in Bihar; and 16 to 28 per cent of those in the Punjab region. In these provinces during 1931, the percentages for untouchables were higher than among the Brahmin girls in this age group.[113] In the female 14–16 age group, over 80 per cent among the outcaste groups were married or widowed, with the exception of three groups in the Punjab—and here the percentages ranged from 62 to 73.

The social reformers who, in the 1890s, began to advocate later marriage for girls were not successful at first; but in contrast to the few isolated voices to be found sporadically in still earlier decades, this minority continued to struggle. Change in the age at marriage has been considerable in India, but it has been an ideological struggle of some intensity in which the laws have been consistently ahead of folk practice.

In the successive laws aimed at raising the age at marriage, three main themes may be seen: the preposterousness (in the view of Western-educated people) of marriage at 8 or 9 years of age; the impropriety of sexual intercourse at an early age; and the tragedy of being a widow in the early teens. (We shall discuss the problem of widow remarriage in a later section.) The first two themes are intertwined closely, because, under the usual pattern, the girl returned to her parents' home after the marriage ceremony. She spent from one to several years there, until the *gauna* ceremony initiated the couple's cohabitation. In the North Indian village of Rampur, Lewis found that most girls married from 12 to 13 years of age, but the *gauna* ceremony did not take place until about three years later. He also found that although the age at marriage was rising, the period between marriage and cohabitation was shortening.[114] Indeed, this delay was sometimes the defense used by Indian apologists, who asserted that since marriage did not ordinarily initiate sexual intercourse, very young ages at marriage were not deplorable.

In fact, however, the girl had little choice in the matter, was taught to obey her husband, and was in no position to oppose him or his family. Indian leaders were aware that, whatever the ideal of restraint, most young men did introduce their wives to sexual intercourse at an early age. One study of only a generation ago, and another more recent one, show clearly that in spite of the delay the Hindu girl began her sex life early. In a relatively late-marrying (13–19 years) middle-class Bombay sample, Ghurye found that in 47 per cent of the marriages sexual intercourse began within a month after the marriage. In this sample, marriage occurred at 13 years or earlier for 17 per cent, and between 14 to 19 years for 70 per cent.[115] In Gunial B. Desai's study of Gujerati women during the 1940s, 40 per cent of the women had had a child within one year of marriage. Five per cent had a child at age 14, 10 per cent at 15, and 16 per cent at 16.[116] There is little reason to suppose that fifty years ago husbands waited until still later ages to begin sexual intercourse, since parents were supposed to send their married daughter to her husband not long after her first menstruation.

The important laws relating to this change are *indexes* of changing values or attitudes among the elite; the most significant appear to be the following:

1860: Indian Penal Code stipulated that sexual intercourse with a wife under 10 years of age was rape.

1894: Mysore government forbade arranging, or helping to arrange, the marriage of a girl who had not completed 8 years of age; the husband was also liable, if over 18 years of age.

1904: Baroda Early Marriage Prevention Act stipulated 12 years as the girl's minimum age, but her guardians might petition for an exception if her age was above 9 years (two thirds of the nearly 700 petitions in the first year were granted).

1918: Indore State proscribed the ages of 14 for boys and 12 for girls, as a minimum.

1921: British India began to consider comparable bills, but none was passed until the Child Marriage Restraint Act of 1929 (Sarda Act), stipulating the ages of 18 for boys and 14 for girls. However, complainants had to post a bond until the Amended Act of 1938.

1929: The Sarda Act of British India and the Baroda Amendment raised ages to 18 and 14 years, respectively.

1933: Indore State produced an amendment to conform to the ages in the British India Act.

1955: The Hindu Marriage Act forbade marriage of girls under 15.

The 1920s was a period of intense debate about the proper age at marriage, and the long delay in passing the British India law was marked by a succession of proposed laws, debates, and counter-proposals, which were crystallized and focused in part by the Age of Consent Committee (Joshi Committee). Using the census data of 1921, the committee calculated that about 39 per cent of girls were married before the age of 10.[117] The 1929 law raised the required ages; on the other hand, it did not cover some 600 Indian states.

At about the same time as the passage of the Sarda Act, Merchant ascertained the views of a sample of young men concerning the proper age of marriage. The age at which it was felt a man should marry was slightly more than 22 years in Bombay, Gujarat, and Poona (22.9, 22.1, and 22.8 years, respectively). The proper age for women was 16.9 for the same states.[118] Fifty to 60 per cent of these men said that the proper marriage age for girls should be 16 to 18 years. In Kapadia's sample of teachers, studied during the 1950s, a slightly lower percentage chose this age period, but 57 per cent asserted that the age should be 18 years and over, as against 20 per cent in Merchant's sample of a generation earlier.[119] A considerable change is thus evident over the generation.

Various surveys taken over the past fifteen years have tried to ascertain what the age at marriage actually is. Their usefulness, however, is limited because such surveys cover only small samples. Among one sample of teachers, as noted earlier, 55 per cent of those who had married before 1920 had done so before age 13, but only 0.4 per cent of those married between 1941 and 1951 had married that young.[120]

Singh reports women's age at marriage by caste (1930s), asserting that upper-caste Hindus marry at 15.1 years on the average, intermediate-caste women at 12.5, and lower-caste women at 11.8. Without doubt, the age at marriage of Brahmin women is rising, because they are now much more likely to receive a formal education.

Rural-urban differences have always been present in India. Sovani reports such differences for the 1930–1939, 1940–1945, and 1946–1951 periods. The age at marriage for rural males remained almost the same over this period, while that of urban males rose. During the same period, the age at marriage for females rose; however, among rural women it rose from only 14.1 to 14.6 years, whereas among urban women it increased from 14.7 to 16.4 years. I have found no data to correspond to Bopegamage's assertion that ". . . there has been a marked rise in the average age of marriage recently in India, i.e., from 15–16 years to an age beyond 20 years which is more or less similar to the condition that existed in the United States in the beginning of this century."[121] This may, however, well be the modal age for the better-educated women.[122]

Since most survey samples include a disproportionate number of middle-class respondents (whose ages at marriage are higher than average) and community studies are usually made in *rural* villages (where ages are lower), the best data on time trends must be taken from the national censuses. Agarwala has derived the age at marriage from the census age distributions by marital status. As Table V-2 shows, there is little change in the age at mar-

Table V-2
Percentage of Single, Indian Males 15–25 Years of Age and Females 5–15 Years of Age, 1891–1951*

Year	Males 15–25 Years, Per Cent Single	Females 5–15 Years, Per Cent Single	MEAN AGE AT MARRIAGE	
			Male	Female
1891	49	72	19.6	12.5
1901	51	74	20.0	13.1
1911	52	75	20.3	13.2
1921	55	78	20.5	13.7
1931	44	70	18.6	12.7
1941	52	85	19.9	14.7
1951	54	85	20.0	15.2

* Shri Nayaran Agarwala, The Mean Age of Marriage in India as Ascertained from Census Data, Ph.D. diss., Princeton University, 1957, Vol. 1, Part 2. The data for these years were calculated from: Census of India, 1891, pp. 155–170 (1901, p. 69, 1911, p. 45, 1921, p. 46, 1931, p. 125), Census of India, 1941, Papers 1–10 on the Y-sample; Census of India, 1951, Paper No. 3 of 1953, pp. 146–156.

riage of men over a sixty-year period. That of females has changed more substantially, but the movement has been slow. The various urban surveys showing very high ages (i.e., 20 or more) at marriage for women do not correspond to the national average.

Since over four fifths of India is nonurban, the rural age norms dominate the national averages, but the urban patterns are an index of change.

There is growing sentiment that the girl should be educated, if only because a better marriage can be arranged, and men with good incomes have come to feel ashamed of an illiterate wife. Legal pressures count for little, of course, except against the extremely young ages. Marriage in rural areas is a family sacrament in which the state does not interfere, and in any event most marriages are now probably within the legal minimum. The increasing political and occupational participation of women in Indian life, and the demand for educated wives, will continue to raise the age at marriage in the cities. Rural areas will probably change slowly, following the lead of the cities.

The discussion has focused on the age of girls at marriage, because there was no religious proscription which required that men marry early. An extremely wide gap between the age of husband and wife was permissible. A man of twenty-five or thirty might marry a girl of twelve or thirteen without any adverse comment. But this discrepancy is narrowing, and in the future it will narrow further as both bride and groom come to express their own choice more openly.

Ross found that in her small middle-class sample the single men and women wanted a lesser age difference between spouses than the married people in the sample had actually achieved. Since parents still arrange marriages, the wishes of the young do not yet determine the age differences. The average age difference between the young married females and their husbands in *joint* families was 10.8 years; in nuclear families, 6.8 years. Ross found out than single men desired a difference of about six years; those from joint families expressing a wish for a slightly higher difference (six years vs. 5.7).[123] Clearly, the ideal that the wife should look up to her husband, who must therefore be considerably older, is weakening slowly even among the middle classes.

As yet, there seems to be no change in the percentage of adults ever married. As Dube comments, "only morons and cripples remain single."[124] Hardly one person in a hundred stays single, because the elders are determined to make a match for all the children. On the other hand, as some freedom of choice is given to the young, there will probably be a small increase in the percentage of those who do not marry at all.

6. Infanticide

Like Japan and China, India did not approve of female infanticide, but it nevertheless continued as a form of family limitation. In all three countries, measurement of either its frequency or presumed decline is difficult. Lacking observational data, vital statistics and census data do not easily yield firm inferences about this practice. A high sex ratio at birth (i.e., the number of males per hundred females) would suggest infanticide, but where females are not welcomed they may, as in Arabic Islam, be simply unregistered. If females exhibit a higher mortality than males in the first few years of life, neglect rather than true infanticide may be the cause; or, these deaths may be unregistered. The available data, however, are worth marshaling in order to see what they may show.

Altekar claims that the custom of female infanticide was adopted by some groups during the medieval period and that even under British rule some lower sections of society practiced it. He goes on to say that the rate of infanticide was much exaggerated, however, and shows that for the 0–5 age group over the forty-year span from 1891 to 1931, there is no apparent shortage of females. He concludes that female infanticide must have been rare during the nineteenth century and that it "has now completely disappeared."[125]

Kapadia asserts that the Todas "do not appear to have given up infanticide completely though they profess to have done so." He also notes that the Rajputs, the Anavils, and the Kulins practiced it, the last group mainly in times of economic difficulties."[126]

Nearly sixty years ago, Risley and Gait commented on the widespread reports of infanticide, and noted that where the proportion of females is lowest, such as in the Punjab, Sind, Rajputana, and the United Provinces, "large sections of the population are, or were formerly, suspected of this practice." It is possible that the Jats still practiced infanticide at that time, and that neglect of females also increased their mortality.[127] The Superintendent of Census in Bombay said that this practice had formerly been followed among some tribes in Sind and Cutch. A similar state of affairs apparently existed in the United Provinces at the turn of the century. On the other hand, the Census Superintendent in Baroda claimed that female infanticide *still* existed in some Kulin villages.

What is interesting with respect to the problem of social change is that Risley and Gait's efforts at that time to use standard tests of the prevalence of female infanticide do not yield any clear results. The variations in sex ratios from age to age are so great as to permit no clear conclusion that infanticide was practiced to any great extent even fifty years ago.[128] In the 1911 Census Report, Gait pursues the subject further, citing various reports of both administrators and travelers in those regions of India where infanticide was still practiced in the nineteenth century. It was indeed the failure of British efforts to stop the practice in the United Provinces, the Punjab, and Rajputana that led to the passage of the 1870 Act (VIII), placing "under police surveillance the communities suspected of this practice."[129] He also asserts that infanticide continued long after the Infanticide Act but that the great shortage of females here and there is more likely due to the neglect of girls, either unconscious or deliberate. He notes that the neglect was ". . . due partly to habit and partly to the parents' great solicitude for their sons. The boys are better clad, and when ill are more carefully tended. They are allowed to eat their fill before anything is given to the girl. In poor families, when there is not enough for all, it is invariably the girls who suffer."[130]

In the communities that were suspected of *once* having practiced infanticide (Jat Sikhs, Hindu Rajputs, Gujars, Hindu Jats), there was an extreme shortage of females. By contrast, among castes or groups that had not been suspected of the practice, and among some that actually charged a bride price, there was an *excess* of girls under five years of age. These comments applied to the Punjabs, but similar statements applied to the United Provinces at that time.

If we consider only the population under age one in the 1951 Census, the sex ratio is about 104 (104 males per hundred females) which is within a normal range. If we look at the more restricted areas of Kutch and the Himalayan Punjab, again the sex ratio is not abnormal (although a bit high—almost 107). Certainly, the evidence seems clear that if the practice survives at all, it is only in tiny areas or groups here and there.

It should be pointed out in this connection that the reports of a half-century or more ago show that the practice was dying out at that time, and in some groups had apparently *already* died out; this occurred before any conceivable consequences of industrialization could have had an impact on this family pattern. Whether the greater impact came from indigenous Indian forces, or from the efforts of the British to suppress the practice, seems impossible to ascertain now.

7. The Joint Family

Since 1911, when Gait commented that in several of the Provincial Reports, "the opinion has been expressed that the joint family shows a growing tendency towards disintegration," almost all observers of Indian family life have accepted this notion. But most observers, like Gait, were also cautious about the speed of this change.[131] It was taken for granted that the forces which had undermined the extended family system in the West would have a similar result in India. Over the past decade, a few Indian sociologists have challenged this view, and some Western analysts have followed them, asserting that industrialization may take a very different form in India.

The data bearing on these issues are fairly complex. To simplify our presentation, the major conclusions of this section are given first:

1. At any given point in time, most Indian households are not joint in composition.
2. This fact in itself, however, does not prove that much change has occurred, since most were not joint in the past, either.
3. Specific surveys have come to divergent conclusions about the prevalence of the joint family. Part of this simply comes from the use of varied definitions. If a rigorous definition is followed, it would probably hold the joint family.

4. Nevertheless, Indian values and attitudes are still generally in favor of the joint family.
5. A number of important structural changes in the joint family are occurring, however. Most of these have to do with the inclusion of all near kin in the joint family, even when they would not have been counted part of the patriline by traditional rules.

Let us consider each of these in turn.

Recent census data seem to prove the common belief that the joint family has been disintegrating; that is, if one assumes it was a *typical* form of the Indian family family in the past. In 1951, 34 per cent of the households in India had three members or less; 43 per cent had four to six members; 17 per cent had seven to nine members; and only 5.7 per cent had ten members or more. Thus, 77 per cent of the households had no more than six members or less, which would allow very little room for a genuine joint family.[132] Change is also suggested by the fact that in most of the population zones, the percentage of *small* households (three members or less) is larger in the urban than in the rural sectors, while correspondingly the percentage of *large* families (seven to nine members) is greater in rural than in urban areas. This might point to some gradual change in family composition under the impact of urbanization.

Unfortunately for this simple interpretation, the 1901 Census *also* showed that the average size of Indian households was relatively modest. In both censuses, the "commensal family," i.e., those dining together, is taken as the unit. In 1901, the average size of a household ranged from 4.4 in Ajmar, 4.6 in Assam, and 4.8 in Berar, to a high of 6 in Kashmir and 6.2 in the Punjab. The average figure is approximately five persons per house.[133] Indeed, the data from the 1901 Census suggest the "disappearance" of the joint family even more firmly, since they present the number of houses or households per hundred married females aged 15 and over ("house" still meaning the "commensal family" rather than a building). If the Indian joint family as classically described had been common, each house or household would have several married females in it. In fact, however, the number of households per hundred married females aged 15 years and over was, at the time, about one hundred, or slightly less, ranging from eighty-five to 119.[134]

It is not surprising then that Gait could write, in the 1911 Census Report, that "in spite of the joint family system, the number of houses corresponds very closely to the number of families in the European sense, i.e., married couples with their children and dependents."[135] He goes on to say that "except among the higher castes, who form but a small fraction of the total population, the joint family is not nearly so common as so frequently supposed."[136] At least with reference to the aboriginal tribes and the lower-caste Hindus, it was the custom, even half a century ago, for sons to set up their own establishment when they married or when their wives began to bear children. Moreover, the family unit usually broke up on the death of the father, and even when family property continued to be held in common, separate dining would begin to take place, under the impact of quarrels among the women, the presure of a man's wife to have a separate control over the earnings, or her wish to be free of the mother-in-law, etc. After carefully considering the Indian definition and practices, Gait asserts that the estimate of the average population of 4.9 persons per household would not be changed much even if one knew all the detailed facts.[137]

What we learn from this datum, however, is merely a confirmation of a subsidiary thesis that has been noted several times in this inquiry, that a majority of the population in *most* societies has lived in a "nuclear household," whatever the ideal family system. The average number of individuals per household in the societies considered in this study would simply not be able to fill all of the statuses that are described in classical descriptions of extended or joint family systems. Although most individuals in India are now living in small or medium-sized families, this was also true a half-century ago. There is, therefore, no basic change in this pattern.[138]

In order to evaluate properly the recent survey materials bearing on the frequency of occurrence of the joint family, we must first consider its traditional ideal structure.

It was not merely a set of nuclear families linked by kinship and possibly headed by an elder male. Structurally, as Gore puts it, the joint family is "a group of adult coparceners [joint heirs] and their dependents," who are wives and young children[139] The new Law of Hindu Succession of 1956 made daughters joint heirs of the family property. This legal change represents a major alteration in the joint family, or at least in the ideology of the elite who have passed this law. In custom, it is unlikely that the legal change will be implemented immediately.

Ideally, the joint family is based on the authority and sharing of relations among adult males rather than on the conjugal bonds between a married couple. The love and affection between *spouses*, which might break the joint unit into nuclear families, does not play a major role, since marriages are arranged before a love relationships can develop. Further threats to the joint family are eliminated by the insistence upon segregating *sexes* within the household both before and after marriage. The relation of respect between elder and younger *generations* makes it improper, if not uncommon, to have an extremely emotional relationship between them. The head of the joint family is supposed to care for all his dependents, not only his own children. A father is not supposed to express great tenderness toward his own sons when elder males are present, and since houses are small it is likely that they will be present much of the time.

The sexes are segregated even in the areas of daily work; this segregation is also a means of teaching children the importance of restraint and chastity. The husband and wife are not supposed to show affection toward one another in public, and have limited opportunities to be alone together, even at night. In traditional households, the men eat first, separate from the women.

Although there are traditional rationalizations for all these rules, as a by-product the rules reduce the intimacy between husband and wife, and thus the likelihood that the small conjugal family will break off from the joint unit.

The authority of the father or eldest brother is not likely to be challenged if he is a great deal older. Nevertheless, in spite of the great solidarity among brothers, many forces tend to break the joint family into separate hearths after the father's death. Individually, wives are likely to feel that their *own* husbands contribute more than they receive, that their *own* children do not receive a fair share, and that they, themselves must adjust to too many ways and personalities. Brothers who would prefer to be apart can always use the rationalization that the fault lies with their wives.

The joint unit can absorb the young girl-wife who is not yet equipped to handle the full-time job of homemaker and mother and to care for the young groom who cannot yet support himself. On the other hand, the joint family cannot escape the responsibility for the incompetent, the helpless, and the parasite. In addition, as Gore astutely points out, the joint family as a system has no clear, institutionalized *point* at which a division into nuclear families should take place. It is likely to take place when the parental couple dies, or when all the younger siblings of the brother's generation are grown up and taken care of. Nevertheless, the division makes Hindus uncomfortable and requires some sort of explanation or rationalization. Ross noted, for example, that if a son lives apart from his family in the same city, there is gossip about a possible family quarrel.[140]

The joint family creates many problems. True, wives are brought in while very young so that they can adjust at a fairly early age. But they also *must* adjust, because they are young and under the authority of elder males and females. The authority of older males to make decisions creates no great problem as long as the reasons for doing things are primarily traditional and ritual ones rather than for the purpose of efficiency. As soon as efficiency or scientific knowledge becomes crucial in decision, seniority and age lose their importance and conflict is much more likely. When there is a considerable amount of class mobility, an individual may earn a good income; it is likely, however, that he attained his post through the support given to him by his joint family. As in other societies, the individual sometimes does not wish to repay this help by aiding others from his joint family. This attitude was supported by the Gains of Learning Act of 1930, which permitted an individual to keep for his own the acquisitions that he made, even though the joint family had paid for his education or the support of his family. The existence of such a law is an index of how linked the individual's wealth was with that of his joint family.

So far, we have described the ideal operation of the joint family. Kapadia asserts, with reference to that pattern, that when the British came, the Hindu family organization was already moving toward the recognition of *bilateral* kinship, and that the British, instead of helping the Hindus to move in their natural direction, crystallized an older tradition of family behavior (the joint family, emphasizing only the patriline).[141] He also claims that the modern extended family no longer prepares food and eats together, worships together, enjoys property in common, and dwells in the same house: "The only feature of the joint family that still exists is the son's interest in the property of the family inherent in the fact of his birth."[142]

In his later analyses, however, Kapadia has sided with I. P. Desai and others who insist that although most families *seem* nuclear, they are actually *joint* in operation. Another analyst classifies as joint all families whose members have not gone through a legal separation and now reside apart. Such differing definitions, which we shall consider in a moment, naturally lead to different assessments of the prevalence of the joint family in India. Some of the findings about the prevalence of the joint family in various villages or regions are summarized here.

Badlapur and *Taluka City* (from Morrison): Joint families, 6 per cent; quasi joint families, 8 per cent; nuclear families, 85 per cent.

Seta Raam (from Elder):   Married sons stay in household until first child is born.

Bangalore (from Ross):   Of 207 brothers of 135 respondents, half live away from home.

Shamirpet (from Dube):   In 120 families, 34 per cent of sons separated within two years after marriage; 36 per cent in two to three years; only one fifth remain after 5 years.

Navsari (from Kapadia):   Of over 1,200 secondary school students, 605 say their uncles live apart; 300 live separately in same village.

Daleke (Sikh) (from Singh):   Report asserts not more than three joint families in village, though some families till the soil cooperatively.

Mahuwa (Saurashtra) (from Desai):   53 per cent residentially nuclear, but author asserts 72 per cent *functionally* joint, i.e., they operate as a joint family even when living apart.

Gokak Taluka (Mysore) (from Kulkarni): Defining "Separate" as families that have *legally* separated off and reside apart, only 9 to 29 per cent are "separate"; all the rest are called "joint." However, the largest single category of family type is "nuclear," 32 to 39 per cent of total.

Poona (from Sovani *et al.*):   Now two thirds nuclear, about same as in 1937.[143]

So variant a set of results points squarely to the problem of definition. Kulkarni defines the "separated family" clearly, but meanings of both "joint" and "nuclear" families remain obscure. Kapadia's and Desai's concept rests on a simple confusion about the conjugal family in the Western World.

Kapadia has insisted that "Even in those cases where the property is divided and the income of the members of the families is not pooled . . .

the constituent families maintain their connections through mutual cooperation and rights and obligations other than those of property. Members of
these constituent families meet on such various occasions as the marriage
feast, etc."[144] He follows this definition by a further clarification: "If a
residential unit of two generations shares with another nuclear or joint
family, with which it has ties of kinship, all or some rights and obligations
shared by the members of the joint family, then it is a joint family functionally."[145]

Defined thus, however, almost all family systems in the major cultural
areas of the world, including the West, become "joint families."

Faced with the fact that 605 students reported that their father's
brothers lived separately from their father, Kapadia attempts to explain
away some of these instances. Over half have left the village, perhaps for
employment. This does not, however, give us any data as to whether in
these cases *all* family income is pooled and distributed by the eldest male.
In a large minority of instances, the father's brother's family has left, but
the property has not been partitioned. Again, this does not prove jointness.
Often, the property is too small to yield any income for the distant brother,
but he wishes to maintain an emotional tie with his village or to have a
distant future claim on the produce. Again, most of these men stay with
their brothers when they return to the village, but this only proves that
their relations are friendly, and that men who have no residence in the
village will stay with their brothers if possible. All of this is quite common
practice in Western society as well. It is no evidence of the continued
strength of the joint family to show that even when there has been partition
"the relations between the two families are cordial."[146] Data on the intensity
of such ties, and their *direction* (whether they link only the male line)
would be more useful in ascertaining how far the traditional joint ties have
disintegrated. For example, an uncle should accept the obligation of caring
for a brother's son while the boy is going to school. A man who works in
the city should send money back to his joint family in the village. Indeed,
Prabhu reports that 41 per cent of his Bombay respondents claimed that
they had actually incurred debts to send money home to the village.[147]

In short, although the obligations are doubtless more intense and the
social interaction more frequent among members of an Indian joint family
than in a Western conjugal family, present data do not show a continuation
of the complete pooling of income, distribution by the eldest male, or
residence of all the appropriate ascendants and collaterals in the contemporary family.

A further clarification of the operation of the joint family in India
will help us to understand the apparent infrequency of large households even
a half-century ago, when we might suppose the joint family to have been
common. Although some large families among the wealthy and powerful
are maintained intact over generations, most families go through a life cycle
in which they change composition to some extent. In one of its phases, it

may be a joint family. Specifically, a couple founds a nuclear unit within the family of the groom's father. Soon after marriage, or after the birth of a child, the young man detaches himself to set up his own household. He does this later or earlier depending on migration opportunities, the availability of land, his education, and so on. If the separation occurs late, for a time his father's household constitutes a joint family. After the son founds his own separate household, he, too, may become the head of a joint household if some of *his* sons remain with him after their marriage.

Consequently, a new nuclear household can be called "temporarily nuclear or conjugal"; or a genuine joint household can be called "temporarily joint," since it soon dwindles to the older parents alone, or is transformed when a single surviving parent joins *his* son's household. This means that even if most people live for *part* of their lives in a joint household, at any given time most households are not joint.

We asserted earlier that in spite of the maintenance of close kin ties in India, there are some important indices of change in the joint family. These are qualitative indices, and do not show what percentage of people have adopted these patterns. Evidence suggests that they are more likely to be found among those who are occupationally mobile and whose prosperity depends, not upon land, but upon education. These alterations point to an important structural change now taking place. Specifically, the modern Indian families most affected by industrialization are much less likely to recognize *only* their traditionally important *patrilineal* kin; they may now interact as much with matrilineal and affinal kin. Increasingly, these ties depend upon mutual congeniality and physical closeness, or the frequency of exchanges or visits with relatives whom they like and who live close by, whether or not these are the relatives who would have been most significant a generation ago as part of the patriline.

Without systematically analyzing these items, let us simply list a few of them.

1. Some Hindus assert that before giving help their relatives should *deserve* it; that is, not all relatives may legitimately demand it unconditionally.
2. Because the young woman now marries later, she develops a more intimate relationship with her parents, and thus continues to have closer ties with them after she marries than in the past.
3. Sometimes young men may seek help from *friends* instead of relatives.
4. In some families, the shift of emotional attention is from the brothers and collaterals through the patriline, to sons, grandsons, daughters, and daughters-in-law.
5. Because of geographic mobility, the mother sometimes lives with her married son and daughter-in-law after her husband dies, so that she is now in *their* home, not *her* home.

Frequency of contacts with kin grow progressively less with longer periods of residence in the city.

Elder reports a difference between the traditional family behavior of the village people and that of those whose lives have been affected by the Seta-Raam Mill. (1) The father in these nuclear mill families now plays a larger role since his own brothers are no longer there as a substitute gratification, and the parental generation is no longer there to prevent a show of affection. (2) Even in the villages, there seems to be some trend towards an emphasis on the social relations with in-laws. And (3) weddings are likely to be less elaborate and relatives less inclined to attend family ceremonials; only the close family members may attend more important ceremonies.[148]

But though such changes in behavior are taking place, showing that some attitudes are shifting, there is as yet no strong ideological attack on the joint family. In other words, there is no firm and active set of values asserting that the joint family should no longer exist.

The Indian justifications for the joint families are many, and they have a rational basis, which does not, however, support its specific traditional structure of emphasis on the *male* line only. Rather, it merely justifies some maintenance of extended kin ties. A joint family gives emotional comfort to the individual, and offers some drama by virtue of its many social relations and functions—its weddings, its funerals, and its rituals. It yields economic insurance to the old, the helpless, and the unemployed. It pools its income to help the young through school, to pay for a marriage, or to begin a commercial venture. Together with the caste organization, it offers many of the services and advantages which an urban and industrial society offers through more impersonal governmental, educational, and financial agencies.

If these agencies are lacking, as to some extent they still are in India, the individual will not easily choose the "nuclear" family as a hypothetical alternative, because to do so is to say that he believes he can stand alone, which the socialization of the Indian does not train him to do. It is a frequent judgment by Western observers that the Indian male does not receive the kind of socialization which would permit him to act independently, show initiative, and function with ease where he must rely completely upon himself.[149]

Consequently, it would be surprising if public opinion surveys or studies of cultural patterns showed that any large percentage of contemporary Indians *actively* preferred to abandon the extended kin network and to move toward a conjugal family system (even though an individual might *personally* wish to escape from his own joint family).

A generation ago, K. T. Merchant studied a group of graduates and a group of nongraduates and found that 41 per cent of the men were in favor of the joint family and 44 per cent opposed to it. More graduates than nongraduates lived in joint families.[150] Among the women, three fourths opposed the joint family. We have found no other study that yields so high a percentage opposed to this system.

In Desai's 1945 study, 57 per cent of the married Gujerati women and 61 per cent of the single women preferred to live separately rather than in joint families.[151]

In Kapadia's study of a group of 513 teachers during the 1950s, 57 per cent lived in joint families and an additional 18 per cent had done so at some time. Sixty-one per cent were in favor of the continuance of the joint family, although one fifth did not answer this question.[152] Moreover, 86 per cent of those who previously lived in joint families now believe it to be a good arrangement and would like to continue living in one.

The much larger 1955 sample taken by the Indian Institute of Public Opinion found that 9 per cent of the urban and 6 per cent of the rural West Bengali, and 24 per cent of the Calcutta respondents said that they would like to have a separate household. By contrast, 60.5 per cent of the urban, 54.5 per cent of the rural West Bengali, and 45 per cent of the Calcutta sample said they preferred to live with a large family. Most of the remainder, 15 to 35 per cent, said that they *had* to live with such a family —thus expressing a strong feeling that custom and social pressure would override any feelings they might have. In Delhi, 32 per cent said they had to live with their family, 24 per cent said they preferred to do so, and only 10 per cent said that they preferred to have a separate household.[153]

In Gore's sample of a merchant caste, urban living seems to make little difference: The preference for the joint family among city dwellers *living* in a joint family is about as intense as the preference for the joint family among members of rural joint families (89 to 93 per cent).[154]

The experience of actually living in a nuclear family does seem to make a difference: 40 per cent of the urban men who were living in nuclear families actually preferred that type of family, while 60 per cent of the urban-born nuclear female sample preferred the nuclear family. Urban *immigrant* women living in a nuclear family were somewhat less inclined (45 per cent) to choose the nuclear family.

Perhaps equally important is the fact that the percentage of those who prefer the nuclear family is much higher if the individuals have had the nuclear family as their own prior family experience. Thus, 89 per cent of those *from* a joint family background preferred that system and only 7 per cent preferred a nuclear family; but only 65 per cent of those of a nuclear family background preferred the joint family, and 28 per cent preferred the nuclear family. Thus the differences are very great between the two types of background even though a majority in both categories prefers the joint family.

The importance of education may also be seen from the difference between Gore's main sample and his additional subsample made up of more highly-educated people. In the main sample, 75 per cent preferred the joint family, and 20 per cent the nuclear; but in his better-educated sample, 62 per cent preferred the joint and 34 per cent the nuclear.

Finally, we can throw some light on the process of fission described above, as well as on change, by focusing on the attitudes in favor of the *lineal* joint family, made up of the direct line of parents and children, as against the *fraternal* (or collateral joint family) made up of adult brothers and their families. The attitudes are linked to differences in behavior; Kulkarni had found that very few legal divisions of family property ever take place between father and son, although a division between brothers seems to be relatively common.[155] In Gore's sample, about three fourths preferred the joint family, but only 54 per cent believed that brothers should continue to live together after the death of the parents. Among nuclear families, only 32 per cent of those born in the city and 37 per cent of the urban immigrants believed brothers should live together. Almost equal percentages expressed some belief that they *ought* to live together, but that this was difficult to do.[156]

The burden of adjustment in the collateral joint family falls primarily on the women.[157] Consequently, we are not surprised that though some 60 per cent of the men believed that brothers should continue to live together (in the sample as a whole), only 48 per cent of the women agreed.[158] Finally, education also plays an important role here, once the level of college graduate is reached. Only 28 per cent of the college men believed that brothers should continue to live together after the death of their parents.[159]

It seems fair to conclude, therefore, that although a majority of Indians still prefer the joint family, the pattern of fission which was common in the past comes to be utilized increasingly by those who for many reasons migrate to the cities and begin to take up other occupations. Those who become highly educated also can use this opportunity to set up an individual household. Women seem to prefer it, and indeed the folklore of India is replete with the objections of women to the joint household when it is made up of brothers. The physical separation of members of the family also decreases the intensity and frequency of social contact, so that the integration begins to reduce after a period of time. Thus, although the changes are not as yet great, the *direction of change* is clear.

8. Role Relations Internal to the Family

Although many of the values and behavior of individuals within the family have already been discussed, a few additional role relationships should be considered. Several of these indicate important changes in the traditionally approved patterns.

Perhaps most central of these is the matter of authority. Ideally, the eldest male made all important decisions, whether he was the grandfather or the eldest brother. Since most decisions were based upon tradition rather than on rational knowledge, age was as effective a basis for authority as any other. The eldest woman in the household, if wise and strong willed, often gained considerable authority over time, and in any event she could control the women. She probably had more to do with the choice of the bride than did the men, although in the actual marriage negotiations the latter took charge of the affair. Thus, even under the traditional system many older individuals *in fact* had considerable authority, but the eldest male could generally succeed in forcing his will upon the others if, as a last resort, he wished to do so.

Although quantitative data are not available, observers seem to agree that the eldest male is no longer the patriarch he was two generations ago. Here, both ideology and new occupational choices make a considerable difference. The ideology of family freedom has affected attitudes in India, as survey data already cited show clearly, and of course when the younger generation obtains new jobs and moves away from the village, it is able to assert its will in a much more effective fashion.

Of her relatively well-educated middle class sample, Miss Ross asked who had possessed the chief authority in their families. Only ten out of 168 asserted that the grandfather had been the main authority, while ninety-three said that the father had made the major decisions. Interestingly enough, however, nineteen maintained that the mother had been chief authority.

On the other hand, many other persons had possessed some authority as well: grandfathers, fathers, mothers, uncles, and aunts. Other relatives were rarely mentioned, and most agreed that after marriage, the new generation no longer accepted the older authority so fully as in the past.[160]

Gore attempted to find out who was central in making major decisions regarding schooling, choice of bride or groom, occupation, and so on, Forty-three per cent of the respondents said that the eldest male (with or without consultation) made the decisions about schooling, and 46 per cent said that the parent, or parents, of the child concerned made the decision.[161] In the joint family (whether urban or rural) far more often than in the nuclear family, the eldest male (that is, not the parent) is likely to make the decisions, either by himself or in consultation with others. It must be remembered that even when a family is residentially nuclear, by Hindu tradition the eldest male has the right to decide, even if he lives in a distant village. In the joint family parents made primary decisions in only 12 per cent of the rural samples as against 19 per cent in the urban samples; in nuclear families, however, parents made decisions in 81 to 88 per cent of the instances.[162]

The American head of household is much more likely to believe that a decision is reached by consultation, when in fact he reaches the decision himself. By contrast, in 73 per cent of the lineal joint families in this Indian sample, the eldest male sees *himself* as making the decisions regarding schooling.[163] In 86 per cent of the nuclear families it is the parent who believes that *he* makes this decision.

As might be expected, in the main sample, persons other than the parents in 77 per cent of the joint families and in 11 per cent of the nuclear families made the decision regarding schooling. In 40 per cent of the joint families and in *none* of the nuclear families within the better-educated subsample did persons other than the parents make these decisions.[164] As might be expected, the women in the household also saw the eldest male as making such decisions.

With respect to the choice of occupation of a member of the family, the relationships are similar. In the joint families, 20 per cent of the respondents believed that parents make the decision concerning the future career, and 73 per cent believe that the eldest male, alone or in consultation with others, makes that decision. Only 4 per cent believe that the person who will enter the occupation makes the decision himself. In nuclear families, two thirds of the parents are seen as making this decision—and again it must be pointed out that tradition gives the eldest male authority in this matter, even if he lives somewhere else. In one fifth of the nuclear families, it was thought that the eldest male made the decision. For 87 per cent of the nuclear families and 44 per cent of the joint families in the better-educated sample the parents were seen as making that decision.

It cannot be supposed that the parents in the nuclear families have made a major ideological decision to *reject* the advice of their elders. The survey data on the general preference for the joint family preclude any such interpretation. Rather, their behavior is inescapable evidence that to the extent that people live in the nuclear family, the frequency and intensity of relations with elders of their own or a prior generation declines somewhat, and they tend to make decisions by themselves. The responses of the more educated stratum, on the other hand, show clearly the direction of the future. It must be emphasized equally that only a small minority of any of these respondents report that the person *about whom* the decision is made takes the matter into his own hands—whether it be choice of occupation, spouse, or schooling.[165]

Perhaps of equal importance in the analysis of the contemporary Hindu joint family is the privilege of discussing or disputing a matter on which a decision has been taken by the father, elder brother, mother-in-law or elder sister-in-law. Sixty-three per cent of the second males said that they did discuss such issues freely while 11 per cent said that they did not; 19 per cent said that they did discuss it but left the final decision to the eldest male.[166] By contrast, only 16 per cent of the women felt that they had that freedom. The differences with respect to sex status are not great as they are between rural-urban families or joint-nuclear families. However, the percentage of men who feel free to discuss such matters with their elders increases from rural families to urban families: 51 per cent of the respondents from rural families and 83 per cent from local urban families said that they felt free to discuss issues with their elders. (All of these are from joint families.)

One index of change with respect to freedom may be found in a 1955 survey of public opinion, which asked whether students now have more freedom from parental control than they used to have. Ninety-one per cent of more than a thousand respondents said "yes" to this question.[167] Kapadia uses both his own data on high school students and those collected by I. P. Desai to show that a considerable proportion of the younger generation does not feel great restraint or awe with parents or guardians. He interprets this, in part, as an indication of the change among elders as well: They do not now attempt so firmly as in the past to impose the traditional ways on their children.

As noted earlier, although about one third said that they could not talk unreservedly with their parents or guardians, 41 per cent said that they could do so. These high school students still seem to pay respect to their elders (as indeed, they are likely to do in Western countries as well) and a majority of them even share in the gossip at dinner. About half expressed some awe of their parents, and nearly four fifths were not willing to comment on their family environments in detail.[168] Kapadia seems to find little if any ideological rebellion among high school students with reference to the family.

Kapadia also obtained data from twelve secondary schools in the town and rural district of Navsari, attempting generally to show that these young people do not wish to break away from their families and that they experience the relations with their elders as pleasant and easy; he does present facts to show that these high school students accept the authority of the family. Only forty-one in the entire sample of 1,233 said that they felt no restraint with any member of the family.[169] Some 38 per cent were "incapable of describing their reaction to their family environment . . . or reported that they did not want to express this reaction."[170] He believes that their uneasiness or rebellion must be low in intensity, since very few ever desire to *leave* the family, a rather radical alternative.

As an additional index of the maintenance of traditional family practices, 58 per cent of these students said that the males eat first in their families and 25 per cent claimed that everyone eats together—a genuine change from the past. On the other hand, Kapadia cites I. P. Desai's study of a comparable high school group in Poona, of which 85 per cent said that the males all ate together, compared with 9 per cent who said that the women ate with the men of the family.

The abolition of purdah is frequently reported in accounts of contemporary Hindu life, and today many women do not follow its rules. Highly-educated professional women are most likely to abandon it, and men who have many contacts with Westerners or with Western patterns may become ashamed of the patterns of restricting and isolating their women. The revolutionary movement in India, as well, drew many Indian women from their homes, causing some of them to ignore the traditional barriers against their participation in social life. Thus, there is no strong *public* defense of purdah, and some families do not practice it.

Nevertheless, purdah continues to be followed by most Hindus to the extent that it is possible. The Westerner feels that the practices of purdah are either ridiculous exhibitions of male domination and jealousy or a violation of the human spirit. The Westerner who thinks about the matter is likely to wonder also *how* it is even possible to maintain the pattern in one-room huts in Indian villages. The customs seem too awkward and inconvenient. Purdah means more, however, than the creation of a separate set of rooms for the women and small children. It also refers to the woman hiding her face from her husband's male friends or elder male kin, usually by drawing her sari over her face or by turning her face away with the eyes downwards.[171] A woman may also draw the sari over her face when she is with her husband and another adult is present (if the brother-in-law or mother-in-law is present, she should not talk to him at all). This pattern of actually hiding the face is found mainly in the northwestern part of India; it is not practiced in the south, the west, and the east.

In general, as noted earlier, the men can maintain this type of control far more effectively in well-to-do families, where space permits a more formal separation of the sexes. But even in villages, some substitute is possible. In Rampur, for example, Lewis found that the preferred arrangement for family living was to have two residences, one for women and children and the other for men and cattle. The men were not ordinarily seen in the home. During the day they worked in the fields and spent their spare time in the men's quarters, where they also slept. They visited their wives at night for sexual purposes.[172] In a shopkeeper's household, the men will normally stay in the front where the shop is, and only rarely go back to the women's and children's quarters.

Only 4 per cent of the 584 Aggarwal female respondents in Gore's sample said that they did not observe purdah (meaning here primarily the symbolic gesture of distance from the elder male and stranger). There is little difference between urban and rural respondents or between those from joint or nuclear families.

The use of separate quarters becomes somewhat more difficult in the urban joint family (not the urban nuclear family, since an elder male relative would not ordinarily be in the household and male visitors would not be frequent). Here is one point at which the sheer physical problems of maintaining a custom undermines the intensity of support for it, as well as inducing change in the behavior itself. Half the rural and the urban fringe families use separate quarters according to Gore's Delhi sample, but only 20 per cent of the *urban* joint families did so. Among *nuclear* families, the situation is still more striking: 57 per cent of the rural families, 41 per cent of the urban fringe families, and only 7 per cent of the urban families have separate quarters for the women.[173]

The pattern of restricting women to separate quarters is not only relatively inconvenient to maintain in the cities, it is also being widely attacked ideologically. Prabhu found that three fourths of his Bombay immigrants stated that women had more freedom of movement and communication in the city, and nine tenths approved this freedom.[174] The use of the sari to cover the face completely when talking to an elder male also has less and less ideological support, and even now it has become often no more than a slight gesture or token of turning away. The Western reader should be reminded that not too many generations ago a proper young lady in the West was supposed to show deference, respect, and demureness, often by lowering the eyes to the ground, when talking with a male stranger or adult.

In the traditional Hindu family, the husband and wife did not go out together for walks or social visits, and the practice is not yet common. In about one third of the urban local families in Gore's sample, however, the wife usually or always went out with her husband; the same held true for 13 per cent of the joint urban immigrant families, and 20 per cent of the nuclear immigrant families. In almost none of the other families was this pattern followed. Going out together is a small index of equalitarianism, but it is not surprising that so few have accepted this custom, especially since some 73 per cent of all the women in this sample said that they still observed the custom of standing in the presence of elder males, and in 87 per cent of these families the women did not eat with the men.[175]

These data are cited primarily to indicate that though the trend of change seems clear, to judge by the ideological discussion in contemporary India and the model set by the most educated stratum, the patterns followed by most Indians have changed only slightly.

The Hindu wife entered the household of her husband's family at a young age and was expected to obey her mother-in-law and to avoid the elder males. As noted earlier, many arrangements of household life had as by-product the avoidance of an intense emotional relation between husband and wife. The woman was revered as mother, not as wife. One consequence was, and is, the intense mother-son relationship in India, a relationship that is not likely to be reduced much in intensity in the near future and which naturally lowers the intensity of the emotional tie between husband and wife.

As to the relationship between husband and wife, the woman is older at marriage now than she was fifty years ago and thus better able to assert her will as well as her claims on her own husband. There is now more ideological sentiment in favor of a relatively close relation between husband and wife, as may be seen in the attitudes in favor of a love relationship on the part of the young. Any change might be expected primarily among the better-educated groups.

In Gore's work, 56 per cent of his main sample, and 32 per cent of his better-educated subsample of men, reported that they felt closer to their mother than to their wife. Nineteen per cent of the main sample felt "equally close to both" and 36 per cent of the educated subsample expressed that sentiment. It may be noted that even to say "equally close" is a change from the traditionally expected sentiments.

In general, with increasing education, a higher percentage of male respondents assert that they feel equally close to their mothers and wives.[176] If one divides the college graduates by whether they followed traditional or newer kinds of *occupations*, a smaller percentage of the men who followed nontraditional occupations felt closer to their mothers, and a larger percentage felt closer to their wives.[177]

Interestingly enough, and perhaps productive of some conflict in the household, is the fact that slightly more than half of the wives believed that their husbands were closer to them, as contrasted with the same proportion among men who felt that they were closer to their mothers than to their wives. The contrast shows the much greater importance of the conjugal tie for the wife (since she is more fully dependent upon it), and perhaps also the rather striking success of Indian men in persuading *both* women that they are the center of his attention!

With reference to the corresponding relationship—the closeness of mothers to their children as against their closeness to their husbands—the ideal is clear but the conflict is not sharp even by traditional standards. That is, the women were supposed to be attentive mothers, but there was no rule that they should not feel very intimate toward their husbands. In some philosophical formulations they were supposed to worship them as gods. About one third of the women said that they felt closer to their children than to their husbands, and about one fifth said the reverse was true. The differences between joint and nuclear families are small, but rural women are less likely to express the sentiment that they feel closer to their husbands (12 per cent).[178]

Ross attempted to tabulate the "affectional relations" in the family and found that the mother-son relationship was mentioned most often (115 cases), and the husband-wife relationship was mentioned with relatively low frequency (sixteen cases).[179] The father-son relationship was striking because it was mentioned most often as one of love (seventy-four mentions) as well as of dislike and hatred (sixteen). The husband-wife relationship was mentioned relatively frequently as one of dislike and hatred (ten).

However, because the traditional ideals do not actually *prescribe* emotional coolness between husband and wife, and because there are no comparable data for a generation or so ago, we cannot use these as an index of change. Certainly the contemporary social definitions among the better-educated Indians place far greater emphasis upon the conjugal relationship than in the past, but these new role definitions maintain the high evaluation of the mother-child relationship. In the tangle of prescribed and real emotions we cannot really tell what the Western ideal is either. Certainly the mother is loved more than the father by both boys and girls, and much is made of the mother-child relationship. Moreover, it is a much more constant emotional tie than that between husband and wife. In the near future little change should be expected in the balance between the husband-wife emotional tie and that of mother-child. Miss Ross has reported one change in the mother-child relationship which seems very likely, although no quantitative data in its support seem to be available. She asserts that "The mother-daughter relationship has probably changed more markedly than any other family relationship since child marriage has been abandoned. The daughter no longer leaves home when a child. . . ."[180] Although even in traditional family patterns the girl's home was an occasional refuge and the focus of much of her nostalgia, the mother-daughter relationship did not continue as long as it does now, when the middle-class girl is not likely to marry until her late teens at the earliest.

Moreover, the gradually increasing emphasis on the mother's side of the family, reported here and there by Indian observers, lends some further foundation for the tie between mother and daughter.

9. Decline of Matriliny

We have made various references to matrilineal family patterns in India, and have already suggested that they are well on the way to disappearance. In fact, reports of half a century ago suggest that many of them had almost disappeared. Among both matrilineal and polyandrous groups, high divorce rates were sometimes found.[181] As these groups have moved toward recognition of the monogamous pattern or toward an emphasis on the male line, we would expect the divorce rates to drop, although no quantitative data seem as yet to be available.

Other patterns also have changed with such alterations in structure. For example, among the Urali of Northern Travencore, the family seems still to be matrilineal, but inheritance by the sisters' sons has been replaced by that of father to son (as has happened in several African societies noted earlier).[182]

Indian observers generally seem to agree that in matrilineal groups, as in the lower castes, the adult female had far more authority than in the Hindu upper-caste patrilineal groups. Consequently, change sometimes expresses itself in a tendency toward patrilineality or at least toward the increasing authority of the father.[183]

Although in certain respects the family pattern was unusual, the changes typical of matrilineal systems may be illustrated by the Nayars, perhaps the most widely studied of these systems.[184] In the central region of the Malabar Coast, or Kerala, the Nayar girl was ritually married before puberty to a man from one of the lineages linked to her own; the man tied a gold ornament (tali) around her neck. After the ceremony the bride and groom were secluded for three days, although sexual relations did not always take place. From that time, the girl was socially mature, had to avoid the men of her lineage, and could begin to receive visiting husbands from men either of her own caste or from a higher caste (Nambudiri Brahmins). These relationships were called sambandham unions. The "husbands" did not live with her nor did they support her or her children. They slept with her at night and left in the morning. When she became pregnant, one of them had to acknowledge paternity or she would become an outcaste or be killed. She had to mourn the death of her ritual husband, the *tali*-tier. All her children called her *sambandham* husbands "lord," but if one was a Brahmin they could not touch him, give him food, or become part of his caste.

The lineages were each made up of four to eight property groups, headed by a male. Thus, the property was passed through the females, but the heads of the lineage and property group were the brothers of the women. The Nambudiri Brahmin husbands did not support either their Nayar wives or children, since these were supported by the *taravad* or property group. Only the eldest Nambudiri son married within his *own* caste, thus keeping the property intact within his patrilineal group. The others entered nonexclusive unions with Nayar women, but could not obtain control over the property.

By the end of the nineteenth century, the sex life of the Nayar women had become less free, and a series of laws was passed both to recognize the peculiarities of the system and the gradual changes toward the usual Hindu system. As early as 1896, for example, the Madras Marriage Act entitled the wife and children of a *sambandham* union to maintenance from the husband, but the wife still had the right to maintenance from her own *taravad*.[185] The Act also provided for "divorce," although the Nayar system had required no specific procedure for the dissolution of such a union. As noted earlier, the Madras Nambudiri Act of 1933 permitted all Nambudiri Brahmins to marry within their own caste, and polygyny (except for special circumstances) was no longer permitted.

The head of the *taravad* was, of course, married to a Nayar woman who was not of his own lineage; but he managed property for the women of his lineage. Consequently, as in all matrilineal systems, some strains developed, compounded here by the presence of the Brahmin men. If the union between husband and wife became overly close, his property group might become suspicious that he might divert gifts or goods from his lineage to her own. He might favor his children as against the children of his lineage. The suspicions were especially strong if the man was head of a property group. Moreover, the suspicions were very likely justified from time to time. One of the consequences that occurred as early as 1878 was a growing demand for partition of the jointly held property, and various acts from that time on dealt with the problem of partition, or granted the right to ask for partition (both males and females inheriting equally).

The gradual fission of all Nayar property rights dissolved the property groups almost completely by the end of the 1930s, and only a few *taravads* had been declared impartible by 1942.[186] The family becomes in effect the ordinary household of two or three generations. Moreover, the old system required that a male *not* living in the household direct the financial and property activities of the *taravad*. As each household becomes separate, i.e., not organized into large property groups, there can be no centralization of authority, and in effect one male or more must be available for each small unit—but the male is likely now to be more interested in running the affairs of his *own* household. Attitudes of bilaterality, recognizing both kin lines, become standard, and the system becomes patrilocal in behavior. The father becomes an accepted element in the matrilineal kinship system.[187] Some children even take their father's personal name.

The polyandrous marital patterns of the Nayar women have disappeared. The mother's brother has lost his power and authority as the property group has dissolved, although he may still manage the property.

Of course, the father does not have the great authority once enjoyed by the male head of a *taravad,* but has more authority over his children and his emotional tie with them is closer than what the ordinary Nayar or in-marrying Nambudiri fathers enjoyed in the nineteenth century.

The decline of matriliny can not be ascribed to industrialization, since it took place mainly in the nineteenth century. It is important, however, that the Nayars were not in an isolated region of India. The many changes in communication, transportation, the use of money, etc. that were part of India's development were also shared by those on the Malabar Coast, who were also under ideological pressure from both the Hindus and the British to change their customs; the system itself generated many strains. We note these facts not as an explanation of the system's decline, but as relevant to the observed changes as well as to the general movement away from matriliny in other regions. That is, as such a system moves into the main stream of Hindu life, it loses its matrilineal structure, and breaks into units where greater recognition is given to the father.

10. Women's Rights

The broad arena of women's rights has been marked in India both by the changes in their role relations within the family and by the alterations in their legal and social disabilities in the larger society. Changes in the latter have been far more radical than in the former. Some of these have already been analyzed, but a few additional ones deserve mention.

The state of affairs that existed before these changes occurred may be summed up by Altekar's assessment, after he concluded his survey of what the status of Hindu women was until very recently: "Their condition has been on the whole deteriorating during the last two thousand years.[188]

Although jurists continue to debate details, generally, under the legal codification that ruled joint family property from about the eleventh century on, the Hindu male was a coparcener in the family property from the moment of his birth. A widow had some rights of maintenance. She also was permitted to own *stridhana,* which was never defined in a general way, but included various movable types of property such as jewels, gifts from her own family, household possessions that came with her to the marriage, gifts by her own husband, and so on. Since these properties sometimes included land as well, *stridhana* often figured in legal decisions about who might inherit it. It was usually held that it did not merge with her husband's family's property. Strictly speaking, the *stridhana* cannot be viewed as the Indian counterpart of the European *dower*.

The unmarried girl did not inherit in the same way as the men of the family. She was expected to be taken care of by her future husband's family, and her share came in the form of the groom price which insured her marriage. The widow did not inherit, since she was entitled to maintenance from the property that her sons inherited. If there had been a separation of the family property, so that in effect her husband had founded an independent family, then she could inherit. Until 1937, only the Bengali permitted the widow to inherit her husband's property if he was still a member of the joint family.[189] In that year, the Hindu Woman's Right to Property Act permitted women the same rights to property that their husbands had had, but they were still not accepted as coparceners. The Act also recognized the inheritance rights of a widow whose son had died before her. An earlier act (1929) also gave some recognition to other categories of females, such as the son's daughter and the daughter's daughter, except where such a right was contrary to local custom. Even so, in 1936 the widow who inherited land did not have full legal power over it. She could not dispose of it except under extreme circumstances. The Hindu Succession Law of 1956 has now given her that right.[190]

Presumably, the Indian Constitution, which came into effect in 1950, itself grants women the right to own property equally with men, but in fact many of these provisions regarding personal law must be spelled out both in statute and in court decisions, since custom has not yet caught up with the idea. In answer to the question: "Do you feel that women should have the same property rights as men?" Forty-five per cent of urban, 60.5 per cent of the rural West Bengali, and 62 per cent of the Calcutta sample said that they did concede that right. Only 33.5 per cent of the Delhi sample conceded it. Thus, only a bare majority of Indian respondents would now concede women property rights even in general terms.[191] Note that the question does not even refer to the equal inheritance by brothers and sisters, which is stipulated in the Hindu Succession Act of 1956; it refers only to the simple ownership of property. Moreover, this sample has an over-representation of middle-class and better-educated Hindus. We would suppose that an adequate sample of the national population would show a clear majority against the notion of equal inheritance by the daughter, especially since at the present time the family must pay for her dowry. There is no evidence that the law is now being followed.

It should not be forgotten, however, that in the matrilineal societies property did go through the females, and although a male usually managed the property (e.g., among the Nayars) the equality of rights of males and females was not attacked. Among both the Nayars and the Nambudiri Brahmins, property could not be divided without the assent of everyone, so that the rights of the female were not disturbed. These Brahmins had a patrilineal family system, but until about a generation ago only the eldest male married a Brahmin. The others usually married a Nayar woman and were supported by the property on her side of the family. Both systems have begun to break up, as has been noted.

Hindu women have taken little part in political life, although since the 1920s a few have begun to participate in the independence movement. Some have tried to improve the status of women through greater education, removal of restrictions on widows, the abolition of purdah, etc. By the 1930s, a few women began to hold high offices in provincial governments when greater autonomy as given to these states. Since that time a few have been governors and ambassadors.

Voting was achieved as a by-product of the suffrage movement in England, which succeeded there in 1918. By 1935, many Indian women were franchised and a few seats were reserved for them in each provincial legislature. Under the new Constitution, of course, women are able to vote.[192]

Again, a description of legal rights does not describe social life at all. Except for the depressed castes, it has always been thought improper for women even to do their own shopping, much less take part in public affairs. In Gore's sample of merchant families, only 4 per cent of the women did household work, handled daily cash, did their own shopping, and looked after children's studies. An additional 8 per cent carried out the first three tasks, but did not look after children's studies. An additional 12 per cent did the first task but not the last two. Seventy-five per cent did household work only.[193] An index of this restriction may be found in Vyas's account of life in his own native village. He notes that at the time of sowing, every able-bodied person worked, and to suggest how urgent the work was, noted that women were no exception. He writes, however, that even under such extreme pressures, the Brahmin and artisan women did not work in the fields.[194]

It must be kept in mind that these restrictions are not merely authoritarian rules imposed by the males; the females are socialized to accept them and to view them as proper. An index of this fact may be found in the materials cited earlier to indicate the difficulty of staffing village schools when most men and women believed that a single woman, alone in an outlying village, would lose her reputation and would not be free from molestation by men. Davis notes a comparable problem with respect to teaching birth control information. During the 1930s, women physicians did not feel easy about discussing birth control methods with men and would not attend demonstrations with male doctors.[195]

Under the traditional governmental system, caste *panchayats* or councils, dominated usually by Brahmins, controlled not only the families in the caste, but also the affairs in the village. Growing criticism of this domination led to the Act of 1939 which established a new type of *panchayat* in villages with 2 thousand population or over, and with taxing powers and civil authority comparable to town councils in the United States. To assure better representation of groups which had hitherto been excluded, seats on the council were reserved for Moslems, for Harijans, and for women. However, in view of the position of women in Indian society at that time, it could not be expected that they would suddenly begin to take an equal part in these new political activities of the councils. Some intelligent and active women took part in them, but only rarely. Mostly, they have been only nominal members.[196] In Rampur, Lewis found that the women had no direct role in the council, and did not attend *panchayat* meetings.[197]

Nevertheless, as any casual newspaper reader will note, many Indian women have taken part in public life, and do so increasingly as a higher proportion of them become educated.

Although schools for girls began in the mid-nineteenth century, the steady growth of education for women only began to gather speed as late as the 1920s, when some 81 thousand girls were in secondary schools. By 1937, the number had risen to 110 thousand, and this was doubled by 1947. By 1951, nearly a million girls were in secondary schools. From 1955 to 1956, 9 million girls were on the rolls of India's educational institutions. By 1951, 44 thousand were even in colleges. The number of women in colleges increased sevenfold between 1937–1938 and 1951.

Although propaganda in favor of female education did not directly attack the joint family, it should be remembered that the male's authority was based to a considerable extent on the fact that the bride was not only very young but uneducated, and had little opportunity to taste the experiences of the outside world. In assessing the problems of social change, it is important to see that although the women have more to gain if they can obtain equal rights and free themselves from restrictions, they are less exposed to all the industrializing and educational influences of modern life that might persuade them to make such demands. By contrast, men are more affected in their ideology by these outside influences, but they, personally, have less to gain from granting such rights. Thus, the paradox often emerges, as in the West, that the more educated men may be ideologically willing to grant many rights which women are not yet able or willing to use.

On the surface, the battle for female education in India would seem to be won. In a sample of Poona high school students, 90 per cent of the girls and 67 per cent of the boys wanted to go beyond high school.[198] In a 1955 public opinion survey, two thirds of the respondents said that it was desirable to give higher education to girls.[199] A more general question as to whether it is a good idea for women to be educated gave still more positive answers. Seventy-two per cent of the urban and 92.5 per cent of the rural West Bengali, and 92 per cent of the Calcutta respondents replied in the affirmative. So did 76 per cent among the Delhi respondents.[200] In Kapadia's sample of teachers 37 per cent wanted women to be matriculated, and 18 per cent wanted them to receive college education.[201]

However, when more specific questions are asked as to what *kind* of an education young Indian girls should have, it becomes clear that there is little serious sentiment in favor of equal education or preparation for a career. Only seventy-six teachers in Kapadia's sample wanted women to obtain the education that men receive, and as many as 284 thought that the woman's place should be in the home. His conclusion that "Men's attitude to women's place in society has not substantially changed,"[202] seems reasonable; since his sample is made up of Hindus who retain this traditional attitude in spite of the fact that they have gone through college and even beyond.

Similarly, in the surveys cited above, 9 per cent of the Delhi sample thought that girls should graduate from college. Nineteen per cent of the urban and 41 per cent of the rural West Bengali sample thought so, as did 34 per cent of the Calcutta sample.[203] The mode of questioning permitted multiple answers which shed additional light on the problem: One fourth to one third of the respondents mentioned needlework or nursing as proper subjects for women, and 10 to 20 per cent expressed the idea that a young daughter should study domestic science. Again we must remember that few lower-class respondents are in these samples, so that these answers represent at best the more enlightened opinions of contemporary India.

These attitudes are linked closely with the Hindu sentiments regarding women working. Among the Harijans or outcastes, women have typically worked, but the higher-caste Hindu women are not supposed to. Among various outcastes, the number of female workers per thousand male workers ranges from about 200 to 800.[204] In Kolhapur City, 12.5 per cent of the working force were women, but these were agriculturalists or members of the outcaste group of sweepers, scavengers, etc. They did not figure at all in specialized or professional work.[205] The association of working women and lower-caste position has been marked in Indian life for centuries. At the same time, the barriers to employment permit the greater domination by males over females, both in general and within the family.

In Gore's sample of a Vaisya caste, 51 per cent of the men and 38 per cent of the women thought that women should not work for money outside the home at all. Thirty-eight per cent of the men and 27 per cent of the women thought that they might do so under special circumstances. That is, about nine out of ten men, and two out of three women, thought that women had no right to work.[206] The meaning of such sentiments should be looked at closely. Ross comments that "The main reason that so many married Hindu middle class women work without reproach is because . . . a wife's income is often essential to the family's standard of living."[207] That is, a professionally-educated woman may work, but it is not viewed as a normal thing to do, and if the husband can afford to support her, she does not.

Public opinion is thus clearly against the idea of women working. In the November 1955 Public Opinion Survey, 24 per cent of the respondents were in favor of a married daughter taking a job; but only 15 per cent of mothers in the sample approved it. Even among the sample's young and better-educated strata, only 28 per cent were in favor (as against 8 per cent among the poorly-educated respondents).[208] In October of the same year, 70 per cent of the Delhi sample said that they would not allow a young, unmarried daughter or sister to go out and work. As in most other areas of family opinion, the West Bengali and Calcutta respondents are more liberal: 46.5 per cent of the rural and 49 per cent of the urban West Bengali were opposed, and only 33 per cent of the Calcutta respondents were so opposed.[209] Although the differences are great, widespread opposition is evident. Ross found that two thirds of the sixty-two men expressing a view in her sample were in favor of women "having a career." This answer is to a much more general question than whether they would permit a young woman in their *own* family to work, and the answers are certainly more favorable than in other surveys. Ross also notes that Gunial B. Desai's study of Gujerati women in the 1940s reported that 80 per cent of the women were against females having a career.[210]

These objections are of great importance in understanding changes in Indian family life, but equally important are the *opportunities* which women may find to use their skills or increase the family income. In the West, too, we noted that sentiment in favor of women's careers is relatively weak, but many women do work. When they do, the men do not seem to oppose it vigorously, because though ideally they might prefer the women to stay at home, they also obtain some benefit from women's work. In India over the last half-century, in spite of the slightly increasing industrialization, there has been a fairly steady decline in the proportion of women engaged in nonagricultural activity. The *proportion* of women workers in agriculture has also declined from 10.8 per cent to 8.7 per cent in the period from 1901 to 1951. In nonagricultural activities, 6 per cent of the workers were women in 1901, but only 2.8 per cent in 1951.[211] In the 1950–1956 period, the absolute number of women working in factories increased, but their share of the total number of factory jobs declined from 11 per cent in 1950 to 10 per cent in 1956. Most female workers are still occupied in agriculture, where their jobs are dependent upon other family members. Since even educated men find great difficulty in obtaining steady employment, the opportunities for women remain minimal. Consequently, both sentiment and opportunity combine to reduce the possible effect of women's employment on their position within the family. Women with special or professional skills do work, and some hold high positions, but as yet there is little evidence of a general movement into independent employment, either before or after marriage. The fact that outcaste or Harijan women work does not affect this conclusion, since they are engaged in lowly activities. But, as every observer has noted, their position in the family has been higher than that of higher-caste women.

11. Divorce, Widowhood, and Remarriage

Divorce was not permitted to Orthodox Hindus. On the other hand, perhaps every one of the depressed castes allowed divorce, although a divorce could not be forced on an unwilling husband.[212] Those who laid claim to a higher rank in the caste system, however, have been known to relinquish divorce as they have other customs which they feel high-caste Hindus supposedly look upon with distaste.[213]

The Hindu Marriage Act of 1955 extended the possibility of divorce to all of the Indian population, extending the right to customary divorce that some four fifths of the Hindu population had had prior to that time. Thus, the Act unified and codified existing practices.

Under traditional Hindu formulations, marriage was sacred and therefore indissoluble. Of course a man could replace his wife or desert her by having nothing to do with her, but he still allowed her to continue living in the household. The wife had no right at all to replace or desert her husband. Only in matrilineal groups, where the marriage bonds were much less tight, could women remarry.

The growing sentiment in favor of divorce was primarily a product of the Women's Rights Movement, and was linked very closely with the growing sentiments against bigamy and against the extreme disability suffered by the widow. Only a tiny minority was in favor of divorce, and the grounds for divorce under all the laws from the 1940s to the Hindu Marriage Act of 1955 seem very harsh by Western standards. A law passed by the State of Baroda in 1942, and the Bombay Hindu Married Woman's Right to Separate Residence and Maintenance Act of 1946, permitted the woman maintenance and residence away from her husband (whatever other custom or law might say) on grounds such as these: loathsome disease contracted by the husband but not from her; such cruelty as would make life with the husband unsafe; desertion without her consent; or his second marriage.[214] Madras passed a divorce law in 1949 and Saurashtra in 1952 with similarly restrictive provisions. Under the 1955 Hindu Marriage Act, divorce is possible if the spouse has been insane for three years, has had leprosy for three years, has disappeared for seven years, or has had a venereal disease for three years. Similarly, if a spouse has converted to another religion, renounced the world, or commited adultery, the other can obtain a divorce. In addition, the wife can sue for divorce on grounds of rape, sodomy, or bestiality, but the marriage has to have lasted three years unless there are some hardships in the specific circumstances of the marriage. Furthermore, no remarriage is permitted for a year after the divorce.[215]

Although the number of divorces will probably rise considerably, if only because there were formerly so few, the grounds enumerated above are not likely to open the floodgates of divorce. At the present time, some strong sentiment still exists against it. Although the data collected by Kuppuswamy are somewhat difficult to interpret for technical reasons, they may be used here as indices of public attitudes in Mysore, one of the more educated areas of India. Sixty-five per cent (71 per cent of the men and 58 per cent of the women) of his sample of over 1,300 agreed that a man might divorce his wife, and 56 per cent (about the same percentages as above for men and women) agreed that a woman might divorce her husband under certain circumstances.[216]

With respect to the many *specific* provisions of the Act of 1955, there is far more disagreement, however. That is, general opinion is in favor of the right to divorce, but the specific grounds are frequently rejected. Three fourths of the group were against dissolution of the marriage on grounds of barrenness; and sex, caste, age, and education do not affect this general pattern. Only half approve divorce "if the man's morals are loose," but four fifths are agreeable to divorce if the *woman* does not conform to the moral rules.[217] Most are in favor of divorce if the husband or wife is incurably insane, but only one fourth of Harijans are of that opinion. Sixty per cent believe that the marriage should not be dissolved even if the husband converts to another religion.[218]

With respect to remarriage, nearly four fifths of the group are in favor of the man's remarriage, but the castes differ with respect to remarriage of the woman: three fourths of the Brahmins are in favor, but only 41 per cent of the Harijans (the difference lies largely in the fact that only 13 per cent of the Harijan *women* approve this).[219]

These data seem somewhat more conservative than those expressed in the November 1955 Indian Public Opinion Survey. At that time, 54.4 per cent of the Delhi respondents said that divorce should not be allowed under any circumstances, and 32.5 per cent of the rural West Bengali agreed. However, only 9 per cent of the urban West Bengali and 13 per cent of the Calcutta respondents expressed that opinion. Over half the West Bengali and Calcutta sample said that divorce should be permitted or that it is a great advance in legislation, contrasted with the 21 per cent of the Delhi sample.[220]

In Gore's merchant group, four fifths were against divorce, but as in Kuppuswamy's data, the more educated are more in favor of divorce.[221]

As noted before, sentiment regarding divorce in India was intertwined with the proscription against remarriage. A remarriage was scandalous; consequently, a divorce law was meaningless. Chastity, dedication to the memory of the husband, and devotion to the children were proper activities for a rejected or widowed woman, although under some rare circumstances a religious life might be permitted. The attitudes toward divorce seem very close to those regarding widow remarriage. That is, the opportunity for divorce is viewed primarily as a possible escape from a difficult situation, rather than the chance to establish a new life because a given marriage has failed. The extension of the divorce privilege is viewed as a way of helping to free the *woman* from an intolerable burden. Similarly, the efforts to give the Hindu widow the right to remarry were viewed as releasing her from an extremely humiliating and depressing situation, rather than the granting of an ordinary human right to live a happily married life. The rule against widow remarriage was strong in India. As noted earlier, Davis was able to show that the Brahmins succeeded relatively well in preventing their widows from remarriage, which is why Brahmins' fertility is lower than that of other castes. The ideal until late in the nineteenth century was that the widow should commit *sati* (i.e., suicide on the funeral pyre of her dead husband). The only acceptable alternative was to live a chaste life until she died. Her head was shaved, and she was required to wear white. She was supposed to eat only one meal a day, and abstain from meat. Her presence was viewed as an ill omen, and no happy gathering or celebration included her. Observers of Indian life generally report that these rules (except for *sati*) were actually followed. Again, this was not so for the depressed castes, among whom a widow re-marriage was always permitted.

The British were especially shocked by *sati*. The custom, however, was given great veneration, and it is even probable that many mounted the funeral pyre willingly. But as Altekar notes, this willingness may have been due to the many formal and informal sanctions visited against a woman who refused to die with her husband. After all, she was a nuisance as well as an economic burden if she continued to live. If she refused to be burned, she might even lose caste and thus be a helpless individual in the society.[222]

Altekar estimates that no more than 2 to 10 per cent of the widows ever committed *sati*, even in the districts most in favor of it. The custom was confined primarily to priestly and noble families—for example, among noble Rajputs among whom, of course, the wife's immolation was much more advantageous to the family than among the lower classes and castes. Altekar estimates that "perhaps one widow in a thousand became a *sati*" in the general population.[223] A sister of Altekar became a *sati* as late as 1946, and the custom had not completely died out even by the 1950s.

The English opposition to *sati* was expressed early but it had relatively little success. The 1829 Act for the Prevention of Sati had little effect, perhaps because it did not also permit widow remarriage, and life as a widow in her former husband's family remained intolerable. The act permitting remarriage was not passed until 1856, and it made no inroad upon either custom or attitude. Successive legislation had only a gradual effect, and many public incidents of repression, outcasting, ostracism, and even violence are recounted as the aftermath of a widow remarriage.

Although the meaning attached to *sati* was religious, widowhood was a serious problem since a girl might well be married as an infant and thus be widowed before she had ever lived as a mature wife. Of course the widower could remarry. In 1901, the Census Report notes that among the upper classes, and in large cities where public opinion was most advanced, some respondents indicated approval of virgin widows remarrying, but their number was still very small.[224]

In 1881, nineteen out of every thousand Indian girls aged 10 to 15 were widowed, and in 1901, eighteen were widowed.[225] Of those aged 20 to 30, ninety-six were widowed in 1881, and ninety-two in 1901. Over the past half-century, more than half of those aged 40 and over have been widowed.

These figures had dropped somewhat by 1911: There were five Indian girls out of a thousand widowed in the 10 to 15 age group, thirteen in the 15 to 20 age group, and thirty-seven in the 20 to 30 age group.[226] The number had dropped still further by 1951 when only 0.32 per cent of the women in the 5 to 14 age group were widowed, 2.8 per cent in the 15 to 24 age group, and 8.0 per cent in the 25 to 34 age group.[227] A lower percentage in the very young age brackets are widows because fewer of them now marry. In the higher ages, the lower mortality of husbands has decreased the percentage of widows. Some widow remarriage, however, has also begun to take place.

The percentage of widows in any given age group is a result of mortality among women, mortality among men, the age difference between the two, and the amount of remarriage among widows. Men have a higher mortality than do women at the same ages, and if the age difference between husband and wife is very great, as it typically was in India, then the problem of widows will be substantial. To the extent that remarriage is not practiced, at any given census most of the women who had become widows earlier are still widows.

The growing approval of widow remarriage seems primarily based upon ethical and ideological arguments, made more intense by the fact that this has been a subject of considerable debate within Hindu legal and philosophical circles for many decades. Permission to remarry is in harmony with the slight but growing sentiment in favor of individual choice, and of course there are economic arguments in favor of it as well. Four out of five of Gore's Vaisya sample were in favor of widow remarriage, although for a wide variety of reasons. Those in a nuclear family, upon whom the burden of maintaining a widow would be greater, were somewhat more in favor of remarriage than were those in a joint family. As might be expected, with greater education there was greater approval of widow remarriage. On the other hand, women were far more against it (31 per cent) than men (7 per cent).[228] Kapadia also found an overwhelming percentage in favor of widow remarriage, and a study by one of his students found well over 90 per cent in favor. Kapadia analyzes his data further, however, to show that only a small proportion of these college graduates actually believe that the widow has a simple human *right* to remarry. Most of them justify it because of possible sexual relations, to avoid being harassed by male relatives, childlessness, etc.[229]

Where public sentiment is favorable, and economic advantage can be supported by ideological argument, we would expect a steady rise in the percentage of widows remarrying, while the lowered mortality of men who are married to women in the marriageable ages should reduce the number somewhat.

In a study of over 11 thousand females aged 13 and over, in six rural communities in Bombay State and part of Hyderabad, some estimate is presented of the amount of current remarriage. In the 23–27 age group, 6 per cent were widows, and in the 38–42 age group, the figure was 25 per cent.[230]

In a sample of over 10 thousand *ever* married, somewhat over 3 thousand *had been* widowed at some time. Of these, 26 per cent had remarried.[231]

If one calculates the percentage of those ever *re*married (once having been widowed) in the age group that is now 13–17 years old, 55 per cent had remarried. In the 18–22 age group, 57 per cent had remarried, and in the 23–27 age group, 50 per cent had remarried. The percentages drop in higher age groups, but even in the 43 and over age group, 18.5 per cent were remarried. Younger women would, of course, have been more willing to remarry, and they would have a greater opportunity to do so.

A more refined calculation is obtained by Dandekar who ascertained the amount of remarriage by *age at widowhood*. (The previous data refer only to the age at the time of the survey.) Eighty-seven per cent of those who were widowed below age 13 had remarried by the time of the survey, as had 60 per cent of those widowed from 13 to 22. Fourteen per cent of those widowed at age 23 to 43 had remarried.[232] His data also suggest, because of the differences between remarriage rates at different ages, that there may be a greater possibility of remarriage now than formerly. Of course, those who were widowed at 43 or over have relatively little chance of remarrying in contemporary India.[233] Lack of children increases the chance of remarriage, probably because childless widows are younger.

Although Dandekar shows the influence of caste on remarriage, it is clear that in his large sample of rural communities the bar is not as absolute as it once was. As might be expected, among the Harijans or depressed castes, non-Hindus, and those of lower status generally, nine out of ten women widowed below age 13 remarried, but an equally large percentage of the intermediate-caste Hindus did so as well. Among the advanced-caste Hindus, 43 per cent of the girls widowed below 13 and 33 per cent of those widowed at 13 to 22 remarried. In this latter age category, 57 per cent of the intermediate-caste Hindus remarried, but about the same percentage is found among the Lingayats. Among the depressed castes, 76 per cent of those widowed in the 13 to 22 age group had remarried.

It seems likely then that at the present time widow remarriage has become relatively common despite disapproval.

Although the values and attitudes against widow remarriage seem to have been intense, a full discussion of widowhood and remarriage requires attention to a further detail of Indian family life. If a woman did remarry, *whom* was she to marry? Karvé comments that there is "no example of widow remarriage in the older literature . . ." but says that "widow remarriage was not necessary because a man could beget children on his brother's widow."[234] Both Altekar and Prabhu discuss this custom, known as *niyoga*, as comparable to the Biblical custom of "raising up seed" for a deceased brother. The child or children were of course part of the deceased man's line.[235] *Niyoga* was, of course, not true marriage. Nevertheless, the evidence seems clear that in many communities in contemporary India, the true levirate has been followed; that is, a marriage of the younger brother with the wife of the deceased elder brother. Moreover, it seems to have a link with still another practice which is mentioned here and there but rarely discussed, the tolerance of some sexual contact between these two persons. Karvé notes that Brahmins, Vaisyas, and other castes deny the existence of the levirate in the northern zone of India, but her observations at least suggest that it is practiced here and there. In Northern Maharashtra in India's central zone, some Kunbi castes practiced the levirate.[236] This pattern is also found among the lower castes of Gujarat. In the central zone, the poor classes practice the junior levirate.[237] In the Southern zone, widow remarriage is found among almost all castes, except the Brahmins, but the levirate is found only where the "Dravidian-speaking population has come in contact with the Northern population."[238]

Such a list is not meant to be complete, and we take note of the custom partly because it has obviously continued to exist in spite of philosophical and religious proscriptions against it. (Karvé notes, p. 153, that lower castes in Gujarat become angry if they are asked about the custom.) The list also throws light on a custom which, although it is a violation of fairly strong taboos, seems to be equally widespread. If there has been a continued custom among many castes and in several regions for the younger brother to marry his deceased brother's wife, then we would expect a high tolerance of at least a joking relationship between these two persons. Indeed, the literature of folk tales about Indian family life attest to the general belief that the young bride finds in her husband's younger brother, her *dewar*, a place of solace and tenderness, which is impossible with her husband before whom she has to show awe. The younger brother, however, might well be closer to her age, and be around the house much more frequently. Nevertheless, the pattern remains somewhat puzzling, because the taboo against extramarital unchastity was, and is, extremely strong in India, and a sexual relation of this kind smacks of incest.[239]

Of course we do not here refer to polyandry, where the brother has actually married the woman, although it is entirely possible that the practice had some remote roots with polyandry, as Gait suggests in his Census report of 1911.[240] Unfortunately, the British civil servant of that time often could not distinguish between a genuine custom, approved by the values of the community, a deviation, or a genuine marriage. Ross, working with a predominantly educated and middle-class group, concedes that "several cases" in her sample suggested that there had been a sexual relation between the brother and sister-in-law, especially in large joint families.[241]

Lewis, too, notes that the woman has a "friendly joking relationship with her *dewar* and that sexual relations may sometimes take place between them." This is "not considered reprehensible," even though fidelity is a virtue. The younger brother is a potential husband. Many of the songs sung by the women refer to the relationship between the two and have many sexual implications. When extramarital relations take place (one informant asserted that nine out of ten in the village had indulged in them at some time or another), they often involve these two.[242]

So high an estimate need not be taken seriously, but the existence of the practice, unapproved by custom, yet recognized in folklore and song, appears undeniable, especially in the groups where the levirate has been practiced. On the other hand, to the extent that this custom is dying out, as indeed are many customs of marriage with close kin, and to the extent that the conjugal relation becomes central in the family system, this special source of solace and tenderness will be both less attractive and less available.

12. Final Comment

The contrast between the most progressive family behavior in India and the family patterns of the overwhelming majority of the population is extreme, matched only perhaps by the Arab countries and a few African nations.

The Indian family systems are not static, however, nor have they been so in the past. Both polyandrous and matrilineal systems have been declining; they had begun to disappear even a half-century ago. The legal changes, which have been substantial, show a gradual evolution over the past century, increasing in pace over the past generation. Although these legal alterations are clearly ahead of public opinion, even when we consider the attitudes and values of only the better-educated strata, they show a steady direction, without regression, toward some form of the conjugal system.

There are, as we noted, many changes other than the legal ones. The gradual shift in the kin network's *focus* is one of the most important of these. Another, increasing approval of remarriage for both divorcees and widows, may be seen as a change in the position of women, but is also an alteration in the traditional family structure. The discarded or widowed wife is no longer relegated to a shameful position in the family, but is permitted to resume a more normal life, with some property rights even being given to her.

Of prime importance, perhaps, is that this amount of change has been taking place in the face of relatively little industrialization. The changes have been too many, and in too many parts of the total kin and family structure, to be attributed solely to industrialization—or, for that matter, to urbanization, since India has had cities for thousands of years. We must recognize the extent to which many indigenous Indian ideological forces have been at work, perhaps usually in the same direction as the forces whose origin was essentially Western.

Yet the reluctance with which Indians are giving up some older family patterns is due to the failure of the emerging social system to provide viable and fruitful alternatives as yet: For example, the opposition to a woman entering paid work is great, but at present her opportunities are few and ill-paid. The cost in social standing is not adequately compensated for by the small income, or the greater richness of her life. Moreover, since marriage still occurs at a relatively young age, if the educated girl attempts to establish a genuine career, she may miss her only chance at a marriage. The meshing of the new alternatives and the demands of the new conjugal system is not at all harmonious.

Similarly, the industrial and urban systems have not yet developed all the cooperative services, aid, and solutions for the individual that were and to some extent still are furnished by the large family network. Consequently, the reluctance of most Indians to move toward the new family type seems understandable.

But though the movement is slow in some areas of action—for example, the real freedom to choose one's own spouse—in others it is more rapid, and there is no evidence of any important movement toward once-discarded but traditional family patterns. The only exception may be found in the actions of a few castes seeking to move upwards in social standing, which imitate one or another of the older Brahmin patterns (the prohibition against divorce, demanding a groom price, etc.). These are numerically few, however, and the massive, if slow, progress of the Indian family systems has been clearly toward some form of the conjugal system.

chapter

VI

China

ひひひひひひ

CONTEMPORARY observers of the Communist Revolution in China often fail to remember that current changes in the family and other areas of Chinese social life were not initiated by the Communist regime. Although Chinese Communists themselves insist on denying this, these changes have been going on over the past half-century. Many merely represent an intensification of social pressures and alterations which began long ago.

The end of the Ch'ing Dynasty in 1911 was preceded, like many revolutions in the West, by a defection of the intellectuals, who ceased to defend and support the old regime and instead began to attack it. In one important respect the fall of this dynasty differed from that of previous ones. In the past, the new leadership typically had called for a *return* to the ancient virtues from which a corrupt rulership had strayed. The usurpers of the Ch'ing Dynasty called on China to *enter* the twentieth century; a new China, they declared, demanded a new family system. The entire Chinese political system was indeed based on the family—ideally it *was* the "great family"—as the Chinese mandarin of the past, from Confucius through the twentieth century, had so strongly insisted.

In the search for new ways to family reform, many alternatives were considered. New solutions were sought, and the civil codes of Switzerland, Germany, Russia, Japan, and many other countries were considered as bases for a Chinese model. The specific changes suggested added up to a gradual adoption of the Western family system, in spite of much anti-Western sentiment and the conscious desire to remain true to Chinese traditions. China moved toward freedom of mate choice, a lessening of the elders' power, a rise in the position of women, a greater freedom of the individual to seek divorce, and the end of footbinding, concubinage, and female slavery.

A fruitful examination can be made of the successive legal changes that ushered in a new era in Chinese family patterns—a movement that progressed steadily toward a conjugal system, even under the Communist Code of 1950 and the new state's communization program. Alterations of family codes, however, do not prove that a population as a whole has accepted the new stipulations in either attitude or behavior. Historical studies of Chinese legal decisions concerning the family show that for centuries certain customs were followed in the face of official disapproval.

Only with the recent drafts of Chinese family codes do we see the new conceptions of the family implemented by leaders who have used their political power and social influence to translate policy into behavior on the part of the populace.

The successive legal drafts show a clear development and prove that the Communist Family Law of May 1, 1950 is not a radical break with past codes. There is also no doubt that new attitudes have come about because the mechanisms used for reformulating family law have made the entire subject an occasion for widespread debate, propaganda, and argument.

It therefore seems useful to present a few of the changes and ideas to be found in the successive formulations of family law that preceded China's most recent family code. These items have not been selected to give a full account of the drafts, but only to note how early some of the "modern" legal formulations began to appear.

THE CH'ING "CODE" AND THE FIRST PEKING DRAFT

The Western reader must first keep in mind that Chinese dynastic law did not typically separate an area of "family law," and that the law itself was not systematized in the Western manner. For the most part, legal decisions, as well as customs, were based upon interpretations of the *li*—"rites," "etiquette," or "proper behavior." Perhaps a roughly comparable pattern would be the commentaries on family behavior of the Talmud, or those based on the Koran. It is as though a Western judge were to base his decisions on common law, equity, and the ideas of Plato (in China, Confucius). Thus, the attempt to produce a specific family code was itself a radical step.

An Imperial Edict of 1907 created a codification commission, two of whose members drew up a draft for a new family law. This was completed in 1911 and published in 1916. During that period, however, the Ch'ing Dynasty fell.[1] The introductory petition to the Throne notes the necessity for integrating Chinese laws and those used abroad, the importance of maintaining the customs of the people, and the importance of making new laws which will help in developing the country. In many ways, this draft is guided by the Japanese Civil Code. The draft begins to accept the necessity of separating the law from *li*. Kinship begins to take on a legal definition that is not based on the traditional mourning charts and the cult of the ancestors. The idea of individual rights, as in the right of the wife to claim divorce, begins to appear. The draft accepts the traditional notion that the state generally should not interfere in family affairs, but asserts the necessity of doing so in such areas as divorce and the family council. The intent of the draft was to define the membership of the council, which was a customary Chinese institution not treated in the official Code, to set the conditions for calling a council meeting, and to specify how decisions were to be reached. Such a council might consist of three to seven elder members of the family (including collateral relatives), and dealt especially with family disputes.

SECOND PEKING DRAFT

This draft is dated 1915 and generally follows the first. It does permit the head of the family to entrust part of his power to another member of the family, and the rights and duties of family members are more clearly defined. Most of the changes are technical, aimed at greater legal clarification.

JUDICIAL INTERPRETATIONS BY THE SUPREME COURT

Decisions by a high court usually involve great people, great issues, or very unusual legal technicalities. Consequently, they cannot be used to understand a family system as a whole. However, the Ta-Li-Yüan (Supreme Court) began in the first decade of the Republic to develop new principles, based on the emerging code and on the new ideas about family and state which were the subject of political discussion at that time. It began to support the general thesis of freedom of marriage. It continued to support the traditional notion that all persons belonging to the same family must live together (for example, a son may not have his own establishment), and followed the traditional reasons which a man could use in divorcing a wife, as well as the three exceptions which prevented such a divorce. The traditional grounds were: barrenness, loquacity, incurable disease, jealousy, adultery, theft from the husband's family, and disobedience or insult to his parents; the bars were: having shared the poverty of a husband who had become well-to-do, having no family to return to, and having mourned three years for the husband's parents.

After divorce the husband could still obtain guardianship of his children as before, but the Court accepted the notion that different arrangements were possible under some conditions: for instance, a mother might become guardian of her children. The Court began to accept the notion that members of the family might own property separately. In the course of several years of decisions, the conception began to be established legally that the intention of the marrying couple was an essential requirement for marriage.

Divorce by mutual consent was to be carried out by the married couple personally (not by the elders) and a quarrel between the husband's ascendants and the wife could not be a basis for divorce.[2]

Finally, it is clear that the Supreme Court came to feel that judicial officials might have great power in interfering in family matters, rather than leaving them to private decisions.[3]

THIRD PEKING DRAFT

This draft is dated 1925 and introduces still more foreign models, especially from the Japanese Code. In general, this draft affords more protection to the individual than the previous ones, following the lead of the Ta-Li-Yüan. Parents and guardians could not dissolve an engagement if a young man and woman persisted in their wish to marry, although in general the classic family system was upheld. References to the *li* are less common than in earlier drafts.

FIRST NANKING DRAFT

This draft was not put into effect, but it does reflect some of the important ideas about family law which were at the center of political discussion taking place in the early period of the Kuomintang around 1928. In this conception, the new laws are seen as specifically important in contributing to the development of the country. One of these, the principle of the equality of sexes, and the absolute freedom of marriage and divorce,[4] had been laid down by the second Congress of the Kuomintang in 1926. In the first Nanking draft, the power of relatives to arrange marriages for the young or those lower in rank was eliminated. Freedom of marriage was affirmed, but a man might not even make an agreement to marry before his 18th year, nor a woman before her 16th. Both husband and wife had the right to demand a divorce, and divorce by mutual consent was permitted. The property of husband and wife could be separated.[5]

KUOMINTANG CIVIL CODE

In the 1931 code, the *li* and the law are almost completely separated. Ancestral worship is ignored. Equality of women is asserted, as well as the principle of the freedom of marriage.[6] Divorce did not have to be based on the specific fault of one spouse, but could be based on the existence of a situation that made the purpose of marriage unattainable. The wife could divorce her husband for adultery, but it still remained possible for a man to take a concubine, and the woman could not use this as a ground for divorce.[7] Following tradition, divorce could be based on the wife's ill treatment of her husband's lineal ascendants, but now she could also ask for divorce if she, herself, had been badly treated by them. A distinction is introduced between legitimate and illegitimate children, but it becomes easy to acknowledge an illegitimate child (following the Soviet Code of Family Law), and with such an acknowledgement the child's position will equal that of the legitimate child.[8] In general, the relation of husband and wife is viewed as central to the family, not their relations with his ascendants. Moreover, the head of the household can no longer require adult members of the family to live in the household.

In May 1931 these family sections of Republican China's Civil Code came into force. It should be kept in mind that somewhat different laws were passed in the so-called Soviet Republic of China, beginning with the 1927–1937 period, and that later, as the Communists took over various parts of China, their own conceptions (for example, the marriage regulations of the Shansi-Hopei-Shahar border region, 1943) began to supersede those of the basic Kuomintang laws.

Most of the changes that the Communist regime has tried to institute represent restatements of the general principles and specific stipulations found in these earlier drafts and codes, with further attempts to integrate them. The new code also takes account of the numerous points at which local custom has not changed greatly, even after years of public pressure. We shall discuss some of these points later. The 1950 law is, then, the culmination of well over half a century of public discussion, ideological argument, philosophical development, and legislative reformulation.

Even in the nineteenth century, some impetus toward a changed status for *women* could be seen in the establishment in China of girls' schools (the kernel of many of these changes) by Western Christians.[9] Some women actually participated in politics by working toward the downfall of the Ch'ing Dynasty. In the nineteenth century, female silk workers in one district in Kwantung took part in an organized movement, which continued throughout the century, against marriage itself, as a protest against the burdens of the old system. Nevertheless, in spite of increasingly liberal laws, family patterns changed only sporadically, and in a small part of the population, over this long period.

More than one new leader who took over the direction of China after the fall of the Ch'ing realized the necessity of changing the family system in order to change the political order. According to Sun-Yat-Sen, it was minimally necessary to supplant the ideal of family and clan unity with the ideal of national unity. Under the old system, if a government order contradicted the command of a father, the son was obliged to obey his father. Under such a system, new reforms were clearly difficult to establish. On purely ideological grounds, any democratic philosophy would inevitably conflict with the old Confucian notion that respect for elders transcended independent judgment and that family ties counted far more than individual worth. By the end of the nineteenth century, ideas stressing individual worth had been strongly expressed, especially by the Reform Movement of 1898, but during the 1920s and 1930s the attack on the old order became especially strong.[10]

Although forces of industrialization and urbanization continued to have an impact on behavior, and the discussions of the generation following the fall of the Ch'ing had their effect, it can be taken as certain that the family patterns of most Chinese had not changed appreciably by the time the Communists took political control. This can be easily deduced from the instructions published in 1953 by the Government Administrative Council (the highest executive agency at that time), urging the full implementation of the 1950 law. These instructions refer to the lack of understanding and even active opposition of officers of the Communist Party itself, who "upheld wicked feudal customs, interfered with the freedom of marriage, oppressed women and thus brought about an uninterrupted series of suicides and even homicides."[11] Marriage reform was seen as an effort to change people's inner thoughts, necessary now that the old system of production and ownership had changed. This would require education, elimination of many misunderstandings, and a directed concentration on the regions of China where little change had taken place up to that point. A massive effort was to begin, therefore, with the aim of establishing in the mind and behavior of the masses the new ideas about marriage and the family. These directives provide evidence, then, that even in the early 1950s the new policies had not succeeded in winning the allegiance of the ordinary Chinese. Let us consider some of these changes in detail.

1. Freedom of Choice in Marriage

Implicitly, the Chinese always recognized that if the young lived apart from the older generation and had independent incomes, the authority of the elders would be undermined. From the T'ang through the Ch'ing Dynasties, living apart from parents and possessing property of one's own was considered unfilial behavior for which punishment was prescribed.[12] Under the old system, marriage was not a personal matter but a family decision, aimed at producing male offspring to assure continued ancestor worship. Consequently, the marital preferences of eligible mates were not considered. Decisions leading to a marriage were made by elders, especially the males (although in fact elder women often carried on much of the negotiation). The authority of the elders to arrange marriage was still recognized in the early years of the Republic.[13] Naturally, then, love was not to play a role in marriage, and considerable effort was made to prevent the kinds of informal interaction that might have led to love relationships. The chances of rebellion against these practices were checked by marriage at a young age.

By the 1930s, however, educated Chinese youth had come to believe that they should be allowed to choose their spouses, and to base their marriages on love. Half the college-educated respondents and almost a fourth of the high-school-educated respondents to a 1925 questionnaire, circulated among readers of a Shanghai newspaper, believed that romantic love was the most important consideration in marriage.[14] Among a college sample of the 1930s, consisting of 482 men and 428 women, Lang found that 54 per cent of the men and 68 per cent of the women wanted to choose their mates themselves and *then* ask for the parents' consent; and 37 per cent of the men and 15 per cent of the women wanted to make the decision entirely by themselves.[15] Only two of the men and three of the women said that they would prefer to have the parents choose the mate. On the other hand, in one of the most modernized districts of North China, a 1932 survey showed that parents ordinarily *had* a free hand in marriage arrangements, and Lang herself found almost no marriages in which the parent had asked the consent of the bride or groom in the villages she investigated.[16] In Shanghai, about one fifth of a small sample of industrial workers' marriages had been consented to by the spouses. The changes toward marriages based on a love relationship seem to have been most evident among professional and educated circles, and to some extent among industrial workers. In the former case, the influence of the new ideology is evident; among the latter, the new independence of the worker from the economic control of elders seems to be of more consequence. In China during the 1930s, as to some extent in contemporary Japan, the new ideology was hampered by the fact that no social arrangement existed that was comparable to the dating pattern in the West; that is, there were no dances, sporting events, parties, and similar informal social settings in which the contact of boy and girl is not defined as a serious involvement.

But freedom of marital choice has gradually come to be accepted in Chinese law and propaganda over the past half-century. Under the new Communist system, it is claimed that "men and women can now build up a life based on real love. They can build up a happy family based on real mutual love, respect, and mutual assistance."[17] The Marriage Law is interpreted to mean that love should be the basis of marriage.[18]

If love and freedom of choice are to be permitted for Chinese youth, then several older institutions of marriage must gradually disappear, although the evidence shows that they have not yet gone. Among these are the bride price, the purchase and pawning of wives and concubines, the *t'ung yang-hsi* (semiadoption of a girl as a later bride for the son), *chui-fu* (adoption of a boy as a future husband for a girl when there is no male heir), *chien t'iao* (a type of polygyny based on the inheritance by one man of two family headships), and, of course, the betrothal of children. All of these patterns are based on the power of the elders to arrange betrothals and marriages for their own purposes. With freedom of love and marriage, young people will no longer honor such agreements, and indeed their very purpose—continuity of the family line and of ancestor worship—will become less important. It is also likely that, as a result, there will be changes in the age and sex distribution of suicides.

Among upper-class families, the girl's family was bound to furnish trousseau and wedding gifts equivalent in value to the bride price itself; indeed, they might well surpass that amount. However, among the lower social strata, the marriage arrangement sometimes approximated actual purchase. As Van der Valk comments: "Sale and pawning of wives and women was, or is, a phenomenon only too well known in the social history of China. It was strictly forbidden and punishable but nevertheless occurred on a wide scale. It ranged from the sale of women publicly and selling married women by fraud, pretending them to be one's sister, to simpler forms such as the demanding of a high price from the man's family if he wished to marry."[19]

One can infer the continuance of these customs in Communist China from the report by Liu Ching-fan, Vice Chairman of the National Commission for the Marriage Law, that the propaganda campaign of March and April 1953 was largely successful in only 15 per cent of the country and completely unsuccessful in 25 per cent; and it was additionally reported that the propaganda itself reached the broad masses of people in only 70 per cent of the country.[20] On the other hand, the reports of the success of the new law and the publicity given to its failure to be extended sufficiently, point to the great effort being expended to persuade or coerce the population to follow the new rules. In the first half of 1954, according to returns from eleven large and medium cities, 97.6 per cent of the applications for marriage registration were granted because they conformed with the provisions of the marriage law and were not forced or arranged. In another report for the first quarter of 1954, the percentage was even higher.[21]

But contrary evidence was reported from rural China: "According to reports in many publications in different areas, rural youths still do not enjoy freedom of marriage, and especially young women are still to a great extent menaced by contracts and arranged marriages."[22] In a report on Shensi province, the charge was made that the Women's Association, the Youth League, the courts, Party branches, and People's Councils did not concern themselves with the Marriage Law and did not refer to the law except when there were homicide cases involving matrimonal problems. The report stated that the masses still considered marriage on a cash basis as a very sensible arrangement, and many girls left their marriage arrangement to their parents. It stressed the need for more publicity about the Marriage Law.[23] In the same report, it is asserted that 90 per cent of the marriages in these rural areas have been arranged by parents. Conceding the fact that an arranged marriage may not involve a genuine sale, the charge is made that in rural areas marriages can become the same thing under various guises: (1) Close kin are used as matchmakers to avoid trouble; (2) the parents conclude a cash deal behind the backs of the matchmakers; (3) two matchmakers are engaged by the buying party—the first one arranges for the cash deal and the second one handles the marriage registration; and (4) noncash gifts are made in the form of clothing and furniture.[24]

Some earlier reports, however, presented a more positive picture of the effects of the Marriage Law: in the 1951–1953 period in Lushan County, Honan Province, 4,600 marriages were reported to have been based on free choice.[25] A report from Kiangsi Province on the period from the promulgation of the Marriage Law until June 1952 stated that 121 thousand marriages were contracted by the free choice of the spouses, and 41 thousand engagements (presumably arranged by parents) were terminated by the individuals concerned. In addition, 16 thousand "child brides" were freed (although no ages for these women were given). Finally, 34 thousand couples were helped to form harmonious homes with the aid of counseling. In certain areas in Shansi Province, 88 per cent of the 2 thousand marriages in 1951 were based on free choice.[26]

In order to stress the evils of the system being supplanted, the Chinese have attempted to emphasize some of its lingering effects. An estimate was made in 1953 that some 70 thousand to 80 thousand women committed suicide or were killed each year because of matrimonial difficulties.[27] For the East China region, from January to August, 1952, over 4 thousand women were killed or committed suicide because of poor marriage relations.[28] In one area of Kiangsu, in January–June, 1952, there were almost 40 thousand betrothals arranged by family elders, three times the number of free engagements, and about 20 thousand arranged marriages, 28 per cent more than the free marriages.[29] In Ninghsia Province, almost 60 per cent of the marriages during the same period were reported to have been arranged by elders. In one county in Fukien, it was charged that 70 per cent of the new wives in 1953 were or had been "child wives," but in Honan 2 thousand "child wives" were reported who had not actually been married.[30]

Considering the relatively undeveloped state of marriage registration, and Chinese statistics in general, such figures cannot be assumed to be dependable, but they do suggest the intensity of interest in the problem and may also be a rough approximation of the facts. The references to "child wives" may refer primarily to the continuing custom of giving a young girl to her future husband's family as a baby, although she is sometimes brought there instead when she is old enough to be of use in the household. This practice is more common among the poor, although in southeast China it can be found among well-to-do families, and the girl is not always very young. The family that takes a *t'ung yang hsi* avoids paying a bride price later, and her family avoids the cost of maintaining her until the time of marriage. The betrothal is thus concluded when the girl is very young. Many legal cases have grown out of arguments which develop between the families later on; for example, the girl's family may try to abduct her when she is of marriageable age, in order to obtain a bride price from another family.[31] The girl may also refuse to go through with the marriage, whereupon a civil suit may arise in which the boy's family demands the costs of maintaining her, while she demands wages for her services while she was growing up. Communist authorities have followed the principle of freedom of marital choice, so that at present the girl does not have to marry the boy, and her family does not have to return either the betrothal presents or the costs of maintenance.

In some areas this type of betrothal amounted to bride sale, but since the judicial authorities will no longer back the boy's family, it may be supposed that this custom has begun to decline.[32]

The Communist Marriage Law prohibits the "exaction of money or gifts in connection with marriage," and the interpretation of the law has distinguished between bride price and ordinary betrothal presents. The former is forbidden as a violation of the principle that love should be the basis of marriage. Such legal disapproval will have far less effect than the increasing economic freedom of the young, who have come to depend far more on their own efforts than on their elders for jobs. This freedom will force the elimination of the bride price. Increasing personal freedom in these matters will eliminate not only the custom of taking a *t'ung yang hsi*, but also the custom of taking a *chui-fu* (the young man who enters the *girl's* home as a future husband for her). The *chui-fu* took the family name of the girl, thus guaranteeing to her family the continuance of the family line in the absence of a son. Ordinarily, this arrangement was made when the boy was young, and as a consequence (which sometimes followed also from the custom of *t'ung yang-hsi*), the girl might be many years older than the boy to whom she was betrothed.

According to the 1931 Code, the cult of the ancestors no longer received legal support, but the institution of *chui-fu* was still recognized.[33] Since the present law recognizes neither betrothal nor marriage when the boy is young, but asserts his freedom to choose a wife when he is of marriageable age (20 years), and since the ancestor cult itself is of far less consequence, it may be supposed that the frequency of this type of marriage will decline considerably.

The same probability applies to the ancient custom of *chien t'iao*, according to which an uncle might establish his brother's son as his own heir, while the boy remained his own father's heir as well, thus being the representative of two cults. Since the wife is in charge of the ordinary ancestor worship, he might, according to custom, marry two wives. Though emperors legislated against this custom during the Ch'ing Dynasty, it nevertheless continued, and in 1953 its bigamous and illegal status still was explicitly pointed out by the Communists.[34] Again, greater governmental control and the lessened importance of the ancestor cult will eliminate this custom, too.

2. Marriages With Relatives

The Chinese case once more illustrates one of our theses, that the *direction* of change may be different from one society to another, since differing systems begin from different points. In China, the new laws permit marriage with a *wider* range of relatives, although this permission in itself will not change contemporary marriage patterns much. In the past some relatives married anyway; and the widening range of marital eligibles *outside* the kin network will be the predominant source of spouses.

There was almost no limit to the prohibition of marriage to someone in the direct line of the male ascendants. The punishment for marrying someone belonging to the same cult of ancestors or male line and *within* the degrees of mourning (all the descendants of a common great-great grandfather) was greater than for marrying outside the degrees of mourning but within the same cult; but both were prohibited.[35] The prohibition generally extended only as far as the fifth Roman degree for persons related through females. Here again, the punishment was heavier if the relative was within the degrees of mourning.

Traditional family law was the subject for centuries of minute debate and analysis on these points of kinship, because of the great emphasis upon the cult of the ancestors. Consequently, successive drafts, beginning with the Civil Code of 1911, devoted great attention to the problem of modernization and included many comparisons with European systems. An effort was made through these drafts to rationalize the system and also to introduce the principle of "equality" into it, by moving toward a system whereby relationships through the female were as important as those through the male.

The present Communist Marriage Law states no rules of kinship, although it does distinguish between lineal and collateral relatives. Marriages between blood collaterals within the fifth degree of relationship were formerly forbidden, but under the new rules, the customs of the people will decide whether they are permissible.[36] Prohibitions by rank or generation were of considerable importance, but it is apparent that the intent of Communist legislation was to eliminate them.[37] Since the cult of ancestors itself has been denounced by Mao Tse-tung, the laws do not accept its importance in the matter of prohibiting marriage between various degrees of relatives, but allow custom to decide on the permissibility of intermarriage between collateral blood relatives. The new legislation avoids many of the legal complexities in the old system, as well as its conflicts between law and custom.

This conflict was most striking in the pattern of cross-cousin or parallel cousin marriage on the maternal side. The earliest known edict against this kind of marriage was introduced in 543 A.D., but the custom was permitted under the T'ang Dynasty.[38] At the core of the conflict surrounding this marriage pattern was the fact that the Chinese emphasis on male kinship meant that connections through females were of less importance, and that ties of friendship and association as well as the advantages of maintaining property intact, made marriages between close relatives seem attractive. On the other hand, such people were definitely within the degrees of mourning, and thus were excluded from marriage. Under Sung law, these marriages were permitted, but in practice some marriages nevertheless were annulled by officials in the Courts. Under Ming law, such marriages were forbidden, but in 1385 a more flexible interpretation was given by the emperor, stipulating that the custom of the people might be followed in this matter.[39] Law and custom continued to conflict with each other through Ch'ing times, and the present Communist legislation shows that the discrepancy is still to be found. It seems clear that marriages between relatives have been very common among ordinary people for hundreds of years, but that their existence has not been given much official attention except in the case of a legal problem. Perhaps most interesting is the fact that in the nineteenth century Van der Valk was unable to find any marriages of this type which had been prosecuted on charges of incest alone.[40] However, the frequency of cousin marriages is not known. Feng expresses his "general impression" that the percentage of cross-cousin marriage is very small.[41] Hsu states that the most favored form of marriage is the matrilateral cross-cousin marriage, that is, of a boy with his mother's brother's daughter.[42] Moreover, he insists that many marriages do occur between families of the same surname, and that there are many marriages between blood relatives in spite of the theoretical prohibition.[43] In addition, in some areas (for example in certain districts of Hopei Province) marriages with father's sister's daughter also are reported.[44]

Finally, some specific relatives by marriage were prohibited from marrying under the old provisions, and similarly were mentioned in earlier Communist legislation, but it is not certain that the contemporary Communist legislation recognizes the group at all, and these prohibitions may not be enforced. Here too, in spite of many legal prohibitions, there were some customs that encouraged or permitted marriages with in-laws—especially, in certain districts, marriage with a deceased brother's widow.[45] Feng also insists that the "junior levirate certainly exists in a few parts of modern China, at least among the poorer classes."[46]

It seems clear, then, that the traditional legal and philosophical prohibitions to marriages among consanguineal, collateral, and affinal kin extended very far in China, and perhaps farther than in any other major society; but legal change over the past decade has been in the direction of ignoring these rules.

Related to these barriers against kin marriages was the prohibition against marriage between two people with the same surname or from the same clan. Since only about 470 surnames were in common use in China, this meant a substantial reduction in the number of marriage combinations possible. Because of this rule, and because a large proportion of the population in a given neighborhood or village often belonged to one clan, marriages in China usually occurred between men and women from different villages or from different areas of a city. In the 1920s, for example, Buck found in the village he investigated that 97 per cent of the farm operators and 94 per cent of the operators' *fathers* were born in the same village. But only 6.6 per cent of their wives were born in the village.[47] Kulp found that the *tsu* or clan sometimes included the entire village.[48] In half the sixty-two villages in the Ting Hsien experimental district in Hopei, the largest clan included over 50 per cent of the families. In 25 per cent of the villages, the largest clan held over 90 per cent of the families.[49] The families named Wang, Chang, and Liu together comprised 30 per cent of the more than 10 thousand families in the sixty-two villages. In eleven of the villages, all the families had the same name.

Yet local customs and the sociologically predictable closeness among families united by blood or marriage created many widespread patterns of marriage within the prohibited degrees of relationship. As a consequence, the new legal provisions permit a *greater* frequency of marriage between kinfolk in various statuses, but the increased geographical and social mobility, and the lessened importance of both the kin line and the need to maintain property and power intact will mean that these local customs of kin marriages will begin to *decline* in frequency.

3. Concubinage and Bigamy

The decline of concubinage in China represents a change of little numerical importance but of great ideological significance. The attack on the institution, which was viewed as a symbol of the corrupt life of the nobility and the degraded position of women, began long before the Communist regime. Dr. Sun Yat-sen himself strongly opposed the system of slaves and concubines and made ordinances against it. Bigamy was prohibited as early as the T'ang Dynasty, and successively through the later Chinese dynasties. Modern legislation has reaffirmed this prohibition.

Both in law and custom, however, there were numerous ambiguities that were never adequately clarified. To begin with, Chinese wives could not claim the exclusive sexual attention of their husbands, and although they might feel and express some jealousy, they had no legal right to object to a concubine, even when she was established in their own household.[50] Since slaves and servants were partly assimilated to a familial status, and the introduction of a concubine into the household was sometimes accompanied by ceremony, the gradation in rank and position among these various women covered a wide range, so that with respect to any particular relationship it was not always clear exactly who was what. Finally, the position of the concubine was defined by many laws.

In addition, marriage itself sometimes occurred with very little ceremony—for example, the *t'ung yang hsi* might very well become a wife long after the childhood ceremony which established her in the home of her husband; or a marriage might take place in childhood, but the girl might return to her own home, to come back to her husband's home in adolescence with little or no ceremony.

As a consequence of these related facts, many law cases arose over the centuries which turned on the problem of who was in fact the wife, and which rights any specific woman had. If the wife died, could the concubine become the wife? Was it possible for a concubine to be charged with adultery? Was incest committed if a man's son had sexual relations with his father's concubine.

Legally, the concubine was not included among her "husband's" relatives, and she was excluded from mourning for most of them.[51] Nor could she be worshipped after death as an ancestor. Both the concubine and her children were under the wife's control, but under some interpretations her children inherited equally with the wife's children.[52] Bigamy itself, in the sense of full marriages with two women, was then of relatively little consequence numerically, and was the point of departure for many legal cases only because of the frequency with which the concubine approached the status of wife. Obviously, if the man had bought the concubine, there was normally no such question. On the other hand, if he desired, she might actually enter his household in wedding dress and sedan chair.[53]

These comments on the approach of the concubine's status to that of a wife do not apply, of course, to the custom of *chien t'iao* noted previously (when one man was the heir of two ancestral lines and actually married two women) or the custom in Kiangsu, Fukien, and Shensi, where certain forms of polyandry seem to have been found.[54] It seems clear that under the traditional code, bigamy without fraud was unlikely, since a man wealthy enough to afford two wives would often be able to establish one as his concubine, without the full formalities of marriage.

Resolving the problem of concubinage is not simple, for a man and woman may decide that they wish to live together without any ceremony. Thus, no charge of bigamy may be brought. If this relationship becomes stabilized, the state has no obvious reason to interfere. The man may still have certain obligations to his wife, but these are minimal. In short, it is difficult to proceed legally against a relationship that has no status under the current law. The official Communist attitude has been the same toward bigamy and concubinage, and the legal solution has also been the same: official opposition to both, but no legal action unless a female party to one of the relationships makes a complaint.

The question can still be raised as to whether China was, and to some extent still is, polygynous.[55] Legally, there was surely no fundamental ambiguity. A man could only have one wife at any one time, and since he and his family relations were investigated carefully before any real marriage, bigamy in the strict sense could not easily occur. The various rights and obligations of wives as against concubines were spelled out clearly. The wife was the concubine's mistress, although legally she could not oppose her husband's choice to introduce one into the household.

In his analysis of marriage types in Singapore, largely among Chinese from southeast China, Freedman has shown the range of ceremonies (civil, Christian, consular, etc.), the types of marriage (monogamy, polygyny, mistress-keeping), and status of the wife, (primary wife, "following wife," secondary wife, and mistress) that continue Chinese mainland practice.

Since most of these relationships are publicly known, one must conclude that to some extent they are supported by the dominant male values now, just as they were in traditional China. In the traditional household, the day-to-day relations among members of the household certainly gave some security to the status of concubine, even though her position was lower than that of the wife. Even in contemporary Singapore, Freedman notes that there may be trouble when a man has two separate households if one "wife" finds out about the other.[56] Finally, it is clear from both traditional and modern accounts that the wife felt great jealousy and hurt when her husband took a concubine.

Thus, the conflict between law and custom seems more apparent than real. What is culturally interesting is the extent to which concubinage does not seem to have been merely a morally deviant behavior, indulged in by those who were strong enough to brave public censure. Rather, it was well integrated into a complex, extended kinship system, in which many non-family positions were assimilated into a quasi family status—not only servants, slaves, and concubines but also friends and even business associates. Moreover, the phenomenon is interesting because of the extent to which the male continued to feel free not only to engage in outside sexual adventures but also to establish a secondary household within his primary one. As Hsu comments, a frequently expressed rationalization was the desire for male offspring, but his factual analysis shows that this cannot have been the main reason for this pattern. The dominance of the male simply permitted him a great freedom in such choices, while the legal system did not permit him to introduce such women (and perhaps he did not wish to accept such a responsibility) as wives.

Although without question the independence of women under the Communist system means a decline in the number of these relationships, we should at least consider for a moment the frequency of concubinage under the older system. Fewer than 0.5 per cent of the families in Ting Hsien reported a concubine.[57] In a survey of some 38 thousand Chinese rural families during the 1930s, there were eighty-one wives to every concubine.[58] In Lang's sample of 1,700 college and high school students, 11 per cent reported that there was a concubine in their home, and the answers of an additional 6 per cent seemed to hint that a concubine was there.[59] Hsu found, by tracing genealogies, that approximately 15 per cent of the households in his sample had had concubines. Such data, of course, go back to the end of the Ch'ing Dynasty.[60] Even if we classify the Chinese system as polygynous, it is similar to other polygynous systems in that few men could have additional "wives." Now, when marriages are based far more on personal ties and women cannot so easily be purchased, and—far more important—the rigidities of class barriers cannot be used as an excuse for refusing to marry (suggesting, instead, a concubinage relationship), this pattern will continue to disappear.

4. Age at Marriage: Conflicting Reports

The most unfilial act, according to Mencius, was to be without descendants. If a man failed to have descendants, then not only would he himself fail to be honored as an ancestor but he would have failed to fulfill his duty to *his* ancestors to see that *they* continued to be worshipped. Consequently, the pressure toward marriage was, and remains, strong in China. The age at marriage was not, however, a subject of legislation. The young married couple was not expected to be independent after marriage, either economically or geographically; they did not even have the right to leave the household of the boy's father. Consequently, little attention was paid to chronological maturity. Under the present Chinese law, men may now marry at 20 years of age, women at 18. As young people gain greater control over their own economic destinies and over their choice of mate, and increasingly obtain posts in the industrial system with little or no family support, the age at marriage will certainly rise. However, the vocabulary of condemnation used by the Communists about the "feudal" past must not be permitted to conceal the facts about age at marriage in the past.

At no time during the historical period has the ideal been "child" marriage, if by that term we mean "preadolescent." The few data we possess from the past generation would suggest that child marriage was not *typical* in the past either.

In the commentary to the first Peking Draft, much discussion is given to the subject of permissible age at marriage because freedom of choice, control by the elders, and emancipation seemed to be tied to a higher age at marriage. The *Li Chi* had stated that a man marries at 30 years of age and a woman at 20 (or 23 under certain circumstances), but Confucius interpreted this statement to mean only that these were *maximum* ages.[61]

In the early part of the T'ang Dynasty, the ages were fixed at 20 and 15 years, and in the early period of the Ming Dynasty the ages were 16 and 14. The first Peking Draft, the first Nanking Draft, and the 1931 Code all set the age of marriage at 18 for men and 16 for women. The 1931 Code also permits a marriage agreement at 17 years for men and 15 years for women. The Communist Code simply raises these ages by two years. These formulations ignored several Chinese customs. One was found especially in the southeast, according to which a woman might well be older than the man. Thus, the wife could be of use in the household very soon. If she was also old enough to be physiologically mature, the possibility of having a son early was increased.[62] In addition, betrothal of children was widespread, and in some areas the marriage itself thus became no more than a formality. One custom permitted two pregnant women to agree upon the future marriage of their progeny if they proved to be a boy and girl (*chi fu*).[63] The custom of *t'ung yang hsi* also made for betrothals at very early age, often with a boy younger than the girl.

Though various prohibitions against these customs and the new rules concerning age at marriage might mean that a marriage performed under those circumstances might now be annulled, Communist authorities do not seem to wish to dissolve these marriages. The parties themselves would have to take the initiative upon attaining marital adulthood, if they wished to dissolve the marriage.

The Communists have taught the harmfulness of early marriage, and on political grounds have attacked "child marriages" as a product of feudal practices. Certainly many girls did marry in their early teens under the old system. On the other hand, the peasant son would usually have to wait until his elders had accumulated enough for an adequate bride price. Since the mortality among female children was high, and some men had both concubine and wife, men of the lower strata often had to delay marriage. As a consequence, we can be sure that modern freedom of choice will eliminate marriages and betrothals at extremely early ages; but the average age at marriage may not rise so sharply as some observers have suggested. Substantial evidence can be cited in support of the contention that unusually early marriage was not common in past generations. Material bearing on this point will therefore be presented here.

Data reported on one Canton clan (Wu) show that the average age of the father at the birth of his *first living* son was 33 years in the period from 1150 to 1500 A.D., 31 years in the 1630–1800 period, and 23 in the 1800–1880 period.[64]

In the early period of the new era after the fall of the Ch'ing Dynasty, one of the groups working to reform the marriage customs, the Ting Hsien Customs Improvement Club, attempted to set the minimum marriage age at 20 years for boys and 16 for girls.[65] The average age at marriage seemed to be rising at the time of the Ting Hsien study in the late 1920s. For the combined samples composed of persons who had married at different times in the past, the average age at marriage in the two samples was 17.2 and 18.7 years, respectively, for the males, and 17.7 in both samples for females. There were only five unmarried women over 21 years of age and 14 per cent of unmarried men in that age group among the 5,255 families.[66] Forty-eight per cent of the 17-year-old girls and 72 per cent of those 18 years of age already had been married in one group of these families.[67]

Before looking at other age distributions, we must note one factor which affects them. The custom of arranged marriages creates a class differential in age at marriage which is the reverse of that in the contemporary conjugal pattern of the West. Where the ideal is that of early fertility, those who are well-to-do can marry off their children at an early age; thus youngsters from wealthier families marry earlier in China, as in Japan and Africa. These families already had sufficient wealth for the bride price and the young man did not need to be independent. The family could thus obtain a grandson quickly, and guarantee the unbroken chain of ancestors for yet another generation.

Since it was the man's family who needed land and wealth in order to marry, the difference in percentages married at given young ages between those with little land and those with more land was greater for males than for females.

In Ting Hsien, the larger the amount of land owned by the family, the lower the age at marriage for both males and females. In most categories of younger ages, a higher proportion of *males* than females were married. On the other hand, among those with very *little* land, some men were unable to marry until relatively late: some 20 per cent of those with less than 50 *mu* of land married later than 22 years of age.[68]

An important regional difference shows up, however, in Ting Hsien: in 70 per cent of a sample of 766 couples, the wife was older than her husband, while in 25 per cent the husband was older.[69] This custom may be widespread in the Shantung-Hopei region. With reference to Shantung, Van der Valk comments: "It was customary for the wife to be much older than the husband, even up to 8 or 9 years, who himself was only 13 or 15 years old and sometimes 12 or 13. It was considered a shame for the parents if their son was not married at 15 or 16."[70] The Communists have poured much scorn on this custom, describing how a young woman might be taking care of an infant who was legally her husband.

This reversal of the presumed ideal Chinese age pattern is also found in southeast China (Hokkien, Teochin, Kiangsu, Kiangsi, etc.). In this region, however, the average age of men at marriage may be slightly lower than that of women because of the widespread custom of *t'ung yang hsi*. This pattern does not seem to have been confined to the poor. Reporting on one village in south China, Kulp found that the age at marriage for girls was approximately 18 years, and for boys from a year to a year and a half younger.[71] In Ting Hsien, as in Lang's sample, among the couples in the free market towns (as contrasted with the rural areas), the average difference in age for the entire group shows the husband to have been 1.8 years *older* than the wife.[72]

Lang also notes that in some localities wives are older as a rule. She found that the husbands were more likely to be older than their wives among the 3 thousand *urban* couples in her sample than among the 370 *rural* couples. She believes that the poorer peasants wanted a woman to be useful in the household.[73]

Another survey from the 1920s yielded an average age of about 18 years at marriage for males, and 17 years for females. The people in this village claimed that young persons in days gone by seldom married before the ages of 23 or 24 years and now were beginning to marry earlier.[74]

Reports of older people are often unreliable, but it is at least interesting to note that in one attempt to ask such people for their ages at marriage, in a sample of persons married in the last quarter of the nineteenth century (that is, fifty years prior to Buck's study), respondents gave an average age of approximately 22 years for males, and 20 years for females.[75] In a 1929–1931 survey taken in twenty-two localities of eleven Chinese provinces, 72 per cent of the women had been married by 15–19 years of age, and 45 per cent of the men had been married by that age, while almost everyone who married had done so by age 25–29.[76]

However, a study based on registration data was carried out in 1932–1935, apparently by the same research team, which showed that only 38 per cent of the females married by age 15–19. This contrast between current registration data and the data from a type of census survey might suggest a slight rise in the age at marriage even by the beginning of the 1930s (since the latter figures are for current marriages and the former figures are for marriages in the past, in some cases dating back two decades). On the other hand, the difference may simply reflect the well-known difficulty of Chinese surveys in ascertaining correct ages.[77] (It should be kept in mind that figures given for Chinese ages are on the average about one year less than those given for Western ages, since a Chinese child is one year old at birth, and adds an additional year each New Year. However, so far as the data permit, all ages given in this section are adjusted to Western ages.) For the period 1931–1935, the mean age at marriage in this Kiangsu community was 22 years for males, and 18.9 for females.

Although each of these figures is based on a small sample relative to the whole Chinese population, they at least show that adolescent or "child" marriage was neither the usual pattern statistically, nor was it the ideal.

In a sample of 2,598 Chengkung couples during the 1940–1944 period, the average age at first marriage was 19.5 years for males and 17.6 years for females. In another region, the average was 20.5 for males and 18.6 for females.[78] These are "registration data."

Survey data for the same period and the same area of Yunnan also suggest the difficulties of obtaining adequate information on this point. As noted previously, a discrepancy of considerable size may sometimes be found between registration and census data. Such a discrepancy in survey-census materials is highly improbable, however, when it shows wide variations for the same area in *successive years*. Thus, for the entire period of these surveys, 44 per cent of the women had been married by age 15–19, but the survey data taken year by year show percentages ranging from 21 per cent to 64 per cent for this group. So great a variation in ordinary census materials taken from one year to the next in a large region suggests very serious shortcomings in the data themselves.[79]

We do have accurate trend data on one substantial population of Chinese, however—those of Taiwan—from which it may be judged that the registration data are really correct in giving somewhat older ages at marriage than commonly supposed—that is, a modal age of 20–21 years for men and 18 years for women. Very early in their occupation of Taiwan, the Japanese instituted an effective registration system. I see no reason, and Barclay suggests none, to suppose that the family behavior of these millions of Chinese deviated much from that on the mainland during this period, except for the exclusion of the upper classes. These Chinese were restricted for the most part to lower-level agricultural work under Japanese domination. Thus, missing from these data are the upper-class Chinese who normally would have married at much younger ages. On the other hand, numerically they would have been few even on the mainland.

In 1905, 47.3 per cent of the women 15–19 years of age were "ever married," while in 1935, only 28.9 per cent of this same age group were "ever married," a definite rise in age at marriage over this period of a generation. Only 10.2 per cent of males were "ever married" by age 15–19 in 1905, and 5.7 per cent in 1935.[80] The 1905 figure for women corresponds roughly to two of the census data reports noted above for China.

The average age at first marriage of Taiwanese males (excluding Japanese) was 24.0 in 1906 and, although it dropped to 22.0 in 1939, by 1943 it was 24.0. That is to say, no trend at all is apparent in the data. For females the age was 18.1 in 1906 and 18.8 in 1907 and then rose very slightly to 20.8 in 1943. This slight rise is probably due to a *decreasing* sex ratio rather than to any change in custom. That is to say, there was a shortage of women in the earlier period of the occupation, but as the ratio approached normalcy, women married slightly later. Thus in about 1940 the age at marriage among Taiwanese Chinese was almost the same as that in the United States over the past two decades.

Hsu's data on Yunnan are not greatly different, although he does not give an age distribution. In West Town, betrothal occurred at young ages during the early 1940s, but the *lowest* age approved for marriages was 17 years for males and 16 for females. More important, "the majority of boys and girls married 2, 3, or 4 years later than that."[81]

One Taiwan trend is similar to those existing in the West, Africa, and Japan: The age difference between husband and wives dropped sharply during the generation from 1906 to 1943, from 5.9 years to 3.3 years.[82]

It should be kept in mind that almost all of the data presented on this point have been from rural areas or small towns. During the generation prior to the Communist success, however, the major changes in marriage and family patterns were taking place in the cities. For these populations, only impressionistic data seem to be available. Thus, Lang found in the 1930s that a sample from Peking and Shanghai was far less likely to have been married at age 15 than Bucks' rural sample.[83] Moreover, she found many working-class girls, as well as male and female college students, who had delayed marriage until well into their 20s. Educated women of the Chinese higher classes always married somewhat later. Ta Chen notes that all women in his sample who had gone abroad for higher education married after age 19.[84] Yang observes that the general practice is for the man to marry after 20 and for the girl to be married after 18 but by the early 20s.[85]

A slight increase in Chinese marriage ages should be expected, as noted before, since very young marriages are criticized by the Communist regime and there is also much less control over the young by elders; furthermore, young men and women are now expected to take their own place in the economic process and must be able to function as adults when they marry. Since almost everyone can obtain a job, this means that the age at marriage will not rise to the European level, but may remain close to that of the United States.

The data from Singapore Chinese marriages—those of urban Chinese who have emigrated, largely from South China—are also relevant here. Their marriage patterns are perhaps more characteristic of urban China just prior to the Communist accession to power. A tabulation of over 5 thousand Singapore brides married by civil and Christian rites in the 1941–1949 period yields an average age at marriage of 21 years. Data calculated from several samples suggest an approximate age of about 23–25 years for grooms, and 19–21 years for brides.[86] In 1947 the Singapore Census showed that 19.7 per cent of Chinese women aged 15–19 had been married (about half as many in this age bracket as in the several mainland samples cited earlier), and 1.8 per cent of men at that age.

The Communists have attacked the practice of early marriage because of its supposed effect upon health, the birth rate, and preparation for a profession. An article which appeared in the Peking *Chung Kuo Min Pao* stated that among young factory workers about four fifths of the females had been married before age 21, in part because of practices surviving from the older society and because veteran workers still play matchmaker. In addition, the statement is made that some of these marriages were caused by premarital sexual relations.[87] This is, of course, a tiny sample, and was used only for editorial purposes. Another editorial published at the same time urged later marriage because early marriage was detrimental to study and work. Among the themes used in the International Women's Day Celebration in 1957 was the discouragement of early marriage.[88] Another editorial in the same month urged late marriage. This was part of the campaign at that time to encourage a limitation on birth. Chung Hui-Lan said, in a 1957 speech, that marrying early was harmful, and the proper age for marriage should be from 25 to 30 years. He declared that the marriage age in the Marriage Law was a minimum only, and urged people not to marry so early.[89] The campaign of persuasion continues, although the Chinese have taken the position that those who have already reached the minimum age prescribed by the 1950 Marriage Law, but were married before that age, should not be disturbed in their marriages. One form that the campaign has taken is a spate of letters to the press. Attempts also have been made to allay fears accompanying the contemplation of delay in marriage and child bearing. For instance, in answer to women's worries that they might have obstetrical difficulties if they had children late, the head of the Chinese medical association said, after an informal meeting of Peking doctors, that 25 years was the best age for having children.[90]

There can be no doubt that the long-time trend in the past toward a slow increase in the age at marriage, especially in the urban areas. Under the new regime, it is likely that the villages will follow. Few data now exist to permit an estimate of the present situation. One datum may be cited, containing a typical Chinese ambiguity, that "in the city of Shanghai, between 1953 and 1955, 70 per cent of the newly married couples fell within the age bracket 18 to 25."[91]

5. Birth Rates and Contraception

The trend in the Chinese birth rate over the past half-century, if one exists, cannot be ascertained. Even the crude birth rate (number of births per thousand population in a given year) is unobtainable, since neither the population base nor the number of births is known for any year. Since in pre-Communist years birth was a concern of the family, not the state, no procedures for registration existed. The attempts during the 1920s and 1930s at developing registration procedures in several localities were frequently hampered by the reluctance of families to report to outsiders the birth of females, because it was no honor to bear a female, and of males, because of the magical and spiritual dangers to the child if the family exhibited pride about having him.

As we have already noted, adult males wanted children in order to have sons who would maintain the system of ancestor worship. Wives wanted children, because in time sons would bring to the household daughters-in-law who would be under their authority. Having sons gave the bride a higher position in the family. The traditional Chinese value system doubtless remained much the same in these respects in rural areas until fairly recently, so that the birth rate has undoubtedly been very high.

One cannot, however, assume, as do some observers, that this rate would have been as high as forty-five to fifty per thousand in the 1950s, when an official Chinese birth rate of thirty-seven births per thousand population was derived from a sample of some 20 million persons. Orleans doubts that the rate could have been that low, because such a rate would seem to be too low "for a country without effective control on fertility."[92] Yet a large error does not seem likely. As in every society, there were various points at which either custom or rationality put some brake upon Chinese fertility.[93]

Many men and women in the lower strata were forced to delay marriage for years because of poverty. Various forms of concubinage and prostitution lowered the birth rate. It was considered improper for husband and wife even to sleep together when their children approached adulthood, and certainly was improper after the marriage of their children. The periodic famines and endemic disease of China killed more infants than adults, and many millions of Chinese died before having children. Widows in the middle and upper strata often did not remarry, a further factor in keeping the birth rate lower than the maximum. An unknown, but large, number of Chinese men engaged in commercial or military operations requiring travel. Since their wives were cared for by the husbands' families, these men could stay away for long periods of time. The extreme poverty of the diet of tens of millions of Chinese certainly reduced fertility still more. All these factors would have kept the birth rate below the maximum, even if no Chinese attempted to control birth by such techniques as *coitus interruptus*.

Chen Ta* estimated China's national birth rate to be thirty-eight per thousand population in 1934, about the same as the 1953 estimate cited above.[94]

An effort was made in Shansi Province to obtain modern population data, but in the twelve years between 1912 and 1923 the recorded birth rate varied from 62.5 (1917) to 12.3 (1919). Such fluctuations are simply not credible. Death rates may vary to that extent, but not birth rates. In the 1920s, the reported birth rates for several cities were also too low to be believable—3.4 in Tientsin (1929), 8.7 in Hankow (1930), and 9.0 in Tsing-tao (1933). From 1929 to 1931, Chiao calculated a birth rate of 35.7 in a sample of over 12 thousand farm families from ten provinces, a figure close to the 38.3 per thousand which Buck found in 1937 in a sample of over 38 thousand farm families.[95] It should be kept in mind that birth rates in Chinese cities, as in any urban agglomeration, are normally affected by the highly skewed age composition of urban populations.

Outside the cities, Chen Ta tabulated the most reliable estimate for the period between 1917 and the 1940s, suggesting that, as in other parts of the world, urban rates have been lower than rural ones, and that Chen Ta's own estimates of the national rate (thirty-eight births per thousand population) is defensible.[96]

Where fertility is greatly desired, as in China, the birth rate is higher among the upper strata. Contraceptive measures are less likely to be used by the rich than by some of the poor, who may try to reduce the number of mouths to feed. On the other hand, the delay in marriage among at least those with higher education (and thus also from the upper stratum) might be somewhat lower than the maximum. Even so, under the traditional system, the total number of surviving children might well be greater than in a poor family.[97]

With increasing urbanization, those who wished to control births would be more likely to become aware of possible techniques for doing so. A rise in the average age at marriage would also have tended to lower the birth rate. Nevertheless, the overwhelming majority of rural Chinese probably did not exhibit any substantial decline in birth rate prior to the past decade.

Westerners are generally convinced, both by arithmetic and by observation, that the nations of the world must reduce their birth rate if they are

* Ta Chen. His name is used differently in different books, and I am here following Orleans.

not to overpopulate the limited surface area of the globe and eventually be unable to feed themselves. Consequently, they greeted with approval the Chinese campaign for birth control which began in late 1956 and continued in the following year. The apparent repudiation of that campaign in 1958 seemed not only puzzling, but irrational. Why was a campaign that had been supported with so great an intensity of propaganda suddenly denounced? Could any reasonably intelligent Chinese leader believe that the unlimited growth of population could be anything but a catastrophe? Let us examine the sequence of events and arguments leading to the brief propaganda campaign in favor of contraception as well as its aftermath. It will be seen that in spite of public cessation of the campaign the Chinese have continued to support contraception, so that the birth rate is undoubtedly beginning to drop and in the future will probably be closer to that of the West.

Although the Chinese announced with great pride in 1953 that their population was then 582.6 million, and that they could take care of it easily, those census figures must have created some anxiety; as early as August, 1953 the Cabinet instructed the Ministry of Public Health to help the public in a program of birth control.[98] At the meeting of the National People's Congress in Peking, September, 1954, the issue of birth control was publicly debated.[99] In December, 1954 one of the important Marxian theorists, Liu Shao-Ch'i, called a conference to discuss the subject of birth control.[100] In March 1955, the Party's Central Committee published an "Instruction on Control of Birth," but this was not released to the public. In September 1956, at the Eighth Party Congress, Premier Chou En-lai made a plea for the "appropriate control of birth."[101]

By 1957, a full-scale propaganda campaign was under way. On March 5, 1957, an editorial in Peking's *People's Daily* discussed the sequence of decisions and events in the development of this campaign ("Births must be well controlled.") The editorial admitted that the aim was to prevent too rapid an increase of population, in contrast to the earlier line of persuasion, which stressed the value of birth control to health, work and study, and the proper care of children.[102]

The Vice-Ministry of Health in discussing contraception and abortion in September 1956, had made these points:

1. Childbirth is not merely a private thing, because it affects the whole nation. The government has some responsibility for childbirth, especially with reference to the health of women.
2. Regular spacing of children is necessary for the health of mothers, and for the improvement of their work and study.
3. The Ministry of Health is considering relaxing the regulation of artificial abortion, but contraception is much more desirable.[103]

An August 1956 editorial in the Peking *Kuang Ming Jih Pao* asserted that the Health Department had not done enough work and that contraceptives were not available in many localities. Moreover, some pharmaceutical plants had stopped the production of contraceptives. The editorial said that the propaganda had not been conducted adequately and had not offered solutions to the problem. Old ideas apparently persisted, since the editorial noted that drugstores would neither sell nor show contraceptives to women. The editorial merely criticized the campaign as inadequate, however; it did not oppose it.[104] The Ministry of Health, in August, 1956, demanded that medical and public health organizations at various levels assume the burden of informing people about contraception, and that provincial and municipal departments of health train groups to give such guidance. Specific contraceptives were mentioned in a speech before the 1957 session of the National Committee, and men were urged to assume some of the responsibility for contraception.[105] The President of Peking University took part in this campaign, and was perhaps the only major speaker to continue his argument after the official Communist position had changed.[106]

The birth control campaign was called off in May, 1958, with the argument, anti-Western in tone, that the strength and wealth of China lay in her population, and although a capitalist country might not be able to expand its production so rapidly as its population grew, China could do so under Communism. There could be no surplus of manpower, because there were jobs for all. The President of Peking University was permitted to write two more articles attacking the Party for dropping the birth-control policy; but the official position was clear: There was no population problem.[107] Both the criticism and the new "policy" permit the outsider to deduce that the campaign did not achieve an immediate and striking success, attacking as it did a rather fundamental value of traditional Chinese life. On the other hand, although fertility is a widespread value in most peasant and primitive societies, demographers who are worried about the world population expansion seem to agree that women in most societies are far more willing to use contraceptives than Westerners—or even the leaders of their societies—have supposed. Certainly the many letters in the Communist newspapers of the period show that there was widespread concern about the problem, especially among women. Naturally, their concern was a personal rather than a national one.

The best interpretation of the succeeding situation seems to be that the political and ideological line then asserted that China as a Communist nation did not need population control. The "spacing of births" was recommended, however, for health reasons and on practical grounds, even if this policy was not expounded in *public*. Birth-control advice and appliances can be obtained in hospitals and from physicians. Newspapers and magazines still advised young people to use contraceptives and not to marry early. It was claimed that as the people come to a higher standard of literacy, they would accept and understand birth control.[108]

The Vice-Minister of Health informed Chandrasekhar that "there seems to be some misunderstanding on this question . . . We don't call it family planning or birth control or planned parenthood . . . We in China call it *planned births*."[109]

Thus, family-planning services may be obtained in hospitals and clinics, and contraceptive factories are in full operation. There seems to be no doubt that over the next few years the birth rate will continue to drop. In the winter of 1962–1963, China again reversed its policy, and espoused birth control openly.

6. Illegitimacy and Prostitution

There seem to be no data by which any trend in Chinese illegitimacy rates can be ascertained. An important change has occurred, however, in the *definition* of illegitimacy, one which would affect the rate, whether known or not. Under the system which continued at least through the 1930s, illegitimacy growing out of the intimacy of dating or courtship—the common origin of illegitimacy in the West—was rare in China. Some prostitutes and tea-house girls had children, but these were of no concern to either law or custom.

Many children were also born to concubines, but although the status of such women was differentiated from wives, their children were certainly not defined as "illegitimate" in any Western sense. Such children took part in household activities, might inherit if the wife herself had no children, were acknowledged to be part of the household, and had a claim on the father for maintenance.

The problem of defining legitimacy was given some attention by the lawmakers attempting to reform the Chinese legal system.[110] Since the 1931 Constitution did not disturb the institution of concubinage, it did not much change the status of this category of children, although it did grant them some rights.[111] The Communist Marriage Law has attempted to define the children born out of wedlock as having the same rights as those born in wedlock, and forbids anyone to discriminate against such children. No such law can achieve its purpose. As long as there is a marriage system, children who are born outside it will have a different social status. The stratification system upon which the older patterns of "illegitimacy" rested is being undermined, however. It is much more difficult for a man to establish his concubine even separately from his household, much less within his household. On the other hand, courtship is becoming more common in China so that the *Western* form of illegitimacy is more likely to occur, in spite of the rather puritanical morality that is preached in contemporary China.[112] The young woman who has a child outside marriage is less likely to be ostracized than under the old system.

Finally, the Communists have made a determined effort to eliminate prostitution. Prostitutes were unproductive, and were a symbol of the corruption of the old system. Moreover, prostitution was defined as a capitalist evil,[113] and prostitutes were viewed as a source of the widespread venereal disease existing in large cities.[114]

The older family system may have depended for its stability in part upon the informal sexual relations that men found among prostitutes; certainly men were permitted to find among prostitutes and concubines the romance not available within the older Chinese family system. Yang remarks that "traditional merchants as well as government officials transacted much of their business, and traditional scholars wrote some of their best lines of poetry in whorehouses."[115] The present Chinese government has tried to stamp out public prostitution. But as long as men are willing to pay, directly or indirectly, for the sexual favors they receive from women, there is bound to be some illegitimacy from this source. In any event, the law requires that both mother and father be responsible for the care and maintenance of the child.

It can be asserted that China is moving toward a new definition of illegitimacy, closer to the Western one and accompanied by new patterns of courtship. With the new pattern, a higher rate of one kind of illegitimacy is developing, while the traditional type of "illegitimacy"—not even defined as true illegitimacy fifty years ago—is disappearing rapidly.

7. From Extended Family and Clan to the Commune

The traditional "ideal" Chinese family contained many generations, all united through the males and all living under one roof. Included were the oldest living male ascendant and his wife, their sons and their sons' wives, the unmarried daughters, all the unmarried grandchildren, the wives of the married grandsons, and so on. Although both Chinese and Western literature have focused on such families, it is now well known that none but the well-to-do was ever able to maintain an extended family network in one household.[116]

In general, the greater the size of the farm, the greater the size of the household.[117] Sons inherited equally, and most families broke up soon after the father's death. As a consequence, average family size in China was only slightly higher than that in the United States, ranging, according to one set of statistics, from 4.1 persons in Jehol Province to a high of 6.9 persons in the frontier province of Kirin in Manchuria.[118] In Ting Hsien, the size of the average family was 3.8 persons at the lowest income level, and 9.3 at the highest income level, with an average for the 5,255 families in the most typical sample being 5.8 persons.[119] And some of the larger households might, in any event, be internally divided into smaller units, as Hsu reports for West Town.

Moreover, this is not a recent "trend." For the past 2 thousand years, the Chinese family has probably had an average size of only about five or six persons.[120] China, therefore, fits the hypothesis we have expressed before, that most of the world's population in major civilizations has lived under some conjugal family pattern, even when the ideal was the extended kin unit.

On the other hand, precisely because the ideal was of a household in- cluding a rather large network of kin, the household would be large when a family obtained sufficient resources. Put another way, the advantages of cooperation and the greater economic and social power of the family head transformed the kinship linkages into workaday and continuous relation- ships.

The mourning grades, or the network of mourning relatives, comprised a symmetrical network of male *ascendants* through ego's great-great- grandfather and ego's lineal *descendants* to his great-great-grandson, plus the *collateral* four degrees from ego at his own generation, three from his father and his son, two from his grandfather and grandson, and one from his great-grandfather and his great-grandson.[121] Since the mourning grades for any individual in a given position in this network would be different from those of any individual in a different position in the network, the mourning grade did not constitute a *corporate* group, although these in- dividuals would be expected to feel some loyalty toward one another. In addition, these positions determined many kinship rules, such as who was forbidden to marry whom.

The largest corporate kin group was the clan, or *tsu*. The *tsu* was viewed as having been founded by a single ancestor, whose sons founded subbranches (*fang*) of the *tsu*. All members of the *tsu* have the same sur- name, since it is a patrilineal system, but not all Chinese with the same surname belonged to the same *tsu*. This corporate kinship unit was of greatest importance in southeast China, in the provinces of Kwangtung, Fukien, Kwangsi, Kiangsi, etc., but was of some importance in the rest of China as well.

The great extension of its activities filled a gap in the Chinese political and social structure under the traditional system, but precisely for that reason it was thought superfluous and a threat to the new Communist regime, and thus had to be destroyed. Among its activities were: (1) helping an individual family to organize and pay for a lavish wedding or funeral; (2) lending money (at standard rates of interest) to *tsu* members; (3) es- tablishing schools; (4) acting as judicial authority within the clan; (5) serv- ing as a corporate parole body, for *tsu* members who had disobeyed the law but had reformed; (5) assuming responsibility for full collection of taxes; (6) protecting by force a *tsu* member from outside aggression.

This list does not exhaust all its activities, and not all *tsu* engaged in every one of these. Perhaps all *tsu* acted to some degree as corporate bodies in maintaining ancestral tablets and ancestral graves, and in general sup- porting ancestral worship. Even with reference to these activities, observers have noted that in central and northern China, the ancestral halls often were left to rot by the *tsu*.[122] The *tsu* was of such importance under the imperial system that individuals were forbidden appointments within their own provinces, because their political power as representatives of the emperor would be bolstered by that of the *tsu*, and the *tsu* could in turn exploit its advantage to the detriment of the welfare of the province.[123]

The *tsu* did not absorb the family. The *tsu* head, elders, and executive body would not ordinarily interfere with behavior within a nuclear family. Instead, it performed the tasks which in modern societies are taken care of by *formal* organizations: banks, subdistrict and village officials (these were not introduced in China until the Republic),[124] police forces, school systems, parole boards, agricultural cooperatives, the local judiciary, and even departments of foreign relations.

Because the corporate body could assemble great economic and political power, it was an important resource, and the rich and powerful families could use it to the disadvantage of the poorer families within it. Thus poorer families had less interest in it, but could not escape its influence. They might well pay more than their share of taxes, and receive far fewer benefits than their richer relatives. In some areas, the *tsu* owned a substantial proportion of the available land; such holdings were supposed to be used for the advantage of all, but the evidence suggests that the poorer families benefited from it less often than a rule of simple equality might suggest. Consequently, developments of the past half-century had helped to weaken the *tsu* even before the Communist regime. During the 1930s in Kwangtung, a province in which the *tsu* was highly elaborated, clan life "seemed to be decaying." Under the Republic, new political authorities, elected by the people, had appeared in the villages. Although they could not at first replace the *tsu*, they were a new political power. Observers have generally conceded that in the cities the *tsu* became much less important.[125] Hsien Chin Hu comments, "The *tsu* is of the greatest importance in rural neighborhoods, in large villages and small towns . . . but in the large cities . . . it becomes lost."[126] In the cities, new agencies for cooperation and the solution of problems formerly taken care of by the *tsu* were created either by the government or by individual enterprise. Of equal importance is that the rich within the cities did not wish to share their advantages with poor relatives of their *tsu*, and could obtain adequate resources by their own efforts. The poor, on the other hand, always felt exploited by the *tsu*, and could be protected somewhat better by state and other formal organizations; consequently, these families expressed their opposition to the landlord and ruling class in a simpler fashion: simply ignoring or rejecting the *tsu*.[127]

It was precisely the aim of the Communists to control all of those areas of life which the *tsu* had under its direction. It became necessary to destroy the *tsu* for simple administrative as well as ideological reasons. Ancestral halls and ancestral groves of trees have now been eliminated. Where possible, ancestral graves have been incorporated into farm lands. Populations have been moved about a great deal, in order to break up the local village ties which united members of the *tsu*. Economic life is to be directed by the state, not the *tsu*. Political power is to be in the hands of the state, not the *tsu*. The Communists attacked the *tsu* as the tool of the rich and of the former corrupt regime, as the basis for dominance by the older generation and by males, and, of course, as the center for "old superstitions."

The Communists intended to supplant the *tsu* by their own local corporate agency—the *commune*.

China entered a new phase in its revolution at the August 1958 meeting of the Central Committee in Peitaiho when it was announced that collective life would be organized into communes. With this step, China had decided to move further toward "pure communism" than any Communist nation ever before had attempted. Since it is argued by some theorists of social change that the cost of radical, swift social change may be no greater over time than the cost of a slower change that successively creates disharmonies among various parts of the society, only time will tell whether the Chinese Communists will be successful in this step. From the time of the Party Congress in May, 1958 until the Peitaiho resolution was published on September 10, many preliminary steps were taken in order to get the communization process under way, but these in no way tempered the program's radical intent and consequences. A show-place commune was formed as early as April, 1958 in Honan; by the end of September it was reported that over 90 per cent of the peasants had been organized into about 24 thousand communes. By November, 1958, 99 per cent of the rural population was said to have been grouped in communes of about 5 thousand households each.[128]

We are here concerned only with the importance of this move for the Chinese family system, but a few further comments are necessary in order to see the magnitude of the phenomenon. Whenever the Communists succeeded in establishing control over any area in China, they initiated land reforms and, where possible, organized agricultural cooperatives. By the middle of 1955, there were over 600 thousand rural cooperatives, covering 14 per cent of the farm population, and by the end of 1956 almost all peasant households were in collectives. These attempted to rationalize farm production, and concentrated primarily on the major crops, leaving garden crops to the individual farmer. Many individual families could continue to take part in buying and selling. Many collectives acted independently of national control, however. The new reforms had undermined the power of clans as well as of the old landlord group, and the new system required far more skill in organization and management. Moreover, the new leaders were often incompetent. Even the state collection of production was not satisfactory to the Communist leaders. The collectives permitted more individual enterprise and less state control than was thought desirable.

A new Five-Year Plan begun in 1958 enormously increased production norms and asserted that the great population of China was not a disadvantage but a great resource. In order to utilize the population, however, far more organization was necessary than was possible under the existing collectives. The planned "great leap forward" was an attempt to solve some of the contradictions and problems in the collectivization process, which was viewed as not having gone far enough. The new commune, already much bigger than the old collective, was to become still larger (perhaps a thousand would include most of the Chinese population). It was to be in charge of almost all of the economic and social life taking place within its borders.[129] Not only were these communes to be in charge of such activities as banking, the building of dams and steel mills, and agricultural production, but they also were to be concerned with the care of children, the utilization of woman power, and even the creation of cheap forms of weddings and funerals. The collectives gave "work points" as income, but under the communes the Chinese would receive a basic amount of services such as feeding in mess halls and so on, and in addition would receive wages.

Under the Draft Regulations of the Weihsing People's Commune (the "Sputnik" People's Commune, which has been used as a show place) the unit was to be responsible for looking after the aged, the weak, orphans, widows, and disabled members "who lack or lose labor power and have no way of living." It also would build communal graveyards.[130]

The Eighth Central Committee of the Communist Party of China in its December 1958 resolution reported on existing developments as well as future aims. The Communist communes had by then set up many "community dining rooms, nurseries, kindergartens, 'homes of respect for the aged,' and other institutions for collective welfare, which have, in particular, completely emancipated women from thousands of years of kitchen drudgery and brought broad smiles to their faces."[131] By assuring the individuals that they need no longer worry about their daily meals, a reliable kind of social insurance had been instituted. Rural areas were to become industrialized. It was conceded that many problems of the rural communes had not been settled and that urban communes were not yet to be established.[132]

Nurseries and kindergartens were to be run so well that any child would be better off in one than at home and "the children [would] want to stay there and the parents [would] want to put them there." The parents were to be able to board the children in such nurseries or kindergartens or to take them home at any time. Moreover, communes would institute universal primary school education as well as various higher levels of schools.[133]

8. Communes and Women's Work

Although the cities had been exempted from communization up to the end of 1958, by July of that year an announcement had been made that housewives in some major cities had organized public dining rooms, nurseries, laundries, etc., in order to be free to work.[134] In August, 1958, 173 urban communes were reported to have been established in Honan.[135] Various experiments at urban communes were reported for 1959. Housewives had organized, according to Chinese reports, more than 400 "street factories" and more than 2,900 "street production units," and in Peking they had set up 670 street mess halls and 1,250 street kindergartens.[136] In another early report in the beginning of 1959, it was asserted that incomplete statistics from twenty-two cities showed that half a million women had started over 40 thousand factories.[137] This report also announced that women had established 180 thousand steel furnaces. By the beginning of 1960, the announcement was made that urban communes were to be developed on a large scale; soon thereafter the total membership of the urban communes was claimed to have reached 20 million,[138] and to have encompassed a majority of most cities in Honan, Hopei, and Heilunkiang. The emphasis in most of these reports was placed on the efficient utilization of labor, especially of female labor. Deputy Li Chieh-po, vice chairman of the All China Federation of Trade Unions, stated in 1960 that the urban communes and neighborhood organizations had provided state enterprises with more than 3.4 million workers, of whom 80 per cent were women.[139] He also claimed that over 50 thousand community dining halls had been established, as well as 42 thousand nurseries and kindergartens for 1.2 million children. Under the new system, not only did the state benefit from the additional work contribution from women, but also the women presumably found their economic position raised within their own families.[140]

In urban areas, the Chinese seem to be proceeding somewhat more slowly than in the rural areas in their search for an effective solution to the problem. In social structural terms, the dilemma is that other facilities already exist for taking care of many of these problems, so that the commune organization necessarily cuts across the lines of authority and planning of such municipal or private agencies. In rural areas, where the *tsu* had been important, the communes furnished far more organization and planning than any existing agencies ever did. As a consequence, urban communes seemed to be formed first from the base of the neighborhood group; although the productivity of such communes might not be great, it was *some* contribution to the system. By initially tying these activities closely to the neighborhoods, the services of women could be utilized far more effectively. In a Chinese report from Chungking in 1961, it was asserted that 80 per cent of the staff in the 680 factories set up by the city were women. Their tasks ranged from ordinary labor up to management and accounting.[141]

These changes in the structural position of the family within the larger society, and of the individual within the family, alter the services that each family member may give to the other, thus affecting the traditional role bargain between any two of them. The family is no longer the main independent unit of economic production. The head of the family is likely not to be the leader or chief manager of production activity. Perhaps of greater importance is that "women and older children within the family may be paid independently for their work, so that they can see what their contribution is, and in addition the possible control by the male head of the family is undermined."[142] Allocation of labor is not made by the family head nor determined by the particularistic kin ties dominant in traditional Chinese society. During the 1930s these ties still were largely operative when Lang embarrassed some of her educated respondents by asking them whether they would prefer to hire a competent person rather than a relative.[143] The center of loyalty can no longer be the family, but becomes instead the various state organizations which increasingly are the areas in which recreation, work, and other activities take place.[144]

The emphasis upon woman power has both a rational and an ideological basis. In the Communist movement within every nation, an appeal has been made to women as to other disadvantaged groups, under the principle of egalitarianism. At the same time, women are a largely unutilized source of cheap productive power in nations undergoing industrialization.

Womanpower cannot be exploited effectively, however, without the development of auxiliary services that permit the family unit to dispense with their contribution to the household while they are working. In the West, the utilization of womanpower occurs under a number of ideological and practical restrictions: (1) A higher proportion of lower-class than of upper-class women take part in the labor force, because the demand for goods increases faster than the income of the individual male worker. (2) *Professional* women in the middle and upper strata may work, but their economic position permits them to pay for both labor and services as substitutes for part of their housewifely duties. (3) Young women, wives without children, and older women participate far more in the labor force than do other categories of women. That is, those women participate most whose household services can most easily be dispensed with.

In certain respects, the development of communal dining halls, nurseries and kindergartens, laundry services, and so on may be more acceptable to the Chinese male than would be any serious attempt to force him to conform to egalitarian values that would direct him to share the household tasks equally or to give up the services which were traditionally his male right. Under the communal system, he may still obtain these services, even though they are not so individualized as they would be in his own household; at least he does not have to take part in such "women's activities," himself. As already noted, after many generations of ideological debate in the West, men have not yet conceded egalitarianism in the home or in the economic life. How much less, then, would Chinese men have accepted such a move. To this degree, then, the communal solution bypasses the still strong insistence on male prerogatives among Chinese men.

Simply put, the Chinese have tried to furnish the material basis for an ideological shift concerning females, whose position was in many ways the foundation stone of the old order. The women have been asked to participate in the new enterprise, but from their shoulders have been taken many of the traditional burdens of individual housework and care for children.

In the West, the working wife typically takes on the double burden of work and household, with some help from her husband. On the other hand, it is unlikely that Chinese women would have been willing to accept the new burden of work if they had already enjoyed the advantages of Western women, who, by remaining at home in traditional activities, enjoy far more social and material benefits and far fewer disadvantages than their Chinese sisters.

As noted earlier, at many points in the past hundred years Chinese women have taken some role in revolutionary activity. Armed women even took part in the Taiping uprising in the early 1850s. There were women political workers in the Kuomintang and in the Communist Party even in the 1920s. As Yang comments, in speaking of the extent to which women were not permitted any political activity under the Ch'ing: "Hence the feminist leaders' enthusiastic participation in China's revolutions, and the fact that despite the many repressions of political interest in the women's movement during its past century of development, this interest always swept up to new heights in every resurging wave of modern Chinese revolution."[145]

The many reports which the Chinese have published on the participation of women in new economic enterprises during the 1950s need not be accepted completely as statements of fact, although they may be no worse than ordinary political exaggeration. They are, in addition, a set of exhortations and persuasions: to the male to adjust to the new situation, to the female to join in this exciting new endeavor. Some of the exhortations result from *active discrimination* against hiring females. As Yang points out, some objections to using them are also *rationally* based, e.g., *the uneconomical aspects of absenteeism.* [146]

When the cooperatives were still in existence, the claim was made that women were then earning about one fourth of the total wage units of the cooperatives and that the principle of equal pay for identical work for men and women was gradually being carried out. Moreover, 70 to 80 per cent of the 756 thousand agricultural producer cooperatives throughout the country were headed by women directors or deputy directors.[147] On the political level, in 1956 one fifth of the delegates at the level of (presumably provincial) People's Congresses and 12 per cent of the delegates to the National People's Congress were women. Indeed, at every level of political administration the number of women was said to be increasing at that time. In the Chang Yun report, it was asserted that more than 850 thousand women were in medical and health work, and there were over 11 thousand women professors, lecturers, and assistant professors.

Statistics reported for 1955 indicate that the largest number (21.3 per cent) of women workers were in cultural, educational, and public health "departments," 18 per cent were in industrial departments, and 17 per cent were in banking and insurance. These figures may be based only on work in Government departments, although this is not specified. An amending footnote does state that private enterprises are not included.[148]

Until the end of 1956, statistics showed that women workers comprised 60 per cent of all textile workers and 25 per cent of the railway system workers. Presumably the base for these figures (for both 1955 and 1956) is close to 3 million women, but since the total number of "workers" (male and female) is reported to be only 15 million, it is difficult to understand what is meant by the category of "worker." It could not, for example, include agricultural workers.[149]

From 1957 to 1961 the number of women research fellows and technicians in the Shanghai branches of the Chinese Academy of Sciences increased over sixfold.[150]

As early as the fall of 1958, many speeches and reports dealt with efforts in the rural provinces to free woman's labor power for farm work by setting up mess halls, nurseries, laundry units, and sewing and knitting units.[151]

Without any doubt, Chinese women have been given far more opportunities than ever in the history of their country to obtain political power, economic advantages, and educational growth. There were more than 5,500 women serving as commune directors or vice directors at the end of 1959.[152] By the academic year 1958, 20 per cent of the students in institutions of higher learning were women,[153] as were 42 per cent of the students in the higher medical and health schools.[154]

Three qualifications should be noted. First, from the standpoint of a democratic ideology, Chinese women and the disadvantaged generally have obtained advantages from the new regime, but they have also submitted to a new and different kind of authoritarianism.

Second, by no conceivable arithmetic or creation of "paper" organizations is it possible for China to have solved so quickly the problem of taking care of its infants and young children while all the women work. To consider only one datum of this kind: there are more than 100 million children aged 0 to 4 years in China. It is not likely that the facilities that have been announced could provide care for so many children. The same statement of course applies to the creation of dining halls and other types of communalized household activities.

With reference to child-care facilities, several types are reported: nurseries, kindergartens, "permanent child care organizations," "youth collective farms," other youth groups, and, of course, regular schools. They are not always separated. An enormous increase in nursery organizations during the harvest season was achieved in 1956[155] and the claim was made in 1960 that in the rural communes, 80 per cent of all preschool children were taken care of.[156] This is possible without the creation of regular nurseries which would permanently free women from taking care of their children. The 5 thousand nurseries in industrial plants in 1956 were taking care of 190 thousand babies and children,[157] a tiny proportion of the number in China. However, a more than fiftyfold increase in the number of kindergartens—a magnitude of increase that suggests improvised facilities rather than adequate ones—between 1957 and 1958 was announced, with the information that these were then taking care of 25.9 million children.[158] If Chinese kindergarten ages were assumed to be the same as those current in the United States, it could be assumed that most children of this group were taken care of. This picture is confused by the fact that in the same year some 47 million children were supposed to be under care in over 3 million "permanent child care organizations."[159] This figure is again announced for 1960.[160] Without knowing what ages are included, no guess can be made as to whether these are schools, orphan asylums, health clinics, or even social work agencies.

With even the loosest interpretation of age groups and the meaning of "child care" by the state, it is impossible that the available *permanent* facilities would cover the total number of children in China. Nevertheless, even with this qualification we assume that the *general* order of magnitude reported is roughly correct, and that the size of the figures (under the least sympathetic interpretation) shows conclusively that the Chinese view child care by the state as an important problem to be solved.

Third, one has only to read between the lines of the denunciations and compliments to understand that great opposition remains to the new women's rights. In two articles and an editorial published in 1961 the theme is the encouragement of the plan to give equal pay to women workers doing the same work as men.[161] In a similar vein, another article expresses the argument that women who do not work have no right to obtain food at the public mess hall or to place their children in a public nursery—though the assertion is made that the people's communes in rural areas have universally set up public mess halls, nurseries, and other facilities.[162] Admitting that when a husband and wife are at work and the children are in public nurseries they cannot spend much time together, the same writer scorned those who want to be together as a "happy family from dawn to dusk" as persons who would prefer a "petty peasant's life."[163]

In one Chinese periodical's discussion of the community mess halls, three types of persons are described: those who insist on the mess halls and want to eat in them (bachelors, young married couples, women in their prime of life); those who are relatively indifferent (those with large families with some working members) who do not save money by using the halls; and large families with few workers, who find it is more economical to eat at home. This last group finds the food in the mess halls too simple; in addition, larger families often include old people or those with chronic illnesses, or children at home, and the halls are inconvenient for them.[164]

Giving women equal pay is still news in China. The proud public announcement that equal pay has been achieved here or there, in some section or brigade, points up how rare the event remains.[165] Various charges of discrimination may still be found in the Chinese press. Moreover, the literature of the past five years contains many statements reminding women that they still have the duty of taking care of members of the family. In one such exhortation, women were reminded that liberation does not mean that all of their tasks have been taken over by the collective. They must still run households industriously and thriftily. This is a patriotic duty and an expression of loyalty to the commune. They should look after household affairs *and* take part in production: "Arrangements made by a housewife in feeding the old and teaching the young, making every member of her family feel comfortable, will naturally lighten the burden on the society and the collective."[166]

To speculate on the future of the family system under the Communists with as little ideological bias as possible, several predictions seem to be valid. First, the commune or some variant of it, will not disappear or be destroyed as a productive or even a distributive system in the course of the next several decades, in spite of its many failures and much dissatisfaction within China about it. Second, without any question, China has seriously and successfully begun to attack the barriers in the way of its industrialization. Chinese achievements in this area are considerable as contrasted with the slow growth of previous decades, even if most of their claims are exaggerated.

Third, many discussions in the Chinese press suggest the abolition of the family "in the old sense," but the Chinese are not "destroying the family" as an economic unit or even as a social unit in which all members participate continuously. The family will remain the basic cell of Chinese society. Chinese discussions of family patterns are not given the weight of resolutions or directives. They are rather to be considered ideological contributions to persuade the people to yield some of their allegiance to one part or another of the old family system.

It seems unlikely that any such directives will ever be issued. At the present time there is no small unit in Chinese social organization which comes between the individual and the state or its agencies. This means that each individual is vulnerable, but it also means that innumerable small problems of daily living are not given to any specific unit as in the past. It is for this reason that so many speeches and editorials point out that individuals still have the responsibility of taking care of one another in the same family. This need will continue under any conceivable kind of society. Moreover, people in all sections apparently feel a psychological need to have a small, emotionally cohesive unit within which they can, in effect, take off their shoes and feel comfortable and protected from the outside. No unit other than the family has ever been evolved for these purposes—unless one perhaps excepts the age graded groupings of men in certain societies, such as the Nyakyusa of East Africa. Conceivably, such a unit could be evolved, but this has not happened in China.

As late as July, 1962 the emphasis on the importance of maintaining family ties continued in the Chinese press. In answer to a young wife's query, the editor of an official magazine of the young communists stated that it is an ancestral custom for the young couple to respect and support their parents. It is further asserted that though custom is not law, it has doubtless a moral authority, which can even be superior to that of the law.[166]

Fourth, we predict that with increasing prosperity and stabilization of the system, there will be, at a minimum, a movement back to the individual responsibility and emotional solace of the family. Moreover, there will be a return to the allocation of many tasks by sex, without a reversion to traditional ways of viewing female tasks. Specifically, it is likely that even after ten or twenty years of the commune system, there will not be equality of men and women, but there will still be an allocation of such tasks as laundry, preparation of food, care of children, and other similar work to the women. This has been the pattern both in Russia and in the Israeli *kibbutzim*, and we predict that this will also occur in China. In all three of these societies, however, ideological equalitarianism between men and women has doubtless gone further than in most Western societies.

9. Infanticide

The Chinese Communists have pointed to the disappearance of female infanticide as one index of the improvement in family life under their system. Infanticide as a practice is mentioned in the historical sources of the feudal period in China and in later dynasties as well.[167]

Ping-ti Ho cites much evidence that infanticide was common in the past, although some of his quotations are obviously exaggerations.[168] It is possible, as Ho claims, that "by the early 20th century the odious custom had almost entirely disappeared." Community studies in this generation do refer to the practice as though it had not disappeared, but in no specific descriptions of Chinese communities have we found any instances in which the author describes families who had killed their female children. Levy states that "in time of famine, drought, high taxes, and the like, it [infanticide] probably reached large proportions."[169] It is not certain to what extent there was *genuine* infanticide (killing a female child at birth by exposing it or abandoning it) or whether, as Ta Chen expresses it, "female children are unconsciously neglected, thereby leading to the higher death rate among them."

Throughout Chinese territory, female infanticide was morally deplored and considered a crime. If the Chinese Communists have actually succeeded in guaranteeing a subsistence for all families, it is likely that female infanticide has nearly disappeared, and that the Chinese people are pleased about it.

Without extremely accurate data of the sex ratio at birth, it is not possible to fix the importance of infanticide. Almost certainly, any correct sex ratio above the range of 103 to 105 (males per hundred females) is due to female infanticide. An increase of any substantial amount in the sex ratio above that point means inevitably that females are dying because they are neglected, since on biological grounds it seems certain that females have greater durability than males. Some light can be thrown on the problem by considering data from Peking from the end of the first decade after the fall of the Ch'ing:

Table VI-1
Sex Ratios, Peking Population, About 1917*

Age Group	Sex Ratio†
1–5	145
6–10	138
11–15	145
16–20	185
21–25	208
26–30	224
31–35	213
36–40	161
41–45	217
46–50	167

* Sidney B. Gamble, *Peking, A Social Survey* (New York: George H. Doran, 1921), p. 415. The sex ratios for the entire table, of which this is a part, were drawn from a sample of over half a million Chinese. Infant mortality rates calculated at that time gave figures of 202 for females and 168 for males (see p. 116).

† Males per hundred females.

Since the female mortality rate (i.e., the number of infants dying in their first year) was nearly 30 per cent higher than that of males, we can suppose that female infanticide was being practiced—always, of course, under the assumption that the data are even approximately correct. The death rate of females from 1 to 5 years of age was 152 per thousand and for males 122 per thousand, so that the supposition of neglect is also strong. Moreover, the sex ratio continues to rise until well into the age group of 30 years and over. We must conclude, then, that both neglect and infanticide were of some importance. As against this conclusion, it must not be forgotten that a high sex ratio would be *normal* in a growing city, because of male inmigration. Nevertheless, male inmigration can not account for all the discrepancy.

The Ting Hsien data of a generation ago unfortunately do not give us the sex distributions at birth, but for all children under 5 years of age the sex ratio was about the same as that in the United States.[170] However, the sex ratio of 104 males per hundred females in the sample of 5255 families rises in the 5 to 9 age group to 110 (thus suggesting neglect) and reaches a peak at the 15 to 19 age group, not returning to a normal sex composition until about ages 30 to 39. Ta Chen obtained an average sex ratio at birth for Cheng Kung during the years 1940 to 1944 that was close to that of the United States, but with extreme variations from one year to the next. The deaths of males and females were about equal during this period within each early age group from 0 to 4 years, suggesting neither neglect nor infanticide.[171] The problem of registration is great, and the most important factor here is a tendency to under-register females. Unfortunately, this raises the sex ratio at birth still further, just as female infanticide would, and we are left with the minor mystery as to which element was of greater importance.[172] Under-registration of female infants would seem to be the cause of the very high sex ratio at the end of the registration period in Cheng Kung. On the other hand, another area, Shao Chi in Kiang Ying, reported a sex ratio *at birth* of 111, indicating either infanticide or under-registration.

The results from the 1953 Chinese Communist census yield some data for the present period. The sex ratio in the group under 1 year old is 104.9, a normal figure. For the 1 to 2 year age group it rises to 106.2. It reaches a peak of 115.8 in the 7 to 13 age group. The normality of the sex ratio in the infant age group is, as we have just noted, to be found in earlier samples as well. It is important to ascertain to what extent there is a rise in the sex ratio in succeeding years as a result of neglect of female children. The 1953 data cannot be used to make such a test, because the older age groups were born in the pre-Communist era, and during periods of many shortages and difficulties, which might have increased the mortality of females still more.[173] These figures suggest that the discrepancy in mortality between young males and females was greater a half-century ago than in any of the later data that we have been able to find.

10. Suicide as a Protest Against the Marriage System

Just how high the suicide rate has been in China, we cannot know. The data will never be available. The *belief* of the Chinese is clear, and may be stated as follows: "In China far more women than men committed suicide. Furthermore, almost no suicide appeared below the age of 15 to 17 and very few appeared after the age of 35 to 40."[174] Levy thus reports as fact what we view as a belief.

The consequences of the belief are equally clear. The young bride has the duty of adjusting to her in-laws, especially to her mother-in-law, and her huband was not supposed to interfere, or even to establish a close emotional tie with his wife. In the case of conflict, he was to support his family against his wife. Since she came from another geographical area, and was not surrounded by her own kin, she had no external kin support (except under extreme conditions).[175] Thus in fact the young woman had no support for her rebellion, and the Chinese viewed this period of adjustment as a difficult one for her. A middle-class bride might be forced to make shoes for her husband's family as a symbol of her subservience, and she was supposed to rise before anyone else and bring tea to her mother-in-law. Even in the 1930s, Lang states that in eighty-six out of 101 families of what she called "traditional strata" (Peking workers, lower middle class, middle class, and upper class), the daughter-in-law was the first to rise in the morning, as against ten families in which the mother got up earliest.[176] Popular belief emphasized the fact that the young woman's only alternatives were adjustment or suicide. It is not, as we shall note, that divorce did not occur, but that the divorce stigma was great, and certainly the *belief* about suicide intensified the motivation to adjust.

It is also important to keep in mind that suicide was a form of protest in China, as it is in a few other societies. In Ch'ü's analysis of law in traditional society, many cases involved a suicide by an *older* person protesting the failure of a younger person to obey orders or to show proper respect. We have not found a general analysis of this phenomenon, but in a society concerned with "face," such a protest was stronger than almost any other act, and invariably had to be investigated by the district magistrate. Almost always, the younger person involved was punished.

The belief about suicide is not upheld by data from the Peking Survey for the end of the decade after the establishment of the Republic. As in the West, a majority of suicides reported in this data was committed by *men*, not women. Almost as many women as men *attempted* suicide, but three out of four successful suicides were male. Again contrary to common belief, suicides were found in older age groups as well. If we calculate the number of suicides by the actual number of persons within each age group, certain age and sex differences appear to qualify the traditional picture (see Table VI-2).

Table VI-2
Suicide Rates by Sex and Age, Peking, 1917*

| Age Group | NUMBER OF SUICIDES PER HUNDRED THOUSAND POPULATION IN SPECIFIC AGE GROUPS | |
	Males	Females
16–20	42	29
21–30	16	53
31–40	47	32
41–50	25	14
51–60	36	15
61 and over	40	13

* Data calculated from Gamble, *Peking* . . . , *op. cit.*, pp. 416, 418.

In the age group presumed to suffer the greatest strain, 16 to 20 (the group in which most Chinese females became wives and thus had to adjust to mothers-in-law), the suicide rate for young men was much higher than that for women. The suicide rate for women in this age group was lower than for the two succeeding age groups. The suicide rate was highest for females aged 21–30, but in most Chinese marriages by this time the women presumably would have had one or more children. In addition, the rate continued to be fairly high for the next decade of life, 31 to 40, although again, the rate was lower than for men of that age. The general distribution by age was different from that of the West (where generally suicides rise with age), but the rate for *men* also remained high in the later decades. With reference to the high rate for females aged 21 to 30, we must conclude that the traditional belief is partly correct, if perhaps not so dramatic as sometimes described.

Among the more than 8 thousand deaths recorded in Cheng Kung (Yunnan) during 1940 to 1944, suicide was not separated, but was placed in the category "poisoning and suicide." There seems to be no sex differential of great consequense, and the number occurring in the age group 40 years and above was more than those occurring in younger age groups.[177]

With reference to a rural population in the early 1920s, Buck claimed that the high ratio for ages 30 to 54 was due to female suicide and to deaths in childbirth, but actually the ratio was fairly low for the most important part of that age group (35 to 39 years). The ratio should have been high in the 20 to 30 age group, but in fact it was low.[178] His data do not therefore show any great influence of the supposedly high female suicide rate in the early years of adjustment to the marriage.

The widespread acceptance of this belief was, however, useful to the Chinese Communists as a way of emphasizing the evils of the old system. As a consequence, in 1953, when they were mapping a widespread propaganda campaign to implement the 1950 Marriage Law, and complaining about the extent to which old customs were still being followed, the charge was made that from 70 to 80 thousand women "are killed or commit suicide on account of matrimonial difficulties" in certain areas in Fukien, Hunan, and Shantung;[179] but the reports do not specify precisely which areas, or what the figures were before 1951–1953. Suicides are not separated from homicides, nor are ages given.

Yang cites the Statistical Abstract of the Republic of China (Nanking, 1935) which, in an incomplete report, gave some information on 1353 suicides from 244 counties. Of these, only about 270 were women whose suicides were "caused" by family conflicts. We do not know how many of these were caused by conflict with the mother-in-law or the husband's family generally. In addition, Yang summarizes Communist reports for 1950 from various regions, but these are like the 1953 reports in that they do not separate homicide and suicide, give no rates by ages, and use isolated reports of violence to bolster an attack on the remnants of the old system. They do not attempt to analyze the facts.[180]

It seems likely that some of these suicides resulted from the frustration of women who saw for the first time some opportunity to break their bonds, but who were prevented from doing so by their more traditional-minded relatives. To what extent these suicides represent a mere continuation of the suicide pattern under the old system, or whether the figures are mere fabrications, we do not know.

In any event, the Communist figures do not show whether there has been a rise in the suicide rate, and we cannot know what the rate was fifty years ago. We are inclined to believe that in all epochs the rate of suicide has been exaggerated by romantic legend, and has functioned to reduce the young bride's motivation to struggle against her in-laws. Conversely, since suicide was a great disgrace for the family that caused it, it is likely that most families *reduced* their pressures on the daughter-in-law when she showed any such intention. Finally, in the areas which have moved toward the new family system, the suicide rate for women in the early period of marriage certainly *has* been reduced. The mother-in-law is less likely to be in the home, the tie between husband and wife is closer, and a far higher proportion of wives work outside the home so that its frustrations may be lessened somewhat.[181]

Nevertheless, a personal humiliation or "loss of face" doubtless was a more frequent motive in suicide than torture by in-laws, and changes in family structure may not greatly affect such a pattern. Thousands of Chinese committed suicide when the government began to round up and to punish those who had expressed their criticism of the government during the period marked by Mao Tse-tung's invitation: "Let a hundred flowers bloom together and a hundred schools of thought contend."

11. Position of the Elders

No elaborate description is necessary to show the extent of change in the position of elders in the Chinese family. These alterations have been described in many books over the past generation, since they began even before the fall of the Ch'ing Dynasty.

Throughout the written history of China, in eloquent and forceful prose, philosophers, judges, and rulers have insisted on the absolute authority of the father or grandfather and the deference to be paid to those who are older and of an older generation.[182] Ch'ü even marshals legal cases to show under what conditions a man might kill his son.[183] The father had absolute authority over the family's property, and even adult children could not live apart from their parents without permission. Only a male could be a family head, but an adult son was supposed to continue to obey his mother.[184] The authority of the *tsu* was in the hands of the elders, and it supported their power within the smaller unit of the household. The family head was responsible for the behavior of individual members, and, for a wide range of offenses, could punish directly, or indirectly through the *tsu*.

Since most Chinese did not read, and the traditional writings did not contain technological information, the elders were indeed a repository of wisdom and useful lore. Not only did they know Chinese custom, but they also knew the solutions to mundane problems such as irrigation, planting, and commerce. It was difficult for a young man to acquire quickly the useful knowledge that was in the heads of the elders. As a result, religious, philosophical, legal, and economic forces were in relative harmony: the elders directed and the young obeyed. The young owed everything to the old, a debt that was never completely discharged. The care that parents gave to their children did not belong to the children by right, but was a payment by the parents to *their* ancestors who earlier had cared for them. The successive changes of power since the fall of the last Chinese dynasty have been, in effect, a revolt by the young against the old. It is not only the Communists who came to power very young. The same may be said for the Kuomintang, and, still earlier, for the leaders of the revolution against the Ch'ing. The basic factors in these revolutions have familial counterparts, and equally have undermined the position of the elders within the family: the rise in the social and economic position of the young, the shift of loyalty away from the family, the freedom of choice in marriage, the establishment of rank on the basis of technical and scientific knowledge rather than tradition, and the increasing chances of obtaining a job as an individual rather than as a member of the family. As Yang remarks: "Thus filial piety, once the most emphatically stressed value in the traditional social order for over 2,000 years, was subjected to open challenge in the 1920's, gradually lost its sacred and binding character among the modern intellectuals by the 1930's, and, by the time the Communists became the ruling power, was publicly discredited by them as feudalistic, designed for the exploitation of the young."[185]

The Communists proclaim that the regime depends upon its children, and a popular slogan in mainland China is "All for the children."[186] Such a change has been dramatic, but primarily because the point from which it began was in such contrast to the Western pattern. Moreover, the degree should not be exaggerated. It is not a campaign to denigrate the old because of their age. It is, rather, an attempt to crystallize and redirect the existing or latent rebellious emotions of the young against their specific parents, in a battle against the landlord, the traditionalist, and the "enemies of the state." After all, by now many of the Communist leaders themselves are no longer young, but it is unlikely that they plan to relinquish authority for that reason. The old are less likely to change, and it is flattering to the young to be told they are important and the wealth of the future.

Even under the traditional system the elders did not maintain their power to the very end, nor was it absolute. The elders' power was balanced to some degree by the fact that it did not truly belong to the father, but flowed from his *own* ancestors. He was their agent, and was under their presumed authority, as the son was under his authority. *Neither* was free to act arbitrarily.[187]

The unfilial son could avoid some censure, at least within a considerable range of behavior, because the family head would not wish in public to admit that he could not control his son. A determined son, then, could go rather far before being stopped by relatives outside the immediate family or the *tsu*, or governmental authority. Finally, as is apparent in every patriarchal system, the informal shift of initiative from father to son could occur without the father being forced to admit that he had lost authority, and without the son ceasing to pay all deference and respect to his father. An active, ambitious, and intelligent man might impose his will on his son until his death; but sons of his mold might be less willing to submit to it, and would gradually assume control over business, planting, or any other activities. The father would retain the final veto, both in custom and in law, but would rarely attempt to exercise it as long as in all ritual and social forms the son and the younger generation continued to pay proper deference.[188]

Still more important is the fact that a government campaign against the aged as such would create many problems of support. Without a small unit like the family to take care of the older people, these would constitute a burden on society and on the state itself. Consequently, official statements have emphasized the obligation of continuing to care for the elders, even though the presence of many generations under the same roof is no longer the Chinese ideal. "Filial piety" has been rejected in the sense of ancestor worship, but even the older notion of filial piety emphasized very strongly the duty of physical care in addition to deference. The duty of children to care for and support parents in their old age is to be distinguished from the older form of respect for the aged which made children the property of their parents.[189]

It has even been claimed that "respect for the old and love for the young is gaining ground on a new basis" because of the democratic revolution and socialist transformation. It is stressed that now young people can take better care of their parents or parents-in-law.[190]

Whether the old people and their children live together will depend upon the needs of production and the best way of bringing up the new Communist generation. Just as infants and children are to be placed in nurseries and schools in order to permit women to produce and to be emancipated, so may the old people be placed in "happiness asylums," although if some old people wish to live with their sons and daughters, they will be permitted to do so.[191] It is up to the individuals concerned whether the old people will be sent to a home for the aged, whether a baby will be placed in a nursery, or whether a person will eat at the mess hall. In the future, it is announced, housing will be constructed so that men and women, old and young in the same family, may come together when they wish. The commune will not give up the family system, but will only abolish the patriarchal system in favor of a "democratic, united family."[192]

Even the mother-in-law is not to be rejected completely: one article, written by a married woman worker who lived with her in-laws, describes her efforts to iron out differences with her mother-in-law and to become friendly with her.[193]

These articles and editorials do not herald a return to the traditional family. They represent no more than official recognition that the propaganda campaign against the power of the elders may lead to misunderstanding on the part of the young, who may at times abandon their filial responsibilities to the State. Such exhortations are a recognition that even when the extended family has disappeared, the conjugal family is a useful servant for the society at large. The communes can more effectively utilize manpower, but even they require that some particular units be responsible for individual problems, and the traditions of the people make the conjugal family the most eligible and available unit. Thus, the Communist efforts to "go beyond the conjugal family" are already being tempered and qualified by the practical demands of daily living.

12. Divorce

Divorce has been generally thought to be very infrequent in the traditional family system of China. Lang comments, ". . . . divorces in old China were rather rare."[194] In discussing divorce, Levy says that the daughter-in-law who found her situation in her husband's family to be intolerable had only two choices, to run away, or to commit suicide. Divorce is not listed as an alternative.[195] Freedman comments, "Chinese often answer to casual inquiry that they do not practice divorce."[196] Kulp's survey of rural life in a village in South China during the 1917–1923 period, found no case of divorce even known to his informants.[197] The category of "divorce" is not even used in the Peking Survey of 1917, although the marital status of the population is recorded. In Ting Hsien, two divorced persons were found in a sample of 515 families.[198]

Some of the structural factors opposing a high rate of divorce have already been mentioned. On the other hand, it is possible that the amount of divorce was underestimated in traditional as well as Republican China. The amount of legal attention devoted to divorce over the centuries certainly hints that divorce may not have been so rare as commonly reported.[199]

If both husband and wife wanted to separate, a divorce by mutual consent has been at least theoretically possible since the T'ang Dynasty.[200] Of course, the woman could not leave her husband, and in perhaps almost all cases it was the husband's family who decided on a divorce, on one of the traditional seven grounds mentioned early in this chapter.

We have discussed the great power of the husband's family, through which the young wife could be kept under control and thus avoid divorce. Two further structural elements would have reduced the *official* divorce rates. If the husband found his wife unbearable, but had no moral grounds for divorce which would satisfy her family, he could solve the problem by taking a concubine if he could afford one; and, if his economic or social position required him to travel, he could stay away from home for years. The wife could not complain about either alternative. Secondly, a considerable amount of marital *instability* was to be found in the relationships with concubines who were part of the household. The man did not have to report the establishment of such a woman in his household, nor did he have to report his expulsion of the woman from his household. If one defines the Chinese marriage system as a "quasi-polygyny," then one must admit that there was a substantial rate of divorce, even if it cannot be quantified.

Finally, the stigma of divorce in China was so great that many who had been divorced would not ordinarily admit to it in the few surveys of forty or fifty years ago.

Without question, the divorce rate in China has risen greatly, over the past generation at least, and had begun to rise in the cities before that time. In Peking, the divorce rate increased from 4.5 per 10 thousand population in 1917 to 28 for the same population in 1932.[201] In his sizeable sample, Notestein found about 0.1 per cent of Chinese males in the marital status of divorced (1929–1931). But this was about the proportion in England and Wales in 1921.[202] That for France in 1926 was 0.5 per cent, to give an additional comparison for roughly the same period. Lang reports that divorces in Shanghai for 1929–1930 were 43 per hundred thousand, about the same as in Germany, Denmark, and Sweden at the beginning of the decade. The comparison is not entirely appropriate, since a city cannot, with complete validity, be compared with a nation.[203] On the other hand, a higher proportion of Chinese marry, and are thus exposed to the risk of divorce.

Chen Ta compares the populations of nine Chinese localities by marital status, the data spanning the decade from the late 1920s to the early 1930s. In Ting Hsein, 3 per cent were divorced. In Lan Hsi, 0.20 per cent were divorced, and in Szechwan and the Kuming Lake region, the percentages were 0.17 and 0.08, respectively.[204] If only the adult population is considered, the percentages are somewhat higher—that is, generally lower than those of Europe for roughly the same period, but high enough, especially in view of the reluctance of Chinese women to admit to divorced status, to suggest that the Chinese divorce rate has been underestimated in the past.

We do have relatively accurate data for the Chinese on Taiwan. In the early period of the Japanese occupation, there was a high sex ratio, and it is possible that under such circumstances, the divorce rate was relatively higher than it would be among a similar population with a different sex ratio.

Professor G. William Skinner suggests (in a private communication) that some of the variations from one Chinese region to another are due to differences in sex ratio. When the sex ratios are high, women are correspondingly less available, and their husbands may try to keep them. However, other men may still be able to tempt them away.

In Taiwan, the percentage of men and women in the marital status of "divorced" was always low, as indeed it is relatively low in the United States (about 2 per cent). However, 14 per cent of the marriages of 1906 were dissolved within five years; 9 per cent of the marriages in 1910 were dissolved within five years.[205] As the sex ratio drops, the percentage of marriages eventually ending in divorce drops gradually. By 1939, only 3.6 per cent of the marriages were dissolved within five years. Since the proportion of marriages dissolved within five years is about two thirds of all divorces which eventually occur for these marriages, the total ending in divorce even in 1939 was over 5 per cent (i.e., fifty divorces per thousand existing marriages).

It seems fairly certain, then, that although the divorce rate did rise with the accession of the Chinese Communists to power, there had been an increase in the divorce rate from at least the time of the founding of the Republic. It is difficult to know to what extent the Chinese figures can be relied upon, because the numbers are used, like the figures on suicide, to prove that many people under the previous regime had wanted to be free but had been forced to stay married. In any event, the Chinese reported 186,167 divorce cases in 1950, 409,500 in 1951, and 398,243 in the first half of 1952.[206] During this same period, Freedman's data for Singapore (1948–1951) also show a rise in the divorce rate.[207]

In a 1956 report, it is stated that from 1950 to the first half of 1952 a total of 933 thousand divorce cases had been dealt with. It is notable that even at that time, no data on divorces after 1952 were presented. This article claims that in one court in Peking only a small part of the divorce judgements were based on a claim that there had been an arranged marriage or a claim of maltreatment of the woman.[208]

At least two patterns characteristic of Western divorce are reported in 1957, but in a much more exaggerated fashion: two thirds of the applications for divorce came from couples married *less* than one year, and in 82 per cent of these cases, *women* took the initiative.[209] It is further asserted, however, that divorce in some instances was due to hasty marriages that had been based on material possessions alone.

The charge that some people have come to take a casual approach to marriage simply because under the new system there is complete freedom of choice,[210] is coupled with the suggestion that the wish of *one* party alone to obtain a divorce may *not* be sufficient ground, and that perhaps special procedures should be set up for divorce hearings in order to guard against hasty and ill-considered ones. In Tientsin, 1955–1956, an increase in the number of divorces handled by the court was reported, although no figures are given. These, too, are asserted to have been caused in part by hasty marriages.[211]

It seems likely that in the near future divorce will become somewhat more difficult under the Communist regime than it has been during the past decade, if only because the state has not been able efficiently to take over family activities (parental care, discipline, etc.), which must still be given to a fairly *stable* unit. This was the experience of the Soviets, and we believe that at the present time the Communists are searching for a middle ground between the ideologically required "freedom of choice" and the equally important ideological demand that each person be "responsible and not self-indulgent" in his private life.

13. Remarriage of Widows and Divorcees

The patriarchal ideal was that the widow would not remarry, and of course the stigma of divorce was so great that the divorced woman also could not remarry. If the woman was deserted she could not find another man to marry her, since the desertion was a bad omen and the new union would be bigamous.[212] Hsu, reporting attitudes for the early 1940s, and Freed, for the late 1940s, state that for widows "remarriage is distasteful and somewhat immoral."[213]

Here, as in so many other areas of Chinese family life, there was a considerable difference between ideal and practice, and the consensus of observers seems to be that the ideal was achieved in the upper strata; that is, divorce and the remarriage of widows were both rare. Looked at from another angle, we find that since most people were poor and *not* in the upper strata, most widows and widowers *did* remarry, and divorcees "disappeared demographically" from the status of divorced by remarrying. A poor family without large funds for a bride price might arrange a marriage with a widow.[214] Indeed, remarriage with a kinsman—even a brother-in-law—occurred.[215] There was apparently some regional variation in China as to who had the right to dispose of the widow,[216] but as most people were relatively poor, and the bride price was a problem, available women did find a market. Levy says, with reference to the remarriage of widows, that "little or nothing was made of it among the peasants."[217]

It seems clear that the remarriage of those who had lost their spouses (for whatever reasons) was likely. We believe that this was so in traditional China, as it is now. Doubtless, the argument as to who gets the bride price has lessened in intensity as well as frequency, but remarriage seems inevitable.

The data from Ting Hsien in the late 1920s show that 17 per cent of the ever-married males in one sample had been widowered, and 16 per cent of the ever-married women had been widowed. But 61 per cent of those men who *had* once been widowers had remarried by the time of the survey, and 12 per cent of the former widows had remarried. Though the sex difference is more extreme than in the United States, the pattern is similar: that is, men have a higher chance to remarry than do women. That a more intense form of this pattern is found in China is probably based on the fact that it was only the *male* who had the property and thus could *choose* to remarry. The widow had no such control. In Ting Hsien, the percentage of widowed males in families with a large amount of property (one hundred or more *mu* [about sixteen acres or more]) was extremely low, simply because they had already remarried. Among the poorest families, some 4 per cent of the males were widowers. The percentage of widows does not show the same variation by amount of property, since these females did not own any. Thus, their marriage chances were not affected as much as the men's.

To the extent that the widow or divorcee in the active years of life can now obtain a job, and thus the equivalent of a dowry, it seems likely that her chances of remarriage will be greater than under the traditional system and, in any event, her chances of a *good* marriage will have increased. The social and legal position of both the widow and the divorcee has changed substantially.

Formerly, the divorcee had no rights that anyone was bound to respect, and the widow could obtain respect only if she remained as the elder mother in the family, without remarrying. She could not take any property away, and her husband's family could block a remarriage if they wanted to do so. Now, however, the government has actively entered the lists on her side, and reports of such support have been given wide publicity.[218]

14. Conclusion

Although the general trend of family change in China seems clear, we have deliberately called attention to the strong resistances which the Communists have encountered—a further indication of the importance of family factors as independent variables.[219] Moreover, we have pointed to a number of areas in which even the Chinese themselves have attempted to break the movement somewhat. Certainly the divorce rate rose too high to please the Chinese and they have receded somewhat from the notion of the "independent woman." Attacks on the ideal of filial piety had to be softened, to prevent the care of the aged being given over to the state. At the same time, numerous reports deal with the "backward" influences that must be combatted, apparent when men refuse to grant equality to able women. The emergence of a new class system and of freedom of choice have meant that women calculate for themselves (instead of having their elders haggle over the matter) which men will furnish the best income as husbands. Of course, the Chinese Communists deplore such a materialistic basis of choice.[220] The separation of husband and wife because of the demands of work is actually an older Chinese pattern, but arouses resentment when the state orders it. Children may now be given to widows or divorced women when the court decides that it is best for the child, but there is no general social acceptance of this principle. On the other hand, the temporary abandonment of the birth-control campaign seems to have been caused partially by its relative failure, and also because of ideological arguments. But it is clear that this was a surface abandonment only; the contraceptives remain available while articles continue to appear in favor of using them, and now the policy is again proclaimed.

This is the first time during the past half-century that the state has actively sought to carry out the family program that was part of the 1911 Revolution. Industrial development will surely occur more rapidly because of these changes—although one may suppose that the social costs of these alterations may still be high. The clan is not supported by either the new economic patterns or the government, and it loses its function to the new communes as well as to lower levels of the Communist organization. The Chinese family goals will not all be achieved quickly, but no great movement "backwards" will occur.

Finally, the family programs will probably become less central in future planning as family patterns, now moving toward the conjugal system, and the emerging Chinese industrial order become better adjusted to one another.

chapter

VII

Japan

JAPAN became an industrialized nation faster than any other nation in the history of the world. As one analyst phrased it:

> They started close to bankruptcy, used almost no foreign capital, established uneconomic heavy industries, organized and maintained a modern military and naval establishment, changed their governmental system radically, altered their system of production and consumption of goods and services to one in which modern industry was strategic, erected and conducted many highly profitable modern enterprises, made literacy virtually universal, and taught their people to operate effectively in terms of types of relationships that had been relatively unimportant and unknown in the Tokugawa period. They did it all with virtually no internal bloodshed or disintegration of major proportions, and they were very far along with the job in no more than five decades.[1]

Japan made radical social and economic structural changes over the near-century after the Meiji Restoration, and for a number of reasons further increased the speed of this alteration after World War II. First, the Allied Occupation deliberately fomented a movement toward the "democratic" patterns of the West. Second, the voices and pressures in favor of change had been stifled from the 1930s to the end of the war, and these were finally released and heard. Third, the prewar leaders had convinced the Japanese that the unique "Japaneseness" of Japan's military greatness and her social and economic traditions were closely interdependent. Her defeat then proved to many the error of those traditions.[2]

Perhaps a single change may be used as an index of the many that have occurred in Japanese family patterns—and also serve to show how different

Japan was from the West. In analyzing the details in a short autobiography of a lower-class Japanese wife who lived during the Meiji period, Lafcadio, Hearn comments about the woman's anxiety about being seen walking with her husband under a borrowed umbrella: ". . . The reader must know that it is not yet considered decorous for a wife and husband to walk side by side in public."[3] By contrast, a Japanese could write in 1954 that in Tokyo, "it is an absolute commonplace for husband and wife to be seen out together, and no one would any longer look askance."[4]

Indeed, the changes have been so striking, and have been reported so widely, that a few responsible scholars have felt it necessary to point out that the old has not given way completely in Japan. One extreme formulation states that "The transformation of the traditional Japanese society . . . has not been correlated with the rise of individualism as in the experience of the West."[5] Insofar as this thesis applies to the family, Matsumoto's own data contradict it. The changes themselves are surprising in so short a time; it would indeed be unbelievable if, in addition, the social patterns had lost their unique qualities or had discarded all of the old. But just as the factory system has assimilated many of the old Japanese social patterns, such as the obligation of the feudal lord to care for his retainers throughout their lifetime, so has the family retained many of its older patterns: it has profoundly changed, like Japanese industrial patterns, but both have retained their Japanese character.

Warnings to the effect that Japan is not yet Western are rather to be viewed as indices of the great alterations in the Japanese system. That is, the Japanese family has moved so far that such warnings may be necessary. By contrast, no one needs to caution that the Indian family system has not as yet become identical with the conjugal family of the industrial West.

Two comments of major importance must precede our more detailed analysis. The first is a reassertion of a thesis which has been expressed throughout this book, that often a particular element to be found in the modern conjugal family system is neither new nor a product of industrialization, but in fact part of an ancient tradition. We shall comment on this in more detail later on, but let it suffice for now to note that in early Meiji and late Tokugawa times it is likely that peasants in rural Japan saw one another prior to marriage, engaged in courtship, probably had sexual relations before marriage, and for the most part chose their own spouses.[6]

A second major orienting correction of many contemporary analyses of family change in Japan is this: Nonfamily relations in Japan were *not* "simulated family relations," in which family behavior and attitudes were applied to social ties outside the family. On the contrary, it is rather that one major *non*family type of relationship, that of lord and retainer, *samurai* and vassal, patron and protegé, was applied to almost every possible social situation *and was even the model for family relations.* Japanese society was feudal, and even the family was feudal in its structure.

Since the term "feudal" has in modern times so frequently been used to mean merely "backward" or "reactionary," a stricter usage must be defined here. In this stricter sense, China was predominantly familial, not feudal; Japan was predominantly feudal rather than familial. A feudal social system approximates the following traits: (1) Its social ranks are closed, at least, ideally; the norms of the society state that people should remain in the position into which they are born. (2) There is a hierarchy of positions of power, so that from the lowest to the highest there is an unbroken chain of obedience upwards and protection downwards. No man is left outside the chain or can avoid it. An individual is related to people outside the direct line of hierarchy through their common overlord. (3) Goods and services, and especially the ownership of land, are distributed on the basis of the social ranks to be found within this hierarchy of power and responsibility.[7]

The importance of the fact that Japan was feudal rather than familial can hardly be overestimated, because it helps to explain why Japan is perhaps the only nation that has been able to use its family system *positively* in the industrializing process. This fact also helps to explain the lack of any serious and widespread family disorganization since 1868, as well as the extent to which not only the upper-class elders but also peasants and lower-class family elders have continued to elicit obedience, deference, and economic support from their grown children.

Several Japanese family characteristics contributed to the industrialization process in Japan, in contrast to China.[8]

1. A single type of family was not the ideal for all the great classes of Japanese society in Tokugawa times, *daimyo* (lord) and *samurai*, peasants, artisans, and merchants. Both norms and behavior differed from class to class as well as from region to region, as folklore and the hundreds of anthropological accounts by Japanese scholars testify. By contrast, the gentry ideal in China seems to have been accepted by all as the proper set of norms, to be followed where possible.

2. Perhaps most important was the fact that the Japanese family was the last link in the chain of hierarchy that led to the *shogun* and cloistered Emperor. By contrast, a Chinese man would ideally follow his father's wishes, even if they conflicted with those of the state; the head of the family acted in the interest of his family, and of his clan, but had no such responsibility to the state. Moreover, the state administration did not extend by unbroken links to the family. There was a large area of informal or family control, and only in crises did the imperial power intervene. This meant, however, that when the lower *samurai* overthrew the *shogunate* and restored the emperor, their decisions could be transmitted directly to every individual, who in fact owed obedience to those who transmitted the orders.

3. Upward class mobility was both fact and ideal in China and a man was expected to bestow upon his relatives the benefits of his position of power and affluence when he achieved them. In Japan, upward mobility was not encouraged, and when it occurred, its most characteristic form was through a widespread system of adoption by which the adopted man moved

into the new family as a protegé, and owed nothing to his blood relatives, whom he no longer considered his.

4. These characteristics interacted with a further element to create consequences for potential industrialization. The norms of both Japanese and Chinese society gave a low social ranking to the merchant, although merchants often had great power and even respect because of their economic position. In China, however, the ideal of the successful merchant family was to leave the business by acquiring land, giving sufficient education to the sons to permit them to move into higher bureaucratic levels through state examinations, and allying themselves by marriage with the gentry. Japanese merchants, by contrast, were not encouraged to do this, with the result that there arose a *continuing* tradition of commerce, trade, and general expertise in precisely the kinds of economic problems that arose with industrialization.[9]

The feudalization of Japanese family relations, in contrast to those of the Chinese, may be further seen in the *oyabun-kobun* relationship, often translated as the "parent-child" relationship (from *oya* for parents and *ko* for child). But in fact its essence is that of patron and protegé or lord and vassal, and that is its original linguistic meaning as well.[10] The protegé owes loyalty and service to his patron, and the patron owes protection and support to his protegé. *Both* kin and nonkin might become protegés of a man, just as *both* kin and nonkin made up the *dozoku*, the near equivalent of the Chinese clan. The members of the family or those of the *dozoku* owed loyalty to the head of the main family (*honke*) who dispensed support and protection. Such a chief might obtain power and influence in his own class, whether fisherman, merchant, or lord, by obtaining many protegés or vassals. The boy who became the family head on the death or retirement of his father was indeed the chief, as he typically was not in China, where this difference was expressed by the equality of inheritance among brothers and the ease with which the extended household broke up soon after the father relinquished his power or died.

This feudalization of all social relationships including those of the family, and the key position of the family structure in Japanese society, are responsible for the fact that at no time in the past hundred years has there been a period in which the demand or rights of the elders have been simply neglected or cast aside by the growing children. One can almost say that not only is there relatively little rebellion of the children against parents or of wives against husbands even now, but to a considerable extent the "source of the push for independence comes from the parents."[11] The lack of familial "disorganization" illustrates a major subsidiary thesis of this book, that those groups or classes are better able to maintain intact their own family system when they can keep their power in the *new* social structure and control new economic and social opportunities. Generally, as in the West, this control has been almost exclusively in the hands of the upper or upper-middle strata, who built the castles, led the military expeditions for colonial empires, or established new regimes after a revolution. Thus, they could control their own young men and women, and it was to their advantage to maintain intact their extended family relations.

However, in Japan to a striking degree, the *oyabun-kobun* relationship, in its pyramidal complexity, meant that a young man did not (and to a large extent, still does not) get a job in the new industrial world without a patron. The patron, in turn, would probably not give him the opportunity unless he could count on the loyalty of both the young man and the young man's father. Such relationships were, and are, of importance in education as well, which becomes a prime key for entering the higher positions in the world of industry as well as government.

It must be emphasized that ability is of consequence here, as it was in Tokugawa Japan. It was, and is, of strategic importance for the patron to acquire a protegé with promise and ability, just as it was, and is, wise for the young Japanese to choose his patron carefully.[12]

Perhaps the single most striking contrast illustrating the difference between the family structures of China and Japan is that the Japanese father, at any class level, could supplant his heir by adopting a son of superior ability—thus further guaranteeing the success of his *ie* (the "house") and obtaining a protegé who discarded his allegiance to his former family—whereas adoption in China was extremely difficult and rare, and viewed as impractical because the young man would always feel loyal toward the family from which he came. That is, a *particularistic* relation between parent and son overrode the new loyalty in China, but not in Japan. Consequently, in each decade since the Restoration the elder generation at every class level has been able to refuse to hand over to its children the new social and economic opportunities; thus, even when many of the family attitudes of the younger generation conformed closely to those of the West, the *behavior* of younger people exhibited far more conformity to the wishes of the older generation. This will be shown in more detail later. It is not so much that the young Japanese is immediately dependent on a family that tries to control him as fully as possible. Rather, he is dependent upon the good will of a *network* of patronage, of which the family links are only one kind. The legal changes in the family code and the ideological influences from the West did not have the disruptive effect upon familial authority that might have been expected, since these did not affect the much more central pattern of protegé and patron.

1. Early Legal Changes

It is now impossible to ascertain all the implicit sociological reasons in the minds of the Japanese leaders who, in the early Meiji period, decided which elements in Japanese society were to be changed. The leaders of the Restoration were determined to maintain the Japanese tradition as completely as possible, yet to move rapidly toward industrialization, which would become the country's sole adequate protection in a world of great colonial powers. Many of the new rules were designed to increase state control over the family and to use it as a means to strengthen the forces the state was marshalling for industrialization. The general goal of Restoration leaders was specific; what we do not know is the process by which they chose the *means*. After all, they might well have altered many family elements in the social structure and witnessed very different consequences. But they were so successful that many family patterns now viewed as "traditionally Japanese" were in fact changes made during the early Meiji period.[13]

Early legislation therefore moved in two directions. One was to extend *samurai* family patterns to the whole society, which meant an intensification of the hierarchy and a strengthening of family controls over the individual. On the other hand, at least a few radical steps were taken to utilize the great potentialities of a system that might permit achievement to all who had talent—i.e., to make the stratification system more flexible.

The new Civil Code, modeled after the German code as being more suitable than other Western codes to the Japanese situation, was not put into effect, however, until 1898. An earlier draft, more liberal and on the French model, was rejected.[14] The preceding three decades had already witnessed a substantial flood of liberal thought, as well as more than one demonstration that the new rulers could keep it in check.[15] The new code, then, represented a selection of ideas that permitted substantial social development in Japan, but under a tight rein. The final formulation of the Code was therefore not just a first burst of enthusiasm about new patterns, but a crystallization of thought and discussion extending over a generation; it was a considered decision to hold certain important things in check and to encourage others. A radical step, never rescinded, was taken as early as 1872, when the government proclaimed that illiteracy would be abolished and that boys and girls should be given equal educational opportunity. Everyone with ability (whatever his class) should be encouraged to learn. But a proclamation alone does not create a school system, and a survey of education and child labor in twenty-two large factories in 1897 showed that 73 per cent of the workers under 10 years of age had no education at all. The mere fact that the survey existed does show that the state was interested in the problem, and the nearly universal literacy of the Japanese is a tribute to its ultimate success.[16]

A government announcement of 1871 freed all classes from the necessity of petitioning for permission to marry (though in fact the rule had applied primarily to the gentry), and another of 1875 required that marriages be reported in the district headman's office.[17] Another notification of the same period permitted marriages between people of different classes as well as the adoption of children of a different class.[18] Both of these provisions permitted more alliances among families of different classes.

Other provisions, however, gave greater power to the head of the *ie*, and imposed the rule of primogeniture on all families where it was possible. This was an extension of *samurai* patterns to families in other classes, where a wide variety of practices existed. For example, when the son of the head of a *samurai* family took over the family authority, it was fairly common for his wife also to be given a symbol of authority, such as the ladle used to serve the family's rice.[19] In rural areas and in lower-class families generally, however, the wife had more authority and scope for action than in *samurai* families. In the discussion centering upon such points before enactment of the laws, the majority of the Legal Committee agreed with the position that "the customs of farmers are not to be made general customs—instead we must go by the practice of *samurai* and noble-man."[20] A member of the *ie* could not choose his residence without the permission of its chief, just as he could not marry without that permission. The goods that a member of the *ie* acquired were to be his own property, but any property about which ownership was in doubt belonged to the head of the household.[21]

The provisions concerning divorce were changed very little. Since divorce was by mutual consent, this meant in essence that the traditional seven reasons for a man's divorcing a woman were permitted (these were taken from the Chinese), as well as the three bars to divorce which the woman could interpose. In addition, however, divorce without consent of the other spouse could be obtained for a number of causes, even (under certain grave circumstances) the man's adultery.[22]

The Code did affect the *public* rate of divorce, however, since it apparently succeeded in doing what the notification of 1875 had failed to do, requiring the registration of marriage for its validity; thereafter divorces were not reported unless the marriage itself had been reported. Since the unrecorded marriages were—and still are—somewhat less stable, a segment of divorces was not to be reported from that time on. Consequently, as will be noted later, the divorce rate dropped very sharply in the year following the adoption of the new Code.[23]

A radical change was intended, as in some of the Chinese code drafts, by the failure to specify any family position for the concubine. But, since Article Two states that all customs have the status of law when no specific law exists, this legalistic device accomplished very little.[24] The discussions regarding this point did have the effect of increased public disapproval of concubinage. In the Code itself, however, a head of household could still recognize his own bastard child and moreover could adopt him.[25]

Most of the provisions in the Code intensified the *samurai* patterns by placing greater emphasis on the male side than was customary in families outside the upper social strata. In lower-class and rural strata, the wife's side of the family was given an appropriate amount of attention in the ceremonies surrounding marriage. The *samurai* were the main body of the elite at that time, however, and were also the leaders of the new changes. Members of social strata who once would have simply practiced the customs of their own group came to regard some upper-stratum patterns as desirable for them and these inclinations were supported by both law and the new elite, who furthermore continued to insist in speeches and discussions that new customs were in fact the "old, traditional Japanese way." New influences, also came from the cities, making many of the older customs, such as the relatively free relations between young men and women, seem crude and countrified by comparison.

Sociologically most interesting, however, is the fact that two great social forces were simultaneously put into motion; first, the *freeing* of the individual in certain ways to find his own position in society with less and less dependence upon the will of his elders; second, the movement toward *greater authority* in the hands of the *ie* head—greater control over mate choice, lessened authority in the hands of the wife, and a tightening of the linkage between the individual family and the state. In the long run, of course, the first of these forces was to be predominant. On the other hand, because Japan was rural, many of the older customs persisted throughout the entire period of nearly a century. For example, divorce was and remains easy in the more isolated areas of Japan, although the gentry strove to impose its own disapproval of divorce upon the Japanese population. The early laws do not, of course, represent majority opinion, but as an expression of the aims and ideals of the ruling class that at least show the direction in which they wanted Japan to move. Moreover, they practiced censorship of publications and speeches, and used the weight of their economic, social, and political power in eliciting the expression of opinions they approved. Consequently, the laws both expressed an important set of attitudes, and to some extent promoted their appearance in a wider segment of the population.

Not until 1948 did a new Japanese Civil Code appear, embodying some legal conceptions of family relations but mostly removing old restrictive articles. These new laws, too, are ahead of contemporary Japanese values, but without any question the difference is narrowing constantly.

2. Choice of Mate: The Return to Freedom

Because the Japanese "common people" (*heinin*) and the upper strata had different family customs at the time of the Meiji Restoration, the trends of different strata in succeeding decades moved in different *directions*, but *toward* similar patterns. The *samurai*, and the successful merchants who imitated them, gave almost no freedom of mate choice to their children, but during the past generation they have come to grant more freedom. The common people who had conceded freedom in the earlier period, but had withdrawn that freedom by perhaps the middle or end of the Meiji Restoration (1912), have more recently begun again to permit younger people to make their own choices.

Regional variations in Japanese courtship and mate-choice customs have been, and remain, plentiful. However, two major forms seem to have been widespread. One of these, found in western and especially in northeastern Japan, was in effect a system of "groom service." The young man married his bride at her house, and lived with her there, not taking her to his home for a long period of time, sometimes as much as three to five years. During that interval, he was expected to work for his parents-in-law.[26] In this, as in the succeeding form of marriage, the bride and groom knew and chose one another prior to marriage.

In a second major form, the marriage took place at the house of the bridegroom, but the bride thereupon returned to her father's house, helping in the work at her father-in-law's house only during very busy periods. Her husband consorted with her and subsequently she moved to his home. In some of the areas where this form of marriage existed—for example, in areas where young women worked as divers—her services were of considerable economic value.[27]

In spite of the many variations, however, it is likely that several common elements found in these rural customs were followed by a majority of the Japanese population. First, most marriages occurred within the village among young people who had known one another for many years. Second, the form of association between young men and women seems to parallel very closely the pattern reported for eighteenth-century Swedish farmers. That is, local boys came to visit girls, and, as part of the courtship pattern, the parents allowed them fairly free sexual access to their daughters. The particular arrangements varied. Sometimes the girl would be allowed to sleep in some place like the kitchen or a hall by the doorway where the boy could visit her at night. Gradually, a young man and woman singled one another out of the group as a future spouse, and married with the permission of their parents. Some variation or another of such a pattern has been reported for widely separated areas in Japan. A remnant of it is reported by Embree in Kyushu,[28] a generation ago, and more recently premarital cohabitation has also been reported for Okinawa.[29] The young man and woman chose each other under the surveillance of their peer group as well as parents. They were likely to be acceptable to the community since they were of the same rank and economic position and, of course, followed the same customs.

A next major common element was the transfer of authority from the young man's father to the young man himself. The young man then had a right to the seat by the hearth. At the same time, usually, the mother-in-law's authority was passed to the bride, symbolized by giving her the family's rice ladle.[30] That is, whether the marriage took place at the home of the bridegroom or of the bride, the couple did not form a domestic unit until they had succeeded to the authority of the household.

The Japanese efforts to extend *samurai* patterns to ordinary people seem to have obtained rather marked success, perhaps because the formula of "democratization" espoused by the Meiji leaders made it possible for common people to follow upper-class norms. Under these norms, the ideal was that the young woman and her groom did not see one another prior to the marriage (in part because they frequently came from different feudal fiefs). The decision was made by the elders, as is common among the nobility, and the aim of any marriage arrangement was the continuation of the family line. So single was this aim, that under the 1898 Code, if a young man and woman were both the sole heirs of their family line, they were not permitted to marry one another since this would mean that one family line would die out. This insistence by the elders on strong control over mate choice, in the interest of the family line, seems to have spread to nearly all Japanese social strata by the Taisho period (beginning in 1912). Even in the distant village of Suye Mura the rural patterns of free courtship had nearly died out by a generation ago, and Norbeck could write in the 1950s that "until about 40 years . . . in-*buraku* marriages based upon mutual attraction are said to have been common."[31]

Such marriages were preceded by negotiations and investigations that were initiated and smoothed by the *nakodo,* the marriage arranger. It was, and still is, considered the duty of a Japanese adult to help arrange a marriage at least once in his lifetime, and the importance of the *nakodo* probably grew considerably in the Meiji period, when a far greater number of families began to follow the new custom of marrying their children to families who did not know one another prior to the marriage negotiations. The *nakodo* was able to find out the facts about the potential bride and groom without either family losing face, so that when the first meeting, the *miai,* occurred, both families were satisfied that the bride and groom were suited to one another—or more accurately, that the two families were suited to one another and that an alliance between their members was appropriate.[32]

Over the period from the Restoration until about World War I, not only did the older traditions fade quickly, but the new patterns came to be accepted as the "true Japanese way," which had been handed down from distant generations. In rural areas, where living adults could describe the past, the new system was viewed as a step forward from uneducated, primitive, and improper methods of contracting marriage.[33]

Obviously, such a great change in mate selection required alterations in sex attitudes. Whether or not the sex attitudes of ordinary Japanese were "looser" than those of the West, their definitions of sexually improper behavior were different. Meiji leaders were concerned that some of these differences might cause Japan to lose the respect of the Western nations, especially during the "ballroom" period when the Japanese elite began to imitate Western customs, such as holding formal dances. The Japanese did not view nakedness as sexual under certain kinds of situations—in the bath house, for example, or women divers in certain areas. Similarly, the premarital sexual behavior of rural youth was not viewed as improper. But with the spread of the elite definition of marriage arrangements, virginity came to be required. Embree quotes one of his respondents as saying that "even a servant girl now has enough education to know that she must keep her virginity."[34] Sexual "misbehavior" came to harm a girl's chance of marriage.[35] By the 1950s, Takashima brides are described as "almost invariably virginal."[36]

The "Japanese" pattern of marriage, initiated by parents or *nakodo*, arranged by *nakodo*, and decided on by both sets of parents, came to be approved as well as followed in practice by most Japanese by about the turn of the century. Voices calling for freedom of choice were not lacking, but they were a tiny minority, and even these voices were forced into silence by the nationalist propaganda of the 1930s. As against this change, it should be remembered that romantic love themes were always common in Japanese popular and classical literature. In addition, the economic expansion and physical dislocation of World War II gave an increasing number of young people a new bargaining position from which to consider the possibility of making an independent decision to marry. Finally, the new Civil Code of 1948 asserted that marriage rested on the consent of the young people themselves.

The public opinion polls after World War II paid considerable attention to the attitudes of people regarding the freedom of mate choice. In a 1949 national sample of Japanese males, 20 per cent stated that parents should choose the mate, and 33 per cent said the individual should choose his own mate. Forty per cent believed that parents and individuals concerned should consult one another, but this is a normal practice in Western countries as well, where freedom of choice is taken for granted. In a national sample of both males and females in 1953, 44 per cent of the respondents asserted that marriage should be the exclusive concern of the individuals, and only 14 per cent thought that it should be exclusively familial.[37]

A report on Okinawan village life claims that there is "almost universal approval of free choice in marriage."[38] Eighty per cent of Baber's university student sample thought that the love of match is ideal *and* practical.[39] Another study of university students reported that 90 per cent claim the right of individual choice.

Dore offers more sophisticated alternatives. He asked 72 adults whether they believed that their sons or daughters should decide for themselves when the time came for marriage. Although these answers do not have the reliability of a national sample, they at least reflect the other side of the parent-child relationship in the matter, and furthermore distinguish between the attitudes toward sons and daughters.

These replies suggest a considerable gap between the aspirations of young people (as evidenced in their answers cited in the previous paragraph) and the parental attitudes they must face. Second, they show that the Japanese parent is not inclined to give so much freedom to the daughter as to the son, and implicitly that the daughter will accept that state of affairs more readily. Evidently, the Japanese parents in Dore's sample expect many of their children to find mates for themselves, but reserve either a veto power or the right to express strong advice.

When the time comes for your son (daughter) to get married, who do you think should decide whom he (she) marries? Yourselves? or he himself (she herself)?[40]

REPLIES	CHILD CONCERNED Son	Daughter
First Answer		
Parents should take the initiative and look for marriage partners	8	32
Second Answer		
Child should be left on own but parents should exercise veto power	24	8
Third Answer		
Child on own, parents should give strong advice, but *no* veto power	23	32
Fourth Answer		
Initiative should be taken by either when opportunity occurs	3	4
Don't know	5	5

A recent national sample (1956) carried out by the Prime Minister's Office asked whether a choice made by parents or by oneself is to be preferred. Sixty-three per cent stated that one's own choice was better, while only 26 per cent said that the parents' choice was better. What is striking about all of these samples is the increasing percentage of the population in favor of individual choice, and the fact that evidence in breakdowns by age and urban residence show more young than old and more urban than rural to favor individual choice. These data indicate that changes are occurring with respect to attitudes.[41]

Attitudes and values, however, are not equivalent to behavior. The love match may be the ideal of the Japanese young, but the social patterns of Japan do not easily lead to such matches. The most important of these barriers is the lack of any simple, natural arrangement by which young people in their teens may meet and go on dates together, away from the immediate surveillance of their elders and without any commitment for the future. Meeting and dating one another away from the family still has a hint of the clandestine about it. An index of this fact may be seen in the answers to a national public opinion survey (1951) which reported that 85 per cent of the respondents saw nothing wrong in husbands and wives going out together, but only 16 per cent thought that it was permissible for a young man and a young woman to walk in the streets together arm in arm.[42]

Nevertheless, the evidence seems clear that young people are increasingly obtaining the decision over their own choice of mate, even though in many instances they go through the formalities of a *miai* and the *nakodo*.

Thus they are obtaining their freedom while expressing their deference to the older generation. Even ten years ago, in one of the *mura* studied by Stoetzel's group, half the younger people were balking at accepting parental decisions about their marriage, and the others were accepting the decision grudgingly.[43] The Welfare Ministry reported in 1957 that love marriages among those married before or during the War constituted only about 13 per cent, but they had increased to 31 per cent among those married *after* the War.[44] Of the nearly 14 thousand marital conciliation cases in the forty-nine Family Courts in 1955, nearly 3 thousand were reported to have been contracted on the basis of romantic love.[45] In Dore's sample, there were 11 per cent of love marriages before 1921, and 23 per cent in the 1921–1930 period. This rose to 33 per cent in 1941–1945 and to 46 per cent in the 1945–1951 period.

It should not be supposed, however, that a "love marriage" means the same in West and East. Japanese parents and children may say that a "love match" was made, or that "the children decided," when by Western standards only a small gesture in the direction of freedom was conceded: a father may show his daughter a picture and ask whether she would like to marry the young man; or the parents may bring the boy and girl together and permit them to spend an afternoon together walking in the park or going to a moving picture. Thus they have "dated" before the marriage. On the other hand, we should not forget that in the West marriages are also not made merely on the basis of random love associations. Only people of roughly the same social and economic position take part in a given marriage market, and both peers and parents exercise as strong a hand in the choice as they dare, especially when they disapprove of the match. Moreover, they are often successful in their disapproval, as noted earlier. Nevertheless, the number of genuinely free choices in Japan is increasing in frequency, and with the increase will come a greater number of cross-class marriages as well as marriages of couples from very different geographical localities.

3. Age at Marriage

The general trend of age at marriage in Japan over the past generation is clear: a rise in the average age at marriage for both men and women. The process involved and the resulting numerical data are rather complex. Although the general rise in average age at marriage fits the textbook predictions, "there was no automatic and proportionate relationship among industrialization, urbanization, and the postponement of marriage."[46]

One source of the difficulty of analysis is that from 1872 until 1918 the marriage data are derived from the family records, the *koseki*. No marriage license is required in Japan, and although a marriage is not valid until it is registered, it need not be registered for some years. Consequently, many marriages began and ended without any official records at all. By the time of the first valid national census data in 1920, over a half-century had passed since the Meiji Restoration. Consequently, we lack data indicating the effect of early urbanization and industrialization.

In 1910, the average age of women at recorded first marriage was 23 years; of men, 27 years. These figures had risen to 24 years for women and 28 years for men by 1935.[47] However, some notion of the regional variation may be seen from the fact that in 1920 the average age at first marriage for women was 25 years in Tokyo and Osaka but 20 years in Aomori and Iwate. The differences are to be found not merely between rural and urban regions. In 1925, 34 per cent of the girls 15 to 19 years of age in rural Iwate were married, as contrasted with only 9.8 per cent in urban Tokyo; but the figures are *lower* in the rural areas of Kagoshima, and lower still in Gumma and Saitama (4.0 per cent and 5.5 per cent, respectively).[48] Taeuber comments that the transition from early to later marriage appears far advanced in the cities by 1920 and 1925, but urbanization had long been going on—indeed, it had long been a focus of complaints by the Tokugawa leaders—and it is possible that *later* marriage had become common in the cities long before the Meiji period.

The rise in age at marriage can be seen more clearly in the proportions of those ever married from 1920 to 1955 at the younger ages (see Table VII-1). As can be seen, there was a steady drop in the proportion marrying at the earlier ages. One exception was found in the year 1950, when there was a temporary drop in the age at marriage for men, reflected in the much higher proportion ever married at ages 20 to 24 for that year. The same trend is visible when the population is divided into rural and urban categories. In general, the rural population married earlier than the urban, although the exceptions are interesting.

Table VII-1
Proportion Ever Married, Females 15 to 19 and Males
20 to 24 Years of Age, 1920–1955*
(in per cents)

	1920	1925	1930	1935	1940	1950	1955
Females	17.7	14.1	10.7	7.5	4.3	3.4	1.8
Males	29.1	27.6	20.4	16.0	10.0	17.1	9.8

* Irene B. Taeuber, *The Population of Japan* (Princeton: Princeton University Press, 1958), p. 211.

If these changes are comparable to those in the West, they conform to the pattern noted earlier in Sweden, England and Wales, and the United States: in other words, there was an *increase* in the age at marriage in the *earlier* period of industrialization. There is no reason to suppose, however, that this change indicates any alterations in the cultural definitions of a proper age for marriage. Lacking adequate data, we may speculate about the several interacting elements that created the regional variations in age at marriage in Japan, the differences between city and rural populations, and the time trends themselves.

First, the Japanese ideal was to marry relatively early, at about 18 years for girls, but early adolescent marriage seems to have been neither an ideal nor a practice. The young wife was expected to be able to shoulder the housework and farm burden of an adult. We have already noted that in at least some, and perhaps many, rural areas, the young man did not marry until he was fully adult. Very likely, he was able to marry only when the older couple felt that they were getting close to retirement, or there was available land for the new couple. If this is so, it would at least partly explain the fact that in the less fully settled northeastern agricultural areas, young people married much earlier than in the southwestern areas like Kagoshima, where the land had been fully occupied for centuries.

Most important, the age at marriage was not a decision made by the couple, but by the parents. The marriage did not take place if in their judgment the time was not appropriate.

As a consequence, the establishment of the early factories did not lead to earlier marriages. The factories were likely to be located in rural areas where labor was cheap, and used young women where possible. These girls were not freed from family controls, and did not even have the right to spend their own money. Their jobs were insecure, and they lived a dormitory life with a factory head as surrogate parent; but they were allowed to court with the local boys. Either their own parents or the surrogate made the decision about marriage; thus their employment did not lead to independence. Moreover, they ceased to work after marriage so that, unlike the contemporary West, the wife's earnings did not serve as a dowry. Consequently, where young women had factory jobs, they were not necessarily able to marry earlier. This may be seen in one such factory area, the prefectures of Gumma and Saitama (north by northeast from Tokyo). The data may be biased somewhat by the inmigration of young, unmarried girls to this area for the purpose of taking jobs, but the correct figures may not have been greatly different: In 1925, the percentage ever married among women aged 15 to 29 was even lower than in the southwestern rural districts.

Since only one male inherited the land and the family headship, the eldest son would usually marry at an earlier age than the other sons.[49] Since there was little local land available, younger sons had to make their own way and, where possible, migrated to cities. In the cities, however, they were still under considerable control, either by their own parents or by their employers. With low wages and little opportunity for advancement, the chances of an early marriage were low.

On the other hand, there was apparently little or no increase (again allowing for the problems in the data themselves) in the proportion *ever* married. In Japan, as in China, almost everyone eventually married; this was the responsibility of the elders. In almost every one of the successive censuses from 1920 to 1955, less than 2 per cent of the male or the female population aged 45 to 49 was unmarried.[50] Men who were fortunate economically were more likely to be married early than other men. A further fact must be kept in mind when looking at these forces in interaction. A higher proportion of unrecorded marriages or couples living together without marrying may be found among those in production and service activities, and among the unemployed. The ages of the man and woman at the *beginning* of such unions are, of course, not known. The socially advanced strata seem to have married earlier (as in China) just as they undoubtedly registered the marriage in the *koseki* soon after the wedding.

Although we are willing to predict that the age at marriage in Japan will *drop* over the next two decades, some public opinion data suggest that there is no great discrepancy between desired and actual age at the present time. In a 1952 public opinion survey, the desired age at marriage for the rural heir was 24.2 years for the male and 20.6 for the female. At that time, in the areas where the survey was taken, the actual age for husbands was 24.6 years and for wives 20.6 years. The respondents also thought that the son who did not inherit should be married slightly older, about one year more.[51] For the sample as a whole, the average desired age for males was 24.7, for females 20.8 years. These data, too, show a lower age for the upper-class husband and wife than for the middle- or lower-class husband or wife.[52]

A further change, similar to a trend in Western marriage patterns, is the *decrease* in the difference between the ages of spouses in areas with substantial industrial opportunities or prosperous agricultural life.[53] Prosperity in the villages permitted a young man to marry a woman who had arrived at about the appropriate age without his having to wait a long time. In a patriarchal society with arranged marriages, it is taken for granted that the bride will be some years younger than her husband, and there is no strong norm which says that a man in his late 30s may not marry a girl in her late teens. Indeed, little attention seems to be paid to such age differences. In addition, since the elders decide upon the alliance on the basis of the interest of the household, family, or lineage, older women may marry younger men. At the same time, however, I believe that in no society is a great discrepancy viewed as desirable by the young people themselves. When there is greater freedom of choice, and the household becomes less dependent upon such alliances, these discrepancies will be reduced somewhat. In addition, during a period of relatively general prosperity when opportunities are widely available, the bargaining situation is such that the woman need not wait too long for an opportunity to marry, nor will the young man. Here again, then, the age discrepancy will be somewhat smaller over time. Finally, however, if *both* processes are occurring—fewer older women marrying younger men, and fewer older men marrying younger women—the difference between the average ages of husbands and wives might well remain fairly stable.

Both these processes seem to be visible in the Japanese data. That is, during the 1904–1936 generation, the average difference in age (*not* considering specifically which age group married into which age group) remained stable at about four years. Over that period, however, there was a trend toward fewer *deviations* from the normal age difference between husband and wife in both categories: older men marrying very young women, or older women marrying younger men. It should be remembered that the latter case was frequently one in which a young man of a poor economic position was adopted and permitted to marry the heiress of a house. In some instances he married her without being adopted, but in either case she was likely to be older. Table VII-2 presents the categories of marriages to show the change over time.[54]

Table VII-2
Reduction in Age-Discrepant Marriages, Japan, 1904–1936*
(in per cent)

AGE OF HUSBAND	AGE OF WIFE			
	15–19	20–24	25–29	30–34
20–24				
1904–1906			6.3	0.7
1914–1916			5.1	0.6
1924–1926			4.6	0.5
1934–1936			5.4	0.4
25–29				
1904–1906	23.4			3.4
1914–1916	25.1			2.9
1924–1926	21.1			1.9
1934–1936	12.6			1.3
30–34				
1904–1906	10.2			
1914–1916	10.1			
1924–1926	8.0			
1934–1936	4.2			
35–39				
1904–1906	3.8			
1914–1916	3.8			
1924–1926	3.2			
1934–1936	1.7			

* Taeuber, op. cit., p. 228.

4. Fertility and Birth Control

The Japanese population expanded in the early Tokugawa period, but for the 125 years prior to the West's intrusion in the 1850s, the population was stable. Thereafter, the population resumed its growth, and did not slow down substantially until about 1950. The Japanese, like many other peasant societies, considered barrenness an adequate reason for divorce. Failure to bear a son was a catastrophe. Consequently, fertility was an ideal, and the Japanese birth rate was high during the nineteeth century, about forty per thousand population, dropping very slightly at the end of the century.[54] By the time of the first national census in 1920, permitting a correct calculation of a population base for ascertaining a crude or an age-specific birth rate, the birth rate had already dropped to 36.1 per thousand population, or 77.6 female births per thousand women aged 15 to 49.

Fertility dropped during the 1920s, and of course continued to drop during the depression of the 1930s. The decline is not great, however, and in the first figures for birth rates at the end of the World War II, the crude birth rate is once more as high as it was in the 1920s (34.3 in 1947). Even in 1947, however, fertility of women aged 15 to 49 was lower than it had been at any time since the depression period.

In the year 1950, which seems to mark a watershed in most data relating to fertility, there is a substantial drop, and in response to a steady pressure by the government to reduce national fertility, the decline continues through the 1950s.

By 1920 important variations in fertility may be seen in comparing regions or rural-urban patterns. It is possible that these differences always existed, and that fertility in Japanese cities was lower than in the country even in Tokugawa times. Fertility was also higher in the more remote areas of the islands and in the less developed agricultural areas (for example, northeastern Japan), but here again these differences may have existed for generations. Whether or not the differences had existed during the past, the decline observed during the 1925–1930 period is to be found in all standard population breakdowns. The birth rate dropped in the cities as well as in villages, and in the more remote agricultural areas as well as in the more settled areas of the southwest. The decline was general in most age groups, and especially among the younger ages. This pattern of general decline is also repeated in the 1950s. Prosperity brought with it some recovery, as in Western nations, but the general trend over more than a generation has been downward.

These facts suggest that industrialization had already begun to have an effect on the Japanese birth rate as early as the 1920s. Without prejudging the direction of cause, it is at least clear that simultaneously with urbanization and industrialization, the birth rate continued to fall off, and the birth control campaign of the 1950s simply gave added impetus to a movement that already had a long history. At the same time, however, there are some interesting complications in this trend. As in age at marriage, there are significant regional differences. Not all urban areas have lower fertilities than all rural areas. For example, the areas of densest agricultural settlement in the south*west* have relatively low fertility. The only large difference attributable to urbanization is found in the comparison between the six large cities of Japan and all the rest of Japan, rather than between all urban and all rural areas. Within a *given* prefecture, the urban rates were lower than the rural rates, but the prefectures themselves differed greatly in fertility.

At the present time, the Japanese crude birth rate, about eighteen per thousand, is less than that of the United States. Japan is the first Asian nation to have reduced its birth rate so far, and in doing so it exhibited the same celerity and effectiveness it had demonstrated in becoming industrialized. The Japanese birth rate has fallen by about one third over the past ten years. The government's decision to move in this direction was taken after World War II, when its colonial empire was smashed and it began to face the problem of space and food for a population that numbered some 3 thousand people per arable acre. During the 1950s the Japanese government mounted a propaganda campaign in favor of limiting births, continued to permit abortion on liberal terms, set up special experimental campaigns in certain villages, and throughout this period watched carefully the results of these various moves. Many studies have been made of this phenomenon, and only a few comments need to be made here.

In the 1950–1959 period, the question was asked, "How many more children do you want in addition to the two children you now have?" The proportion wanting *no more* increased from 30 per cent to 58 per cent. As another indication of the change during this decade, the proportion answering that contraception is "good" increased from 61 per cent in 1950 to 74 per cent in 1959. Moreover, the percentage currently practicing contraception increased from 20 to 42.5 in the 1950–1959 period.[55]

As might be expected, the rural groups lagged slightly behind the big city areas, and the upper occupational and educational levels are more in favor of contraception than the lower. Also, younger people tend to favor it far more than the older people. There are no important differences between husbands and wives on these points.[56]

In a special study of a seven-year program of the Japanese government in three villages, it was ascertained that 75 per cent of the couples had practiced contraception by the end of that period and 97 per cent of those with five children had done so. On the other hand, almost 10 per cent had chosen sterilization instead. During the 1948–1955 period, the birth rate dropped from 26.7 to 13.6 births per thousand population. Moreover, during this period the number of abortions had also dropped,[57] indicating that contraception was being used.

It seems likely that a large part of the heavy decline in the Japanese birth rate during the 1950s was due—at least at the beginning of the 1950s—to the increased use of abortion: in 1950 there were 209 abortions per thousand live births, 398 in 1952, and 572 in 1953. In the group of women aged 40 to 44, there were 2,259 abortions per thousand live births in 1953, and 4,877 per thousand live births in the 45 to 49 age group.[58] A very tiny minority of Japanese oppose abortion on religious grounds, and only about

11 to 12 per cent on grounds of social morality. The opposition against contraception seems to be no stronger than that.

Moreover, this is not a spread of "urban" attitudes or even of "modern industrial" attitudes. In one Japanese village, it was found that "at least 43 per cent of local pregnancies ended in abortion."[59] On the other hand, by 1954, some of the families had begun to use contraception.[60]

In Tokugawa times the Japanese practiced abortion, contraception, and infanticide. Obviously, it is not now possible to ascertain numerically precise rates for any of these, but the frequency of comments by Japanese philosophers and historians suggests that the practices were known to everyone, and that they must have played a substantial role in keeping the effective fertility down—especially during the latter part of the Tokugawa period when the population apparently remained stable. It is possible that abortion was more common in the great cities and infanticide more common among the peasants, for whom the midwife usually performed the task of "thinning" (i.e., getting rid of the excess plants, so that the remainder might grow better).[61]

Under certain reasonable assumptions of mortality and fertility, Taeuber concludes that the very low reported birth rates for feudal Japan are simply not believable and that there has been some exaggeration of the extent of infanticide. As she points out, the first born male was not destroyed, and the youthful mortality was so great that several children were in fact necessary to assure the continuation of the house. On the other hand, of course, the importance of maintaining the *ie* intact through the generations meant that the Japanese did pay great attention to the fertility level and at least had national attitudes about controlling the number of children who were to survive. Since at all times there will be some moral disapproval of such an action, it is entirely possible that the actual *rate* of infanticide was not extremely high but was resorted to whenever family security seemed to make it necessary.

Thus the Japanese entered the modern era with no strong religious or ethical attitudes that abortion was improper, and, in rural regions at least, infanticide was considered necessary if deplorable. In addition, however, they were accustomed for generations to the national government's attempts to change their behavior in various ways—by food allowances, grants of land rights, and even subsidies. The 1948 authorization of abortion, then, merely gave official sanction to practices and attitudes that were centuries old.[62] Thus, the first result of the government campaign was to increase the number of abortions without lowering the birth rate. The campaign also attempted to persuade people to use contraceptives, however, and that movement has become more successful during the past decade. The resort to abortion, when contraceptives can prevent the necessity for it, is, in fact, old-fashioned. It seems likely, then, that in the future the Japanese will respond in their fertility behavior to higher or lower opportunity levels very much as Western families now do. Of course, for some time to come, the residents of mountain and fishing villages may prefer abortion, and perhaps there may even be some continued use of infanticide, but in most of Japan, the limitation of birth will be the result of the increasing acceptance of contraceptives.

5. Illegitimacy and Concubinage

As is clear from the preceding discussion of the Japanese family system, there were several classes of infants who might be labeled "illegitimate" by Western standards, but which had very different statuses in Japanese society. Since the Japanese marriage was not usually registered at once in the *koseki*, the first child might be born before the marriage was registered, at least in Meiji and modern times. The child of a concubine might be recognized by the father (under the old Civil Code, his wife could not prevent that), the child thereby becoming a legal member of that household. Since polygyny was not permitted, the Japanese husband could not marry his concubine. On the other hand, for various reasons a man might not wish to recognize his own illegitimate child, and of course there were many children born of casual relationships or liaisons which the society viewed as improper.

The stigma of social illegitimacy seems to have been great. In *Suye Mura*, Embree reports that if the girl became pregnant, her parents arranged a marriage for her as quickly as possible, and not usually with her secret lover but with a man in a class somewhat lower than that of the girl. Moreover, he states that when a first son was given out for adoption, it was usually an illegitimate child of the mother (that is, born before she married).[63] In a report on a Japanese village of the 1950s, the author asserts that "sexual misbehavior plays havoc with the girl's chances of marriage."[64] The child who was "officially" illegitimate in that he was born before a genuine marriage had actually been registered, was of course not socially defined as illegitimate, and his position did not suffer at all. The child born of a concubine, but accepted by his father as part of the *ie*, may have suffered somewhat, but was nevertheless part of the household. The child who was not recognized was, however, recorded in the household of his mother, or perhaps in a new *koseki* that was established by the mother for herself and the child. The child was located in the social structure, but at a low level.

Due to the peculiarities of the registration system as it reflected the social system, the percentage of illegitimate births was thus not high in Japan, and it has steadily dropped over the past half-century, as Table VII-3 shows.

During the 1920–1947 period, the percentage of strictly illegitimate births also dropped, from more than half of the 1920 illegitimacy rate (4.8 per cent of the total were strictly illegitimate) to 1.6 per cent in 1947. Thereafter, the figure is not reported, since under the new Civil Code the status of

Table VII-3
Illegitimate Births as Percentage of Total Live Births, 1890–1954*

1890	8.2
1920	8.2
1930	6.4
1940	4.1
1950	2.5
1954	1.7

* 1920–1954 figures from Taeuber, *The Population of Japan, op. cit.,* p. 261. Half or more of the total illegitimate births are recognized by the father.

concubine is not recognized at all. Consequently, there is no distinction made between the "recognized illegitimate" and the "strictly illegitimate" births.

The cause of this decrease is not clear. The modern decline in concubinage, as a result of changing attitudes regarding older customs, would cause the rate of illegitimacy to drop only negligibly, since concubinage was generally confined to men with wealth and thus was not common.[65] The spread of contraceptives during the past decade would cause the illegitimacy rates to drop somewhat, just as the increased social freedom of the young might cause it to increase a bit, but neither factor can account for the apparently steady decline over the past period of nearly half a century. (It should be noted from Table VII-3 that there seems to be no change from 1890 to 1920). Elders cannot now successfully insist that the young man of position cast aside a girl who has conceived a child by him and whom he wishes to marry, but this factor would also be of little importance in reducing the rate of illegitimacy over such a long period of time.

Certainly two factors seem worthy of some consideration here, although it would be difficult to prove their importance. The first is the spread of the aristocratic family pattern to the rural or to the lower social strata, which meant essentially that the head of the household obtained much greater control over the behavior of members of his family—greater supervision as well as the ability to force a quick marriage. Thus, illegitimacy could be forestalled by a speedy marriage, and in any event the attitudes of vigilance about virginity would have had an effect on illegitimacy.

Second, and somewhat more speculative, is the possibility that the Japanese who came to dwell in cities also came to recognize that under these new conditions the family and the girl could no longer trust the social controls of household and neighborhood to force a marriage if a girl became involved in a liaison. The family could be somewhat more tolerant in rural areas, where the young man could not easily escape. He was known, and known to have been seeing the girl. The difference, however, meant that both families and the girls themselves would then become more alert to the dangers involved in free social relations. Thus, the anonymity and lack of neighborhood control in the city may have led to increasing family control over the girl. A partial support of this interpretation is that the percentage of *recognized* illegitimate births *outside* the large cities remained constant from 1923 to 1938 (3.1 to 3.7 per cent), whereas the category drops very sharply in the cities.

The position of the concubine in Japan shaded off toward that of mistress without recognition by the family. As in China, the wife had no legal basis on which to object to a concubine, but did so nevertheless. The range of relationships with the unrecognized mistresses in turn shaded off toward various emotional and sexual alternatives which of course were explicitly part of the system of prostitution and female entertainers for which Japan has been famous.

Although, on a formal level, these patterns were similar to those of China, certain differences seem to appear which cannot easily be demonstrated. The Japanese appear to have been far more clearly "monogamous," at least in the sense that the status of concubine did not often become a matter for legal argument. In addition, although it is arguable as to whether China was not in spirit polygynous, this cannot be said of Japan. A partial index to this difference may be found in the rationalization given by the Chinese for taking a concubine—the barrenness of the wife. By contrast, adoption was so fully accepted in Japan that a concubine could not easily be justified on this basis, and thus could not have so much support in the institutional structure as in China. In addition, the class lines were so much more sharply drawn in Japan than in China, that there could be less chance of a concubine becoming acceptable as a later wife. In China, many legal opinions hinged on this problem.

The Japanese wife could object to a man's wasting his money on gambling or women, but she had little institutional support for objecting to his seeking outside sexual or social pleasures with women if he met his familial obligations adequately. It must be emphasized, however, that the difference between Japan and the West in this area may not at all lie in the *frequency* of such relationships. No such data exist for the West, except for Kinsey's recent data, and certainly in the Latin countries as well as in the lower classes of all Western countries there has always been considerable tolerance of the male who seeks pleasure with prostitutes. The difference lies rather in the fact that in Japan the relations with entertainers or with mistresses could be acknowledged without any great public shock or disapproval and that the injured wife could only grieve in private; she had little social or moral support for her emotional objections.

If these comments are correct, the few relevant postwar data show great changes. Dore asked a small Tokyo sample whether it was all right for a married man to have a mistress, and three out of four said no. Three fifths found this practice objectionable even if the wife was properly taken care of.[66] In one study in a national survey, it was ascertained that three fourths or more of the women said that they preferred chastity in men they were to marry. It need not be said that the men, without exception, preferred virgins.[67]

Legalized prostitution was abolished in 1946, but there has been little enforcement of the law, and later attempts to pass further legislation designed to strengthen the law have not been successful, in part because licensed public prostitution had much institutional support, especially through its connections with respectable society and business practices (e.g., for entertainment). The Yoshiwara district was famous not merely for the delights it contained but also as a locale for romantic literature and classical drama, and it was not until 1872 that a cabinet ordinance prohibited the sale of human beings and liberated prostitutes from slave contracts. Thus the abolition of publicly licensed prostitution in 1947 was simply followed by the opening of private houses and the transformation of such houses into ostensible hotels, teashops, cafes, and so on.

In one survey taken in the Tokyo area in 1948, over three fourths felt that street-walkers should not be permitted, but only one fourth were unsympathetic to girls in organized houses. Moreover, three fourths or more of the sample thought that organized houses might be necessary. As might be expected, women were much less convinced of this than were men.[68] Perhaps a small index of the difficulty of changing the position of women, which was the foundation for the system of prostitution in Japan, is the news item of 1956 which reported that 782 daughters had been "sold into prostitution by poverty-stricken families in Hokkaido."[69]

In any civilization there will of course be some prostitution, but the attacks on both prostitution and concubinage in Japan are changing their character. A more flexible marriage and job market certainly will permit some women an alternative mode of living, and fewer will wish to enter these statuses since by doing so they lose their former semirespectability. On the other hand, of course, the unrecognized mistress will always be one form of adjustment to the problems of marriage, and the very complex ties of entertainment and business, the separation of a husband's social life from his home, and the considerable freedom of Japanese men will preserve at least some part of organized prostitution for the indefinite future.

6. Husband-Wife Relations

Any assessments of the changes in husband-wife relations in Japan must be concerned in part with the dominance of the husband over the wife. However, several complex factors prevent a precise estimate at this time.

First, without doubt, the laws—both the Constitution and Civil Code which came into effect in 1947 and the Family and Inheritance Law which came into effect in 1948—are far in advance of both public opinion and actual behavior, and the former is still in advance of the latter.

Second, the subtleties of social expectation, reward, and punishment in the intimate relations between husband and wife permit the wife to express her objections without openly denying the husband's authority. A Japanese wife who walks deferentially behind her husband on a city street may have scolded him vigorously half an hour before. A wife may feel compelled to go through the proper formal leave-taking when her husband goes out for an evening of girls or gambling, but her slowness and reluctance are also a protest. She may massage him, prepare his bath, or wait on him silently while he eats first, but may perform these tasks less conscientiously and carefully than usually. The Japanese husbands may then feel the implied criticism as keenly as the United States husband might if his wife were to dissect his behavior in front of friends.

Third, of perhaps more importance, is the subtle and difficult problem of ascertaining husband-wife relations of a century or a half-century ago with any reasonable assurance. The 1898 Code did not describe actual husband-wife relations, any more than the present one does. Both, on the other hand, foreshadowed and accelerated the coming trends. A few cautious generalizations can be made however. Men from the upper strata did not know their wives before marriage, especially as the bride was likely to come from some distance away. She left her family *ie* and became part of her husband's and husband's father's *ie*. She had to adjust to the wishes of her elder in-laws. Especially since her husband was young, without much influence, and was not in love with her, she could not expect any support from him if she objected to her treatment. Divorce was defined by both her family and his as *her* failure. The husband could adjust to the wife with ease, doubtless at times too easily to suit his parents. With much greater difficulty, his wife learned to adjust to his idiosyncrasies and those of his family. Whatever pleasure they shared as they grew older was not undermined by overly high expectations on either side. Expecting little from marriage except traditional responsibilities, Japanese spouses probably enjoyed a higher likelihood of achieving contentment than husbands and wives in many contemporary Western countries. As they took over the leadership of *ie* and home, they did not become equal in authority, but the wife did achieve a considerable authority in the home itself. She conducted the rituals to the ancestors, disciplined the children, took part in seeking a spouse for her adult children, and made household purchases. Her actions and her activities outside the home were restricted, but her place in it was secure.

But though the realities of even upper-class life required the head of the household to permit his wife some areas of decision, both ideal and law pressed her to subordinate herself fully to his wishes and needs and to those of the *ie*. Neither the law nor ideal could force a complete subordination, but whatever respect she received for herself as a *person* (i.e., aside from the respect she enjoyed as consort of the household head), she had to create *individually*, without institutional support. She had little with which to bargain. Even for sexual and emotional solace her husband could dispense with her; aside from commercial women well trained for this purpose, concubines could be obtained.

Although this pattern began to change in Meiji days as women came to be educated, and the somewhat more egalitarian European customs were imitated, such as ballroom dancing, banquets, foreign travel, and even a movement for female suffrage, each of these was held in tight rein by the social and economic control in the hands of the elder upper-class males. Even education was not an opening of intellectual or social opportunity, but an attempt to teach the refinements of upper-class life (as, to a great extent was the pattern in Western finishing schools until about World War I). The changes were slow and halting, more radical in the realm of ideas than in behavior.

Husband-wife *relations* in rural or lower-class households were very different. It is not, however, clear just how different were their *values* and *attitudes* regarding family life. As in other old civilizations, there are persistent hints of a by-gone matrilineal system, but no such pattern was to be found in the Meiji times. Men made the important decisions, especially in matters concerning the *dozoku* or clan. The elders were powerful enough to send the young bride back if she did not quickly adjust, and moreover—unlike upper-class families—actually did so. The bride and the groom chose one another, but the tie was not strong enough to resist the authority of elders.

Yet descriptions of lower class and especially peasant behavior do suggest that the wife was somewhat more of a partner and less of an obsequious supporting servant than in upper-strata families. As in the other family systems we have been analyzing, male dominance in Japan was (and doubtless still is) greater toward the upper strata.

The subordination of the wife to her husband or his family is a function of the bargaining position allotted to her by her individual qualities and the social structure. Strong-willed women, wise women, beautiful women, are not easy to dominate in any society or in any period. The bargaining position of any given segment of women, leaving aside their individual differences, is determined by the extent to which the society gives them opportunities for production, decision, and action outside the control of their men. Their wishes must be respected more, because husbands and families wish to continue receiving the benefits of this outside activity, whether it is money, power, or prestige.

In Japanese fishing villages, farm work was done by women. They also helped prepare for the fishing expedition and later took part in processing the catch. In some coastal areas, women were also divers. In mountain villages devoted to forestry, again the women did much of the farming and helped the men in their work. Where silk culture was important, before the industry moved to the cities, women did much of that work. Indeed, Koyama comments on the strong position of the woman, "Only fifty years ago, the wife who was gainfully employed in the early stage of the silk textile industry was known for her *Kakadenka* (petticoat) government."[70]

Although wives in farmer villages may only recently have begun to obtain the benefits of the new family reforms, and their bargaining position was not so strong as that of wives in other types of villages, it is possible that their position was less subordinate than their city sisters' throughout the period since the Restoration. In his study of a generation ago, Embree states that "In farm work land and wife are equal, so that in a farmer's household a woman has a comparatively higher status than in a shop-keeper's home."[71]

But although the peasant or lower-class wife was less dominated by her husband than was the upper-class wife by hers, several questions remain to be answered. Most important, were there any substantial *changes* in relations between husband and wife in the rural or urban lower classes until the past two decades? If so, can they be tabulated and charted systematically by regions over the period since 1868?

Both Westerners and Japanese tend to assert that little change has occurred in rural areas, and a few suppose that the observed family practices are simply ancient custom. One team of Western observers in the period after World War II asserted that the status of women in Japan is lower than in Western countries. They go on to state that "This is particularly true in rural areas, where feudal traditions have survived the longest and change to modern practices has been slowest."[72] This team also reports the greater power in the hands of the women in one fishing village, where the women control the financial management of the household as well as farm cultivation.[73] In another fishing village, however, the analysts state that "there is little evidence of change in the position of women," but does note that the relations between *young* spouses are changing.[74]

Certainly, as already noted, *some* changes did occur, e.g., in courtship practices over this period. It is possible that the main outlines of change may have been the following: (1) Both urban and rural lower-class women at the beginning of Meiji were less subordinate than upper-class women. (2) The rural pattern of dominance did not generally change until recently, although in certain specific areas there were some changes. (3) Middle- and lower-class *urban* segments have changed more rapidly, so that by the late 1940s these women had come to enjoy much freer relations with their husbands than had rural women. (4) Middle and upper strata families have come to accept the *values* and attitudes of a more egalitarian relation between husband and wife, but their *behavior* has not changed as much as their attitudes.

Data from post war studies shed some more light on the possible patterns of change in recent times. The young, the better-educated, and the urban segments are more inclined to voice attitudes of egalitarianism. In Stoetzel's Kyoto and Sapporo samples, most of the students asserted that they expected "spouses would have equal influence in the direction and control of family affairs." Sixty-six per cent of the Kyoto men, 75 per cent of the women, and 82 per cent of the Sapporo sample gave that answer.[75] In a national opinion study, only a tiny minority of respondents disapproved of certain Western customs such as "exaggerated esteem for women" and "the humiliating position of men."[76]

When housewives in a 1955 national sample were asked about the planning of their household economy, 46 per cent asserted that they mainly worked out the plan, while 34 per cent asserted that their opinion was always asked. Only 18 per cent said that their opinion was sometimes asked, or that they never made the plans themselves.[77] Even in farm families, it was learned that 63 per cent of the wives were in charge of household expenditures. With reference to the more specific question as to "handing over the wages to wives," 86 per cent of the husbands in a Ministry of Labor study said that they did so, but in farm families 91 per cent of the husbands controlled these expenditures.[77] The figure of 63 per cent of wives "in charge of household expenditures" refers to a fringe area near Tokyo, which presumably would be different from other farm families.

The participation of Japanese men in housework may be seen as an index of change in relations between husband and wife. In one national sample, 32 per cent of the respondents approved of a man assisting in kitchen work (note that this percentage is higher than in Norway) and 45 per cent disapproved. Dore ascertained, however, that in over two thirds of the households in his small Tokyo sample, the husband actually did help once in a while, and another fourth helped in emergencies. It should be noted that these data contrast attitudes and behavior. It is quite possible that many men who help do not really approve of doing so, while in rural households men often help—and probably always did help to some extent with household activities. Men also helped with children in fishing and in silk villages half a century ago.[78]

Perhaps a more positive expression may be found of the increasing importance of the husband-wife relationship as against the relationship of husband with his parents. In interpreting several types of answers to probing questions regarding the importance to be given to the wishes of a mother-in-law as against those of the wife, Dore comments that in both his sample and in Tokyo society, the majority opinion is that "a man's relation with his wife is of more importance than his relations with parents."[79] The new family laws have removed the former restrictions on the financial independence and the rights of inheritance of the wife, and have given her equality in such areas as grounds for divorce and in the exercise of parental powers. But laws themselves do not create equality. In many farm areas, the elders may still be the predominant influence, especially at the beginning of a marriage; or, as one report states it: "The people in this village and the rest of Japan agree that the bride's relationship to her mother-in-law determines the duration of marriage."[80]

An intuitively persuasive pattern seems to emerge from two of Dore's samples. With reference to *traditional* matters, the Japanese still give greater importance to the male. Some 45 per cent of housewives stated that they followed the customs of their husband's family with reference to the preparation of foods and decoration for annual festivals. Only 26 per cent said that they followed their own family's customs. However, 19 per cent said that they had paid no attention to the problem, and another 5 per cent said that they had learned from neighbors how to do things. The second question asked whether the wife saw more of her husband's relatives (brothers and sisters) than her own relatives, but 78 per cent did not indicate a difference at all. About 14 per cent said that they saw more of their own relatives, and 9 per cent the husband's. Thus the pattern of adhering to the influence of the male is fading somewhat, perhaps not so much because it is rejected, but because other activities and customs supersede the old. Since the urban family does not interact constantly with a range of close relatives who have a strong interest in maintaining old family patterns, the wife is likely to be influenced in her frequency of daily social interaction with kin by such matters as geographical nearness, or the kind of problem being faced.[81]

Another index of the growing importance of the husband-wife relationship is the shortening period of time between the marriage ceremony and registration of the marriage in the *koseki*. This is because there is no reason to delay registration until it is decided how well a bride fits into a household. Both the young man and the young woman are more likely to have chosen one another, and the continuity of the marriage is not dependent on the judgment of the man's elders. From 1947 to 1957 the percentage registered within one month after the ceremony nearly doubled, rising from 9.6 to 17.8 per cent.[82] The delay is greater in rural than in urban areas.

On the basis of the few data available, some of which have been cited earlier, it must be concluded that the husband-wife relationship in Japan has become more clearly the center of family relations, and the two spouses are expected to be emotionally closer to one another in their interaction.

7. Women and Occupations

In the first stages of Japan's industrialization, women were recruited into factory work. By 1900, about 342 thousand laborers were working in factories, about 60 per cent of them in textile mills. Sixty-five per cent of the workers were women. In cotton spinning factories in 1901, 73 per cent were women, about half of them under 20 years of age.[83] Most of these were young farm girls, who were not permitted to have control over their wages. When heavy industry began to develop, the percentage of male factory workers increased, but by World War II, Japanese women held a wide range of jobs and worked in war production factories just as Western women did during that period.

The growing utilization of farm machinery, insecticides, and chemical fertilizers made farm work somewhat easier, and permitted a shift in the pattern of work distribution on the farm. In 1955, about half of the working women in Japan were farm women, but only about a third of the working men were farm men. That is, the women were working primarily as unpaid family workers, while the men were working part time or full time at non-agricultural occupations. Consequently, although 54.5 per cent of all women 14 years of age and over were in the labor force in 1955, about half were in agriculture and thus did not have independent jobs.

A smaller percentage of women are in such unpaid family work now than a decade ago.[84] Most of the females who work outside the home are young and unmarried. The percentage of women who continued to work after marriage rose from 9.0 per cent in 1948 to 17.4 per cent in 1957.[85]

This pattern expresses the strong Japanese opposition to the married woman continuing at her job. (We have already noted how important this factor is in both the age at marriage within a country, and the relations between husband and wife.) In one small student sample taken about a decade ago, and thus representing rather liberal opinions, 54 per cent of the men and 19 per cent of the women stated that they disapproved of "any career or occupation outside the home."[86] Tokyo female workers in 1952, interviewed by the Women's and Children's Bureau, were asked how long they wished to work. Only 21 per cent said that they wished to continue working as long as possible. Thirty-six per cent wanted to work until marriage. The remainder (33 per cent) wanted either to quit as soon as possible or under certain circumstances.[87] In Stoetzel's Kyoto sample, also an extremely liberal group, 22 per cent of the men and 25 per cent of the women were opposed to employing married women.[88]

A different form of this question was asked of a small sample of middle-class mothers having at least one child in school. Seventy-eight per cent of the urban women and 84 per cent of the rural women said that it was not a good thing for a mother to hold a job outside her home.[89] In the Tokyo survey noted above, only 12 per cent of the working women and 21 per cent of the housewives unequivocally asserted that it was all right for both husband and wife to be working.[90]

It seems to be assumed that when a Japanese working woman is married, she will quit her job, with little likelihood that she will be rehired. The Japanese woman who works is likely to be either at the bottom of the heap economically speaking and forced to work at minimum wages, or else is exceptionally skilled. Even in teaching, traditionally an occupation for Japanese women, there are pressures to resign if the woman marries.[91]

In Japan, women's wages are less than men's for a similar task. They are the last to be hired and the first to be let go. Since they do not remain long on the job, they rarely rise to higher positions. Their commitment to the job is low, and they do not have the moral support of the men. In 1952, there were over 1,300,000 women in labor unions[92]—but almost no women were in important positions within the unions themselves.[93] In 82 per cent of a sample of unions studied in 1957, there was a special section for women, and this alone indicates the relatively low position of women in the working force. That is to say, they were not accepted as fellow workers, but treated as a separate group. In a study done in 1948, it was ascertained that over 40 per cent of the women who had taken jobs did not know the content or salary of the job when they took it. That is to say, the women did not feel they had a right to inquire into such matters. Professional women, by contrast, knew these data about their jobs.[94]

Perhaps a striking index of the failure of Japanese society to utilize its well-trained women may be seen in the activities of college and university graduates in 1957. Fifty-five per cent of the women graduates were working or studying in 1957, as against 83 per cent of the male graduates. Thirty-five per cent of the women graduates were neither working nor studying after graduation as against 5 per cent of the men.[95] As Fujita comments, "The male graduates of newly established universities of the post-war era are so numerous that it is rather natural for the employer to hesitate to employ women graduates who are a completely new labor force for them."[96]

Thus, the evident move toward a more egalitarian relation between men and women is slowed perceptibly by the unwillingness of men to concede higher positions to Japanese women, and especially to married women. At the present time, women have obtained the vote. They hold a percentage of legislative seats characteristic of most legislatures of the world, about 3 per cent. They have been given positions as principals in many public elementary and junior high schools. In 1952, about 6 per cent of college teachers were women. They even have some judgeships, especially in the field of law involving women and children. At least by law, they have a right to equal inheritance as children, and as widows they have a right to part of their husband's property. Nevertheless, their entrance into any but the most menial jobs has been slow and accompanied by considerable resistance.

8. Parents and Children

The relations between Japanese parents and their older children have been changing since the Restoration, possibly at a more rapid pace since World War II. The change is evident when one looks at such indices as freedom of mate choice, and the balance of power relations of the elder mother or father when contrasted with those of the young spouse. Moreover, almost every Japanese child of primary school age attends school (99 per cent). And over half attend middle school, whereas only a tiny minority did so at the time of the Restoration. Thus, a child is removed from parental influences for a large segment of his time. About four fifths of the public high schools are coeducational. The child learns to respect new information and ideas that may not conform with his parents' attitudes. He may now even fail to learn the traditional Japanese mythology in the school.[97]

If the relations of parents and adult children are different, presumably those in the earlier stages of childhood are too. As in the West, however, systematic observations of this interaction were not collected half a century ago which would serve as a basis for comparison with the modern period. It is possible that these patterns of interaction have not changed much and that the alterations to be observed in the relations of parents and adult children arise not so much from differences in early childhood experiences as from influences of adolescence and later.

A hint of this may be found by comparing comments and reports made over the past fifty years. After giving his report on "The Bringing Up of Japanese Girls" to the Japan Society of London in 1904, Chokuro Kadono was asked, "We read that children never cry in Japan. Is there any reason for that?"[98] It is equally interesting that in Kadono's Japanese view the answer was that he saw *no difference* in this respect between Japanese and English children. A generation later, the American, Embree, observed that a child is "the favored one in the family" during the first year and, "in general, children are very much spoiled. They can and do strike their parents in a rage and call them the favorite Japanese epithet of *baka!* (fool)."[99] Embree asserted that a child will get almost anything he wants if he cries for it long enough, and is shaped to Japanese standards by patience and endless repetition. Of course, both standards and correction become stricter with each passing year.

Several studies from the 1950s report similar behavior. One observer comments with respect to a mountain village, "I never saw an adult strike a child during my stay in Kurusu." The child was not severely scolded for mistakes or lapses in the control of elimination, and the women did not remember any instances of punishment. "Ceaseless patient demonstration was used as a method of instruction in adult techniques, and permissiveness extended even to the area of sexual activity: Infant sexuality was accepted unless it occurs in what is regarded as inappropriate surroundings."[100] Another team reported a rice village in western Honshu where the child "receives attention when he cries," and "someone picks the baby up, and soon the breast is offered."[101] The village point of view approved of a minimum of "early punishment or negative discipline. Before his mother gets around to conscious discipline," the child may be several years of age. "The principle of violence and severe scolding seems to be absent."[102] Nor was this only a rural pattern. Dore makes a similar judgment about his urban families.[103]

This combination of great initial affection and indulgence with a subsequent unremitting insistence on treating the group as dominant conforms with a common result of socialization, perhaps more extreme in Japan than in other major civilizations: one's security and satisfaction depend primarily on *groups* rather than individuals, and especially on *superiors* in age and position. Moreover, these basic relations begin within the family. The result may be seen in several areas of action. For example, in writing of Meiji times, when various travel barriers had been removed, Yanagida writes that the Japanese tended to travel in groups, and when they returned they were welcomed by the villagers at the outskirts of the community. Westerners are sometimes struck when a Japanese speaker says he agrees with a previous speaker but the content of his statement is in fact a violent contradiction. Before World War II, Japanese school classes were promoted as a group, with none left behind—and this was *not* an importation of Western "progressive school ideas."[104] In their postwar survey of Takashima, a fishing village, Norbeck and Norbeck also comment that in competitive games everyone receives some kind of present.[105] The simple pleasures of the *donen* or age-group relations formed in the earliest years remain important throughout the Japanese man's life.

Thus, many elements in the early parent-child relationship and in its extensions to other social interaction may, as suggested above, have changed only little over the past half-century.

The great emotional dependence of the Japanese child on his parents is not very surprising, whatever new ideas he learn at school. As Vogel comments, they "are very close to their parents, spend little time away from home even in their late teens, participate in very few extra-curricular activities in high school, spend relatively little time at friends' houses during the high school age, and make most major decisions only on very close consultation with their parents."[106]

From such a relationship, little rebellion of children against parents or of wives against husbands could be expected. Family members are likely to sleep in the same room, even when there are unused bedrooms. The Japanese child learns to believe that he cannot solve his problems himself, but needs his mother, and is not likely to want to leave his home.[107] In going to a new situation, the Japanese prefers to have things already arranged for him. Even on the job, the Japanese employee receives a low wage (so that he cannot become independent) but often receives the equivalent of, or even more than, his wage in special bonuses, social security, and other services.[108]

Consequently, even in adult years, the married couple may be emotionally dependent upon their parents, as the parents are upon them. The dominance by parents is not, then, mere authoritarianism, but is rather a reluctance or a lack of satisfaction in making independent decisions. The elderly parent "feels isolated and rejected unless he is living with one of his children."[109] If one parent is dead the surviving parent, in four fifths of the cases, will live with one of the children.

It is within this social context that the contemporary data on parent-child relations must be understood. Several reports indicate a lesser dependence of children on their parents. In a sample of one hundred young Tokyo people, Stoetzel reports that fifty thought there was a gulf between themselves and the preceding generation, and an additional fourteen thought that a break existed but it was not wide.[110] Sixty-six per cent of a national sample in the 1950s felt that "the number of children who pay no attention to their parents has increased of late." Perhaps more striking is the answer of one of Stoetzel's samples to the question as to whether children should obey their parents. About one third of both the urban and rural samples said that they should obey their parents, "but not when they are independent." What is more striking, however, is the fact that about half the sample gave no reply to the question. This is, then, an area of conflict where a clear response is difficult to make.[111]

A 1953 national sample asked whether, given the alternative, the respondents would prefer to live in a household in which the parents and the children got along well, or one in which the husband and wife were happy together. Fifty-four per cent laid greatest emphasis on the husband-wife relationship, while 21 per cent favored the parent-child relationship.[112] Perhaps of greater importance, however, is the question asked of the Kyoto and Sapporo student sample in Stoetzel's study: 25 per cent of the Kyoto males felt that help from their family and future in-laws would be "regular and indispensable" in their lives, while 45 per cent stated that they expected these elders to be of assistance "whenever necessary." Twenty-two per cent gave the answer, "in the event of money difficulties only." Only 7 per cent of the Kyoto males, 2 per cent of the Kyoto females, and 23 per cent of the Sapporo sample said that they expected no assistance from the parental generation.[113] That is, the emotional dependence is supported by expected economic dependence or help.

A national sample of married persons was asked in 1950 whether they planned to be dependent on their children when they grew old. Only 11 per cent stated that they would not be dependent at all, and another 10 per cent said that they would live with the children but be financially independent.[114] A 1952 sample was asked about their personal preferences, and 82 per cent said that they would prefer to live with their children or grandchildren when they grew old; 90 per cent of a 1950 rural sample gave the same preference.[115] Thus, we see that the parents reciprocate the feeling of dependence expressed by the children.

A somewhat different wording was used in a series of surveys from 1950 to 1959, as to the *wish* to depend upon the children. Fifty-five per cent expressed that wish in 1950, but this steadily dropped to 39 per cent in 1959. The old are more likely to give this answer than the young, men are more likely to express this wish than women, and rural people more than urban people. In addition, lower-strata persons are more likely to give this answer than upper-strata persons.[116]

Filial piety is expressed by caring for the parents, but it is also a source of satisfaction to both the old and the young. As a result, Japan has relatively little development of old-age pensions and social security systems. Moreover, there is some sentiment that to accept such help is not quite proper.[117] Ideally, the oldest son will assume this responsibility, although Baber found that 60 per cent of his male students and 85 per cent of his female students thought that the care of the old parents ought to be the *equal* responsibility of the children.

On the other hand, urban housing conditions make joint living somewhat more difficult, and the help of the old in housekeeping matters is likely to be viewed—by both generations—as irrelevant. The new norms of independent decision as to mate, place of residence, and the relative importance of the husband-wife relationship all mean that some conflict is inevitable; some voices have even been raised in *defense* of the mother-in-law, asserting that the modern daughter-in-law ought to be more tolerant and understanding.

This assumption of control by the young has deep roots and is not new. It should be remembered that in rural Japan during Meiji times when the wife finally took over the authority of the household from her mother-in-law, she had full authority to make all household decisions, and the mother-in-law had to ask permission about a wide range of matters, even minor ones such as ladling out the rice.

The position of the eldest son in the family has also changed in several ways. First, the eldest son may have been the most usual heir to the family land even in Tokugawa times, but many other patterns of inheritance were also found. Elder and younger sisters, as well as younger brothers, could inherit. The1898 Code imposed the *samurai* pattern of primogeniture, under which the eldest son inherited and was responsible for the household. Younger sons could make their way in the cities, learn a trade, find a bride who was the sole heiress of the family land, or perhaps receive some help from the elder brother in starting an independent farm. Parents gave the eldest son considerable authority over his siblings at an early age, so that he became accustomed to ruling them. Traditionally, younger sons were treated with more indulgence, and were given more freedom in choice of occupation. In Japanese folk wisdom, it is the younger sons who are the innovators. Usually, the eldest son continued the management of the family property, often after the formal or semiformal retirement of his father.

This pattern had become standard in rural Japan by World War II. The Family and Inheritance Law in 1948 required equality of inheritance, but rural Japanese rejected it. In one postwar survey, four out of five families said that the eldest son was the sole heir.[118] Two thirds of the villagers thought that equality of division would jeopardize the family's livelihood. Indeed, most of the cases coming before the family court during the 1949–1953 period were petitions to yield up the rights of succession; two thirds of these were filed by women.[119]

Since about two thirds of the Japanese population now lives in cities, for an increasing part of the population there is no family landed property to inherit. A majority of Baber's student sample believed in equal inheritance, but of course these were urban educated people for whom, perhaps, a plot of rural land had little meaning.

Japanese youth who return to the village are likely to be elder sons (i.e., they return to take over the land), but some elder sons remain in the city. Dore has offered an interesting interpretation of the flow. Some younger sons migrate to the cities because there is no opportunity for them on the land, and some Japanese analysts comment that the younger son is likely to get more education because he has to make his own way. On the other hand, the eldest son is the favorite in many respects.[120] Dore suggests, then, that if the eldest son does well in school, almost certainly his family (if it can afford the cost) will allow him to go as far as he can so that he may have a career in an urban occupation. Thus he will be reluctant to return to the village.[121]

In the city itself the eldest son is not groomed for family leadership. To the extent that he makes his own way, however, he has less reason to feel that he alone should take care of his parents, and is more likely to prefer sharing that burden with the other children. Finally, because he is not now so clearly the only responsible person, the shared interests of the daughter and her mother come to increase the weight of that tie and thereby the importance of relations with *her* side of the family. Thus the pattern of flow ultimately affects the internal relations of the kin group.

9. Extended Kin: The Dozoku

The revised Civil Code of 1947 did not, strictly speaking, abolish the *ie*, but it did *ignore* it; the Japanese apparently felt that the Code abolished the household system. In a 1947 national sample, 58 per cent said that they favored this "abolition." As might be expected, students were more frequently in favor (almost four fifths) and farmers and fishermen least in favor (43 per cent).[122] Most of the answers reflect the belief at that time that abolition of the household system would give greater freedom to individuals.

The household system, however, was only part of an extended family system. Strictly speaking, the Japanese family was a "stem" family, that is, one person inherited the headship along with some responsibility for other members of the immediate family. It was not expected that all the males of one generation should stay in the home, but if conditions were ideal younger sons might found a "branch family," or *bunke*. In rural areas especially, and in upper-stratum urban families, the *honke* (main family) and *bunke* families linked together to form the *dozoku*. But these varied from one region to another. In all, only one *honke* was to be found. Where land was available, there might be one or more *bunke* of varying historical depth. These kin, together with the wives of the men, formed the true blood kin within the *dozoku*. In some areas, the *dozoku* was formed entirely of such people. However, in forest and fishing villages especially, the *dozoku* also included some "ritual kin."

These ritual kin did not inherit membership in the *dozoku* by birth, but had to validate their status by working for the true blood kin. They did not inherit land or authority, and were linked with the true kin members of the *dozoku* by exchanges of labor, by landlord-tenant relationships, and other ritual ties. The relationship was not one of contract, but largely of ascription. And on certain ritual occasions such as the Buddhist All Souls' Day (*bon*), all the members of the *dozoku* would reaffirm their bonds and solidarity.[123]

Once more the intrusion of the feudal superordinate-subordinate relationship into Japanese family patterns is evident. The "ritual kin" in the *dozoku* obtained security and protection; in return, they gave loyalty and service. Consequently, the system was useful to the national authorities in holding rural unrest to a minimum and keeping individuals in their respective statuses. The *honke* kept its privileges, and each generation permitted the subordinate members of the *dozoku* to receive some benefits in exchange for the labor they gave.

The structural parallel between this and the *oyabun-kobun* system mentioned earlier is obvious. The latter type of system, somewhat more individualized in form, has been more common in urban areas, where the *dozoku* began to decline even in Meiji times. In the cities the "clan" could not be land-based. The extended family could not control a sufficiently wide number of *occupations* to be able to hold intact both its members and its subordinates. On the other hand, *oyabun-kobun* ties may still be found in the traditional arts, where the master-apprentice relationship is so important. In addition, one may appropriately refer to one of the great families of Japan, such as the Mitsui, as a *dozoku*.

Most families could not obtain sufficient advantage from maintaining the *dozoku* in the city, so that even in the Meiji period the city (as contrasted with villages) was marked by a lack of cooperation in vital matters between *honke* and *bunke*.[124]

The *oyabun-kobun* relationship substitutes in part for the *dozoku* relationship, but it is created by the individuals concerned during their *own* lifetimes; it may not be an inheritance from kinship relations of the past. Even in rural areas, the *dozoku* lost much of its foundation at the end of World War II. In 1892, 40 per cent of Japanese farmers were tenants. When the Allied Occupation began in 1945, 60 per cent were tenants and thus dependent on others. By the completion of the land reform, between 80 and 90 per cent were either owners, or owners *and* tenants.[125]

Consequently under the new land system neither the individual nor his family depended primarily upon the *dozoku* for his land. New and independent power bases for social control as well as for obtaining justice also developed. Nevertheless, as already noted, the patron-protegé relationship remains an important part of Japanese social structure. Interestingly, although almost every observer describes this relationship, an urban survey of 1947 disclosed that 58 per cent of the sample thought that the *"oyabun-kobun* society" was bad.[126]

But if the *dozoku* as a working organization has declined in importance, this does not mean that the sentimental and expressive ties among extended kin have declined. Even forty years ago, three fifth of the Japanese lived in "nuclear families," but their extended kin ties were important to them.[127] Moreover, even in late Tokugawa times, about half of the households were actually nuclear. The hierarchical links between the head of the main household and the branch household have of course declined, but personal and affectional links remain. Dore asserts that after three generations in the city, the ritual links between branch and main family "have almost completely disappeared."[128] The number of *new* branch houses had begun to decline even before World War II. The extended kin relations are not important enough to make the establishment of *honke-bunke* worthwhile to either family. Dore concludes that "the range of kin recognized by urban Japanese today is now little, if at all, wider than in England."[129] We saw earlier that this extension in England is of considerable size but, of course, much smaller than under the former Japanese system. On the other hand, when Japanese do refer to their extended kin relations, they are likely to use the traditional *vocabulary* and, at least in ritual activities within the household, they pay some deference to ancestors. In rural areas, the kinship links are between houses, not persons.[130] In daily relationships, however, villagers will deal with relatives as they deal with neighbors, and distant relatives may be considered less important than closer neighbors.[131] All descriptions of family patterns, whether urban or rural, do show that members keep up the ancestral tablets of the immediate ascendants.

The extended family certainly functioned, as it did in China, to enable young people to establish themselves in the city or in new occupations, to make certain that if matters should go badly they could return to the main household for help. Whether the *dozoku* was made up of only blood relatives or included ritual kin as well, it formed an effective cooperative work group. The group maintained order and dispensed justice according to its norms, without calling on governmental help. To this degree, the *dozoku* offered one kind of solution for certain of the problems in traditional Japan.

10. Divorce

The Japanese conception of divorce is different from that of the West or even of China. Even before marriage became a sacrament in the West, divorce was disapproved both theologically and socially. The Church, and later the state, permitted divorce only under rare circumstances. Japan followed the traditional Chinese grounds for divorce and, as noted earlier, also accepted the three possible female barriers to divorce (having mourned for the husband's parents, having no home to return to, and having shared early poverty with the husband). In Japan and China, marriage and divorce were neither sacramental affairs nor a concern of the state. The relation between generations was more significant than that between husband and wife, and the young bride had to satisfy her elder in-laws, not primarily her husband. To be sent home as an unsatisfactory bride was presumably a disgrace in both cultures. Nevertheless, divorce rates were high in Japan during the early Meiji period and perhaps for generations prior to that, while divorce was apparently uncommon in China. The difference remains puzzling, although we shall explore its meaning here.

The time trend of divorce rates in Japan conforms to our general thesis, that in the process of industrialization the breakdown of a family system that creates high divorce rates may lower divorce rates. Even though the Japanese system is moving toward some form of the conjugal family, a system of relatively high fragility, it begins with so high a rate of marital dissolution that the long-time trend is *downward* during industrialization, not upward. We saw this same phenomenon in Arabic Islam. Table VII-4 shows the trend of divorce rate from 1887.

Table VII-4
Number of Divorces per Thousand Marriages, 1887–1950*

Year	Divorces	Year	Divorces
1887	320	1910	131
1890	335	1920	100
1897	340	1930	98
1898	210	1940	76
1900	184	1950	100
1905	173		

* *Marriage and Divorce,* 1867–1906, Part 1, U.S. Bureau of the Census, Washington, 1909, p. 386. I have not been able to obtain official Japanese figures for the years through 1905, but every figure from this publication which I have been able to check against official sources for the period did tally exactly. The figures for 1910 onward were calculated from Taeuber, *The Population of Japan,* op. cit., p. 223.

Table VII-4, however, contains many complexities. First, it presents the ratio of divorces to marriages in the same year, but not the number of divorces to existing marriages. No such data for married couples existed in the earlier generations of the new regime, and no modern population census was taken until 1920. The number of divorces per thousand *population* shows the same trend, however.[132]

Second, the rate begins to drop before any likely impact on the Japanese family system from industrialization. A hint of the real reason for the early decrease, and for part of the decrease in the early twentieth century, may be found in the very sharp drop in 1898 when the new Civil Code was put into effect. As early as 1871, in an Imperial notification that freed all classes from petitioning for permission to marry, it was required that a marriage had to be reported to the *kocho* or headman if it was to be valid.[133] Since that rule was apparently not enforced until 1898, when the Code began to lay far greater stress on the *ie* or household and thus upon the *koseki* or household records from which all vital statistics data were summarized, its enforcement meant that there was a failure to register divorces when the marriage had not been registered. This would account for the sharp drop in divorce rate in 1898–1899.

This did not mean, however, that a significant change had taken place in divorce behavior by 1900. The change reflected no more than a shift in recording procedures. This means that we must be extremely cautious in interpreting the various trends in divorce patterns over the past half-century. The changes may be only statistical. Moreover, it is even possible that some of the *regional* differences which have been reported reflect differences in recording procedure rather than differences in actual divorce behavior.

A further puzzle must be considered. The official divorce rate was higher in Japan during the 1880s than it has been in the United States during most of its history, and very likely the real rate was still higher. But divorce was a disgrace, and in the early Meiji period most rural marriages were made within the community. Over time, of course, the geographic range of mate choice was widened somewhat. This should have meant, however, that much ill feeling was once engendered between families who would be part of the same social network in the same small village. What mechanism existed to decrease this tension, or to make the return of the girl less annoying? Moreover, wherever there is a high rate of divorce, there is a high rate of remarriage. It follows that a very high percentage of settled married spouses must have been married at least once before their final choice. This means, then, that contrary to common belief, the second marriage of the girl could not have *usually* been with a "less desirable" young man: There would not have been enough available in any community.

Moreover, the pattern cannot have been, as commonly supposed, based in any substantial way on the wife's "failure to bear progeny."[134] In fact, repudiation of the young bride occurred far too early in the marriage for this issue to have been seriously raised. We must now consider, without being able finally to choose among them, three alternative hypotheses: (1) The decline in the divorce rate was a result of the trend toward industrialized patterns (individualism, emphasis on the husband-wife relationship, love marriages, etc.). (2) Among rural Japanese, the majority of the population, the decline of the divorce rate was essentially a spread of *samurai* ideals and behavior, unfavorable to divorce. (3) Rural-urban differences over time are primarily a function of registration behavior. Unfortunately, if the last of these is correct, neither it nor the other two can properly be tested—after all, these are the only data obtainable. Nevertheless, let us consider these possibilities.

The first hypothesis has some plausibility since the drop in the divorce rate is fairly substantial even at the turn of the century and continues steadily downward until the postwar period. In the earlier years of this period, industrialization had made relatively few changes in the family system as a whole, and the changes that were observable were primarily in the direction of a tightening of control by elders, following upper-class patterns. The influence of the 1898 Civil Code was in that direction also. We have found no quantitative data for that period (although very likely they could be obtained), but all accounts seem to agree that the *upper strata* rarely divorced. Most lower-strata people were rural, and followed the rural patterns of marriage and easy divorce we have already noted.

In a system which permits rather free divorce, the lower strata will have a higher divorce rate than the upper strata.[135] Kawashima and Steiner located some data on divorce rates in different Tokyo wards for 1930, and found that the divorce rates in two white-collar districts were about half as high as those in two lower-income wards. A similar relationship appeared in 1951, although the difference had narrowed somewhat.[136] When the divorce rates by occupation are calculated for 1957, a similar result appears, as Table VII-5 shows.

Table VII-5
Number of Divorces per Thousand Married Male Workers
15 Years and Over, Japan, July, 1957*

Occupation	Number of Divorces
Technicians and engineers	7
Professors and teachers	3
Medical and public health technicians	15
Managers and officials	4
Clerical and related workers	8
Farmers, lumbermen, fishermen, and related workers	10
Workers in mining and quarrying	18
Craftsmen, production process workers, and laborers not elsewhere included	18
Domestic workers	238

* Calculated from: *1955 Population Census of Japan*, Vol. II (Japan: Bureau of Statistics, Office of the Prime Minister), One Per Cent Sample Tabulation, Part III, Occupation, July, 1957; Table 3, "Occupation (Intermediate Group) of Employed Persons 15 Years Old and Over by Marital Status and Sex, for All Japan, All *Shi* and All *Gun*," pp. 136–137 (males only).

We would suppose that as the middle and upper strata in modern times have become affected by nontraditional values, the difference between lower- and upper-stratum divorce rates has diminished, and will certainly diminish more in the future. In any event, the hypothesis that the early drop in the the divorce rates was due primarily to the spread of *samurai* family ideals and behavior is a likely one.

It seems equally likely, however, that the rural divorce rate was higher than the urban one during the Meiji period, and the data calculated by Kawashima and Steiner show that it is only since the 1950s that urban rates appear to have risen above the rural. This is not entirely clear because of the problems in the data themselves and because the 1917 data they present suggest that the twenty-six *capital* cities had higher rates than the surrounding countryside.[137] On the other hand, it is possible that in the urban areas, families did not follow the custom of relatively free choice and easy divorce by the in-laws, in part because the elders could not count on the support of a surrounding community that would accept these values and have new mates available. Very likely, urban elders insisted on registration of the marriage and thus of the divorce as well, so that the official divorce rate was closer to the *real* rate than in rural areas. In rural areas, by contrast, the girl's reputation would not be harmed, and she would simply be placed back in a pool of marriage eligibles of the same class position. Thus, neither marriage nor divorce would be recorded, and the official rate of divorce might be lower than the real one.

I have not been able to find quantitative data bearing on this interpretation, but nonquantitative comments do suggest that in Japanese rural areas the actual rate of divorce continued at an extremely high rate well into the period in which Kawashima and Steiner believe they see evidences of industrialization. Thus, for example, Embree comments that "the marriage itself is as likely as not to break up before a child is born." If Embree means what he says, this means roughly half the marriages entered into ended in divorce.[138] This observation was made a generation ago. In the 1950s, Norbeck comments that in his fishing village divorce is "uncommon"—but he goes on to say that "unions which are dissolved before official entry is made in city records are not ordinarily considered as divorces."[139] Norbeck's observations may be thought of as negative evidence, since apparently such divorces are rare, and the additional historical comments that he makes (chap. 6) show how fully the *samurai* ideals of chastity, surveillance, and marital stability had been accepted in this village. In a rice village reported on in the 1950s, the authors comment that "nearly half of the first attempts at marriage fail. Figures are uncertain, for men tend to gloss over or forget their early failure, but even though the marriage is not officially recorded until clear sailing is in prospect, the village records . . . show that six of the present 24 households have divorce-ending marriages. In four other houses at least the bride whose name finally was registered was the second or third girl taken into the house."[140]

In another postwar study of a mountain community, the author states: "That the above is a somewhat over-idealized picture in Yasuhara is indicated by the number of unsuccessful adoptions and arranged marriages. Unfortunately the family register does not record the majority of these broken contracts, because a period of waiting during which time the arrangement is tested, has become the rule. Should the union prove unsuitable, it can then be dissolved without taking legal steps."[141]

Undoubtedly, the real rate of divorce in rural Japan has fallen. The discrepancy between the *real* rate and the *official* rate, however, is much greater than in urban areas, so that comparison of time trends may not be possible.

Even the complex data now available do show clearly that contradictory trends were going on over the past half-century or more in Japan: the spread of the *samurai* low divorce patterns to lower-strata and rural people; the continuation, but perhaps with a slow diminution, of failure to register potentially fragile marriages in rural regions; the increased registration of marriages in urban regions; and the gradual spread from industrial and urban regions outward, since the 1920s, of more modern attitudes of individualized marriage, intensified after World War II. This last element, of course, reduces the divorce rate from *traditional* causes (elder in-laws sending the bride back), but may *increase* the number of divorces due to individual incompatibility between husband and wife.

In addition, doubtless there were important *regional* trends. In an ingenious and elaborate attempt to locate these differences, Kawashima and Steiner attempt to classify the Japanese prefectures as having high or low divorce rates at different time periods since the 1880s. The data are not entirely consistent, perhaps because of the complexities of recording already noted, but the authors conclude that the northern Japanese region (Hokuriku) excluding Niigata, central Honshu (Kinki), and the southern areas of Shikoku and Kyushu, which were *once* low divorce rate areas, have now become *high* divorce rate areas. By contrast, the area around Tokyo (Kanto), northeastern Honshu (Tohoku), and the mountainous areas of central Japan, together with the prefectures of Niigata and Shimane started out with a high divorce rate and now have a relatively low one.[142]

Earlier, we cited data to show that there has been a trend toward the earlier registration of marriages. The unregistered marriages continue to be more fragile and concentrated toward the lower strata.

Of course, if the divorce rate drops steadily and there is no change in the basic statistical distribution of marriage duration, the average duration of marriage will continue to increase. Naturally, this means only the recorded marriages. This increase was observable during the 1920s and 1930s, when the hazards of divorce were greatest in the *second* year of marriage.[143] The percentage of marriages ending during the sixth to twelfth month of marriage decreased from 9.4 per cent to 7.6 per cent; the percentage of divorces ending within the first five years of marriage decreased from 61 per cent to 53 per cent. On the other hand, during the same period, divorces of marriages lasting five to ten years increased slightly from 23 per cent to 26 per cent; and for longer durations of marriage there were increases during this decade as well.[144]

Another change over time should be the *increasing* proportion of divorces involving children. When divorce takes place in the earlier years, and primarily upon the initiation of the elder in-laws, it is much less likely that any children have been born to the marriage. Indeed, as in China, bearing a child early in the marriage, especially a son, was often a way by which the young wife established the security of her marriage. When marriage begins with a love relationship, and becomes a matter of individual incompatibility, there will be a longer period of time, *during which a conception can take place,* before divorce is desired. Of course, as in the West, childlessness will be much more common among marriages ending in divorce, especially now that contraceptives have become common. Western sociologists generally interpret this relationship to mean that the conflicts or doubts in both spouses early in the marriage lead them to put off having children until their adjustment is more complete. Consequently, most divorces occur to couples without children. However, in Japan, the percentage of divorced marriages with children should have increased somewhat over the past generation.

Another recent change that may be seen as an index of new attitudes is the growing percentage of divorces that come to the divorce courts. Under both the old and new systems, divorce by mutual agreement was the pattern, which essentially meant that the husband or his elders decided on the divorce, and the decision was entered in the family record. As early as 1873, a woman could sue for divorce under certain conditions, but few divorces came to the divorce court. Prior to World War II, only about 400 divorce actions took place each year out of the approximately 50 thousand divorces in Japan.[145] For the most part, these court actions were begun by women. In nearly 80 per cent of the divorce applications, the court action was initiated by the wife in 1950. Although this dropped to 73 per cent in 1957, it is likely that the percentage of *women* filing such actions will always be a majority. The action itself is nontraditional and individualistic, since it represents either the woman's desire to obtain a divorce when her husband does not want it, or an opposition to her husband's wish for a divorce. Alternatively, it may mean that the wife simply wants the protection of the court, rather than being left without any aid from her husband and his family.

We believe that legal actions initiated by wives will remain a majority. Although, in an industrial society, we think it is the husband who more often first *wants* the divorce, he is undoubtedly prevented by institutional pressures from initiating it himself. Therefore, we believe the process emerging in Japan to be similar to the one found in the West—i.e., the husband makes himself obnoxious enough to compel the wife to initiate the divorce. Nevertheless, to go to the court at all is an individualistic act as defined by the traditional Japanese system.

A final change in divorce patterns should be noted, although once again it must be qualified by reference to class patterns. Under traditional *samurai* norms, a woman did not divorce and a widow did not remarry. Properly, the widow remained part of her husband's household, and continued to carry out her duties after her husband had died. In any event, if she wished to remarry, her own family and her husband's family would not permit it, and she would have no independent resources with which to enter a marriage.

It is evident, however, that in Japan as in China, the divorced and the widowed did remarry, and that remarriage is not a new phenomenon. Obviously, the remarriage rate must have been very high in rural Japan in Meiji times, since a high proportion of all young people married and divorced after a short period. Had they not remarried, the family system would simply not have continued at all. As we approach the more modern period of the 1920s, when more accurate data become available, a calculation of the "demographic disappearance" of the divorce can be carried out; and Taeuber has shown, by following up populations in successive age groups, that the divorced must have remarried even at that time. A similar result appears for data from the 1930s.[146] Similarly for Suye Mura of the 1930s, Embree comments that "a widow usually remarries" (sometimes a younger brother of the husband).[147] Apparently, the upper-class norms in this matter did not spread to the rest of the population. In most of the Japanese population, widows and divorcees did remarry—granting, of course, that their chances of remarriage depended on their relative value in the marriage market (e.g., whether they had individual wealth, were pretty, had good reputations, etc.).

We would expect one trend to appear, at least during the postwar period, although we have found no data as yet to corroborate the hypothesis: With the increasing emphasis on individual choice, and the right of the widow to some part of the family property, we would expect an increase in the rate of remarriage among middle- and upper-strata Japanese. Moreover, the increasing focus on the husband-wife relationship has, as already noted, given a lesser importance to the elder mother and mother-in-law. Without a realm of action of her own, it is likely that remarriage for even somewhat older divorced or widowed Japanese men and women will become more common in the future.

Conclusion

✧✧✧✧✧✧✧✧✧✧✧✧

THE DIFFICULTIES of obtaining adequate data on world changes in family patterns over the past half-century are many and often insurmountable. As is so often true in social research, the time series that we can locate (for example, the number of marriages per thousand population), are of only modest relevance for important social relationships. Most often, precise data on significant relationships are missing and we have to substitute reports of travelers and explorers, foreigners who lived a long time in the country, or educated citizens who are amateurs in sociology.

It might therefore be concluded that the wise course would have been to defer our inquiry for another decade when the volume of expert studies has increased, as it undoubtedly will in the next few years. Precise research information is needed and is being produced, as pressure is being exerted by leaders of newly emerging nations, who are all, perhaps for the first time in history, trying to solve social and economic problems on a large scale.

But although the new data will be of great importance as a mirror of the contemporary period, any researcher would nevertheless have to delve into the past in order to obtain an adequate baseline, a measure of the extent of change that has been going on. It cannot be assumed that merely because people say things are changing greatly that they have indeed changed much from the past. Moreover, it is useful to describe what is going on at the present time so that the changes in the coming decade can be measured too.

This inquiry may also serve another function, the stimulation of historical research in the field of the family. Historians have neglected this area, being far more concerned with larger economic or political processes. Also, the difficulty of obtaining adequate data has undoubtedly made such inquiries less attractive. By historical research we do not mean merely references to historical events or reading history books, but genuinely archival investigation, and specifically the testing of sociological propositions with historical data.

The amount of work that needs to be done is great, and few sociologists in Europe and the United States have been properly trained for historical research. The importance of such research in this field can not be overemphasized, simply because so many "facts" need to be corrected: ideal patterns of family behavior have been thought to be real ones, and a hypothetical harmony in past family relations has been assumed, rather than treated as an hypothesis to be tested. Even for the recent period we have pointed out various illustrations of incorrect assumptions about the past—for example, the supposed pattern of youthful marriage in Western family systems, or the frequency of extremely large families living under one roof in many other cultures. The work of the family sociologist would be enriched greatly if historical research in this area were expanded greatly.

We have also noted that some family behavior thought to be a recent change is, in fact, simply a continuation of older patterns. For example, urban family behavior has always been somewhat different from rural, and the difference is not to be found only in the modern era. In Japan we found that freedom of mate choice, now viewed as a new family pattern, is really a re-emergence of an old one: it was common among most of the population a hundred years ago, and is once more being accepted as the norm.

Another warning grows out of our inquiry. We have concentrated upon change, and thus have necessarily eliminated from consideration the very great *stability* in all family systems. There have been periods of relatively rapid social change within the family patterns of some small groups like the Mormons during the nineteenth century or the Israelis during the twentieth century, but family patterns often resist the pressures of many outside circumstances. Since we do not have adequate *measures* of family change, it is difficult to say whether change in one epoch is much more rapid than in another, or that change in *one* institution in the total social structure is more rapid than in another institution.

Moreover, even when two family systems are changing in the same direction, the *absolute* rates may be very different. For example, all Western family systems seem to be experiencing a substantial growth in the divorce rates. A system that is moving from two to four divorces per thousand marriages is experiencing an increase of 100 per cent, while another may perhaps be increasing its divorce rate from 100 to 102 divorces per thousand marriages. The percentage *increase* is much higher in the first case, but the rate is still relatively low.

For every culture we have been investigating, there are some commentators who claim that a revolution in family behavior is taking place. We believe this is a correct judgment. On the other hand, those who experience the events of any given decade often claim that change is going on at a rapid rate. We suppose that if we could interview the English of seven centuries ago, they would tell us that "things are not the same as in our father's day." At the time of the colonial period in the United States, our Pilgrim Fathers asserted that the family was changing rapidly, that the children insisted upon choosing their own spouses, and that parents were losing control over children.

It is almost certainly incorrect to assume that both society and family were relatively static prior to industrialization and that the recent changes have occurred only because the modern world has begun to share in a new technology. We shall never know the details of earlier social structures, especially family relations in many regions, but whenever we are able to obtain concrete historical reports about adjacent periods of a specific culture, such as the tenth and eleventh centuries in Europe, it is quite clear that substantial changes in social relations have sometimes occurred in the past. An example may be found in Stone's study of the expansion of the marriage market and the changes in dowry relationships among the English nobility during the sixteenth and seventeenth centuries.[1]

In the modern era, many commentators have remarked on the increasing power of the wife in family relationships, but it is at least arguable that from the fourteenth to fifteenth centuries the European wife experienced an equal change in the opposite direction: She *lost* authority. A wife once had the right of assuming her husband's authority when he was absent or insane, but in France, by the sixteenth century, she was legally incapable of an independent act.[2] Although the Consulate and the Empire were short lived in France, important changes in family patterns were at least initiated under the banner of egalitarianism. The major family systems have not remained static for centuries, nor did they begin to change only with industrialization. Neither can we assume that where Western powers have ruled a region, as in the Arab world or India, all the changes came solely from the West. Indigenous changes are also important. We noted earlier, for example, the decline of the traditional marriage system among the Nayar. The English, believing that system to be immoral, did not approve of it, but their disapproval cannot be assumed to be the cause of change; they made no great campaign against it, and other family patterns persisted that they disliked. Changes that occurred under Western powers deserve specific attention, but we cannot assume *a priori* that it was the Western world that created them.

It is clear, however, that at the present time a somewhat similar set of influences is affecting all world cultures. All of them are moving toward industrialization, although at varying speeds and from different points. Their family systems are also approaching some variant of the conjugal system. We have stated as an initial point of view, validated throughout by data, that the *direction of change* for each characteristic of the family might be very different from one culture to another even though the pattern of movement for the system as a whole is toward a variant of the conjugal type. For example, the divorce rate has dropped in Japan during the past half-century, whereas it has risen in the Western world; in both instances the move is toward a conjugal pattern. The illegitimacy rate has increased in urbanizing and industrializing Africa, but it has been dropping in the Western world.

Even though all systems are more or less under the impact of industrializing and urbanizing forces, we have not assumed that the amount of change is a simple function of one or the other, or even of combinations of both. On the contrary, we have asserted that we do not believe that the theoretical relations between a developing industrial system and the conjugal family system are entirely clear. On the empirical side we suggest that the changes that have taken place have been far more rapid than could be supposed or predicted from the degree of industrialization alone. We have insisted, instead, on the independent power of ideological variables. Everywhere the ideology of the conjugal family is spreading, even though a majority does not accept it. It appeals to the disadvantaged, to the young, to women, and to the educated. It promises freedom and new alternatives as against the rigidities and controls of traditional systems. It is as effective as the appeal of freedom or land redistribution or an attack on the existing stratification system. It is radical, and is arousing support in many areas where the rate of industrialization is very slight. Yet, the ideology of the conjugal system would have only a minimal effect if each newly emerging system did not furnish some independent base for implementing the new choices implicit in the ideology. We believe that the crucial points of pressure from industrialization on the traditional family structure are the following:

1. It calls for physical movement from one locality to another, thus decreasing the frequency and intimacy of contact among members of a kin network—although at the stage of full industrialization this is partly counteracted by greater ease of contact at a distance (telephone, letter, etc.).

2. Industrialization creates class-differential mobility. That is, among siblings or kindred, one or more persons may move rapidly upward while the others do not, thus creating discrepancies in styles of life, taste, income. etc., and making contact somewhat less easy and pleasant.

3. Urban and industrial systems of agencies, facilities, procedures, and organizations have undermined large corporate kin groupings since they now handle the problems that were solved within the kin network before industrialization: political protection, pooling funds to educate bright youngsters, defending a locality, lending money, etc.

4. Industrialization creates a value structure that recognizes achievement more than birth; consequently, the kin have less to offer an individual in exchange for his submission. He has to make his *own* way; at best his

kin can give him an opportunity to show his talent. Without rewards, control is not possible. The success of the Japanese family in keeping the kin group intact proves the rule more effectively, since some family control over jobs has been maintained. On the other hand, as industrialization has moved forward, the individual is more likely to be able to make his own way without his kin so that he need not consult them in important decisions. Note too that such a change brings new attitudes as well: Kin are less *willing* to call upon one another for such help because they would be embarrassed; they too accept the values of achievement.

5. Because of specialization, by which thousands of new jobs are created, it is statistically less likely that an individual can obtain a job for his kinsman. He may not be in a suitable sector of the occupational sphere, or at a level where his influence is useful.

We have noted the apparent theoretical harmony between the conjugal family system and the modern world and the modern industrial pattern, but have also pointed out some disharmonies. We stressed that though the conjugal system serves the needs of the industrial system, it is not at all clear that the latter serves the needs of the *family* pattern. The creation of a new family structure in China, which would further reduce the kinship ties that are part of the conjugal system, might well be more effective in industrialization; but it also has its costs.

To point to another theoretical and empirical obscurity—contemporary theory asserts that a society based on achievement is likely to have a conjugal system, but we suggest that various periods of the past—such as the twelfth and thirteenth centuries in Europe, or the beginnings of the four major Chinese dynasties prior to the 1911 Revolution—were to a considerable extent based on achievement, with no measurable trend toward a conjugal system.

Perhaps equally important, we have insisted that although some type of conjugal pattern and the ideology that often precedes it begins to emerge along with industrialization, we cannot suppose that only the industrializing elements are causally important. We must also entertain the hypothesis that the changes in the family itself may facilitate the process of industrialization. We have suggested, for example, that earlier changes in the Western family system, beginning perhaps with the seventeenth century, may have made that transition to industrialization easier than in other cultures. That is, the family variables are themselves independent and have an impact on the total social structure. The mere fact of their resistance suggests some independent power but we believe that in addition they may facilitate or retard the acceptance of industrialization. It is perhaps at this point that the ideology of the family plays an important role by opening the way to the new family behavior as well as to the industrial role pattern.

We have also emphasized that the conjugal family system is not equivalent to a "nuclear family" composed only of parents and children. We have shown on both empirical and theoretical grounds that the conjugal family has far more kinship ties and correlatively is under far more kinship control than is sometimes supposed by Western observers or non-Western analysts. It seems impossible to cut down the size of the effective conjugal family to its nuclear core only, either in the West or in any other society, without some type of political or coercive force. The additional kin who are included are there because of a direct emotional tie with some members of the nuclear core, a tie supported by the institutional structure: Siblings are necessarily involved with their siblings-in-law; husbands and wives are tied to their parents-in-law; grandparents are emotionally attached to their grandchildren and vice versa. The ties among these kin may be traced through some member of the nuclear core and it is impossible to eliminate these additional kin ties without disrupting the nuclear family itself. Thus, the corporate kindred or lineage may lose most of its functions under urbanization and industrialization, but these extensions of kin ties continue to remain alive and important in social control, through reciprocal gifts and exchanges, visits, and continual contacts.

But although we must not commit the error of *minimizing* the extension of kin in a conjugal family system, we must also avoid *exaggerating* the ties of the extended family which preceded the modern conjugal family. It seems empirically clear that prior to the modern era in the Western world, and in all of the cultures we have been examining, several generations of one family did not live under the same roof, and did not carry on all of their productive activities there. If only because of the brute facts of mortality and the necessity of gaining a living on small plots of land, this was true for both urban and rural strata. On the other hand, the extended kin played a substantial role in non-Western cultures even when they did not live together, and the *ideal* remained that of a common household. When an individual attained sufficient wealth and social standing, he succeeded in creating and maintaining a large assemblage of kin under his leadership.

Even when an extended family was created, as we suggested for India and the Arab world, this was often a *phase* in the development of a single family between the initial fission by which a man established a conjugal unit separated from his father's household and the next generation of fission when the man's grown married siblings began to break off from their father, or from the household after their father died. This was undoubtedly a common historical process in the past, and the present merely accentuates and intensifies it, since now there are more and earlier opportunities for the younger generation to break off and set up independent households.

With reference to the question of *how* the impact of industrialization occurs on the family, we have suggested that the primary process hinges on the control by elders of the new opportunities under industrialization. That is, do *they* create the new jobs and can *they* hand them out to the younger generation or to their women? A crucial difference between upper- and lower-class elders lies in the fact that the new opportunities are typically created and developed by upper-class elders, who can thus control their own sons or women and thus maintain their lines of authority long after these have begun to disintegrate among lower-strata families. Elders in lower-strata families cannot generate these opportunities. Consequently, they have little to offer the younger generation to counteract their normal tendency to independence. As a result, even in the modern Western world, upper-strata families maintain a far larger extension of kin and far greater control over their own young than do lower-strata families.

This central variable is qualified somewhat by the factor of ideology. Those who hold power cannot keep it unless they believe in the *rightness* of their authority. It is especially difficult to hold to that belief in the face-to-face relations of the family, because of the inherent love and affectional ties among its members. When that faith weakens under the impact of the new ideology, the normal push of the disadvantaged, the young, and women may become sufficiently strong to change family relations if new opportunities are available through which these younger people can obtain an independent social and economic base.

This same evidence of a role bargaining process may be found in the radically changing position of women in all of the cultures under examination. The fundamental transformation of woman's estate is sometimes overlooked, because in certain past epochs women had a considerable amount of *personal* freedom. The modern industrial world is the first cultural system, however, to permit women to occupy independent jobs. They have become independent of members of their family. They obtain their work by themselves, and also control the money they earn. This has meant an enormous increase in the economic productivity of populations that have made use of their women in this fashion. At the same time, it has changed the bargaining position of women within the family system. Needless to say, this is a reciprocal process. It is by virtue of a change in the general evaluation of women and their position in the large society that the permission is granted to work independently; but once women begin to take these positions in the large society, then they are better able to assert their own rights and wishes within the family. This process need not be, and probably rarely is, rational or even conscious.

Class differences remain, and so do their inherent paradoxes. Toward the lower strata, in all of these cultures, it is evident that the woman actually has had somewhat more authority. The sheer lack of funds and services at these levels has given the woman a key position within the family. This has been especially so in areas and places where she has held independent or semi-independent jobs: Japanese women divers in the coastal or forestry villages are an illustration of this pattern. Toward the upper strata, men have had less need of a particular wife, and could obtain almost any service a wife could perform by using alternative women as concubines, servants, housekeepers, and so on. The funds were available to seclude or protect the wife more, and the discrepancy between the man's economic and social power and her own was much greater.

Ideological *differences* in the modern world run in the opposite direction. Toward the upper strata, men who are better educated and more strongly affected by the new philosophy of the family are somewhat more willing on a philosophical level to concede rights, and women are somewhat more eager to demand them, although their behavior may in fact be less free than toward the lower strata. Men in the lower strata, by contrast, are much more traditional-minded than their counterparts in the upper strata, and are less willing to concede the new rights being demanded; but they have to do so because of the increased bargaining power of their women.

Thus, in the age-old war between the sexes and between generations, the entrance of a new ideology of the family plays a crucial role. It validates and speeds the emergence of some minority patterns into majority patterns; but it slows others down. It strengthens and gives bargaining power to some kinship positions, and weakens still others. It does this not only because of the demands on the part of those who seek new rights, or because of the values of those who resist the concession of the new rights, but also, and perhaps centrally, because the third parties, that is, other people involved in their role network, may support the recalcitrants or weaken the innovators.

However, we do not believe that any family system now in operation, or likely to emerge in the next generation, will grant full equality to women, although throughout the world the general position of women will improve greatly. The revolutionary philosophies which have accompanied the shifts in power in Communist countries or in the Israel *kibbutzim* have asserted equality, and a significant stream of philosophic thought in the West has asserted the right to equality, but no society has yet granted it. Nor does the movement in Western countries, including the Communist countries, suggest that the future will be greatly different. We believe that it is possible to develop a society in which this would happen, but not without a radical reorganization of the social structure. The family base upon which all societies rest at present requires that much of the daily work of the house and children be handed over to women. Doubtless, men can do this nearly as well, but they have shown no eagerness to assume these tasks, and families continue to rear their daughters to take only a modest degree of interest in full-time careers in which they would have equal responsibilities with men.

A subsidiary thesis in our analysis has been that different relations within the family, and between the family and the larger society, are under a differential tension even in the *traditional* system. Some relations are well-buttressed, while others contain great strains which are overborne by the dominant social patterns. When new elements enter, however, such as a new ideology, or differential opportunities, then the relations under greatest strain are likely to give way first. Still, many relations may continue with undiminished vigor. We noted, for example, that in China the mother-in-law's domination over the daughter-in-law was a theme for literary and philosophical comment, and that the pattern continued although people deplored it. The new forces at work in China, from the 1911 Revolution on, had undermined the strength of this traditional relationship, and the Communists merely implemented the change further. In the new social system that has been emerging in China and Japan, the mother-in-law is less useful in the new household. Her husband, the father of her son, no longer has the same power over *his* son, and thus can no longer threaten the daughter-in-law to the same degree. The young man is more likely to have become emotionally attached to his wife even before marriage, so that he is less willing to support his mother in a dispute between the two. The young wife is more likely to be working, and thus making a real contribution to the prosperity of the household. At many points, then, the daughter-in-law can resist the mother-in-law more easily, and has been reared to believe that resistance is proper. The mother-in-law, on the other hand, does not feel the same certainty of success. Consequently, this relationship has changed substantially.

Yet, the intense mother-son relationship in the traditional Indian and Arab family systems was not under great strain, and has not been under any ideological attack. The newly emerging family patterns do not seem, therefore, to weaken it at any important point.

Since the world is becoming industrialized and urbanized simultaneously, it may not be possible to isolate these two processes as separate sets of causal factors. As we emphasized earlier, a common theoretical error is to treat "urbanization" as *a single variable*, but to include in that variable almost all of the social changes that are now going on. Since these are the changes that are taking place, one cannot treat them as causal variables. Indeed, they are the phenomena to be explained. Or, alternatively, by including under this category almost every conceivable social change, one can say that "urbanization causes everything" simply because urbanization is so loosely defined as to include everything.

Similarly, industrialization cannot be defined as the *impact* upon the "social structure" of the factory system, rapid communication and transportation, a high level of scientific training, and so on. These are all part of the same complex. The former set of phenomena cannot come into being unless the social structure is being transformed somewhat. They are not, strictly speaking, to be viewed as a set of *causal* variables working on a static and passive set of social patterns. Rather, they *are* the changes to be explained. We cannot find cases in which suddenly there is a full industrial complex in interaction with a so-far unchanged social structure. Machines do not make social structures; people with specific social patterns make machines. At present, we see no great clarity emerging from these theoretical arguments, although we have tried to suggest various points at which industrialization may have an impact on the family, and have thereby selected from the total phenomena of industrialization a few of the key variables.

From time immemorial philosophers and observers have noted differences in the social relationships in the city as against those in the country.
This observation points to the need to distinguish between two aspects of
urbanization, the urbanization of an *individual* or an individual family, and
the increase in the *percentage* of people in a society who are urbanized or
living in an urban context. The individual family that becomes urbanized
is doubtless more likely to utilize the urban agencies of social control,
finance, transportation, help, and so on, because these are available and because they may be easier to deal with in the long run than the required
reciprocal exchanges with kin. Thus, in the cities the large corporate or kin
groups or lineages are reduced in importance. This merely creates an urban-
rural difference in family patterns, however.

Cities came to be part of man's heritage about 6 thousand years ago,
but urbanized *nations*—nations in which a majority of the population lives
in cities—did not emerge until recently. The urbanizing of a nation leads to
somewhat different consequences than the mere existence of one or more
urban centers in a nation. When a large part of the nation begins to urbanize, there are many new opportunities in the cities for *most* people who
move there. People flock to the cities, and thus undergo individually or as a
family the social processes by which many older, traditional kin ties or
obligations are undermined. The urban patterns begin to be viewed as
dominant and proper, even by rural people. The cities expand economically
and often industrially, so those who move are justified by their success.
The traditional class composition shifts because of this expansion. People are
attracted by the new realms of experience available in the city. The city becomes the carrier of new ideologies, thus giving a moral validation to these
alterations in social patterns. Thus, the urban-rural differences begin to
decline, since the thinking of those who live in rural areas is shaped by the
forces that urbanize the nation.

One aspect of the movement to the city ought to be briefly noted. The
industrial world is not based on family ownership of land; it has become the
first civilization not based upon landholding. Land is no longer the major
source of production, and man's relationship to it is no longer correlated
with his social position.

Thus, a major change has taken place. The transformation in modern
times is that the elders give the young man and woman an education. This
is their inheritance, their dower or dowry. Elders are left with only education, maintenance, and love as levers for controlling their young. Love is
not a sufficient lever, because in the modern world it is a reciprocal relationship, and the young as well as the older generation can wield the threat of
withdrawing love. Education cannot be used so easily, because it is not
exclusive, as land is; it can be given to all the siblings equally. Moreover,
most people feel that even the worthless child should be educated, because
without education he might be still worse. There is no widespread view that
such an educational patrimony can be lost, misspent, or wasted as fully as

can money or land. There is thus no great social support for withholding an education from the young, and almost no one does. Those who do are criticized by their peers. Less able to control their young by withdrawing social or economic benefits from them, the elders lose some of their ability to maintain the family line itself, as well as the family traditions of the society against which the young of each generation always rebel, if only briefly and with little success.

These factors are causally related to the decline in the control over the marriage choice of the young. With reference now primarily to the upper strata, where control still remains firm in most cultures, the advantages of a family alliance have declined with the lessened importance of land and the increased importance of occupation. The family cannot easily guarantee the young man's future through a job, because his ability and work, over which they have little control, count so much. They can give him an opportunity, but he has to make that opportunity good by his own efforts. Neither side of the family can count on the continuance of the alliance, since the decision lies in the couple's hands: the high rate of divorce in a conjugal system may undo the alliance. Neither, then, is willing to invest so much in a union as they once would. Consequently, the elders have less motivation for making an alliance, and leave it increasingly in the youngsters' hands. They are less willing to bend their efforts toward maintaining it for so precarious a gain, while empirically their actual control has weakened.

Another aspect of this greater freedom may be seen in the greater liberty to remarry. In an earlier work, I suggested the general hypothesis that whenever there is a high divorce rate, there is a high remarriage rate.[3] I have found no reason as yet to change this conclusion. Both Japan under the old system and Islam have had very high rates, coupled with a nearly universal "settling down" to a stable marriage. Very few adults continue to live outside the marriage state in spite of a high rate of marital disruption.

A change in the marriage of widows was also noted in India, where it was formerly forbidden, and in China, where it was strongly opposed. Such opposition had many roots, differing of course from culture to culture. Some were economic: A widow, as contrasted with a divorcee, normally has certain property rights—for example, the money which she brought to the marriage and which may remain hers under some legal definition, the inheritance from her husband, or simply a customary right to receive some support from her husband's family. Since she is now a member of her husband's family, her parental family has little right to arrange a new marriage for her; her husband's family may have a strong material interest in opposing a new marriage which might either alienate some property which they enjoy or confuse the matter of inheritance. She may also have to leave her children behind if she remarries. In addition, of course, remarriage suggests disrespect to the memory of the dead.

In the West, widows may remarry, although it seems safe to say that there always was some feeling against remarriage, partly because of the sentiment (backed by the Church) that a woman properly remains forever married to her first husband, and partly based on the notion that older women ought not to respond to the promptings of sexual feeling. Pitt-Rivers, for example, found the custom of the *vito* in Andalusia, an at least half-serious charivari directed against widow remarriage. He suggests that it can be found as a rather widespread custom here and there in rural areas.

However, when the ideology of the conjugal family begins to assert that each individual, even though a female, has a right to her own life choices, and as the prevalence of joint-family property declines, neither sentiment nor economic interest supports the celibacy of widows. Moreover, the husband's family no longer cares to assume the obligations of support for the widow as she is increasingly able to support herself. As the bride price or groom price becomes less important, neither her family nor his has any interest in hindering her free choice. In industrialized nations, she also becomes somewhat more independent through insurance, pensions, and social security provisions.

Thus a general trend, rapid in some areas and slow in others, is toward an increase in the remarriage of both widows and divorcees where there had been some opposition in prior generations. Both may now enter the marriage market independently, free from the social stigma which they once had to suffer.

Both freedom of choice and equalitarianism are of importance in another step toward the conjugal family: a reduction in the proportion of the adult population living under concubinage or some form of polygamy. Several factors are at work in this process. Most important, the emotional demands which each spouse can legitimately make on the other preclude the acceptance of polygamous arrangements. Under this system, wives are less inclined to share the emotional intensity of the family with other women, and husbands do not wish to share a single wife with cohusbands. Polygyny itself was generally confined to those men who had considerable wealth or prestige, and under most systems it was expensive. Africa was an exception to some degree, since an additional wife might add economic wealth and sometimes even represented an investment. Wives were acquired by paying out a bride price, but in turn they engaged in agricultural work which brought additional income. Of course the wives of chiefs were in another category, for they represented an investment in prestige.

The female's bargaining position has also improved, since now she has alternative modes of employment. She does not have to accept the "protection" of a male in order to survive.

Concubinage, the acquisition of additional women without the formality of true marriage, is a somewhat more complex matter, although both arguments also apply to it. Youngsters have more sexual freedom in the conjugal system than in most systems prior to the modern era, although certainly they have less than in most primitive societies. But sexual freedom is not necessarily associated with concubinage. The equalitarian ideology that accompanies this system denies an overwhelming importance to class or caste rules, so that it is much less possible now for the male to suggest a concubinal arrangement with the woman whom he claims to love. He is less able to assert that he would "love to marry" a woman but cannot because of social restrictions. Under present conditions in most Western countries, and increasingly in others, this excuse is an empty one.

Perhaps more important, however, is the fact that the relative advantages—including time, attention, and even money—that the modern male of high standing can give to a concubine are far less than once were possible. His rank does not permit him easily to avoid the scorn and criticisms of her friends or class equals. She *can* earn a living alone. He cannot, in the older phrase, "protect her." In addition, the man's legitimate wife objects to such arrangements.

The equalitarianism of the conjugal system applies to the man as well: for although some men may enjoy a feeling of possession when they pay the expenses of a concubine or mistress, others are much less willing to do so because increasingly they feel that *they* are giving as much of themselves as the woman is, and that it is therefore somewhat demeaning for a man to pay her expenses. In China these aspects of equalitarianism are especially important, since the Communists want to draw *everyone* into the productive system regardless of sex, and the concubine is a symbol of the pampered and loose life of the old regime.

In our analyses, we have attempted to bring together as adequate a body of data as possible to test a considerable number of hypotheses about past or present changes in family patterns in the major cultures of the world. At many points, however, it seems clear that the data miss some of the most significant aspects of family life. Structural changes can often be noted by the passing observer. For example, a tiny shift in Japanese family behavior permits the woman to walk along side her husband in public. What, however, of the tone, the *timbre*, of feelings and emotions that are changing? Most Japanese marriages are still arranged by the parents, but the fact that some are not, and that the new values do not approve of so vigorous a control over mate choices, means that there are more dreams about possible romantic courtships among young adults, which gives a character and a flavor to contemporary Japanese relations between young men and women that is qualitatively different from the recent past. Another example—the elderly Japanese widow is still being taken care of by her sons, but if she was reared in a rural household in which she saw her own mother achieve greater authority with age, ruling as a matriarch behind the public authority of her husband, then the modern widow cannot have that same experience and may experience a lack of fulfillment—but we cannot capture such nuances with the crude measuring instruments at our disposal.

In this investigation, we have, in a very deep sense, pointed to both the present and the future, while attempting to make a sociological analysis of the past half-century: As an illustration, in suggesting that various of these family changes are now taking place in India and the Arab world, we are pointing in effect to data that *will* appear, behavioral patterns that *will* become more pronounced, attitudes that are emerging but *will* become dominant in the future. In a fundamental way, we have offered again and again some hypotheses as to family behavior and values in the next ten or twenty years. We are suggesting that processes are at work which will lead to the changes indicated. We have tried to stay within available descriptions, but we have not hesitated to make predictions about the immediate future on the basis of available materials, and where we have gone beyond our data, we have noted that fact.

We have not evaluated these changes. We have attempted to describe them, to analyze them, to lay bare the sociological processes that are at work in producing them. For the evaluation of such changes the individual reader must rely on his own philosophy. Some will see them as the advent of a new and fruitful era, a period in which men and women will find a richer personal life, in which they will have a greater range of choices in their own emotional fulfillment. They will rejoice to learn that young Chinese brides do not have to bring tea to their mothers-in-law in the morning or wash their feet, that young Chinese grooms and brides may openly express their love for one another. They will be pleased that the Indian husband who has tired of his wife may not take an additional secondary mate into his household, or that the Arab husband finds divorce a much more tedious, awkward, and expensive affair than it once was. They will be glad that it is only the rare young European woman who now has to acquire a dowry in order to make a desirable marriage, and they will be pleased that increasingly in the major family systems, when either a husband or a wife finds no happiness in marriage, either can break it and perhaps find happiness with someone else.

But still others will view all these processes with suspicion, skepticism, or dismay. They may see them as the breakdown of major civilizations. They will see the Western pattern of the conjugal family spreading like a fungus over other societies, leading inevitably to a decline in their quality and the ultimate destruction of the achievements of our time. They will know that although under a system of arranged marriages some people did not find love, but almost everyone had a chance at marriage; and more pain and trauma can come from the disruption and dissolution of love under the conjugal family system. They will insist, moreover, that although the older systems weighed heavily upon the young and upon women, the elders did, in fact, have more wisdom, and the young in time grew older and took their place in the community, while both men and women in their turn, and according to their positions, received the honor, respect, and power to which they once had to submit.

Finally, under the old system everyone at least knew what his obligations were, and learned to carry them out over many years. Now, increasingly, each person must work out an individual system of role relationships—some of them perhaps even more burdensome than the older ones would have been, but in any event somewhat difficult to adjust to, simply because there has been little prior socialization and experience that might fit them to assume those burdens easily and willingly.

For my own part, I side with those who are pleased to see these processes taking place, although I am aware of the pain, bitterness, and frustration which they may engender in the older as well as the younger generation; and I do not believe for a moment that the system now emerging can be shown to yield greater "happiness" or "adjustment."

I am personally in favor of these changes, even though I do not believe we shall ever know how to balance the ecstasy and agony of the family systems now coming into being against that of older systems. Driven to judge, I suspect that on the average, the older family patterns did yield greater contentment to the people who lived out their lives under them, but any careful reading of the folklore and literature of those cultures reveals countless instances of extreme pain and happiness as well. Indeed, pressed by argument, I might concede that perhaps most people under the conjugal family systems in the West also lead lives of grey contentment with no great emotional color. Perhaps, as a still gloomier calculation, one might claim that most people in all cultures achieve at best a life of quiet desperation in their family relations.

Yet I welcome the great changes now taking place, and not because it might be a more efficient instrument of industrialization, for that is irrelevant in my personal scheme. Rather, I see in it and in the industrial system that accompanies it the hope of greater freedom: from the domination of elders, from caste and racial restrictions, from class rigidities. Freedom is *for* something as well: the unleashing of personal potentials, the right to love, to equality within the family, to the establishment of a new marriage when the old has failed. I see the world revolution in family patterns as part of a still more important revolution that is sweeping the world in our time, the aspiration on the part of billions of people to have the right for the first time *to choose* for themselves—an aspiration that has toppled governments both old and new, and created new societies and social movements.

For me, then, the major and sufficing justification for the newly emerging family patterns is that they offer people at least the potentialities of greater fulfilment, even if most do not seek it or achieve it.

Notes

✚✚✚✚✚✚✚✚✚✚✚✚

Preface

1. Opladen Westdeutscher Verlag, 1960; *American Sociological Review*, 25 (August, 1960), 483–496; *American Journal of Sociology*, 66 (November, 1960), 246–258; and Robert K. Merton, Leonard Broom, and Leonard S. Cottrell (eds.), *Sociology Today* (New York: Basic Books, 1959), pp. 178–196.

2. The first three are found in *American Sociological Review*, 24 (February, 1959), 38–47; *loc. cit.*, 25 (February, 1960), 21–30; *loc. cit.*, 26 (December, 1961), 910–925. The last is published in *International Social Science Journal*, 14, No. 3 (1962), 507–526.

Chapter I World Changes in Family Patterns

1. For a concise statement of nineteenth-century family theory, see René König, "Familie und Familiensoziologie," in W. Bernsdorf and Friedrich Bülow (eds.), *Wörterbuch der Soziologie* (Stuttgart: Enke, 1955), pp. 114–126.

2. E. B. Tylor, "On a Method of Investigating the Development of Institutions: Applied to Laws of Marriage and Descent," *Journal of The Royal Anthropological Institute*, 18 (1888), 245–272.

3. See George P. Murdock, *Social Structure* (New York: Macmillan, 1949), pp. 226–227. Not all Eskimo groups fall into the same kinship category: See Charles C. Hughes, "An Eskimo Deviant from the 'Eskimo' Type of Social Organization," *American Anthropologist*, 60 (December, 1959), 1140–1147.

4. Attempting to locate underlying variables by scalogram analysis, Robert F. Winch and Linton C. Freeman found that two variables would not "fit" into a scale of societal complexity: those relating to family and religion; see "Societal Complexity: An Empirical Test of a Typology of Societies," *American Journal of Sociology*, 62 (March, 1957), 461–466. Recently, Meyer F. Nim-

koff has begun a cross-cultural attempt to fit different forms of the family with different economic and technological traits.

5. Marx's analysis of the process may be found in *Capital* (New York: Modern Library, 1936), chap. XV.

6. Neil Smelser, *Social Change in the Industrial Revolution* (Chicago: University of Chicago, 1959).

7. Ogburn's earlier formulation may be found in *Social Change* (New York: Viking, 1922; rev. ed., 1952). See his more mature analysis in *Technology and the Changing Family* (New York: Houghton Mifflin, 1955), chaps. 11 and 12; and *The Social Effects of Aviation* (New York: Houghton Mifflin, 1946), chap. 15.

8. Ogburn, *Technology* . . . , *op. cit.,* pp. 99–100.

9. *Ibid.,* p. 152.

10. William J. Goode, *After Divorce* (New York: The Free Press of Glencoe, 1956), p. 3; cf. Ernest W. Burgess and Harvey J. Locke, *The Family,* 2nd ed. (New York: American Book, 1953), chap. 3.

11. It is an ideal type in the Weberian sense; cf. Max Weber, " 'Objectivity' in Social Science and Social Policy," in Edward A. Shils and Henry A. Finch (trans.) *The Methodology of the Social Sciences* (New York: The Free Press of Glencoe, 1949), pp. 89 ff.; also a brief summary in William J. Goode, "Note on the Ideal Type," *American Sociological Review,* 12 (August, 1947), 473–475.

12. For a list of additional variables for comparing family systems, see William J. Goode, "The Sociology of the Family," in Robert K. Merton, Leonard Broom, and Leonard S. Cottrell (eds.), *Sociology Today* (New York: Basic Books, 1959), pp. 178–191.

13. For an analysis of love-control in various societies, see William J. Goode, "The Theoretical Importance of Love," *American Sociological Review,* 24 (February, 1959), 38–47.

14. Additional help patterns are described in Marvin B. Sussman, "The Help Pattern in the Middle Class Family," *American Sociological Review,* 18 (February, 1953), 18–28.

15. For other kinship characteristics of this "Eskimo" type, see Murdock, *op. cit.,* pp. 226–228.

16. See, e.g., Sussman, *op. cit.,* 22–28.

17. See also Wilbert E. Moore's report on the relation between traditional family

patterns and industrial demands in Mexico: Wilbert E. Moore, *Industrialization and Labor* (Ithaca: Cornell University Press, 1951), chaps. 9, 10, and 11.

18. See however, Smelser, *op. cit.,* chaps. 9, 10, and 11.

19. Talcott Parsons, in *The Social System* (New York: The Free Press of Glencoe, 1949), chap. 5, has analyzed some parts of this relationship between role needs of job and family, and has particularly used the two pattern variables of ascription-achievement and universalism-particularism to differentiate among four types of societies.

20. For a good analysis of mobility rates in a kin-based society, see Robert Marsh, *The Mandarins* (New York: The Free Press of Glencoe, 1961).

21. See Mirra Komarovsky, *Women in the Modern World* (Boston: Little, Brown, 1953), chap. 4. Time-budget data will be presented in a later chapter.

22. Marx, *op. cit.,* p. 405.

23. See Theodore M. Caplow, *The Sociology of Work* (Minneapolis: University of Minnesota, 1954), chap. 15. For France and Belgium: *Sociologie Comparée de la Famille Contemporaine* (Paris: Colloques Internationaux du Centre National de la Recherche Scientifique, 1955), p. 68.

24. William J. Goode, Mary Jean Huntington, and Robert K. Merton, *The Professions in Modern Society,* unpublished manuscript, chap. 2; U.S. Bureau of the Census, *Statistical Abstract of the United States: 1961,* 82d ed. (Washington, D.C., 1961), p. 124; United States Department of Health, Education, and Welfare, Office of Education, *Biennial Survey of Education in the United States, Statistics of Higher Education: 1955–56,* chap. 4, Sect. 1, p. 30.

25. For a review of the data on the amount of mobility under different dynasties in China, see Marsh, *op. cit.;* his independent study of the Ch'ing shows a similarly high amount of mobility. See also his "Bureaucratic Constraints on Nepotism in the Ch'ing Period," *J. Asian Studies* (February, 1960), 117–119. For a more generalized treatment of China as a society that was both particularistic and achievement oriented, see Parsons, *op. cit.,* chap. 5.

26. As William L. Kolb has cogently argued, those who oppose romantic love as a basis for marriage often base their arguments on principles which are "anti-democratic"; see his "Sociologically Established Family Norms and Democratic Values," *Social Forces,* 26 (May, 1948), 451–456.

27. Arthur Phillips has written a useful summary of the application of native law in his "Marriage Laws in Africa," in Arthur Phillips (ed.), *Survey of African Marriage and Family Life* (London: Oxford University Press, 1953), chap. 2.

28. See Gerhardt Baumert, *Deutsche Familien Nach Dem Kriege* (Darmstadt: Roether, 1952), p. 162; see also P. Fougeyrollas, "Predominance du mari ou de la femme dans le ménage," *Population*, 6 (January–March, 1951), 91.

29. Its connections with science have been most ably investigated by Robert K. Merton, in his "Science, Technology, and Society in Seventeenth Century England," *Osiris* (1938). See also his further analyses and later bibliographical comment in *Social Theory and Social Structure*, 2d ed. (New York: The Free Press of Glencoe, 1957), chaps. 18 and 19.

30. A good compendium of industrial developments during this period may be found in A. Wolf, *A History of Science, Technology, and Philosophy in the Eighteenth Century* (New York: Macmillan, 1939).

31. See Edmund S. Morgan, *The Puritan Family* (Boston: Public Library, 1944).

32. Smelser, *op. cit.*, chaps. 9, 10, and 11.

Chapter II   Family Changes in the West

1. Ernest W. Burgess and Harvey J. Locke, *The Family*, 2nd ed. (New York: American Book, 1953), chap. 13. At that time more than a hundred such studies had been done in the United States alone.

2. Robert F. Winch, *The Modern Family* (New York: Holt, 1952), chap. 15; and *Mate Selection* (New York: Harper, 1958).

3. See Bernard Barber, *Social Stratification* (New York: Harcourt, Brace, 1957), chap. 14.

4. For a cross-cultural analysis of love, see William J. Goode, "Theoretical Importance of Love," *American Sociological Review*, 24 (February, 1959) 38–47. See also Ernest W. Burgess and Paul Wallin, *Engagement and Marriage* (Philadelphia: J. B. Lippincott, 1953), chap. 7, where the authors show how coolly the engaged partners view each other's characteristics and prospects.

5. Lawrence Stone, "Marriage Among the English Nobility in the Sixteenth and Seventeenth Centuries," *Comparative Studies in Society and History*, 3 (January, 1961), 195.

6. Alain Girard, "Une enquete en France sur le choix du conjoint," International Population Union Conference Paper No. 16, New York, 1961, pp. 3–4.

7. Jean Sutter, "Evolution de la distance separant le domicile des futurs époux," *Population*, 13 (January–March, 1958), 227–258. See especially tables on 235–244.

8. Gerhardt Baumert, *Jugend der Nachkriegzeit* (Darmstadt: Roether, 1952), pp. 91, 93.

9. *Patterns of Sex and Love: A Study of the French Woman and Her Morals* (New York: Crown Publishers, 1961), p. 60.

10. For example, see comment by I. Stanojčic in *Transactions of the Third World Congress of Sociology*, Vol. 8 (London: International Sociological Association, 1957), p. 115; or Gerhardt Baumert, "Einige Beobachtungen zur Wandlung der familialen Stellung des Kindes in Deutschland" in Nels Anderson (ed.), *Recherches Sur La Famille* (Gottingen: Vandenhoeck and Ruprecht, 1957), p. 14.

11. Girard, *op. cit.*, p. 5.

12. See, for example, L. Bernot and R. Blancard, *Nouville* (Paris: Institut d'ethnologie, 1953).

13. Jan Lutynski, "A Preliminary Draft of the Study of Marriages in Poland," unpublished manuscript (Poland: University of Lodz, 1959), p. 13.

14. J. A. Pitt-Rivers, *The People of the Sierra* (New York: Criterion Books, 1954), p. 106.

15. Laurence Wylie, *Village in the Vaucluse* (Cambridge, Mass.: Harvard University Press, 1957), p. 126.

16. Joel M. Halpern, *A Serbian Village* (New York: Columbia University Press, 1958), p. 189.

17. Claire Le Plae, *Les Fiançailles* (Louvain: Institut de Recherches Economiques et Sociales, 1947), p. 91.

18. *Ibid.*, p. 143.

19. *Ibid.*, p. 152.

20. *Ibid.*, p. 153.

21. K. H. Connell, *The Population of Ireland, 1760–1845* (Oxford: Clarendon Press, 1950), pp. 53–56. See also Conrad M. Arensberg and S. T. Kimball, *Family and*

Community in Ireland (Cambridge: Harvard University Press, 1940).

22. Elizabeth Noelle and Erich Peter Neumann, (eds.), *Jahrbuch der Oeffentlichen Meinung 1947–1955* (Allensbach am Bodensee: Verlag fur Demoskopie), p. 18.

23. Edward C. Banfield, *The Moral Basis of a Backward Society* (New York: The Free Press of Glencoe, 1958), p. 55.

24. Halpern, *op. cit.*, pp. 191–192.

25. Baumert, "Einige Beobachtungen, ..." *op. cit.*, p. 14.

26. In *Sociologie Comparée de la Famille Contemporaine* (Paris: Centre National de la Recherche Scientifique, 1955), p. 153.

27. Jean Baugniet, "Le Statut Juridique de la Femme," in *La Condition Sociale de la Femme* (Brussels: Solvay Institute of Sociology, XXV Semaine Sociale Universitaire, 1956), p. 111.

28. Wesley D. Camp, *Marriage and the Family in France Since the Revolution*, Ph.D. diss. (New York: Columbia University, 1957), p. 80.

29. H. Cantril and Mildred Strunk (eds.), *Public Opinion 1935–1946* (Princeton: Princeton University Press, 1951), p. 483.

30. *Ibid.*, p. 482.

31. *Patterns of Sex and Love, op. cit.*, p. 109.

32. Girard, *op. cit.*, p. 6.

33. A. C. Kinsey, W. B. Pomeroy, and C. E. Martin, *Sexual Behavior in the Human Female* (Philadelphia: Saunders, 1953), pp. 240–244, 298–301; see also *Sexual Behavior in the Human Male* (Philadelphia: Saunders, 1948), pp. 395–414.

34. See Thomas D. Eliot *et al.*, *Norway's Families* (Philadelphia: University of Pennsylvania Press, 1960), chap. 11. See also Udo Deutsch, "Comparative Incidence of Pre-marital Coitus in Scandinavia, Germany and the United States," in Jerome Himelhoch and Sylvia Fleis Fava (eds.), *Sexual Behavior in American Society* (New York: W. W. Norton, 1955), pp. 360–363. For similar reports on the Netherlands, see K. Ishwaran, *Family Life in the Netherlands* (The Hague: Uitgeverij van Keulen, N.V., 1959), p. 192.

35. In "old-fashioned" Portugal, the regions of Lisboa, Beja, Evora, and Setubal have illegitimacy rates of from 20 to 30 per cent. Of the New World countries, most of them Iberian in their attitudes but with very different social structures, a majority have illegitimacy rates of over 30 per cent. A recent estimate for West Germany asserts that from 20 to 30 per cent of the German females are pregnant when they are married, and this percentage is increasing. And from 1939 to 1954, 58 per cent of the Finnish couples had births within less than eight months after marriage. See K. Horstmann, "Schwangerschaft und Eheschlieszung," given at the International Population Congress of Vienna, 1959 and reported in *Population*, 14 (October–December, 1959), p. 619; and Rollin Chambliss, "Contributions of the Vital Statistics of Finland to the Study of the Factors that Induce Marriage," *American Sociological Review*, 22 (February, 1957), 33–48. Since 1946, conception preceded about 36 per cent of all marriages. In England, 30 per cent of all mothers conceive their first born outside wedlock. See Eliot Slater and Moya Woodside, *Patterns of Marriage* (London: Cassell & Co., 1951), p. 111. The illegitimacy rate in Iceland has been over one fourth in the past decade; the rate was 19 per cent in 1956 in Steiermark, Austria and was 18.5 per cent in 1954 in Obernbayern, Germany.

36. Le Plae, *op. cit.*, pp. 230–231.

37. For a series of studies on premarital conception and illegitimacy rates, see the following: Jean Morsa, "Notes sur La Famille dans Une Localité du Brabant Wallon," in Nels Anderson (ed.), *Recherches sur La Famille* (Tubingen: J. C. B. Mohr [P. Siebeck], 1956), p. 178; Pierre Girard, "Aperçus de la Demographie de Sotteville-Les-Rouen vers la Fin du XVIIIᵉ Siècle," *Population*, 14 (July–September, 1959), 494; Harold Christensen, "Cultural Relativism and Premarital Sex Norms," *American Sociological Review*, 25 (February, 1960), 31–39; Sidney H. Kroog, "Aspects of the Cultural Background of Premarital Pregnancy in Denmark," *Social Forces*, 39 (December, 1951), 215–219; and Andrée Michel, *Famille Industrialisation, Logement* (Paris: Centre National de la Recherche Scientifique, 1959), p. 164.

38. P. Chombart de Lauwe, "La Naissance des Aspirations a des formes nouvelles de la Famille," in Nels Anderson (ed.), *op. cit.*, pp. 99–100.

39. Eliot *et al.*, *op. cit.*, pp. 276–277.

40. Angelo Serra and Antonio Soim, "La consanguinité d'une Population," *Population*, 14 (January–March, 1959), 50–59. See also Table 43 in Camp, *op. cit.*, p. 154. In addition, see Jean Sutter and Leon Tabah, "Frequence et Repartition des Marriages Consanguins en France, *Population*, 3 (Oc-

tober–December, 1948); 607–630; N. Freire-Maia, "Inbreeding Levels in Different Countries," *Eugenics Quarterly*, 4 (September, 1957), 127–138; and Carl Henry Alstrom, "First Cousin Marriages in Sweden 1750–1844...," *Acta Genet. Stat. Med.*, 8 (1958), 296–369.

41. Gerhardt Baumert, *Deutsche Familien Nach dem Kriege* (Darmstadt: Roether, 1954), p. 28.

42. In 1853–1857, the French husband was four years and four months older than his wife; in 1876–1880 the figure rose to four years and eight months. It then dropped to four years and three months in 1901–1905, and in 1953 had declined to three years and two months. See Camp, *op. cit.*, p. 57.

43. Thomas C. Monahan, *The Pattern of Age at Marriage in the United States*, 2 vols. (Philadelphia: Stephenson Brothers, 1951).

44. Gerard Duplessis-Le Guelinel, *Les Marriages en France* (Paris: Coln, 1954), p. 21.

45. For figures on pre-Revolutionary France, see Claude Levi and Louis Henry, "Ducs et Pairs sous L'Ancien Regime," *Population*, 15 (October–December, 1960), p. 818.

46. See the comments by Gemaehling and Aries, in *Sociologie Comparée de la Famille Contemporaine, op. cit.*, p. 52.

47. Duplessis-Le Guelinel, *op. cit.*, pp. 14–20. See also John T. Krause, "Some Recent Implications of Recent Research in Demographic History," *Comparative Studies in Society and History*, 1 (November–January, 1959), 178 ff.; John T. Krause, "The Medieval Household: Large or Small?" *Economic History Review*, 2d series, 9 (November, 1957), 420–433; George C. Homans, *English Villagers of the Thirteenth Century* (Cambridge: Harvard University Press, 1941); Conrad Arensberg, *The Irish Countryman* (New York: Macmillan, 1957), chap. 3.

48. Connell, *op. cit.*, pp. 49–60.

49. *Ibid.*, pp. 51–53.

50. See the summary of United States data on class and marriage patterns, in Ruth S. Cavan, *The Family* (New York: Crowell, 1953), chaps. 5, 6, and 7.

51. Franco Archibugi, "Recent Trends in Women's Work in Italy," *International Labor Review*, 81 (April, 1960), 287.

52. Paul H. Jacobson, *American Marriage and Divorce* (New York: Rinehart, 1959), pp. 35–36. See also Ogburn, *Tech-nology and the Changing Family* (New York: Houghton Mifflin, 1955), p. 93.

53. Camp, *op. cit.*, pp. 57–58. Unfortunately, prior to 1938, recording was by five-year age groups, and included all ages, including the very old; thus there may be some inclusion of remarriages.

54. C. E. V. Leser, "Trends in Women's Work Participation," *Population Studies*, 2 (November, 1958), 101.

55. Eliot *et al.*, *op. cit.*, p. 161.

56. Robert Boudet, "La Famille Bourgeoise," in *Sociologie Comparée de la Famille Contemporaine, op. cit.*, p. 144.

57. In these data, as in all census data on marital status, some unknown number of men and women claim to be married who never were, and some claim to be single who were divorced. How many will make such a claim depends on whether the truth is thought to be worth hiding. The amount of error could not be great in the West.

58. Although I believe this relationship to be valid, contrary evidence should be noted: Elizabeth R. Kramm and Dorothy S. Thomas, "Rural and Urban Marriage in Relation to the Sex Ratio," *Rural Sociology*, 7:1 (March, 1942), 33–39.

59. Neil Smelser, *Social Change in the Industrial Revolution* (Chicago: University of Chicago, 1959), chap. 9.

60. Connell, *op. cit.*, chaps. 1–2.

61. See the comment by Alain Girard, in *Sociologie Comparée de la Famille Contemporaine, op. cit.*, p. 55.

62. Kingsley Davis, *Human Society* (New York: Macmillan, 1949), pp. 599–600.

63. For these and other changes, see Clyde V. Kaiser, "Changes in Fertility by Socio-Economic Status during 1940–1950," *Milbank Memorial Fund Quarterly*, 33 (October, 1955), 393–430. See also Conrad Taeuber and Irene V. Taeuber, *The Changing Population of the United States* (New York: Wiley, 1958), p. 262. Although the Taeubers point out that fertility has nearly always been higher in rural than in urban areas of the United States, they also note that the urban birth rate was 22.0 in 1950, and the rural 24.5, a relatively small difference.

64. See John T. Krause, "Some Implications of Recent Work in Historical Demography," *Comparative Studies in Society and History*, 1 (January, 1959), 184–187.

65. Slater and Woodside, *op. cit.*, pp. 212–213.

66. Alfred Sauvy, "La Prevention des Naissances dans la Famille," *Population*, 15

(January–March, 1960), 117. In Sweden the drop may have been due to a lowered marriage rate.

67. Mary S. Calderone (ed.), *Abortion in the United States* (New York: Hoeber-Harper, 1958), p. 180.

68. The newspaper *Vecerni Praka* reported that in Prague alone abortions outnumbered live births in 1961. Approximately 9,000 abortions compared with only 8,500 births were recorded. See "Marriages Slowed for Czechs by Work and Housing Needs," *New York Times Magazine* (February 18, 1962).

69. Of the young Polish married couples in Lutynski's study, only 62.5 per cent began to live together after their wedding. Lutynski, *op. cit.*, p. 20.

70. "Marriages Slowed for Czechs," *op. cit.*

71. Halpern, *op. cit.*, pp. 201–202. He reports that in his village the proportion of abortions seemed higher today than formerly.

72. I have developed a more extensive theoretical analysis of this idea in my two articles, "Norm Commitment and Conformity to Role-Status Obligations," *American Journal of Sociology*, 66 (November, 1960), 246–248; and "A Theory of Role Strain," *American Sociological Review*, 25 (August, 1960), 483–496. I have applied the theory in several analyses, some previously cited. See also "At What Points Do Urbanization and Industrialization Have an Impact on Family Systems?," UNESCO Conference, September, 1961, Opatija, Yugoslavia, to be published in *Current Sociology*.

73. Andrée Michel, "La Femme dans la Famille Française," *Cahiers Internationaux*, 12 (March–April, 1960), 61–76.

74. *Ibid.*, p. 62.

75. *Ibid.*, p. 64.

76. Pierre de Fissher, *Attitudes Antiféministes et Milieux Intellectuals* (Louvain: Editions Nauwelaerts, 1956).

77. de Fissher cites the series of studies that Clifford Kirkpatrick carried out. Here the relevant article is "A Comparison of Generations in Regard to Attitudes Toward Feminism," *Journal of Genetic Psychology*, 49 (December, 1936), 343–361.

78. Leser, *op. cit.*, p. 101.

79. Archibugi, *op. cit.*, 288–300.

80. Livia Forniciari, "Osservazioni Sull'Andamento del Lavoro Femminile in Italia negli Ultimi 50 Anni," *R. Intern. Sci. Soc.*, 17 (May–June, 1956), 222–240; and "The Employment of Women in Italy 1881–1951," *Comparative Studies in Society and History*, 2 (April, 1960), 369–374; see also Forniciari's "Il Lavoro Femminile in Francia," *R. Intern. Sci. Soc.*, (January–February, 1957), 45–51, which gives some explanation for rises and falls; but her explanations would often apply to both negative and positive cases. I have not been able to interpret the data adequately.

81. Elisabeth Pfeil, "An Empirical-Sociological Study on the Employment of Married Women in Western Germany," Hamburg, Germany, International Population Union Conference Paper #101, 1961, p. 4.

82. Ishwaran, *op. cit.*, p. 82.

83. Eliot *et al.*, *op. cit.*, pp. 181 ff.

84. Statements 2 to 5 are from *Womanpower* (New York: Columbia University Press, 1957), pp. 10 ff. I have corrected the first statement to present a recent figure.

85. Eliot *et al.*, *op. cit.*, p. 182.

86. Jean-Claude Chasteland and Paul Paillat, "Les Femmes dans L'Activité Nationale," *Esprit*, 5 (May, 1961), 811.

87. Nicholas DeWitt, *Education and Professional Employment in the U.S.S.R.* (Washington, D.C.: National Science Foundation, 1961).

88. *Ibid.*

89. Arthur Olsen, "Polish Chiefs Pay Women a Tribute," *New York Times*, March 9, 1962.

90. *Newsyear: 1960*, compiled from *Facts on File* (New York: Facts on File, 1961), 490.

91. In Poland the reported sex ratio is 107 women to 100 men, with a partially war-created surplus of 1 million women in a population of 30 million. *Ibid.*

92. David C. Marsh, *The Changing Social Structure of England and Wales, 1871–1951* (London: Routledge and Kegan Paul, 1951), p. 208.

93. Eliot *et al.*, *op. cit.*, p. 181.

94. *Sociologie Comparée de la Famille Contemporaine*, *op. cit.*, p. 67. See also Chombart de Lauwe's "L'homme et la Promotion de la Femme," *L'Ecole des Parents*, 10 (September–October, 1959), 3–9.

95. *Sondages*, 19, no. 3 (1957), 42.

96. Rolf Fröhner, Maria von Stackelberg, and Wolfgang Eser, *Familie und Ehe* (Bielefeld: Maria von Stackelberg Verlag, 1956), p. 355.

97. Ishwaran, *op. cit.*, p. 189.

98. *Ibid.*, p. 213.

99. David R. Mace, "The Employed Mother in the U.S.S.R.," *Marriage and*

Family Living, 23 (November, 1961), 330–333.

100. Alain Girard and Henri Bastide, "Le Budget-temps de la femme mariée a la Campagne," *Population,* 14 (April–June, 1959), 281–284.

101. Gerhardt Baumert, *Jugend der Nachkriegszeit* (Darmstadt: E. Roether, 1952), p. 180.

102. See *New York Times,* June 10, 1961, for a survey by the Young Catholic Workers and directors of a marriage preparation course, covering 300 parishes in twenty dioceses of Quebec, New Brunswick, and Ontario.

103. M. J. Morsa, "La Population Feminine Active et son Evolution en Belgique," in *La Condition Sociale de la Femme,* (Brussels: University of Brussels, Solvay Institute of Technology, XXV° semaine sociale universitaire, 1956), pp. 45–46.

104. Pfeil, *op. cit.,* p. 4.

105. *A Social Profile of Detroit, 1956* (Ann Arbor: Department of Sociology and the Survey Research Center, University of Michigan, 1957), pp. 43, 47.

106. *A Social Profile of Detroit, 1956, op. cit.,* p. 43.

107. Ilija Stanojčic, "Facteurs Fondementaux agissant sur les Changements des Rapports Familiaux en Yougoslavie," in *Transactions of the Third World Congress of Sociology* vol. 8 (Amsterdam: International Sociological Association, 1957), p. 226.

108. Sophie Grinberg-Vinaver, "The Status of Women Throughout the World," *Marriage and Family Living,* 17 (August, 1955), 197–198.

109. Fröhner, Stackelberg, and Eser, *op. cit.,* pp. 397–401.

110. Cantril and Strunk, *op. cit.,* p. 99.

111. Ishwaran, *op. cit.,* p. 156.

112. *Sociologie Comparée de la Famille Contemporaine, op. cit.,* pp. 101–102; Geoffrey Gorer, *Exploring English Character* (London: Cresset Press, 1955), pp. 131–132. See also Michael Young, "Income Within the Family," *British Journal of Sociology,* 3 (December, 1952) 305–321.

113. Cantril and Strunk, *op. cit.,* pp. 60–61, 433.

114. Baumert, *Deutsche Familien Nach Dem Kriege, op. cit.,* p. 4.

115. David M. Heer, "Dominance and the Working Wife," in *Social Forces,* 36 (May, 1958), 341–347; Robert O. Blood and Robert M. Hamlin, "The Effect of Wife Employment on the Family Power Structure," in *ibid.,* 347–52. The authority of the male is also higher with an increasing number of children.

116. See René König, "Changes in the Western Family," *Transactions of the Third World Congress of Sociology,* Vol. IV (London: International Sociological Association, 1956), p. 72. A full citation of materials on authoritarianism up to 1950 may be found in O. Jean Brandes, *Aspects of the German Family in the War and post-War Periods,* M.A. Thesis, Columbia University, 1956.

117. Cantril and Strunk, *op. cit.,* p. 207.

118. A survey on the simple equalitarian matter of husband helping with housework, ascertains that in Norway, less than one third do so regularly, though a higher proportion reported for younger people and city dwellers suggests that the situation is changing. Eliot *et al., op. cit.,* p. 187.

119. *Ibid.,* p. 206.

120. Baumert, *Deutsche Familien Nach Dem Kriege, op. cit.,* pp. 151–152; however, his figures are somewhat confusing.

121. Fröhner, Stackelberg, and Eser, *op. cit.,* pp. 394–397.

122. Olsen, *op. cit.*

123. Raymond Firth (ed.), *Two Studies of Kinship in London,* London School of Economics, Monographs on Social Anthropology, No. 15 (London: The Athlone Press, 1956), p. 76.

124. *A Social Profile of Detroit: 1955, op. cit.,* p. 26.

125. Morris Axelrod, "Urban Structure and Social Participation," *American Sociological Review,* 21 (February, 1956), 15.

126. Scott Greer, "Urbanism Reconsidered: A Comparative Study of Local Areas in a Metropolis," *American Sociological Review,* 21 (February, 1956), p. 22.

127. *A Social Profile of Detroit: 1955, op. cit.,* pp. 17–18. Totals did not add up to 100 per cent, since a family may have given or received more than one kind of help.

128. *Ibid.,* p. 25.

129. Ethel Shanas, *Family Relationships of Older People* (New York: Health Information Foundation Research Series 20, 1961), pp. 27–28.

130. Michael Young and H. Geertz, "Old Age in London and San Francisco: Some Families Compared," *British Journal of Sociology,* 12 (June, 1961), 128.

131. Pfeil, *op. cit.,* p. 4.

132. Lutynski, *op. cit.,* p. 24.

133. Eugene Litwak, "Geographical Mobility and Extended Family Cohesion,"

American Sociological Review, 25 (June, 1960), 385–394; and "Occupational Mobility and Extended Family Cohesion," *American Sociological Review*, 25 (February, 1960), 9–20.

134. Marvin B. Sussman, "Parental Participation in Mate Selection and Its Effects Upon Family Continuity," *Social Forces*, 32 (October, 1953), 77–79.

135. Marvin B. Sussman, "The Help Pattern in the Middle Class Family," *American Sociological Review*, 18 (February, 1953), 23.

136. Lutynski, *op. cit.*, p. 14.

137. *Ibid.*, p. 27.

138. *Ibid.*, p. 15.

139. Sussman, "Parental Participation," *op. cit.*

140. Elaine Cumming and David M. Schneider, "Sibling Solidarity: A Property of American Kinship," *American Anthropologist*, 63 (June, 1961), 501.

141. Michael Young, "The Role of the Extended Family in a Disaster," *Human Relations*, 7 (July, 1954), 383–391.

142. A suggestion of this pattern may be found in W. M. Williams Gosforth, *The Sociology of an English Village* (New York: The Free Press of Glencoe, 1956), chap. 7.

143. See Eliot *et al.*, *op. cit.*, pp. 194 ff., for a discussion of this doctrine in Norway.

144. Fröhner, Stackelberg, and Eser, *op. cit.*, p. 410.

145. Seymour S. Bellin, *Extended Family Relations in Later Years of Life*, Ph.D. Diss., Columbia University, 1962.

146. *Ibid.*, pp. 45, 52.

147. *Ibid.*, p. 64. Although I have not cited Bellin's relevant figures, the frequency with which parents and children saw one another confirms the data cited earlier in this section.

148. Willem Steigenga, "Family Structure, Age-Composition, and Housing Needs," New York, International Population Congress, 1961, Paper #35 (Mimeo), p. 5.

149. Lutynski, *op. cit.*, p. 27.

150. *Ibid.*, p. 29.

151. Alain Girard, "Aspects statistiques du Probleme Familial," *Sociologie Comparée de la Famille Contemporaine, op. cit.*, 63.

152. Baumert, "Einige Beobachtungen . . .," *op. cit.*, p. 10.

153. Michel, *Famille, Industrialisation, Logement, op. cit.*, p. 174.

154. Ishwaran, *op. cit.*, p. 71. On the other hand, see Eliot *et al.*, *op. cit.*, pp. 76–80, 90–92, 167–168, for the Norwegian rules in rural areas that still protect the rights of the eldest son.

155. These comments are taken from the article by Kingsley Davis, "The Sociology of Parent-Youth Conflict," *American Sociological Review*, 5 (August, 1940), 523–535. The article is rich with insights that are still applicable to the current situation.

156. See the discussion in Goode, *After Divorce*, (New York: The Free Press of Glencoe, 1956), chap. 1; and "Family Disorganization," in Robert K. Merton and Robert A. Nisbet (eds.) *Contemporary Social Problems* (New York: Harcourt, Brace, 1961).

157. Pierpaolo Luzzatto Fegiz, *Il Volto Sconsciuto Dell'Italia* (Milano: A. Giuffre, 1956), pp. 397–398.

158. *Ibid.*, pp. 398–400.

159. *Ibid.*, pp. 400–403.

160. Domenico Riccardo Peretti-Griva, *La Famiglia e el Divorzio*, (Bari: Editori Laterza, 1956), pp. 142–143.

161. *Official Yearbook of the Commonwealth of Australia*, No. 43, (Canberra: Commonwealth Bureau of Census and Statistics, 1957), p. 588.

162. For Holland, see *Echtscheidingen In Nederland, 1900–1957*, Central Bureau voor de Statistiek (Zeist: W. De Haan, 1958), p. 14.

163. *Ibid.*, pp. 23–25.

164. See William J. Goode, "Marital Satisfaction and Instability: A Cross-Cultural Analysis of Divorce," *International Social Science Journal*, XIV, no. 3 (1962), 507–526.

Chapter III   Changing Family Patterns in Arabic Islam

1. See H. A. R. Gibb's comments on this modernist movement in *Modern Trends in Islam* (Chicago: University of Chicago Press, 1947) chap. III. For a still more nostal-

gic view of early Islam, see S. Khuda Bukhsh, *Marriage and Family Life Among the Arabs*, 2d ed. (Lahore: Orientalia, 1953). See also Sayed Kotb, *Social Justice in Islam*,

John B. Hardie (trans.) (Washington: American Council of Learned Societies, 1945), chaps. 3, 4, and 6; Henri Laoust, "Le Reformisme Musulman dans la litterature Arabe Contemporaine," *Orient*, 3 (June, 1959), 81–107; and Kenneth Cragg, "The Modernist Movement in Egypt," in Richard N. Frye (ed.), *Islam and The West* (The Hague: Mouton, 1956), pp. 159–160.

2. Afif I. Tannous, *The Arab Village Community of the Middle East* (Washington: Smithsonian Institution Pub. 3760, 1944), p. 538; H. R. P. Dickson, *The Arab of the Desert*, 2d ed. (London: Allen & Unwin, 1921) pp. 154–155. Many tribes on the peninsula did not wear veils. In Pakistan, of course, the burka covers the entire body.

3. E. W. Lane, *Manners and Customs of the Modern Egyptians* (London: J. M. Dent & Sons, 1954), p. 51. (The text is that of 1860.)

4. His book, *The Emancipation of Women*, was published in 1901. See Ilse Lichtenstadter, "The Muslim Woman in Transition," *Soziologus*, 7, no. 1 (1957), 23 ff. Gibb, *op. cit.*, pp. 92–93, also cites the poem, "Unveil!" published in the 1920s by the Iraqi poet az-Zahawi. Such reformers were in the minority until the past decade.

5. Kazem Daghestani, *La Famille Musulmane Contemporaine en Syrie* (Paris: Leroux, 1932), p. 127.

6. *Ibid.*, p. 129.

7. *Ibid.*, p. 130.

8. *Ibid.*, p. 139. More rarely, a friend or relative of the two families might arrange a meeting between the young people.

9. *Ibid.*, p. 140. See also Jacques Weulersse, *Paysans De Syrie Et Du Proche-Orient*, 2d ed. (Paris: Gallimard, 1946), p. 221.

10. Daghestani, *op. cit.*, pp. 129–130.

11. For the fellahin, based on materials from the 1930s or earlier, see Henry Ayrout, *Fellahs D'Egypte*, 6th ed. (Cairo: Editions du Sphynx, 1952).

12. Daghestani, *op. cit.*, p. 138.

13. Lane, *op. cit.*, pp. 162 ff.

14. Khaled Chatila, *Le Mariage Chez Les Musulmans En Eyrie* (Paris: Presses Modernes, 1933), pp. 185, 194.

15. The first two statements are from George L. Harris (ed.), *Egypt* (New Haven: Human Relations Area Files, Country Survey Series, 1957), p. 297; the second is from Marie Karam Khayet and Margaret C. Keatinge, *Lebanon Land of the Cedars* (Beirut: Khayats, 1956), p. 36. Both are intended to describe the present.

16. Chatila, *op. cit.*, pp. 39–40.

17. Raphael Patai, in his "Cousin Right in Middle Eastern Marriage," *Southwestern Journal of Anthropology*, 11 (Winter, 1955), 390, has summarized the reports from various regions, although some of them are untrustworthy. See also Millicent R. Ayoub, *Endogamous Marriage in a Middle Eastern Village*, Ph.D. diss., Radcliffe College, 1957, pp. 152–162, for another summary from both Biblical and Islamic reports.

18. Kazem Daghestani, "Evolution of the Moslem Family in the Middle Eastern Countries," *UNESCO International Social Science Bulletin*, 5, no. 4 (1953), 687.

19. Lane, *op. cit.*, pp. 161–162. The latter conclusion is also reported by Ayoub, *op. cit.*, p. 85, for a Druze group.

20. Daghestani, *La Famille . . .*, *op. cit.*, pp. 21–22.

21. Weulersse, *op. cit.*, pp. 217, 221.

22. Patai, *op. cit.*, p. 377.

23. Henri de Montety, *Les Femmes de Tunisie* (Paris: Mouton, 1958), p. 119. An official of the Tunisian government informs me privately that no one among the educated people considers the claim to the father's brother's daughter as serious any more.

24. Jean Cuisenier, "Structures parentales et structures vicinales en Tunisie," *Revue de L'Institut des Belles Lettres Arabes a Tunis*, 23 (November, 1960), 421–424.

25. Ayoub, *op. cit.*, pp. 65, 67–68, 76. The citations are: Frederik Barth, *Principles of Social Organization in Southern Kurdistan* (Oslo: Brodrene Jorgensen, 1953), pp. 167–169; and Hilma Granqvist, *Marriage Conditions in a Palestinian Village* (Helsingfors: Societas Scientiarium Fennica, 1931), pp. 81, 92, 194–195.

26. Ayoub, *op. cit.*, p. 38.

27. Raphael Patai, *The Kingdom of Jordan* (Princeton: Princeton University Press, 1958), p. 139.

28. Frederik Barth, "Father's Brother's Daughter's Marriage in Kurdistan," *Southwestern Journal of Anthropology*, 10 (Summer, 1954), 167–169.

29. Anne H. Fuller, *Buarij: Portrait of a Lebanese Muslim Village* (Cambridge: Harvard Middle Eastern Monographs No. 6, 1961), p. 67.

30. De Montety, *op. cit.*, p. 60.

31. Morroe Berger, *The Arab World Today* (New York: Doubleday, 1962), pp. 75–76.

32. *Ibid.*, pp. 200–201.

33. *Akhbar El-Yom*, (Cairo: January 6, 1960), 10; (January 16, 1960), 10.
34. Chatila, *op. cit.*, pp. 187–191.
35. *Ibid.*, p. 192.
36. See also Weulersse, *op. cit.*, pp. 220–221, for bride prices among Syrian peasants in 1930 and 1935, and for references to the exchange of brides and the pattern of having a particular sister named for a particular brother as his bride price.
37. Daghestani, *La Famille . . .*, *op. cit.*, p. 139.
38. Chatila, *op. cit.*, pp. 21–23.
39. *Ibid.*, pp. 47–48.
40. De Montety, *op. cit.*, pp. 13, 84–85.
41. *UNESCO: Observations of Governments Under Draft Convention and Draft Recommendation on the Minimun Age of Marriage, Consent to Marriage, and Registration of Marriages*, January 13, 1961, p. 15.
42. "Interview with Mlle. Sid Cara," *International Council of Women Quarterly Review* (January, 1959), 52.
43. Daghestani, "Evolution . . . ," *op. cit.*, 686.
44. George L. Harris (ed.), *Iraq* (New Haven: Human Relations Area Files Press, 1958), p. 272.
45. Khayet and Keatinge, *op. cit.*, pp. 38–42.
46. Harris, *Iraq*, *op. cit.*, p. 273.
47. Patai, *The Kingdom of Jordan*, *op. cit.*, p. 150.
48. Frantz Fanon, *L'an V de la Revolution Algerienne* (Paris: François Maspero, 1959), p. 27.
49. *Ibid.*, pp. 35–45.
50. *Ibid.*, pp. 94–97.
51. *Ibid.*, p. 98.
52. *Ibid.*, pp. 104–105.
53. Thomas Hammerton, *Tunisia Unveiled* (London: Robert Hale, 1959), p. 14.
54. André de Meerseman, *Tunisie Sève Nouvelle* (Paris: Casterman, 1957), p. 212.
55. M. K. Nahas, "Married Life in Iraq," Nels Anderson (ed.), *Recherches Sur la Famille* (Tubingen: J. C. B. Mohr [Paul Siebeck], 1956), p. 185.
56. *Ibid.*, p. 194.
57. *Ibid.*, p. 195.
58. Nadia Haggag Yussef, *Changes in Egyptian Family Life* (American University at Cairo, M.A. thesis, 1958), p. 93.
59. *News from Tunisia*, Bulletin No. 51 (January 15, 1960), 3.
60. Cragg, *op. cit.*, pp. 159–160.
61. Gibb, *op. cit.*, pp. 93–94.
62. Lane, *op. cit.*, p. 188.

63. *Ibid.*, p. 189.
64. Daghestani, "Evolution . . . ," *op. cit.*, p. 687.
65. *Study of the Role of Women: Their Activities and Organizations in Lebanon, Egypt, Iraq, Syria and Jordan* (New York: The International Federation of Business and Professional Women, 1956), p. 65.
66. *Ibid.*, p. 56.
67. Chatila, *op. cit.*, pp. 240–245.
68. *Ibid.*, p. 247.
69. Weulersse, *op. cit.*, p. 220.
70. Chatila, *op. cit.*, pp. 256–259.
71. Harris, *Jordan*, *op. cit.*, p. 190.
72. *Vital Statistics—1951-II*, Cairo, 1957, p. 1155.
73. Daghestani, *La Famille . . .*, *op. cit.*, pp. 71, 74.
74. *Ibid.*, p. 76.
75. Lefter Mboria, *La Population de L'Egypte*, University of Paris, Faculty of Law Thesis (Cairo: Procaccia, 1938), p. 105.
76. Data kindly supplied to me by Statistical Department, Cairo, September, 1960.
77. *Statistique Generale de L'Algerie*, 1904, p. 66; *Annuaire Statistique de L'Algerie*, Service Centrale de Statistique, Alger, 1937, p. 139; *Annuaire Statistique de L'Algerie*, 1955, p. 45.
78. Jacques Breil, *La Population en Algerie* (Paris: Imprimerie Nationale, 1957), p. 54.
79. *Ibid.*
80. *Ibid.*, pp. 20–23.
81. Lane, *op. cit.*, p. 161.
82. Mboria, *op. cit.*, p. 104.
83. Chatila, *op. cit.*, pp. 26–27.
84. Horace M. Miner and George De Vos, *Oasis and Casbah: Algerian Culture and Personality in Change* (Ann Arbor; University of Michigan, 1960), p. 76.
85. *Statistique Generale de L'Algerie* (Alger: Direction de L'Agriculture, du Commerce, et de la Colonisation, 1904), pp. 66–67.
86. H. V. Muhsam, "Some Notes on Bedu Marriage Habits," in Corrado Gini (ed.), *XIV International Congress of Sociology* (Roma: Societa Italiana di Sociologia, 1950), pp. 6, 17.
87. Charles W. Churchill, *The City of Beirut, Lebanon* (Beirut: Dar El-Kitab, 1954), pp. 32–33.
88. Raphael Patai, "The Family," in Raphael Patai (ed.), *The Republic of Lebanon* (New Haven: Human Relations Area Files, 1956), p. 274.
89. Nahas, *op. cit.*, p. 186.

90. *Annuaire Statistique de L'Egypte,* 1955–1956, p. 31.

91. *The Hashemite Kingdom of Jordan Statistical Yearbook 1960,* p. 51.

92. *Census of Egypt* (Cairo: Census Department, 1909), p. 91.

93. Wendell Cleland, *The Population Problem in Egypt* (Lancaster, Pennsylvania: Science Press, 1936), p. 42.

94. *Annuaire Statistique de L'Algerie, 1954–1955, 1955–1956,* p. 45.

95. Breil, *op. cit.,* pp. 99–101.

96. See the discussion and references on this point in David Yaukey, *Fertility Differences in a Modernizing Country* (Princeton: Princeton University Press, 1961), pp. 121–129.

97. *Ibid.,* p. 125. The following women were excluded from the total sample, which included over 900 women: Those married before 1920, those extremely slow in becoming pregnant, those who used some method to delay the first pregnancy or were separated from their husbands for more than three consecutive months, or those married very early or very late.

98. *Ibid.,* p. 128.

99. Females married at age 11 to 13 years in Yaukey's sample did not have a live birth until 25.5 months later on the average, as against 16.6 months later for those married at ages 14 to 17. On the other hand, both age groups bore more children over their total reproductive span (see *Ibid.,* pp. 48, 189) than those married still later.

100. Weulersse, *op. cit.,* p. 247.

101. H. V. Muhsam, "Fertility and Reproduction of the Bedouins," *Population Studies,* 4 (March, 1951), 357–360.

102. M. A. El-Badry, "Some Demographic Measurements for Egypt Based on the Stability of Census Age Distribution," *Milbank Memorial Fund Quarterly,* 33 (July, 1955), 269.

103. Mboria, *op. cit.,* p. 34.

104. Cleland, *op. cit.,* p. 39.

105. M. A. El-Badry, "Some Aspects of Fertility in Egypt," *Milbank Memorial Fund Quarterly,* 34 (January, 1956), 30 ff.

106. Richard Stephens, *Population Factors in the Development of North Africa* (Washington, D.C.: George Washington University, 1960), p. 5.

107. Weulersse, *op. cit.,* p. 247.

108. Breil, *op. cit.,* pp. 110–111.

109. Hamed Ammar, *Growing Up in an Egyptian Village* (London: Routledge and Kegan Paul, 1954), p. 97.

110. Mboria, *op. cit.,* p. 182.

111. Daghestani, *La Famille . . . , op. cit.,* p. 101.

112. *New York Times,* June 1, 1962.

113. For a description of the clinics established, see Nefissa Hussein Eissa, "Family Planning in Egypt," *Journal of Family Welfare,* 3 (March, 1957), 86–87; see also, Seklani, *op. cit.,* pp. 851–852.

114. Ilse Lichtenstadter, *Islam and the Modern Age* (New York: Book Man Association, 1958), p. 138.

115. "In the Arab World," *New Outlook,* 1 (June, 1958), 57–58.

116. *The Moslem World,* 36, no. 1 (January, 1946), 89.

117. See the summary of these opinions by G. H. Bosquet, "L'Islam et la Limitation Volontaire des Naissances," *Population,* 5 (January–March, 1950), 121–128.

118. Mahmoud Seklani, "La Fecondité dans les Pays Arabes: Données Numeriques, Attitudes et Comportements," *Population,* 15 (October–December, 1960), 851–854, presents some of the favorable views that have been expressed.

119. Mohamed Kamal Abdel-Razzax, "Contraceptive Methods Applied in Family Planning Clinics in Egypt," *Journal of Family Welfare,* 3 (March, 1957), 87–89.

120. This argument has been offered by El Sayed Abdel Hamid El Daly, *Birth Rates and Fertility Trends in Egypt* (Cairo, 1952), p. 2, with some evidence in favor of it.

121. Hannah Rizk, *Fertility Patterns in Selected Areas in Egypt,* Ph.D. diss. Princeton University, 1959. Since Rizk's study has not been published, I am citing here the relevant materials from Yaukey.

122. Yaukey, *op. cit.,* p. 31.

123. *Ibid.,* p. 36.

124. *Ibid.,* p. 37.

125. *Ibid.,* pp. 66, 70.

126. See J. N. Finha, "Differential Fertility and Family Limitation in the Urban Community of Uttar Pradesh," *Population Studies,* 11 (November, 1957), 157–159.

127. Yaukey, *op. cit.,* p. 114.

128. *Ibid.,* p. 78.

129. Yussef, *op. cit.,* p. 103.

130. James M. Gillespie and Gordon W. Allport, "Youth's Outlook on the Future," *Doubleday Papers in Psychology,* No. 15 (New York: Doubleday & Co., 1955), p. 54.

131. Ammar, *op. cit.,* p. 192.

132. L. Sayed Abdel Hamid El Daly, *op. cit.,* p. 3.

133. Arthur Jeffrey, "The Family in

Islam," Ruth Nanda Anshen (ed.), in *The Family*, rev. ed. (New York: Harper, 1959), p. 221.

134. Louis Milliot, *Introduction à l'étude du droit Musulman* (Paris: Recueil Sirey, 1953), p. 390.

135. *Ibid.*, pp. 387–388.

136. *Ibid.*, p. 389.

137. Article 60, *News From Tunisia*, Bulletin No. 61, January 15, 1960, p. 9.

138. Breil, *op. cit.*, pp. 74 ff.

139. Republic of Egypt, *Vital Statistics*, Vol. 2-1951 (Cairo, 1957), pp. 920–921.

140. Raymond Pearl, *The Biology of Population Growth* (New York: Knopf, 1925), pp. 98–104.

141. Hashemite Kingdom of Jordan, Department of Statistics, *Statistical Yearbook 1960*, Amman, pp. 23, 26.

142. Gouvernement Cherifien, Service Central de Statistiques, *Aspects de Demographie Marocaine* (n.d., about 1950).

143. Mboria, *op. cit.*, pp. 43–45.

144. Harris, *Egypt*, *op. cit.*, p. 292.

145. Patai, *The Republic of Syria, op. cit.*, p. 373.

146. Daghestani, *La Famille . . . , op. cit.*, pp. 136–137, 154–155.

147. Weulersse, *op. cit.*, p. 218.

148. Daghestani, "Evolution . . . ," *op. cit.*, p. 684.

149. *A Demographic Study of an Egyptian Province* (London: London School of Economics and Political Science Monographs on Social Anthropology No. 8, 1942), pp. 42–46.

150. *Annuaire Statistique de l'Egypte, 1951–1952, 1952–1953, 1953–1954* (Cairo, 1956), pp. 10, 23.

151. Muhsam, "Fertility . . . ," *op. cit.*, pp. 357–358.

152. Gouvernement Cherifien, Service Central de Statistiques, *Aspects de Demographie Marocaine, op. cit.*

153. Seklani, *op. cit.*, pp. 846–849.

154. *Population Legale ou de Residence Habituelle* (Alger: Service de Statistique Generale, 1954).

155. Patai, *The Kingdom of Jordan, op. cit.*, p. 136.

156. Patai, *Jordan, op. cit.*, pp. 281–282.

157. Churchill, *op. cit.*, p. 31.

158. Lincoln Armstrong and Gordon K. Hirabayashi, "Social Differentiation in Selected Lebanese Villages," *American Sociological Review*, 21 (August, 1956), 433.

159. Ayoub, *op. cit.*, p. 14.

160. See the summary by Lucie A. Wood, *An Inquiry Into the Preference for*

Parallel Cousin Marriage Among the Contemporary Arabs, Ph.D. diss., Columbia University, 1959, p. 48.

161. Henry Rosenfeld, "Processes of Structural Change Within the Arab Village Extended Family," *American Anthropologist*, 60 (December, 1958), 1127.

162. *Ibid.*, 1129–1130.

163. *Ibid.*, 1128–1129.

164. *Ibid.*, 1133.

165. *Ibid.*, 1134.

166. *Ibid.*, 1135–1137.

167. The expert in Arab kinship structure will recognize that I am paying little attention to well known works, and am leaning most heavily on Daghestani, *La Famille . . . , op. cit.*, and at various points am checking his observations with more recent authors.

168. Harris, *Iraq, op. cit.*, p. 68.

169. *Ibid.*

170. Raphael Patai (ed.), *The Republic of Syria* (New Haven: Human Relations Area Files, 1956), pp. 181–182. See also diagrams on pp. 183–184.

171. Raphael Patai (ed.), *Jordan* (New Haven: Human Relations Area Files, 1957), pp. 195–199.

172. Harris, *Egypt, op. cit.*, chap. 19.

173. Daghestani, *La Famille . . . , op. cit.*, pp. 154–155.

174. Weulersse, *op. cit.*, pp. 216–217.

175. E. Bräunlich, "Beiträge zur Gesellschaftsordnung der Arabischen Beduinenstämme," *Islamica*, 6, no. 2 (1933), 78.

176. Patai, in *Syria, op. cit.*, p. 182.

177. Patai, in Harris, *Iraq, op. cit.*, p. 68.

178. Patai, *Jordan, op. cit.*, pp. 194–195.

179. Daghestani, *La Famille . . . , op. cit.*, p. 150.

180. Patai, *Jordan, op. cit.*, p. 203; Daghestani, *La Famille . . . , op. cit.*, pp. 156–198.

181. H. R. P. Dickson, *The Arab of the Desert*, 2d ed. (London: Allen & Unwin, 1951), pp. 114–116.

182. Alois Musil, *The Manners and Customs of the Rwala Bedouins* (New York: American Geographical Society, Oriental Explorations and Studies No. 6, 1928), pp. 46–47.

183. Patai, *The Republic of Syria, op. cit.*, p. 185; and *Jordan, op. cit.*, p. 195.

184. Ammar, *op. cit.*, pp. 44–45.

185. Ammar, *op. cit.*, p. 44.

186. *Ibid.*, p. 47.

187. Patai, *The Republic of Syria, op. cit.*, p. 257.

188. Patai, *Republic of Syria, op. cit.*, p. 340.

189. Berger, *op. cit.*, p. 81.

190. *Preliminary Report on the World Social Situation* (New York: United Nations Secretariat Department of Social Affairs, New York, 1952), p. 162. In 1939, *wakfs* controlled more than 10 per cent of the total cultivated area in Egypt.

191. Patai, *The Republic of Syria, op. cit.*, p. 277. The data are from Doreen Warriner, *Land and Poverty in the Middle East* (London: Royal Institute to International Affairs, 1948), p. 85.

192. Patai, *Jordan, op. cit.*, p. 246.

193. Bräunlich, *op. cit.*, p. 188.

194. Bräunlich, *op. cit.*, p. 227.

195. Josef Henninger, "Die Familie bei den Heutigen Beduinen Arabiens und Seiner Randgebiete," *Internationales Archiv. Fur Ethnographie*, 42 (1943), 133–135.

196. Bräunlich, *op. cit.*, p. 80. For a compendious listing of the relationships and apparent genealogies to be found in these tribes over the past eighty years, see Max Freiherr von Oppenheim, *Die Beduinen*, 2 vols. (Leipzig: Otto Harrassowitz, 1939); his comments on organization are in vol. 1, pp. 22–27, 39. See also, H. Charles, *Tribus Moutonnieres du Moyen-Euphrate, Documents d'Etudes Orientales*, vol. 8, Institute Français de Damas, n.d. (the date of the study was 1936).

197. Ammar, *op. cit.*, pp. 189–199; Violette Dickson, "A Wedding in Kuwait" (1939), in H. R. P. Dickson, *Kuwait and Her Neighbors* (London: Allen & Unwin, 1956), p. 421. See also Daghestani, *La Famille ..., op. cit.*, pp. 58–59.

198. Daghestani, *ibid.*

199. Henry Ayrout, *op. cit.*, p. 148. For considerable detail on the conditions under which a married woman goes to stay in her father's or brother's house for a while when she quarrels with her husband, see Hilma Granqvist, *Marriage Conditions in a Palestinian Village II.* Societas Scientiarum Fennica. Commentationes Humanarum Litterarum 6, No. 8, Helsingfors, 1935, Chapter 9.

200. Winifred S. Blackman, *The Fellahin of Upper Egypt* (London: George A. Harrap, 1927), pp. 38 ff.

201. For the Bedouins, see H. R. P. Dickson's comment on this in *op. cit.*, pp. 143–145.

202. Lane, *op. cit.*, p. 194.

203. Daghestani, *La Famille Musulmane ..., op. cit.*, p. 84.

204. *Ibid.*, p. 84.

205. Granqvist, *op. cit.*, p. 149.

206. Weulersse, *op. cit.*, pp. 223–224.

207. See Lane, *op. cit.*, p. 194, for a description of the leisure hours of the well-to-do Egyptian woman a hundred years ago.

208. Daghestani, *La Famille ..., op. cit.*, p. 80.

209. Miner and DeVos, *op. cit.*, p. 82.

210. Ayrout, *op. cit.*, p. 147, whose data come largely from the 1920s and 1930s in Egypt, noted that the fellah women had more freedom in the city.

211. Fanon, *op. cit.*, pp. 85–86, 101–103.

212. United Nations, *Legal Status of Married Women* (New York: Commission on Status of Women, 1958), pp. 48, 51.

213. Miner and DeVos, *op. cit.*, p. 58.

214. Ammar, *op. cit.*, pp. 53–54.

215. *Ibid.*, p. 55. See also, Ayoub, *op. cit.*, pp. 126–127.

216. The Rwala were, however, much more given to chastising the son (see Musil, *op. cit.*, p. 256); see also the reports in Henninger, *op. cit.*, pp. 103–104.

217. Tovia Ashkenazi, *Tribus Semi-Nomades de la Palestine du Nord* (Paris: Librarie Orientaliste, Paul Geunther), p. 74.

218. See Fanon, *op. cit.*, pp. 98–99, for a change in the relationship between elder and younger brother as a result of the Algerian experience.

219. Ammar, *op. cit.*, pp. 63–66, 83, 94.

220. Kotb, *op. cit.*, chap. 3. See also Gibb, *op. cit.*, pp. 94 ff., for some comments on these modernist attitudes.

221. Kotb, *Ibid.*, p. 53.

222. Jacques Baulin, "Lutte Contre Les Stupefiants et Reformes Sociales en Egypte," *Orient*, 3 (June, 1959), 92–93.

223. Jacques Berque, *Histoire Sociale d'un Village Egyptien au Xieme Siècle* (Paris: Mouton, 1957), p. 44.

224. See Baulin, *op. cit.*, p. 94, for commentaries about whether the various schools did or did not make clitoridectomy a duty. Berque, *op. cit.*, pp. 44–45, describes the decline and the re-emergence of clitoridectomy in the village of Sirsal-Layyan. The practice was disappearing, but about 1911 the women in the village managed to gain a temporary financial advantage, to which the men reacted by reverting to the practice. Again, the exact sequence of events is not so relevant as that the practice did exist, and was used as a tool for social control.

225. United Nations Secretariat, *Newsletter on Status of Women*, Nos. 13, 21; September, 1956 and September, 1960; *International Council of Women Quarterly*

Review, October, 1958, p. 34; *Women of Tunisia*, Secretariat of State for Information and Commerce, Tunisia, April, 1961.

226. Nada Tomiche, "Changing Status of Egyptian Women," *New Outlook*, 1 (September, 1957), pp. 39–40.

227. Aziza Hussein, "Role of Women in Social Reform in Egypt," *Middle East Journal*, 7 (Autumn, 1953), 445.

228. Daghestani, *La Famille . . .* , *op. cit.*, pp. 102–122.

229. *United Nations Statistical Yearbook, 1960.*

230. *Women of Tunisia, op. cit.*

231. Berger, *op. cit.*, p. 152; data from: Muhammad Abd Elmoneim S. Mito, *The Social Change of Daughters' Position in Egyptian Moslem Middle Class Families in Alexandria*, unpub. thesis, Institute of Sociology and Social Science, Alexandria University, 1953.

232. UNESCO: *Access of Girls and Women to Education Outside the School* (January 14, 1960), 60.

233. *Ibid.*, pp. 18, 57.

234. *Time*, June 1, 1962, p. 28.

235. Ibrahim Abdulla Muhyi, "Women in the Arab Middle East," *Journal of Social Issues*, 15, no. 3 (1959), 48, 51.

236. *Ibid.*, pp. 53–54.

237. Berger, *op. cit.*, p. 278.

238. *Ibid.*, p. 279.

239. Michel Lelong, "Femmes Tunisiennes d'Aujourd'hui," *IBLA (L'Institut des Belles Lettres Arabes)*, 22, no. 87 (3ᵉ trimestre, 1959), 355.

240. Pergrouhi Najarian, "Adjustment in the Family and Patterns of Living," *Journal of Social Issues*, 15, no. 3 (1959), 38.

241. Nelly Forget, "Attitudes Towards Work by Women in Morocco," *International Social Science Journal*, 14, no. 1 (1962), 100.

242. *Ibid.*, 110, 117.

243. *Ibid.*, 101–106.

244. *Ibid.*, 109.

245. UNESCO, *Women in Public Services and Functions* (December 8, 1959), 5, 33.

246. *Women of Tunisia, op. cit.*, 30.

247. UNESCO, *Implementation of the Convention on the Political Rights of Women by the States Parties Thereto* (January 11, 1960).

248. Tomiche, *op. cit.*, p. 43.

249. Mboria, *op. cit.*, p. 69.

250. Lane, *op. cit.*, pp. 101–103.

251. For still another kind of case of the ill-advised divorce, see Blackman, *op. cit.*, pp. 95–96.

252. See various examples of this in Granqvist, *op. cit.*, pp. 257 ff.

253. Dickson, *op. cit.*, p. 144.

254. Patai, *Jordan, op. cit.*, p. 295.

255. Harris, *Egypt, op. cit.*, p. 298.

256. *New York Times*, February 22, 1960.

257. United Nations, *Newsletter on Status of Women*, no. 19 (September, 1959).

258. *News from Tunisia*, Bulletin No. 15, January 15, 1960.

259. *Women of Tunisia, op. cit.*, 43.

260. Anne H. Fuller, *op. cit.*, p. 68.

261. Granqvist, *op. cit.*, p. 268.

262. Henry Rosenfeld. "An Analysis of Marriage and Marriage Statistics for a Moslem and Christian Arab Village," *International Archives of Ethnography*, Part II, 48 (1958), 55.

263. Mboria, *op. cit.*, pp. 69–70.

264. See Mboria, *op. cit.*, p. 68, where he criticizes the Egyptian marriage and divorce data.

265. *Lebanon*, (New Haven: Human Relations Area Files Press, 1956), p. 285.

266. United Arab Republic-Syrian Region, *Statistical Abstract 196*, p. 104.

267. The Hashemite Kingdom of Jordan, *Statistical Yearbook, 196*, pp. 53, 58.

268. *Ibid.*, p. 56.

269. United Arab Republic-Syrian Region, *Statistical Abstract*, 1960, p. 104.

270. *Ibid.*, p. 104.

271. *Vital Statistics—1951—II* (Cairo: Republic of Egypt, 1957).

272. Edward Wakin, "Veiled Revolution," *Midstream* (Autumn, 1959) 81.

273. Mboria, *op. cit.*, p. 179.

274. Rosenfeld, "An Analysis of Marriage . . . ," *op. cit.*, p. 55.

275. Goode, *After Divorce, op. cit.*, p. 303.

276. *Vital Statistics, op. cit.*, pp. 1118–1119.

277. Rosenfeld, "An Analysis of Marriage . . . ," *op. cit.*, p. 49.

278. Granqvist, *op. cit.*, pp. 303 ff.

279. Rosenfeld, "An Analysis of Marriage . . . ," *op. cit.*, pp. 56–57.

280. Harris, *Egypt, op. cit.*, p. 293; see also, Ammar, *op. cit.*, p. 42.

281. Daghestani, *La Famille Musulmane . . .* , *op. cit.*, pp. 98–99; and Ashkenazi, *op. cit.*, p. 69.

282. See Rosenfeld, "An Analysis of Marriage . . . ," *op. cit.*, p. 58; and Maurice Gaudefroy-Demombynes, in John P. McGregor (trans.) *Muslim Institutions* (London: Allen & Unwin; second printing, 1954), p. 130.

Chapter IV   Sub-Saharan Africa

1. For a recent summary of the relations among the five distinct language families of major importance and the seven of minor importance, see Joseph H. Greenberg, "Africa as a Linguistic Area," in William R. Bascom and Melville J. Herskovits (eds.), *Continuity and Change in African Culture* (Chicago: University of Chicago Press, 1959), pp. 15–27.

2. Claude Tardits, *Porto-Novo* (Paris: Mouton, 1958), p. 11. (My translation.)

3. For example, George P. Murdock, *Africa* (New York: McGraw-Hill, 1959), pp. 24–32; Simon and Phoebe Ottenberg, *Cultures and Societies of Africa* (New York: Random House, 1960), pp. 28–60; also Arthur Phillips (ed.), *Survey of African Marriage and Family Life* (London: Oxford University Press, 1953), Part I (by L. P. Mair); and *Social Implications of Industrialization and Urbanization in Africa South of the Sahara* (Paris: UNESCO, 1956).

4. George P. Murdock, *Social Structure* (New York: Macmillan, 1959).

5. See the article by Morris Zelditch on the distribution of expressive and instrumental roles in family systems in "Role Differentiation in the Nuclear Family: A Comparative Study," in Talcott Parsons and Robert F. Bales (eds.), *Family, Socialization and Interaction Process* (New York: The Free Press of Glencoe, 1955), chap. 6.

6. Murdock, *Africa, op. cit.*, p. 27.

7. Population estimates for this second largest continent of the world suggest that it contains no more than about 250 million people.

8. L. P. Mair, in Phillips (ed.), *op. cit.*, p. 1.

9. A. R. Radcliffe-Brown, "Introduction," in A. R. Radcliffe-Brown and Daryll Forde (eds.), *African Systems of Kinship and Marriage* (London: Oxford University Press, 1956). Professor Gutkind of Brandeis University has informed me, however, of current work in East Africa that suggests a wider range of marital arrangements, including some types of apparently informal unions. It remains to be seen whether these are individual deviations from the norm in a given society, or socially approved but less formal unions.

10. Murdock, *Africa, op. cit.*, p. 25.

11. As can be seen, at least some of these characteristics may be found individually here and there in the work organization of tribal societies: see Stanley H. Udy, "Three Industrial Forms of Organized Work" in Wilbert E. Moore and Arnold S. Feldman (eds.), *Labor Commitment and Social Change in Developing Areas* (New York: Social Science Research Council, 1960), pp. 78–91.

12. In this context, I believe that the most useful outline of this theory can be found in my two articles, "Norm Commitment and Conformity to Role-Status Obligations," *American Journal of Sociology*, 65 (November, 1960), 246–258; and "A Theory of Role Strain," *American Sociological Review*, 25 (August, 1960), 483–496. A much more elaborate development of some implications of these ideas can be found in George C. Homans, *Social Behavior* (New York: Harcourt Brace, 1961).

13. Immanuel Wallerstein, *Africa* (New York: Vintage Books, 1961), p. 31.

14. *Ibid.*, p. 34.

15. Tanya Baker and Mary Bird, "Urbanization and the Position of Women," *The Sociological Review*, 7 (July, 1959), 107.

16. Arthur Phillips, "Marriage Laws in Africa," in Arthur Phillips (ed.), *op. cit.*, Part 2.

17. Georges Balandier has tabulated the great increase in urbanization in some of Africa's major areas, especially on the West Coast, during the 1940–1950 period in his "Social Changes and Problems in Negro Africa," in Calvin W. Stillman (ed.), *Africa in the Modern World* (Chicago: University of Chicago Press, 1955), p. 56.

18. Georges Balandier, *Brazzaville Noire* (Paris: Cahiers de la Fondation Nationale des Sciences Politiques, Number 67, 1955), p. 135. He says earlier (p. 121) that "The ties of ethnic identity at least in Potopoto are not sufficiently strong to impose identity on the urban population."

19. I. Schapera, "Kinship and Marriage Among the Tswana," in Radcliffe-Brown and Daryll Forde (eds.), *op. cit.*, p. 151.

20. See Mair, in Phillips (ed.), *op. cit.*, pp. 78, 121–124.

21. See Phillips (ed.), *op. cit.*, chap. 4.

22. See J. C. D. Lawrance, *The Iteso* (London: Oxford University Press, 1957), p. 94.

23. Edward C. Hopen, *The Pastoral Fulbe Family in Gwandu* (London: Oxford University Press for the International African Institute, 1958), p. 76.

24. J. H. M. Beattie, "Nyoro Marriage and Affinity," *Africa*, XXVIII (January, 1958), 5.

25. Michael Banton, *West African City: A Study of Tribal Life in Freetown* (London: Oxford University Press, 1957), p. 208.

26. K. L. Little, *The Mende of Sierra Leone: A West African People in Transition* (London: Routledge and Kegan Paul, 1951), p. 149.

27. Godfrey Wilson, "An Essay on the Economics of Detribalization in Northern Rhodesia," Part II, *Rhodes-Livingstone Papers*, No. 6 (Livingstone, Northern Rhodesia: Rhodes-Livingstone Institute, 1942), 52–53; see also Mair, in Phillips (ed.), *op. cit.*, p. 84; and J. A. Barnes, "Marriage in a Changing Society," *Rhodes-Livingstone Papers*, No. 20 (London: Oxford University Press, 1951), pp. 61–62.

28. Ruth Levin, "Marriage in Langa Native Location," *Communications from the School of African Studies* (Cape Town: University of Cape Town, 1947), p. 12.

29. F. Tardits, *op. cit.*, pp. 59–60.

30. For the Kxatla, see I. Schapera, *Married Life in an African Tribe* (New York: Sheridan House, 1941), pp. 43 ff., 56, 352; for southern Nyasaland and the Fort Jameson Ngoni, see Mair, in Phillips (ed.), *op. cit.*, p. 84; and Barnes, *op. cit.*, pp. 61–62.

31. Günter Wagner, *The Changing Family Among the Bantu Kavirondo* (London: Oxford University Press, 1939), pp. 17, 20–21, 22, 25–26, 34, 49, 52.

32. Monica Wilson, Selma Kaplan, Theresa Maki, Edith M. Walton, *Keiskammahoek Rural Survey* (Pietermaritzburg: Shuter and Shooter, 1952), p. 81.

33. Monica Wilson, *The People of the Nyasa-Tanganyika Corridor* (Cape Town: University of Cape Town, Communications from the School of African Studies, 1958), pp. 29, 60; and Edwin Ardener, "Coastal Bantu of the Cameroons," *Ethnographic Survey of Africa*, Western Africa, II (1956), 62.

34. Levin, *op. cit.*, p. 57; Ellen Hellmann, *Rooiyard*, *Rhodes-Livingstone Papers*, No. 13 (Livingstone, Northern Rhodesia: Rhodes-Livingstone Institute, 1958), p. 81; see also Phillips, *Survey*, *op. cit.*, pp. 26, 36–37, 38, 58, 67, 70, 104, 110, 146–147, 148, See *Social Implications*, *op. cit.*, pp. 186, 197,

405 ff., 411 ff., 567–568, 620. For Livingstone, see Meran McCulloch, *A Social Survey of the African Population of Livingstone* (Manchester: Manchester University Press, 1956), p. 19.

35. Pierre Clément, "Social Patterns of Urban Life," in *Social Implications*, *op. cit.*, p. 404.

36. Gray has devoted extensive analysis to the economic aspect of these "purchases." See Robert F. Gray, "Sonjo Bride-Price and the Question of African 'Wife Purchase'," *American Anthropologist*, 62 (February, 1960), 34–57.

37. A. Phillips, "Marriage and Divorce Laws in East Africa," *Journal of African Law*, 3 (Summer, 1959), 95.

38. Edward H. Winter, *Bwamba: A Structural-Functional Analysis of a Patrilineal Society* (Cambridge: W. Heffer & Sons, 1956), p. 21. Note also, however, that another change among the Bwamba has been the substitution of bride wealth for the exchange of women. Formerly both systems were used.

39. Wilbur C. Hallenbeck (ed.), *The Baumanville Community: A Study of Family Life of Urban Africans* (University of Watal: Institute for Social Research, 1955), pp. 92–93.

40. Mair, in Phillips (ed.), *op. cit.*, p. 130.

41. Arthur Phillips, "Recent French Legislation Concerning African Marriage," *Africa*, 22 (January, 1952), 66 ff.; Mair, in Phillips (ed.), *op. cit.*, pp. 67 ff., notes a number of places in East Africa where the amount of marriage payment has increased. Eveline R. G. King, "On Educating African Girls in Northern Rhodesia," in *Human Problems in British Central Africa*, 10 (1950), 66, notes that fathers expect a higher bride price for educated daughters. Monica Wilson et al., *op. cit.*, p. 84, describes the rural Keiskammahoek pattern of elopement with the connivance of the bride's father in order to avoid an expensive marriage ceremony. Schapera also reports, in "Kinship and Marriage Among the Tswana," in Radcliffe-Brown and Forde, *op. cit.*, p. 150, that among two tribes bride cattle were abolished toward the end of the last century, and that many Christians in other tribes have also abandoned it.

42. P. P. Howell, "Observation on the Shilluk of the Upper Nile," *Customary Law: Marriage and the Violation of Rights in Women*, *Africa*, XXIII, no. 2 (April, 1953), 94–109.

43. *Ibid.*, p. 149.

44. Leonard W. Doob, *Becoming More Civilized* (New Haven: Yale University Press, 1960), p. 302.

45. Schapera, in Radcliffe-Brown and Forde, *op. cit.*, pp. 158, 163. The aim of such marriages was not so much to "keep the blood clear" as to obtain political advantage.

46. *Ibid.*, p. 151.

47. Meyer Fortes, "Kinship and Marriage Among the Ashanti," in Radcliffe-Brown and Forde, *op. cit.*, p. 282.

48. Laura Longmore, *The Dispossessed: A Study of the Sex-Life of Bantu Women in Urban Areas in and Around Johannesburg* (London: Jonathon Cape, 1959), p. 30.

49. Hopen, *op. cit.*, p. 53.

50. A. Phillips, "Marriage and Divorce Laws in East Africa," *Journal of African Law*, 3 (Summer, 1959), 95.

51. Doob, *op. cit.*, p. 302.

52. Banton, *op. cit.*, p. 199; and Little, *op. cit.*, p. 147. See also Kenneth Little, "Some Patterns of Marriage and Domesticity in West Africa," *The Sociological Review*, 7 (July, 1959), 69.

53. See Levin, *op. cit.*, pp. 16–17; Ellen Hellmann, *Rooiyard*, *op. cit.*, pp. 11, 112.

54. We shall probably never know what the United States figure was, either, although the usual estimate is 26 years. Marriage registration was in an undeveloped state at the turn of the century. For a full scale critique of United States data, see Thomas C. Monahan, *The Pattern of Age at Marriage in the United States*, 2 vols. (Philadelphia: Stevenson Brothers, 1951). See also Paul H. Jacobson, *Marriage and Divorce* (New York: Rinehart, 1959), pp. 21 ff., 75.

55. See Kingsley Davis and Judith Blake, "Social Structure and Fertility," *Economic Development and Social Change*, 4 (April, 1956), 211–235, for the many ways by which the customs of a society not using contraceptives may reduce fertility below the maximum.

56. Vernon Dorjahn, "The Factor of Polygamy in African Demography," in Bascom and Herskovits (eds.), *op. cit.*, p. 110.

57. H. V. Muhsam, "Fertility of Polygamous Marriages," *Population Studies*, 10 (July, 1956) 3–16.

58. A. M. Carr-Saunders had noted Africa's relatively low birth rate during the 1930s in *World Population* (Oxford: Clarendon Press, 1936), pp. 300 ff.

59. A. W. Southall, "The Position of Women and the Stability of Marriage," in Aiden Southall (ed.), *Social Change in Modern Africa* (London: Oxford University Press, 1961), p. 46.

60. For the Ibo, see Phoebe V. Ottenberg, "The Changing Economic Position of Women Among the Afikpo Ibo," in Bascom and Herskovits (eds.), *op. cit.*, pp. 20–21; and for a comparison of the Agni with the Ashanti, see Robert A. Lystad, "Marriage and Kinship Among the Ashanti and the Agni: A Study of Differential Acculturation," in *ibid.*, pp. 193, 198.

61. J. Lombard, "Cotonou, ville africaine," *Bull. IFAN*, 16 (July–October, 1954), 341–377.

62. K. L. Little, *op. cit.*, pp. 10–11; A. W. Southall, "Determinants of the Social Structure of African Urban Populations, With Special Reference to Kampala (Uganda)," in *Social Implications, op. cit.*, p. 568; Georges Balandier, *op. cit.*, p. 145.

63. I have described this process in some detail in "Illegitimacy in the Caribbean Social Structure," *American Sociological Review*, 25 (February, 1960), 21–30. Judith Blake has given an intensive analysis of the situation in Jamaica in her *Family Life in Jamaica* (New York: The Free Press of Glencoe, 1961). For the New World generally, see my "Illegitimacy, Anomie, and Cultural Penetration," *American Sociological Review*, 26 (December, 1961), 910–925. Southall, *op. cit.*, p. 47, describes a similar pattern for urban Africa.

64. Southall, *op. cit.*, p. 48.

65. A. I. Richards, *Economic Development and Tribal Change* (Cambridge University Press, 1953), pp. 265, 267.

66. Gordon Wilson, "Mombasa—A Modern Colonial Municipality," in Southall, *op. cit.*, p. 111.

67. See my previously cited article, "Illegitimacy, . . ."

68. Meran McCulloch, "Survey of Recent and Current Field Studies on the Social Effects of Economic Development in Inter-Tropical Africa," in *Social Implications, op. cit.*, p. 197. See also A. W. Southall, "Determinants of the Social Structure of African Urban Populations," with special reference to Kampala (Uganda), in *ibid.*, p. 568; E. Hellmann, "The Development of Social Groupings Among Urban Africans in the Union of South Africa," in *ibid.*, pp. 734–736. See Mair, *op. cit.*, in Phillips (ed.), pp. 22–24 (Kxatla), 26–27 (Pondo), 30–31 (urban South Africa), 104 (Central Africa: Bemba); but note, pp. 108–109, how much control the Bemba in urban Broken Hill still retained over the young as late as the 1930s.

69. Pierre Clément, "Social Patterns of Urban Life," in *Social Implications, op. cit.*, p. 419. See also pp. 405 ff., 420–421, 620.

70. Monica Wilson *et al., op. cit.*, pp. 126–127.

71. Miriam Janisch, "A Study of African Income and Expenditure," (City of Johannesburg: Non-European and Native Affairs Department, December, 1941), p. 7.

72. E. Hellmann, "The Development of Social Groupings, . . ." in *Social Implications, op. cit.*, pp. 731–732.

73. Balandier, *op. cit.*, pp. 138–140.

74. Janisch, *op. cit.*, pp. 8–9. See also a study of the Lakeside Tonga, cited in J. Clyde Mitchell, "Labor Migration and the Tribe," in *Listener*, 56 (October, 1956), 646–647.

75. Vernon R. Dorjahn, *op. cit.*, pp. 102–105. He also reports (p. 100) that polygyny in Swaziland and Basutoland is decreasing.

76. Banton, *op. cit.*, p. 217, notes that women are critical of polygyny.

77. Wilbur T. Hallenbeck (ed.), *The Baumanville Community* (Natal: University of Natal Institute for Social Research, 1955), p. 89. In the Freetown sample, out of the 252 males aged 25 years and over, 137 had one wife, ten had two, and only two men had three wives (*ibid.*, p. 98). In the African center at Elisabethville in 1950, only 4 per cent of 4 thousand men were in polygynous unions; and in the urban slum area of Rooiyard there was only one polygynous household (Meran McCulloch, "Survey of Recent and Current Field Studies, . . ." in *Social Implications, op. cit.*, p. 164). The Elizabethville study is by M. Grévisse, *Le Centre Extra-Coutumier d'Elizabethville*, Centre d'Etude des Problemes Sociaux Indigènes, Bulletin No. 15, Hellmann, *op. cit.*, p. 80. Only 6 per cent of 3,500 women in Broken Hill were polygynously married (Godfrey Wilson, *op. cit.*, p. 64). The influence of the missions also has had some effect on the decline of polygyny (Edwin Ardener, "Coastal Bantu of the Cameroons," *Ethnographic Survey of Africa, West Africa*, 11 [1956], 65) as indicated in a study of the Kpe (British Cameroons).

78. Kenneth Little, "Some Patterns of Marriage and Domesticity in West Africa," *The Sociological Review*, 7 (July, 1959), 72–73.

79. *Ibid.*

80. Mair, in Philips (ed.), *op. cit.*, p. 137.

81. Hopen, *op. cit., p.* 145.

82. J. Davidson, "Protestant Missions and Marriage in the Belgian Congo," *Africa*, 18 (April, 1948), 125.

83. Mair, in Phillips (ed.), *op. cit.*, pp. 112–113; and J. Van Wing, "La Polygamie aux Congo Belge," *Africa*, 17 (1947), 93–102. These reports are from the World-War-II period.

84. Banton, *op. cit.*, p. 202.

85. Hellman, "The Development of Social Groupings, . . ." in *Social Implications, op. cit.*, pp. 732–733.

86. Little, *op. cit.*, pp. 65–67.

87. Balandier, *op. cit.*, p. 130.

88. Hopen, *op. cit.*, p. 79. He is speaking of the Fulbe here.

89. P. C. Lloyd, "The Yoruba Town Today," *The Sociological Review*, 7 (July, 1959), 51, 58–59.

90. J. van Velsen, "Labor Migration as a Positive Factor in the Continuity of Tonga Tribal Society," in Southall, *op. cit.*, pp. 230–241.

91. Baker and Bird, *op. cit.*, p. 114.

92. Acquah, *op. cit.*, p. 81.

93. Balandier, *op. cit.*, p. 126, asserts however, that such links are not common.

94. *Ibid.*, p. 127.

95. Hopen, *op. cit.*, p. 105.

96. *Ibid.*

97. *Ibid.*, p. 108; and Tanya Baker and Mary Bird, "Urbanization and the Position of Women," *The Sociological Review*, 7 (July, 1959), 118.

98. Michael Banton, *West African City* (London: Oxford University Press; 1957), p. 217.

99. Phillips, *Survey, op. cit.*, pp. 71–72. Phillips also records an example of the typical exaggeration of men in these matters, by noting that the Nkundo (Belgian Congo) men claim that European authorities have so restrained the men that Nkundo wives have become insolent and their husbands have become slaves (*ibid.*, p. 111).

100. Brazzaville, *op. cit.*, p. 134.

101. The Keiskammahoek Rural Survey asserts, however, that whereas women formerly controlled a field and its produce, since land has become scarcer it is allocated to and inherited by men (see *ibid.*, pp. 107–108).

102. Baker and Bird, *op. cit.*, p. 111, also note that this process has been taking place among the Yoruba. It is also reported, with reference to inheritance in Busia's study of Sekondi-Takoradi. Note also Phillips, *Survey, op. cit.*, p. 261, for the French territories.

103. Ione Acquah, *Accra Survey* (London: University of London Press, 1958), p. 85. S. Hofstra has reported such associations for British West Africa, French West Africa, and Equatorial Africa in his "Die Betekenis van Enkele nieuwere Groupsverschijnselen vor de Sociale Integratie van Verandenend Africa," *Mededeling Konig. Nedenl. Akad. Wetensch*, 18, no. 14 (1955), 343–377.

104. J. F. Holleman, "The African Woman in Town and Tribe," *Listener*, 56 (October, 1956), 496.

105. Pius Okigbo, "Social Consequences of Economic Development in West Africa," *Annals of the American Academy of Political and Social Science*, 305 (May, 1956), 127. Here, the mechanization of palm oil extraction has been a threat to the wife's income from hand processing of oil. See also the Keiskammahoek survey noted earlier (in Brazzaville, *op. cit.*, p. 108), which found that women have lost some of their rights over land and must now accept more fully their husbands' supervision.

106. See David M. Schneider and Kathleen Gough (eds.), *Matrilineal Kinship* (Berkeley: University of California, 1961).

107. A. St. J. J. Hannigan, "The Present System of Succession Amongst the Akan People of the Gold Coast," *Journal of African Administration*, 6 (October, 1954), 166–171. See also Meyer Fortes, "Kinship and Marriage Among the Ashanti," in Radcliffe-Brown and Forde (eds.), *op. cit.*, p. 271.

108. J. Comhaire, "Some Aspects of Urbanization in the Belgian Congo," *American Journal of Sociology*, 62 (July, 1956), 8–13.

109. Daryll Forde, "Double Descent Among the Yakö," in Radcliffe-Brown and Forde (eds.), *op. cit.*, p. 309. Since the Yakö recognize both lineages, they have tried to resolve the conflict by having the boy marry a girl of another lineage within his own matriclan.

110. *Ibid.*, p. 331.

111. Meran McCulloch, "The Ovimbundu of Angola," in Darryll Forde (ed.), *Ethnographic Survey of Africa* (London: International African Institute, 1952), p. 23.

112. N. De Cleene, "La Famille dans L'Organisation Sociale du MaYombe," *Africa*, 10 (January, 1937), 5–6, 8–10.

113. Mair, in Phillips (ed.), *op. cit.*, p. 77.

114. Meyer Fortes, "Time and the Social Structure: An Ashanti Case Study," in

M. Fortes (ed.), *Social Structure* (Oxford: Clarendon Press, 1949), pp. 66, 75, 77.

115. C. L. Bohannan, "Dahomean Marriage, A Reevaluation," *Africa*, 19 (1959), 273–278.

116. J. C. Mitchell, "Social Change and the Stability of African Marriage in Northern Rhodesia," in Southall, *op. cit.*, p. 318.

117. L. A. Fallers, "Some Determinants of Marriage Stability in Busoga: A Reformulation of Gluckman's Hypothesis," *Africa*, 27 (April, 1957), 106–121.

118. In Southall, *op. cit.*, p. 328. He presented some data on this point in "Aspects of African Marriage on the Copper Belt of Northern Rhodesia," *Rhodes-Livingstone Journal*, No. 22, 1957, p. 10.

119. Elizabeth Colson, *Marriage and the Family Among the Plateau Tonga of Northern Rhodesia* (Manchester: Manchester University Press), pp. 175–181.

120. Clément, *op. cit.*, p. 423.

121. Mair, in Phillips (ed.), *op. cit.*, p. 144, from an unpublished report by M. G. Smith; for other regions, see pp. 26, 42–44, 67, 71, 99, 104–106.

122. J. C. Mitchell, *Yao Village* (Manchester: Manchester University Press, 1956), p. 186.

123. Godfrey Wilson, *op. cit.*, p. 41; and Mitchell, in Southall (ed.), *op. cit.*, p. 322.

124. Mitchell, in *Human Problems*, 22 (September, 1957), *op. cit.*, p. 8.

125. Edwin Ardener, "Social and Demographic Problems of the Southern Cameroons Plantation Area," in Southall, *op. cit.*, pp. 51–52, 93–94. See also his "Coastal Bantu of the Cameroons," *Ethnographic Survey of Africa, Western Africa*, 11 (1956), 65.

126. Alison Izzett, "Family Life Among the Yoruba, in Lagos, Nigeria," in Southall, *op. cit.*, pp. 314–315. See also P. Marria, "Slum Clearance and Family Life in Lagos," *Human Organization*, no. 19 (Fall, 1960), 126–128, where he notes that the relocation in a housing estate actually caused a higher divorce rate because of the greater difficulty of making a living so far from the main commercial area.

127. A. L. Epstein, "Divorce Law and the Stability of Marriage Among the Lunda of Kazembe," *Human Problems in British Central Africa*, 14 (1954), 12.

128. Elliot P. Skinner, "Labor Migration and its Relationship to Socio-Cultural Change in Mossi Society," *Africa*, 30 (October, 1960), 388–391.

129. Mair, in Phillips (ed.), *op. cit.*, p. 145.

130. Meyer Fortes, *The Web of Kinship Among the Tallensi* (London: Oxford University Press, 1949), p. 84.

131. Gustave Jahoda, "Love, Marriage, and Social Change: Letters to the Advice Column of a West African Newspaper," *Africa*, 31 (April, 1959), 177–189.

132. A. Phillips, "Marriage and Divorce Laws in East Africa," *Journal of African Law*, no. 3 (Summer, 1959), 97. He is writing especially of Kenya, Uganda, and Tanganyika.

133. Lloyd A. Fallers, "Changing Customary Law in Busoga District of Uganda," *Journal of African Administration*, 8 (July, 1956), 142.

134. Lloyd A. Fallers, *Bantu Bureaucracy* (Cambridge: W. Heffer & Son, 1956), p. 122. See also his discussion, cited earlier, on the determinants of marriage stability in *Africa*, 32 (April, 1957), p. 106–121.

135. Rhona Sofer, "Adaptation Problems of Africans in an Early Phase of Industrialization at Jinja (Uganda)," in *Social Implications*, *op. cit.*, pp. 620–621.

136. "Determinants of the Social Structure of African Urban Populations, With Special Reference to Kampala (Uganda)," by A. W. Southall, in *Social Implications*, *op. cit.*, p. 569.

137. Monica Wilson, "Nyakyusa Kinship," in Radcliffe-Brown and Forde, *op. cit.*, p. 135.

138. Pamela Gulliver and P. H. Gulliver, in Daryll Forde (ed.), *The Central Nilo-Hamites, Ethnographic Survey of Africa* (London: International African Institute, 1953), p. 24, Part 7.

139. P. P. Howell, "Some Observations on Divorce Among the Nuer," *Journal of the Royal Anthropological Institute*, 83 (July-December, 1953), 136–146. See also E. E. Evans-Pritchard, "Bride-Wealth and the Stability of Marriage," *Man*, no. 122 (May, 1953), 80.

140. A. W. Southall, "The Position of Women and the Stability of Marriage," in Southall (ed.), *op. cit.*, p. 66.

141. Colson, *op. cit.*, p. 214.

142. A. Phillips, "Marriage and Divorce, . . ." *op. cit.*, p. 97.

143. W. Brown, "Status of Uganda Women in Relation to Marriage Laws," *African Woman*, 4 (December, 1960), 60.

144. Lloyd A. Fallers, *Bantu Bureaucracy* (Cambridge: W. Heffer, 1956), p. 85.

145. Keiskammahoek Rural Survey, *op. cit.*, p. 92.

146. Doob, *op. cit.*, p. 302.

147. See the use of categories for specifying "anomie" in my "Illegitimacy, Anomie, and Cultural Penetration," *op. cit.*, pp. 919–920.

148. Jahoda, *op. cit.*, I and II, *passim*.

149. *Ibid.*, I, pp. 43–44.

Chapter V   Changing Family Patterns in India

1. On the differences between the rapidly built cities of the West and the more settled ancient cities like Lahore, Timbuktu, or Samarkand, see Gideon Sjöberg, *The Preindustrial City* (New York: The Free Press of Glencoe, 1960).

2. Kingsley Davis, *The Population of India and Pakistan* (Princeton: Princeton University Press, 1951), pp. 1–7.

3. Philip M. Hauser (ed.), *Urbanization in Asia and the Far East* (Calcutta: UNESCO, 1957), pp. 99, 101.

4. Hauser, *op. cit.*, pp. 167, 183.

5. Davis, *op. cit.*, p. 215.

6. See the comparisons in *Statistical Abstract of the United States 1961* (Washington, D.C.: U.S. Government Printing Office, 1961), p. 930.

7. Davis, *op. cit.*, chap. 18.

8. Davis, *op. cit.*, pp. 216–218; see also

Joseph W. Elder, *Industrialism in Hindu Society*, Ph.D. diss., Harvard University, 1959, pp. 336 ff., for the various ways in which the English hampered industrialization.

9. H. Gray, "Education," in A. R. Caton (ed.), *The Key of Progress* (London: Oxford University Press, 1930), p. 11.

10. Elder, *op. cit.*, p. 50.

11. Hauser, *op. cit.*, p. 136.

12. Davis, *op. cit.*, p. 72.

13. Hauser, *op. cit.*, p. 124. See also pp. 16 ff.

14. See A. S. Altekar, *The Position of Women in Hindu Civilization* (Banaras: Motilal Banarsidas, 1956), pp. 35–49; and Pandhari-Nath Prabhu, *Hindu Social Organization*, rev. ed. (Bombay: Popular Book Depot, 1954), pp. 153–155, for a description of these types.

15. Altekar, *op. cit.*, pp. 32–34.
16. See Mohinder Singh, *The Depressed Classes* (Bombay: Hind Kitabs, 1947), pp. 170–171, for other courtship practices among outcastes.
17. E. Kathleen Gough, "The Nayars and the Definition of Marriage," *Journal of the Royal Anthropological Institute*, Part I, 89 (1959), 23–25; see also M. S. A. Rao, *Social Change in Malabar* (Bombay: Popular Book Depot, 1957), chaps. 4, and 5.
18. See Singh, *op. cit.*, pp. 165–166, for the rule as well as some exceptions.
19. For comments on this group, see Irawati Karvé, *Kinship Organization in India* (Poona: Deccan College Monograph Series No. 11, 1953), pp. 58 ff.; K. M. Kapadia, *Marriage and Family in India*, 2d ed. (Bombay: Oxford University Press, 1959), pp. 127 ff.; and Altekar, *op. cit.*, pp. 73–74.
20. S. C. Dube, *Indian Village* (London: Routledge and Kegan Paul, 1955), pp. 42–44.
21. Kapadia, *op. cit.*, pp. 1–9.
22. Milton Singer (ed.), *Traditional India* (Philadelphia: American Folklore Society, 1959), p. xviii.
23. Karvé, *op. cit.*, p. 117.
24. For a diagram of the traditional counting method, see Karvé, *op. cit.*, p. 56.
25. Kapadia, *op. cit.*, p. 130.
26. Oscar Lewis, "Peasant Culture in India and Mexico: A Comparative Analysis," in McKim Marriott (ed.), *Village India* (Chicago: University of Chicago Press, 1955), p. 163.
27. See Kapadia, *op. cit.*, pp. xxvi–xxvii, 143, 172.
28. See Prabhu, *op. cit.*, pp. 180–181; as well as Altekar, *op. cit.*, pp. 68–69.
29. Altekar, *op. cit.*, p. 71.
30. Aileen D. Ross, *The Hindu Family in Its Urban Setting* (Toronto: University of Toronto Press, 1961), pp. 261–264, cites several figures within this range, and notes that in a debate in the United Provinces Legislative Council various dowry levels were mentioned for men in different kinds of occupations: 4 to 5 thousand rupees for lecturers in colleges and universities, as against 30 to 40 thousand for officials in the national bureaucracy.
31. Singh, *op. cit.*, p. 163.
32. Dube, *op. cit.*, pp. 190–191, asserts that the price might vary between 500 and one thousand rupees.
33. Singh, *op. cit.*, p. 164; and Dube, *op. cit.*, p. 119.
34. Ross, *op. cit.*, pp. 239–240.

35. Gray, *op. cit.*, p. 16.
36. G. S. Ghurye, *Caste and Class in India* (Bombay: Popular Book Depot, 1957), p. 238.
37. Kapadia, *op. cit.*, p. 119.
38. K. M. Kapadia, "Changing Patterns of Hindu Marriage and Family II," *Sociological Bulletin*, 3 (September, 1954), 136–137.
39. *Ibid.*, pp. 139–140.
40. Elder, *op. cit.*, pp. 411, 415, 439.
41. Kapadia, *Marriage and Family . . . , op. cit.*, p. 119.
42. Ross, *op. cit.*, p. 270.
43. *Monthly Public Opinion Surveys of the Indian Institute of Public Opinion*, 1 (October, 1955), 1, 2.
44. It should be kept in mind that Calcutta is in Bengal and the Bengal area is perhaps the most literate of the major Indian states.
45. *Monthly Public Opinion Surveys . . . , op. cit.*, pp. 18–19.
46. *Ibid.*, p. 30.
47. *Ibid.*, pp. 19–31.
48. K. M. Kapadia, "Changing Patterns of Hindu Marriage and Family," *Sociological Bulletin*, 3 (March, 1954), 79.
49. William A. Morrison, "Family Types in Badlapur: An Analysis of a Changing Institution in a Maharashtrian Village," *Sociological Bulletin*, 8 (September, 1959), 47.
50. Noel P. Gist, "Caste Differentials in South India," *American Sociological Review*, 19 (April, 1954), 126–127; and "Mate Selection and Mass Communication in India," *Public Opinion Quarterly*, 17 (Winter, 1953), 481–495.
51. E. Kathleen Gough, "The Social Structure of a Tanjore Village," in Marriott, *op. cit.*, p. 49.
52. See Ghurye, *op. cit.*, chap. 10, for a commentary on such incidents.
53. Ross, *op. cit.*, p. 252.
54. K. M. Kapadia, "Changing Patterns of Hindu Marriage . . . ," *op. cit.*, 70–71.
55. *Monthly Public Opinion Surveys . . . , op. cit.*, 8, 23.
56. *Monthly Public Opinion Surveys of the Indian Institute of Public Opinion*, 1 (November, 1955), 35.
57. See Kapadia's summary of some of these relationships in "Changing Patterns of Hindu Marriage . . . ," *op. cit.*, 80 ff.
58. Ghurye, *op. cit.*, pp. 205–222.
59. *New York Times*, Wednesday, May 10, 1961.
60. *Monthly Public Opinion Surveys*

of the Indian Institute of Public Opinion, 1 (November, 1955), 40.

61. K. T. Merchant, *Changing Views of Marriage and Family* (Madras: B. G. Paul, 1935), pp. 109, 111.

62. Karvé, *op. cit.*, p. 117.

63. Dube, *op. cit.*, pp. 40 ff., 119.

64. Altekar, *op. cit.*, p. 75.

65. See also other relevant commentaries in Kapadia, *Marriage and Family* ..., *op. cit.*, pp. 125 ff.

66. *Ibid.*, p. 130.

67. *Ibid.*, p. 133; according to Kapadia, the Chit Pavan Brahmins seem to have stopped cross-cousin marriage only recently.

68. Ghurye, *op. cit.*, p. 136. However, he cites as his authority for this statement the *U.P. Census Report, 1911.*

69. Karvé, *op. cit.*, pp. 144, 152, 154, 156. On p. 154 she lists others among whom this pattern may exist.

70. Karvé, *op. cit.*, pp. 142, 192.

71. Here I am following the suggestions of George C. Homans and David M. Schneider, *Marriage, Authority, and Final Cause* (New York: The Free Press of Glencoe, 1955). They are generally commenting on unilateral cross-cousin marriage where a society's *explicit* values are in favor of it (see especially pp. 23–25).

72. Gough, "The Nayars and the Definition of Marriage," *op. cit.*, p. 24.

73. Prabhu, *op. cit.*, pp. 197–199.

74. *Ibid.*, pp. 197–199; Altekar, *op. cit.*, pp. 84–87, 104 ff.; and Kapadia, *op. cit.*, pp. 97 ff.

75. *Census of India, 1901*, Vol. I, Part 1 (Calcutta: Office of the Superintendent of Government Printing, India, 1903), p. 447.

76. See report by E. A. Gait in *Census of India, 1911*, Vol. I, Part 1 (Calcutta: Superintendent of Government Printing, India, 1913), p. 246.

77. Dube, *op. cit.*, pp. 122, 132.

78. D. N. Kale, *Agris* (Bombay: Asia Publishing House, 1952), pp. 210–211, 242–244.

79. In this section, I am following Kapadia's summary, in *Marriage and Family* ..., *op. cit.*, pp. 113–115.

80. Altekar, *op. cit.*, p. 87.

81. *Monthly Public Opinion Surveys of the Indian Institute of Public Opinion*, 1 (October, 1955), 14, 27–28.

82. *Census of India, 1901, op. cit.*, p. 447.

83. Kapadia, *Marriage and Family* ..., *op. cit.*, p. 91.

84. *Census of India, 1901, op. cit.*, p. 448.

85. *Census of India, 1911, op. cit.*, p. 239.

86. *Ibid.*, p. 241.

87. Kapadia, *Marriage and Family* ..., *op. cit.*, p. 63.

88. S. Chandrasekhar, *Population and Planned Parenthood in India*, 2d ed. (London: Allen & Unwin, 1961).

89. Davis, *op. cit.*, pp. 71–73. See also Abram J. Jaffe, "Urbanization and Fertility," *American Journal of Sociology*, 48 (July, 1942), 48–60, for a demonstration of this difference in other nations in the past.

90. Davis, *op. cit.*, pp. 73–74.

91. *Ibid.*, pp. 75–76.

92. N. Z. Sovani, *The Social Survey of Kolhapur City*, Part 1—"Population and Fertility" (Poona: Gokhale Institute of Politics and Economics), Publication No. 18, 1948, and V. M. Dandekar and Kumudini Dandekar, *Survey of Fertility and Mortality in Poona District*, Publication No. 27 (Poona: Gokhale Institute of Politics and Economics, 1953), p. 67.

93. Davis, *op. cit.*, p. 226.

94. *Ibid.*, p. 227. In the middle 1930s Margaret Sanger also toured India.

95. Chandrasekhar, *op. cit.*, pp. 95–99 ff.

96. *Ibid.*, p. 117.

97. Davis, *op. cit.*, p. 227, cites this study, which had not been published at the time.

98. Gunial B. Desai, *Women in Modern Gujarati Life*, unpub. M.A. thesis, University of Bombay, 1945. For these materials I am indebted to Pravin M. Visaria, Demographic Training and Research Center, Chembur, Bombay.

99. Chandrakant S. Patil, *A Socio-Economic Survey of the Middle-Class in Bombay*, unpub. M.A. thesis, University of Bombay, 1956. Data sent to me by Pravin M. Visaria.

100. Ashish Boz, "The Population Puzzle in India," *Economic Development and Cultural Change*, 7 (April, 1959), 244. For further relevant data, see Dandekar and Dandekar, *op. cit.*, pp. 144, 172, 173.

101. J. N. Sinha, "Differential Fertility and Family Limitation in an Urban Community of Uttar Pradesh," *Population Studies*, 11 (November, 1957), 165 ff.

102. A. S. Patel, "A Study of Attitudes of University Students," *Journal of the Maharaja Sayajirao, University of Baroda*, 9 (March, 1960). These data were supplied to me by Pravin M. Visaria.

103. William A. Morrison, *The Relation of Family Size and Social-Cultural Variables to Attitudes Toward Family Planning*

in a Village of India, Ph.D. diss., University of Connecticut, 1957, pp. 29–31.

104. William A. Morrison, "Attitudes of Females Towards Family Planning in a Maharashtrian Village," *Milbank Memorial Fund Quarterly*, 35 (January, 1957), 69–71.

105. *Ibid.*, p. 74.

106. William A. Morrison, "Attitudes of Males Towards Family Planning in a Western Indian Village," *Milbank Memorial Fund Quarterly*, 34 (July, 1956), 274–281.

107. *Monthly Public Opinion Surveys of the Indian Institute of Public Opinion*, 4 (December, 1958), 1.

108. *Ibid.*, pp. 14–16.

109. See, for example, S. Chandrasekhar, "Attitudes of Baroda Mothers Towards Family Planning," in *Proceedings of the Third International Conference on Planned Parenthood* (Bombay: Family Planning Association of India, 1953), pp. 68–72; B. Singh, "Action Research in Family Planning," in *Proceedings of the Fifth International Conference on Planned Parenthood* (London: International Planned Parenthood Federation, n.d.), pp. 71–74; R. Vasatahni, "Acceptance of Family Planning in a Rural Study," *Journal of Family Welfare*, 3 (January–February, 1957), 14–19; and the account of "Family Planning in Asia," given by Marshall C. Balfour at the Population Association meetings in New York, May 5–6, 1961, reported in *Population Index*, 27 (July, 1961), 212.

110. G. S. Ghurye, "Social Change in Maharashtra, Part II," *Sociological Bulletin*, 3 (March, 1954), 42–50. This study is based on fictional and biographical materials.

111. Shri Nayaran Agarwala, *The Mean Age at Marriage in India as Ascertained from Census Data*, Ph.D. diss., Princeton University, 1957, Vol. 1, Part 2; the data are calculated from *Census of India, 1891*, pp. 155–170.

112. Kapadia, "Changing Patterns of Hindu Marriage ...," *op. cit.*, 68.

113. Singh, *op. cit.*, Appendix XVI, presumably calculated from the 1931 Census of India.

114. Oscar Lewis, *Village Life in Northern India* (Urbana: University of Illinois Press, 1958), pp. 159–160.

115. G. S. Ghurye, "Sex Habits of a Sample of Middle Class People of Bombay," Second All-India Population and Family Hygiene Conference, 1939, cited in Kapadia, *Marriage and Family ...*, *op. cit.*, p. 160.

116. G. B. Desai, *Woman in Modern Gujarati Life*, 1945, cited in Kapadia, *idem*, p. 161.

117. Altekar, *op. cit.*, p. 62; for comment on the development of the laws, see Kapadia, *Marriage and Family ...*, *op. cit.*, pp. 149–156.

118. Merchant, *op. cit.*, pp. 99–100.

119. Kapadia, *Marriage and Family ...*, *op. cit.*, pp. 164–165.

120. Kapadia, "Changing Patterns of Hindu Marriage ...," *op. cit.*, 68.

121. A. Bopegamage, "India's Population Grows Young," *Sociological Bulletin*, 8 (March, 1959), 81. Of course, this age is incorrect for the United States, too.

122. Altekar, *op. cit.*, p. 62, asserts that middle-class women now marry at about 20 to 21 years of age.

123. Ross, *op. cit.*, pp. 249–250.

124. Dube, *op. cit.*, p. 132. See also Singh, *op. cit.*, p. 158.

125. Altekar, *op. cit.*, p. 8.

126. Kapadia, *Marriage and Family ...*, *op. cit.*, pp. 91, 110.

127. *Census of India, 1901*, Vol. 1, Part 1, Report, pp. 115–116.

128. *Ibid.*, pp. 115–121.

129. *Census of India, 1911*, Vol. 1, Part 1, Report, pp. 215–216.

130. *Ibid.*, p. 218.

131. *Ibid.*, p. 47.

132. *Census of India, 1951*, Vol. 1, Part 2-A, Demographic Tables (Delhi, 1955), p. 153.

133. *Census of India, 1901*, Vol. 1, Part 1, Report, p. 33.

134. *Ibid.*

135. *Census of India, 1911*, Vol. 1, Part 1, Report, p. 46.

136. *Ibid.*

137. *Ibid.*, p. 47. The figure of 4.9 persons was also the average for the British Isles; it ranged from 4.8 in Scotland, to 5.2 in England and Wales.

138. Marion J. Levy of Princeton University has recently informed me that he is attempting, by analyzing mortality, fertility, and age distributions, to ascertain the likelihood (under the assumption of normal distributions) that *any* large segment of a population could have lived in an extended kin household. Preliminary calculations seem to suggest that under most demographic conditions the likelihood was low. That is to say, under most ordinary demographic patterns, most people have lived in a nuclear household.

139. Madhav S. Gore, *The Impact of Industrialization and Urbanization on the*

Aggarwal Family in Delhi Area, unpub. Ph.D. diss., Columbia University, 1961, p. 8.
140. Ross, *op. cit.*, p. 47.
141. Kapadia, *Marriage and Family* . . . , *op. cit.*, pp. 248–249.
142. *Ibid.*, pp. 249–250.
143. Morrison, "Family Types in Badlapur . . . ," 53; Elder, *op. cit.*, p. 284; Ross, *op. cit.*, p. 41; Dube, *op. cit.*, p. 133; K. M. Kapadia, "The Family in Transition," *Sociological Bulletin*, 8 (September, 1959), 74–75, 79; Indera P. Singh, "A Sikh Village," in Singer, *op. cit.*, p. 297; I. P. Desai, "The Joint Family in India—An Analysis," *Sociological Bulletin*, 5 (September, 1956), 144–156; M. G. Kulkarni, "Family Patterns in Gokak Taluka," *Sociological Bulletin*, 9 (March, 1960), 70.
144. Kapadia, *Marriage and Family* . . . , *op. cit.*, p. 261.
145. Kapadia, "The Family in Transition," *op. cit.*, p. 73.
146. *Ibid.*, p. 81.
147. Cited in M. F. Nimkoff, "The Family in India," *Sociological Bulletin*, 8 (September, 1959), 35, from P. N. Prabhu, "Bombay, A Study on the Social Effects of Urbanization," in *UNESCO: The Social Implications of Industrialization and Urbanization South of Sahara* (Paris: The International African Institute, 1956).
148. These items are from Kapadia, *Marriage and Family* . . . , *op. cit.*, pp. 264–265; Singh, *op. cit.*, p. 297 ff.; Ross, *op. cit.*, pp. 47, 50, 75, 78, 84–86, 89, 95–96; Kapadia, "The Family in Transition," *op. cit.*, 82; Elder, *op. cit.*, p. 288; A. Aiyappan, "In Tamilnad," *Sociological Bulletin*, 4 (March, 1955), 121; Gore, *op. cit.*, p. 177.
149. See the personality data presented by Elder, *op. cit.*, chap. 5; as well as Gitel P. Steed, "Notes on an Approach to a Study of Personality Formation in a Hindu Village in Gujarat," in Marriott, *op. cit.*, pp. 102–144.
150. Merchant, *op. cit.*, pp. 123–126; and Kapadia, *Marriage and Family* . . . , *op. cit.*, p. 259.
151. Cited in Ross, *op. cit.*, p. 47, from *Women in Modern Gujerati Life*, M.A. thesis, University of Bombay, 1945.
152. K. M. Kapadia, "Changing Patterns of Hindu Marriage and Family III," *Sociological Bulletin*, 4 (March, 1955), 161, 163.
153. *Monthly Public Opinion Surveys of the Indian Institute of Public Opinion*, 1 (October, 1955), 8, 23.
154. Gore, *op. cit.*, p. 191.

155. Kulkarni, *op. cit.*, p. 60.
156. Gore, *op. cit.*, p. 207.
157. *Ibid.*, p. 208.
158. *Ibid.*, p. 212.
159. *Ibid.*, p. 215.
160. Ross, *op. cit.*, pp. 103–104.
161. Gore, *op. cit.*, p. 232.
162. *Ibid.*, p. 233.
163. *Ibid.*, p. 235.
164. *Ibid.*, p. 237.
165. See *ibid.*, pp. 247 ff.; see also pp. 375–377.
166. *Ibid.*, p. 271.
167. *Monthly Public Opinion Surveys of the India Institute of Public Opinion*, 1 (November, 1955), 39.
168. Kapadia, "The Family in Transition," *op. cit.*, pp. 86–89.
169. *Ibid.*, p. 86.
170. *Ibid.*, p. 89.
171. Gore, *op. cit.*, pp. 291–293.
172. Lewis, *Village Life in Northern India*, *op. cit.*, pp. 52, 308–309.
173. Gore, *op. cit.*, pp. 298–299.
174. Cited by Nimkoff, *op. cit.*, p. 35.
175. Gore, *op. cit.*, pp. 301, 305–306, 310.
176. *Ibid.*, pp. 324, 329.
177. *Ibid.*, p. 331.
178. *Ibid.*, pp. 345, 347.
179. Ross, *op. cit.*, p. 137.
180. *Ibid.*, p. 151.
181. D. N. Majumdar, "Demographic Structure in a Polyandrous Village," *Eastern Anthropologist*, 8 (March–August, 1955), 161–175; see also *idem* (December–February, 1954), 85–110. Majumdar estimates, for example, that in one polyandrous village, divorce had dissolved more marriages than death had, and similar patterns were found in another village in Uttar Pradesh.
182. B. N. Mukherjee, "Family Structure and Laws of Residence, Succession and Inheritance Among the Urali of Travencore," *Vanyajati*, 3 (July, 1955), 91–104. Citation taken from *Sociological Abstracts*, 6, no. 1 (1958), No. 4131.
183. Singh, *op. cit.*, p. 157, comments on the "equality" of women in the depressed castes, which often also show "traces of matrilineality." See also "The Changing Status of a Depressed Caste," based on Bernard Cohen's work in Marriott, *op. cit.*, p. 67 ff.; for a matrilineal group see M. S. A. Rao, "Social Change in Kerala," *Sociological Bulletin*, 2 (September, 1953), 124–134; and "In Kerala," *idem* 4 (March, 1955), 123–129. See also V. Souza, "Mother Right

in Transition," *idem*, 2 (March, 1953), 135–142.

184. See E. Kathleen Gough, "Changing Kinship Usages in the Setting of Political and Economic Change among the Nayars of Malabar," *Journal of the Royal Anthropological Institute*, 82 (1952), 71–87; and "The Nayars and the Definition of Marriage," *idem*, 89, Part I (1959), 23–34; and M. S. A. Rao, *Social Change in Malabar* (Bombay: Popular Book Depot, 1957).

185. M. S. A. Rao, *Social Change in Malabar, op. cit.,* p. 98.

186. Kapadia, *Marriage and Family . . . , op. cit.,* pp. 273–275.

187. M. S. A. Rao, *Social Change in Malabar, op. cit.,* pp. 121–122.

188. Altekar, *op. cit.,* p. 359.

189. *Ibid.,* p. 269.

190. Kapadia, *Marriage and Family . . . , op. cit.,* "Appendix."

191. *Monthly Public Opinion Surveys of the Indian Institute of Public Opinion,* 1 (October, 1955), 17, 29.

192. Altekar, *op. cit.,* pp. 191–192.

193. Gore, *op. cit.,* p. 281.

194. G. C. Vyas, " 'Avidha'—A Narration of a Changing Life in a Gujerat Village," *Sociological Bulletin,* 2 (March, 1953), 21–22.

195. Davis, *op. cit.,* p. 229.

196. See the survey carried out in the late 1940s by A. V. Rao, *Structure and Working of Village Panchayats* (Poona: Gokhale Institute of Politics and Economics, Pub. No. 28, 1954), p. 7.

197. Lewis, *Village Life in Northern India, op. cit.,* p. 150.

198. Data from Desai's study cited in Ross, *op. cit.,* p. 212. See also pp. 210, 211, 227.

199. *Monthly Public Opinion Surveys of the Indian Institute of Public Opinion,* 1 (November, 1955), 38.

200. *Loc. cit.,* 1 (October, 1955), 11, 26.

201. Kapadia, "Changing Patterns . . . II," *op. cit.,* p. 155.

202. *Ibid.,* pp. 155–157.

203. *Monthly Public Opinion Surveys of the Indian Institute of Public Opinion,* 1 (October, 1955), 11, 29.

204. Singh, *op. cit.,* chap. 9, Appendix 10.

205. N. V. Sovani, *Social Survey of Kolhapur City, Vol. 3—Family Living and Social Life* (Poona: Gokhale Institute of Politics and Economics, Pub. No. 24, 1952), p. 112.

206. Gore, *op. cit.,* pp. 284 ff.

207. Ross, *op. cit.,* p. 198.

208. *Monthly Public Opinion Surveys of the Indian Institute of Public Opinion,* 1 (November, 1955), 35.

209. *Ibid.* (November, 1955), 13, 27.

210. Ross. *op. cit.,* pp. 201–203.

211. Unpublished data from Registrar General and Census Commissioner for India, New Delhi, in "Women in Employment in India," *International Labor Review,* 79 (January–June, 1959), 440–441.

212. Singh, *op. cit.,* p. 168.

213. P. V. Kane, *Hindu Custom and Modern Law* (Bombay: University of Bombay, 1950), p. 82.

214. Kapadia, *Marriage and Family . . . , op. cit.,* p. 258.

215. *Ibid.,* pp. 178–179.

216. B. Kuppuswamy, *A Study of Opinion Regarding Marriage and Divorce* (Bombay: Asia Publishing House, 1957), pp. 48–49.

217. *Ibid.,* pp. 61–63.

218. *Ibid.,* p. 64.

219. *Ibid.,* p. 69.

220. *Monthly Public Opinion Surveys of the Indian Institute of Public Opinion,* 1 (November, 1955), pp. 18, 29.

221. Gore, *op. cit.,* pp. 385–387. See also the attitudes expressed by Ross' sample, *op. cit.,* p. 274.

222. Altekar, *op. cit.,* pp. 132–139.

223. *Ibid.,* p. 138.

224. *Census of India, 1901,* Vol. 1, Part 1, Report, pp. 445–446.

225. *Ibid.,* p. 454; see also Davis, *op. cit.,* p. 36.

226. *Census of India, 1911,* Vol. 1, Part 1, Report, p. 275.

227. *Census of India, 1951,* Vol. 1, Part 2A, pp. 168–172 (includes *both* divorced and widowed, but few were divorced).

228. Gore, *op. cit.,* pp. 391–396.

229. K. M. Kapadia, "A Perspective Necessary for the Study of Social Change in India," *Sociological Bulletin,* 6 (March, 1957), 40–49.

230. Kumudini Dandekar, "Widow Remarriage in Six Rural Communities in Western India," International Population Union Conference, New York, 1961, unpub. paper no. 56, p. 1.

231. *Ibid.,* p. 3.

232. *Ibid.,* p. 9.

233. *Ibid.,* p. 10.

234. Karvé, *op. cit.,* p. 73.

235. Altekar, *op. cit.,* pp. 143 ff.; and Prabhu, *op. cit.,* p. 200.

236. Karvé, *op. cit.*, pp. 131-136 for the northern zone, and 153, 156 for the central zone.

237. *Ibid.*, p. 172.

238. *Ibid.*, p. 193.

239. In the 1911 Census, pp. 246-248, various comments on the levirate are noted, as well as the sexual freedom sometimes given to the widow.

240. *Ibid.*, pp. 239, 240.

241. Ross, *op. cit.*, p. 174.

242. Lewis, *Village Life in Northern India*, *op. cit.*, pp. 189-193.

Chapter VI   China

1. In this section I am following M. H. Van der Valk, *An Outline of Modern Chinese Family Law* (Peking: Catholic University of Peking, 1939), p. 25.

2. *Ibid.*, p. 37.

3. *Ibid.*, p. 39.

4. *Ibid.*, p. 49.

5. *Ibid.*, p. 52.

6. *Ibid.*, p. 57.

7. *Ibid.*, pp. 114-115.

8. *Ibid.*, pp. 128-133.

9. Olga Lang, *Chinese Family and Society* (New Haven: Yale University Press, 1946), p. 104. Catholics opened a school for girls in 1800 and the Protestants began to open schools in the 1840s. By the 1880s many such schools had started. By 1905, the Chinese government had officially recognized the need for women's education.

10. *Ibid.*, p. 108.

11. M. H. Van der Valk, *Conservatism in Modern Chinese Family Law* (Leiden: E. J. Brill, 1956), p. 1.

12. T'ung-Tsu Ch'ü, *Law and Society in Traditional China* (Paris: Mouton, 1961), pp. 29-30.

13. *Ibid.*, p. 99.

14. Lang, *op. cit.*, pp. 121-122.

15. *Ibid.*, pp. 287-288.

16. *Ibid.*, pp. 122-123.

17. Yu Ming, "We Must Adopt a Solemn Attitude Towards the Problem of Love and Marriage," *Peking Ta Kung Pao* (December, 1956), translated and reprinted in *Survey of China Mainland Press* (To be abbreviated SCMP throughout chapter), no. 1406 (February, 1957), 5.

18. Van der Valk, *Conservatism . . . , op. cit.*, p. 62.

19. *Ibid.*, p. 60.

20. His statement is to be found in *Current Background* (To be abbreviated as *CB* throughout chapter), no. 322 (March 20, 1955); the latter statement (originally stated July 23, 1953) is to be found in *CB*, no. 323 (March 25, 1955), 10.

21. Tzu Chi, "In the Handling of Divorce Cases, We Must Struggle against Bourgeois Ideology," *Hua Tung Cheng Fa Hsüeh Pao*, reprinted in *Extracts from China Mainland Magazines* (hereafter referred to as *ECMM*) no. 65 (January, 1957); and Ku Chou, "Principles for Handling Divorce Cases During the Years Since Promulgation of Marriage Law," *Cheng Fa Yen Chiu (Political and Legal Studies)*, no. 5 (October, 1956), *ECMM*, no. 57 (September, 1956), 16.

22. "Give Correct Guidance to the Marriage and Love Problems of Rural Youth," a comment on local Youth Leagues papers and periodicals, *Chung Kuo Ching Nien (China Youth)*, no. 21 (November, 1956), reprinted in *ECMM*, no. 66 (January, 1957), 13.

23. Feng Yu-Ching, "Arranged Marriages Getting Serious in Rural Areas in Shensi Province," *Chung Kuo Ching Nien Pao* (August 30, 1956), reprinted in *SCMP*, no. 1372 (September, 1956), 16.

24. *Ibid.*, pp. 14-15.

25. "China's Emancipated Women," *New China News Agency* (Kaifeng: March, 1953), reprinted in *SCMP*, no. 527 (March, 1953), 15-16.

26. "Implementation of Marriage Law in Different Parts of the Country Very Uneven," *New China News Agency* (Peking: January, 1953), *CB*, no. 236 (March, 1953), 4-7.

27. *Jen Min Jih Pao (Peoples' Daily)*, (Peking: February 25, 1953), as cited in Van der Valk, *Conservatism . . . , op. cit.*, p. 1.

28. "Implementation of Marriage Law . . . ," *op. cit.*, 4-7.

29. "Feudal Marriage Systems and Malpractices Still Found in Most Parts of China," *New China News Agency* (Peking: February, 1953), *CB*, no. 236 (March, 1953), 14-15.

30. *Ibid.* These were presumably *t'ung yang-hsi*.

31. Van der Valk, *Conservatism . . . , op. cit.*, p. 49.

32. See *ibid.*, pp. 49–50, for a list of some of the major provinces in which various forms of the *t'ung yang-hsi* are to be found.

33. Van der Valk, *An Outline* . . . , *op. cit.*, pp. 93–94.

34. Van der Valk, *Conservatism* . . . , *op. cit.*, pp. 45–47, lists the ten Chinese provinces in which this custom was found.

35. For a discussion and analysis of mourning grades, see Han-yi Feng, *The Chinese Kinship System* (Cambridge, Massachusetts: Harvard University Press, 1948); and T'ung-Tsa Ch'ü, *op. cit.*

36. Van der Valk, *Conservatism* . . . , *op. cit.*, p. 25.

37. *Ibid.*, p. 29.

38. T'ung-Tsu Ch'ü, *op. cit.*, p. 95.

39. Van der Valk, *Conservatism* . . . , *op. cit.*, p. 72.

40. *Ibid.*, p. 28.

41. Han-yi Feng, *The Chinese Kinship System* (Cambridge, Massachusetts: Harvard University Press, 1948), p. 44.

42. Francis L. K. Hsu, *Under the Ancestors' Shadow* (New York: Columbia University Press, 1948), pp. 81–82.

43. See also Hsu's "Observations on Cross-Cousin Marriage in China," *American Anthropologist*, 42 (January–March, 1945), 85–103.

44. Van der Valk, *Conservatism* . . . , *op. cit.*, p. 28.

45. See *ibid.*, p. 30.

46. *Ibid.*, p. 51.

47. J. Lossing Buck, "An Economic and Social Survey of 150 Farms, Yenshan County, Chihli Province, China," *University of Nanking Bulletin*, 13 (June, 1926), 61.

48. Daniel H. Kulp, *Country Life in South China*, Vol. 1 (New York: Teachers College, 1925), p. 145.

49. Sidney D. Gamble, *Ting Hsien* (New York: Institute of Pacific Relations, 1954), pp. 6–7. This study was made in the 1920s.

50. Maurice Freedman, *Chinese Family and Marriage in Singapore* (London: H.M.F.O., 1957), p. 57.

51. Ch'ü, *op. cit.*, p. 125.

52. Van der Valk, *An Outline* . . . , *op. cit.*, p. 23.

53. Kulp, *op. cit.*, pp. 151, 181.

54. Van der Valk, *Conservatism* . . . , *op. cit.*, p. 46.

55. Professor G. William Skinner, in a personal communication, says that Chinese society is polygynous, "no matter how the legalist might look at it."

56. Freedman, *op. cit.*, pp. 57, 103.

57. Gamble, *op. cit.*, p. 7.

58. Frank Notestein, "A Demographic Study of 38,256 Rural Families in China," *Milbank Memorial Fund Quarterly Bulletin*, 16 (January, 1938), 63–64.

59. Lang, *op. cit.*, p. 221.

60. Hsu, *Under the Ancestors' Shadow*, *op. cit.*, p. 106.

61. These comments on various suggested ages at marriage are taken from Van der Valk, *Conservatism* . . . , *op. cit.*, p. 52, who derives them from the commentaries to Article 6 of the first Peking Draft.

62. These are rationalizations of custom, and would apply to girls from 15 to 17 years as well as to very young girls. I have not found a satisfactory explanation of the custom.

63. Van der Valk, *Conservatism* . . . , *op. cit.*, p. 53.

64. W. Eberhard, "Research on the Chinese Family," *Sociologus*, 9, no. 1 (1959), 1–11.

65. Gamble, *op. cit.*, pp. 44, 385.

66. *Ibid.*, pp. 7, 385.

67. *Ibid.*, p. 39.

68. *Ibid.*, p. 44. One *mu* is about one sixth of an acre.

69. *Ibid.*, p. 45.

70. Van der Valk, *Conservatism* . . . , *op. cit.*, p. 52.

71. Kulp, *op. cit.*, p. 175.

72. Gamble, *op. cit.*, p. 45.

73. Lang, *op. cit.*, p. 129.

74. Buck, *op. cit.*, 81.

75. Chi-Ming Chiao, Warren S. Thompson, and D. T. Chen, *An Experiment in the Registration of Vital Statistics in China* (Oxford, Ohio: Scripps Foundation, 1938), p. 39.

76. Chi-Ming Chiao, "A Study of the Chinese Population," *Milbank Memorial Fund Quarterly Bulletin*, 11 (October, 1933), and 12 (January, April, July, 1934), 31–32; Frank W. Notestein, *op. cit.*, 57–59.

77. Chiao, Thompson, and Chen, *op. cit.*, pp. 36, 39, 45.

78. Ta Chen, *Population in Modern China* (Chicago: University of Chicago Press, 1946), p. 42.

79. Ta Chen, *op. cit.*, p. 92.

80. George W. Barclay, *Colonial Development and Population in Taiwan* (Princeton: Princeton University Press, 1954), p. 211.

81. Hsu, *Under the Ancestors' Shadow*, *op. cit.*, p. 888.

82. Unpublished data furnished to me by Dr. Barclay.

83. Lang, *op. cit.*, p. 128.

84. Ta Chen, *op. cit.*, p. 30.

85. C. K. Yang, *The Chinese Family in the Communist Revolution* (Cambridge, Massachusetts: Harvard University Press, 1959), p. 41.

86. Freedman, *op. cit.*, pp. 112–114, 118.

87. Huang Lien-Hai, "Surveys of Early Marriages among Young Factory Workers" (September, 1956), reprinted in *SCMP*, no. 1389 (October, 1956).

88. *Jen Min Jih Pao* (March, 1957), reprinted in *SCMP*, nos. 1475, series 5; 1488, series 10; and 1497, series 17 (October, 1956).

89. "Population and birth control," delivered to the Third Session of the Second CPPCC National Committee, March 1957. See *Jen Min Jih Pao* (Peking: March, 1957), reprinted in *CB*, no. 445 (April, 1957).

90. *China News Analysis*, no. 172 (March 15, 1957), 2, 5.

91. Leo A. Orleans, "Birth Control: Reversal or Postponement?", *The China Quarterly* (July–September, 1960), 63.

92. Orleans, *op. cit.*, p. 59.

93. Kingsley Davis and Judith Blake have penetratingly outlined the many points at which the customs of even a high-fertility society may raise *or* lower the rate of reproduction. See "Social Structure and Fertility: An Analytic Framework," *Economic Development and Cultural Change*, 4 (April, 1956), 211–235.

94. Orleans, *op. cit.*, p. 59, says that in 1957 Chen Ta expressed his dissatisfaction with the vital statistics registration work of China. Chen Ta is the former director of the State Statistical Bureau. For the 1934 estimate, see Chen Ta, *op. cit.*, p. 29.

95. Chen Ta, *op. cit.*, pp. 28–29.

96. *Ibid.*, Tables 16, 17.

97. Lang, *op. cit.*, pp. 152–153.

98. *China News Analysis* (hereafter referred to as *CNA*), no. 172 (March 15, 1957), 1.

99. S. Chandrasekhar, "China's Population Problem," in E. Stuart Kirby (ed.), *Contemporary China*, Vol. 3 (Hongkong: Hongkong University Press, 1960), pp. 22–23.

100. *CNA*, *op. cit.*, 1; and Chandrasekhar, *op. cit.*, p. 23.

101. *CNA*, *op. cit.*, 1.

102. *Idem*, no. 173, 1; and Orleans, *op. cit.*, pp. 60–61.

103. Fu Lien-Chang, "Correct Attitudes to the Question of Contraception and Artificial Abortion," *Chung Kuo Ching Nien Pao* (Peking: August, 1956), reprinted in *SCMP*, no. 1365 (September 7, 1956), 7–9. In May, the Chinese Medical Association had voiced some objections to relaxing the control over abortion. (*CNA*, no. 172, 1, gives the *People's Daily* editorial date as March 5, 1957.)

104. "For Active Dissemination of Contraception Knowledge," *SCMP*, no. 1352 (August, 1956).

105. Chung Hui-lan, "Population and Birth Control," Third Session of the Second CPPCC National Committee, March 14, 1957, reported in *Jen Min Jih Pao* (Peking: March, 1957), and reprinted in *CB*, no. 445 (April, 1957), 2, 5, 21.

106. See Ma Yin-chu, "A New Theory of Population," statement to the First National People's Congress, reported in *Jen Min Jih Pao*, *op. cit.*, and reprinted in *CB*, no. 469 (July, 1957), 13–15.

107. See Orleans, *op. cit.*, pp. 68 ff.; and Sri Pati Chandrasekhar, *Red China* (New York: Praeger, 1961), chap. 7.

108. Orleans, *op. cit.*, pp. 69–70.

109. Chandrasekhar, "China's Population Problem," *op. cit.*, pp. 31–32.

110. See Van der Valk, *An Outline . . .*, *op. cit.*, pp. 129–131.

111. *Ibid.*, p. 131, 171.

112. Pregnancy from illicit sexual intercourse is named as one of the consequences of the attitude of young people freed from the feudal system. See Tzu Chi, "In the Handling of Divorce Cases, We Must Struggle Against Bourgeois Ideology," *East China Journal of Political Science and Law* (in Chinese), no. 3 (December 15, 1956), in *ECMM*, no. 65 (January, 1957), 7.

113. See the amusing account by Chandrasekhar, *Red China*, *op. cit.*, pp. 83 ff., of his visit to the prostitutes' reformation institute in Shanghai.

114. Chang-tu Hu, *et al.*, *China* (New Haven: HRAS Press, 1960), pp. 402–403.

115. Yang, *op. cit.*, p. 57.

116. Francis L. K. Hsu, "The Myth of Chinese Family Size," *American Journal of Sociology*, 48 (May, 1943), 555–562. For a more general comment on the relations between fact and ideal in the Chinese family, see Rose Hum Lee, "Research on the Chinese Family," *American Journal of Sociology*, 54 (May, 1949), 497–504.

117. Buck, *op. cit.*, p. 63.

118. The date is 1942–1943. See Yang, *op. cit.*, pp. 7–8.

119. Gamble, *op. cit.*, p. 25. In another

smaller sample of over 2 thousand families, the average was 5.6 persons.

120. Morton H. Fried, "The Family in China: The People's Republic," in Ruth N. Anshen (ed.), *The Family*, rev. ed. (New York: Harper, 1959), p. 148. See also Maurice Freedman, *Lineage Organization in Southeastern China* (London: Athlone Press, 1958), p. 3, which cites several additional studies on the size of the Chinese household.

121. Feng, *op. cit.*, p. 42: Hsien Chin Hu, *op. cit.*, p. 9.

122. See Fried, *op. cit.*, p. 93: "Ancestral halls are frequently found to be in a state of decay." Lang, *op. cit.*, p. 178, states that "beautiful and well-kept ancestral temples are rare."

123. Hsien Chin Hu, *op. cit.*, p. 95.

124. Lang, *op. cit.*, p. 177.

125. *Ibid.*, pp. 178, 180.

126. Hsien Chin Hu, *op. cit.*, p. 10.

127. *Ibid.*, pp. 98–99. The various modes and techniques for exploitation at different levels are detailed by Freedman, *Lineage Organization . . . , op. cit.*, chaps. 8, 9, and 10.

128. E. S. Kirby, "The Enigma of the Communes" in E. Stuart Kirby (ed.), *Contemporary China*, Vol. 3 (Hongkong: Hongkong University Press, 1960), pp. 156–157.

129. *Ibid.*, p. 158.

130. "Draft Regulations of the Weihsing People's Commune," in Kirby, *op. cit.*, p. 246.

131. "Resolution on some Questions Concerning the People's Communes," Eighth Central Committee of the Communist Party of China at its Sixth Plenary Session on December 10, 1958, in *idem*, p. 214.

132. *Ibid.*, p. 215.

133. *Ibid.*, pp. 227–228.

134. D. E. T. Luard, "The Urban Commune," *The China Quarterly* (July–September, 1960), 74.

135. *Ibid.*, p. 75.

136. Chang Hsiao-Mei, "The Broad Masses of the Housewives Take up the Posts of Social Labor" (speech to First Session of Second National People's Congress), *Jen Min Jih Pao*, *op. cit.*, reprinted in *CB* (May, 1959).

137. "Women, an Important Force to Socialist Construction," *Shih-Shih Shou-Ts'e* (*Current Events*), no. 5 (March, 1959), reprinted in *ECMM*, no. 168 (May, 1959).

138. Luard, *op. cit.*, pp. 76–77.

139. *New China News Agency*, Peking, April 8, 1960, in *CB*, no. 625, July, 1960.

140. Speech by Deputy Liao Su-hua, "How is the People's Economic Life Organized in Chungking Municipality," Peking, *Jen Min Jih Pao* (Peking: April, 1960) reprinted in *CB*, no. 625 (July, 1960).

141. *Rural China News Agency*, no. 2454, (Chungking: Survey of China Mainland Press, March, 1961).

142. Yang, *op. cit.*, pp. 161–164.

143. Lang, *op. cit.*, chap. 16.

144. See Yang, *op. cit.*, chap. 9, "The Shifting Center of Loyalties."

145. Yang, *op. cit.*, p. 119.

146. *Ibid.*, pp. 150–154.

147. Chang Yun, "Build the Nation and Manage Household with Industry and Thrift, and Struggle for Building Socialism," report to Third National Congress of Chinese Women, September, 1957, reported in *Jen Min Jih Pao* (Peking: September, 1957), and reprinted in *CB*, no. 476 (October, 1957).

148. "China's Workers in 1955: Their Number, Composition and Distribution," *Tung Chi Kung Tso Tung Hsin* (*Statistical Work Bulletin*), no. 23 (December 14, 1956), reprinted in *ECMM*, no. 68 (February, 1959).

149. "How Many Women Workers, Women APC Members and Women Cadres in China," *Shih-Shih Shou Ts'e* (*Current Events*), no. 5 (March 6, 1957), reprinted in *ECMM*, no. 83 (March 20, 1957).

150. *New China News Agency* (Shanghai: March, 1961), reprinted in *SCMP*, no. 2454 (March, 1961), 16. As so often in Communist data, the percentage increase is given, but not the base figures.

151. See the various articles in *Hung Ch'i* (*Red Flag*) titled "People's Communes in Communist China," no. 5 (August, 1958), reprinted in *CB*, no. 517 (September, 1958).

152. "Party's General Line Illuminating Road of Thorough Emancipation of Women in our Country," by Ts'ai Ch'ang, President of Women's Federation of Peking, *Jen Min Jih Pao* (Peking: October, 1959), reprinted in *CB*, no. 609 (January, 1960).

153. *Ten Great Years: Statistics of the Economic and Cultural Achievements of the People's Republic of China* (Peking: Foreign Languages Press, 1960); translated from Chinese Edition, 1959.

154. Chang Yun, *op. cit.*, p. 15.

155. *Ibid.*

156. *SCMP*, no. 2454 (March 13, 1961), 17.

157. *SCMP*, no. 1300 (June, 1956), 11.

158. *Ten Great Years, op. cit.*, p. 202.

159. *Ibid.*, p. 221.

160. Tsai Chang, "Party's General Line Illuminates the Path of Emancipation for our Women," *Women of China*, no. 1 (January, 1960), reprinted in *ECMM*, no. 201 (January, 1960), 28.

161. *Chung-Kuo Fu-nü (Women of China)*, no. 11 (1961), reprinted in *ECMM*, no. 291 (December, 1961), 13–15.

162. Hu Sheng, "Concerning the Family—A Letter to a Friend," *Chung-Kuo Fu-nü (Women in China)*, no. 18 (December, 1958), reprinted in *ECMM*, no. 159 (March, 1959), 14.

163. *Ibid.*, p. 17.

164. Ting Tzu-hui, "Try to Run the Community Mess Halls Well, Seriously Try to Follow the Principle of Voluntariness," *Hsin-hua Pan-yueh-k'an (New China Half-Monthly)*, no. 12 (June 25, 1959), reprinted in *ECMM*, no. 179 (August 5, 1959).

165. "A Production Brigade in Kwangtung Insists on Same Pay for Men and Women Doing Same Kind of Job," *Nanfang Jih-pao* (Canton: May 24, 1961), reprinted in *SCMP*, no. 2560 (May 24, 1961), 5.

166. Liu Hsi-Chun, "Properly Arranging the Life is an Important Task," *Ta Kung Pao* Peking: reprinted in *SCMP*, no. 2651 (January 4, 1962), 20.

166. *L'Express*, no. 579 (July 19, 1952), 32.

167. See Lang, *op. cit.*, p. 42, for some of the historical references to this practice.

168. *Studies on the Population of China, 1368–1953* (Cambridge, Massachusetts: Harvard University Press, 1959), pp. 58–62. For example, one local history states that "some 80 or 90 percent of the baby girls are drowned."

169. Levy, *op. cit.*, p. 99. See also pp. 69, 81, 226, 290.

170. Gamble, *Peking, A Social Survey* (New York: George H. Doran, 1921), p. 57.

171. Ta Chen, *op. cit.*, p. 83; see also his life tables, pp. 105–106.

172. S. Chandrasekhar suggests that there may actually be more female children born in some areas. In fact, however, wherever good registration data are achieved such a phenomenon disappears. See *Population and Planned Parenthood in India* (London: Allen & Unwin, 1955), pp. 21–22.

173. For the sex ratio of various age groups, see S. Chandrasekhar, *China's Population*, 2d ed. (Hongkong: Hongkong University Press, 1960), pp. 46–47.

174. Levy, *op. cit.*, p. 117.

175. See *ibid.*, pp. 116–117, for the claim that sometimes her family would use or threaten force if she was not treated reasonably well.

176. Lang, *op. cit.*, p. 232.

177. Ta Chen, *op. cit.*, Tables 25 and 26.

178. Buck, *op. cit.*, p. 84.

179. From the *Jen Min Jih Pao* (Peking: February, 1953), 2, cited in Van der Valk, *Conservatism . . . , op. cit.*, p. 1.

180. Yang, *op. cit.*, pp. 107–108. It should be kept in mind that both homicide and suicide are "family caused" for the most part.

181. Chandrasekhar, *China's Population, op. cit*, p. 61.

182. Because a man might have more than one wife in his lifetime, his youngest son might be far younger than anyone else in that filial generation, and indeed some males in the grandchild generation might be older than the man's youngest son. At times, then, the generation principle conflicted with the age principle and required adjustment in decisions as to who was in authority over the clan activities.

183. Ch'ü, *op. cit.*, pp. 20 ff.

184. *Ibid.*, p. 21.

185. Yang, *op. cit.*, p. 91.

186. Chang-tu Hsü, *op. cit.*, p. 396.

187. See Hsü, *op. cit.*, p. 258, who views this as one of the "safety valves" for the strains generated by the Chinese system.

188. *Ibid.*, pp. 245–248.

189. Yuan Po, "What Attitudes Should one Take Towards one's Parents?", *Chung Kuo Ch'ing Nien Pao* (Peking: December, 1954), *SCMP*, no. 973 (January, 1955), 30–32.

190. Chang Yun, *op. cit.*, p. 27.

191. Chai Shang-tung, "How Should we Regard Communist Family Life?", *Chung-kuo Ching-nien (China Youth)*, no. 22 (December, 1958), reprinted in *ECMM*, no. 155 (January, 1959).

192. "The People's Communes: Questions and Answers," *Chung-kuo Kung-jin (Workers of China)*, no. 24 (December, 1958), in *ECMM*, no. 161 (March, 1959).

193. Shui Chieh, "How I Managed to Improve my Relations with my Mother-in-Law," *Chung-kuo Fu-niu (Women of China)*, no. 4 (February, 1959), reprinted in *ECMM*, no. 167 (May, 1959).

194. Lang, *op. cit.*, p. 41.

195. Levy, *op. cit.*, p. 186.

196. Freedman, *Chinese Family and Marriage in Singapore, op. cit.*, p. 176.
197. Kulp, *op. cit.*, p. 184.
198. Ting Hsien, *op. cit.*, p. 38.
199. Perhaps the best analysis of the legal interpretations of the grounds for divorce from historical times through the Republican era is to be found in Wang Tse-sin, *Le Divorce en Chine* (Paris: Leviton, 1932).
200. See the citations given in Ch'ü, *op. cit.*, p. 118. See also his analysis of the seven conditions for divorce, pp. 118 ff.
201. E. Stuart Kirby, *Contemporary China*, Vol. 1 (Hongkong: Hongkong University Press, 1956), p. 121.
202. Notestein, *op. cit.*, p. 64.
203. Lang, *op. cit.*, p. 217.
204. Chen Ta, *op. cit.*, p. 112, Table 43.
205. Barclay, *op. cit.*, p. 221.
206. These figures are given in Liu Ching-Fan, "The Thorough Implementation of the Marriage Law," *New China News Agency* (Peking: March, 1953), reprinted in *CB*, no. 243 (May, 1953), 3–12. Another comment on this phenomenon may be found in Wen-hui C. Chen, "The Family Revolution in Communist China," no. 6, Series 3 (1953), in *Studies in Chinese Communism* (Texas: Lackland Air Force Base, Human Resources Research Institute, January, 1955). However, neither data nor analysis appears to be sound.
207. Freedman, *Chinese Family and Marriage in Singapore, op. cit.*, p. 182.
208. Ku Chou, "Principles for Handling Divorce Cases During the Years Since Promulgation of the Marriage Law," *Cheng*

Fa Yen Chiu (Political and Legal Studies), no. 5 (October, 1956), reprinted in *ECMM*, no. 57 (November, 1956).
209. Most of the article shows the advances that have been made in marital harmony and the implementation of the new law: Tzu Chi, "In the Handling of Divorce Cases, We Must Struggle Against Bourgeois Ideology," *Hua Tung Cheng Fa Hsueh Tao (East China Journal of Political Science and Law)*, no. 3 (December, 1956), reprinted in *ECMM*, no. 65 (January, 1957).
210. Wu Ch'ang-chen, "The Principle of Freedom of Marriage Should Not Be Abused," *Kuang Ming Jih Pao*, (Peking: February, 1957), reprinted in *SCMP*, no. 1509 (April, 1957), 7–8.
211. "Some Young People in Tientsin Involved in Hasty Marriages, Divorces," *Jen Min Jih Pao* (Peking: March, 1957), reprinted in *SCMP*, no. 1509 (April, 1957), 9.
212. Hsu, *op. cit.*, p. 105.
213. Fried, *op. cit.*, p. 45. Hsu, *op. cit.*, p. 251, also comments that "the remarriage of widows is treated with much social and ritual censure."
214. Levy, *op. cit.*, p. 96.
215. See Ch'ü, *op. cit.*, pp. 97–99, for a discussion of the "levirate."
216. See Freedman, *Lineage Organization in Southeast China, op. cit.*, pp. 31–32.
217. Levy, *op. cit.*, p. 46.
218. Yang, *op. cit.*, pp. 44–54.
219. See *ibid.*, chap. 13, "Recession of the 'High Tide' and long-term trends," for a good summary of this situation.
220. See Fried, in Anshen, *op. cit.*, p. 159.

Chapter VII   Japan

1. Marion J. Levy, "Contrasting Factors in the Modernization of China and Japan," in Simon S. Kuznets, Wilbert E. Moore and Joseph J. Spengler (eds.), *Economic Growth: Brazil, India. Japan* (Durham, North Carolina: Duke University Press, 1955), pp. 528–529.
2. See Ronald P. Dore, *City Life in Japan* (Berkeley: University of California Press, 1958), p. 152, for a commentary on the disruption of beliefs immediately after World War II.
3. Lafcadio Hearn, "A Woman's Tragedy; The Diary of a Japanese Woman," *Transactions and Proceedings of the*

Japanese Society (London: October, 1902), 131.
4. Dore, *op. cit.*, p. 163, cites from Kawashima Takeyoshi.
5. Yoshiharu Scott Matsumoto, "Contemporary Japan," in *Transactions of the American Philosophical Society*, N.S. 50, part I (Philadelphia: 1960) p. 7.
6. Perhaps the most easily available analysis of these customs may be found in Kunio Yanagida, *Japanese Manners and Customs in the Meiji Era*, trans. Charles S. Terry (Tokyo: Obunsha, 1957), chaps. 4, 6, and 10.
7. I am here following Levy, *op. cit.*,

p. 498, but I believe that any rigorous usage of "feudalism" would have to conform closely to his definition.

8. In several papers, Levy has described the differences between the Japanese and the Chinese family as an important factor in the industrialization of the two countries. The most important is the one already cited. See especially, however, *ibid.*, pp. 502 ff. Levy does not state my central thesis: the feudalization of family relations; but he has singled out in this essay the crucial differences between the two countries in their various stages of modernization. His treatment may be contrasted with the otherwise useful monograph by Norman Jacobs, *The Origin of Modern Capitalism and Eastern Asia* (Hongkong: Hongkong University Press, 1958). See especially chap. 7, "Kinship and Descent," where he simply misses some of the major factors seized upon by Levy.

9. As Robert N. Bellah points out in his *Tokugawa Religion* (New York: The Free Press of Glencoe, 1957), the Japanese merchants were even distinguished by a special religious sect: *Shingaku*.

10. For a discussion of these terms, see Yanagida, *op. cit.*, pp. 113–117.

11. Ezra F. Vogel, "The Democratization of Family Relations in Japanese Urban Society," *Asian Survey*, 1 (June, 1961), 19; and Ezra F. and Susanne H. Vogel, "Family Security, Personal Immaturity, and Emotional Health in a Japanese Sample," *Marriage and Family Living*, 23 (May, 1961), 165.

12. See Dore, *op. cit.*, pp. 207–209, for the ramifications of this system.

13. Richard K. Beardsley, John W. Hall, Robert E. Ward, *Village Japan* (Chicago: University of Chicago Press, 1959), p. 478.

14. Marquis de la Mazelière, "L'évolution de la famille japonaise," *Bulletin et Mémoires de la Société d'Anthropologie de Paris*, 5 (September, 1904), 665:

15. For the main terms of argument, and especially the moves toward the popular assembly, see Masaaki Kosaka (ed.), *Japanese Thought in the Meiji Era*, trans. David Abosch (Tokyo: Pan-Pacific Press, 1958), especially chap. 1, Part 3.

16. Shibusawa Keizo, *Japanese Life and Culture in the Meiji Era*, trans. Charles S. Terry (Tokyo: Obunsha, 1958), pp. 294–298.

17. L. W. Küchler, "Marriage in Japan," *Transactions of the Asiatic Society of Japan*, 13 (July, 1885), 117.

18. *Ibid.*, p. 117.

19. Yanagida, *op. cit.*, p. 118.

20. *Ibid.*, p. 119. The statement was made by Hozumi Yatsuka.

21. Mazelière, *op. cit.*, p. 666.

22. *Ibid.*, p. 670.

23. I am indebted to Takeji Kamiko for his comments on this point. See also Toshio Fueto, "The Discrepancy Between Marriage Law and Morals in Japan," *The American Journal of Comparative Law*, 5 (Spring, 1956), 256–266.

24. Mazelière, *op. cit.*, p. 667.

25. *Ibid.*, p. 667.

26. Yanagida, *op. cit.*, pp. 161–162.

27. *Ibid.*, p. 163.

28. John F. Embree, *Suye Mura* (Chicago: University of Chicago Press, 1939), p. 211. See also the citations in Irene B. Taeuber, *The Population of Japan* (Princeton: Princeton University Press, 1958), p. 207.

29. Clarence J. Glacken, *The Great Loochoo* (Berkeley: University of California Press, 1955), p. 221.

30. Ichiro Kurata, "Rural Marriage Customs in Japan," *Contemporary Japan*, 10 (March, 1941), 371.

31. Edward Norbeck, *Takashima* (Salt Lake City: University of Utah Press, 1954), p. 175. Yanagida, *op. cit.*, p. 162, says that almost the whole country had begun to follow this pattern by the middle Meiji.

32. Ezra S. Vogel, " 'O-nakohdo-san': the Japanese Marriage Arranger," unpublished paper (mimeo.), Yale University, 1961, p. 2.

33. Norbeck, *op. cit.*, p. 175.

34. Embree, *op. cit.* p., 194.

35. Beardsley, Hall, Ward, *op. cit.*, p. 316.

36. Edward and Margaret Norbeck, "Child Training in a Japanese Fishing Community," in Douglas G. Haring (ed.), *Personal Character and Cultural Milieu*, 3d ed. (Syracuse: Syracuse University Press, 1956), p. 673.

37. Matsumoto, *op. cit.*, p. 17; and Jean Stoetzel, *Without the Chrysanthemum and the Sword* (New York: Columbia University Press, 1955), p. 256.

38. Glacken, *op. cit.*, p. 221.

39. Ray E. Baber, *Youth Looks at Marriage and the Family* (Tokyo: International Christian University, 1958), p. 108.

40. Dore, *op. cit.*, p. 139.

41. Takashi Koyama, *The Changing*

Position of Women in Japan (Paris: UNESCO, 1961), p. 41.

42. Dore, *op. cit.*, p. 70.

43. Stoetzel, *op. cit.*, p. 82.

44. Nobuo Shinozaki, *Report on Sexual Life of Japanese* (Tokyo: Institute of Population Problems, Welfare Ministry, July 1957), p. 34. Apparently, this was mainly an urban sample.

45. Tatsuo Sameshima, "The Japanese Family Court," *First International Congress of Comparative Law of the International Association of Juridical Sciences*, (mimeo.), San Juan de Compostela, September 5–7, 1958.

46. Irene B. Taeuber, *The Population of Japan* (Princeton: Princeton University Press, 1958), p. 213.

47. *Ibid.*, p. 227.

48. *Ibid.*, p. 210.

49. *Ibid.*, p. 210.

50. *Ibid.*, p. 211.

51. *Family Systems and Calculations of Farming Communities in Japan*, Population Problems Series No. 6 (Tokyo: The Population Problems Research Council, Mainichi Newspapers, 1952), pp. 30, 46.

52. In Stoetzel's Sapporo sample, the *expected* age at marriage was 29 years for men. It was 27 years for Kyoto men, and 24 years for girls. This figure, of course, does not represent an ideal but represents only a calculated anticipation. See Stoetzel, *op. cit.*, p. 181.

53. Taeuber, *op. cit.*, p. 227.

54. In *ibid.*, chap. 3, Taeuber has made a signal contribution to the understanding of Japanese population patterns during this period by analyzing the official figures and presenting some plausible substitutes. Nonregistration of births was common and there was no complete census at all, so that neither the numerator nor the denominator of a correct birth rate can be more than approximated.

55. Tatsuo Honda, *Fifth Public Opinion Survey on Birth Control in Japan*, Population Problems Series No. 16 (Tokyo: Population Problems Research Council, Mainichi Newspapers, 1959).

56. See also the summary of these changes during 1950–1959 in Jean-Louis Riallin, "La Prévention des Naissances au Japon," *Population*, 15 (April–June, 1960), 333–351.

57. Yoshio Koya, "Seven Years of a Family Planning Program, in Three Typical Japanese Villages," *Milbank Memorial Fund Quarterly*, 36 (October, 1958), 363–

372. Other public opinion data on these points may be found in Matsumoto, *op. cit.*, pp. 20–23.

58. The data are from Tatsuo Honda, "A Survey of the Spread of Birth Control," which is a report of the *Third Public Opinion Survey on Birth Control in Japan*. The data are cited by Irene B. Taeuber, "Recent Population Developments in Japan: Some Facts and Reflections," *Pacific Affairs*, 29 (March, 1956), 27.

59. Beardsley, Hall, Ward, *op. cit.*, p. 335.

60. For a study of the abortion histories of 1,500 Japanese wives, see Yoshio Koya, "A Study of Induced Abortion in Japan and Its Significance," *Milbank Memorial Fund Quarterly*, 32 (July, 1954), 282–293.

61. See Taeuber, *The Population of Japan*, *op. cit.*, pp. 29–31.

62. For comment on the historical background of fertility control in Japan, see Thomas K. Burch, "Induced Abortion in Japan," *Eugenics Quarterly*, 2 (September, 1955), 140–151.

63. Embree, *op. cit.*, pp. 62, 84, 194–195.

64. Beardsley, Hall, Ward, *op. cit.*, p. 316.

65. Kizaemon Ariga, "The Contemporary Japanese Family in Transition," *Transactions of the Third World Congress of Sociology*, Vol. 4 (Amsterdam: International Sociological Association, 1956), pp. 219, 221.

66. Dore, *op. cit.*, p. 179.

67. Shinozaki, *op. cit.*, p. 28.

68. *The Japanese People Look at Prostitution* (Tokyo: National Opinion Research Institute, n.d), pp. 1, 3, 5, 6.

69. Matsumoto, *op. cit.*, p. 26.

70. Koyama, *op. cit.*, p. 79.

71. Embree, *op. cit.*, p. 97.

72. Arthur F. Raper *et al.*, *The Japanese Village in Transition* (Tokyo: General Headquarters, Supreme Commander for the Allied Powers, 1950), p. 217. They, too, note that most rural women are housewives, not independent members of the labor force.

73. *Ibid.*, p. 218.

74. Norbeck, *op. cit.*, p. 210.

75. Stoetzel, *op. cit.*, p. 177.

76. *Ibid.*, p. 117.

77. Cited in Koyama, *op. cit.*, p. 59.

77. *Ibid.*, p. 60.

78. Chokuro Kadono, "The Bringing Up of Japanese Girls," *Transactions and Proceedings of the Japan Society*, London, 6 (1903–1904), 308–315.

79. Dore, *op. cit.*, p. 128.

80. Beardsley, Hall, Ward, *op. cit.*, p. 330.

81. Dore, *op. cit.*, pp. 142, 153.

82. Cited by Koyama, *op. cit.*, p. 44, from data published by the Ministry of Health and Welfare.

83. Shibusawa, *op. cit.*, pp. 316–317.

84. Koyama, *op. cit.*, pp. 104–107.

85. *Ibid.*, from Ministry of Labor Annual Report of Labor Statistics.

86. James M. Gillespie and Gordon W. Allport, *Youth's Outlook on the Future*, Doubleday Papers in Psychology, No. 15 (New York: Doubleday, 1955), p. 60.

87. Matsumoto, *op. cit.*, p. 28. Ten per cent were D.K.'s or unclassified answers.

88. Stoetzel, *op. cit.*, p. 176.

89. Chiye Sano, *Changing Values of the Japanese Family* (Washington, D.C.: Catholic University of America Press, 1958), p. 54.

90. Matsumoto, *op. cit.*, p. 28, from interview survey by Women's and Children's Bureau.

91. Taki Fujita, *Japanese Women in the Post-War Years*, Twelfth Conference, Institute of Pacific Relations, Kyoto, Japan, September–October, 1954 (Tokyo: Nihon Taiheiyo Mondai Chosakai, 1954), p. 9.

92. *Statistical Materials Relating to Japanese Women* (Tokyo: Women's and Minors' Bureau, Japan, 1953), p. 11.

93. Koyama, *op. cit.*, pp. 121–123.

94. Matsumoto, *op. cit.*, p. 27.

95. Koyama, *op. cit.*, pp. 30–31.

96. Fujita, *op. cit.*, p. 9.

97. John B. Cornell, "Matsunagi," in Robert J. Smith and John B. Cornell, *Two Japanese Villages* (Ann Arbor: University of Michigan Press, 1956), p. 74.

98. Kadono, *op. cit.*, p. 320.

99. Embree, *op. cit.*, pp. 184–195.

100. Robert J. Smith, *Kurusu*, in Smith and Cornell, *op. cit.*, p. 73.

101. Beardsley, Hall, Ward, *op. cit.*, p. 292.

102. *Ibid.*, pp. 294–296.

103. Dore, *op. cit.*, pp. 7–8.

104. With reference to the imposition of existing group relations and obligations even on foreign visitors, see the perceptive account by John Sykes, *A Japanese Family* (London: Allan Wingate, 1957).

105. Norbeck and Norbeck, *op. cit.*, p. 666.

106. Vogel, "The Democratization of Family Relations in Japanese Urban Society," p. 19.

107. Vogel and Vogel, *op. cit.*, p. 163.

108. See the analysis by James Abegglen, *The Japanese Factory* (New York: The Free Press of Glencoe, 1958), chaps. 3, 4, and 5.

109. Vogel, "The Democratization of Family Relations in Japanese Urban Society," *op. cit.*, p. 21.

110. Stoetzel, *op. cit.*, p. 166.

111. *Ibid.*, p. 171.

112. Cited by Dore, *op. cit.*, p. 445.

113. Stoetzel, *op. cit.*, p. 169.

114. Cited by Matsumoto, *op. cit.*, p. 18; the study was done by Mainichi.

115. *Ibid.*, pp. 18–19.

116. *Fifth Public Opinion Survey on Birth Control in Japan*, Population Problems Series No. 16 (Tokyo: Population Problems Research Council, Mainichi Newspapers, 1959), pp. 4–5.

117. See Dore's comment on this point, in *op. cit.*, pp. 74–75.

118. See Raper, *op. cit.*, p. 211; and Stoetzel, *op. cit.*, p. 53.

119. Fujita, *op. cit.*, pp. 3–4.

120. See *Family System and Population of Farming Communities in Japan*, Population Series No. 6 (Tokyo: Population Problems Council, Mianichi Newspapers, 1950), p. 43, for data on this point.

121. Dore, *op. cit.*, pp. 123–124.

122. Yasuo Tatsuki, *General Trend of Japanese Opinion Following the End of War* (Tokyo: Japan Institute of Pacific Studies, 1948), pp. 43–44.

123. In this section, I am following largely the work of Kizaemon Ariga, *Dozoku: A Preliminary Study of the Japanese "Extended Family" Group and Its Social and Economic Functions* (Columbus, Ohio: Office of Naval Research Project, NR 176-110 and Rockefeller Foundation, Interim Technical Report No. 7, September 1953). See also the related comments by Yanagida, *op. cit., passim.*

124. Yanagida, *op. cit.*, p. 104.

125. L. I. Hewes and Laurence Ilsley, *Japan: Land and Men; An Account of the Japanese Land Reform Program 1945–51* (Ames, Iowa: Iowa State College Press, 1955), pp. 191 ff.

126. Cited in Matsumoto, *op. cit.*, p. 39; the study was done by the newspaper *Asahi*. There was far less disapproval in Kyushu. Note also the survey cited in *idem*, p. 40, according to which respondents denied the existence of such relationships in *their* towns and villages.

127. Masao Ueda, *Families and House-*

holds in Japan (New York: International Population Union Conference, 1961), p. 2.

128. Dore, *op. cit.*, p. 149.

129. *Ibid.*, p. 150.

130. Beardsley, Hall, Ward, *op. cit.*, p. 266. In this village, people did not absorb unrelated people into their *dozoku.*

131. *Ibid.*, p. 265.

132. See Tables 1 and 2 in Takeyoshi Kawashima and Kurt Steiner, "Modernization and Divorce Rate Trends," *Economic Development and Cultural Change,* 9 (October, 1960), pp. 2, 14–15.

133. Küchler, *op. cit.*, p. 172.

134. *Ibid.*, p. 223.

135. For a more extensive analysis of this point, including time trends in many nations, see my forthcoming article "Marital Satisfaction and Instability: Class Differentials Over Time," *International Sociological Bulletin,* UNESCO. See also Kadono, *op. cit.*, p. 310 ff. and Küchler, *op. cit.*, for a description of exhortations for a stable marriage given to upper-class Japanese girls.

136. Kawashima and Steiner, *op. cit.*, p. 239.

137. Kawashima and Steiner, *op. cit.*, pp. 236–239.

138. Embree, *op. cit.*, p. 213.

139. Norbeck, *op. cit.*, p. 52.

140. Beardsley, Hall, Ward, *op. cit.*, p. 332.

141. Cornell, *op. cit.*, p. 76.

142. Kawashima and Steiner, *op. cit.*, pp. 229–235.

143. Taeuber, *The Population of Japan, op. cit.*, p. 228.

144. Kawashima and Steiner, *op. cit.*, p. 221.

145. Taeuber, *The Population of Japan, op. cit.*, p. 228.

146. Taeuber, *The Population of Japan, op. cit.*, p. 230.

147. Embree, *op. cit.*, p. 89.

Conclusion

1. Lawrence Stone, "Marriage Among the English Nobility in the 16th and 17th Centuries," *Comparative Studies in Society and History,* 3 (January, 1961), 182–206; see also my "Comment" in *loc. cit.*, 207–214.

2. See Pierre Petot, "La Famille en France Sous l'Ancienne Regime," *Sociologie* *Comparée de la Famille Contemporaine* (Paris: Editions du Centre Nationale de la recherche scientifique, 1955), 9–18.

3. William J. Goode, *After Divorce,* (New York: The Free Press of Glencoe, 1956), p. 216.

Index

Page numbers in italic refer to material from tables or charts.

CUSHING-MARTIN LIBRARY
STONEHILL COLLEGE
NORTH EASTON, MASSACHUSETTS